RETHINKING PAUL'S RHETORICAL EDUCATION

Society of Biblical Literature

Early Christianity and Its Literature

Gail R. O'Day, General Editor

Editorial Board

Warren Carter
Beverly Roberts Gaventa
Judith M. Lieu
Joseph Verheyden
Sze-kar Wan

Number 10

RETHINKING PAUL'S RHETORICAL EDUCATION
Comparative Rhetoric and 2 Corinthians 10–13

RETHINKING PAUL'S RHETORICAL EDUCATION

COMPARATIVE RHETORIC
AND 2 CORINTHIANS 10–13

Ryan S. Schellenberg

Society of Biblical Literature
Atlanta

RETHINKING PAUL'S RHETORICAL EDUCATION
Comparative Rhetoric and 2 Corinthians 10–13

Copyright © 2013 by the Society of Biblical Literature

All rights reserved. No part of this work may be reproduced or transmitted in any form or by any means, electronic or mechanical, including photocopying and recording, or by means of any information storage or retrieval system, except as may be expressly permitted by the 1976 Copyright Act or in writing from the publisher. Requests for permission should be addressed in writing to the Rights and Permissions Office, Society of Biblical Literature, 825 Houston Mill Road, Atlanta, GA 30329 USA.

Library of Congress Cataloging-in-Publication Data

Schellenberg, Ryan S.
  Rethinking Paul's rhetorical education : comparative rhetoric and 2 Corinthians 10–13 / by Ryan S. Schellenberg.
     p. cm. — (Early Christianity and its literature ; 10)
  Includes bibliographical references and indexes.
  ISBN 978-1-58983-779-9 (paper binding : alk. paper) — ISBN 978-1-58983-780-5 (electronic format) — ISBN 978-1-58983-781-2 (hardcover binding : alk. paper)
  1. Bible. N.T. Corinthians, 2nd—Criticism, interpretation, etc. 2. Rhetoric in the Bible. 3. Paul, the Apostle, Saint. I. Title. II. Series: Early Christianity and its literature ; no. 10.
  BS2675.52.S344 2013
  227'.306—dc22   2013004944

Printed on acid-free, recycled paper conforming to
ANSI/NISO Z39.48-1992 (R1997) and ISO 9706:1994
standards for paper permanence.

For Rick Schellenberg

What governs the inflections that make any utterance unmistakably the words of one speaker in this whole language-saturated world?

—Marilynne Robinson, *Absence of Mind*

Contents

Acknowledgments xi
Abbreviations xiii

Introduction 1

Part 1: Paul's Rhetorical Education in Recent Scholarship

1. From Unschooled Tentmaker to Educated Rhetorician 17
    "No Mere Tentmaker" 18
    "Kein Klassiker, kein Hellenist hat so geschrieben" 22
    Paul, the Educated Rhetorician 26
        Soundings 28
        The Rise of Rhetorical Criticism 31
        "Comparison, Self-Praise, and Irony" 34
        A Developing Consensus 36
        Paul and the Diatribe 42
        Paulus und das antike Schulwesen 45
    Dissenting Voices 52
    Conclusion 55

2. Second Corinthians 10–13: A Historical and
    Literary Introduction 57
    Second Corinthians 10–13 and Recent Evaluations
        of Paul's Rhetoric 57
    The "Letter of Tears" 62
    Paul and the Corinthians 68
    Putative Evidence of Rhetorical Education in
        2 Corinthians 10–13 76

Part 2: Querying Rhetorical Criticism of 2 Corinthians 10–13

3. Forensic Rhetoric, Epistolary Types, and Rhetorical Education 81
   Epistolary Theory and Paul's Rhetorical Education   81
      Letter Types in 2 Corinthians 10–13   83
      Epistolary and Rhetorical Training in Greco-Roman
         Antiquity   88
      Conclusion   96

4. Paul's (In)appropriate Boasting: *Periautologia* 97
   Plutarch, *De laude ipsius* (*Moralia* 539A–547F)   99
      Boasting by Necessity   103
      Self-Defense   105
      Misfortune   108
      Usefulness; Benefit to Hearers   109
      Comparative Boasting   110
      Conclusion   114
   Quintilian, *Institutio oratoria* 11.1.15–26   116
   Hesitancy and *Prodiorthōsis*   118
   Conclusion   120

5. *Peristasis* Catalogues: Rhythm, Amplification, *Klangfiguren* 123
   Lists and Catalogues in Greco-Roman Antiquity   123
   Catalogues, *Auxēsis*, and Rhetorical Education   136
   Conclusion   140

6. Not a Fool, a Fool's Mask: *Narrenrede* and *Prosōpopoiia* 141
   Hans Windisch and Paul's So-Called *Narrenrede*   141
   Narrenrede, *Prosōpopoiia*, and Rhetorical Education   144
   Conclusion   148

7. *Synkrisis* in Corinth 149
   Sophistry in Corinth?   151
   Συγκρίνω and Rhetoric   157
   Paul's Comparison in 2 Corinthians 11:21b–23   160

8. Not a Fool, It's (Only) Irony 169
   Glenn Holland's Boastful Ironist   170
   Disclaiming Boastfulness   175

Conclusion 179

PART 3: RHETORIC AS INFORMAL SOCIAL PRACTICE

9. Toward a Theory of General Rhetoric 185
   - A Theory of General Rhetoric 186
   - Rhetoric in the New World 192
   - Categories for Comparison 197

10. Attending to Other Voices 201
    - Red Jacket's Self-Defensive Boasting 202
      - Sagoyewatha, or Red Jacket 202
      - Red Jacket's *Periautologia* 206
      - Conclusion 211
    - Informal *Prodiorthōsis* 212
      - Anticipating Social Constraints 213
      - "You Must Not Think Hard If We Speak Rash" 217
      - "Feigned Reluctance"? 218
    - *Prosōpopoiia* and the Use of Interlocutors' Voices 223
      - *Prosōpopoiia* in 2 Corinthians 10–13 227
      - "The Tree of Friendship" 229
    - The Ubiquity of Catalogue Style 231
    - Conclusion 239

11. The Acquisition of Informal Rhetorical Knowledge 243
    - The Nature of Language Socialization 243
    - An Analogy: *The Singer of Tales* 245
    - Mexicano Rhetorical "Education" 247
    - Conclusion 251

12. Ἰδιώτης τῷ Λόγῳ 255
    - Untempered Vigor 256
    - Epistolary Style: A Red Herring 258
    - Τὸ ἐν Λόγῳ Ἰδιωτικὸν τοῦ Ἀποστόλου 261
    - "Confused and Insufficiently Explicit" 263
    - 2 Corinthians 10:10; 11:6 277
      - "His Letters are Forceful and Bold" 277
      - "Boorish in Speech" 286
    - Envy and Foolishness: The Social Locations of Self-Praise 294

>   Boasting in Weakness 304

Conclusion: "Where Is the Voice Coming From?" 309
>   Voice, *Habitus*, and the Individual Speaker 311
>   Toward a Reading of 2 Corinthians 10–13 315
>   "Where Is the Voice Coming From?" 317
>   A Weak Apostle in Corinth 320

Bibliography 325
>   1. Ancient Texts and Translations 325
>   2. Secondary Literature 328

Index of Ancient Texts 373
Index of Modern Authors 392
Index of Subjects 401

Acknowledgments

This book is a revision of my doctoral dissertation, completed in 2012 at the University of St. Michael's College in the University of Toronto. A project of this nature can, of course, be an arduous undertaking, and I would like to express my gratitude to a number of teachers, colleagues, and friends whose generous contributions have enriched the final product, not to mention the experience of writing it.

First, I am profoundly grateful to Leif Vaage, my advisor, who provided invaluable guidance along the way. I have benefited much from his insightful questions and incisive criticism, as well as his consistent warmth, support, and enthusiasm for this study. Although I owe him a substantial intellectual debt, I am grateful too for his commitment to helping me cultivate my own academic voice.

Among the faculty of the Toronto School of Theology, two additional teachers and mentors deserve special thanks. First, John Kloppenborg has both taught and modeled consistent excellence in scholarship as in collegiality. He also served as a member of my dissertation committee, which task he undertook with characteristic thoughtfulness and care. Chapter 2 in particular is better for his interaction with it. Second, Colleen Shantz has simply been far more generous with her help and support than I have had any right to expect.

I am grateful, too, for the helpful comments and corrections offered by the other members of my dissertation committee, Scott Lewis, Judith Newman, and Dean Anderson. In particular, Dr. Anderson's very close reading saved me from numerous errors.

Dr. Glenn Holland was gracious enough to comment on an early draft of chapter 8. I appreciate his willingness to engage my work, and I hope to continue the conversation.

Supportive colleagues at Fresno Pacific University are too numerous to name. Still, I am especially grateful to Mark Baker and Brian Schultz for their counsel and encouragement in bringing this project to fruition. Special thanks also to my immediate colleagues in the Biblical and Religious Studies division, as well as to Tim Geddert of the FPU Biblical Seminary. Thanks also to Nicole Erickson for her assistance with indexing.

This research was supported by a Doctoral Fellowship from the Social Sciences and Humanities Research Council of Canada.

Finally, deepest thanks to Susan, who has been encouraging always, and always ready to celebrate milestones along the way.

Abbreviations

Abbreviations follow, in order of priority: Patrick H. Alexander et al., eds., *The SBL Handbook of Style: For Ancient Near Eastern, Biblical and Early Christian Studies* (Peabody, Mass.: Hendrickson, 1999); *L'Année philologique on the Internet*. Cited 14 July 2011. Online: http://www.annee-philologique.com; Simon Hornblower and Anthony Spawforth, *The Oxford Classical Dictionary* (3rd ed.; Oxford: Oxford University Press, 2003). Exceptions and additional abbreviations are provided below.

BSGRT	Bibliotheca scriptorum graecorum et romanorum teubneriana
ESEC	Emory Studies in Early Christianity
HTKNTSup	Herders theologischer Kommentar zum Neuen Testament Supplementband
LNTS	Library of New Testament Studies
PaSt	Pauline Studies
Colloquy	Protocol of the Colloquy of the Center for Hermeneutical Studies in Hellenistic and Modern Culture
RG	*Rhetores Graeci*. Edited by Leonhard von Spengel. 3 vols. BSGRT. Leipzig: Teubner, 1854–1885.
SBLECL	Society of Biblical Literature Early Christianity and Its Literature
SGLG	Sammlung griechischer und lateinisicher Grammatiker
SNTW	Studies of the New Testament and Its World
SSCFL	Studies in the Social and Cultural Foundations of Language
TCH	Transformation of the Classical Heritage
UTB	Uni-Taschenbüch für Wissenschaft
WGRW	Society of Biblical Literature Writings from the Greco-Roman World

WGRWSup   Society of Biblical Literature Writings from the Greco-Roman World Supplement Series
ZKNT   Zahn-Kommentar zum Neuen Testament

Introduction

A century ago now, Adolf Deissmann observed, "The older study of Paul with its one-sided interest in its bloodless, timeless paragraphs of the 'Doctrine' or the 'Theology' of Paul did not trouble itself about the problem of the social class of Paul."[1] Since that time, social-scientific methods have become standard fare in the guild, and study of the social history of early Christianity has proliferated: we have Malina and we have Meeks;[2] we have the Context Group; we cite the likes of Geertz, Bourdieu, and Mary Douglas. And what have we done with Paul?

In one sense, we have made significant progress. Recent studies of 1 Thessalonians and especially the Corinthian correspondence have highlighted the specific social and religious contexts addressed by Paul in each instance.[3] Paul's letters, such research emphasizes, are not disinterested theology; they represent instead his rhetorical engagement of particular social realities. Indeed, the last decade or two of Pauline scholarship generally could be characterized as the study of Paul's rhetoric in its social context.

---

1. Adolf Deissmann, *Paul: A Study in Social and Religious History* (trans. William E. Wilson; New York: Harper & Row, 1957), 47; orig. *Paulus: Eine kultur- und religionsgeschichtliche Skizze* (Tübingen: Mohr, 1911).

2. Bruce J. Malina, *The New Testament World: Insights from Cultural Anthropology* (3rd ed.; Louisville: Westminster John Knox, 2001); Wayne A. Meeks, *The First Urban Christians: The Social World of the Apostle Paul* (New Haven: Yale University Press, 1983).

3. On Thessalonians, see esp. Richard S. Ascough, "The Thessalonian Christian Community as a Professional Voluntary Association," *JBL* 119 (2000): 311–28; Ascough, *Paul's Macedonian Associations: The Social Context of Philippians and 1 Thessalonians* (WUNT 2/161; Tübingen: Mohr Siebeck, 2003). On Corinthians: Gerd Theissen, *The Social Setting of Pauline Christianity: Essays on Corinth* (trans. John H. Schütz; SNTW; Edinburgh: T&T Clark, 1982); Dale B. Martin, *The Corinthian Body* (New Haven: Yale University Press, 1995); Edward Adams and David G. Horrell, eds., *Christianity at Corinth: The Quest for the Pauline Church* (Louisville: Westminster John Knox, 2004).

But in one key respect it appears we are right where Deissmann left us: we have not sufficiently troubled ourselves about the problem of *Paul's* "social class"—or, to use language with less ideological baggage, Paul's place in ancient society. Indeed, although what we have learned about life in the cities of first-century Achaia and Asia Minor has certainly enriched our understanding of the so-called "Pauline communities," it has not had much influence on our conception of Paul himself. Paul now speaks into a social context, but the exigencies of his own existence are seldom explored.

And, paradoxically, it seems the study of Paul's social rhetoric is complicit in our failure to attend more carefully to his social location. Just as Deissmann bemoaned how Paul the human being was obscured by scholarly constructions of Paul the theologian, now it seems Paul the rhetorician cloaks whatever of the man himself might yet be uncovered. It is not Paul but Paul's rhetorical strategy that our work in this realm has sought, and so, in the absence of any explicitly articulated portrait, the man behind the text becomes, by default, a strategist, carefully selecting persuasive words in order to manage his converts from afar.[4]

"In no other of the Apostle's Epistles," said F. C. Baur of 2 Corinthians, "are we allowed to look deeper into the pure humanity of his character."[5] Yes, until the recent rise of rhetorical criticism, 2 Corinthians—and especially the "letter of tears" in 2 Cor 10–13—was read as an outburst of profound emotion.[6] Paul was dismayed and distraught, it was agreed, and the striking rhetorical features of 2 Cor 10–13 were considered artifacts of affect, the fossilized record of Paul's subjectivity at this one moment in time.

In contrast, recent treatments of the passage tend to leave the nature of Paul's own investment in the Corinthian community unremarked, focusing instead on his apparently dispassionate use of rhetorical strategies. Now Paul does not boast, he "uses boasting";[7] he does not plead, he "uses

---

4. See Colleen Shantz, *Paul in Ecstasy: The Neurobiology of the Apostle's Life and Thought* (Cambridge: Cambridge University Press, 2009), 209.

5. Ferdinand Christian Baur, *Paul the Apostle of Jesus Christ: His Life and Work, His Epistles and His Doctrine* (ed. Eduard Zeller; trans. Allan Menzies; 2 vols.; 2nd ed.; London: Williams & Norgate, 1876), 1:302. Cf. Frederic W. Farrar, *The Life and Work of St. Paul* (2 vols.; New York: Dutton, 1879), 2:99.

6. See further the first section of chapter 2 in the present volume.

7. Duane F. Watson, "Paul and Boasting," in *Paul in the Greco-Roman World: A Handbook* (ed. J. Paul Sampley; Harrisburg, Pa.: Trinity, 2003), 90.

many of the means rhetoricians recognized as ways to affect the πάθος of his hearers."⁸ What such readings accomplish, it is important to note, is the erasure of precisely that "humanity" that so fascinated Baur. Paul has been reduced to the sum of his rhetorical intentions.

Likewise, for example, in his analysis of Gal 4:19, where Paul appears to express anguished concern for his Galatian converts ("My little children, for whom I am again in the pain of childbirth until Christ is formed in you"), Troy Martin gives no consideration at all to Paul's experience of his relationship with the Galatian community or what it might tell us about Paul's social and religious subjectivity. No, Martin's Paul simply chooses "pathetic persuasion" as a "strategy" that allows him "to achieve his ends."⁹ Certainly this is one way to account for such a text, but it represents an interpretive decision—specifically, the decision to read Pauline discourse as a series of tactical maneuvers—that surely cannot go unexamined.

In practice, then, the last few decades of rhetorical criticism have facilitated the evasion of a whole set of questions concerning the nature of Pauline discourse—namely, all those questions that concern Paul himself as a human subject. In short, with the rise of rhetorical criticism Paul has gone from being a mind to being a mouth; we still pay scant attention to the rest of him.¹⁰ Indeed, despite all our effort to understand Paul's rhetoric, too often we ignore the fundamental problem: Who speaks?—or, if I may borrow the evocative question posed by Canadian novelist Rudy Wiebe, "Where is the voice coming from?"¹¹

---

8. Jerry L. Sumney, "Paul's Use of Πάθος in His Argument against the Opponents of 2 Corinthians," in *Paul and* Pathos (ed. Thomas H. Olbricht and Jerry L. Sumney; SBLSymS 16; Atlanta: Society of Biblical Literature, 2001), 159.

9. Troy W. Martin, "The Voice of Emotion: Paul's Pathetic Persuasion (Gal 4:12–20)," in *Paul and* Pathos (ed. Thomas H. Olbricht and Jerry L. Sumney; SBLSymS 16; Atlanta: Society of Biblical Literature, 2001), 201.

10. There are, as always, exceptions: e.g., Ronald F. Hock, *The Social Context of Paul's Ministry: Tentmaking and Apostleship* (Philadelphia: Fortress, 1980); John Ashton, *The Religion of Paul the Apostle* (New Haven: Yale University Press, 2000); David J. A. Clines, "Paul, the Invisible Man," in *New Testament Masculinities* (ed. Stephen D. Moore and Janice Capel Anderson; SemeiaSt 45; Atlanta: Society of Biblical Literature, 2003), 181–92; Jennifer A. Glancy, "Boasting of Beatings (2 Corinthians 11:23–25)," *JBL* 123 (2004): 99–135; Shantz, *Paul in Ecstasy*; and, of course, Deissmann, *Paul*.

11. Rudy Wiebe, *Where Is the Voice Coming From?* (Toronto: McClelland & Stewart, 1974).

Although he used the language of "social class," it was something akin to this question of voice that fascinated Deissmann: When we read the letters of Paul, he asked, do we find the sort of discourse we would expect from the likes of "Origin, Thomas Aquinas, and Schleiermacher," or do we rather hear a voice akin to "the herdman of Tekoa, the shoemaker of Görlitz, and the ribbon-weaver of Müllheim"?[12] For Deissmann, the answer was clear: "St. Paul's mission was the mission of an artisan, not the mission of a scholar."[13]

In contrast, the bulk of current scholarship argues—and often simply assumes—that Paul's discourse is most aptly compared to that of ancient philosophers and rhetors—a point adequately illustrated by a quick survey of titles currently on my bookshelf: *Philo and Paul among the Sophists*, *Paul and the Popular Philosophers*, *Der Apostel Paulus und die sokratische Tradition*, *Paul and Philodemus*, *Ancient Rhetoric and Paul's Apology*, and so forth. Implicit in such comparative studies is the notion that Paul's letters are, in essence, intellectual discourse.[14]

Bolstering this perspective—or perhaps deriving from it[15]—are recent claims that Paul was the beneficiary of formal education in classical rhetoric. What is more, it is this putative rhetorical education that now sponsors most assertions that Paul was a man of relatively high social status. Dale Martin's verdict illustrates the logic:

---

12. Adolf Deissmann, *Light from the Ancient East: The New Testament Illustrated by Recently Discovered Texts of the Graeco-Roman World* (trans. Lionel R. M. Strachan; London: Hodder & Stoughton, 1927), 381. The translator's note here is worth reproducing: "The prophet Amos is fairly recognizable, but English readers may be reminded that Jakob Böhme, the mystic, 1575–1624, lived and died at Görlitz, Gerhard Tersteegen, the devotional writer, 1697–1769, at Mülheim" (381 n. 2).

13. Ibid., 385.

14. The extent to which this is a reflection of our own discursive context is surely worthy of consideration. When Albert Schweitzer, for example, calls Paul "the patron saint of thought," one suspects that Paul has become—despite Schweitzer's own oft-cited warning against such projection in historical Jesus research—a cipher for his own self-understanding (*The Mysticism of Paul the Apostle* [trans. William Montgomery; London: Black, 1931], 377).

15. The circular nature of the implicit argument is noted by C. J. Classen: "Es wird vom Text ausgegangen, um auf die Bildung zu schließen, und dann das erschlossene Bildungsniveau genutzt, um den Text zu interpretieren" ("Kann die rhetorische Theorie helfen, das Neue Testament, vor allem die Briefe des Paulus, besser zu verstehen?" *ZNW* 100 [2009]: 155).

The best evidence for Paul's class background comes from his letters themselves. In the past several years, study after study has shown that Paul's letters follow common rhetorical conventions, certain rhetorical topoi, figures, and techniques, and are readily analyzable as pieces of Greco-Roman rhetoric. To more and more scholars … it is inconceivable that Paul's letters could have been written by someone uneducated in the rhetorical systems of his day. Paul's rhetorical education is evident on every page, and that education is one piece of evidence that he came from a family of relatively high status.[16]

As we will see in chapter 1, this conception of Paul's rhetorical ability represents a break with previous scholarly consensus. As Mark Edwards has quipped, "Commentators from the patristic era to the present have acknowledged that the New Testament teems with literary devices; only in recent years has it been customary to argue that the authors must have acquired these arts at school."[17] Paul's earliest exegetes simply could not imagine a tentmaker with rhetorical training. And although for nineteenth- and early twentieth-century scholars Paul's tentmaking was overshadowed by his prestigious Roman citizenship, still his letters sounded more like "rhetoric of the heart" than the careful compositions of an educated orator. Only in the last few decades have we seen confident claims that Paul was the recipient of a formal rhetorical education.

An initial problem with these claims is that much of the evidence adduced does not withstand careful scrutiny. Using as a test case 2 Cor 10–13, a text that is widely lauded for its creative manipulation of rhetorical conventions, part 2 of this study takes recent rhetorical criticism on its own terms and examines the credibility of its proposals. Here I demonstrate that many of the alleged parallels between Paul and the rhetoricians derive from superficial or misleading treatments of the rhetorical manuals and exemplars, and, further, do not adequately describe what we find in Paul. Those parallels that remain are few—I isolate four—and rather general; nevertheless, they do merit further explanation.

I seek to provide such explanation in part 3, where I examine the possibility that such figures, tropes, and rhetorical strategies as are found in Paul's letters derive not from formal education but from informal

---

16. Martin, *The Corinthian Body*, 52.
17. Mark J. Edwards, "Gospel and Genre: Some Reservations," in *The Limits of Ancient Biography* (ed. Brian McGing and Judith Mossman; Swansea: Classical Press of Wales, 2006), 51.

socialization. I am not the first to raise this possibility; indeed, its proponents represent a substantial minority among Pauline scholars, and it has been a persistent thorn in the flesh of those who would attribute to Paul a formal education in rhetoric. But it has not been examined critically, and thus assertions to this effect have amounted simply to that: assertions.

I get methodological leverage on this problem by using George Kennedy's work on comparative rhetoric as a starting point for a discussion of what he calls "general rhetoric"—that is, the basic human propensity for persuasive communication—and a description of its instantiation as an aspect of informal social practice. Important here is the sociolinguistic insight that it is not only or even primarily formal training that instills in speakers conventional patterns of language use. On the contrary, participation in particular speech communities necessarily involves and indeed inculcates competence in conventional "ways of speaking"[18]—that is, the ability appropriately to use established genres, forms, tropes, and figures. "Communicative competence," therefore, requires mastery not only of grammar but also of "a repertoire of speech acts"[19]—in other words, the ability to utilize what I will refer to as informal rhetoric.

This repertoire differs, of course, from one speech community to another. Nevertheless, as the work of Kennedy and others makes clear, there are a number of informal rhetorical features that are, if not universal, at least ubiquitous, recurring, albeit with local variation in usage and meaning, across a range of societies. Importantly, among these aspects of what Kennedy calls "general rhetoric" we find many of the same tropes and figures as those codified in the classical rhetorical tradition. Indeed, using diverse comparators from a variety of cultures, I demonstrate that the four rhetorical features identified in part 2 as being common to 2 Cor 10–13 and the formal classical tradition in fact belong to the domain of general rhetoric. Sensitivity to the inappropriateness of self-praise (what Plutarch called περιαυτολογία), use of warnings or disclaimers prior to potentially offensive speech (what the classical rhetorical tradition knows as προδιόρθωσις), strategic use of an interlocutor's voice (the broader strategy of which προσωποποιία is a single instance), and the use of figures

---

18. Dell Hymes, "Ways of Speaking," in *Explorations in the Ethnography of Speaking* (ed. Richard Bauman and Joel Sherzer; 2nd ed.; SSCFL 8; Cambridge: Cambridge University Press, 1989), 433–54.

19. Dell Hymes, "On Communicative Competence," in *Linguistic Anthropology: A Reader* (ed. Alessandro Duranti; 2nd ed.; Malden, Mass.: Blackwell, 2001), 60.

associated with "catalogue style" (figures known to rhetorical theorists as anaphora, isocolon, asyndeton, etc.) all are found in speakers who demonstrably have no formal rhetorical training. Accordingly, lacking specific indicators in the mode or manner of their use, their appearance in Paul's letters does not constitute evidence of formal rhetorical education. Yes, this is rhetoric, but there is no evidence that it is formal rhetoric.

There are, further, a number of positive indicators in 2 Cor 10–13 that Paul's voice should be located elsewhere—not least his own confession to that effect in 2 Cor 10:10 and 11:6. In addition to providing a detailed exegesis of these contested verses, chapter 12 addresses two key indicators that are often ignored in current scholarship. First, as patristic readers already recognized, Paul's train of thought frequently must be read into the text and his usage is sometimes suspect. Indeed, until the recent rise of rhetorical criticism, it was all but universally acknowledged that Paul's letters lacked rhetorical polish. Analysis of Paul's syntax in 2 Cor 10–13 shows why.

Second, Paul's "voice"—that is, his rhetorical comportment—differs tellingly from that cultivated among recipients of formal rhetorical education. Here I revisit a number of the comparators introduced in parts 2 and 3, attending to the way each voice negotiates his or her particular social location. In this regard, Paul does not resemble self-possessed aristocrats like Plutarch, Quintilian, or Demosthenes, or, for that matter, the Iroquois orator Red Jacket, who, though he received no formal education, occupied what was in one key way an analogous social location: he was accustomed to deference. Paul, on the contrary, speaks as one accustomed to ridicule, derision, and subjugation. His is an abject rhetoric, characterized by insecurity and self-abasement—and vigorous bursts of defiance.

I expect it will already be evident that in pursuing the argument outlined above I make a number of moves uncommon in New Testament scholarship, thus it may be useful to clarify from the outset precisely what it is I think I am doing. Parts 1 and 2 of this study are, although perhaps contrarian in content, perfectly conventional in their mode of argumentation: I take recent scholarship on Paul's rhetoric on its own terms, examining the viability of its claims by reassessing the very pool of evidence upon which it relies—namely, ancient rhetorical manuals and exemplars. My argument is historiographical, or, more precisely, philological and literary-critical, in the most traditional sense. On these grounds I demonstrate that the bulk of what has been taken as evidence in 2 Cor 10–13 for Paul's rhetorical education has in fact been misconstrued as such.

It is in part 3 that I seek to develop my own proposal for evaluating Paul's rhetorical "voice" and thus leave the conventional methodological domain of rhetorical criticism. Here I conspicuously and intentionally press beyond the mode of argumentation that has been prevalent in New Testament rhetorical scholarship.

First, and most basically, I expand the pool of evidence by adducing rhetorical performances that have no historical connection to the Greco-Roman tradition. This sort of move demands an explanation, since it runs counter to what is often considered a basic precept of rhetorical criticism as a historical discipline: If we intend to make historical claims about Paul's rhetoric, says Margaret Mitchell, we must study his letters "in the light of the Greco-Roman rhetorical tradition which was operative and pervasive at the time of the letter's composition."[20] Synchronic studies of Paul's rhetoric may be legitimate in their own right, but they are by definition ahistorical, and thus, Mitchell insists, should not be confused with historical criticism.[21] On what grounds, then, do I justify comparing Paul with the likes of Red Jacket, and, what is more, basing historical conclusions on such a comparison?

Mitchell's method represents the historiographical approach conventional among New Testament scholars, and certainly it has the appearance of rigor. In my view, however, the lacunae in our evidence finally make such an approach untenable. The rhetorical exemplars that have been preserved represent but a minute fragment of the rhetorical discourse of the ancient world, and belong almost exclusively to one rarefied corner thereof. We simply do not have the data we should need to construct a full taxonomy of ancient rhetorical practice; indeed, there are entire domains of human speech that elude the grasp of traditional philology. Therefore, we lack the comparative perspective that would allow us confidently to locate and describe the rhetoric of Paul's letters. Attempting to do so without acknowledging the inadequacy of our evidence is a dangerous procedure indeed. If we had no knowledge of other insects, it would not be surprising if we were to mistake a butterfly for a peculiar species of bird. We are apt to make a similar mistake, I suggest, if all we have with which to compare Paul's rhetoric are the performances of the Greco-Roman aris-

---

20. Margaret M. Mitchell, *Paul and the Rhetoric of Reconciliation: An Exegetical Investigation of the Language and Composition of 1 Corinthians* (HUT 28; Tübingen: Mohr Siebeck, 1991), 6.

21. Ibid., 7.

tocracy and their cultural retainers. In other words, given the state of the evidence, Mitchell's model provides no way of knowing what is particular to the formal Greco-Roman tradition; and, until we know what is particular to this tradition, we are in no position to determine the manner and extent of Paul's indebtedness to it.

Put another way, what confronts us here is a question of comparative method. As is adequately demonstrated by a glance at the studies listed above—*Der Apostel Paulus und die sokratische Tradition* et alia—the attempt to locate Paul's place in the ancient world necessarily involves comparison. But what, exactly, is the descriptive work such comparison accomplishes? And what are the theoretical assumptions that underlie it?

These questions seldom rise to the surface of the discussion, but it seems to be taken for granted in much New Testament scholarship, as in ancient historiography more generally, that a significant comparison is one that establishes a relationship of historical dependence. In other words, what we find probative is the mode of comparison Jonathan Z. Smith, following Deissmann, calls genealogical.[22] It is on account of this methodological presupposition that, whereas my comparison of Paul with Red Jacket is sure to be deemed idiosyncratic and thus demanding of an explanation, comparison of Paul with Plutarch, say, is seldom thought to require theoretical justification. Of course, this is not because Plutarch is thought to have influenced Paul directly; rather, the underlying logic is that similarities between Paul and Plutarch can be attributed to shared intellectual inheritance. In other words, both are located on the same branch of a history-of-ideas family tree, and we can establish the precise nature of their kinship by means of comparison.

But there is a fundamental problem with this genealogical mode of comparison, at least as usually practiced in the study of ancient history

---

22. On the distinction used herein between genealogical and analogical modes of comparison, see Deissmann, *Light from the Ancient East*, 265–66; Ashton, *Religion of Paul*, 11–22; Jonathan Z. Smith, *Drudgery Divine: On the Comparison of Early Christianities and the Religions of Late Antiquity* (CSJH; Chicago: University of Chicago Press, 1990), 46–53; Gregory D. Alles, *The Iliad, the Rāmāyaṇa, and the Work of Religion: Failed Persuasion and Religious Mystification* (Hermeneutics: Studies in the History of Religions; University Park: Pennsylvania State University Press, 1994), 4–7. A similar distinction is made, independently, it would seem, by Karel van der Toorn, "Parallels in Biblical Research: Purposes of Comparison," in *Proceedings of the Eleventh World Congress of Jewish Studies, Jerusalem, June 22–29, 1993: Division A, The Bible and Its World* (Jerusalem: World Union of Jewish Studies, 1994), 1–8.

and the New Testament, for embedded within it are unstated anthropological presuppositions that govern our conceptualization of the relationship between the extant sources and the ancient lives to which they attest—presuppositions that, being unexamined, inevitably do so anachronistically. In particular, we have failed to interrogate our conception of the role of literary activity in human societies, and to reflect on the specific social space it occupies within the broader phenomenon of human communication. We tend to operate with the assumption that this one realm of discourse serves as an adequate proxy for the whole. But what do we actually know when we know the literary sources of societies like those of the ancient Mediterranean?[23] In a discipline such as ours, the question surely merits consideration; and, to address it, we should need to undertake not genealogical but what Smith calls analogical comparison.[24] That is, we should need comparisons that enable us to establish adequate theoretical categories for conceptualizing those realms of human communication to which our sources do not directly attest.

What I am advocating, then, and attempting in this study, is an anthropologically informed extension of traditional historiographical methods. The particular oversight I seek to rectify concerns our conceptualization of the relationship between persuasive speech in Greco-Roman antiquity—the vast majority of which disappeared from the historical record immediately it was uttered—and the formal rhetorical tradition to which most of our sources attest. Until we have some notion of the relationship between these two domains, arguments regarding the nature of Paul's rhetoric proceed in anthropological—and therefore also historiographical—ignorance.

Within the confines of this study, it is not possible to provide a complete theorization of the problem I have named in the preceding paragraph. That would demand a much fuller discussion than can be attempted here. What I will offer, however, informed by recent work in sociolinguistics and comparative rhetoric, is a theoretical overview that provides a sufficient foundation for the more specific comparative task that constitutes the bulk of part 3—namely, a set of (analogical) comparisons that illuminate four

---

23. Cf. Justin J. Meggitt, "Sources: Use, Abuse and Neglect," in *Christianity at Corinth: The Scholarly Quest for the Corinthian Church* (ed. Edward Adams and David G. Horrell; Louisville: Westminster John Knox, 2004), 241–53.

24. See esp. Smith, *Drudgery Divine*, 50–53; Alles, *The Work of Religion*, 4–7.

specific rhetorical practices Pauline scholars otherwise have located in 2 Cor 10–13.

The comparators I introduce here have been selected on the basis of three simple criteria: each speaker is persuasive, in her or his own way; each lacks formal rhetorical education; and each makes at least one of the rhetorical moves Pauline scholars have identified in 2 Cor 10–13. But how, exactly, do these comparisons function? I understand them to accomplish three distinct but related tasks.

First, they falsify the logic by which scholars have inferred formal education from the resemblance between Paul's letters and ancient rhetorical theory and practice. To illustrate with an example, if Red Jacket, who demonstrably had no formal education in the classical rhetorical tradition, used *prodiorthōsis* as clearly as did Paul, then its appearance in Paul's letters cannot in itself serve as evidence of his formal rhetorical education. Since the resemblance between Red Jacket and formal Greco-Roman rhetoric in this regard evidently derives not from genealogy but from analogy—specifically, from an analogous response to a similar social exigency—we cannot deduce from Paul's use of *prodiorthōsis* the direct influence of rhetorical theory unless first we rule out the possibility that it too represents an analogical similarity—in other words, that it too derives from what Kennedy would call general rhetoric or attests to Paul's familiarity with an informal rhetorical tradition. Therefore, in order to conclude that Paul was directly dependent on formal rhetorical theory, it is not sufficient for us to observe that he uses *prodiorthōsis*; no, we should need also to identify specific indicators of formal education in the manner of Paul's use thereof. At the very least, his rhetorical usage would have to resemble the ancient exemplars more closely than does that of Red Jacket.[25]

But this set of comparisons does more than falsify the prevailing mode of argumentation; it also has a second and constructive role, providing an alternative context within which to conceptualize Paul's rhetoric. More precisely, having demonstrated the untenability of locating Paul's rhetoric within a particular genealogical context—namely, the formal tradition of classical rhetoric—I use comparison to establish for it an analogical context and thus to sponsor its redescription by means of the theoretical category of informal rhetoric.

---

25. On the comparative logic here, see further the final section of ch. 9 in this volume.

These comparisons shed indirect light, then, as if by refraction, on that for which we have little direct evidence—namely, the informal rhetoric of the ancient world. Or perhaps a better metaphor is that of triangulation: If individual rhetorical tropes and figures are found in our ancient sources and are also ubiquitous in other societies—and, specifically, those societies uninfluenced by the classical tradition—then we can deduce that they were characteristic not only of the formal rhetorical tradition but also of the informal rhetoric of the Greco-Roman world. Lacking direct evidence, we may be unable to describe with precision their use in Greco-Roman antiquity; however, our analogical data allow us to observe a range of informal usages and thus to map the possibilities. Since, again, we lack direct evidence, it is only thus, I submit, that we can locate the rhetoric of Paul.

Third, the comparisons I undertake in this study undergird my effort to describe what I will call Paul's "voice." Before elaborating on the nature of this final mode of comparison, it will be useful briefly to explain what I intend "voice" to indicate.[26] Here Pierre Bourdieu's conception of *habitus* provides a useful starting point: Like other modes of comportment, speech is structured by what Bourdieu refers to as "systems of durable, transposable dispositions" that represent the embodiment of social history.[27] Bourdieu refuses to ascribe significance to the comportment of individual subjects, preferring instead to speak of "structural variants,"[28] but of course he cannot deny the existence of individual difference: If comportment is, as Bourdieu insists, the embodiment of the history of social relations, and if, as he acknowledges, "it is impossible for all members of the same class (or even two of them) to have had the same experiences, in the same order,"[29] then no two individuals will comport themselves identically. Therefore, even after sociology (thus conceived) has done its explanatory work, during the process of which such individual difference is, as a matter of principle, ignored, we are left with a remainder of human behavior—a remainder that I, for one, find interesting, and think it worthwhile to describe, if not to explain.

---

26. For further discussion see the conclusion in this volume.
27. Pierre Bourdieu, *Outline of a Theory of Practice* (trans. Richard Nice; Cambridge Studies in Social Anthropology 16; Cambridge: Cambridge University Press, 1977), 72.
28. Ibid., 86.
29. Ibid., 85.

Thus, by speaking of Paul's voice I mean to indicate the discursive dispositions, correlative of his social location but also distinctly his own, that characterize his letters as artifacts of social practice. Paul's voice comes from Paul's body; Paul's body inhabits a particular social location, and it does so in its own peculiar way.

Those speakers selected as comparators in this study have a range of voices, as, of course, do the ancient rhetorical theorists and practitioners discussed in part 2. As I will emphasize, each seeks room to maneuver within the constraints of a given social location; each adopts a persuasive *ethos* that is available within those bounds. I use these diverse voices as a comparative sounding board, noting particular similarities and differences, in order to highlight specific characteristics of Paul's voice that tend otherwise to escape notice. What I undertake here, then, is the sort of "kaleidoscope-like" comparison that, says Smith, "gives the scholar a shifting set of characteristics with which to negotiate the relations between his or her theoretical interests and data stipulated as exemplary."[30]

Of course, my group of comparators by no means provides me with an exhaustive catalogue of rhetorical dispositions, nor do I attempt a thorough taxonomy. Instead, I attend to a few salient characteristics that arise from the comparisons themselves. Clearly, then, I cannot claim fully to describe Paul's voice; nevertheless, in the light of rhetorical criticism and using comparison as a lens, I do highlight significant and often neglected aspects of it. And, by doing so, I offer a challenge to prevailing views of Paul and his letters.

---

30. Smith, *Drudgery Divine*, 53.

Part 1
Paul's Rhetorical Education in Recent Scholarship

1
From Unschooled Tentmaker to Educated Rhetorician

For patristic interpreters, Paul's social location was uncontroversial: he was a tentmaker. Paul was not "distinguished by great ancestors," observed Chrysostom, "for how could he be, having such a trade?"[1] Moreover, Chrysostom and his peers had no difficulty inferring from Paul's trade his *paideia*—or, rather, his lack thereof: Paul was a "leatherworker (σκυτοτόμος), a poor laborer (πένης), ignorant (ἄπειρος) of outer wisdom" (*Hom. 2 Tim.* 4.3 [PG 62:622]); he was ἰδιώτης ... καὶ πένης καὶ ἄσημος (*Laud. Paul.* 4.13). Indeed, in the social imagination of Paul's early readers, to be a manual laborer was, by definition, to be devoid of learned culture (cf. Celsus 3.55).[2]

Modern scholarship has rejected this straightforward inference from Paul's trade of his social location and attendant education—though, as we will see, conclusions regarding his social location and his education have remained interdependent. For nineteenth- and early twentieth-century scholars, it was above all Paul's purported Roman citizenship that spon-

---

[1]. Chrysostom, *Laud. Paul.* 4.10 (trans. Mitchell). See also Chrysostom, *Scand.* 20.10; *Hom. 1 Cor.* 15.5 (PG 61:128); *Hom. 1 Cor.* 3.4 (PG 61:28); *Hom. Heb.* 1.2 (PG 63:16); *Stat.* 5.6 (PG 49:71); *Hom. 2 Tim.* 4.4 (PG 62:624); 5.2 (PG 62:626); Ps.-Chrysostom, *Hom. 2 Cor 12:9* 1 (PG 59:509); Gregory of Nyssa, *Ep.* 17.11; Theodoret, *Affect.* 5.67. Although I disagree with her conclusion regarding the implications for evaluating Paul's social location, I am heavily indebted to Margaret Mitchell's excellent treatment of Chrysostom on Paul's labor in *The Heavenly Trumpet: John Chrysostom and the Art of Pauline Interpretation* (HUT 40; Tübingen: Mohr Siebeck, 2000), 240–48, 374–77.

[2]. On patristic evaluation of Paul's social status, see further the third section of ch. 12 below and my "τὸ ἐν λόγῳ ἰδιωτικὸν τοῦ Ἀποστόλου: Revisiting Patristic Testimony on Paul's Rhetorical Education," *NovT* 54 (2012): 354–68.

sored the argument—or, more often, the assumption—that he possessed significantly higher status than his earliest readers imagined. Still, unlike many rhetorical critics of recent years, these scholars generally concurred with patristic exegetes that Paul's letters did not display the marks of a formal education in rhetoric.

"No Mere Tentmaker"

As Deissmann complained, the scholarship of his time had little to say about Paul's social location. But since these scholars were interested in Paul's upbringing for other reasons—primarily as a means of gaining leverage on the pressing Jewish Paul versus Hellenistic Paul debate—they often included a short evaluation of the evidence for the social level of his family. Though often frustratingly vague,[3] these paragraphs ran along consistent lines. Indeed, the same argument appears almost invariably until at least the 1950s: although his work as an artisan might seem to suggest a life of poverty, Paul was a Roman citizen, and thus must have come from a notable family.[4]

---

3. So, e.g., William Wrede: "Die soziale Schicht, der sie angehörte, dürfen wir nicht hoch, aber auch nicht allzu niedrig denken" (*Paulus* [2nd ed.; Tübingen: Mohr Siebeck, 1907], 5).

4. Most famously W. M. Ramsay: "According to the law of his country, he was first of all a Roman citizen. That character superseded all others before the law and in the general opinion of society; and placed him amid the aristocracy of any provincial town" (*St. Paul the Traveller and the Roman Citizen* [London: Hodder & Stoughton, 1895], 30–31). For Theodor Mommsen, "Dass er, wenngleich ein gelernter Handwerker, einem ansehnlichen Bürgerhaus angehörte, geht daraus hervor, dass er von Kind auf die römische Civität gehabt hat; denn nur die hervorragenden Municipalen wurden in dieser Weise ausgezeichnet" ("Die Rechtsverhältnisse des Apostels Paulus," ZNW 2 [1901]: 82). So also Adolf Jülicher, *Einleitung in das Neue Testament* (5th & 6th ed.; Grundriss der theologischen Wissenschaften 3.1; Tübingen: Mohr Siebeck, 1906), 25; Olaf Moe, *The Apostle Paul: His Life and His Work* (trans. L. A. Vigness; Grand Rapids: Baker, 1968), 34; Edgar J. Goodspeed, *Paul* (Nashville: Abingdon, 1947), 5. Often no explicit argument relating Paul's citizenship to his aristocratic status is made, yet a note regarding his citizenship stands beside and lends credibility to an otherwise unsupported claim of high-class origins. So Karl Adam: "Die Familie des Paulus besass ausserdem das römische Bürgerrecht und gehörte den begüterten und angesehenen Kreisen an" ("Der Junge Paulus," in *Paulus-Hellas-Oikumene: An Ecumenical Symposium* [Athens: Student Christian Association of Greece, 1951], 12). Similarly, Anon., *The Life and Travels of the Apostle Paul* (Boston: Lilly, Wait, Colman

Nineteenth- and early twentieth-century scholarship generally acknowledged that Paul's manual labor appeared to indicate low-status origins but avoided this conclusion in one of two ways. First, scholars adduced rabbinic texts that commended the learning of a trade—either as a child (*t. Qidd.* 1:11) or combined with study of Torah (*m. 'Abot* 2:2)—and concluded that a well-to-do Pharisee learning to make tents was simply abiding by Jewish convention.[5] F. W. Farrar's treatment is typical:

> As the making of these *cilicia* was unskilled labour of the commonest sort, the trade of tentmaker was one both lightly esteemed and miserably paid. It must not, however, be inferred from this that the family of St. Paul were people of low position. The learning of a trade was a duty enjoined by the Rabbis on the parents of every Jewish boy.[6]

Building on Jacob Neusner's reevaluation of the rabbinic traditions,[7] Ronald Hock discredited this line of interpretation as retrojection of sec-

---

& Holden, 1833), 16–17; Eduard Meyer, *Ursprung und Anfänge des Christentums* (3 vols.; Stuttgart: Cotta, 1923), 1:308; F. J. Foakes-Jackson, *The Life of Saint Paul: The Man and the Apostle* (New York: Boni & Liveright, 1926), 63–64; A. D. Nock, *St. Paul* (London: Butterworth, 1938), 21; Josef Holzner, *Paul of Tarsus* (trans. Frederic C. Eckhoff; St. Louis: Herder, 1946), 14; Alfred Wikenhauser, *New Testament Introduction* (trans. Joseph Cunningham; New York: Herder & Herder, 1958), 352–53; Hans Lietzmann, "Paulus," in *Das Paulusbild in der neueren deutschen Forschung* (ed. Karl Heinrich Rengstorf; Wege der Forschung 24; Darmstadt: Wissenschaftliche Buchgesellschaft, 1964), 381.

5. This interpretation is as old as Bengal, *Gnomon of the New Testament* (trans. Andrew R. Fausset; 7th ed.; 2 vols.; Edinburgh: T&T Clark, 1873), 2:671; orig. *Gnomon Novi Testamenti* (Tübingen: Schrammii, 1742). So also Max Krenkel, *Paulus: Der Apostel der Heiden* (Leipzig: Duncker & Humblot, 1869), 11, 217–18; Adolf Hausrath, *A History of New Testament Times: The Time of the Apostles* (trans. L. Huxley; 4 vols.; London: Williams & Norgate, 1895), 3:44–45; Jülicher, *Einleitung*, 25; Anon., *Life and Travels*, 17; H. J. Holtzmann, *Die Apostelgeschichte* (3rd ed.; Hand-Commentar zum Neuen Testament 1.2; Tübingen: Mohr Siebeck, 1901), 114; Hans Hinrich Wendt, *Die Apostelgeschichte* (9th ed.; KEK 3; Göttingen: Vandenhoeck & Ruprecht, 1913), 263; F. J. Foakes-Jackson, *The Acts of the Apostles* (MNTC 5; London: Hodder & Stoughton, 1931), 170; Nock, *St. Paul*, 21–22; Goodspeed, *Paul*, 11–12; Martin Dibelius, *Paul* (ed. Werner Georg Kümmel; trans. Frank Clarke; Philadelphia: Westminster, 1953), 37.

6. Farrar, *St. Paul*, 1:23.

7. Jacob Neusner, *The Rabbinic Traditions about the Pharisees before 70* (3 vols.; Leiden: Brill, 1971).

ond-century ideals onto the pre-70 Judean world.⁸ It generally, and rightly, has been discarded.⁹

A second way of ameliorating the status implications of Paul's manual labor was subtler: Paul's father was portrayed not as a laborer, but rather as the owner of the shop—a "well-to-do cloth merchant and tentmaker."¹⁰ Thus Paul's knowledge of the trade could be easily explained: "There is nothing improbable if his father were wealthy, that the son should learn the practical part of the business."¹¹ Although such argumentation persists,¹² it is obviously fueled not by its inherent probability but rather by scholars' prior conclusion on other grounds that Paul was not brought up a "mere artisan."¹³

One factor here is surely Luke's portrait of Paul the citizen of Rome and Tarsus (Acts 21:39; 22:25–29; 23:27). Luke's Paul is evidently a man of elevated status:¹⁴ he is always aristocratically self-possessed;¹⁵ he comfort-

---

8. Hock, *Social Context*, 22–23. Cf. Wolfgang Stegemann, "War der Apostel Paulus ein römischer Bürger?" *ZNW* 78 (1987): 228. Indeed, not only the notion of combining Torah study with labor, but the whole construct of "rabbinic education" that fuels the notion of Paul as a budding young Torah scholar has been shown by Catherine Hezser to result from "uncritical understanding of later Talmudic texts which are … anachronistic in associating the educational institutions of the amoraic period with pre-70 times" (*Jewish Literacy in Roman Palestine* [TSAJ 81; Tübingen: Mohr Siebeck, 2001], 39).

9. But see Martin Hengel, *The Pre-Christian Paul* (trans. John Bowden; London: SCM, 1991), 16–17; Rainer Riesner, *Paul's Early Period: Chronology, Mission Strategy, Theology* (trans. Doug Stott; Grand Rapids: Eerdmans, 1998), 154–55; Udo Schnelle, *Apostle Paul: His Life and Theology* (trans. Eugene M. Boring; Grand Rapids: Baker Academic, 2005), 61; Joachim Gnilka, *Paulus von Tarsus: Apostel und Zeuge* (HTKNT-Sup 6; Freiburg: Herder, 1996), 25.

10. Holzner, *Paul of Tarsus*, 14. Cf. Foakes-Jackson, *Acts*, 170; Meyer, *Ursprung und Anfänge*, 1:308.

11. Foakes-Jackson, *Acts*, 170.

12. Ronald Dubay, "Paul, Citizen and Prince" (Ph.D. diss., University of California, Irvine, 2009), 22; Hengel, *Pre-Christian Paul*, 15; Bruce Chilton, *Rabbi Paul: An Intellectual Biography* (New York: Doubleday, 2004), 12–13.

13. The phrase is from Foakes-Jackson, *Acts*, 169.

14. John Clayton Lentz, *Luke's Portrait of Paul* (SNTSMS 77; Cambridge: Cambridge University Press, 1994); Jerome H. Neyrey, "Luke's Social Location of Paul: Cultural Anthropology and the Status of Paul in Acts," in *History, Literature, and Society in the Book of Acts* (ed. Ben Witherington; Cambridge: Cambridge University Press, 1996), 268–76; Neyrey, "'Teaching You in Public and from House to House' (Acts 20.20): Unpacking a Cultural Stereotype," *JSNT* 26 (2003): 69–102; Robert L. Brawley,

ably converses with the likes of Felix and Festus;[16] he capably addresses the Athenians in the Areopagus (Acts 17:16–34). Such a man could only have been a tentmaker incidentally. And, indeed, this is precisely how Luke, like many subsequent biographers, deals with Paul's labor: he mentions it in passing (Acts 18:3).[17]

What was ultimately at stake in the marginalization of Paul's labor—in nineteenth-century discussions and perhaps in Luke's portrait as well—is apparent in the telling evaluation of Conybeare and Howson, who remain unusually agnostic as to the economic status of Paul's family of origin, but leave no doubt as to its "respectability":

"Paul in Acts: Lucan Apology and Conciliation," in *Luke-Acts: New Perspectives from the Society of Biblical Literature* (ed. C. H. Talbert; New York: Crossroad, 1984), 139–40; Richard I. Pervo, *Profit with Delight: The Literary Genre of the Acts of the Apostles* (Philadelphia: Fortress, 1987), 77–81.

15. See esp. Paul's deportment in Acts 27, and the comments thereon by Lentz, *Luke's Portrait of Paul*, 94–95; Ernst Haenchen, *The Acts of the Apostles: A Commentary* (trans. Bernard Noble and Gerald Shinn; Oxford: Blackwell, 1971), 710–11; Ramsay, *St. Paul the Traveller*, 332–33.

16. See Neyrey, "Luke's Social Location of Paul," 260–62; Lentz, *Luke's Portrait of Paul*, 156–57. Note also Steven J. Friesen, "Paul and Economics: The Jerusalem Collection as an Alternative to Patronage," in *Paul Unbound: Other Perspectives on the Apostle* (ed. Mark D. Given; Peabody, Mass.: Hendrickson, 2010), 42–45.

17. Although the accuracy of Luke's portrait has been defended vigorously (e.g., F. F. Bruce, "Is the Paul of Acts the Real Paul?," *BJRL* 58 [1976]: 282–305; Stanley E. Porter, *Paul in Acts* [Library of Pauline Studies; Peabody, Mass.: Hendrickson, 2001], 187–206), there remain striking differences between the Paul of Acts and the Paul of the letters. (For a convenient summary, see Richard I. Pervo, *The Making of Paul: Constructions of the Apostle in Early Christianity* [Minneapolis: Fortress, 2010], 150; for a cautious recent study, see Thomas E. Phillips, *Paul, His Letters, and Acts* [Library of Pauline Studies; Peabody, Mass.: Hendrickson, 2009].) To give an example relevant to the text here under discussion, can we imagine Luke's Paul being treated by his converts with anything other than unwavering deference? Luke, at least, does not. As Lentz suggests (*Luke's Portrait of Paul*, 171–72), it appears that Luke's honorable Paul is part of the apologetic—or, better, "propagandistic" (Pervo, *Profit with Delight*, 79)—fabric of his narrative, which portrays Christianity as a respectable religion with ancient roots and honorable adherents. Perhaps Luke's Paul functions as a metonym for his idealizing depiction of Christianity in his own time: his accusers are either envious Jews or the troublemaking rabble—they are not to be credited; governors, however, recognize him as respectable and virtuous, if not altogether benign. In any case, for the purposes of this study, I am concerned only with Paul as attested by his undisputed letters.

Whatever might be the station and employment of his father or his kinsmen, whether they were elevated by wealth above, or depressed by poverty below, the average of the Jews of Asia Minor and Italy, we are disposed to believe that this family were possessed of that highest respectability which is worthy of deliberate esteem.[18]

We will do well to watch for signs of this subtext—the need for a respectable Paul—in current scholarship as well.

"Kein Klassiker, kein Hellenist hat so geschrieben"

Along with an honorable family, a respectable education was almost universally assumed in nineteenth- and early twentieth-century studies. Thus any debate concerned not whether Paul was well educated, but whether his education was Jewish or Hellenistic in orientation:[19] for advocates of a "Hebraist" Paul like F. W. Farrar, Paul spent his formative years as a rabbinical student;[20] for those, like Hans Böhlig, who emphasized Hellenistic influences, Paul had eagerly imbibed the Greek learning for which Tarsus was famous.[21] W. C. van Unnik's *Tarsus or Jerusalem* stands as a fitting testament to this discussion: the assumption throughout is that Paul was a budding young scholar; the only question is where he studied.[22]

---

18. W. J. Conybeare and J. S. Howson, *The Life and Epistles of St. Paul* (new ed.; London: Longmans & Green, 1870), 39–40. Note here the more recent suggestion of Martin Hengel: "Here we may with justification speak of 'lay nobility by birth,' even if his family was not very rich" (*Pre-Christian Paul*, 17).

19. This is evident from even the title of an early treatment of the question: Christian Wilhelm Thalemann, "De eruditione Pauli apostoli Iudaica, non Graeca" (diss., Leipzig, 1708).

20. Farrar, *St. Paul*, 1:44–45. So also Anon., *Life and Travels*, 16–17; Charles R. Ball, *The Apostle of the Gentiles: His Life and Letters* (London: SPCK, 1885), 9–10; Holzner, *Paul of Tarsus*, 1–22; Conybeare and Howson, *St. Paul*, 49–52, 56–63; Goodspeed, *Paul*, 10; Nock, *St. Paul*, 21–27; Moe, *Apostle Paul*, 47–50. The durability of this image is evident from, e.g., Chilton, *Rabbi Paul*, 1–27.

21. Hans Böhlig, *Die Geisteskultur von Tarsos im augusteischen Zeitalter: Mit Berücksichtigung der paulinischen Schriften* (FRLANT 2/2; Göttingen: Vandenhoeck & Ruprecht, 1913), 153. Cf. Alphons A. Steinmann, *Zum Werdegang des Paulus: Die Jugendzeit in Tarsus* (Freiburg: Herder, 1928). R. Reitzenstein proposed that Paul took up the study of Greek texts after his commissioning as apostle to the Gentiles (*Die hellenistischen Mysterienreligionen nach ihren Grundgedanken und Wirkungen* [3rd ed.; Leipzig: Teubner, 1927], 419).

22. W. C. van Unnik, *Tarsus or Jerusalem, the City of Paul's Youth* (trans. George

Nevertheless, the possibility of a specifically *rhetorical* education was seldom raised[23]—and, given the prevailing evaluation of Paul's compositional style, this is perhaps not surprising. Throughout this period, there was wide agreement among biblical scholars and classicists alike that Paul's prose was not sophisticated. Eduard Norden's famous formulation—"der Rhetorik des Herzens in ungefeilter Sprache"—expressed the prevailing judgment.[24] Indeed, even Johannes Weiss and C. F. G. Heinrici, cited by advocates of rhetorical criticism as forebears of the method, were well aware of the peculiarity of Paul's diction.

Weiss concurred with his predecessors that Paul had an "eminently personal style," notable above all for its "directness."[25] However, he questioned the consensus that Paul's writings therefore represented a wholly artless outpouring of powerful emotions—a view, he suggested, that was based solely on impressionistic sketches.[26] Weiss himself was fascinated by the rhythmic properties of Paul's letters, which, he asserted, must be read

---

Ogg; London: Epworth, 1962). Similarly Klaus Haacker, "Zum Werdegang des Apostels Paulus: Biographische Daten und ihre theologische Relevanz," *ANRW* 26.2:852–60; Hengel, *Pre-Christian Paul*, 18–62; Raymond A. Martin, *Studies in the Life and Ministry of the Early Paul and Related Issues* (Lewiston, N.Y.: Mellen Biblical Press, 1993), 7–102.

23. For a notable exception, see Johannes Weiss, *Earliest Christianity: A History of the Period A.D. 30–150* (ed. Rudolf Knopf; trans. Frederick C. Grant; 2 vols.; New York: Harper & Row, 1959), 1:183–84. Cf. Farrar, *St. Paul*, 1:625–30. Also worth noting is a 1961 article by Robert M. Grant wherein he seeks to trace Hellenistic influences in 1 Corinthians. Commenting on 1 Cor 13, Grant concludes with a prolepsis of the argument that would become prominent in coming decades: "The rhetorical skill with which Paul has worked out his clauses and his sentences in this chapter is by no means spontaneous. It reflects a careful study either of rhetorical manuals or of some literary model or models" ("Hellenistic Elements in 1 Corinthians," in *Early Christian Origins: Studies in Honor of Harold R. Willoughby* [ed. Allen Paul Wikgren; Chicago: Quadrangle, 1961], 65).

24. Eduard Norden, *Die antike Kunstprosa vom VI. Jahrhundert V. Chr. bis in die Zeit der Renaissance* (5th ed.; 2 vols.; Stuttgart: Teubner, 1958), 2:502: "the rhetoric of the heart in unpolished language." See further ch. 12 below.

25. Weiss, *Earliest Christianity*, 2:400.

26. Johannes Weiss, "Beiträge zur Paulinischen Rhetorik," in *Theologische Studien* (ed. Caspar René Gregory; Göttingen: Vandenhoeck & Ruprecht, 1897), 165. See, however, his comments on 1 Cor 13: "This work of art came into existence as a result of the deepest reflection and through the impetus of an almost unconscious feeling for form and literary style" (Weiss, *Earliest Christianity*, 2:407).

"with the ear."²⁷ So although he could not deny that Paul's prose lacked the elegant periodic structure of the Greek classics, Weiss insisted that it nevertheless had artistic qualities: "Was dem Paulus so an Kunstprosa fehlt, ersetzt er, wenigstens in den sorgfältiger geschriebenen Briefen, durch eine gewisse rhetorische Bewegung, die entschieden packend und häufig durch Symmetrie, Rhythmus, Schwung und Vollklang nicht unkünstlerisch wirkt."²⁸

Weiss sought to demonstrate that Paul's particular style derived from two well-balanced influences, the "Cynic-Stoic diatribe" on the one hand and the Jewish Scriptures on the other.²⁹ To account for this, he posited that Paul received instruction from "a Jewish rhetorician with a Hellenistic education."³⁰ Tellingly, though, Weiss made the jump from observation of stylistic affinities to assertion of formal education not by carefully comparing Paul with the rhetorical sources—something he advocated but never undertook³¹—but rather on the basis of his general incredulity that an uneducated person could write such compelling letters: "More than an elementary education is needed for the simplest English essay that will be readable; how much more then is needed for works of permanent spiritual and literary importance."³² But surely this is the sort of assertion that needs to be tested; otherwise, despite all his commendable sensitivity to the characteristics of Paul's style, Weiss's argument concerning Paul's education reduces to a Western academic conceit.

Heinrici was not persuaded by Weiss's argument. Although he agreed that various rhetorical devices could be detected in Paul's letters, for Heinrici the assumption that Paul employed them self-consciously was unwarranted.³³ Moreover, he felt that Weiss told only one side of the story,

---

27. Weiss, "Beiträge zur Paulinischen Rhetorik," 166.
28. Ibid., 167: "What Paul lacks in artistic prose, he replaces, at least in the carefully written letters, with a certain rhetorical movement, which is definitely compelling, and frequently, through symmetry, rhythm, liveliness, and resonance, has a not inartistic effect."
29. Ibid., 167–68.
30. Weiss, *Earliest Christianity*, 184. On this suggestion, see now Hengel, *Pre-Christian Paul*, 18–62; Andrew W. Pitts, "Hellenistic Schools in Jerusalem and Paul's Rhetorical Education," in *Paul's World* (ed. Stanley E. Porter; PaSt 4; Leiden: Brill, 2008), 19–50.
31. Weiss, "Beiträge zur Paulinischen Rhetorik," 165–67.
32. Weiss, *Earliest Christianity*, 183.
33. C. F. Georg Heinrici, *Der zweite Brief an die Korinther: Mit einem Anhang,*

and thus produced superficial and misleading analogies. Weiss neglected, for example, to observe the striking difference between what Heinrici considered Paul's *volkstümlich* use of the chreia and the formal usage recommended by the teachers of rhetoric.[34]

Like Weiss, Heinrici did assert the relevance of an understanding of ancient rhetoric for interpreting Paul's epistles, but this was not because Paul was rhetorically trained.[35] Rather, he suggested that a scholar sensitive to ancient speech patterns would be better equipped to recognize Paul's cogeniality or affinity with the Hellenistic milieu in which he lived.[36] So, after providing a summary of the rhetorical devices and *Klangfiguren* (figures of sound) in 2 Cor 10–13, Heinrici concluded: "Aber all' diese Momente geben dem Abschnitte nicht den Eindruck einer abgecirkelten Prunkrede; der Fluss ist natürlich, mancher Ausdruck verletzend und gewöhnlich. … Sie erwächst ihm aus der Sache, aus der inneren Ergriffenheit von seiner Aufgabe."[37] In the end, then, Heinrici's evaluation of Paul's style is not unlike Norden's:

> Des Paulus Stil ist individuell und packend. … Kein Klassiker, kein Hellenist hat so geschrieben, auch kein Kirchenvater. Der von seinem Herrn überwältigte hellenistische Jude steht für sich da. Seine Ausdrucksweise ist nicht durch Nachahmung ($\mu i\mu\eta\sigma\iota\varsigma$) bedingt, sondern durch die ursprüngliche plastische Kraft seiner Gedankenbildung.[38]

Zum Hellenismus des Paulus (8th ed.; KEK 6; Göttingen: Vandenhoeck & Ruprecht, 1900), 457–58.

34. Ibid., 442.

35. Ibid., 39: "Ich … sonst aufmerksam gemacht, ohne ein Missverständnis darüber offen zu lassen, dass ich P[aulus] nicht als studirten Gerichts-, Prunk- oder Lehrrhetor fasse."

36. Ibid., 39–41, 314, 437. Note Heinrici's awareness that rhetorical sensitivity is something the *scholar* brings to the table: "Wer die virtuos ausgebildeten Methoden und die technisch festgelegten Ueberzeugungsmittel ($\kappa o\iota\nu\alpha\grave{\iota}\ \pi\acute{\iota}\sigma\tau\epsilon\iota\varsigma$) der antiken Rhetorik kennt, wird sowohl durch das ganze, wie auch im einzelnen vielfach an sie erinnert, so fern auch des P[aulus] Weise von jeder schulmässigen Entlehnung oder Nachahmung ist" (39).

37. Ibid., 314: "But all these elements do not give the passage the impression of a calculated eloquence; the flow is natural, many an expression offensive and common. … It arises from the subject at hand, from the inner emotion of his task."

38. Ibid., 453: "Paul's style is unique and compelling. … No classicist, no Hellenist has written thus, nor any church father. The Hellenistic Jew, overpowered by his Lord, stands alone. His mode of expression is not determined by imitation (*mimēsis*), but by

Paul, the Educated Rhetorician

It would be an exaggeration to say that current scholarship has reached a consensus on Paul's social location. Still, the pattern is clear, and, despite our greater sophistication in social-scientific theory, our conclusions differ little from those reached in the nineteenth century: Paul is still of "relatively high status,"[39] and we continue to insist that his manual labor is not

---

the original, versatile power of his thought process." See also Heinrici, *Der litterarische Charakter der neutestamentlichen Schriften* (Leipzig: Dürr, 1908), 65–66.

39. So Martin, *The Corinthian Body*, 52. For Bruce Longenecker, Paul belonged with the likes of Erastus, Gaius, and Phoebe at "ES4" on his "economy scale"—that is, enjoying a "moderate surplus" of resources—prior to the intentional "downward mobility" he undertook as an apostle in order to identify with the poor to whom he proclaimed the gospel (*Remember the Poor: Paul, Poverty, and the Greco-Roman World* [Grand Rapids: Eerdmans, 2010], 301–10). Elsewhere Paul is, e.g., the "offspring of better-situated diaspora Jews" (Jürgen Becker, *Paul: Apostle to the Gentiles* [trans. O. C. Dean; Louisville: Westminster/John Knox, 1993], 36; cf. F. F Bruce, *Paul, Apostle of the Heart Set Free* [Grand Rapids: Eerdmans, 1977], 36; Gnilka, *Paulus von Tarsus*, 25–26), a "retainer" (Neyrey, "Social Location of Paul"), or even an "aristocrat" (Jerome Murphy-O'Connor, *Paul: A Critical Life* [Oxford: Oxford University Press, 1997], 40–41; Ronald F. Hock, "The Problem of Paul's Social Class: Further Reflections," in *Paul's World* [ed. Stanley E. Porter; PaSt 4; Leiden: Brill, 2008], 40–41). See, similarly, Theissen, *Social Setting*, 36; Morna D. Hooker, *Paul: A Short Introduction* (Oxford: Oneworld, 2003), 19; Ben Witherington, *The Paul Quest: The Renewed Search for the Jew of Tarsus* (Downers Grove, Ill.: InterVarsity, 1998), 70, 89–129; Brian Rapske, *The Book of Acts and Paul in Roman Custody* (vol. 3 of *The Book of Acts in Its First Century Setting*; ed. Bruce W. Winter; Grand Rapids: Eerdmans, 1994), 71–112; Nils A. Dahl, *Studies in Paul: Theology for the Early Christian Mission* (Minneapolis: Augsburg, 1977), 35; Bert Jan Lietaert Peerbolte, "Paul and the Practice of *Paideia*," in *Jesus, Paul, and Early Christianity: Studies in Honour of Henk Jan de Jonge* (ed. Rieuwerd Buitenwerf, Harm W. Hollander, and Johannes Tromp; NovTSup 130; Leiden: Brill, 2008), 261–62. Some have him a little lower on the scale—a member of the "urban middle class" (Schnelle, *Apostle Paul*, 63; E. P. Sanders, *Paul*, Past Masters [Oxford: Oxford University Press, 1991], 10–11) or an independent artisan (Hengel, *Pre-Christian Paul*, 17; Meeks, *First Urban Christians*, 9, 64). Anthony Saldarini locates him "on the border of the upper and lower classes" (*Pharisees, Scribes and Sadducees in Palestinian Society: A Sociological Approach* [Biblical Resource Series; Grand Rapids: Eerdmans, 2001], 141. Those who insist that Paul's status as a laborer decisively places him among the lower strata include Calvin J. Roetzel, *Paul: The Man and the Myth* (Studies on Personalities of the New Testament; Columbia: University of South Carolina Press, 1998), 23–24; Justin J. Meggitt, *Paul, Poverty and Survival* (SNTW; Edinburgh: T&T Clark, 1998), 75–97; Wolfgang Stegemann, "Zwei sozialgeschichtliche Anfragen an unser Paulusbild," *Der*

indicative of his social standing.[40] However, whereas for older scholarship it was Paul's putative Roman citizenship that sponsored such arguments, it is now Paul's rhetorical education that is seen as the key to understanding his social location.

As the following discussion will demonstrate, assertions that Paul received a formal rhetorical education have relied almost exclusively on the observation of rhetorical features in his letters. (A noteworthy exception, which avoids the difficulties inherent in this approach, is C. J. Classen's "Philologische Bemerkungen zur Sprache des Apostels Paulus";[41] however, as I have argued at length elsewhere, the evidence Classen adduces that Paul uses formal rhetorical terminology is too meager to be convincing.)[42] In its basic form, the prevailing argument consists of two propositions:

(1) Paul's letters can be analyzed according to the dictates of Greco-Roman rhetoric; therefore, Paul was well educated in rhetoric.
(2) Rhetorical education was available only among the wealthy elite; therefore, Paul was brought up among the elite.[43]

---

evangelische Erzieher 37 (1985): 480–90; Stegemann, "War der Apostel Paulus ein römischer Bürger?"; Simon Légasse, *Paul apôtre: Essai de biographie critique* (2nd ed.; Paris: Cerf, 2000), 49.

40. See esp. Ronald F. Hock, "Paul's Tentmaking and the Problem of his Social Class," *JBL* 97 (1978): 555–64; Hock, "Paul's Social Class"; Heike Omerzu, *Der Prozeß des Paulus: Eine exegetische und rechtshistorische Untersuchung der Apostelgeschichte* (BZNW 115; Berlin: de Gruyter, 2002), 45–47. And note the mode of argumentation in Haacker, "Werdegang des Apostels Paulus," *ANRW* 26.2:831; Ben Witherington, *Conflict and Community in Corinth: A Socio-Rhetorical Commentary on 1 and 2 Corinthians* (Grand Rapids: Eerdmans, 1995), 20–21; Schnelle, *Apostle Paul*, 62–63; Hooker, *Paul*, 19; Murphy-O'Connor, *Paul: A Critical Life*, 40–41; Martin, *The Corinthian Body*, xv–xvi; Gnilka, *Paulus von Tarsus*, 25; Tor Vegge, *Paulus und das antike Schulwesen: Schule und Bildung des Paulus* (BZNW 134; Berlin: de Gruyter, 2006), 452–55.

41. Carl Joachim Classen "Philologische Bemerkungen zur Sprache des Apostels Paulus," *Wiener Studien* 107/108 (1994–1995): 321–35; repr. in *Rhetorical Criticism of the New Testament* (WUNT 128; Tübingen: Mohr Siebeck, 2000).

42. Ryan S. Schellenberg, "Rhetorical Terminology in Paul: A Critical Reappraisal," *ZNW* 104 (2013): 177–91.

43. See Martin, *The Corinthian Body*, 51–52; Longenecker, *Remember the Poor*, 306–7; Witherington, *The Paul Quest*, 70, 89–129; Witherington, *Conflict and Community in Corinth*, 20–21; Schnelle, *Apostle Paul*, 63; Murphy-O'Connor, *Paul: A Critical Life*, 40, 47–51; Hengel, *Pre-Christian Paul*, 17. More tentative is Abraham J. Mal-

Whatever one makes of the second proposition, the first is clearly problematic. In short, to anticipate my argument in part 3, it provides no theoretical space for conceptualizing rhetoric as informal social practice, and thus fallaciously equates rhetoric with formal rhetoric. What I would like to highlight now, though, is that this argument presupposes a very different assessment of Paul's rhetoric from that of earlier scholars. It is worth asking, then, how we got here. What has fueled this reevaluation of Paul's rhetorical competence?

SOUNDINGS

The work of E. A. Judge marks a turning point in Pauline scholarship, not so much because of his conclusions—in fact, few of his specific proposals have been widely accepted—as because of the new questions he posed. Informed by a detailed knowledge of the Roman world, Judge sought to uncover what he referred to in the title of his groundbreaking 1960 study as *The Social Pattern of the Christian Groups in the First Century*.[44] His forays into the social description of the early Christian assemblies were harbingers of the explosion of social-historical study of the New Testament that began in the 1970s and 1980s, and they continue to shape the discipline. Indeed, many ongoing debates owe their existence to questions first formulated or re-formulated by Judge: At what social level or levels do we find the first Christian communities? On what social models were the early assemblies structured? What contemporary analogies illuminate the role of Paul?

In answer to this latter question, Judge famously proposed that Paul was a "sophist." Since he has been accused of imprecision on this point, it is worth considering to whom, precisely, Judge thought he was thereby comparing Paul:

---

herbe, *Social Aspects of Early Christianity* (Baton Rouge: Louisiana State University Press, 1977), 29–59.

44. E. A. Judge, "The Social Pattern of the Christian Groups in the First Century," in *Social Distinctives of the Christians in the First Century: Pivotal Essays* (ed. David M. Scholer; Peabody, Mass.: Hendrickson, 2008); repr. from *The Social Pattern of the Christian Groups in the First Century: Some Prolegomena to the Study of New Testament Ideas of Social Obligation* (London: Tyndale, 1960).

> We may for our present purposes safely lump [Aelius Aristides and Dio Chrysostom] together with the philosophers, ranging from the Stoic Epictetus to the vagabond Cynic preachers, and the more religious teachers from the neo-Pythagorean sage Apollonius of Tyana to the charlatan Peregrinus, call them all sophists, and say that this is the class to which St Paul belonged.[45]

This is, as has been noted, a rather diverse group of peers,[46] and we should certainly like to know whether Paul was more like Dio or Epictetus, Apollonius or Peregrinus. Still, although Pauline scholars have not found the term *sophist* palatable, Judge's suggestion has become the starting point for all further discussion of Paul's social location. Abraham Malherbe, Ronald Hock, and Stanley Stowers have all acknowledged their debt to his work; indeed, each has sought to describe with more specificity how to locate Paul among the analogues Judge proposed.[47]

Judge himself continued to ruminate on the question of Paul's social location for decades. Two collections of articles have appeared recently, and, reading his essays in turn, it is illuminating to watch him grapple with the problem of where Paul fit in the ancient world.[48] Paul's education and literary level play a prominent role as Judge seeks to carve out a space for Paul somewhere between the "metropolitan aristocracy" and the uneducated urban poor.[49] Perhaps the clearest statement comes in a 1974 essay:

---

45. E. A. Judge, "The Early Christians as a Scholastic Community," in *The First Christians in the Roman World: Augustan and New Testament Essays* (ed. James R. Harrison; WUNT 229; Tübingen: Mohr Siebeck, 2008), 540.

46. So Stanley K. Stowers, "Social Status, Public Speaking and Private Teaching: The Circumstances of Paul's Preaching Activity," *NovT* 26 (1984): 74 n. 82; Mark D. Given, *Paul's True Rhetoric: Ambiguity, Cunning, and Deception in Greece and Rome* (ESEC 7; Harrisburg, Pa.: Trinity, 2001), 9–10.

47. See Malherbe, *Social Aspects*, 45–59; Ronald F. Hock, "The Workshop as a Social Setting for Paul's Missionary Preaching," *CBQ* 41 (1979): 440 n. 6; Stowers, "Social Status," 74.

48. E. A. Judge, *The First Christians in the Roman World: Augustan and New Testament Essays* (ed. James R. Harrison; WUNT 229; Tübingen: Mohr Siebeck, 2008); E. A. Judge, *Social Distinctives of the Christians in the First Century: Pivotal Essays* (ed. David M. Scholer; Peabody, Mass.: Hendrickson, 2008). All citations herein are from these volumes. See the bibliography for original publication information.

49. Judge, "St. Paul and Classical Society," in *Social Distinctives*, 86.

> He was familiar in the ordinary educated way with a range of ideas that circulated in Hellenic society. But at the same time he was altogether removed from any tight professional involvement with the classical method of discussion, which was very much the special province of philosophy and the literary *élite*. He would never have been recognized as a man of letters or a philosopher in the technical sense within the Greek tradition. Yet he remains very securely placed amongst the ordinary educated classes, the Hellenized rabbi, freely using the full resources of standard, technical Greek for his own purposes.[50]

Paul, then, was well educated, though he did not belong among the elite literati. But how are we to describe this middle ground? Who are these "ordinary educated classes"?

On the specific question of Paul's *rhetorical* education—a question to which he is among the first to give serious consideration—Judge points, tentatively, not to the *gymnasion* but to the school of hard knocks. In an early essay, he admits, "Whether or not Paul was given a rhetorical education at Tarsus cannot be determined"; still, he deems it most likely that "for Paul the art was acquired by hard experience rather than by training."[51]

He sounds the same tone in his influential article on Paul's boasting in 2 Cor 10–13: The arguments concerning Paul's rhetorical education are "inconclusive," but "it is beyond doubt that Paul was, in practice at least, familiar with the rhetorical fashions of his time."[52] Notably, Judge's influential reconstruction of Paul's contentious relationship with the Corinthians is predicated on this conclusion: Paul "had not in fact had the full classical training himself," but his rivals were "fully trained professionals, and Paul was ridiculed by them for his poor performance."[53]

In later work, Judge is less certain on this point, and he begins to consider the possibility that Paul's refusal to engage in "platform rhetoric"[54] was not a matter of his competence but rather of his principles: It is "not clear" whether or not Paul had a rhetorical education, but "it is certain that

---

50. Judge, "St. Paul as a Radical Critic of Society," in *Social Distinctives*, 100–102.
51. Judge, "Scholastic Community," 541. Cf. E. A. Judge, "The Conflict of Educational Aims in the New Testament," in *The First Christians in the Roman World*, 700.
52. E. A. Judge, "Paul's Boasting in Relation to Contemporary Professional Practice," in *Social Distinctives*, 60–61.
53. Judge, "Educational Aims," 700.
54. E. A. Judge, "First Impressions of St Paul," in *The First Christians in the Roman World*, 415.

he refused absolutely to practice it if he did."55 So Paul is either untrained or unwilling. In 2001, Judge was still equivocating:

> The language and style of St Paul annoyed even his own converts. His being "an amateur" in speech (*idiotes* 2 Cor 11:6) was part of the problem. His "bodily presence" was "weak" and his speech "contemptible", yet (strangely) his letters were "weighty and strong" (*bareiai kai ischyrai* 2 Cor 10:10). I take this to mean that he knew well how to make a rhetorical impact, but refused to impose himself in the desired manner when actually present. His admirers were embarrassed and his critics dismissed him as professionally incompetent. Presumably he had not had a formal tertiary education before leaving Tarsus.56

THE RISE OF RHETORICAL CRITICISM

While for Judge it was social-historical questions that prompted inquiry into Paul's rhetorical education, it would soon become a pressing issue from the perspective of form criticism as well. This was due, above all, to Hans Dieter Betz's treatment of 2 Cor 10–13 and especially Galatians as "apologetic letters" that could be analyzed according to the rhetorical dictates of Quintilian and the *Rhetorica ad Herennium*.57 What Betz initially conceived as a form-critical exercise quickly took on a life of its own as New Testament scholars eagerly explored the possibility that more precise

---

55. E. A. Judge, "Cultural Conformity and Innovation in Paul: Some Clues from Contemporary Documents," in *Social Distinctives*, 165. Cf. Judge, "The Reaction against Classical Education in the New Testament," in *The First Christians in the Roman World*, 714–16. Here Judge is apparently influenced by the work of his student Christopher Forbes (see the section "Comparison, Self-Praise, and Irony" below), whose then-forthcoming work he cites with approval.

56. E. A. Judge, "Ethical Terms in St Paul and the Inscriptions of Ephesus," in *The First Christians in the Roman World*, 368.

57. Hans Dieter Betz, *Der Apostel Paulus und die sokratische Tradition: Eine exegetische Untersuchung zu seiner "Apologie" 2 Korinther 10–13* (BHT 45; Tübingen: Mohr, 1972); Betz, "The Literary Composition and Function of Paul's Letter to the Galatians," *NTS* 21 (1975): 353–79; Betz, *Galatians: A Commentary on Paul's Letter to the Churches in Galatia* (Hermeneia; Philadelphia: Fortress, 1979). Also appearing in 1979, but much less influential, was a short article by Wilhelm Wuellner arguing that Paul's digressions in 1 Corinthians in fact evince Paul's rhetorical sophistication ("Greek Rhetoric and Pauline Argumentation," in *Early Christian Literature and the Classical Intellectual Tradition* [ed. William R. Schoedel and Robert L. Wilken; ThH 54; Paris: Beauschesne, 1979], 177–88).

knowledge of Paul's rhetorical toolbox could illuminate the exegesis of his letters.

Betz posited for Paul a considerable degree of rhetorical sophistication: yes, Galatians was composed in accordance with the handbooks' recommendations for forensic rhetoric,[58] but, he insisted, "the letter does more than simply conform to convention."[59] Noting the difficulty of clarifying the rhetorical disposition of chapters 3 and 4, Betz suggested that Paul was clever enough to hide his tracks: "One might say that Paul has been very successful—as a skilled rhetorician would be expected to be—in disguising his rhetorical strategy.... In fact, for the rhetoricians of Paul's time there could be nothing more boring than a perfect product of rhetorical technology."[60]

Betz himself showed no real interest in the question where Paul may have acquired these skills,[61] but reviewers were quick to notice the need for an explanation.[62] For the method to be tenable it was necessary to provide a credible account of Paul's exposure either to the handbooks themselves or at least to the rhetorical tradition they exemplify. In an early rhetorical-critical study of Philemon, F. Forrester Church was content simply to assert, "Whether [Paul] was trained in school or acquired his talent through a natural course of observation and imitation, Paul was a master of persuasion."[63] Reviewing Betz's *Galatians*, David Aune emphasized the latter possibility, highlighting Paul's "exposure to the structures and styles of trained rhetoricians" and his "ample opportunity to make speeches." For Aune, Paul's use of rhetoric could be explained as the result of a rhetorical trickle-down effect: "In spite of the sophistication of speeches and speakers trained in traditional Greco-Roman rhetorical schools, many shared features and structures must have linked high rhetoric with its more vulgar counterpart."[64]

---

58. Betz, *Galatians*, 59.
59. Betz, "Literary Composition and Function," 356.
60. Ibid., 369.
61. Note his agnosticism in the "Minutes of the Colloquy," *Paul's Apology II Corinthians 10–13 and the Socratic Tradition* (ed. Wilhelm H. Wuellner; Colloquy 2; Berkeley: Center for Hermeneutical Studies, 1975), 26.
62. See David E. Aune, review of Hans Dieter Betz, Galatians: A Commentary on Paul's Letter to the Churches in Galatia, *RelSRev* 7 (1981): 326.
63. F. Forrester Church, "Rhetorical Structure and Design in Paul's Letter to Philemon," *HTR* 71 (1978): 21.
64. Aune, review of Betz, 326.

George Kennedy argued similarly in his foray into New Testament rhetoric. To Kennedy's mind, the evidence for Paul's education was "ambivalent"; but, so far as the legitimacy of the method was concerned, the question was immaterial:

> Even if he had not studied in a Greek school, there were many handbooks of rhetoric in common circulation which he could have seen. He and the evangelists as well would, indeed, have been hard put to escape an awareness of rhetoric as practised in the culture around them, for the rhetorical theory of the schools found its immediate application in almost every form of oral and written communication.[65]

The notion that Paul's letters reflect the conventions of Greek rhetoric because rhetoric was, to use Bruce Longenecker's phrase, "in the air" was for a time the prevailing view, and it continues to command influence.[66]

---

65. George A. Kennedy, *New Testament Interpretation through Rhetorical Criticism* (Studies in Religion; Chapel Hill: University of North Carolina Press, 1984), 9–10.

66. Richard N. Longenecker, *Galatians* (WBC 41; Nashville: Thomas Nelson, 2003), cxiii. See also Burton L. Mack, *Rhetoric and the New Testament* (GBS; Minneapolis: Fortress, 1990), 31; Douglas A. Campbell, *The Rhetoric of Righteousness in Romans 3.21–26* (JSNTSup 65; Sheffield: JSOT Press, 1992), 75–76; Stanley E. Porter, "The Theoretical Justification for Application of Rhetorical Categories to Pauline Epistolary Literature," in *Rhetoric and the New Testament: Essays from the 1992 Heidelberg Conference* (ed. Stanley E. Porter and Thomas H. Olbricht; JSNTSup 90; Sheffield: JSOT Press, 1993), 104–5; Porter, "Paul of Tarsus and His Letters," in *Handbook of Classical Rhetoric in the Hellenistic Period, 330 B.C.–A.D. 400* (ed. Stanley E. Porter; Leiden: Brill, 1997), 563; Murray J. Harris, *The Second Epistle to the Corinthians: A Commentary on the Greek Text* (NIGTC; Grand Rapids: Eerdmans, 2005), 108; Ivar Vegge, *2 Corinthians—a Letter about Reconciliation: A Psychagogical, Epistolographical and Rhetorical Analysis* (WUNT 2/239; Tübingen: Mohr Siebeck, 2008), 40–41; Hengel, *Pre-Christian Paul*, 58; E. Randolph Richards, *The Secretary in the Letters of Paul* (WUNT 2/42; Tübingen: Mohr Siebeck, 1991), 151; Johan S. Vos, "Die Argumentation des Paulus in 1 Kor 1,10–3,4," in *The Corinthian Correspondence* (ed. Reimund Bieringer; BETL 125; Leuven: Leuven University Press, 1996), 27–28. Cf. Classen, *Rhetorical Criticism*, 29; A. Duane Litfin, *St. Paul's Theology of Proclamation: 1 Corinthians 1–4 and Greco-Roman Rhetoric* (SNTSMS 79; Cambridge: Cambridge University Press, 1994), 137–40; Wilhelm H. Wuellner, "Der vorchristliche Paulus und die Rhetorik," in *Tempelkult und Tempelzersörung (70 n. Chr.): Festschrift für Clemens Thoma zum 60. Geburtstag* (ed. Simon Lauer and Hanspeter Ernst; Judaica et Christiana 15; Bern: Lang, 1995), 133–65; Steven J. Kraftchick, "Πάθη in Paul: The Emotional

But the implications of Kennedy's next assertion have largely gone unnoticed:

> Though rhetoric is colored by the traditions and conventions of the society in which it is applied, it is also a universal phenomenon which is conditioned by basic workings of the human mind and heart and by the nature of all human society.... What is unique about Greek rhetoric, and what makes it useful for criticism, is the degree to which it was conceptualized. The Greeks gave names to rhetorical techniques, many of which are found all over the world.[67]

This universal dimension of rhetoric continued to fascinate Kennedy, as we will see in more detail below. Among New Testament scholars, however, it has not been allowed to disrupt the neat logic that Paul's use of rhetorical techniques is straightforward evidence of his rhetorical education.[68]

"COMPARISON, SELF-PRAISE, AND IRONY"

Second Corinthians 10–13 has played a particularly significant role in the discussion concerning Paul's rhetorical education, and not only because of the contested evaluations of Paul's speech reported in 2 Cor 10:10 and 11:6. For Judge, these chapters in particular attested to Paul's role as an unwilling participant in a battle of rhetorical wits. And it was an evaluation of their conformity to Hellenistic rhetorical conventions that prompted his student Christopher Forbes to inquire, more directly than previous scholars, into the implications of rhetorical criticism for our conception of Paul's education.

For Forbes, "the key to the whole 'boasting' passage" lies in Paul's ostensible refusal in 2 Cor 10:12 to classify (ἐγκρῖναι) or compare (συγκρῖναι)

Logic of 'Original Argument,' " in *Paul and* Pathos (ed. Thomas H. Olbricht and Jerry L. Sumney; SBLSymS 16; Atlanta: Society of Biblical Literature, 2001), 39–68.

67. Kennedy, *New Testament Interpretation*, 10–11.

68. Note, however, the work of C. J. Classen, who has emphasized that our ability to find rhetorical figures, tropes, and strategies in the letters of Paul does not in itself imply that Paul had formal rhetorical education. See esp. *Rhetorical Criticism*, 29. Also "St. Paul's Epistles and Ancient Greek and Roman Rhetoric," *Rhetorica* 10 (1992): 319–44. But Classen's own attempt to isolate evidence of Paul's formal knowledge of rhetorical theory by identifying his use of technical terminology (*Rhetorical Criticism*, 29–44) is not convincing. See further p. 27 above.

himself with his rivals.⁶⁹ Comparison (σύγκρισις), Forbes notes, was a topic of frequent discussion among Greek rhetorical theorists, eventually appearing in the *Progymnasmata* of Aelius Theon as well as that of Hermogenes. Moreover, authors such as Plutarch went to great lengths, Forbes explains, to describe how the sort of self-praise (περιαυτολογία) undertaken by Paul could be accomplished without causing offense. Finally, Forbes suggests that Paul used irony—another technique frequently discussed by the rhetoricians—to avoid unseemly self-promotion and to parody the sort of rhetorical comparisons (συγκρίσεις) apparently being undertaken by his rivals.⁷⁰

At this point Forbes moves from literary criticism to biographical inquiry: "If my analysis of Paul's rhetoric is correct, we must ask where he acquired the subtlety and skill which he here displays."⁷¹ Although he acknowledges the possibility that Paul simply learned from experience, Forbes's real interest is to consider an alternative explanation, namely, that Paul received "a full education in formal Greek rhetoric."⁷² As Forbes correctly argues, the assumption that Paul's Judean background rules out Hellenistic education is insupportable.⁷³ Thus, on the grounds of Paul's rhetorical prowess, Forbes suggests: "His education reached at least beyond the level of the grammatici, and into rhetorical school."⁷⁴

---

69. Christopher Forbes, "Comparison, Self-Praise, and Irony: Paul's Boasting and the Conventions of Hellenistic Rhetoric," *NTS* 32 (1986): 1. Forbes (25 n. 4) acknowledges his debt here to the work of his fellow student Peter Marshall, whose then forthcoming work also treats Paul's use of *synkrisis* and other rhetorical devices and also concludes, tentatively, that Paul "may have been trained in rhetoric but had deliberately set it aside" (*Enmity in Corinth: Social Conventions in Paul's Relations with the Corinthians* [WUNT 2/23; Tübingen: Mohr Siebeck, 1987], 390).

70. Forbes, "Comparison, Self-Praise, and Irony," 2–22. For an extended evaluation of this interpretation of Paul's boasting, see chs. 4, 7, and 8 below.

71. Ibid., 22–23.

72. Ibid., 23.

73. The inviability of such an assumption has been demonstrated most thoroughly by Martin Hengel, who insists that Jerusalem, like other Hellenized provincial cities, provided opportunities for Greek education (*Pre-Christian Paul*, 54–62). Hengel, however, fails to justify his assumption that Paul was a well-off "young scholar" (p. 60), and therefore could and would have availed himself of such opportunities. Cf. Pitts, "Hellenistic Schools in Jerusalem," 48–50.

74. Forbes, "Comparison, Self-Praise, and Irony," 24. But see now Forbes, "Ancient Rhetoric and Ancient Letters: Models for Reading Paul, and Their Limits," in *Paul and Rhetoric* (ed. J. Paul Sampley and Peter Lampe; New York: T&T Clark, 2010),

Notably, Forbes is quick to draw the attendant conclusion that such education "bespeaks a certain social standing." Thus Paul's manual labor, he explains, should not be considered indicative of his social status; rather, it should be understood as voluntary self-abnegation.[75] This is a well-worn argument, as we have seen, but now with one key modification: Paul's rhetorical education has neatly stepped into the argumentative role long filled by his Roman citizenship, mitigating the apparent status implications of Paul's labor and thus ensuring that Paul is respectably insulated from the ignominy of (involuntary) poverty.

A Developing Consensus

Subsequent treatments of Paul's rhetorical education have followed the basic contours of Forbes's argument. Although prior to 2003 there had been no full-length study dedicated to the subject, scholars asserted with growing confidence that Paul's rhetorical ability must have been acquired through formal training.[76]

The decisive role of rhetoric in evaluating Paul's social location is particularly evident in Dale Martin's *The Corinthian Body*. Building on Gerd

---

148, where he apparently retracts his earlier suggestion, now asserting: "It seems very unlikely that his formal education extended to the upper levels."

75. Forbes, "Comparison, Self-Praise, and Irony," 24.

76. In addition to those discussed below, see Marshall, *Enmity in Corinth*, 390; Georg Strecker, "Die Legitimität des paulinischen Apostolates nach 2 Korinther 10–13," *NTS* 38 (1992): 567; Bruce C. Johanson, *To All the Brethren: A Text-Linguistic and Rhetorical Approach to I Thessalonians* (ConBNT 16; Stockholm: Almqvist & Wiksell, 1987), 34; David Hellholm, "Enthymemic Argumentation in Paul: The Case of Romans 6," in *Paul in His Hellenistic Context* (ed. Troels Engberg-Pedersen; SNTW; Minneapolis: Fortress, 1995), 179 n. 226; Mario M. DiCicco, *Paul's Use of Ethos, Pathos, and Logos in 2 Corinthians 10–13* (Mellen Biblical Press Series 31; Lewiston, N.Y.: Mellen Biblical Press, 1995), 23–28; Dieter Kremendahl, *Die Botschaft der Form: Zum Verhältnis von antiker Epistolographie und Rhetorik im Galaterbrief* (NTOA 46; Freiburg: Universitätsverlag, 2000), 30–31; Kieran J. O'Mahony, *Pauline Persuasion: A Sounding in 2 Corinthians 8–9* (JSNTSup 199; Sheffield: Sheffield Academic Press, 2000), 179–80; Gnilka, *Paulus von Tarsus*, 25; Schnelle, *Apostle Paul*, 53; Marcus J. Borg and John Dominic Crossan, *The First Paul: Reclaiming the Radical Visionary Behind the Church's Conservative Icon* (New York: HarperOne, 2009), 61–62; Hooker, *Paul*, 36–37; Phillips, *Paul, His Letters, and Acts*, 85–86. Cf. Margaret M. Mitchell, *Paul, the Corinthians and the Birth of Christian Hermeneutics* (Cambridge: Cambridge University Press, 2010), 94 and passim.

Theissen's pioneering work, Martin argues that the various body-oriented conflicts that characterize the relationship between the "strong" and the "weak" in Corinth—divisions at the Lord's Supper, and disputes regarding meat offered to idols, the use of civil courts, Paul's acceptance of financial support, glossolalia, and the resurrection of the body—reflect the different social locations of the two groups. In other words, each group's beliefs about the body correlate to that group's social status and level of education: the strong claim to possess esoteric knowledge and assert their indifference toward the physical body; the weak fear bodily and social pollution and are thus concerned to maintain "firm corporal and social boundaries."[77]

Martin identifies a consistent pattern in Paul's response to these disputes: although initially he identifies himself rhetorically with the strong, in each case Paul finally sides with the weak.[78] So, for example, although Paul at first concedes, with the strong, that "no idol in the world really exists" (1 Cor 8:4), he ultimately shares the more popular view that "what pagans sacrifice [to idols], they sacrifice to demons and not to God" (10:20).[79] In sum, Paul does not subscribe to an upper-class moral-philosophical understanding of the body; no, "for whatever reason, [Paul's] view of the body is more in harmony with views generally held by lower-class, less-educated members of Greco-Roman society."[80]

But Martin does not draw what would seem to be the obvious conclusion, namely, that Paul *was* one of the lower class, less-educated members of Greco-Roman society. On the contrary, Martin is convinced that Paul "grew up in a relatively privileged milieu and viewed his manual labor as voluntary self-abasement for the sake of his ministry."[81] Why? Because of Paul's rhetorical competence. For Martin, "Paul's rhetorical education is evident on every page [of his letters], and that education is one piece of evidence that he came from a family of relatively high status."[82]

Likewise, Jerome Murphy-O'Connor posits upper-class origins for Paul on the grounds of "[his] educational attainments, which suggest a

---

77. Martin, *The Corinthian Body*, 197. A convenient summary of the argument appears on p. xv.
78. Ibid., 103.
79. Ibid., 182–89.
80. Ibid., xvi.
81. Ibid., xv–xvi.
82. Ibid., 52.

background infinitely superior to that of the average artisan."[83] There is some circularity in Murphy-O'Connor's argument here, for when he comes to treat Paul's education itself in more detail, it is Paul's "social position" that bears the weight of the argument and justifies the assumption that Paul would have had the opportunity to benefit from Tarsus's educational opportunities.[84] Murphy-O'Connor is finally rescued from this circular argumentation by "the evidence of rhetorical arrangement" in Paul's letters, which provides independent internal evidence to support his interdependent biographical claims.[85]

The apologetic potential of such an argument—specifically, its usefulness in asserting Paul's respectability and serious intellectual credentials—becomes explicit in the work of Ben Witherington. For Witherington, Paul's elevated social status as attested by his knowledge of rhetoric provides the primary justification for accepting Luke's assertion that Paul was a Roman citizen.[86] Although he does not speculate further regarding the precise nature of Paul's education, Witherington argues that the rhetorical features of Galatians, Philippians, and 1 and 2 Corinthians "reflect significant learning, skill, organization and preparation."[87] In Witherington's hands, this underlying rhetorical training becomes a means of asserting the intellectual significance of Pauline discourse: "Paul," he assures us, "was no rustic backwoods preacher rattling off whatever exhortations came to mind."[88]

In 2003, two independent studies of Paul's rhetorical education appeared, both arriving at the conclusion already anticipated by scholars such as Martin, Murphy-O'Connor, and Witherington. The basic thrust of Jerome Neyrey's article is readily discernable from its title: "The Social Location of Paul: Education as the Key." As one would expect, the argument is an elaboration of the proposal of Forbes: Paul knows rhetoric; rhetorical education is available only among the elite; Paul must therefore belong among the elite.[89]

---

83. Murphy-O'Connor, *Paul: A Critical Life*, 40.
84. Ibid., 50.
85. Ibid.
86. Witherington, *The Paul Quest*, 70.
87. Ibid., 126.
88. Ibid.
89. See Neyrey, "Social Location of Paul," 130, 160–61.

The bulk of Neyrey's article consists of a summary of the findings of the previous few decades of rhetorical criticism, with the implications for Paul's education appended to each section: scholars have found that Paul's letters can be classified according to the letter types described by Pseudo-Demetrius; therefore, Paul must have been educated in epistolary composition.[90] Scholars have described the rhetorical arrangement of various Pauline letters and letter sections according to the canons of ancient rhetoric; therefore, Paul "knew sophisticated rhetorical theory."[91] Scholars have identified "progymnastic genres" such as comparison, encomium, and speech-in-character (*ēthopoiia*) in Paul's letters; therefore, Paul must have been "educated in progymnastic learning."[92] Scholars have found in Paul's letters various philosophical themes, styles, and *topoi*; therefore, Paul must have had "an education beyond that of progymnastic rhetoric, even some training in popular philosophy."[93]

Neyrey then proceeds to correlate this portrait of Paul with Gerhard Lenski's model of social stratification in advanced agrarian societies. Since Paul's letters evince familiarity with aspects of the Greek curriculum that were "exclusively the prerogative of the wealthy and elites … it seems that the minimum level at which we might locate Paul is in the retainer class."[94] In other words, Neyrey concludes, Luke got it right: Paul is "an elite who was educated for a life of leisure and who learned the art and craft of rhetoric and philosophy."[95]

Ronald Hock's article on Paul's education takes much the same shape. He begins with a survey of recent scholarship on Greco-Roman education, describing the standard schema of primary, secondary, and tertiary curricula.[96] He then superimposes Paul's literary capacities onto this schema: His primary education is attested by his basic literacy and his use of poetic maxims.[97] His interaction with literary texts—in this case, the Sep-

---

90. Ibid., 130–33.
91. Ibid., 140.
92. Ibid., 141, 148.
93. Ibid., 150.
94. Ibid., 160.
95. Ibid., 161.
96. Ronald F. Hock, "Paul and Greco-Roman Education," in *Paul in the Greco-Roman World: A Handbook* (ed. J. Paul Sampley; Harrisburg, Pa.: Trinity, 2003), 198–208. On the inadequacy of this model of ancient education, see "Epistolary Theory and Paul's Rhetorical Education" in ch. 3 below.
97. Ibid., 208.

tuagint—provides evidence of his secondary education.⁹⁸ Finally, Paul's eloquent letters "clearly point to an author who had received sustained training in composition and rhetoric, and it was only during the tertiary curriculum that such instruction was given."⁹⁹ Therefore, "it is hard not to draw the conclusion that Paul had formal rhetorical training."¹⁰⁰

Like Neyrey, Hock readily infers Paul's elevated social standing from his rhetorical education. But it is worth noting the circularity of Hock's argument here: he begins by asserting that Paul's "status as an aristocrat makes education a given," then goes on to argue that his "educational achievement ... put Paul into a very tiny elite indeed."¹⁰¹ It is also worth noting that this description of a well-educated Paul conveniently vindicates the portrait of an aristocratic Paul Hock himself had outlined in his previous work.¹⁰² What we have here, it seems, is the elaboration of a paradigm, not a deductive argument demonstrating Paul's education. That does not in itself invalidate Hock's proposal—his paradigm may indeed be accurate—but it is important to see that his assertions of Paul's elite status and elite education are in fact interdependent.

This becomes particularly evident in a 2008 article wherein he revisits the question of Paul's social status. Although Hock's earlier work is often cited as the last word on Paul's manual labor, critics had noted an apparent contradiction: on the one hand, Hock claims that Paul had an aristocratic upbringing that taught him to despise manual labor; on the other, he argues that Paul learned his trade the way most other laborers did—from his father.¹⁰³ Hock attempts to resolve this tension by correcting his earlier assertion: Paul did not learn his trade from his father but rather acquired it after his conversion in order to address his newly "reduced economic circumstances."¹⁰⁴

---

98. Ibid.
99. Ibid., 209. Hock elaborates this latter claim by describing Paul's use of the forms of the *Progymnasmata*, particularly *ēthopoiia*, and the rhetorical arrangement of Galatians.
100. Ibid., 215.
101. Ibid., 198, 215.
102. See Hock, "Paul's Tentmaking"; Hock, *Social Context*, 35.
103. Hock, "Paul's Tentmaking"; Hock, *Social Context*, 22–25. The contradiction had been remarked by Meggitt, *Paul, Poverty and Survival*, 87 n. 54; Todd D. Still, "Did Paul Loathe Manual Labor? Revisiting the Work of Ronald F. Hock on the Apostle's Tentmaking and Social Class," *JBL* 125 (2006): 785 n. 22; Roetzel, *Paul*, 191 n. 73.
104. Hock, "Paul's Social Class," 16.

Hock attempts to demonstrate that Paul's decision to learn a trade when faced with social marginalization was "consistent with aristocratic conventions,"[105] but he manages to cite only one case of an adult learning a τέχνη, and that a fictional one (Xenophon, *Eph*. 5.1.4–5.1.11). The other texts cited by Hock demonstrate, as he himself admits, that portrayals of down-and-out aristocrats generally have them fall back on unskilled labor or even brigandry, a pattern that would seem to suggest a lack of appetite or opportunity for mid-life apprenticeships. Perhaps Hock has shown that it is possible for Paul to have learned his trade postconversion; he has by no means demonstrated that it is probable.

What Hock falls back on to bolster his argument is, then, Paul's schooling: Paul must have learned his trade after his conversion, since as a boy he was far too busy pursuing his literate education.[106] So, in the end, we may summarize the structure of Hock's argument like this: Paul was an aristocrat, so he spent his youth in school; Paul was busy in school during his youth, so he can only have learned his trade as an adult; learning a trade as an adult is something aristocrats do, therefore—and now we have come full circle—Paul was an aristocrat.

Hock seeks to ground exegetically this otherwise circular argument for Paul's elite status in three ways: first, he reiterates his claim that Paul betrays an aristocratic attitude toward manual labor; second, he cites his own work on Paul's education; third, he bookends the discussion with brief but allusive references to Paul's citizenship.[107] Restricting ourselves to evidence from the Pauline corpus itself, that leaves Hock's argument with two pillars: Paul's disdain for labor and his rhetorical prowess.

Hock first argued that Paul had an aristocrat's disdain for manual labor in his 1978 "Paul's Tentmaking and the Problem of His Social Class." Paul, Hock noted, referred to his engagement in manual labor in terms that were hardly positive: "I enslaved myself" (ἐμαυτὸν ἐδούλωσα [1 Cor 9:19]); "I demeaned myself" (ἐμαυτὸν ταπεινῶν [2 Cor 11:7]). Moreover, Paul included labor in his hardship catalogues alongside beatings, homelessness, and hunger (1 Cor 4:12). In sum, Hock concluded, "Paul experienced his working as we should expect an aristocrat to have done, namely, as something slavish and demeaning."[108]

---

105. Ibid., 17.
106. Ibid., 15–16.
107. Ibid., 8, 18.
108. Hock, "Paul's Tentmaking," 562. Hock's argument has been taken up by

Hock's exegesis has recently been challenged by Todd Still, who denies that Paul had such a negative view of his trade.[109] But even if Hock is correct and Paul considered his labor slavish, the conclusion that Paul was an aristocrat does not follow, for it surely does not require an aristocratic upbringing to resent hard work. Hock adduces a few inscriptions that highlight the pride of artisans in their work, but this is not sufficient to justify his sweeping claim that, unlike Paul, "those who practiced trades had positive attitudes about their prospects and reputations."[110] As Justin Meggitt notes, the reality was rather more complex: "Both the disparagement of physical work, and unabashed pride in it, can be found in élite and non-élite Graeco-Roman and Jewish sources."[111] There simply is no reason to imagine that the elite had a monopoly on resenting the drudgery of hard labor. And this leaves Hock with only Paul's putative education, as evidenced by his rhetorical prowess, upon which to ground his portrait of an aristocratic apostle.

Paul and the Diatribe

Like Neyrey and Hock, Stanley Stowers has argued that it is the characteristics of Paul's prose that best indicate the level of his education, but he has come to a different conclusion. For Stowers, the key is Paul's long-noted stylistic affinity to the diatribe. Unlike Rudolf Bultmann, who sought the diatribe's *Sitz im Leben* in street-corner moral preaching, Stowers argues that it represents the schoolroom discourse of various popularizing philosophers.[112] The diatribe-like style of Paul's letters, then, suggests that his

---

Sanders, *Paul*, 11; Murphy-O'Connor, *Paul: A Critical Life*, 40; Dale B. Martin, *Slavery as Salvation: The Metaphor of Slavery in Pauline Christianity* (New Haven: Yale University Press, 1990), 123; Longenecker, *Remember the Poor*, 305.

109. Still, "Did Paul Loathe Manual Labor?"

110. Hock, "Paul's Social Class," 11. Cf. Timothy B. Savage, *Power through Weakness: Paul's Understanding of the Christian Ministry in 2 Corinthians* (SNTSMS 86; Cambridge: Cambridge University Press, 1996), 84–86.

111. Meggitt, *Paul, Poverty and Survival*, 88. For an excellent recent treatment, see Catharina Lis, "Perceptions of Work in Classical Antiquity: A Polyphonic Heritage," in *The Idea of Work in Europe from Antiquity to Modern Times* (ed. Josef Ehmer and Catharina Lis; Burlington, Vt.: Ashgate, 2009), 33–68. Note especially Lis's emphasis on stratification *among* manual laborers, and thus the impossibility of identifying *the* attitude of ancient laborers toward their work (50–56).

112. Stanley K. Stowers, *The Diatribe and Paul's Letter to the Romans* (SBLDS 57;

ministry too had a schoolroom setting—"an audience of disciples, taught privately."[113] Indeed, for Stowers, the common notion that Paul was a public preacher is untenable, since Paul lacked the requisite status for public speaking: "Paul was a Jew and a leather-worker. It is doubtful that he could have overcome the stigma of these roles even if he had sought to do so."[114]

In his early work, Stowers did not address the question of Paul's social background in any depth, nor did he speculate on where he might have learned the philosophical discourse of the diatribe. But, like Neyrey and Hock, he weighed in on the question of Paul's education in 2003. Stowers resists the notion that Paul belonged among the tiny fraction of the population that constituted the elite: Paul's prose simply lacks the aesthetic sophistication sought by Cicero or Quintilian.[115] But neither are his letters completely devoid of rhetoric. No, they occupy a middle ground; and, for Stowers, it is study of the diatribe that "illuminate[s] just such an alternative tradition of rhetoric nourished by moral teachers and philosophers who may or may not have had high rhetorical educations."[116]

Stowers describes Paul's education accordingly, quoting his own *Rereading of Romans*:

> "Paul's Greek educational level roughly equals that of someone who had primary instruction with a *grammaticus*, or teacher of letters, and then studied letter writing and some elementary rhetorical exercises."

Chico, Calif.: Scholars Press, 1981), 45–78. Cf. Rudolf Bultmann, *Der Stil der paulinischen Predigt und die kynisch stoische Diatribe* (FRLANT 13; Göttingen: Vandenhoeck & Ruprecht, 1910).

113. Stowers, "Social Status," 63.

114. Ibid., 74. Admittedly, some Cynics managed to command a public audience, but, according to Stowers, "the hit-and-run tactics of the Cynic do not fit [Paul]" (80). Although he does not cite Theissen at this point, it appears to be the notion of Paul as a "community organizer" (see *Social Setting*, 27–67) that, for Stowers, distinguishes him from such Cynics.

115. Elsewhere, Stowers rightly remarks: "Such aestheticism belonged to an extremely small group of writers, who lived in a rarefied world of elite sensitivities. It was the study of rhetoric which developed these sensitivities, and it was the cultivation of these classical aesthetic interests that most distinguishes the letter writing of certain later Christian authors … from Paul or Ignatius" (*Letter Writing in Greco-Roman Antiquity* [LEC 5; Philadelphia: Westminster, 1986], 34).

116. Stanley K. Stowers, "Apostrophe, ΠΡΟΣΩΠΟΠΟΙΙΑ and Paul's Rhetorical Education," in *Early Christianity and Classical Culture* (ed. Thomas H. Olbricht and L. M. White; NovTSup 110; Leiden: Brill, 2003), 368.

This clearly excludes higher rhetorical theory. ... The same teacher who taught him the skills in letter writing that make his letters literarily and rhetorically far above the common papyrus letters may also have trained him in some progymnastic exercises useful to letter writers.[117]

I am in wholehearted agreement with the thrust of Stowers's argument: Paul's letters may be illuminated in various ways by the documentary papyri, but they certainly stand out in that crowd. And they clearly lack the niceties of elite epistles. A map of the middle ground would be welcome indeed. But is the diatribe the answer?

As Stowers is aware, there has been considerable debate over the years regarding whether or not the diatribe existed as an identifiable *Gattung*, and, if so, which authors are most representative of it.[118] But even if we side with Stowers on this point, still it is clear that the stylistic features we generally consider "diatribal" were not restricted to any single genre.[119] Why then should we assume that they were restricted to a single social setting? Even H. B. Gottschalk, arguing that the ancients did indeed call certain books diatribes, must conclude:

> These tricks of style are not confined to "diatribes"; they are found, for example, in Seneca's letters, in Lucretius, in Horace's *Satires* and many other kinds of later literature. ... The evidence is very slender, but such as it is, it suggests that this style predominated in the things called diatribes,

---

117. Ibid., 368–69; citing Stowers, *A Rereading of Romans: Justice, Jews, and Gentiles* (New Haven: Yale University Press, 1994), 17.

118. See Stowers, *Diatribe*, 26–48; Stanley E. Porter, "The Argument of Romans 5: Can a Rhetorical Question Make a Difference?" *JBL* 110 (1991): 656–60. H. D. Jocelyn and H. B. Gottschalk go back and forth on the major issues: Jocelyn, "Diatribes and Sermons," *LCM* 7 (1982): 3–7; Jocelyn, "'Diatribes' and the Greek Book-Title Διατριβαί," *LCM* 8 (1983): 89–91; Gottschalk, "Diatribe Again," *LCM* 7 (1982): 91–92; Gottschalk, "More on DIATRIBAI," *LCM* 78 (1983): 91–92.

119. Porter, "The Argument of Romans 5," 660–61; Barbara Price Wallach, *Lucretius and the Diatribe against the Fear of Death: De rerum natura III 830–1094* (Mnemosyne Supplement 40; Leiden: Brill, 1976), 7–8; Helmut Rahn, *Morphologie der antiken Literatur: Eine Einführung* (Die Altertumswissenschaft; Darmstadt: Wissenschaftliche Buchgesellschaft, 1969), 156. A. A. Long judiciously describes the "so-called diatribe tradition" as "a practice, both oral and written, of ethical training to which professional teachers and didactic writers contributed in ways that were both generic and individual" (*Epictetus: A Stoic and Socratic Guide to Life* [Oxford: Clarendon, 2002], 49).

while other genres might make use of it as one among a larger repertory of styles.[120]

If "diatribal style" is so amorphous that it can show up in the poetry of Lucretius and find echoes in rabbinic midrash,[121] it seems rather adventurous to infer from its appearance in Paul that he belongs in the moral-philosophical classroom.

PAULUS UND DAS ANTIKE SCHULWESEN

By far the most substantial study of Paul's education to date is Tor Vegge's *Paulus und das antike Schulwesen*, a dissertation completed under David Hellholm in 2004 and published in *Beihefte zur Zeitschrift für die neutestamentliche Wissenschaft* in 2006. Despite its length—575 pages—and its broad scope, the basic structure of Vegge's argument is by now familiar: "Seine Texte zeigen ... daß er Form und Stil so beherrscht, wie sie in 'griechisch-hellenistischen' Rhetorikschulen unterrichtet wurden"; therefore, Paul must have come from a high-status family.[122]

Vegge begins with an almost encyclopedic study of education in the Hellenistic world, addressing everything from the structure of schools, the role of teachers, and the various curricula to the sociological function of literate education. Both rhetorical and philosophical education receive detailed treatment; both will be of significance when Vegge gets to Paul. But what Vegge tends to overlook, as Thomas Kraus notes, is the value of documentary papyri for illuminating the sort of pedestrian educational

---

120. Gottschalk, "Diatribe Again," 92. Paul's letters, we might note, are clearly among those texts that make use of "diatribal style" as one of a larger repertory of styles. See Stowers, *Diatribe*, 25.

121. Wallach, *Lucretius and the Diatribe*; Rivka Ulmer, "The Advancement of Arguments in Exegetical Midrash Compared to That of the Greek ΔΙΑΤΡΙΒΗ," *JSJ* 28 (1997): 48–91. Stowers critiques Wallach for allowing her understanding of the genre to be unduly swayed by sources that are "atypical of the diatribe" (*Diatribe*, 36), but the fact that such borderline texts even exist makes the point. Such texts may not be evidence for what the ancient diatribe—if there was such a thing—was like, but that does not render them irrelevant for understanding the stylistic features with which we are concerned.

122. Vegge, *Paulus und das antike Schulwesen*, 357, 455: "His writings indicate ... that he has mastered form and style as they were taught in 'Greek-Hellenistic' schools of rhetoric."

practices that Quintilian and his ilk surely would have considered hopelessly provincial but that were, nevertheless, likely quite representative outside elite circles.[123] This amounts, unfortunately, to stacking the deck: By the time Vegge begins to address Paul—on page 341!—we are liable to have forgotten that a world outside that of budding elite orators and philosophers exists. And if the only mode of education we can imagine is elite formal education, we simply have nowhere else to place Paul.

It is no surprise, then, when Vegge unreservedly locates Paul among the educated elite, insisting "daß Paulus eine literarische Ausbildung in ihrer allgemeinen griechisch-hellenistischen Form erhielt und daß er danach bei einem Redelehrer die Progymnasmata durchlief, wodurch er sich die Grundlage seiner literarischen Virtuosität verschaffte."[124] The grounds for this conclusion are twofold: first, Paul's letters feature the sort of rhetoric that could only have been learned in school; second, what we know of Paul's origins makes his exposure to rhetorical education probable.

This latter argument centers on Tarsus's reputation as a seat of higher learning. Vegge argues, contra van Unnik, that Paul was a Tarsan through and through, since Luke's emphasis on Paul's time in Jerusalem (cf. Acts 22:3) can be ascribed to his own theological and literary interests.[125] And, if it was in Tarsus that Paul went to school, Paul must have benefited from the unparalleled educational environment to which Strabo famously attests (*Geogr.* 14.5.13).[126]

---

123. Thomas J. Kraus, "Schooling and School System in (Late) Antiquity and Their Influence on Paul" (review of Tor Vegge, *Paulus und die antike Schulwesen: Schule und Bildung des Paulus*, *ExpTim* 118 (2007): 617. Kraus notes, for example, that Herbert Youtie does not appear in the bibliography. Neither does Rafaella Cribiore's *Gymnastics of the Mind: Greek Education in Hellenistic and Roman Egypt* (Princeton, N.J.: Princeton University Press, 2001), though it was published three years before Vegge defended his dissertation. Theresa Morgan's *Literate Education in the Hellenistic and Roman Worlds* (Cambridge Classical Studies; Cambridge: Cambridge University Press, 1998) is occasionally consulted, but not really digested.

124. Vegge, *Paulus und das antike Schulwesen*, 462: "that Paul received a literary education in its general Greek-Hellenistic form and that he then went through the *Progymnasmata* with a teacher of rhetoric, whereby he acquired the foundation of his literary virtuosity."

125. Ibid., 425–41. Likewise Murphy-O'Connor, *Paul: A Critical Life*, 32–33. Cf. Van Unnik, *Tarsus or Jerusalem*.

126. Vegge, *Paulus und das antike Schulwesen*, 458.

But even if we grant, as most are inclined to do, that Luke had accurate information regarding Paul's city of origin and that Strabo's hyperbolic description possesses a kernel of truth, the relevance of Tarsus's academic life to Paul is by no means self-evident. As Richard Wallace and Wynne Williams wryly observe:

> Although Paul's city Tarsus was famous for its philosophers, there is no reason to suppose that a Jewish tentmaker born in Tarsus would therefore have a better than average knowledge of philosophical ideas, any more than we would expect someone who worked in a car factory in Oxford to have for that reason a better knowledge of Wittgenstein than one whose workplace was in Coventry.[127]

That is, in order for Tarsus's famed rhetorical schools to be at all relevant, Paul must have had the requisite social status to attend them. Vegge insists that he did, but his argument for Paul's status rests on precisely the issue that is at stake here, namely, Paul's education.[128] In the end, then, we know Paul was elite because of his education, which in turn we can infer from his elite status. Vegge's biographical argument, like that of Hock, is beset by circularity. Thus the whole structure finally rests upon Vegge's assertion that Paul's letters contain indisputable marks of formal education in rhetoric.

Aware of claims that Paul could have learned his persuasive speech informally, Vegge is eager to clarify that, for the purposes of his study, rhetoric means school rhetoric—"die schulisch erlernten Formen der Sprache."[129] And he adduces two texts as evidence of this unambiguously *schulische* rhetoric: 1 Cor 7 and 2 Cor 10–13. I will address his treatment of them in turn.

According to Vegge, Paul in 1 Cor 7 elaborates a *thesis* as recommended by Aelius Theon (*Progymn.* 11 [*RG* 2:120–128]).[130] In his treatment of the exercise, Theon had listed the various *topoi*—fourteen in all, by Vegge's count—which could be used in such elaboration (*RG* 2:121–122). Vegge finds eleven of these in Paul's discussion of marriage. To Vegge it seems

---

127. Richard Wallace and Wynne Williams, *The Three Worlds of Paul of Tarsus* (London: Routledge, 1998), 133. Cf. Norden, *Die antike Kunstprosa*, 495.
128. Vegge, *Paulus und das antike Schulwesen*, 455.
129. Ibid., 365, cf. 357.
130. Ibid., 389–406.

clear, then, that Paul composed 1 Cor 7 as a thesis; "und wenn an dieser Stelle glaubhaft gemacht werden kann, daß Paulus die Gymnasmatatform der Thesis in seinem Unterricht verwendet und in seinen Schriften eingesetzt hat, ist darin ein Indiz für die von ihm genossene literarische Bildung zu sehen."[131]

It cannot be denied that certain aspects of this text are reminiscent, at least, of some of the *topoi* described by Theon. Paul's assertion that the unmarried woman is fully attentive to the Lord and therefore holy (ἁγία [1 Cor 7:34]) perhaps accords with Theon's advice to argue from the *topos* "that [the proposed course of action] is reverent (ὅσιος)," or, more specifically, that it is "pleasing to gods."[132] Theon suggests arguing that a proposed action is beneficial (λυσιτελές) and establishes security (πρὸς ἀσφάλειαν ... ἐπιτήδειον [*RG* 2:122]); Paul writes, "Those who marry will experience distress in this life, and I would spare you that…. I say this for your own benefit" (7:28b, 35a).

But others of Vegge's instances are less persuasive. I do not see how Paul's "concession" in 1 Cor 7:2–4—"Because of cases of sexual immorality, each man should have his own wife and each woman her husband"—can be construed as an argument that restraining from sexual intercourse "entspricht ... nicht der Physis und dem allen Menschen gemeinsamen Ethos und den gemeinsamen Gesetzen."[133] It may be that this is what Paul thinks, that such an assumption lies behind his brief διὰ δὲ τὰς πορνείας, but if so he does not tell us. In fact, although Paul does argue from "nature" elsewhere when discussing sexual mores (cf. 1 Cor 11:14), here the emphasis is not on what is natural or customary but rather on the vulnerability of the Corinthians' self-control to the tempting of Satan (v. 5). And although the logic of vv. 3–4 does involve an implicit appeal to what is customary—note especially the language of conjugal "duty" (ὀφειλή)—if our goal is to uncover unambiguous evidence of rhetorical education, it simply will not

---

131. Ibid., 405: "And if it can be substantiated here that Paul utilized the progymnastic form of the thesis in his teaching and has inserted it into his writings, we thus see one indicator of the literary education he enjoyed."

132. Theon, *Progymn.* 11 (*RG* 2:122): ὅτι ὅσιον· διττὸν δὲ τοῦτο· ἢ γὰρ θεοῖς κεχαρισμένον ἢ τετελευτηκόσιν. I use Patillon's Budé edition here and throughout this study, and provide numbering from Spengel's *Rhetores Graeci* for ease of reference.

133. Vegge, *Paulus und das antike Schulwesen*, 394. Theon (*Progymn.* 11 [*RG* 2:121]) recommends arguing from the *topos* that a certain course of action "is in accordance with nature and according to the common manners and customs of all mankind" [trans. Kennedy].

do to equate an implicit appeal to custom with the use of a progymnastic *topos*. Implicit appeals to custom can be found far from the Greco-Roman rhetorical tradition, and we clearly would not want to ascribe a progymnastic education to every orator who employed one.[134]

Verses 2–5 highlight another problem with Vegge's formal analysis: We do not have a proof here at all, as we would expect if Paul were elaborating a thesis, but rather paranesis, as the use of the imperative throughout the passage indicates. Indeed, it is difficult to see how Paul's direct instruction accords with Theon's definition of a thesis as "a verbal inquiry admitting controversy without specifying any persons and circumstance; for example, whether one should marry, whether one should have children; whether the gods exist" (*RG* 2:120 [trans. Kennedy]). No, Paul has very specific persons in view—namely, his Corinthian readers—and he enumerates a whole series of specific situations regarding which he provides concrete instructions.

Vegge seeks to avoid the problem this creates by suggesting that Paul alternates between "thetical" speech, which is generally applicable, and "hypothetical" speech, which addresses a particular situation.[135] But this is still a mischaracterization of the passage, which in fact consists of a series of thematically interrelated instructions to which the sort of argumentative *topoi* described by Vegge are occasionally appended as ad hoc justifications. And this brings us to the truly fatal problem with Vegge's analysis: how can this be the elaboration of a thesis when there is no thesis to elaborate?

Vegge himself takes 1 Cor 7.1b—"It is well for a man not to touch a woman"—as Paul's thesis. But this simply does not work, for, as scholars have long noted, "the principle contained in this statement does not serve to further Paul's argument in 1 Cor. 7.1–24."[136] Rather, the bulk of the chapter takes the form of what H. Chadwick called "qualifying foot-

---

134. See, e.g., the argument from ancient practice in Red Jacket's speech at the Council of Newtown Point, 1791 (Granville Ganter, ed., *The Collected Speeches of Sagoyewatha, or Red Jacket* [The Iroquois and Their Neighbors; Syracuse, N.Y.: Syracuse University Press, 2006], 29–30). For more on Red Jacket, see pt. 3 below.

135. Vegge, *Paulus und das antike Schulwesen*, 396–404. On the distinction between thesis and hypothesis, see Hermogenes, *Progymn.* 24–25.

136. John Coolidge Hurd, *The Origin of 1 Corinthians* (New York: Seabury, 1965), 67.

notes" that explain why such a thesis is impracticable.[137] In fact, as such diverse interpreters as Dale Martin and Gordon Fee agree, what we have here is not Paul's own statement at all; this is a citation from the Corinthians' letter.[138] As elsewhere in 1 Corinthians, Paul expresses agreement in principal with the ("strong") Corinthians' slogan, but in fact undermines their position by counseling concession to the "weak."[139] Clearly, this rhetorical procedure has little in common with the elaboration of a thesis as described in the *Progymnasmata*.

Vegge himself recognizes that what Paul does here is different from what Theon and Hermogenes recommend. Like Betz, however, he takes Paul's deviation from the standard as evidence that Paul is not composing trite schoolboy prose:

> Stellt der Teiltext ... keine Thesis dar, die den straff gehaltenen Übungsbedingungen eines schulischen Progymnasmas entspräche, denn bei Texten, die nicht innerhalb schulischer Disziplin erstellt wurden, galt für geschickte Autoren die freie Handhabung der Formmerkmale als Ideal.[140]

But this sort of statement in fact undermines the whole argument, for what Vegge has been claiming is that Paul's rhetoric is so clearly informed by formal schooling that no other explanation of its source is adequate. If it now turns out that 1 Cor 7 doesn't look much like a progymnastic thesis after all, what are the grounds for asserting that this is in fact educated rhetoric? It is possible, of course, that Paul was trained in the elaboration of a thesis but chose to do something more complex here; it is also possible that 1 Cor 7 doesn't look like a thesis simply because it isn't one. Jazz players trained at Juilliard may be excellent improvisers, but that does not mean that deviation from the score is evidence of a Juilliard education. If our goal is to isolate educated discourse, we will clearly need sharper tools.

---

137. H. Chadwick, "'All Things to All Men' (1 Cor. IX. 22)," *NTS* 1 (1955): 265.

138. Martin, *The Corinthian Body*, 205; Gordon D. Fee, *The First Epistle to the Corinthians* (NICNT; Grand Rapids: Eerdmans, 1987), 270–71. For discussion and a survey of scholarship, see Hurd, *Origin of 1 Corinthians*, 65–74.

139. See Martin, *The Corinthian Body*, 103, 227–28.

140. Vegge, *Paulus und das antike Schulwesen*, 405: "The passage is not a thesis that complies with the strictly maintained formal requirements of a scholastic progymnastic exercise, because, in texts that were not constructed in the context of academic discipline, the free handling of formal features was considered the ideal for skillful authors."

Vegge's second example of Paul's educated rhetoric is 2 Cor 10–13, a passage with which we will be concerned at length in subsequent chapters. For much of this section, Vegge simply lists the rhetorical features that others have identified in the passage; I treat these arguments in part 2 below. In addition, however, Vegge follows his teacher David Hellholm in emphasizing Paul's use of enthymemes,[141] which, for Vegge, attests to his philosophical education.

The logic of Vegge's argument, stated syllogistically, is as follows: Philosophically trained writers (like Seneca and Plutarch) use enthymemes; Paul's letter contains enthymemes; ergo, Paul was philosophically trained.[142] But this is fallacious, for Vegge has not inquired whether such enthymemic argumentation as Paul's can be found in nonphilosophical texts as well. It can. In fact, it is generally accepted that the use of enthymemes is a ubiquitous element of human communication.[143] Jesse Delia argues that this results from the basic nature of human cognition: People seek in general to avoid cognitive dissonance, and the enthymeme persuades by activating that instinct—that is, by encouraging people to accept the implications of their presuppositions.[144]

Vegge's ability to locate enthymemes in Paul is therefore hardly evidence that he was educated in philosophical rhetoric. In order for this argument to be at all persuasive, Vegge would need to identify the particular stylistic features of enthymeme use in Hellenistic philosophical texts,

---

141. Hellholm, "Enthymemic Argumentation." Cf. Paul A. Holloway, "The Enthymeme as an Element of Style in Paul," *JBL* 120 (2001): 329–43.

142. Vegge, *Paulus und das antike Schulwesen*, 413, 423.

143. See Anders Eriksson, "Enthymemes in Pauline Argumentation: Reading between the Lines in 1 Corinthians," in *Rhetorical Argumentation in Biblical Texts: Essays from the Lund 2000 Conference* (ed. Anders Eriksson, Thomas H. Olbricht, and Walter G. Übelacker; ESEC 8; Harrisburg, Pa.: Trinity, 2002), 245–46. George Kennedy locates enthymemes in speech embedded in aboriginal Australian myths (*Comparative Rhetoric*, 48–49), and hypothesizes that enthymemes were among the earliest forms of human persuasion (41, 224–25). For their use among Tikopians, for example, see Raymond Firth, "Speech-Making and Authority in Tikopia," in *Political Language and Oratory in Traditional Society* (ed. Maurice Bloch; London: Academic Press, 1975), 42.

144. Jesse G. Delia, "The Logic Fallacy, Cognitive Theory, and the Enthymeme: A Search for the Foundations of Reasoned Discourse," *QJS* 56 (1970): 140–48. Cf. J. Scenters-Zapico, "The Social Construct of Enthymematic Understanding," *RSQ* 24 (1994): 71–87.

and then demonstrate similarities in Paul's usage. As it stands, his observation that Paul used enthymemes tells us nothing more than that Paul was making an argument.

Dissenting Voices

Not all are persuaded by the line of argument traced by Forbes and elaborated by Neyrey, Hock, and Vegge, but opposing views, though frequently expressed, have seldom been carefully argued. Two exceptions are worthy of note.

Justin Meggitt has generated considerable discussion with his *Paul, Poverty, and Survival*, a frontal attack on the "new consensus" in which Meggitt unhesitatingly places the first urban Christians in the context of ancient urban poverty.[145] By Meggitt's account, the reality of the ancient world was such that "the non-élite, over 99% of the Empire's population, could expect little more than abject poverty."[146] For Meggitt, that includes Paul. As a manual laborer, Paul would have "suffered the … long hours of labour (and the … feelings of hunger) that characterised artisan life."[147] And Meggitt is not at all convinced by arguments that Paul had a privileged childhood but, later, as a result of his conversion and newfound calling, voluntarily subjected himself to poverty. Although he accepts Paul's citizenship of both Rome and Tarsus, he considers neither to be evidence

---

145. Justin J. Meggitt, *Paul, Poverty, and Survival* (SNTW; Edinburgh: T&T Clark, 1998). For a glimpse into the ensuing discussion, see Dale B. Martin, "Justin J. Meggitt, Paul, Poverty and Survival," *JSNT* 84 (2001): 51–64; Gerd Theissen, "The Social Structure of the Pauline Communities: Some Critical Remarks on J. J. Meggitt, *Paul, Poverty, and Survival*," *JSNT* 84 (2001): 65–84; Meggitt, "Response to Martin and Theissen," *JSNT* 84 (2001): 85–94.

146. Meggitt, *Paul, Poverty and Survival*, 50. It is Meggitt's undifferentiated treatment of the non-elite 99 percent that has been the most frequently criticized aspect of his work, with a number of scholars insisting, rightly, I think, that this is an oversimplification. Stephen Friesen has led the charge toward greater nuance and precision: "Poverty in Pauline Studies: Beyond the So-Called New Consensus," *JSNT* 26 (2004): 323–61; Walter Scheidel and Steven J. Friesen, "The Size of the Economy and the Distribution of Income in the Roman Empire," *JRS* 99 (2009): 61–91. See also Bruce W. Longenecker, "Exposing the Economic Middle: A Revised Economy Scale for the Study of Early Christianity," *JSNT* 31 (2009): 243–78.

147. Meggitt, *Paul, Poverty and Survival*, 76.

of elite status, and, to his mind, Hock's notion that Paul had an aristocratic attitude toward manual labor is "extremely ill thought out."[148]

Moreover, for Meggitt the claim that Paul received an elite education is founded on a false presupposition, namely, the idea "that education and wealth are immutably bound together."[149] This assumption, though accurate with regard to the formal ἐγκύκλιος παιδεία, neglects to consider the opportunities for informal education in the ancient city. According to Meggitt: "Graeco-Roman culture was widely disseminated and displayed (it was not solely the preserve of the élite): quotations from authors such as Virgil, Ovid, Lucretius, much more complex than the one example we have from Paul, were found scratched on walls in Pompeii."[150] In short, the assumption that "only the formally educated can display signs of learning," like the idea that "only the rich consider work slavish," reveals only "the prejudices, biases, and perhaps, the socio-economic contexts of the scholars themselves"; it does not help us understand Paul.[151]

Whereas Meggitt addresses the question of Paul's education from the perspective of social history, R. Dean Anderson challenges the assertion that Paul's letters were shaped by firsthand knowledge of rhetorical theory.[152] Reviewing a large swath of rhetorical-critical treatments of Paul's letters, Anderson concludes that Paul's alleged conformity to the dictates of ancient rhetorical theory evaporates upon careful investigation.

First, with regard to form—what Quintilian would call *dispositio*—Anderson argues that Paul's letters do not in fact contain the expected divisions of a speech, a conclusion that seems to be borne out by the difficulty of arriving at anything like a consensus regarding their rhetorical structures.[153] For Anderson, any structural features that Paul's letters do

---

148. Ibid., 80–83, 88.
149. Ibid., 84.
150. Ibid., 86 n. 49. On this point, see further F. Gerald Downing, "A Bas Les Aristos: The Relevance of Higher Literature for the Understanding of the Earliest Christian Writings," *NovT* 30 (1988): 212–30; Nicholas Horsfall, "The Cultural Horizons of the 'Plebs Romana,'" *Memoirs of the American Academy in Rome* 41 (1996): 101–19.
151. Meggitt, *Paul, Poverty and Survival*, 96. See also Roetzel, *Paul*, 23.
152. R. Dean Anderson, *Ancient Rhetorical Theory and Paul* (rev. ed.; CBET 18; Leuven: Peeters, 1999). See also Philip Kern's *Rhetoric and Galatians: Assessing an Approach to Paul's Epistle* (SNTSMS 101; Cambridge: Cambridge University Press, 1998).
153. Anderson, *Ancient Rhetorical Theory*, 130; cf. Fairweather, "Galatians and

share with works of formal rhetoric can be attributed to what I will later call "general rhetoric," that is, the basic capacity of humans to persuade:

> The fact that we have been able to make some remarks drawn from the rhetorical theory connected with the *partes orationis* has more to do with the fact that most literary productions have a beginning, middle and an end, than that Paul was thinking in terms of specifically rhetorical προοίμιον, πίστεις and ἐπίλογος.[154]

With regard to argumentation—Quintilian's *inventio*—Anderson draws a similar conclusion: Yes, Paul occasionally uses παραδείγματα in his argumentation, but they often function differently from what rhetorical theorists would prescribe; moreover, "the use of examples is common in all literate societies."[155] There is no evidence here of the influence of rhetorical education.

Finally, Paul's style—*elocutio*—does not resemble that of a formal orator. In addition to being paratactic rather than periodic or hypotactic,[156] it lacks the fundamental rhetorical virtue of clarity (σαφήνεια).[157] In short, then, "it seems highly unlikely that Paul received any formal training in rhetorical theory."[158]

Classical Rhetoric," 220; Classen, *Rhetorical Criticism*, 23–27; Kern, *Rhetoric and Galatians*, 90–166.

154. Anderson, *Ancient Rhetorical Theory*, 280. Likewise Stanley K. Stowers, review of Hans Dieter Betz, *2 Corinthians 8 and 9: A Commentary on Two Administrative Letters of the Apostle Paul*, JBL 106 (1987): 730; Classen, *Rhetorical Criticism*, 24; Vegge, *A Letter about Reconciliation*, 42.

155. Anderson, *Ancient Rhetorical Theory*, 280. Anderson's intuition here is sound: see further George A. Kennedy, *Comparative Rhetoric: An Historical and Cross-Cultural Introduction* (New York: Oxford University Press, 1998), 6, 42, 126, 225.

156. Anderson, *Ancient Rhetorical Theory*, 281.

157. Ibid., 279–81. Similarly, Marius Reiser, *Sprache und literarische Formen des Neuen Testaments: Eine Einführung* (UTB 2197; Paderborn: Schöningh, 2001), 73.

158. Anderson, *Ancient Rhetorical Theory*, 277. E. Randolph Richards comes to a similar conclusion on the basis of Paul's frequent anacolutha and uneven grammar (*Paul and First-Century Letter Writing: Secretaries, Composition, and Collection* [Downers Grove, Ill.: InterVarsity Press, 2004], 139).

Conclusion

In reaching the conclusion that Paul did not have the benefit of a rhetorical education, Anderson is now in the minority. As we have seen, however, until a few decades ago, his would have been an uncontroversial assertion. Patristic exegetes, responding to the ridicule of Celsus and his ilk, conceded that Paul's prose did not satisfy the aesthetic criteria of the Greco-Roman literati. And modern critical scholars, until recently, concurred: Paul's manner of expression was perhaps passionate and personal, but it certainly was not cultured.

Despite this agreement, patristic and modern interpreters parted ways in the explanations they put forward for the peculiar forcefulness of Paul's letters. For Origen, Chrysostom, and Augustine, it was the inspiration of the Holy Spirit that explained the treasure of divine wisdom hidden in the clay vessel of Paul's diction.[159] Modern critical scholarship could not countenance this conception of inspiration, but was long enamored of the romantic idea of natural eloquence: Paul, it was argued, escaped the empty formalism of the rhetorical schools; his was the unruly but authentic rhetoric of the heart.

Current scholarship is wary of both explanations. Inspiration is generally considered a matter of private belief to which no explanatory value should be attributed, and appeal to the "natural" looks suspiciously like a way to sneak inspiration in the back door, to insist that Paul's letters are not "mere rhetoric," or to keep him safely insulated from "pagan" influence.[160] So, faced with a growing mountain of literature highlighting the rhetorical dimensions of Paul's letters, recent scholars have now put forward their own explanation: Paul writes persuasively because he learned how to do so at school.

Part 2 of this study will examine the adequacy of this hypothesis for explaining the nature of Paul's prose. What lends this task particular urgency is the role Paul's putative education currently plays in discussions concerning his social location. As we have seen, although Paul's alleged

---

159. See esp. Chrysostom, *Laud. Paul.* 4.13; *Hom. 1 Cor.* 3.4 (PG 61:27–28); Augustine, *Doct. chr.* 4.7.11. Cf. Origen, *Comm. Jo.* 4.2. See further the section Τὸ ἐν Λόγῳ Ἰδιωτικὸν τοῦ Ἀποστόλου, ch. 12 below.

160. See esp. the insightful comments of Margaret M. Mitchell, "Le style, c'est l'homme: Aesthetics and Apologetics in the Stylistic Analysis of the New Testament," *NovT* 51 (2009): 369–88.

Roman citizenship and his ostensibly aristocratic attitude toward labor continue to exert influence, above all it is the conviction that Paul demonstrates the sort of rhetorical prowess that he can only have derived from elite education that sponsors the current consensus—namely, that Paul was a man of relatively high social status, and that his manual labor is not decisive for determining his social location. If it can be demonstrated that what Paul knows of persuasion need not have been learned in school, then we evidently must reconsider this consensus, and, with it, the nature of Paul's mission and the letters that are its legacy.

2
SECOND CORINTHIANS 10–13:
A HISTORICAL AND LITERARY INTRODUCTION

As C. J. Classen has remarked, since the work of Betz and Kennedy there has come such a flood of rhetorical-critical publications that not even the specialist can hope to master them all.[1] Clearly, then, it would not be practicable to attempt to evaluate all the evidence scholars have adduced of Paul's knowledge of classical rhetoric. Instead, I will use 2 Cor 10–13, a text widely considered emblematic of Paul's rhetorical prowess, as a test case.

SECOND CORINTHIANS 10–13 AND
RECENT EVALUATIONS OF PAUL'S RHETORIC

Those familiar with the history of the rhetorical criticism of Paul's letters may be surprised by this selection. It was, after all, Hans Dieter Betz's commentary on Galatians that sparked the recent resurgence of interest in the relationship between Paul's letters and ancient rhetorical theory. But Betz's legacy here is an odd one: although many scholars enthusiastically have endorsed Betz's premise—that is, the notion that Galatians is best understood by comparison with ancient rhetorical theory—they have been unable to agree with Betz, or with one another, what, precisely, rhetorical criticism of the letter should give us to understand.[2] Significantly, this lack

---

1. Classen, "Kann die rhetorische Theorie helfen?" 146.
2. For further discussion, see Porter, "Paul of Tarsus and His Letters," 541–47, 561; Anderson, *Ancient Rhetorical Theory*, 129–42; Kern, *Rhetoric and Galatians*, 90–119; Duane F. Watson, "The Three Species of Rhetoric and the Study of the Pauline Epistles," in *Paul and Rhetoric* (ed. J. Paul Sampley and Peter Lampe; New York: T&T Clark, 2010), 36–39. See also Classen, "St. Paul's Epistles and Ancient Greek and Roman Rhetoric," 339–42; Classen, "Kann die rhetorische Theorie helfen?" 156–69. A number of significant contributions to the discussion are conveniently collected

of agreement concerns not only the finer details of rhetorical analysis but also the basic matters of rhetorical species and arrangement.

This has not dissuaded advocates of the method. According to Jerome Neyrey, "Even if scholars subsequently challenge this or that part of Betz's arrangement, they only prove that the initial insight was right."[3] But why should this be, exactly? Can we really measure the success of a method by the number of competing claims it generates? At what point, one wonders, has it simply failed to be probative?

Notably, Betz himself recognized that the relationship between any prescribed rhetorical τάξις and the arrangement of Galatians was far from straightforward. He admitted that the paranetic material in Gal 5–6 could not be explained on the basis of rhetorical theory.[4] And, when faced with the difficulty of wrestling the disparate material of Gal 3–4 into the outline required by his rhetorical analysis, he was forced to suggest, "Paul has been very successful—as a skilled rhetorician would be expected to be—in disguising his argumentative strategy."[5] Comments of this sort have proliferated in Pauline scholarship, and have served Betz and his followers well, for, in addition to being compellingly counterintuitive, they insulate their claims from any attempt at falsification: By this logic, the more clearly it be demonstrated that Paul did not follow rhetorical expectations, the more certain we should be that he was a rhetorical genius.

This is not to say that our inability confidently to locate the *partes orationis* in Paul's letters in itself demonstrates his unfamiliarity with rhetorical theory. As Margaret Mitchell in particular has emphasized, we often have the same difficulty if we seek the prescribed rhetorical τάξις in orations produced by speakers who we know on other grounds to have been trained rhetors.[6] But notice what such a statement implies: For Paul, as for Demosthenes, if we seek evidence of rhetorical training, we must rely on what can be determined *on other grounds*. Close conformity to the prescribed arrangement of the handbooks may perhaps provide evidence of rhetorical training. But lack of conformity, such as even Betz agrees we find in Galatians, is simply inconclusive: it

---

in Mark D. Nanos, ed., *The Galatians Debate: Contemporary Issues in Rhetorical and Historical Interpretation* (Peabody, Mass.: Hendrickson, 2002).

3. Neyrey, "Social Location of Paul," 134.
4. Betz, "Literary Composition and Function," 375–76.
5. Ibid., 369.
6. Mitchell, *Rhetoric of Reconciliation*, 8–11.

may indicate the artful flexibility of a trained master, or it may simply indicate ignorance.

At best, then, the relationship between ancient rhetorical theory and the arrangement of Galatians is either enigmatic or disguised. Thus it proves difficult to argue—or, again, to falsify the argument—that the structure of Galatians provides meaningful evidence of Paul's rhetorical education.

Prior to his work on Galatians, however, Betz sharpened his rhetorical-critical teeth on 2 Cor 10–13.[7] And it is here, in fact, that rhetorical criticism has produced what are generally thought to be assured results. Indeed, 2 Cor 10–13 has recently been called "Paul's rhetorical tour de force," a "magnificent composition," and "a brilliant piece of text."[8] As we will see, these judgments have not arisen from assessment of rhetorical τάξις but rather from analysis of specific forms, figures, and rhetorical strategies embedded in the letter.

For previous generations of scholarship, what was most remarkable about this passage was its ability to convey Paul's spirit, capturing his heartfelt indignation and his fiery passion. A strange but compelling flow of words, it was agreed, had erupted from the intensity of Paul's emotion. Thus Hans Windisch observed how "die Leidenschaft verwandelt mit einem Mal den ἰδιώτης τῷ λόγῳ in einen δεινότατος τὸν λόγον."[9] Others described the passage in similar terms: For Edgar Goodspeed, this was "a passage of the most amazing force and vigor … [that possesses] a power and effectiveness seldom equaled in any literature."[10] And Alfred Plum-

---

7. Betz, *Der Apostel Paulus und die sokratische Tradition*. See also Betz, "Rhetoric and Theology," 126–27 n. 1.

8. Witherington, *Conflict and Community in Corinth*, 373; Margaret M. Mitchell, "A Patristic Perspective on Pauline περιαυτολογία," *NTS* 47 (2001): 354; Betz, "Rhetoric and Theology," 155.

9. Hans Windisch, *Der zweite Korintherbrief* (9th ed.; KEK 6; Göttingen: Vandenhoeck & Ruprecht, 1924), 349: "passion all at once transformed the one 'untrained in speech' into the most powerful of speakers." See also Anton Fridrichsen, "Sprachliches und Stilistisches zum Neuen Testament," in *Exegetical Writings: A Selection* (ed. Chrys C. Caragounis and Tord Fornberg; WUNT 76; Tübingen: Mohr Siebeck, 1994), 289; repr. from *Kungliga Humanistiska Vetenskaps-Samfundet i Uppsala, Årsbok* 1 (1943); Heinrici, *Der zweite Brief an die Korinther*, 314.

10. Edgar J. Goodspeed, *An Introduction to the New Testament* (Chicago: University of Chicago Press, 1937), 61.

mer spoke of "a rhythmical and rhetorical swing that sweeps one away in admiration of its impassioned intensity."[11]

In recent decades, though, a new consensus has emerged that explains this passage not as a function of Paul's emotional intensity but rather as a manifestation of his mastery of the classical rhetorical tradition. In fact, 2 Cor 10–13 has become the text most frequently cited as evidence of Paul's rhetorical prowess.[12] It was this passage that led Judge to inquire into the social context of Paul's boasting, and this passage that is the lynchpin in the arguments of Christopher Forbes, Peter Marshall, and now Tor Vegge that Paul received formal training in rhetoric.[13]

The extent to which 2 Cor 10–13 has shaped scholarly imagination concerning Paul's rhetoric is particularly evident from Jerome Murphy-O'Connor's treatment in his *Paul: A Critical Life*. According to Murphy-O'Connor, Paul ordinarily restrained himself from rhetorical display so as not to distract from the message of the gospel (cf. 1 Cor 2:5), but "his conscious control … collapsed in the heat of anger, and in the Fool's Speech (2 Cor. 11:1 to 12:13) deeply engrained qualities become evident,"[14] namely, "the masterful facility and freedom with which he employs a number of the techniques of rhetoric"—techniques, says Murphy-O'Connor, that he can only have learned in school.[15] The implication, of course, is that if it were it not for 2 Cor 10–13, scholars might be taken in by Paul's self-characterization as a rhetorical amateur (2 Cor 11:6). But thanks to Paul's passionate outburst, the truth is out.

So, if there is one text regarding which all seem to agree that Paul is dependent on knowledge of the formal tradition of ancient rhetoric, it is 2 Cor 10–13. There are quibbles regarding how, precisely, Paul manipulates rhetorical conventions—that is, the extent to which he conforms to or subverts the established protocol—but there is essential agreement that the passage is a rhetorically astute response to his opponents' claims.[16]

---

11. Alfred Plummer, *A Critical and Exegetical Commentary on the Second Epistle of St. Paul to the Corinthians* (ICC; Edinburgh: T&T Clark, 1915), xlviii.

12. Witness, e.g., Duane Watson, "Second Corinthians 10–13 as the Best Evidence That Paul Received a Rhetorical Education" (paper presented at the annual meeting of the Society of Biblical Literature, Chicago, 17 November 2012).

13. Judge, "Paul's Boasting"; Forbes, "Comparison, Self-Praise, and Irony"; Marshall, *Enmity in Corinth*, 390; Vegge, *Paulus und das antike Schulwesen*, 406–23.

14. Murphy-O'Connor, *Paul: A Critical Life*, 51.

15. Ibid., 320.

16. See esp. Judge, "Paul's Boasting"; Forbes, "Comparison, Self-Praise, and

This contrasts strikingly with the inconclusiveness that has beset rhetorical studies of Galatians and suggests that it is here, if anywhere, that we will find evidence of Paul's rhetorical education.[17]

Irony"; Frederick W. Danker, "Paul's Debt to the *De Corona* of Demosthenes: A Study of Rhetorical Techniques in 2 Corinthians," in *Persuasive Artistry: Studies in New Testament Rhetoric in Honor of George A. Kennedy* (ed. Duane F. Watson; JSNTSup 50; Sheffield: Sheffield Academic Press, 1991), 262–80; Scott J. Hafemann, "'Self-Commendation' and Apostolic Legitimacy in 2 Corinthians: A Pauline Dialectic?" *NTS* 36 (1990): 66–88; Mitchell, "Patristic Perspective"; Glenn S. Holland, "Speaking Like a Fool: Irony in 2 Corinthians 10–13," in *Rhetoric and the New Testament: Essays from the 1992 Heidelberg Conference* (ed. Stanley E. Porter and Thomas H. Olbricht; JSNTSup 90; Sheffield: Sheffield Academic Press, 1993), 250–64; Duane F. Watson, "Paul's Boasting in 2 Corinthians 10–13 as Defense of His Honor: A Socio-rhetorical Analysis," in *Rhetorical Argumentation in Biblical Texts: Essays from the 2000 Lund Conference* (ed. Anders Eriksson, Thomas H. Olbricht, and Walter G. Übelacker; ESEC 8; Harrisburg, Pa.: Trinity, 2002), 260–75; Scott B. Andrews, "Too Weak Not to Lead: The Form and Function of 2 Cor 11.23b–33," *NTS* 41 (1995): 263–76; Antonio Pitta, "Il 'discorso del pazzo' o periautologia immoderata? Analisi retoricoletteraria di 2 Cor 11,1–12,18," *Bib* 87 (2006): 493–510; Michael Wojciechowski, "Paul and Plutarch on Boasting," *Journal of Greco-Roman Christianity and Judaism* 3 (2006): 99–109; John T. Fitzgerald, "Paul, the Ancient Epistolary Theorists, and 2 Corinthians 10–13," in *Greeks, Romans, and Christians: Essays in Honor of Abraham J. Malherbe* (ed. David L. Balch, Everett Ferguson, and Wayne A. Meeks; Minneapolis: Fortress, 1990), 190–200; Charles A. Wanamaker, "'By the Power of God': Rhetoric and Ideology in 2 Corinthians 10–13," in *Fabrics of Discourse: Essays in Honor of Vernon K. Robbins* (ed. David Gowler, Gregory Bloomquist, and Duane F. Watson; New York: Trinity, 2003), 194–221.

17. Following Margaret M. Mitchell (*Rhetoric of Reconciliation*), many have been persuaded that 1 Corinthians too provides compelling evidence of Paul's formal rhetorical capacity, in particular his ability to compose a letter that conforms to the generic expectations governing deliberative rhetoric. According to Mitchell, "1 Corinthians is a single letter of unitary composition which contains a deliberative argument persuading the Christian community at Corinth to become reunified" (1); its thesis is 1 Cor 1:10. This argument depends for its force on the appearance in Paul's letter of four features she deems characteristic of deliberative rhetoric: (a) a focus on action to be undertaken in the future; (b) appeal to what is advantageous (τὸ συμφέρον); (c) proof by example; and (d) an appropriate (political) subject of deliberation, often factionalism and civic concord (23). The first and third of these features are simply too general to serve as evidence of Paul's knowledge of rhetorical conventions—that is, in the terminology that will be introduced in ch. 9 below, they are aspects of general rhetoric. If we knew on other grounds that Paul's letter was composed in accordance with one of Aristotle's three species, such features would perhaps help us choose (cf. 25, 42). But of course they are widespread also in texts uninformed by Aristotle's scheme. Appeal to

The "Letter of Tears"

It is not necessary to detain ourselves here with a detailed discussion of the composition history of 2 Corinthians. Indeed, although on occasion the exegetical proposals of this study are enriched by the compositional hypothesis I adopt, the primary argument is in no way dependent on it. So I offer only a brief summary of the position taken here, as well a few critical comments on recent efforts to defend the unity of 2 Corinthians on the basis of its rhetorical plausibility.

The theory that 2 Corinthians is a composite letter was first advanced by J. S. Semler in his 1776 commentary and achieved considerable influence through the work of A. Hausrath and J. H. Kennedy around the turn of the previous century.[18] Although there is continued debate regarding the number of letters that canonical 2 Corinthians comprises, as well as

---

what is advantageous is, if not particular to, at least especially characteristic of deliberative rhetoric; however, as Dean Anderson notes, none of Paul's references to the concept of advantage concern what is ostensibly the thesis of the letter (*Ancient Rhetorical Theory*, 256): Paul does not tell the Corinthians that it is in their best interest to avoid factions; instead, he argues that it is advantageous for them to avoid fornication (6:12), to stay unmarried in the short time before the eschaton (7:35), and not to give offense in eating idol food (10:23, 33). And although of course each of these issues has the potential to create conflict in Corinth, Paul simply does not, *pace* Mitchell, integrate his treatment of them into a unified argument for unity. Paul's discussion of marriage in ch. 7 provides a useful example. Mitchell is right, surely, that marriage and sexuality can be sources of contention (121–25), but Paul shows no concern about this. The two things that do concern Paul are the potential for fornication, which he abhors (vv. 2, 5, 9, 36–37), and the need for single-minded focus in light of the impending eschaton (vv. 26–35). (A detailed evaluation of Mitchell's proposal appears in the dissertation on which this study is based: "'Where is the Voice Coming from?': Querying the Evidence for Paul's Rhetorical Education in 2 Corinthians 10–13" [Ph.D. diss., University of St. Michael's College, 2012], 79–88.)

18. Johann Salomo Semler, *Paraphrasis II: Epistolae ad Corinthios* (Halle: Hemmerde, 1776); Adolf Hausrath, *Der Vier-Capitel-Brief des Paulus an die Korinther* (Heidelberg: Bassermann, 1870); James Houghton Kennedy, *The Second and Third Epistles of St. Paul to the Corinthians: With Some Proofs of Their Independence and Mutual Relation* (London: Methuen, 1900). On the history of interpretation, see esp. Hans Dieter Betz, *2 Corinthians 8 and 9: A Commentary on Two Administrative Letters of the Apostle Paul* (ed. George W. MacRae; Hermeneia; Philadelphia: Fortress, 1985), 3–36; Margaret E. Thrall, *A Critical and Exegetical Commentary on the Second Epistle to the Corinthians* (2 vols.; ICC; Edinburgh: T&T Clark, 1994–2000), 1:3–49; L. L. Welborn, "The Identification of 2 Corinthians 10–13 with the 'Letter of Tears,'" *NovT* 37 (1995):

their relative chronology, most would concur that chapters 10–13 constitute an independent letter.[19]

The most conspicuous piece of evidence here is Paul's abrupt change of tone. Chapters 10–13 are famously agonized and polemical—a striking change from chapters 1–9, where Paul is conciliatory and, his anxiety having been relieved by Titus's welcome report from Corinth, effusive in his gratitude for God's consolation.[20] Indeed, as Kirsopp Lake opined, "If 2 Cor. x.–xiii. had existed in a separate form, no one would ever have dreamt of suggesting that it was the continuation of 2 Cor. i.–ix."[21]

Both Hausrath and Kennedy took the theory one step further, identifying 2 Cor 10–13 with the "tearful letter"—or, at least, the bulk thereof—to which Paul refers in 2 Cor 2:3–4 and 7:8–12. Paul's general description of this letter, written, he says, ἐκ πολλῆς θλίψεως καὶ συνοχῆς καρδίας and διὰ πολλῶν δακρύων (2:4), is in accord with Paul's evident anguish in 2 Cor 10–13. But even more telling are a number of verbal echoes or "cross-references" in 2 Cor 1–9 that show Paul taking up motifs from his earlier letter.[22] I note only three: (1) Chapters 10–13 contain Paul's self-conscious and reluctant self-commendation (10:12, 18; 12:11). In 3:1 and 5:12, Paul insists that he is not *again* commending himself. (2) In chapter 10, Paul warns that from now on he will be as forceful in person as he is in his letters (10:1–2, 9–11)—a motif that culminates in 13:1–4, when Paul threatens a visit to the Corinthians in which he will not spare them discipline (οὐ φείσομαι). In what appears to be an attempt to justify his decision not to undertake this punitive visit after all (1:15–2:4), Paul tells the Corinthians: "It was to spare you (φειδόμενος ὑμῶν) that I did not come again

---

136–43; Francis Watson, "2 Cor. X–XIII and Paul's Painful Letter to the Corinthians," *JTS* 35 (1984): 324–31; Vegge, *A Letter about Reconciliation*, 7–34.

19. For an excellent and succinct statement of the evidence, see L. L Welborn, *An End to Enmity: Paul and the "Wrongdoer" of Second Corinthians* (BZNW 185; Berlin: de Gruyter, 2011), xix–xxviii.

20. See Watson, "2 Corinthians X–XIII and Paul's Painful Letter," 324; Günther Bornkamm, "The History of the Origin of the So-Called Second Letter to the Corinthians," *NTS* 8 (1962): 258; Plummer, *Second Epistle*, 269–70. Note also the more specific discrepancies identified by Welborn, *An End to Enmity*, xx.

21. Kirsopp Lake, *The Earlier Epistles of St. Paul: Their Motive and Origin* (London: Rivingtons, 1911), 157. Cf. Hausrath, *Der Vier-Capitel-Brief*, 1.

22. For what follows, see the classic statements of Kennedy, *Second and Third Epistles*, 89–98; Plummer, *Second Epistle*, xxix–xxxiii; Lake, *Earlier Epistles*, 155–62; as well as Welborn, *An End to Enmity*, xxii–xxiv.

to Corinth" (1:23). (3) In retrospect, Paul can say that his earlier letter functioned to prove the Corinthians' obedience (2:9), whereas at the time of that previous letter, Paul had been preparing to punish disobedience (10:6). In short, the conflictual situation reflected in 2 Cor 10–13 recurs, now in the past tense, in chapters 1–9[23]—which themselves, many argue, comprise multiple letters.[24]

---

23. The two major objections to this thesis, that it fails to make sense of what is said about Titus's visits and that there is no explicit reference in chs. 10–13 to the offense discussed in 2:5–11, have been refuted by Francis Watson ("2 Corinthians X–XIII and Paul's Painful Letter," 332–35) and Larry Welborn ("Identification of 2 Corinthians 10–13"), respectively.

24. As was noted initially by Johannes Weiss, 2 Cor 2:14–7:4 interrupts Paul's ongoing account of his encounter with Titus in Macedonia, from whom he heard consoling news concerning the Corinthians; thus 2 Cor 1:1–2:13; 7:5–16 appears to be a separate, self-contained "Letter of Reconciliation" that postdates the "Letter of Tears" (*Earliest Christianity*, 1:349; see also Bornkamm, "So-Called Second Letter," 259–60). Weiss considered the intervening section—2:14–6:13; 7:2–4 (6:14–7:1 appears to be an interpolation)—to be, together with chs. 10–13, this tearful letter (*Earliest Christianity*, 1:348–49; cf. Rudolf Bultmann, *Exegetische Probleme des zweiten Korintherbriefes* [2nd ed.; Darmstadt: Wissenschaftliche Buchgesellschaft, 1963], 14 n. 16). But the considerable difference in tone between the two fragments makes such an identification doubtful, as noted by Dieter Georgi, *The Opponents of Paul in Second Corinthians: A Study of Religious Propaganda in Late Antiquity* (Philadelphia: Fortress, 1986), 13–14; Bornkamm, "So-Called Second Letter," 260; Watson, "2 Corinthians X–XIII and Paul's Painful Letter," 330. It is preferable to see two independent letters in 2 Cor 1–7, both of which were composed after 2 Cor 10–13. Note that here I disagree with Bornkamm, who argues that 2:14–6:13; 7:2–4 was "written in an earlier moment when Paul heard for the first time of the appearance of his opponents, but when the community had not yet fallen prey to them" ("So-Called Second Letter," 260; cf. Georgi, *Opponents of Paul*, 14; Margaret M. Mitchell, "The Corinthian Correspondence and the Birth of Pauline Hermeneutics," in *Paul and the Corinthians: Studies on a Community in Conflict; Essays in Honour of Margaret Thrall* [ed. Trevor J. Burke and J. K. Elliott; NovTSup 109; Leiden: Brill, 2003], 21, 27–30). There is simply no textual evidence for this theory; it rests solely on the general plausibility of an escalating conflict and ignores the way in which Paul's touchiness about self-commendation in 3:1 and 5:12 seems clearly to recollect his boasting in 2 Cor 10–13. So N. H. Taylor, "The Composition and Chronology of Second Corinthians," *JSNT* 44 (1991): 73–74; Welborn, *An End to Enmity*, xxiii–xxv. The status of 2 Cor 8 and 9, which are quite clearly two separate letters, remains disputed. I find persuasive, however, Margaret Mitchell's argument that the mention of Titus in 12:18 refers back to the collection visit announced in 8:6, 22. This would make 2 Cor 8 the earliest of the letters that comprise 2 Corinthians, and the only one to precede Paul's painful

But although a majority of scholars continue to view 2 Cor 10–13 as an independent letter or letter fragment, and many would identify it with Paul's "letter of tears," a number of recent interpreters have attempted to reassert the compositional unity of 2 Corinthians—and they have done so precisely on rhetorical grounds.[25] Works by J. D. Hester (Amador) and Frederick J. Long can be taken as representative of the two major modes of argumentation that have developed.

Hester criticizes proponents of partition hypotheses for what he considers a naïve view of the relationship between a text and its rhetorical exigency. "Traditional historical critics," he argues, resort to partition into discrete letters because they presume that a text should straightforwardly address a single situation and, further, should reveal "a logical, progressive development of events and circumstances."[26] A rhetorical approach, he argues, recognizes "the freedom with which argumentative and persuasive composition is conceptualized and arranged in the face of the dizzying array of circumstances that can confront an author/rhetor."[27] When the text is analyzed with this in mind, Hester insists, the underlying unity of the complex rhetorical production that is 2 Corinthians comes into view.

Hester's work offers a salutary reminder that history is inevitably more complicated than historians would prefer and that we often seek in vain for a easily narratable chain of cause and effect. But his methodological critique misses the mark. Partition theories of 2 Corinthians have been prompted not by the perceived need for a plausible rhetorical situation—simple or

---

second visit. See "Paul's Letters to Corinth: The Interpretive Intertwining of Literary and Historical Reconstruction," in *Urban Religion in Roman Corinth: Interdisciplinary Approaches* (ed. Daniel N. Schowalter and Steven J. Friesen; HTS 53; Cambridge: Harvard University Press, 2005), 307–38. 2 Cor 9 would then be the latest of the letters—a reprise, post-conflict and post-reconciliation, of Paul's request for participation in the collection.

25. See esp. Frances M. Young and David F. Ford, *Meaning and Truth in 2 Corinthians* (Biblical Foundations in Theology; London: SPCK, 1987), 27–44; Witherington, *Conflict and Community in Corinth*, 327–52; J. David Hester Amador, "The Unity of 2 Corinthians: A Test Case for a Re-discovered and Re-invented Rhetoric," *Neot* 33 (1999): 411–32; Hester Amador, "Revisiting 2 Corinthians: Rhetoric and the Case for Unity," *NTS* 46 (2000): 92–111; Fredrick J. Long, *Ancient Rhetoric and Paul's Apology: The Compositional Unity of 2 Corinthians* (SNTSMS 131; Cambridge: Cambridge University Press, 2004).

26. Hester Amador, "Revisiting 2 Corinthians," 94.

27. Ibid.

complex—but rather by observance of specific textual details, such as the "cross-references" discussed above, that have demanded some sort of explanation.[28] Certainly many have sought also to uncover a "logical, progressive development of events and circumstances," but this generally has been a way of testing various hypotheses, not of generating them.

It is not surprising, then, that where Hester's own reading of the evidence most clearly falters is in his treatment of such textual details. He is able, arguably, to provide a plausible account of how, in general terms, the rhetoric of 2 Cor 10–13 could be said to draw on themes introduced in chapters 1–9.[29] But he simply fails to attend to the specific details that convinced scholars like Kennedy, Hausrath, and Lake that 2 Cor 1–9 in fact recalls chapters 10–13 retrospectively.

The same is true of the recent monograph by Fredrick Long, who, like Hester, elects to bypass any meaningful engagement with the studies that convinced most twentieth-century interpreters of the composite nature of this text. Long seeks to argue that 2 Corinthians as a whole conforms to the conventions of epistolary forensic rhetoric—that it is, in other words, a "letter of apology," comparable to Demosthenes's *Ep. 3* and *Ep. 4* and Plato's *Ep. 7*. For Long, then, 2 Cor 10–13 comprises the *refutatio* (10:1–11:15), self-adulation (11:16–12:10), and *peroratio* (12:11–13:10) of this unified letter, which was called forth by "two interrelated charges of inconsistency": Paul failed to visit the Corinthians as he had promised, and behaved κατὰ σάρκα with respect to his use of rhetoric and pursuit of financial gain.[30]

One serious difficulty with Long's proposal has already been diagnosed incisively by Ivor Jones: 2 Cor 12:11–13:10 cannot credibly be read as the *peroratio* of the whole of 2 Corinthians.[31] Such a reading misconstrues the verses in question by ignoring the role they play in their immediate context and constructing false parallels to chapters 1–9. Or, as Jones

---

28. See, e.g., Lake, *Earlier Epistles*, 160.

29. Hester Amador, "Revisiting 2 Corinthians," 98–100. Still, I find Plummer's comments on the rhetorical implications of having chs. 10–13 follow 1–9 far more compelling than those of Hester, even if they are unadorned with theoretical terminology: "It is strange policy, immediately after imploring freshly regained friends to do their duty, to begin heaping upon them reproaches and threats" (*Second Epistle*, xxx; cf. Georgi, *Opponents of Paul*, 9).

30. Long, *Ancient Rhetoric*, 125–35.

31. Ivor H. Jones, "Rhetorical Criticism and the Unity of 2 Corinthians: One 'Epilogue,' or More?" *NTS* 54 (2008): 500–512.

puts it, "the theory of a reversed recapitulation of the letter's material [such as would be suitable to a peroration] has displaced careful exegetical work ... and encouraged inattention to distinctive features of chs. 10–13."[32]

Importantly, Jones's critique here exposes a larger difficulty with Long's method: Rather than emerging from a careful reading of the letter, Long's exegetical conclusions derive precisely from the hypothesis he is attempting to demonstrate. Let us look at just two examples, each of which concerns one of the two main charges against which Long believes Paul to be defending himself.

First, according to Long, "the theme of failing to visit (and writing instead) is a unifying theme for Paul's defense in 2 Corinthians."[33] Of course, few would deny that this theme is pervasive throughout the canonical letter. But Long's description of it simply ignores what exegetes have seen for over a century: Paul's discussions of his plans to visit Corinth are not all of a piece; instead, they presuppose different stages in Paul's less than successful attempt to exercise apostolic authority.[34] In 2 Cor 10–13 there is no indication that Paul has been criticized for his absence, or for his vacillating travel plans. Certainly he has been criticized for writing bold and forceful letters from afar (10:9–11), but this is a problem not because he has failed to visit, but because precisely because he *had* visited Corinth—and had failed while there to live up to the expectations his letters had raised (10:1; 13:2–4, 10). Contrarily, in 2 Cor 1–9 there is no hint of the παρών vs. ἀπών motif prominent in 2 Cor 10–13; instead, the problem evidently is the variability of Paul's travel plans (1:15–2:1). What we have here, then, are two quite different situations: In 2 Cor 1:15–2:13, Paul is justifying the postponement of a visit; in 2 Cor 10–13, Paul is dealing with the fallout of a disastrous one. Evidently, it is not the text itself but the presupposition that 2 Corinthians is a single apology that is driving Long's exegesis here.

Second, Long notes Paul's insistence both in 1:17 and 10:2–4 that he has not been operating κατὰ σάρκα, and thus deduces that throughout the entire letter Paul is responding to the accusation that he has "worldly intentions."[35] Oddly, though, having found an overlap in vocabulary here, Long pays no attention at all to what Paul might mean in each instance

---

32. Ibid., 508.
33. Long, *Ancient Rhetoric*, 126.
34. Cf. Plummer, *Second Epistle*, xxxi–xxxii; Lake, *Earlier Epistles*, 157–58.
35. Long, *Ancient Rhetoric*, 127.

and elects instead, ignoring the two texts he has cited, to argue, on other grounds, that Paul's alleged worldliness concerned his use of rhetoric and his financial trickery. Given the frequency and variable usage of the phrase in Paul's letters, surely one must do more than find two occurrences of the phrase κατὰ σάρκα to demonstrate that one is an echo of another. Again, the presupposition of unity seems to have displaced careful exegesis.

Finally, it is worth noting that Long does not, in fact, argue for Paul's familiarity with rhetorical conventions. No, his is the inverse argument: Paul's rhetorical knowledge is taken for granted, and the case for the unity of 2 Corinthians proceeds on the basis of this assumption. If, as this study will attempt to demonstrate, the assertion that Paul had formal knowledge of rhetorical theory cannot be sustained, such rhetorical-critical arguments for the unity of 2 Corinthians must be abandoned, or, at the very least, thoroughly reconceived.[36]

Paul and the Corinthians

That 2 Cor 10–13 is a remarkable piece of writing all agree. This text sur-

---

36. Also deserving of mention here is Ivar Vegge's recent monograph (*A Letter about Reconciliation*), which argues for the unity of 2 Corinthians on the grounds of its psychogogical coherence. What Vegge sees as the key impetus behind partition theories is the interpretive assumption that Paul's description of his "complete confidence" in the Corinthians' "obedience" (7:14–15) accurately reflects the status of their relationship. If Paul and the Corinthians are so completely reconciled, Vegge acknowledges, it is indeed difficult to see how 2 Cor 1–9 could be said to reflect the same situation as 2 Cor 10–13, which presupposes a considerable breach in their relationship. But Vegge observes that in Hellenistic psychagogy such praise as Paul offers in 2 Cor 7 is often idealized and thus serves a "hortative function," summoning the audience more fully to actualize the characteristics for which its members have been praised. Despite its very different tone, then, Paul's hortative praise, says Vegge, serves essentially the same function as his criticism of the Corinthians in 2 Cor 10–13—namely, it summons the Corinthians to complete the reconciliation with Paul that had already begun during Titus's visit. Vegge's point concerning the hortative function of praise is well taken, and he does show that Hellenistic psychagogues recommended a careful combination of both praise and criticism. But he fails to adduce any examples of a comparable combination to that putatively used by Paul—that is, praise and censure that occur in two clearly delineated segments of a discourse, and, what is more, appear not to complement but to contradict one another. Though compelling in theory, his psychagogic solution does not adequately address the specific difficulties scholars have noted with reading 2 Corinthians as a unified composition.

passes even Galatians in urgency and forcefulness, and also in vituperation. Paul, it appears, had increasingly been sidelined by the Corinthians, and in 2 Cor 10–13 he pulls out all the stops in an attempt to reassert his apostolic status. A brief overview of the situation that called for such measures will help to set the stage for the detailed exegesis offered in subsequent chapters.

First, we know from 2 Cor 13:1–2 that Paul had visited Corinth a second time prior to writing 2 Cor 10–13, and it appears that things had not gone well for him. His frustration and humiliation are evident from the tone of the letter as a whole, and his repeated reference to claims that he is bold when absent but weak or lenient when present suggest that an attempt to assert his authority in person was unsuccessful, perhaps even ridiculed (10:1–2, 8–11; 12:21; 13:2, 10; cf. 11:21a).

Paul's later recollection of this visit in the "Letter of Reconciliation" (2 Cor 1:1–2:13; 7:5–16) is short on details, but confirms this general impression. Paul explains that he had delayed his third trip to Corinth in order to avoid "another painful visit" (τὸ μὴ πάλιν ἐν λύπῃ πρὸς ὑμᾶς ἐλθεῖν [2:1]). Instead, he had sent the letter that I have identified with 2 Cor 10–13, a letter written "out of much distress and anguish of heart and with many tears" (2:4). "Someone" (τις, τοιοῦτος, αὐτός) had offended Paul deeply, behaving in the sort of way that now engendered, in retrospect, the language of punishment and forgiveness (2:5–11).[37]

There is some conflict between Paul's retrospective reference here to a solitary "wrongdoer" (ὁ ἀδικήσας [7:12]) and the plural language that he had used in the heat of battle, language that sometimes seems to refer to a body of opposition (10:2, 11b–12; 11:12–15, 18, 22–23a; 12:21; 13:2; but cf. 10:7, 10–11a; 11:20, 21b), perhaps to be equated with those Paul calls the "super-apostles" (11:5; 12:11) plus those in their sway. The evidence does not admit of a detailed reconstruction, but it seems best to assume that by the time Paul wrote the "Letter of Reconciliation," the most egregious offender—the "rebel leader," as Welborn puts it[38]—had relented, become isolated, or both, and thus Paul no longer faced what once had looked like a large-scale defection.[39]

---

37. See Welborn, *An End to Enmity*, 50–51, 63–64, 69–70.
38. Ibid., 67.
39. Ibid., 31 and passim. Welborn provides a detailed reconstruction indeed, arguing that the "wrongdoer" was Gaius, the host of the Corinthian assembly, and

It is usually thought that 2 Cor 10–13 attests to a new conflict, not to the exacerbation of the tension already evident in 1 Cor 1–4. This reading is more often asserted than argued,[40] and, in fact, it appears to depend on two highly ambiguous pieces of evidence. First, interpreters seem to assume that Paul's extremely caustic characterization of his rivals in 2 Cor 10–13 cannot be directed at the same people that he had treated with relative deference in 1 Corinthians. But Paul's treatment of Peter in Galatians would suggest that this argument is based on rather tenuous assumptions regarding his character; and, in any case, from everything we know of Paul's second visit to Corinth, it was easily disastrous enough to provide fodder for Paul to reevaluate his previous opinion. Second, it is asserted that whereas 1 Corinthians concerns tensions within the Corinthian community, 2 Cor 10–13 is written to address the influence of outsiders.[41] But this very widespread assertion inexplicably overlooks the fact that the work of other apostles was already at the root of what Paul denounced as factionalism in 1 Cor 1:12. Moreover, there is no evidence that Paul's rivals in 2 Cor 10–13 are recent arrivals,[42] only that Paul's own status is now more tenuous. (Note, in particular, that 2 Cor 11:4 gives no indication of how recently the one in question [ὁ ἐρχόμενος] had arrived). There simply are no grounds for introducing an entirely new group of rivals.

Moreover, there is considerable continuity in the nature of the problems faced by Paul. In 1 Corinthians, Paul had insisted that the mystery of God is not comprehended by human wisdom (1:17–2:13); that the mind of Christ is not grasped by those who are merely σαρκικοί (2:14–3:3); that the kingdom of God is not a matter of λόγος but of δύναμις (4:20; cf. 2:4). He uses similar terms in 2 Cor 10:3–5, contrasting his own divine-power-fueled weapons with the merely fleshly λογισμοί he combats (τὰ ὅπλα τῆς

---

narrating the history of his friendship with Paul. This is intriguing indeed but requires too many layers of speculation to be persuasive.

40. E.g., Georgi, *Opponents of Paul*, 6–7, who mistakenly attributes to Kirsopp Lake the "discovery" that 1 and 2 Corinthians address different opponents. Lake in fact argues that "it is impossible not to think that [the opponents of 2 Corinthians] were identical with the persons to whom he refers in the opening chapters of 1 Corinthians" (*Earlier Epistles*, 234).

41. So, e.g., Jerry L. Sumney, "Paul and His Opponents: The Search," in *Paul Unbound: Other Perspectives on the Apostle* (ed. Mark D. Given; Peabody, Mass.: Hendrickson Publishers, 2010), 60; Thrall, *Second Epistle*, 2:926; Hester Amador, "Revisiting 2 Corinthians," 96–97.

42. So, rightly, Mitchell, "Paul's Letters to Corinth," 334 n. 90.

στρατείας ἡμῶν οὐ σαρκικὰ ἀλλὰ δυνατὰ τῷ θεῷ). As in 1 Cor 1:17 and 2:1–5, here too Paul apparently must account for the fact that his proclamation lacks the sophistication of his rivals' (2 Cor 11:5–6). In 1 Cor 3:8, Paul had insisted upon the principle that each worker would be rewarded according to his own labor (κατὰ τὸν ἴδιον κόπον); in 2 Cor 10:15 he bitterly deplores those who boast ἐν ἀλλοτρίοις κόποις. Finally, just as in 1 Cor 4:21, where Paul offers the Corinthians a choice between his coming with discipline (ἐν ῥάβδῳ) or with gentleness (πραΰτης), so Paul announces at the outset of 2 Cor 10–13 that he writes διὰ τῆς πραΰτητος καὶ ἐπιεικείας τοῦ Χριστοῦ but is prepared to punish any disobedience when he comes (10:6; cf. 13:1–4, 10).

But if 2 Cor 10–13 represents an intensification of the same conflict that generated 1 Cor 1–4, nevertheless it is clear that Paul's relationship with the Corinthians has deteriorated significantly in the interim. This is evident above all from Paul's touchiness about the esteem shown to his rivals. Whereas in 1 Corinthians Paul had been content to suggest that another (ἄλλος) could legitimately build on the foundation he had laid—albeit with the somewhat threatening proviso that this builder's work would be tested with fire, and the builder himself liable to punishment (3:10–17)—now he scorns those who have the audacity to boast of work done in someone else's κανών (10:12–16) and dismisses their teaching as insidious proclamation of another Jesus, a different spirit, a different gospel (11:4). Whereas earlier Paul could call Apollos and himself coworkers (συνεργοί [1 Cor 3:9]), now Paul speaks angrily of those who would consider themselves his equals (11:12; cf. 10:7):[43] they are false apostles, deceitful workers, ministers of Satan who disguise themselves as ministers of Christ (11:13–15). He insists that he is not at all inferior to these

---

43. On the significance of Paul's relationship with Apollos, see Joop F. M. Smit, "'What Is Apollos? What Is Paul?' In Search for the Coherence of First Corinthians 1:10–4:21," *NovT* 44 (2002): 231–51; Ker, "Paul and Apollos," 83–84; Gerhard Sellin, "Das 'Geheimnis' der Weisheit und das Rätsel der 'Christuspartei' (zu 1 Kor 1–4)," *ZNW* 73 (1983): 69–96; Charles A. Wanamaker, "A Rhetoric of Power: Ideology and 1 Corinthians 1–4," in *Paul and the Corinthians: Studies on a Community in Conflict; Essays in Honour of Margaret Thrall* (ed. Trevor J. Burke and J. K. Elliott; NovTSup 109; Leiden: Brill, 2003), 115–37. Cf. Peter Richardson, "The Thunderbolt in Q and the Wise Man in Corinth," in *From Jesus to Paul: Studies in Honour of Frank Wright Beare* (ed. Peter Richardson and John C. Hurd; Waterloo, Ont.: Wilfred Laurier University Press, 1984), 101–7.

"super-apostles" (11:5; 12:11). What has prompted this outburst of ire, this renewed concern for his own relative status?

The details of Paul's unpleasant second visit are obscure,[44] but at four points in 2 Cor 10–13 Paul appears to quote or refer to accusations made against him, thereby providing useful clues about what has upset him:

(1) 2 Cor 10:10: ὅτι αἱ ἐπιστολαὶ μέν, φησίν, βαρεῖαι καὶ ἰσχυραί, ἡ δὲ παρουσία τοῦ σώματος ἀσθενὴς καὶ ὁ λόγος ἐξουθενημένος. Paul, it appears, is accused of being bold from afar but weak in person—an accusation, I will argue, that derives from his failure to exercise the authoritative discipline with which he had threatened the Corinthians (cf. 1 Cor 4:20–21). Though often translated as plural, φησίν here is singular, corresponding to ὁ τοιοῦτος in v. 11 and perhaps τις in v. 7. Given Paul's similar usage to refer to the chief offender in 2 Cor 2:1–5 and 7:12, this should probably be seen as a response to a specific person and perhaps a specific occurrence, not a "diatribe" style generalized attribution (contra BDF §130.3)—especially since 2 Cor 10–13 is not among those few Pauline texts in which we find a fictive interlocutor or other indicators of diatribe style.[45] This verse will be the subject of a thorough exegesis in chapter 12. For now, it is enough

---

44. Certainly there is not sufficient evidence to support Welborn's hypothesis of a charge made against Paul during a "quasi-judicial proceeding in the Corinthian assembly" ("'By the Mouth of Two or Three Witnesses': Paul's Invocation of a Deuteronomic Statute," *NovT* 52 [2010]: 217). Welborn's attempt to argue that Paul invoked Deut 19:15 in his own defense fails to account for the immediate context of the citation: Paul is threatening judgment, insisting he will not again be lenient (13:2–4). Moreover, immediately before the citation, Paul notes that this will be his third visit (13:1a); immediately afterward, he enumerates his two previous warnings (προείρηκα καὶ προλέγω [13:2]). Using Deut 19:15 as a threat may be contrary to its original purpose, and the analogy of visits/warnings and witnesses may be strained, but this remains the only reading that makes sense of the text as it stands. The cost of this interpretation, as Welborn rightly notes, is that it "requires us to assume that Paul used a citation of Scripture contrary to its stated purpose and without consideration of its context" (210). To quote Welborn again, a little mischievously, "We should not be surprised if this cost were too high for many interpreters to bear" (220). Margaret Mitchell's delightfully clever reading (*Birth of Christian Hermeneutics*, 79–94) likewise neglects the most immediate context of Paul's citation; moreover, I find it difficult to see how the Corinthians can be expected to be counting up Paul's "witnesses"—the textual demarcation of which is, by any account, far from transparent—prior to being told that their number is at issue. Mitchell wonderfully "comments with" the text, to use her phrase (12), but I am not persuaded that this is credible exegesis.

45. See esp. Welborn, *An End to Enmity*, 102–3.

to note that, whatever the specific occurrence, Paul has been treated with derision.

(2) 2 Cor 10:1: ὃς κατὰ πρόσωπον μὲν ταπεινὸς ἐν ὑμῖν, ἀπὼν δὲ θαρρῶ εἰς ὑμᾶς. Although, unlike 2 Cor 10:10, there is no explicit citation formula here, the fact that Paul interrupts himself to offer this self-deprecating characterization is widely taken as evidence that he is paraphrasing a derisive evaluation of him made by another.[46] In support of this reading we may note the repetition of this present-absent antithesis throughout the letter (cf. 10:11; 13:2, 10), which is difficult to account for unless Paul is echoing language with which the Corinthians are familiar. Importantly, this accusation appears to be related to the antithetical characterization of Paul's letters as forceful but his bodily presence as weak (10:9–11). Indeed, it may be that 10:1 and 10:10 amount to two iterations of a single complaint.

(3) 2 Cor 11:6a: εἰ δὲ καὶ ἰδιώτης τῷ λόγῳ, ἀλλ' οὐ τῇ γνώσει. We have already noted that in 1 Corinthians Paul finds himself defending his "foolish" (μωρία [1 Cor 1:18–23]) proclamation, which apparently seemed neither as wise nor as eloquent as that of his rivals (1 Cor 1:17; 2:1–5). It is not clear whether the phrasing of 2 Cor 11:6 reflects a specific characterization of Paul, but he obviously worries that he is being deemed their inferior (cf. 11:5). Again, the verse will be treated in full in chapter 12 below.

(4) 2 Cor 12:16: ἀλλὰ ὑπάρχων πανοῦργος δόλῳ ὑμᾶς ἔλαβον. In 1 Cor 9 Paul had provided what he called his ἀπολογία for those who would examine him—that is, presumably, examine his financial conduct (v. 3). The gist is this: Paul claims the right (ἐξουσία), like the other apostles, to "refrain from working for a living" (v. 6) and to reap τὰ σαρκικά from the Corinthians in exchange for τὰ πνευματικά (v. 11); however, he has not used this "right," so he says, because he wants to preserve his alternate μισθός, namely, the satisfaction of having offered the gospel free of charge (v. 18) and thus without unnecessary obstruction (v. 12). It seems strange that Paul should argue at such length in order to prove his entitlement to recompense he insists he would rather die than accept anyhow.[47] Indeed,

---

46. So already John Chrysostom, *Hom. 2 Cor.* 21.1 (PG 61:542). Also Plummer, *Second Epistle*, 273; Ralph P. Martin, *2 Corinthians* (WBC 40; Waco, Tex.: Word, 1986), 303; Victor Paul Furnish, *II Corinthians* (AB 32A; Garden City, N.Y.: Doubleday, 1984), 460.

47. The passage begins, apparently, as an attempt to illustrate, from his own expe-

the fact that Paul has to insist on this right so strenuously undermines the common interpretation that Paul was forced to defend himself precisely for *not* accepting payment.[48]

Such interpretations rely for their credibility on Paul's rhetorical questions in 2 Cor 10–13, questions that seem to imply that Paul was somehow seen to be in the wrong for not accepting support:

> Did I commit a sin by humbling myself so that you might be exalted, because I proclaimed God's news to you free of charge? … I refrained and will refrain from burdening you in any way. As the truth of Christ is in me, this boast of mine will not be silenced in the regions of Achaia.… How have you been worse off than the other churches, except that I myself did not burden you? Forgive me this wrong! … I will most gladly spend and be spent for you. If I love you more, am I to be loved less? (11:7–9; 12:12–14)

Note first that this is evidently a continuation of the same tension we observed in 1 Corinthians. As in 1 Cor 9, here too Paul insists he will be no burden (ἐγκοπή [1 Cor 9:12]; καταναρκάω [2 Cor 11:9; 12:13, 14]) but will retain his boast (καύχημα [1 Cor 9:15, 16]; καύχησις [2 Cor 11:10]) that he offers the gospel free of charge (ἀδάπανος [1 Cor 9:18]; δωρεάν [2 Cor 11:7]). Whatever forced Paul to offer an ἀπολογία in 1 Cor 9 clearly remains contentious (cf. 2 Cor 12:19). And it appears from what Paul goes

---

rience, the principle of refraining from the exercise of one's right (ἐξουσία) as elucidated in 1 Cor 8, but it does not in fact make a very good object lesson, since the example itself is controversial and thus in the end distracts from the principle it sought out to illustrate. Note here how Margaret Mitchell's emphasis on Paul's self-exemplification fails to reckon with the ambivalence of Paul's own status in Corinth (*Rhetoric of Reconciliation*, 49–60). The basic logic of the use of παραδείγματα, as Mitchell explains, is that people like to follow the examples of those they esteem (cf. Aristotle, *Rhet.* 1.6.29). Accordingly, in deliberative rhetoric it was common to adduce as examples the deeds of illustrious men and renowned cities. Paul cannot count on being thus esteemed, which renders his use of his own example rhetorically problematic—hence the notorious convolutions of 1 Cor 9.

48. E.g., Theissen, *Social Setting*, 40–49; Marshall, *Enmity in Corinth*, 165–258; Hock, *Social Context*, 50–65. Hock bypasses this problem with a startlingly misleading characterization of Paul's insistent argument: According to Hock, Paul in 1 Cor 9 "admitted" that he had the right to receive support (61).

on to say that the problem arose from suspicion that his collection project was duplicitous:[49]

> Let it be assumed that I did not burden you. Nevertheless (you say) since I was crafty, I took you in by deceit. Did I take advantage of you through any of those whom I sent to you? I urged Titus to go, and sent the brother with him. Titus did not take advantage of you, did he? (2 Cor 12:16–18)

Titus, we know from 2 Cor 8:6, had been sent to Corinth by Paul twice in relation to the collection, and had been accompanied by "the brother" at least on the second of those trips (2 Cor 8:18).[50] So there can be no doubt that it is Paul's collection project that lies in the background here, and, once we know this, it is not difficult to reconstruct the nature of the accusation. As Wilfred L. Knox explained some time ago, "The suspicion was expressed that Paul's previous refusal to accept support from his converts at Corinth was a mere pretext for exacting larger sums on a later date on the score of the alleged collection, which, it was hinted, might very well fail to find its way to those for whom it was destined."[51] Paul was incredulous that despite having worked for his living he was now accused of financial misconduct, hence the barrage of rhetorical questions cited above.

We have identified, then, the gist of a number of accusations against Paul, each of which represents an exacerbation of tensions already evident in 1 Corinthians. Perhaps these demeaning characterizations were suggested by his rivals and accepted to a greater or lesser extent by some of the Corinthians. Perhaps they were promulgated by the "wrongdoer" of 2 Cor

---

49. See esp. Hurd, *Origin of 1 Corinthians*, 205–6.

50. The fact that 2 Cor 8:18 and 2 Cor 12:18 appear to be references to the same visit by Titus and "the brother," the former prior to the event and the latter afterward, is one piece of evidence adduced by Margaret Mitchell in her cogent argument that 2 Cor 8 was sent after 1 Corinthians but prior to 2 Cor 10–13. See "Paul's Letters to Corinth," 326.

51. Wilfred L. Knox, *St Paul and the Church of Jerusalem* (Cambridge: Cambridge University Press, 1925), 328; cited in Hurd, *Origin of 1 Corinthians*, 205–6. Cf. Welborn, *An End to Enmity*, 166–81. Further support for this reading comes from Paul's insistence in 2 Cor 8:20–21 that he will behave such that no one blame him with regard to the collection, an assertion that makes little sense if there was no suspicion in the air.

7:12, who was not one of Paul's rival apostles but was under their sway.[52] In any case, Paul evidently found the whole affair humiliating, and, in 2 Cor 10–13, fought to reassert his primacy in Corinth. If Paul had the capacity for winning rhetoric, this clearly would have been the time to deploy it.

Putative Evidence of Rhetorical Education in 2 Corinthians 10–13

What evidence, then, have interpreters adduced of Paul's rhetorical prowess? More specifically, what features of Paul's rhetoric in 2 Cor 10–13 have been thought to reflect familiarity with the formal tradition of Greco-Roman rhetoric? There are six prominent arguments to consider here, and it is these with which I will be concerned in the subsequent six chapters. At this point, it will be helpful briefly to summarize the evidence that has been brought forward:

> (1) First, it has been asserted that the form of 2 Cor 10–13 as a whole corresponds to the formal prescriptions of epistolary theory.
> (2) More frequent are claims that Paul's "boasting" in this passage attests to his familiarity with ancient rhetorical conventions for self-praise (περιαυτολογία) as described above all in Plutarch's *De laude ipsius*.
> (3) Paul's list of tribulations in 2 Cor 11:23–30 is generally taken as an example of a *peristasis* catalogue, which, we are told, was a literary form common in the "diatribes" of moral philosophers. According to some, Paul used the form, conventionally enough, to assert his status as an ideal sage; for others, Paul's boasting in weakness amounts to a parody, a *reductio ad absurdum* of his opponents' boasting in their achievements.
> (4) Interpreters almost uniformly refer to 2 Cor 11:1–12:10 (or thereabouts) as Paul's "Fool's Speech" or *Narrenrede*, and suggest, explicitly or implicitly, that the *Narrenrede* was an established literary or dramatic form that Paul adapted to his situation.
> (5) It is frequently argued that in 2 Cor 10–13 Paul engages in a rhetorical *synkrisis*, comparing himself with his rivals as prescribed by rhetorical convention.

---

52. So Welborn, *An End to Enmity*, passim.

(6) Underlying the majority of rhetorical-critical approaches to 2 Cor 10–13 is the conviction that Paul's rhetoric here is ironic, and thus attests to his rhetorical sophistication.

In addition to these six main rhetorical features, exegetes have identified a variety of minor rhetorical figures in these chapters. Particular attention has been paid to Paul's litany of hardships in 2 Cor 11:16–12:10, wherein already J. Weiss identified such figures as parallelism, anaphora, antistrophe, homoioteleuton, homoioptoton, and isocolon.[53] As we will see in our discussion of *peristasis* catalogues below, all of these stylistic features correspond to what has been called "catalogue style" and thus need not receive independent treatment.

---

53. Weiss, "Beiträge zur Paulinischen Rhetorik," 185–87. Cf. Heinrici, *Der zweite Brief an die Korinther*, 313–14; Josef Zmijewski, *Der Stil der paulinischen "Narrenrede": Analyse der Sprachgestaltung in 2Kor 11,1–12,10 als Beitrag zur Methodik von Stiluntersuchungen neutestamentlicher Texte* (BBB 52; Cologne: Hanstein, 1978), passim.

Part 2
Querying Rhetorical Criticism of 2 Corinthians 10–13

3
Forensic Rhetoric, Epistolary Types, and Rhetorical Education

As we saw in part 1, in recent decades interpreters of Paul have concluded with increasing confidence that his letters attest to the sort of rhetorical sophistication that can only have been learned in school. This is, we noted, a reversal of what had been the dominant view until well into the twentieth century. Prior to the recent rise of rhetorical criticism, scholars were all but agreed that Paul's letters, though forceful in their own peculiar way, differed markedly from those of the rhetorically trained literati, and thus that their persuasive force, such as it was, must be explained on grounds other than rhetorical education.

The burden of part 2 of this study, then, is to examine the evidence that has sponsored the overthrow of this long-held consensus. As the review of recent scholarship above has demonstrated, arguments for Paul's rhetorical education—and thus his elevated social status—depend all but exclusively on alleged correspondence between Greco-Roman rhetorical conventions and various rhetorical features in Paul's letters. What, then, is the nature of this correspondence? Do Paul's letters in fact evince familiarity with this formal rhetorical tradition? Or, to put the question another way, does formal rhetorical education provide an adequate explanation for the nature of Paul's persuasive voice?

Epistolary Theory and Paul's Rhetorical Education

Unlike rhetorical-critical studies of Galatians, which have been concerned above all with demonstrating the ostensible conformity of the structure of the letter to the *partes orationis* described by ancient rhetorical theorists, treatments of Paul's rhetoric in 2 Cor 10–13 have focused primarily on rhetorical forms and figures embedded within the letter. In fact, most seem to agree that 2 Cor 10–13 is not amenable to formal description in terms of rhetorical disposition.¹ This is really no surprise: 2 Cor 10–13 is not a speech; it is a letter. More immediately plausible, then, than analysis in terms of rhetorical τάξις is John Fitzgerald's assertion that Paul's letter has affinities with the letter types described by ancient epistolary theorists—affinities that, for Fitzgerald, attest to Paul's rhetorical education:

> Inasmuch as … instruction in epistolary style was provided by teachers of rhetoric, the correspondence of Paul's letters to the styles and letter types given by Ps.-Demetrius and Ps.-Libanius … provides another piece of evidence that Paul's educational level was high and that he had received training in rhetoric.²

As we will see, however, Fitzgerald's argument misconstrues both the nature of the epistolary handbooks and their role in ancient rhetorical education.

In addition to assessing the viability of Fitzgerald's argument, I intend the following discussion to play a second role also—namely, to establish a historical context in which to evaluate the evidence for Paul's rhetorical education. Specifically, I hope to untangle the conflation, common in current New Testament scholarship, of literate education with formal rhetorical training. Although it is true that literary *paideia*, which included formal education in rhetoric, generally was available only among the elite, basic literacy and rudimentary letter-writing ability were more widespread, and those who possessed them need not have had any meaningful exposure to advanced literary curricula.

---

1. So, e.g., Bruce W. Winter, "The Toppling of Favorinus and Paul by the Corinthians," in *Early Christianity and Classical Culture: Comparative Studies in Honor of Abraham J. Malherbe* (ed. John T. Fitzgerald, Thomas H. Olbricht, and L. Michael White; NovTSup 110; Leiden: Brill, 2003), 303. Cf. Jan Lambrecht, "The Fool's Speech and Its Context: Paul's Particular Way of Arguing in 2 Cor 10–13," *Bib* 82 (2001): 305–24. Although they have not commanded much influence, there have been attempts to describe the arrangement of 2 Cor 10–13 in terms of rhetorical theory: Hans-Georg Sundermann, *Der schwache Apostel und die Kraft der Rede: Eine rhetorische Analyse von 2 Kor 10–13* (Europäische Hochschulschriften Series 23, Theologie 575; Frankfurt: Lang, 1996); Brian K. Peterson, *Eloquence and the Proclamation of the Gospel in Corinth* (SBLDS 163; Atlanta: Scholars Press, 1998), 75–139. Both suffer from a failure to engage actual specimens of the rhetorical genres to which they assign Paul's letter, and are dependent almost exclusively on the handbooks' functional descriptions.

2. Fitzgerald, "Ancient Epistolary Theorists," 193; cf. Neyrey, "Social Location of Paul," 130–33.

Letter Types in 2 Corinthians 10–13

In his influential commentary, Hans Windisch noted that 2 Cor 1–7 and 10–13 bore resemblance, "im Ganzen oder auf einzelne Abschnitte," to a number of letter types described by Pseudo-Demetrius and Pseudo-Libanius.[3] The "apologetic" letter (Ps.-Demetrius 18) was one such type, but so were the "accusing" (17), the "reproachful" (4), the "censorious" (6), the "vituperative" (9), the "admonishing" (7), and the "threatening type" (8). "Es ist für den Griechen bezeichnend," Windisch remarked, "dass er für den Typus des Streitbriefes so viel Nuancen zur Verfügung hat."[4]

Windisch did not, apparently, delve any deeper into the matter than consideration of the labels Pseudo-Demetrius and Pseudo-Libanius assigned to their letter types. And Fitzgerald's essay does not get us much further. Consigning almost all discussion of what Pseudo-Demetrius actually says to the footnotes, Fitzgerald simply undertakes a reading of 2 Cor 10–13 that characterizes what Paul seeks to do in terminology drawn from these ancient letter manuals. Thus when Paul "entreats" the Corinthians (10:1–2), Fitzgerald invokes Pseudo-Demetrius's "supplicatory" letter (12), when he threatens punishment, this is deemed comparable to the "threatening" letter type (8), and so on. In total, Fitzgerald suggests that 2 Cor 10–13 evinces familiarity with seven letter types,[5] and thus concludes that it is a "mixed" letter.[6]

---

3. Windisch, *Der zweite Korintherbrief*, 8.

4. Ibid.: "It is characteristic of the Greek that for the disputative letter-type he has so many nuances at his disposal."

5. (1) "Supplicatory" (Ps.-Demetrius 12; cf. Ps.-Libanius 7, 54); (2) "threatening" (Ps.-Demetrius 8; cf. Ps.-Libanius 13, 60); (3) "apologetic" (Ps.-Demetrius 18); (4) "counteraccusation" (Ps-Libanius 69); (5) "accusation" or "reproach" (Ps.-Demetrius 17; Ps.-Libanius 64); (6) "ironic" (Ps.-Demetrius 20; cf. Ps.-Libanius 9, 56); (7) "provoking" (Ps.-Libanius 24, 71).

6. Note that Ps-Libanius describes a "mixed" letter as one composed ἐκ διαφόρων χαρακτήρων—that is, from "different" or perhaps "various" styles, not, as Malherbe's translation has it, "from many styles." Indeed, Ps.-Libanius's sample certainly does not contain more than two: "I know that you live a life of piety, that you conduct yourself as a citizen in a manner worth of respect, indeed, that you adorn the illustrious name of philosophy itself, with the excellence of an unassailable and pure citizenship. But in this one thing alone do you err, that you slander your friends. You must avoid that, for it is not fitting that philosophers engage in slander" (92 [trans. Malherbe]). And the one letter Malherbe designates as "mixed" from P.Bon. 5 col. 11.6–27 likewise involves only two styles. Still, this has not prevented Pauline scholars

What such analysis actually involves is evident from the few instances where Fitzgerald's references to the handbooks go beyond the mere naming of letter types. What he says concerning the "apologetic" letter (18) is particularly illuminating:

> The situation presupposed in 2 Corinthians 10–13 ... conforms to the typical apologetic *Sitz im Leben*. The case involves three parties: Paul, the Corinthians, and the opponents. The accusations against Paul have been raised by the opponents (the third party), but Paul (the first party) does not respond directly to them. The apology is instead directed to the Corinthians (the second party). Ps.-Demetrius presupposes precisely this situation in an example of an apologetic letter, with the first party's response to the third party's charges being directed to the second party.[7]

It is important to see that what such a comparison has in view is not the form, nor the style, nor the method of Pseudo-Demetrius's and Paul's letters. Instead, it simply notes the similarity of the historical exigency presupposed by Pseudo-Demetrius and that faced by Paul: Paul considered himself the victim of slander, as did Pseudo-Demetrius's fictive letter writer.[8] It hardly takes training in epistolary theory to attempt a defense of oneself under such conditions, and it is not at all remarkable that such a defense should be directed at those whose esteem one covets (the "second party") and not the slanderers themselves (the "third party"). Put another way, since Pseudo-Demetrius's goal, as outlined in his preface, was to provide a sample letter appropriate to every social circumstance in which a letter might be employed,[9] it stands to reason that he managed to provide something of relevance to the situation Paul faced in Corinth. Unless

---

from using Ps.-Libanius's "mixed letter" as a convenient catchall category in which to place letters that do not correspond to any of the individual types. Of course, it is not difficult to imagine a simpler explanation for this lack of correspondence, and one that does not necessitate treating the handbook evidence like a nose of wax.

7. Fitzgerald, "Ancient Epistolary Theorists," 197.

8. Likewise, concerning the accusing or reproachful letter, Fitzgerald notes: "Just as Paul accuses the Corinthians of receiving those who malign him, so also Ps.-Demetrius's letter writer complains that the recipient has caused him grief by befriending someone who has unjustly accused him of improper conduct. Again, just as Paul reproaches the Corinthians for failing to be properly appreciative of his sacrifices for them, Ps.-Libanius's letter of reproach castigates the recipient for lack of gratitude toward his benefactor" ("Ancient Epistolary Theorists," 198–99).

9. See esp. Stanley K. Stowers, "Social Typification and the Classification of

Paul can be shown to have addressed this situation in a manner akin to what Pseudo-Demetrius recommended, the fact that he faced a similar exigency does not constitute evidence of Paul's familiarity with the handbook tradition.

Here it is important to be clear regarding what, precisely, this letter manual was intended to accomplish.[10] Pseudo-Demetrius's goal evidently was not to promote the mastery of formal elements such as salutations and farewells. His sample letters contain the bodies of the letters only; apparently, ability to append the basic epistolary elements was taken for granted.[11] And although Pseudo-Demetrius does say that he will provide a sample of the appropriate arrangement (τάξις [pr.]) of each letter, it would be misleading to suggest that his primary concern was to break each type down into its formal elements.[12] No, what he sought to instill had more to do with appropriate style, tone, and etiquette. As Carol Poster summarizes the function of his handbook:

> Its utility lies in its provision of phrases that can be reused and its modeling of how a secretary should compose elite correspondence in a tone appropriate to an educated man of *paideia*. The secretary who owned a copy of this manual would not need to work up an admonishing or congratulatory letter *ex nihilo*, but instead could look up the pertinent letter type, and either copy verbatim or embellish the model.[13]

Ancient Letters," in *The Social World of Formative Christianity and Judaism* (ed. Jacob Neusner; Philadelphia: Fortress, 1988), 82.

10. My analysis will focus on the work of Ps.-Demetrius, for which scholars generally give a date range of second century B.C.E.–third century C.E. See Abraham J. Malherbe, ed., *Ancient Epistolary Theorists* (SBLSBS 19; Atlanta: Scholars Press, 1988), 4; Carol Poster, "A Conversation Halved: Epistolary Theory in Greco-Roman Antiquity," in *Letter-Writing Manuals and Instruction from Antiquity to the Present: Historical and Bibliographic Studies* (ed. Carol Poster and Linda C. Mitchell; Studies in Rhetoric/Communication; Columbia: University of South Carolina Press, 2007), 24. Ps.-Libanius's handbook likely dates from the fourth century C.E. (Poster, "A Conversation Halved," 27), and thus should be used only cautiously as evidence for the nature of first-century epistolary training.

11. So Hans-Josef Klauck, *Ancient Letters and the New Testament: A Guide to Context and Exegesis* (trans. Daniel P. Bailey; Waco, Tex.: Baylor University Press, 2006), 201.

12. See Stowers, "Social Typification," 79–80.

13. Poster, "A Conversation Halved," 27. Cf. Malherbe, *Ancient Epistolary Theorists*, 4; Klauck, *Ancient Letters and the New Testament*, 201–2.

In other words, the goal was not that Pseudo-Demetrius's readers would write letters of certain genres or types—how, indeed, could they do otherwise?—but that, whatever type of letter they were writing, they would write it well, that is, appropriately for men of their standing and in keeping with the social mores relevant to the situation at hand.[14] Accordingly, if we seek evidence that Paul was familiar with the sort of epistolary practice Pseudo-Demetrius reflects, we will have to consider not just the basic social situation Paul's letter presupposes but also its conformity with the aristocratic social codes embedded in Pseudo-Demetrius's samples.[15] One potential indicator of such conformity, of course, would be similarly refined deployment of rhetorical tropes.

Since the "apologetic" letter is the type most frequently adduced as relevant to 2 Cor 10–13,[16] it will provide a useful example for undertaking this mode of comparison. In keeping with what we should expect from Poster's characterization of his handbook, Pseudo-Demetrius's sample letter, which "adduces, with proof, arguments which contradict charges that are being made" (18 [trans. Malherbe]), derives its force from skillful manipulation of the conventional rhetoric of friendship:

---

14. As Stanley Stowers has rightly explained, "An elaborate letter of recommendation written by a highly educated person and a crude commendation by a barely literate Egyptian peasant are essentially of the same genre because they are both attempting to effect the same social transaction. The elaborations of the one letter make it cultured and aesthetically pleasing, not of a different genre" ("Social Typification," 85).

15. Ps.-Demetrius clearly expects his audience to consist of those "in prominent positions" (ἐν ὑπάρχοις κείμενοι [1]; cf. 11). See further Poster, "A Conversation Halved," 25; Klauck, *Ancient Letters and the New Testament*, 200.

16. See esp. Betz, *Der Apostel Paulus und die sokratische Tradition*, 41. Note that despite Betz's reference to apologetic letters, Betz himself was not really interested in epistolary apologies: After demonstrating that such things existed, he promptly left them behind and went on to compare Paul's letter to a variety of *literary* apologies. In fact, he produces no exemplars of the form to which he assigns the letter, save a passing reference, in a footnote, to Plato's *Ep.* 3. Likewise, in his treatment of Galatians as another such "apologetic letter," Betz adduces, again in passing, Plato's *Ep.* 7, misleadingly citing A. Momigliano's reference to that text as "apologetic" (Betz, "Literary Composition and Function," 354–55; Betz, *Galatians*, 14–15; citing Momigliano *The Development of Greek Biography* [Cambridge: Harvard University Press, 1971], 60–62). On Betz's misuse of Momigliano, see Aune, review of Betz, 324; Anderson, *Ancient Rhetorical Theory*, 124.

> Fortune has served me well in preserving for me important facts to be used in the demonstration of my case. For at the time that they say I did this, I had already sailed for Alexandria, so that I happened neither to see nor meet the person about whom I am accused. Since there has been no disagreement between you and me, it is absurd for you to accuse someone who has wronged you in no way. But those who brought the accusation appear themselves to have perpetrated some foul deed, and, suspecting that I might write you something about them, they (took care) to slander me in anticipation. If you have believed their empty accusations, tell me. On the other hand, if you persevere with me as you should, you will learn everything when I arrive. In fact, one could be confident that, if I had at any time spoken against other people to you, I would also have spoken against you to others. So, wait for my arrival, and everything will be put to the proof, so that you may know how rightly you have judged me to be your friend, and I may prove you by your actions. I dare say that those who accused us will rather attack each other and choke themselves. (18 [trans. Malherbe])

What makes this exemplar particularly effective is its deft deflection of attention from the guilt of the sender to the moral character of the recipient. For Pseudo-Demetrius, less is more: The charges themselves are addressed casually, almost in passing; they are simply too absurd to focus on. Thus, by the end of the letter, we can hardly help but presume the sender's innocence, being interested instead in whether the recipient will act as befits a true friend. Indeed, the sample letter's conventional friendship language is not merely a function of the handbook format, but in fact performs an important part of the social "work" of the letter. By using the traditional language of friendship, Pseudo-Demetrius locates the relationship of sender and recipient within a well-defined and therefore suasive moral framework, and thus the sender's "apology" becomes in fact an invitation for the recipient to act as a true friend ought.

Paul's letter, on the contrary, remains essentially focused on Paul himself. There are only a few glancing references to the impure motives of his rivals (10:12; 11:12–13) and the lack of loyalty among his addressees (12:11). What Paul returns to again and again is the question of his own status (10:1–2, 7–11, 14–18; 11:5–6, 7–12; 11:17–12:10; 12:11–13, 15–19; 13:3–4, 6–8). He is unable, it seems, to resist the urge to self-defense. Were Pseudo-Demetrius consulted about this letter, he would surely suggest to Paul that by protesting too much he in fact lends credibility to the charges against him. In any case, such insistent self-vindication is clearly not what this handbook recommends for an apologetic letter.

Further, these letters are strikingly different in tone: Pseudo-Demetrius is confident and reassuring toward his addressee and relatively mild toward his accusers. His is a magnanimous posture: he is willing to give his friend the benefit of the doubt. Paul, contrarily, is famously impassioned, sarcastic, and vituperative. He pleads and he threatens. In short, his comportment is altogether different from that of Pseudo-Demetrius's ideal aristocratic letter writer.

Such differences in comportment are seldom remarked in Pauline scholarship. If, however, as Stowers asserts, ancient epistolary practice represented precisely the reinscription of social norms—an "implicit sociology," he calls it[17]—then this is exactly the level of comparison that is required. What such comparison demonstrates is clear: There is no evidence in 2 Cor 10–13 of Paul's participation in the professional epistolary tradition to which Pseudo-Demetrius attests. This conclusion will be reinforced in the next section, wherein I consider the nature of exposure to epistolary conventions and *topoi* in Greco-Roman antiquity.

Epistolary and Rhetorical Training in Greco-Roman Antiquity

Epistolary theory was a latecomer to the field of rhetoric, and, when it did arrive, it continued to occupy a peripheral place. As Abraham Malherbe notes, "The discussion in Demetrius is an excursus, [the consummate letter writer] Cicero makes no room for a systematic discussion of it in his works on rhetoric, and the references in Quintilian and Theon are casual."[18] But if we have little evidence of systematic theorization, nevertheless it appears that, in practice, letter writers sought to abide by fairly well-established epistolary conventions of style and content, as is evidenced above all by a fairly predictable set of standard formal elements and recurrent *topoi*.[19] How, then, were these conventions learned?

---

17. Stowers, "Social Typification," 87.
18. Malherbe, *Ancient Epistolary Theorists*, 3. Cf. Klauck, *Ancient Letters and the New Testament*, 206–10; George A. Kennedy, *Greek Rhetoric under Christian Emperors* (History of Rhetoric 3; Princeton, N.J.: Princeton University Press, 1983), 70–73.
19. See esp. John L. White, *Light from Ancient Letters* (FF; Philadelphia: Fortress, 1986), 189 and passim; Francis Xavier J. Exler, *The Form of the Ancient Greek Letter of the Epistolary Papyri (3rd c. B.C.–3rd c. A.D.): A Study in Greek Epistolography* (Chicago: Ares, 1976); Heikki Koskenniemi, *Studien zur Idee und Phraseologie des griechischen Briefes bis 400 n. Chr.* (Helsinki, 1956).

Certainly we must dispense with Fitzgerald's assignation of epistolary training to rhetorical school,[20] which, it appears, is based either on a selective or a mistaken reading of Malherbe. Fitzgerald bases his conclusion on Malherbe's assertion that "letters were written as an exercise in style early in the tertiary stage of the educational system."[21] What one would not guess from Fitzgerald's use of Malherbe is that what Malherbe argues, in fact, is that "epistolary form was taught on the basis of model letters in the *secondary* stage of education."[22] What Malherbe says concerning letter writing during the tertiary stage is that here we first observe evidence of interest in epistolary *style*,[23] a specification that is obscured by Fitzgerald. Malherbe goes on:

> It should be noted that the purpose of the [tertiary] exercise was not to learn how to write letters, but to develop facility in adopting various kinds of style. One might expect that it was at this point that epistolary theory would be introduced, but the evidence is too slender to make a confident judgment. *Nor can we assign the handbooks of 'Demetrius' and 'Libanius' to this point in the curriculum.*[24]

We would never suspect from reading Fitzgerald that Malherbe in fact relegates the letter-writing manuals to a place outside the scope of the tripartite literary curriculum altogether, suggesting instead that they were used to train professional letter writers.[25]

In any case, we would be sorely mistaken to imagine that competence in letter writing could serve, in itself, as evidence of rhetorical education. On the contrary, as Carol Poster explains, "epistolary theory … [permeated] a far greater portion of ancient society than rhetorical training."[26] Direct evidence for letter writing in schools is not extensive, but what evi-

---

20. Fitzgerald, "Ancient Epistolary Theorists," 193.
21. Malherbe, *Social Aspects*, 59.
22. Malherbe, *Ancient Epistolary Theorists*, 6 (my emphasis).
23. Ibid., 7.
24. Ibid. (my emphasis).
25. Ibid.
26. Poster, "A Conversation Halved," 41. For a thorough treatment, see also her "The Economy of Letter Writing in Graeco-Roman Antiquity," in *Rhetorical Argumentation in Biblical Texts: Essays from the 2000 Lund Conference* (ed. Anders Eriksson, Thomas H. Olbricht, and Walter Ubelacker; ESEC; Harrisburg, Pa.: Trinity, 2002), 112–24.

dence we do have suggests that its rudiments were taught at a much earlier stage than Fitzgerald or even Malherbe allows.[27] The letters preserved in P.Bon. 5, which appear to be schoolroom exercises, are relatively crude and certainly betray little in the way of rhetorical sensibility.[28] Similarly, our best evidence for ancient knowledge of letter-writing skills—that is, the extant letters themselves—are, for the most part, "written in the kind of school language used by persons of average, superficial education, who painfully attempted to write in an educated manner."[29] Indeed, any theory regarding the place of letter writing in ancient education must account for the fact that the rudiments of epistolography were widely familiar even among those who had not yet mastered grammar. John Muir provides a sensible, though necessarily speculative explanation:

> The outline of the basic family letter with its regular constituents of wishes for good health, thanks for gifts received, assurances of remembrance in prayers and final greetings to friends and relations was probably taught as a part of elementary education, and preserved and consolidated by that social expectation which still shapes such letters today.[30]

Clearly, then, the basic formal elements of Paul's letters—greetings, farewells, and epistolary *topoi*—provide no evidence of advanced education, rhetorical or otherwise. In fact, they provide no evidence of education at all, for they appear also in letters sent by the illiterate, whose letters were written, like Paul's, by secretaries.[31]

The evidence that letter writing occurred in the *rhetorical* schools of Paul's time is extremely sparse, consisting of little more than an isolated mention in Theon's *Progymnasmata* (8 [*RG* 2:115]), where Theon men-

---

27. See esp. Raffaella Cribiore, *Gymnastics of the Mind: Greek Education in Hellenistic and Roman Egypt* (Princeton, N.J.: Princeton University Press, 2001), 215–19.

28. Text and translation in Malherbe, *Ancient Epistolary Theorists*, 44–57. See also P.Paris 63.1–7 (= UPZ I 110). Discussion in Klauck, *Ancient Letters and the New Testament*, 204–5.

29. Malherbe, *Ancient Epistolary Theorists*, 6.

30. John Muir, *Life and Letters in the Ancient Greek World* (London: Routledge, 2009), 22. For an ethnographic treatment of the social expectation to which Muir refers, see Keith H. Basso, "The Ethnography of Writing," in *Explorations in the Ethnography of Speaking* (ed. Richard Bauman and Joel Sherzer; 2nd ed.; SSCFL 8; Cambridge: Cambridge University Press, 1989), 425–32.

31. See esp. Richards, *Secretary in the Letters of Paul*.

tions letter writing as a possible avenue for practicing personification (προσωποποιία).³² The focus here, it should be noted, was not on letter writing per se, but rather on the student's mastery of another exercise, the strategic inhabitation of another's voice.³³ We may presume that this would have had as a welcome byproduct the improvement of epistolary style, but it was obviously assumed that students undertaking the *Progymnasmata* already knew how to write a letter. Moreover, there is no evidence that students in rhetorical school were ever taught to write in their own voices or to compose "real" letters—that is, the sort of letters that bureaucrats, statesmen, and family members sent to one another. There were, certainly, well-educated men—Cicero, Seneca, and Gregory of Nazianzus, for example—who brought their rhetorical training to bear on the writing of letters, but this should not be taken to imply that they learned to write letters at a school of rhetoric.

Further, as noted above, it is certain that the handbooks of Pseudo-Demetrius and Pseudo-Libanius were not designed for use in rhetorical school. Instead, they were explicitly directed at professionals—bureaucrats and statesmen—for whom competent letter writing was essential to a "brilliant" (λαμπρός [Ps.-Demetrius, pr.]) career.³⁴ Presumably their secretaries, whom Pseudo-Demetrius castigates for their careless compositions, would likewise have benefited.

---

32. Theon's comment is paralleled in the fifth century by Nicolaus of Myra (*Progymn.* 10 [Felten 67]). Theon is usually dated to the first century C.E. So, e.g., Michel Patillon, ed., *Aelius Théon: Progymnasmata* (Budé; Paris: Les belles lettres, 1997), viii–xvi; George A. Kennedy, trans., *Progymnasmata: Greek Textbooks of Prose Composition and Rhetoric* (WGRW 10; Atlanta: Society of Biblical Literature, 2003), 1. Note, however, that Malcolm Heath has recently challenged this consensus, advocating instead a fifth-century date ("Theon and the History of the Progymnasmata," *GRBS* 43 [2002]: 129–60). I am not in a position to comment on this question, except to note that Heath's dating would make good sense of the fact that reference to the ἐπιστολικῶν εἶδος appears in Theon and Nicolaus but not in the *progymnasmata* of Ps.-Hermogenes or Apthonius. A fifth-century date for both of these references would be in keeping with a general trend of increasing interest in letter writing by rhetoricians in late antiquity, evinced above all by Libanius. See Raffaella Cribiore, *The School of Libanius in Late Antique Antioch* (Princeton, N.J.: Princeton University Press, 2007), 169–73.

33. Malherbe, *Ancient Epistolary Theorists*, 7.

34. See Poster, "A Conversation Halved," 25; Klauck, *Ancient Letters and the New Testament*, 200; Malherbe, *Ancient Epistolary Theorists*, 7.

And these secretaries introduce a further complicating factor: Many of those who were expected to write letters competently were slaves.[35] Here rhetorical and epistolary training decisively part ways, a phenomenon for which there is a relatively simple explanation: whereas only the cultured elite encountered circumstances that demanded displays of formal rhetorical prowess, people of all social strata found it socially and economically necessary to send one another letters. In other words, although the literati attempted—chiefly by using the moral power of ridicule, it would appear—to restrict meaningful public speech and cultural activity to the rather closed circle of the *pepaideumenoi*,[36] the basic tools of literacy, including letter writing, were far too useful to be subject to such restraint. So, while rhetorical education "remained accessible mainly to the rich and upper class,"[37] training in basic literacy went wherever it was economically and socially advantageous.[38]

Here it is important to distinguish between the sort of *paideia* to which the elite aspired and the functional literacy of slaves, clerks, and secretaries. This distinction has been neglected in much classical scholarship—and thus much biblical scholarship as well—largely because we generally have taken elite discussions of education as representative. Elite sources do give the impression of a universal curriculum, the *enkyklios paideia*, which consisted of the fundamental elements of literary education and culminated in the study of rhetoric.[39] And scholars of ancient education have provided a convenient and intuitive systematization of the elite testimony, according to which students passed through three separate stages of this single curriculum: primary instruction, focusing on the fundamentals of literacy, was provided by a γραμματιστής; secondary education dealt with advanced grammar and literary studies under the

---

35. Poster, "Economy of Letter Writing," 122; Richards, *Secretary in the Letters of Paul*, passim.

36. See esp. Morgan, *Literate Education*, 234–36. Also William A. Johnson, *Readers and Reading Culture in the High Roman Empire: A Study of Elite Communities* (New York: Oxford University Press, 2010), esp. 17–31.

37. Teresa Morgan, "Rhetoric and Education," in *A Companion to Greek Rhetoric* (ed. Ian Worthington; Blackwell Companions to the Ancient World; Malden, Mass.: Blackwell, 2007), 310.

38. See esp. Alan D. Booth, "The Schooling of Slaves in First-Century Rome," *TAPA* 109 (1979): 11–19.

39. Cf. Quintilian, *Inst.* 1.10.1; Morgan, *Literate Education*, 33–36.

tutelage of a γραμματικός; and tertiary education, provided by a σοφιστής or ῥήτωρ, consisted in the study of rhetoric.⁴⁰

Proponents of this model recognize, of course, that not all students who began the *enkyklios paideia* made their way through the entire curriculum. Indeed, it is generally agreed that only a small proportion of students advanced to the level of tertiary, that is, rhetorical education.⁴¹ Still, despite the concession that some people made it further along the track than others, the model, like the elite texts on which it is based, implies that literate education in the ancient world was a single endeavor. *Paideia* was *paideia*, and either one had a little of it or a lot.

In recent scholarship, however, the adequacy of this model increasingly has come into question. This is due, in large part, to a new focus on the testimony of documentary papyri. Armed with these pedestrian texts, recent studies have shed light on a hitherto obscure realm of literate activity that is quite different from what the elite would have considered true *paideia*⁴²—a realm wherein, for example, students might master handwriting without being able to read the texts they produced.⁴³ As Teresa Morgan has noted, in contrast to the ideal promulgated by the likes of Quintilian, "the contents of the papyri suggest a much more flexible system [of education] adaptable to a wide range of social contexts."⁴⁴

The key finding here is one that unmasks the myth of a universal curriculum: as one would expect, "pupils from different social groups learnt what was appropriate, or deemed appropriate, to their backgrounds and expectations."⁴⁵ That is, they learned what it was worth their while to

---

40. So Henri I. Marrou, *A History of Education in Antiquity* (trans. George Lamb; New York: Sheed & Ward, 1956), 160. This schema has made its way into biblical studies as well. See, e.g., Hock, "Greco-Roman Education," 199–208; Neyrey, "Social Location of Paul," 158–59.

41. So Marrou, *History of Education*, 123; Hock, "Greco-Roman Education," 204.

42. See esp. Morgan, *Literate Education*; Raffaella Cribiore, *Writing, Teachers, and Students in Graeco-Roman Egypt* (ASP 36; Atlanta: Scholars Press, 1996); Cribiore, *Gymnastics of the Mind*; Herbert C. Youtie, "ΑΓΡΑΜΜΑΤΟΣ: An Aspect of Greek Society in Egypt," *HSCP* 75 (1971): 161–76; Youtie, "Βραδέως γράφων: Between Literacy and Illiteracy," *GRBS* 12 (1971): 239–61; Nicholas Horsfall, "Statistics or States of Mind?" in *Literacy in the Roman World* (ed. J. H. Humphrey; Journal of Roman Archaeology Supplement Series 3; Ann Arbor: University of Michigan, 1991), 59–76.

43. See Cribiore, *Gymnastics of the Mind*, 161–62.

44. Morgan, *Literate Education*, 52.

45. Ibid., 51.

learn. Certainly students at all levels of society were proud to display what literary culture they did master,[46] but, for all but the aristocratic elite, the primary motivation and reward was economic advantage:[47] a village boy did not learn to read and write so that he could do a poor job of being Cicero; he learned to read and write so that he could do an adequate job of being a scribe.[48]

It is perhaps not surprising, then, that the notion of a coherent tripartite curriculum does not hold up under scrutiny.[49] As Rafaella Cribiore emphasizes, there simply was no uniform system of education.[50] In general, however, at least in Rome and the major cities of the empire, "a two-track system prevailed," Cribiore argues, "that served different segments of the population: while schools of elementary letters provided a basic literacy to slaves and freeborn individuals of the lower classes, schools of liberal studies offered a more refined education to children of the upper classes."[51]

Let me put this in terms of statistics, imprecise as they must be: William Harris declines to give a specific percentage, but his literacy estimates put us somewhere in the range of 10 percent for the cities of the Greek East.[52] By Cribiore's reckoning, the majority of students learned only the rudiments of reading and writing[53]—that is, they would not have been

---

46. See esp. ibid., 109–18.

47. See Horsfall, "Statistics or States of Mind?" 63–65; Horsfall, "'The Uses of Literacy' and the 'Cena Trimalchionis,'" *GR* 2/36 (1989): 202–6.

48. Note that the existence of multiple literacies that generally correspond to various social locations—and therefore have varying degrees of relationship to the formal educational system—is precisely what recent ethnographic work on literacy should have us expect. See esp. Shirley Brice Heath, *Ways with Words: Language, Life, and Work in Communities and Classrooms* (Cambridge: Cambridge University Press, 1983); Brian V. Street, *Literacy in Theory and Practice* (Cambridge Studies in Oral and Literate Culture; Cambridge: Cambridge University Press, 1984).

49. See esp. Booth, "Schooling of Slaves"; Booth, "Elementary and Secondary Education in the Roman Empire," *Florilegium* 1 (1979): 1–14; Robert A. Kaster, "Notes on 'Primary' and 'Secondary' Schools in Late Antiquity," *TAPA* 113 (1983): 323–346.

50. Cribiore, *Gymnastics of the Mind*, 36. See also Kaster, "Primary and Secondary Schools."

51. Cribiore, *Gymnastics of the Mind*, 37. See also Kaster, "Primary and Secondary Schools," 346.

52. William V. Harris, *Ancient Literacy* (Cambridge: Harvard University Press, 1989), 329–30.

53. Cribiore, "Gymnastics of the Mind," 187.

on the "liberal education" track at all. Again, accepting the impossibility of anything like precision, that means that in a city like Ephesus, between five and nine percent of the population would have had only rudimentary training in reading and writing, and an additional one to four percent would have had varying degrees of real *paideia*. This one to four percent, it is worth noting, corresponds well to the three percent or so of the population that, by Steven Friesen's calculations, constituted the aristocracy of a typical urban center.[54]

So, within this basic framework, where does one find the ability to write letters? Certainly not restricted to the *pepaideumenoi*. On the contrary, as Carol Poster concludes:

> Letter-writing skills were scattered among various levels and types of instruction, from basic grammar classes to advanced professional training courses.... Slaves and women could profitably be trained in the mechanical skills of tachygraphy and calligraphy. Freedmen or nonelite metropolitan Greeks could, by limited literacy and professional letter-writing education, take advantage of plentiful employment opportunities as lower-level clerks, but might not have the social qualifications (or fees) appropriate to elite rhetorical courses. Sophistic education would provide access to elite secretarial positions.[55]

In sum, then, even if Paul could be shown to have written letters in accordance with contemporary epistolary standards, this would prove nothing more than that he, or the secretary to whom he had access, had some basic clerical training. Only if we were also to encounter what were for his contemporaries the essential indicators of true *paideia*—specifically, refined diction, learned literary references, elegant use of conventional tropes and *topoi*, and elite moral and social values[56]—would we have

---

54. According to the calculations of Steven Friesen, the wealthy aristocracy made up about 1.23% of the empire, amounting to just under 3% of the population of larger urban centers ("Poverty in Pauline Studies," 340; cf. Meggitt, *Paul, Poverty and Survival*, 50 n. 49).

55. Poster, "Economy of Letter Writing," 120.

56. On these as indicators of *paideia*, see esp. Marrou, *History of Education*, 98–100; Tim Whitmarsh, "Reading Power in Roman Greece: The *paideia* of Dio Chrysostom," in *Pedagogy and Power: Rhetorics of Classical Learning* (ed. Yun Lee Too and Niall Livingstone; Ideas in Context 50; Cambridge: Cambridge University Press, 1998), 193–98; Joy Connolly, "Problems of the Past in Imperial Greek Education," in *Education in Greek and Roman Antiquity* (ed. Yun Lee Too; Leiden: Brill, 2001),

grounds for asserting that Paul had received advanced literary education, or, more specifically, formal training in rhetoric.

Conclusion

The general resemblance of 2 Cor 10–13 to certain of the letter types described by Pseudo-Demetrius cannot be regarded as evidence for Paul's formal education. Its use as such derives from a misconstrual of the nature and function of this epistolary handbook. Indeed, the classification of Paul's letters among Pseudo-Demetrius's letter types has involved surprisingly superficial comparison, glossing over telling differences in manner and comportment. When we take the time to look at *how* Paul apologizes, rebukes, admonishes, and so forth, it becomes difficult to sustain the argument that Paul is a participant in the epistolary tradition to which Pseudo-Demetrius attests. Moreover, given what we can discern concerning the place of letter writing in ancient education, Paul's more general epistolary competence can by no means be considered evidence of formal literary, let alone rhetorical, education.

339–72; W. Martin Bloomer, "Schooling in Persona: Imagination and Subordination in Roman Education," *ClAnt* 16 (1997): 57–78; Robert A. Kaster, "Controlling Reason: Declamation in Rhetorical Education at Rome," in *Education in Greek and Roman Antiquity* (ed. Yun Lee Too; Leiden: Brill, 2001), 317–37; Ruth Webb, "The Progymnasmata as Practice," in *Education in Greek and Roman Antiquity* (ed. Yun Lee Too; Leiden: Brill, 2001), 289–316; Hezser, *Jewish Literacy*, 185; Charles A. McNelis, "Greek Grammarians and Roman Society during the Early Empire: Statius' Father and His Contemporaries," *ClAnt* 21 (2002): 87–90; Maud W. Gleason, *Making Men: Sophists and Self-Presentation in Ancient Rome* (Princeton, N.J.: Princeton University Press, 1995), xxi–xxv, 164; Osvaldo Padilla, "Hellenistic παιδεία and Luke's Education: A Critique of Recent Approaches," *NTS* 55 (2009): 421–23; Mitchell, *The Heavenly Trumpet*, 242; Thomas Schmitz, *Bildung und Macht: Zur sozialen und politischen Funktion der zweiten Sophistik in der griechischen Welt der Kaiserzeit* (Zetemata 97; Munich: Beck, 1997), 39–66.

4
Paul's (In)appropriate Boasting: *Periautologia*

Paul's boasting in 2 Cor 10–13 has been a source of consternation for generations of pious readers. Not only has the passage given many the impression that he was "pathologically concerned about his own status,"[1] but in this text Paul appears to engage in precisely the sort of behavior of which he accuses his rivals. As Alfred Plummer notes, "seeing that he has just been maintaining that self-praise is no recommendation, it seems grossly inconsistent [that he should go on to describe his own accomplishments]."[2]

Not surprisingly, the posture of preachers and exegetes has long been almost as defensive as Paul's own. One tack has been to stress that Paul really had no other choice—at least, not if the truth of the gospel was to be preserved. Thus Ambrosiaster assures us that Paul "is not really boasting" (*non ergo vere ad gloriam suam haec loquitur*), because he was constrained by the accusations against him to defend himself (*Comm.* 200 [PL 17:342; trans. Bray]). In a similar vein, F. C. Baur stresses Paul's reluctance to tell of his revelatory experiences: "Willingly he would have avoided speaking of them at all, in order to escape every appearance of vain self-exaltation, yet here it behooved him to be silent on nothing which might serve for

---

1. Quip from Judge, "Paul's Boasting," 66. Note that Judge himself does not share this perspective. But see C. H. Dodd, *New Testament Studies* (Manchester: Manchester University Press, 1953), 79; S. H. Travis, "Paul's Boasting in 2 Corinthians 10–12," in *Studia Evangelica VI* (ed. Elizabeth A. Livingstone; TUGAL 112; Berlin: Akademie-Verlag, 1973), 527.

2. Plummer, *Second Epistle*, 291. See also Hafemann, "Self-Commendation," 71; Nigel M. Watson, "'Physician, Heal Thyself'? Paul's Character as Revealed in 2 Corinthians, and the Congruence between Word and Deed," in *The Corinthian Correspondence* (ed. Reimund Bieringer; BETL 125; Leuven: Leuven University Press, 1996), 671–78.

the vindication and establishment of his apostolic authority."[3] The implication, of course, is that Paul either had to reassert his position in Corinth or stand idly by as the gospel was perverted by false apostles.

Other, more sophisticated defenses of Paul's boasting have been proffered. Plummer resolves the apparent contradiction between Paul's anti-boasting talk and his self-promoting walk by stressing that he is self-consciously playing his opponents' game: "The difference between him and his critics is this; that they, without being aware of it, are fools ceaselessly, because folly has become a second nature to them; whereas he deliberately plays the fool for a few minutes, because their folly can be met in no other way."[4] R. H. Strachan resorts to splitting hairs: "Paul boasts, not that he is an apostle, but that God had made him one."[5] In short, the history of the interpretation of 2 Cor 10–13 has consisted, in large part, of a series of excuses for Paul's unseemly demeanor.

This apologetic endeavor has received fresh vigor in recent decades from the rediscovery of Windisch's observation that Plutarch provides a nearly contemporaneous discussion of how to indulge in self-praise without arousing offense. Windisch, noticing a number of interesting parallels between Plutarch's *De laude ipsius* (*Mor.* 539A–547F) and Paul's dilemma, had concluded:

> Die ganze Abhandlung verdeutlicht uns die psychologischen Voraussetzungen der hier vorliegenden Situation, die Notlage, in der P[aulus] sich befindet, wie die Stimmung, die er bei den Hörern voraussetzt. P[aulus] teilt durchaus die Anschauungen Plutarchs und des Griechentums, in dessen Namen Plutarch spricht.[6]

---

3. Baur, *Paul*, 1:280.
4. Plummer, *Second Epistle*, 291.
5. R. H. Strachan, *The Second Epistle of Paul to the Corinthians* (MNTC; London: Hodder & Stoughton, 1935), 16. Cf. Rudolf Bultmann, "καυχάομαι," *TDNT* 3:650–52; Luke Timothy Johnson, *The Writings of the New Testament: An Interpretation* (rev. ed.; Minneapolis: Fortress, 1999), 316.
6. Windisch, *Der zweite Korintherbrief*, 345: "The whole treatise clarifies for us the psychological preconditions of the present situation, the plight in which Paul finds himself, and the disposition he expects from his hearers. Paul shares fully the outlook of Plutarch and of the Greeks as whose representative Plutarch speaks."

In other words, Paul shared the cultural assumptions of his contemporaries. What was particularly interesting to Windisch was that these contemporaries were Greek.

Windisch's appeal to Plutarch was taken up by Hans Dieter Betz in his 1972 monograph *Der Apostel Paulus und die sokratische Tradition*, but now the discussion was transposed into the key of rhetoric. Where Windisch referred rather vaguely to a shared "outlook," Betz spoke of Paul's conformity to rhetorical dictates: "Paulus hält sich strikt an die Vorschriften, wie sie die Rhetorik für die 'περιαυτολογία' aufgestellt hatte."[7] From here, using the fallacious but attractive reasoning we noted throughout chapter 1, it was but a short path to the conclusion that Paul's use of *periautologia* betrays his rhetorical education.[8] And, as an added bonus, those troubled by Paul's boasting could newly be assured that, however overblown it may appear to modern readers, Paul's self-praise is "completely inoffensive when measured by ancient standards."[9]

Plutarch, De laude ipsius (Moralia 539A–547F)

It is necessary first to dispel the notion that Plutarch's treatise is a summation of established rhetorical dictates. In fact, this is not a rhetorical work at all; it is an ethical tractate. Like elsewhere in the assorted writings we call the *Moralia*—and in his *Parallel Lives*, for that matter—Plutarch is advising ὁ πολιτικὸς ἀνήρ how he may conduct his public career honorably and virtuously (*De laude* 539F).[10] Indeed, as L. Radermacher long ago observed, *De laude ipsius* is perfectly at home in Plutarch's moralizing corpus: "Die

---

7. Betz, *Der Apostel Paulus und die sokratische Tradition*, 75: "Paul adheres strictly to the rules that rhetoric had established for *periautologia*."

8. So Marshall, *Enmity in Corinth*, 355.

9. George Lyons, *Pauline Autobiography: Toward a New Understanding* (SBLDS 73; Atlanta: Scholars Press, 1985), 72. See also Witherington, *Conflict and Community in Corinth*, 432.

10. Cf. Plutarch, *An seni* 783C–E; *Praec. ger. rei publ.* 798A–825F. See further Dana Fields, "Aristides and Plutarch on Self-Praise," in *Aelius Aristides Between Greece, Rome, and the Gods* (ed. W. V. Harris and Brooke Holmes; Columbia Studies in the Classical Tradition 33; Leiden: Brill, 2008), 155–60. On the centrality of moral philosophy throughout Plutarch's work, see also D. A. Russell, "On Reading Plutarch's 'Moralia,'" *GR* 2/15 (1968): 135. On the moralizing program of the *Lives*, see esp. Timothy E. Duff, *Plutarch's Lives: Exploring Virtue and Vice* (Oxford: Oxford University Press, 2002).

Frage, ob und wann man sich selber loben dürfe, ist eine ethische, und so ist es weiter nicht auffallend, wenn wir eine erbauliche Abhandlung darüber unter den moralischen Schriften des Plutarch finden."[11] In short, what interests Plutarch is not eloquence but virtue; hence he seeks to isolate self-praise that is "good and helpful, teaching admiration and love of the useful and profitable rather than of the vain and superfluous" (546B [De Lacy and Einarson, LCL]; cf. *Comp. Dem. Cic.* 2.3).

Betz too had to admit that "it was the ethical implications [of self-praise] in which Plutarch was primarily interested," but he argued that Plutarch was thereby developing an idea that "had long been a topic of discussion by rhetoricians."[12] In other words, Plutarch took existing rhetorical precepts and elaborated their moral foundation and ethical implications. For Betz, then—and the ensuing discussion of *periautologia* among New Testament scholars—whatever Plutarch's own interests and intent, the important thing is that he bore witness to an established rhetorical tradition.[13]

Betz's recruitment of Plutarch as a witness for preexisting rhetorical *Vorschriften* was undertaken on Radermacher's authority. Radermacher had noticed parallels between Plutarch's treatise and discussions of self-praise by rhetoricians, and thus argued that Plutarch must have been influenced by rhetorical sources:[14] Alexander Numenius's fragmentary Περὶ

---

11. L. Radermacher, "Studien zur Geschichte der greichischen Rhetorik, II: Plutarchs Schrift de se ipso citra invidiam laudando," *RhM* 2/52 (1897): 419: "The question whether and when one may praise oneself is an ethical one, and so it is not really surprising that we find an edifying treatise on the subject among the moral writings of Plutarch." See also Laurant Pernot, "*Periautologia*: Problèmes et méthodes de l'éloge de soi-même dans la tradition éthique et rhétorique gréco-romaine," *REG* 111 (1998): 110.

12. Hans Dieter Betz, "De laude ipsius (Moralia 539A–547F)," in *Plutarch's Ethical Writings and Early Christian Literature* (ed. Hans Dieter Betz; SCHNT 4; Leiden: Brill, 1978), 367; Betz, *Der Apostel Paulus und die sokratische Tradition*, 75–76.

13. So Forbes, "Comparison, Self-Praise, and Irony," 8–9; Marshall, *Enmity in Corinth*, 353; DiCicco, *Ethos, Pathos, and Logos*, 58–63; Sundermann, *Der schwache Apostel*, 35–36; Dennis C. Duling, "2 Corinthians 11:22: Historical Context, Rhetoric, and Ethnicity," *HvTSt* 64 (2008): 828–30; repr. from *The New Testament and Early Christian Literature in Greco-Roman Context: Studies in Honor of David E. Aune* (ed. John Fotopoulos; NovTSup 122; Leiden: Brill, 2006); Watson, "Paul's Boasting in 2 Corinthians 10–13," 269–75; Mitchell, "Patristic Perspective"; Wojciechowski, "Paul and Plutarch on Boasting," 109; Pitta, "Il discorso del pazzo," 501–3.

14. Radermacher, "Plutarchs Schrift," 420–23.

ῥητορικῶν ἀφορμῶν reportedly included a discussion of περιαυτολογία that explained πῶς ἄν τις ἑαυτὸν ἀνεπαχθῶς ἐπαινέσειεν (*RG* 3:4); and Pseudo-Hermogenes, noting that praising oneself (τοῦ ἑαυτὸν ἐπαινεῖν) is "offensive and easily detested," gives three methods for doing so ἀνεπαχθῶς (*Meth.* 25 [Rabe 441–442; trans. Kennedy]). As Radermacher noted, such resemblances to Plutarch's subject matter and indeed his title are certainly striking. The difficulty, however, is that these works, like every other substantive rhetorical treatment of the matter, postdate Plutarch: Alexander can be dated with some precision to the middle of the second century C.E., and Pseudo-Hermogenes cannot have written prior to the authentic Hermogenes's late second-century acme.[15] Of course, one would normally conclude from this sort of chronology that it was Plutarch's work that spawned rhetorical treatments of *periautologia*, not vice versa.

Prior to 100 C.E.—about when Plutarch composed his text[16]—the odium of self-praise was mentioned in passing, but no extant work treated the subject at length—certainly not in sufficient detail to qualify as a real predecessor to Plutarch's discussion.[17] Christopher Forbes avers that "self-praise was discussed as early as Aristotle,"[18] and he is correct, though perhaps guilty of some exaggeration: Aristotle mentions, with no elaboration, that Iphicrates once gave his own encomia (αὐτὸν ἐνεκωμίαζε [*Rhet.* 1.7.32]); elsewhere he briefly notes that when one is developing *ethos*,

---

15. For Alexander, see Mervin R. Dilts and George A. Kennedy, eds., *Two Greek Rhetorical Treatises from the Roman Empire: Introduction, Text, and Translation of the* Arts of Rhetoric, *Attributed to Anonymous Seguerianus and to Apsines of Gadara* (Mnemosyne Supplement 168; Leiden: Brill, 1997), xii. For Ps.-Hermogenes, see E. Bürgi, "Ist die dem Hermogenes zugeschriebene Schrift Περὶ μεθόδου δεινότητος echt?" *WS* 48 (1930): 187–97; 49 (1931): 40–69. Other handbooks including relevant discussions are Ps.-Aristides, *Rhet.* 1.12.2.7 (*RG* 2:506) and Apsines, *Rhet.* 3.6. Neither predate Plutarch.

16. So Pernot, "*Periautologia*," 109. See also C. P. Jones, "Towards a Chronology of Plutarch's Works," *JRS* 56 (1966): 73. Pernot makes the plausible suggestion that the topic was suggested to him while working on the paired lives of Cicero and Demosthenes. Indeed, his comparison of the two leads Plutarch to similar reflections on Demosthenes's ability to praise himself ἀνεπαχθῶς and Cicero's offensive περιαυτολογία (*Comp. Dem. Cic.* 2).

17. The one possible exception, Quintilian's discussion of boasting in *Inst.* 11.1.15–26, will be discussed below.

18. Forbes, "Comparison, Self-Praise, and Irony," 8.

insidious comments about oneself (ἐπίφθονον), like harsh comments about someone else, are best attributed to another (3.17.16).

The *Rhetorica ad Herennium* (1.5.8) and Cicero's *De inventione* (1.16.22) both briefly mention the value of lauding one's own conduct. But neither treats self-praise as a subject in its own right; instead, both mention it in passing as a stratagem for gaining an audience's goodwill at the outset of an oration.[19] Moreover, neither have anything resembling Plutarch's detailed treatment of the dangers of self-praise or delimitation of specific situations in which it is appropriate. Both handbooks simply caution that praise of one's own services should be done without arrogance. This hardly amounts to precepts for *periautologia*.

In fact, it is worth noting that the word περιαυτολογία appears only once prior to Plutarch.[20] Moreover, this single extant occurrence comes not in a rhetorical context, but, tellingly, in a moral-philosophical tractate: Philodemus's fragmentary *De bono rege secundum Homerum* (col. 21), a text wherein, using examples drawn from Homer, Philodemus provides "a description of the duties and moral behaviour of a *princeps* in private and public life."[21] Here we have interests that clearly are akin to those of Plutarch. Like Plutarch, Philodemus's concern is not eloquence but virtuous and effective public service. Moreover, like Plutarch, Philodemus addresses the outspoken self-praise of the Homeric heroes (Olivieri cols. 16, 18, 20,

---

19. Likewise Ps-Dionysius, *Rhet.* 5.6. In his reading of 2 Cor 10–13 alongside *Rhet. Her.* and Cicero's discussion of goodwill, J. Paul Sampley ignores the fact that both of the latter specifically discuss exordia, and thus obscures the fact that providing an exordium calculated to arouse goodwill is precisely what Paul *does not* do in this letter (cf. 10:6) ("Paul, His Opponents in 2 Corinthians 10–13, and the Rhetorical Handbooks," in *The Social World of Formative Christianity and Judaism* [ed. Jacob Neusner; Philadelphia: Fortress, 1988], 162–77).

20. It also appears only seldom afterward—and only once in a rhetorical handbook (Alexander, Περὶ ῥητορικῶν ἀφορμῶν [*RG* 4:9]). A *TLG* search locates 30 occurrences up to and including Chrysostom. Of those, fully half are from Plutarch: 11 from *De laude* (539C; 539E; 540B; 540F; 544C; 546B bis; 546C; 546D; 546E; 547C), 3 from elsewhere in the *Mor.* (*Rect. rat. aud.* 41C; 44A; *Adol. poet. aud.* 29B) and one from *Comp. Dem. Cic.* 2.1. With such sparse attestation, it is curious that the word has become a technical term among New Testament scholars. It is as if we are convinced that possessing a name for something—preferably a Greek or Latin name; German will do in a pinch—is equivalent to understanding it.

21. Oswyn Murray, "Philodemus on the Good King according to Homer," *JRS* 55 (1965): 178.

22;[22] cf. *De laude* 540F; 541B-D; 542E; 543F-544B), including Nestor's notoriously self-aggrandizing speech to Patroclus (fr. 9; cf. *Il.* 11.655-762), which very incident is later discussed by Plutarch (*De laude* 544D; cf. Dio Chrysostom, *Nest.*). As a predecessor to *De laude ipsius*, Philodemus's treatise clearly is a more viable candidate than any extant rhetorical work.

Plutarch is a moralist—a grammarian of decorum, to borrow Bourdieu's useful phrase[23]—in this case playing the role of a political advisor. Accordingly, *De laude ipsius* provides moral and strategic reflections on a particular exigency of statesmanship. This is not a collection of rhetorical techniques. Treating it as such promotes a cursory reading of the treatise that divorces Plutarch's recommendations for inoffensive self-reference from the moral values that inform them—which is precisely the sort of thing that has been endemic among Pauline scholars. Indeed, as we will see, interpreters of 2 Cor 10-13 have drawn a number of superficial parallels between Paul's boasting and Plutarch's discussion, and have done so without attending at all to the social values that animate the treatise. When we read Plutarch on his own terms, what stands out is not what he shares with Paul but rather the profoundly different place he occupies in ancient society. Thus a careful reading of *De laude ipsius* does shed light on Paul's rhetoric, but it calls into question the facile conclusion that Paul praised himself according to the dictates of ancient rhetorical theory.

Boasting by Necessity

Most frequently adduced by Pauline scholars is Plutarch's general observation that self-praise is excusable when it is absolutely necessary (539E; 541A), which purportedly illuminates Paul's insistence that he boasts only by compulsion (2 Cor 12:11; cf. 11:30; 12:1). So Duane Watson asserts, "As convention advises, Paul demonstrates the necessity of boasting."[24] In

---

22. On Olivieri col. 16, see Jeffrey Fish, "The Good King's Giving Credit Where Credit is Due: *P.Herc.* 1507, Col. 34," in vol. 1 of *Atti del XXII Congresso internazionale di papirologia: Firenze, 23-29 agosto 1998* (ed. Isabella Andorlini et al.; 3 vols.; Florence: Istituto papirologico G. Vitelli, 2001), 469-74. On cols. 18, 20, and 22, see Murray, "Philodemus on the Good King," 166, 171-72.

23. Bourdieu, *Theory of Practice*, 8.

24. Watson, "Paul and Boasting," 91; likewise Windisch, *Der zweite Korintherbrief*, 345; Betz, *Der Apostel Paulus und die sokratische Tradition*, 79; DiCicco, *Ethos, Pathos, and Logos*, 80; Duling, "2 Corinthians 11:22," 829; Furnish, *II Corinthians*, 552; Wojciechowski, "Paul and Plutarch on Boasting," 106.

fact, however, Plutarch says nothing at all about *demonstrating* that self-praise is necessary; he simply says that one should only praise oneself if it is necessary.

It is not surprising, perhaps, that in the process of transforming *De laude ipsius* into a collection of rhetorical techniques Pauline scholars have introduced this misreading, for otherwise there is no rhetorical device here at all, but simply a moral criterion. Further, the very nature of this criterion makes it impossible to know whether speakers who seem to employ it are in fact aware that they are doing so. If speakers must by necessity indulge in self-praise, they will do so whether or not they know that it is permissible. That is what necessity means.

In any case, the concept of necessity is far too general a criterion to be a meaningful point of comparison. If self-praise was widely considered unseemly (cf. *De laude* 539A–B), it is not difficult to imagine why someone who engaged in it would claim to have no other choice. Certainly we need not posit knowledge of rhetorical precepts.

The point can be demonstrated by a survey of what was said in justification of Paul's boasting before discussion of *periautologia* came into vogue. Independently of any reference to Plutarch's treatise or putative rhetorical precepts for self-praise, older commentators frequently invoked the urgency of Paul's situation, thus excusing his boasting. So Calvin remarked on Paul's behalf: "Not as if he were a fool in glorying; for he was constrained to it by necessity."[25] Likewise, F. W. Robertson observed: "It is evident … that he has been forced to speak of self only by a kind of compulsion. Fact after fact of his own experiences is, as it were, wrung out, as if he had not intended to tell it."[26] This sort of argument was ubiquitous.[27] Clearly, we do not need Plutarch to tell us that people can, when in dire necessity, get away with behavior that otherwise would be deemed inappropriate.

---

25. John Calvin, *Commentary on the Epistles of Paul the Apostle to the Corinthians* (trans. John Pringle; 2 vols.; Edinburgh: Calvin Translation Society, 1849), 2:338; cf. 2:352, 381.

26. F. W. Robertson, *Sermons on St. Paul's Epistles to the Corinthians* (Boston: Ticknor & Fields, 1860), 418.

27. See, e.g., Joseph Agar Beet, *A Commentary on St. Paul's Epistles to the Corinthians* (London: Hodder & Stoughton, 1882), 452, 466; James Denney, *The Second Epistle to the Corinthians* (Expositor's Bible; London: Hodder & Stoughton, 1894), 312; Charles Hodge, *An Exposition of the Second Epistle to the Corinthians* (New York: Hodder & Stoughton, 1858), 249; Plummer, *Second Epistle*, 291.

Self-Defense

Plutarch's more specific argument concerns the necessity of defending oneself (ἀπολογούμενος) in the case of slander or false accusation (διαβολὴν ἢ κατηγορίαν [540C]), and here we are justified, I think, in speaking of the influence of rhetorical tradition: Quintilian defends Cicero's boasting on similar grounds (*Inst.* 11.1.18, 22–23), as does Cicero himself (*Har. resp.* 17; *Dom.* 92–95), and the basic argument is put to use by Demosthenes (*Cor.* 4), Isocrates (*Antid.* 1–8), and Dio Chrysostom (*Pol.* 2). So, although Paul likely could not have encountered instruction on this matter in a rhetorical handbook—Quintilian's is the first extant "textbook" to refer to such an argument (ca. 93–95 C.E.)—nevertheless an astute student of rhetorical tradition would have been able, should he be faced with such an exigency, to draw on the practice of his predecessors.

It is widely agreed that Paul had been the object of various accusations in Corinth, and it is clear that in 2 Cor 10–13 he was fighting for his reputation. Thus it is frequently asserted that, on these grounds, "Paul would have received Plutarch's permission to engage in self-praise."[28] As we will see, however, such a claim is founded on a misleadingly superficial reading of Plutarch's concerns. Moreover, even if it were true, it would not yet provide evidence of rhetorical education. The fact that this was a traditional argument among rhetoricians does not by any means prove that only trained rhetoricians would have thought to employ it.

In fact, Paul's behavior here is perfectly understandable without positing knowledge of rhetorical precepts: Paul's reputation and therefore his influence among the Corinthians were on the wane, so he responded, predictably enough, by reminding them of his divine mandate and his peerless qualifications. As far as I can see, the only real parallel between Paul and Plutarch here is that Plutarch described the same general situation in which Paul would later find himself—that of a man whose stock was in danger of falling. Most people would speak in their own defense in such situations, and it would not be surprising if they found it useful

---

28. Charles H. Talbert, *Reading Corinthians: A Literary and Theological Commentary on 1 and 2 Corinthians* (New York: Crossroad, 1987), 118; cf. Betz, *Der Apostel Paulus und die sokratische Tradition*, 78–79; Sundermann, *Der schwache Apostel*, 35–36; Watson, "Paul and Boasting," 82, 90; DiCicco, *Ethos, Pathos, and Logos*, 80; Thrall, *Second Epistle*, 2:835; Furnish, *II Corinthians*, 554; Wojciechowski, "Paul and Plutarch on Boasting," 108; Marshall, *Enmity in Corinth*, 354.

to recite their own merits.[29] Thus the simple fact that Plutarch's exemplars and Paul both spoke on their own behalf when under fire is not particularly remarkable.

Perhaps a more compelling case could be made if Paul—like Demosthenes (*Cor.* 3) or Isocrates (*Trap.* 1) or Cicero (*Har. resp.* 17; *Phil.* 14.13), for example—drew explicit attention to the fact that he had to boast in order to defend his own reputation. But the only time Paul addresses the question of self-defense (πάλαι δοκεῖτε ὅτι ὑμῖν ἀπολογούμεθα [2 Cor 12:19]), it is to deny that he is undertaking it. If there were a rhetorical advantage to be gained by reminding the Corinthians that only in self-defense would he speak so boastfully, Paul has let it pass him by.

Finally, no one who adduces Plutarch's discussion here has paid the least attention, apparently, to his explanation of *why* self-praise works when one is speaking in one's own defense. What Plutarch says is, in fact, most telling, providing considerable insight into both the logic of his treatise and the sort of discourse he admires:

> [When one has been slandered,] not only is there nothing puffed up, vainglorious, or proud in taking a high tone about oneself at such a moment, but it displays as well a lofty spirit and greatness of character which by refusing to be humbled humbles and overpowers envy (μὴ ταπεινοῦσθαι ταπεινούσης καὶ χειρουμένης τὸν φθόνον). For men no longer think fit even to pass judgement on such as these, but exult and rejoice and catch the inspiration of the swelling speech, when it is well-founded and true. (540D [LCL])

If there is a rhetorical principle inscribed here, it is important to see that it is inseparable from its exercise within a particular social milieu and by a particular sort of aristocratic speaker. It is not the rules of rhetoric, but rather the social dynamics that inhere in a specific set of political relationships that, for Plutarch, make self-defensive boasting effective and therefore justifiable: If he possesses adequate gravitas, Plutarch explains, a beleaguered statesman can overawe his hearers by confidently asserting his power, thus moving himself beyond the range of his hearers' envy.

---

29. So already Norden, responding to Heinrici's suggestion that Paul was familiar with ancient apologetic conventions: "Jeder Mensch, der sich zu verantworten hat, verwandte Töne anschlägt, aber muss er die von anderen erlernen?" (*Die antike Kunstprosa*, 2:494).

Paul is not this sort of speaker. Although he certainly boasts in his own defense, his boasting does not appear to activate the social mechanism—the overpowering of envy—to which Plutarch refers. Indeed, I think it is safe to say that no one would confuse the sort of "swelling speech" Plutarch describes with 2 Cor 10–13. Far from "refusing to be humbled," Paul famously puts his weakness on display. What this confession of weakness signifies will be the subject of further discussion below. In the current context, a comparison of Paul's demeanor with that depicted in Plutarch's examples of self-defensive μεγαλαυχία will suffice.

Epaminondas, so the story goes, convinced the other Theban generals serving with him not to return home at the end of their term as the law prescribed, but rather to seize their advantage and keep fighting. Though they orchestrated a very successful campaign, upon their return home the generals were impeached for their unauthorized action.[30] Epaminondas, apparently, boldly took all the blame upon himself, then defiantly undertook an unconventional self-defense:

> When Epameinondas expatiated on the glory of his acts and said in conclusion that he was ready to die if they would admit that he had founded Messenê, ravaged Laconia, and united Arcadia—[the very acts for which he stood on trial]—they did not even wait to take up the vote against him, but with admiration for the man commingled with delight and laughter broke up the meeting. (540E; cf. Nepos, *Epam.* 8.2–5)

A self-assured man like this does not dignify slander by becoming indignant; he simply rises above it.[31] Indeed, it is the impression that one's dignity and self-possession are unfazed by petty accusations that lends such a defense particular force and undeniable charm—or perhaps the infuriating impression of patriarchal conceit, I suppose, depending on your perspective. In any case, Plutarch, who shared Epaminondas's values, was charmed.

---

30. In addition to the summary account at *De laude* 540D–E, see also Plutarch, *Pel.* 25.1–2; Nepos, *Epam.* 7–8; Diodorus Siculus 15.66–72.

31. Thus Seneca *Ira* 3.25.3: "There will be no doubt about this—that whoever scorns his tormentors removes himself from the common herd and towers above them. The mark of true greatness is not to notice that you have received a blow. So does the huge wild beast calmly turn and gaze at barking dogs, so does the wave dash in vain against a mighty cliff" (Basore, LCL). See also Seneca, *Const.* 13.5; 14.3; *Clem.* 1.10.3; Quintilian, *Inst.* 11.1.17.

Paul's demeanor is strikingly different. As is frequently remarked, his boasting is halting and reluctant, and although such reluctance may have its own way of mitigating the negative impression of self-praise, it certainly does not make for the sort of overawed and admiring response evoked by Epaminondas and his ilk. Paul, Chrysostom quipped, shrank from self-praise like a horse rearing back from a precipice (*Laud. Paul.* 5.12; *Hom. 2 Cor. 11:1* 4 [PG 51:305]). What Plutarch envisioned was more like a horse charging through an enemy line.

In sum, then, although there is certainly a superficial similarity here—Plutarch speaks of self-defense; Paul defends himself—attention to the values and social assumptions that fuel Plutarch's treatment reveals that 2 Cor 10–13 has little in common with what Plutarch actually commends. Paul simply does not carry himself with the sort of dignity and "loftiness of spirit" that "humiliates and overpowers envy" (540D). In fact, what comparison of Paul's self-praise with Plutarch's discussion of self-defense does highlight is the tenuousness of Paul's claim to status. Unlike Epaminondas, who can pretend disregard for the verdict of his jury (cf. Demosthenes, *Cor.* 10; Dio Chrysostom, *Pol.* 12), Paul wears his desperation on his sleeve.

Misfortune

Plutarch's discussion of why the unfortunate can indulge in μεγαλαυχία more appropriately than the fortunate—sometimes adduced as a parallel to Paul's boasting of shipwrecks, beatings, and the like[32]—is predicated on the same values (541A–C). Here the image Plutarch provides is that of an indomitable boxer holding his head up high: Unlike a vain man walking with his nose in the air, the boxer's bold posture evinces courage, not fatuous arrogance. Likewise, the unfortunate, "far removed from ambition by their plight, are looked upon as breasting ill-fortune, shoring up their courage, and eschewing all appeal to pity and all whining and self-abasement (ταπεινούμενον) in adversity" (541A [LCL]). Paul, I think all will agree, does not "[use] self-glorification to pass from a humbled and piteous state to an attitude of triumph and pride" (541B [LCL]); on the contrary, he puts his ignominy on display—he wallows in it, I suspect Plu-

---

32. Heinrici, *Der zweite Brief an die Korinther*, 313; Betz, "De laude ipsius," 388; Watson, "Paul and Boasting," 92.

tarch would say.³³ And this sort of posture ultimately nullifies what for Plutarch makes the self-glorification of the unfortunate inspiring.

Usefulness; Benefit to Hearers

Plutarch concludes his treatise by reiterating the moral criterion that underlies the entire discussion: self-praise, in order to be legitimate, must be useful. In his words, "We will abstain from speaking about ourselves unless we are going to provide some great benefit to ourselves or to our hearers" (547F).³⁴ The ἑαυτούς here comes as a bit of a surprise, since throughout the work Plutarch has emphasized that it is concern for the well-being of others that might motivate a statesman to speak on his own behalf (539E–F; 544D). Presumably this is a reference to the sort of self-defense when facing calumny or hardship that we have just discussed. In any case, one thing is clear: the desire for glory is not, for Plutarch, sufficient cause for self-praise; one must have some further—and noble—end in view.

This would also seem to be the assumption of Dio Chrysostom. Dio never provides anything resembling a systematic discussion of self-praise, but he does, on one occasion, set out to defend Homer's Nestor against charges of braggadocio (ἀλαζονεία [*Nest.* 3; cf. *Il.* 1.260–268; 273–274]).³⁵ Dio justifies Nestor's self-praise—without once using the word *periautologia*, we might note—by means of a single observation: Nestor's boasting, like a doctor's unpleasant drug, was intended to have a salutary effect, namely, the end of Agamemnon and Achilles's quarrel (4–8).

Still, there are no grounds for asserting that Plutarch and Dio reflect rhetorical precepts here. Dio is not commenting on the rhetorical efficacy of Nestor's speech—in fact, the speech did not, he admits, have its intended effect (9)—but is rather considering whether or not Homer had made Nestor a braggart. This is a question of character, not rhetoric. As we have seen, the acceptability of Nestor's self-adulation had been discussed under the rubric of moral philosophy at least since Philodemus (*Hom.* fr.

---

33. Note Plutarch's observation that although speakers may confess minor faults in order to blunt the edge of envy, they should not report what is truly "degrading or ignoble" (αἰσχραὶ μηδ᾽ ἀγεννεῖς [544B; LCL]). See Glancy, "Boasting of Beatings," 119–21.

34. Cf. Betz, *Der Apostel Paulus und die sokratische Tradition*, 76.

35. Dio's *Nestor* is adduced as background to Paul's boasting by Forbes, "Comparison, Self-Praise, and Irony," 9; Watson, "Paul and Boasting," 78.

9), and the consensus seems to have been that in this case Nestor's boasting was the lesser of two evils.

It is also noteworthy that from what Plutarch says, as from Dio's example, we should expect the criterion of usefulness to operate entirely in the background, helping a statesman decide whether or not it is appropriate to indulge in self-praise, but not having any observable impact on how it is articulated. For Plutarch, self-praise is risky whether it is useful or not; however, if it is useful, then it just might be worth the risk (544D–F). There is nothing to suggest that he was recommending a rhetorical strategy of seeking to attenuate the risk by drawing attention to the benefit one's self-praise would provide for one's audience. Nestor did not explain that he was boasting for Agamemnon and Achilles's own good; no, that was Dio's retrospective justification.

Comparative Boasting

Plutarch obviously does not like self-praise, but what really irritates him is self-praise motivated by vain ambition (φιλοτιμία), particularly when it involves rivalry with others:

> When those who hunger for praise cannot find others to praise them, they give the appearance of seeking sustenance and succour for their vainglorious appetite from themselves, a graceless spectacle. But when they do not even seek to be praised simply and in themselves, but try to rival the honour that belongs to others and set against it their own accomplishments and acts in the hope of dimming the glory of another, their conduct is not only frivolous, but envious and spiteful as well.... Here then is something we clearly must avoid. (540A–C [LCL]; cf. Quintilian, *Inst.* 11.1.16)

At this juncture Pauline interpreters generally abandon their treatment of Paul's boasting and commence with a discussion of how Plutarch's treatise informs our portrait of his opponents. Thus for Duane Watson, "This warning illumines Paul's statement about his opponents' comparisons with each other and with himself as not 'show(ing) good sense' (10:12), because they were based on working in his sphere of action and trying to undermine his authority and honor (10:13–16)."[36] Whereas Paul followed

---

36. Watson, "Paul and Boasting," 90; see also Watson, "Paul's Boasting in 2 Corinthians 10–13," 272; Betz, "De laude ipsius," 385–86; Harris, *Second Corinthians*, 707–8.

Plutarch's conventions for self-praise, his rivals, on the contrary, "were the sort of arrogant self-boasters the culture despised."[37]

It is an open question whether Paul's rivals really were so shamelessly competitive and self-adulating as interpreters of 2 Cor 10–13 are wont to imagine: we have no independent evidence, and Paul's testimony is far from disinterested. What we do know, from sound documentary evidence, is that *Paul* perceived the status gained by others as a threat to his honor and fought back by indulging in self-praise. Whatever he says in 2 Cor 10:12 about not daring to compare himself with his rivals, comparative boasting is precisely what he goes on to do.

That Paul here is in direct contravention of the one precept for *periautologia* regarding which Plutarch is most insistent seems to have escaped notice. So far as I can see, the only explanation for this interpretive myopia is our presupposition that Paul was in the right—that he was the (capital A) Apostle to the Gentiles and therefore that anyone seeking to discredit him or gain influence in "his" communities was a self-interested meddler. But the fact that Paul went on to become St. Paul must not be allowed to obscure the reality of the Corinthian community in the mid-50s: This was a group of Christ-believers that had been shaped by a number of charismatic leaders, among whom Paul was but one. Paul claimed a special position by virtue of having founded the community (1 Cor 3:6; 4:15; 2 Cor 10:14), but, in the ongoing competition for influence in Corinth, this apparently was no trump card. As David Horrell recently has argued, despite Paul's claims, the Corinthian community was no "Pauline church."[38] Labeling it such mires our work in anachronistic conceptions of Paul's apostleship and blinds us to the fact that legitimacy was precisely what was up for grabs in Corinth.

Reading 2 Cor 10–13 without presupposing Paul's primacy enables us to see just how egregiously Paul violates Plutarch's proscription of com-

---

37. Craig S. Keener, *1–2 Corinthians* (New Cambridge Bible Commentary; Cambridge: Cambridge University Press, 2005), 222.

38. David G. Horrell, "Pauline Churches or Early Christian Churches? Unity, Disagreement, and the Eucharist," in *Einheit der Kirche im Neuen Testament* (ed. Anatoly A. Alexeev, Christos Karakolis, and Ulrich Luz; WUNT 218; Tübingen: Mohr Siebeck, 2008), 193, and, more generally, 186–96. I am also indebted here to Steven Friesen's comments during "After the First Urban Christians: The Social Scientific Study of Pauline Christianity Twenty Five Years Later" (panel discussion at the meeting of the Society of Biblical Literature, New Orleans, La., 21 November 2009).

parative boasting. Plutarch had made room for stripping honor from those deemed unworthy, but insisted that it be done without indulging in self-praise: "If we hold them undeserving and of little worth, let us not strip them of their praise by presenting our own, but plainly refute their claim and show their reputation to be groundless" (540C [LCL]). In contrast, Paul's refutation is comparative throughout, contrasting his own praiseworthy behavior with what he insists are his rivals' false claims. Ironically, it begins with the assertion that he, unlike "some people," will not compare himself with others (10:12)—an assertion that is, of course, precisely an implicit comparison. Paul insists that he will not boast εἰς τὰ ἄμετρα; he will not overreach himself; he will not boast in the labors of others or in another's κανών (10:13–16). Again, comparison with the behavior he imputes to his rivals is implied throughout. Likewise, "It is not those who commend themselves"—read, "my rivals"—"that are approved, but those whom the Lord commends"—read, "me" (10:18). So when Paul insists that he is not inferior to the super-apostles (11:5), and then proceeds to his series of κἀγώ's (11:22–23), he is only making explicit the comparative mode that has been dominant throughout. By Plutarchian standards, Paul is clearly out of line.

Plutarch does, however, later in his treatise, qualify his resistance to rivalrous boasting: "Yet where mistaken praise injures and corrupts by arousing emulation of evil and inducing the adoption of an unsound policy where important issues are at stake, it is no disservice to counteract it" (545D). Again, interpreters have latched on to the superficial parallel, asserting that Paul's boasting passages "meet the requirements of this test":[39] Paul, we are assured, only seeks to dissuade the Corinthians from his rivals' corrupting influence.

Paul indeed does portray the influence of his opponents as a sinister force threatening to contaminate or destroy the Corinthian community (11:2–4, 13–15), but he by no means seeks to counteract this influence in the way Plutarch recommends. For Plutarch, the way to censure vice without merely looking envious of those who indulge in it is straightforward: "It is not ... with the praise of persons but with that of acts, when they are vicious, that the statesman must wage war" (545E). For his part, Paul never manages to explain how, specifically, his opponents are leading the Corinthians astray, nor which vicious acts the Corinthians are in danger of

---

39. Talbert, *Reading Corinthians*, 118; also Marshall, *Enmity in Corinth*, 354–55.

emulating. Instead, he vaguely insinuates that his rivals pollute the Corinthians' chastity (11:2-3) and accuses them of being disguised ministers of Satan (11:13-15). Clearly, this is an attack on persons, not on deeds. Nor is it an attack on bad theology. If the issue were a theological or a moral one, Paul should, if he were following Plutarch's advice, have explained the dangers of the Corinthian's present course of action, and done so without self-reference. He did not. Instead, he sought to reassert his authoritative role whilst undercutting the influence of his rivals.

Interpreters have worked hard to uncover the theological or ideological controversy that purportedly underlies the dispute between Paul and his rivals in 2 Corinthians,[40] but all they have managed to do, I submit, is to elevate the means of the controversy into its substance: Paul polemically insists that the opponents have "another spirit" (11:4), so, his interpreters conclude, the dispute must have concerned the role of pneumatic experience;[41] Paul seeks to defuse the accusation that he is a layman in speech, hence this must be a disagreement about the value of rhetoric;[42] Paul defends himself for not receiving financial support from the Corinthians, hence he must have differed from his opponents insofar as he had counter-cultural ideas about patronage.[43]

What each of these reconstructions does, I suggest, is confuse the argumentative strategies Paul employs with his ultimate goal. Certainly Paul and his rivals have various differences of opinion, but these are the means through which the conflict between them is negotiated, not its fundamental grounds. To argue that what we see here is a conflict about rhetoric, or patronage, or pneumatism is like saying that people engage in duels to prove the superiority of their favorite pistols. No, the real grounds of the controversy are far less subtle: What is perfectly clear from reading 2 Cor 10-13—though apparently unpalatable to many interpreters—is that the primary thing on Paul's mind is his own status in the Corinthian

---

40. See Jerry L. Sumney, *Identifying Paul's Opponents: The Question of Method in 2 Corinthians* (JSNTSup 40; Sheffield: JSOT Press, 1990), 15-67.

41. E.g., Lake, *Earlier Epistles*, 222-35; Georgi, *Opponents of Paul*.

42. Judge, "Paul's Boasting"; Betz, "Rhetoric and Theology"; Winter, *Philo and Paul*.

43. Marshall, *Enmity in Corinth*, 173-258. See also Scott Bartchy's argument that Paul's "new creation" leadership values contrasted with his rivals' "old creation" values ("'When I'm Weak, I'm Strong': A Pauline Paradox in Cultural Context," in *Kultur, Politik, Religion, Sprach—Text: Wolfgang Stegemann zum 60. Geburtstag* [ed. Christian Strecker; vol. 2 of *Kontexte der Schrift*; Stuttgart: Kohlhammer, 2005], 49-60).

community. Only through the casuistry of apologetic interpreters have we learned of a theological or ideological controversy.

Conclusion

Other parallels between Paul and *De laude ipsius* have been proposed, but they do not warrant detailed treatment. It is occasionally suggested that Paul's theological grounding of his apostolate (10:8) is in accord with Plutarch's suggestion that one can minimize the appearance of hubris by giving some credit for one's achievement to chance and some to God (542E). But there is no similarity here: For Plutarch, giving credit to God allows one to set aside the burden of glory (φορτίον τῆς δόξης ... ἀποτίθεσθαι); for Paul, on the contrary, to invoke God's commissioning is precisely to make a status claim. As we have seen repeatedly, the superficial similarity erodes under further examination.

Likewise, a number of interpreters have followed Betz in asserting that Paul's narration of his trip to the third heaven in the third person (12:2-4) evinces his familiarity with a rhetorical precept expressed by Plutarch: When possible, praise someone who shares your laudable traits rather than praising yourself, and then hope your audience can put two and two together (542C-D).[44] Aside from the fact that Paul does not really praise someone else, it is important to see that for Plutarch's ruse to work, the audience must not suspect the speaker's self-promoting intention; for, if it is evident that one is really trying to praise oneself, one fails to avoid the appearance of boastfulness (cf. 542C). For his part, Paul had introduced

---

44. Betz, *Der Apostel Paulus und die sokratische Tradition*, 95. So also Andrew T. Lincoln, "'Paul the Visionary': The Setting and Significance of the Rapture to Paradise in II Corinthians XII.1-10," *NTS* 25 (1979): 208-9; Jerry W. McCant, *2 Corinthians* (Readings; Sheffield: Sheffield Academic Press, 1999), 143; Long, *Ancient Rhetoric*, 190. Cf. Mitchell, "Patristic Perspective," 366. Mitchell's invocation of the rhetorical device *prosōpopoiia* to describe Paul's procedure here is particularly misleading. As Mitchell herself explains, Paul "does not speak the words of his new character so much as he denies that his own words, allegedly spoken about another, are really about himself." That is, the speaking voice is Paul's throughout; it is the object, Paul the visionary, not the subject, Paul the speaker, who is masked. Hence there is no fictive speaker here, and no *prosōpopoiia*. Moreover, Chrysostom, whose reading Mitchell claims to be elucidating here, makes no clear reference to this rhetorical figure: His προσωπεῖον ἕτερον ὑπελθεῖν (*Laud. Paul.* 5.15) is surely an attempt to describe how Paul-as-visionary disguises himself (cf. 5.12 [κρύπτει ἑαυτόν]), not a periphrastic reference to *prosōpopoiia*.

this very section by explaining that he would proceed to boast of "visions and revelations of the Lord" (12:1). His intentions are transparent, thus there can be no real resemblance here to what Plutarch recommends.[45]

I conclude this section by reiterating the argument: The notion that Paul evinces knowledge of rhetorical precepts for *periautologia* is founded on a misleading treatment of Plutarch's treatise. *De laude ipsius* is not a collection of rhetorical precepts, and there is no evidence that it is dependent on previous rhetorical discussions of *periautologia*. In fact, there are no previous rhetorical discussions of *periautologia* attested. What Plutarch's treatise provides is an example of the use of moral suasion to control the sort of self-assertion—in this case self-assertion in the form of self-praise—that threatens to disrupt the social order by inciting envious rivalry. His is a conservative project: he seeks to justify the limited use of self-praise by a certain sort of speaker—namely, the traditional aristocrat who already has elevated status and its accompanying gravitas—whilst denouncing the self-praise of those who aspire to clamber up the social ladder. Self-praise that preserves the social order is acceptable; self-praise that would alter it is not. In the end, the question is not how one speaks so much as who speaks—and Paul does not appear to be the sort of speaker that would gain Plutarch's approval.

Nevertheless, Paul's comments in 2 Cor 12:11 are reminiscent of two very general aspects of Plutarch's discussion: it is better to be praised by others than to praise oneself; self-praise is appropriate when done in legitimate self-defense. But this reminiscence is more credibly explained (with Windisch and contra Betz) as resulting from overlapping social mores than from shared dependence on rhetorical tradition. Moreover, as I will demonstrate in part 3, these assumptions are hardly unique to Paul and Plutarch, and can be detected in discourse that certainly has no connection to the classical rhetorical tradition.

---

45. I have left unresolved the question why Paul refers to himself in the third person, one of many puzzling aspects of his narration of this experience. I favor the explanation that this manner of speaking derives from a subjective ambiguity inherent in the ecstatic experience itself—an explanation that seems particularly credible after Colleen Shantz's recent work on the neurobiology of altered states of consciousness like that described in 2 Cor 12:1–4. See *Paul in Ecstasy*, 93–101. Cf. Furnish, *II Corinthians*, 543; Thrall, *Second Epistle*, 2:782.

QUINTILIAN, *INSTITUTIO ORATORIA* 11.1.15–26

If there is one rhetorical work from which Plutarch could theoretically have gleaned material for his reflections on self-praise, it is the *Institutio oratoria* of his contemporary Quintilian.[46] Quintilian begins his eleventh book with a long section dedicated to the topic of speaking appropriately (*apte* [11.1.1]), the bulk of which elaborates on his insistence that one must consider "not merely what it is expedient, but also what it is becoming to say" (11.1.8 [Butler, LCL]). Although it is true that usually the two criteria go hand in hand—to speak unbecomingly is seldom to one's advantage, and becoming speech is usually also expedient (11.1.8)—there are exceptions: It would have been expedient for Socrates, for example, to "[employ] the ordinary forensic methods of defence" (11.1.9 [LCL]), but it also would have been a betrayal of his noble character. "This instance alone," Quintilian concludes, "shows that the end which the orator must keep in view is not persuasion, but speaking well (*non persuadendi sed bene dicendi*), since there are occasions when to persuade would be a blot upon his honour" (11.1.11 [LCL]; cf. 2.15). Therefore, what is becoming trumps what is expedient every time: "There are two things which will be becoming to all men at all times and in all places, namely, to act and speak as befits a man of honour, and it will never at any time beseem any man to speak or act dishonourably" (11.1.14 [LCL]).[47]

Quintilian's primary example of unseemly speech is boasting about one's own eloquence. This, he insists, is always a mistake (11.1.15). But here Quintilian gets himself into difficulty, for the one orator most consistently censured for such behavior is Quintilian's beloved Cicero.[48] Hence

---

46. George Kennedy dates the work to the final years of Domitian, probably between 93 and 95 C.E., a few years before the turn-of-the-century date we have proposed for Plutarch's *De laude ipsius*. See Kennedy, *Quintilian* (New York: Twayne, 1969), 27–29. See also Tobias Reinhardt and Michael Winterbottom, eds., *Quintilian, Institutio Oratoria, Book 2* (Oxford: Oxford University Press, 2006), xxiii. Note that Plutarch claims to have had a rudimentary grasp of Latin, acquired late in life (*Dem.* 2). See D. A Russell, *Plutarch* (London: Duckworth, 1973), 54; C. P. Jones, *Plutarch and Rome* (Oxford: Clarendon, 1971), 80–87.

47. See further Arthur E. Walzer, "Moral Philosophy and Rhetoric in the Institutes: Quintilian on Honor and Expediency," *RSQ* 36 (2006): 273–77.

48. For Quintilian's admiring evaluation of Cicero, see *Inst.* 10.1.105–114, 123; 12.1.16–21. On Cicero's notorious arrogance, see Walter Allen, "Cicero's Conceit," *TAPA* 85 (1954): 121–44; Robert A. Kaster, "Self-Aggrandizement and Praise of Others

his entire discussion of the propriety of self-praise consists of a defense of Cicero's notorious boastfulness (11.1.17–26).

Notably, there is little in his defense of Cicero to suggest that Quintilian is dependent upon previous discussions of self-praise; on the contrary, these appear to be mostly ad hoc justifications. Indeed, if there had been such widely accepted criteria for self-praise as Pauline scholars would have us believe, and if Cicero abode by them, it is difficult to fathom why he should have been so frequently censured for his boasting (11.1.17). No, Quintilian finds himself defending Cicero precisely because the appropriateness of self-praise is a matter of taste and judgment, not the simple application of established rhetorical rules (cf. 11.1.91).

Still, Quintilian does seem to assume that his audience shares some basic presuppositions concerning good rhetorical etiquette. First, he stresses that Cicero's boasting was "due quite as much to the necessities of defense as to the promptings of vainglory" (11.1.18 [LCL]), which sort of argument I have treated in detail above. Second, he observes that Cicero, in his private letters,[49] regularly quotes the remarks of others about his eloquence in order to mitigate the appearance of boasting. This strategy presumably stems from Aristotle's advice (*Rhet.* 3.17.16), and had other practitioners too (cf. Pliny, *Ep.* 9.23.5–6), but it annoys Quintilian: "Yet I am not sure that open boasting is not more tolerable, owing to its sheer straightforwardness, than that perverted form of self-praise" (11.1.21 [LCL]). In any case, unlike Cicero, Paul seems to have had no one in Corinth to quote in his favor.[50] Finally, Quintilian notes that Cicero deflected some credit for his success to the senate and some to providence (11.1.23). As noted above, Plutarch makes a similar point, but this has little in common with Paul's claim to divine backing.

Quintilian's discussion goes on to treat other instances of unbecoming speech—an "impudent, disorderly, or angry tone" (11.1.29 [LCL]), immodesty in speaking of shameful things (11.1.30), an indecorous attitude toward one's opponents (11.1.57), and so forth. He does provide some rhetorical strategies for dealing with various courtroom exigencies

---

in Cicero," *Princeton/Stanford Working Papers in Classics*, no. 120502 (2005). Cited 14 July 2011. Online: http://www.princeton.edu/~pswpc/pdfs/kaster/120502.pdf.

49. Quintilian seems to presume that there is more scope for self-praise in letters to intimate friends than in public oratory (11.1.21). Cf. Cicero, *Att.* 1.16.8, and see Roy K. Gibson, "Pliny and the Art of (In)offensive Self-Praise," *Arethusa* 36 (2003): 243–45.

50. So Watson, "Paul's Boasting in 2 Corinthians 10–13," 273.

along the way, but it is Quintilian's moralizing that sets the dominant tone. Indeed, as we might have expected from the definition of the aim of rhetoric with which he began the section—*non persuadendi sed bene dicendi* (11.1.11)—the discussion is exemplary of Quintilian's own particular emphasis, the notion that the ideal orator is not merely persuasive, but virtuous—a "good man speaking well" (*vir bonus dicendi peritus* [12.1.1; cf. 2.15.34]).

There may have been ancient precedent for this marriage of morality and rhetoric, but here Quintilian is self-consciously treading on what, in his time at least, was presumed to be the philosophers' turf (1 pr. 10–18; 12.2.6–9).[51] Indeed, he begins book 12 by claiming that whereas his technical discussion has been largely a matter of collating the best existing work, in his attempt to nurture the virtuous speaker he is peerless (12 pr. 2–4). It appears, then, that Quintilian's discussion of the inappropriateness of boasting derives not from prior codification of precepts for *periautologia* but rather from his own preoccupation with the moral formation of his ideal orator. Moreover, the only possible connection to Paul is Quintilian's excusing of Cicero's boasting on the grounds that it was necessary for his self-defense—hardly sufficient grounds, as we have seen, for asserting that Paul and Quintilian reflect a common rhetorical tradition.

Hesitancy and *Prodiorthōsis*

Interestingly, Plutarch says much less about giving the impression of hesitancy or reluctance when indulging in self-praise than do interpreters of 2 Corinthians. That is, he says nothing at all. Neither does Quintilian. To my knowledge, the nearest we get to a rhetorical recommendation of such a practice comes somewhat later in Pseudo-Herodian's treatment of προδιόρθωσις. According to Pseudo-Herodian, we should soften our words when we are about to say something shameful concerning our adversary or something vainglorious (μεγάλαυχα) concerning ourselves by first forewarning our hearers (*Fig.* 33 [*RG* 3:95]). And this is just what Paul does, repeatedly pleading for his hearers to bear with him before he begins

---

51. See Michael Winterbottom, "Quintilian the Moralist," in vol. 1 of *Quintiliano: Historia y actualidad de la retórica* (ed. Tomás Albaladejo, Emilio del Río, and José Antonio Caballero; 3 vols.; Logroño: Ediciones Instituto de Estudios Riojanos, 1998), 318–20. Cf. Arthur E. Walzer, "Quintilian's 'Vir Bonus' and the Stoic Wise Man," *RSQ* 33 (2003): 25–41; Walzer, "Moral Philosophy and Rhetoric in the Institutes."

to boast (11:1, 17; 12:1). As Margaret Mitchell has noted, Paul's attempt to preempt the judgment that he was a fool was deemed an instance of *prodiorthōsis* as early as John Chrysostom.[52] Heinrici recognized it as such; so did E. A. Judge.[53] I do not disagree. However, I would like to add two points of clarification.

First, it should be noted that Pseudo-Herodian, writing no earlier than the second century,[54] stands alone in linking *prodiorthōsis* with speech about oneself.[55] Other descriptions of the figure make clear that it was construed very generally as warning the audience of something unpleasant to come (Alexander, *Fig.* 1.3 [*RG* 3:14–15]; Tiberius, *Fig.* 8; cf. Ps.-Hermogenes, *Inv.* 4.12). When more specific usages are discussed, they vary widely—from warning the audience that one is about to cite poetry (Hermogenes, Περὶ ἰδεῶν, 2.4) to notifying judges that one is about to say something ill-omened concerning their potential fate (Apsines, *Rhet.* 10.34 [*RG* 1:399]). The rhetoricians, like Plutarch, clearly saw no inherent connection between *prodiorthōsis* and *periautologia*. Thus Paul's expressions of reluctance to boast may perhaps be rhetorically appropriate, but it would be an exaggeration to say they are done in conformity with rhetorical precepts for self-praise.

Second, we need hardly posit that Paul was rhetorically educated in order to account for his use of *prodiorthōsis*. Again, the history of interpretation of Paul's boasting helps put things in perspective: even if they

---

52. *Laud. Paul.* 5.12; *Hom. 2 Cor.* 23.1 (PG 61:553); 24.1 (PG 61:564); 25.1 (PG 61:569); *Hom. 2 Cor. 11:1* 4 (PG 51:305). See further Mitchell, "Patristic Perspective," 363–64.

53. Heinrici, *Der zweite Brief an die Korinther*, 313; Judge, "Paul's Boasting," 67. So also Sundermann, *Der schwache Apostel*, 83–84; Furnish, *II Corinthians*, 499; Pitta, "Il discorso del pazzo," 496; Thrall, *Second Epistle*, 2:659.

54. *De figuris* in fact consists of two separate writings pieced together by a redactor. Neither part can be dated with precision, but Ps.-Herodian's description of *prodiorthōsis* comes in the second part, for which the earliest proposed origin is the time of Hadrian. See Kerstin Hajdú, *Ps.-Herodian, De figuris: Überlieferungsgeschichte und kritische Ausgabe* (SGLG 8; Berlin: de Gruyter, 1998), 21–23.

55. Nearest to Ps.-Herodian is probably the discussion of Ps.-Aristides (1.12.2.7 [*RG* 2:506]), although he does not speak explicitly of *prodiorthōsis*, nor does he refer to self-praise. Rather, in the context of a discussion of epideictic, he lists six ways of avoiding praise (of another) that irritates one's audience (τοῦ μὴ φορτικῶς ἐπαινεῖν), the third of which is to begin by asking an audience's indulgence (ὅταν πρὶν εἰπεῖν τι συγγνώμην ἐφ' οἷς ἂν μέλλῃ λέγειν αἰτῆται παρὰ τῶν δικαστῶν).

have not always known its name, interpreters of Paul have had no difficulty whatsoever describing the function of the figure, and, until recently, they were content to consider it an expression of Paul's sincere reluctance to boast. Charles Hodge's remark is typical: "So repugnant was this task to his feelings, that he not only humbly apologizes for thus speaking of himself, but he finds it difficult to do what he felt must be done."[56] Whether or not Hodge accurately describes Paul's feelings on the matter, the point is that Paul's hesitancy is perfectly comprehensible without positing rhetorical training: Paul knows that boasting is unseemly, and is either embarrassed to do it or is worried about how his hearers will respond—indeed, where personhood is constructed corporately,[57] the two amount to the same thing: Paul fears he will be derided as a fool. As will be demonstrated in part 3, speakers without formal rhetorical education also resort to *prodiorthōsis* in such situations; hence this cannot be adduced as evidence of Paul's rhetorical education.

Conclusion

Contrary to the prevailing view, we must conclude that there is nothing in Paul's boasting to warrant the conclusion that he was familiar with rhetorical principles governing self-praise. First, the notion that Plutarch and Quintilian based their writings on established rhetorical dictates for *periautologia* cannot be sustained. Both may occasionally reflect existing rhetorical practice, but Plutarch's is a work of moral philosophy with only incidental rhetorical observations and Quintilian, in his treatment of what is "becoming," is self-consciously innovating. Writing forty-some years after Paul, these authors provide no evidence of clearly defined rhetorical principles for self-praise.

---

56. Hodge, *Second Epistle*, 249. Cf. Calvin, *Corinthians*, 2:365; Baur, *Paul*, 1:280; Robertson, *Sermons*, 418; Strachan, *Second Epistle*, 16; Beet, *Corinthians*, 439, 447.

57. See Pierre Bourdieu, "The Sentiment of Honour in Kabyle Society," in *Honour and Shame: The Values of Mediterranean Society* (ed. J. G. Peristiany; Chicago: University of Chicago Press, 1966), 211; Bruce J. Malina and Jerome H. Neyrey, "First-Century Personality: Dyadic, Not Individualistic," in *The Social World of Luke-Acts: Models for Interpretation* (ed. Jerome H. Neyrey; Peabody, Mass.: Hendrickson, 1991), 67–96; Zeba Crook, "Honor, Shame, and Social Status Revisited," *JBL* 128 (2009): 598–99.

Why, then, has Betz's invocation of *De laude ipsius* been so well received? Why does nearly every recent commentary on 2 Corinthians refer to Plutarch's precepts for *periautologia*—and do so without bothering to mention what actually interested Plutarch? The explanation, I suggest, is evident from the brief history of interpretation with which this chapter began: We simply have been unable to come to terms with a Paul who really does boast, a Paul who fights tooth and nail to defend his own status. Like the picture of Paul donning a fool's mask—an interpretive chimera we will consider in a subsequent chapter—the image of Paul manipulating rhetorical conventions allows us to posit for Paul a degree of self-consciousness that keeps him safely at arm's length from the shameless speaker the passage otherwise implies. Hence Duane Watson's odd but telling periphrastic usage: for Watson, Paul does not boast, Paul "uses boasting."[58] The implication, of course, is that the whole thing is merely a clever stratagem and that therefore we can keep our theologian, our intellectual, our rhetorician—in short, our respectable Paul.

---

58. Watson, "Paul and Boasting," 90.

5
Peristasis Catalogues:
Rhythm, Amplification, *Klangfiguren*

There is no evidence that ancient rhetorical education involved training in the composition of hardship catalogues per se. Nevertheless, Paul's lists of hardships are generally taken as evidence of his familiarity with contemporary rhetorical strategies, and, more specifically, with the propagandistic techniques employed by popular moral philosophers. Jerome Neyrey, for example, describes 2 Cor 11:23–28 as "a literary device known as a *peristasis* catalogue" that attests "indubitably" to Paul's knowledge of Stoic tradition.[1] An assessment of the extent of Paul's familiarity with contemporary popular philosophy is beyond the scope of this study; however, insofar as his so-called *peristasis* catalogues are associated with rhetorical amplification or *auxēsis* and attendant figures such as anaphora, asyndeton, and assonance, it is necessary to assess whether they provide evidence of formal education in rhetoric.

Lists and Catalogues in Greco-Roman Antiquity

One might infer from Neyrey's reference to "a literary device known as a *peristasis* catalogue" that we are dealing here with a literary form that was named and theorized by ancient literary critics—in other words, the sort of thing that would have been discussed in schools of rhetoric. This is not in fact the case.[2] On the contrary, the use of *Peristasenkatalog* as a *termi-*

---

[1]. Neyrey, "Social Location of Paul," 151–52.
[2]. John T. Fitzgerald asserts, correctly, that "the term *peristasis* was well-established in rhetorical circles by the first century" (*Cracks in an Earthen Vessel: An Examination of the Catalogues of Hardships in the Corinthian Correspondence* [SBLDS 99; Atlanta: Scholars Press, 1988], 37). Its rhetorical usage, however, had none of the

nus technicus in Pauline scholarship tends to obscure the fact that until the twentieth century there was no literary device known by such a name.

As noted above, Johannes Weiss was among the few scholars prior to Betz to suggest that Paul had received formal rhetorical training. For Weiss, the similarity of Paul's prose with the "Cynic-Stoic diatribe" was particularly compelling. As one example, he set Rom 8:38–39 alongside a similarly structured text from Epictetus:[3]

καὶ ἁπλῶς
  οὔτε θάνατος
  οὔτε φυγὴ
  οὔτε πόνος
  οὔτε ἄλλο τι τῶν τοιούτων
αἴτιόν ἐστι τοῦ πράττειν τι
ἢ μὴ πράττειν ἡμᾶς,
ἀλλ' ὑπολήψεις καὶ δόγματα
     (*Diatr.* 1.11.33)[4]
	πέπεισμαι γὰρ ὅτι
	  οὔτε θάνατος
	  οὔτε ζωὴ
	  οὔτε ἄγγελοι
	  οὔτε ἀρχαὶ
	  οὔτε ἐνεστῶτα
	  οὔτε μέλλοντα
	  οὔτε δυνάμεις
	  οὔτε ὕψωμα
	  οὔτε βάθος
	  οὔτε τις κτίσις ἑτέρα
	δυνήσεται ἡμᾶς χωρίσαι ἀπὸ τῆς ἀγάπης
	τοῦ θεοῦ τῆς ἐν Χριστῷ Ἰησοῦ τῷ
	κυρίῳ ἡμῶν
	     (Rom 8:38–39)

Weiss's comparison was taken up by his student Ruldolf Bultmann, who termed such texts *Peristasenkataloge*—lists of the vicissitudes of fate.[5]

Bultmann's term, it should be noted, is not merely descriptive, for it implies a particular interpretation of the meaning of Paul's lists of tribulations, which, for Bultmann, derives from Stoic indifference to one's

---

connotations of fortitude in adversity that Fitzgerald emphasizes, but referred quite simply to the circumstances of the case at hand, from which proofs may be derived. See, e.g., Ps.-Hermogenes, *Inv.* 3.5; Quintilian, *Inst.* 3.5.5–18.

3. Weiss, "Beiträge zur Paulinischen Rhetorik," 196. On earlier comparative treatments of Paul's hardship catalogues, see Fitzgerald, *Cracks in an Earthen Vessel*, 7–8 n. 2.

4. "And, in brief, it is neither death, nor exile, nor toil, nor any such thing that is the cause of our doing, or of our not doing, anything, but only our opinions and the decisions of our will" (Oldfather, LCL).

5. Bultmann, *Stil der paulinischen Predigt*, 19, 71.

external circumstances—one's περιστάσεις, as Epictetus and his ilk would say:[6] "Wie der griechische Weise, so zählt auch Paulus die Fügungen des Schicksals oder der Mächte, denen der Mensch unterworfen ist, auf und verkündet begeistert seine Überlegenheit über Freuden und Leiden, über Ängste und Schrecken."[7] As Bultmann's question-begging terminology has become standard, so has his interpretive framework.

This is particularly evident in John T. Fitzgerald's *Cracks in an Earthen Vessel*, which remains the most influential treatment of these texts to date. Armed with the conventionality of Bultmann's term, Fitzgerald is able to take a shortcut on the road from form to function: he begins with a study of philosophical use of the term περίστασις, which we are apparently to adjudge relevant simply because the texts he is discussing are, after all, "called" *peristasis* catalogues.[8] Hence Fitzgerald unaccountably treats Bultmann's interpretive conclusion—the notion that Paul's lists of hardships are illuminated by Stoic discussion of περίστασις—as the starting point for his discussion, not noticing, apparently, that the connection between Stoic περίστασις and so-called "*peristasis* catalogues" only seems self-evident because of the terminology he has inherited.[9]

Nevertheless, a connection did exist in certain philosophical circles between the idea that virtue must endure the unpredictable circumstances supplied by fate and illustrative lists of those same circumstances. Epictetus provides the clearest example:

> Who, then, is the invincible man? He whom nothing that is outside the sphere of his moral purpose can dismay. I then proceed to consider the

---

6. On the term, see Fitzgerald, *Cracks in an Earthen Vessel*, 33–46.

7. Bultmann, *Stil der paulinischen Predigt*, 71: "Like the Greek sage, so also Paul enumerates the twists of fate or the powers to which man is subject and announces enthusiastically his mastery over joys and sorrows, over worries and fears." It is interesting to observe how Bultmann himself, in the final words of this quotation, adopts the beguiling rhythm of the texts he is treating.

8. Says Fitzgerald, with no further ado, "The first step … is an examination of the key term '*peristasis*'" (*Cracks in an Earthen Vessel*, 31).

9. Note Fitzgerald's undefended assertion that "for the purposes of this investigation, the most important of the various types [of *peristasis* catalogue] is *the* [hardships *of the*] *wise man*"—an assertion by which he bypasses any discussion of "catalogues of occupational hardship," "catalogues of punishments," or "woes of the wanderer"—all of which would appear to be relevant to a discussion of 2 Cor 11 (*Cracks in an Earthen Vessel*, 47–49).

circumstances one by one (ἑκάστην τῶν περιστάσεων), as I would do in the case of the athlete.... If you put a bit of silver coin in a man's way, he will despise it. Yes, but if you put a bit of a wench in his way, what then? Or if it be dark, what then? Or if you throw a bit of reputation in his way, what then? Or abuse, what then? Or praise, what then? Or death, what then? All these things he can overcome. (*Diatr.* 1.18.21–22 [Oldfather, LCL])

This, I think all will agree, is justly described as a *peristasis* catalogue—whether or not anyone before Bultmann would have thought to call it that.

And, although Fitzgerald himself has little to say concerning form or style, he does draw our attention to Stoic catalogues that have striking formal similarities to Paul's lists of tribulations. Plutarch's description of Stoic self-understanding provides a fine example:[10]

ὁ δὲ τῶν Στωικῶν σοφὸς
  ἐγκλειόμενος
    οὐ κωλύεται
  καὶ κατακρημνιζόμενος
    οὐκ ἀναγκάζεται
  καὶ στρεβλούμενος
    οὐ βασανίζεται
  καὶ πηρούμενος
    οὐ βλάπτεται
  καὶ πίπτων ἐν τῷ παλαίειν
    ἀήττητός ἐστι
  καὶ περιτειχιζόμενος
    ἀπολιόρκητος
  καὶ πωλούμενος ὑπὸ τῶν
    πολεμίων
    ἀνάλωτος
    (*Stoic. abs.* 1057E)[11]

ἐν παντὶ
  θλιβόμενοι
  ἀλλ' οὐ στενοχωρούμενοι
  ἀπορούμενοι
  ἀλλ' οὐκ ἐξαπορούμενοι
  διωκόμενοι
  ἀλλ' οὐκ ἐγκαταλειπόμενοι
  καταβαλλόμενοι
  ἀλλ' οὐκ ἀπολλύμενοι
  (2 Cor 4:8–9)

---

10. Cited by Anton Fridrichsen, "Zum Thema 'Paulus und die Stoa': Ein stoische Stilparallele zu 2 Kor 4,8f.," *ConBNT* 9 (1944): 31; Fitzgerald, *Cracks in an Earthen Vessel*, 100.

11. "The sage of the Stoics is not impeded when confined and under no compulsion when flung down a precipice and not in torture when on the rack and not injured when mutilated and is invincible when thrown in wrestling and is not blockaded by

The most striking formal similarity here is the shared antithetical structure, which occurs also in 1 Cor 4:10–13a, 2 Cor 6:8–10, and Phil 4:12, as well as in Epictetus (e.g. *Diatr.* 2.19.24).[12] Also striking is the patterned use of conjunctions and verb forms to generate a compelling rhythm. Paul and Plutarch use different conjunctions—Plutarch prefaces each clause with καί but has no adversative within the clauses, whereas Paul connects his clauses asyndetically but uses ἀλλά within them—but each do what they do consistently. Likewise with verb forms: Paul uses the same participial form throughout, whereas Plutarch begins each clause with a concessive participle and concludes it with the indicative—at least until the fifth clause, when a new rhythm emerges.[13]

Such similarities are compelling, and would seem to necessitate the conclusion that Paul was dependent, both ideologically and stylistically, on the *peristasis* rhetoric of popular philosophy. However, when we begin to cast our net a little wider, we find these same stylistic features attested in a wide range of texts and put to a variety of different uses. But let us start where Weiss started: with Epictetus.

It is hardships (περιστάσεις), says Epictetus, that show what men are (*Diatr.* 1.24.1). And, given the influence of Bultmann's work, it is not surprising that the catalogues most often adduced in Pauline scholarship are those most in keeping with this dictum.[14] But what this selective mode of comparison obscures is the fact that Epictetus's *Peristasenkataloge* are but

---

circumvallation and in uncaptured while his enemies are selling him into slavery" (Cherniss, LCL).

12. This is not, however, characteristic of all Paul's hardship catalogues nor those of his contemporaries. In fact, the majority consist of simple lists: Rom 8:35b; 2 Cor 6:4b–5; 2 Cor 11:23b–29; 2 Cor 12:10; Epictetus, *Diatr.* 2.10.17; Seneca, *Const.* 6.3. See further Robert Hodgson, "Paul the Apostle and First Century Tribulation Lists," *ZNW* 74 (1983): 62–67.

13. Plutarch's fifth clause differs from the previous four both in the elaboration of the participial clause and the use of the privative alpha rather than the particle οὐ to provide negation. The privative alpha recurs in each of the final three clauses, and the participial clause is extended in the fifth and seventh, thus generating an a-b-a pattern.

14. Esp. *Diatr.* 1.1.22–24; 1.11.33; 1.18.21–23; 2.1.35; 2.16.42; 2.19.18, 24. Cf. Plato, *Resp.* 361E–362A; Horace, *Sat.* 2.7.83–87; Seneca, *Const.* 6.3; 8.3; *Ep.* 71.25–29; 82.10–14; Dio Chrysostom, *Virt.* (*Or.* 8) 15–16; Plutarch, *Stoic. abs.* 1057D–E. For a full list of texts cited by Pauline scholars, see Markus Schiefer Ferrari, *Die Sprache des Leids in den paulinischen Peristasenkatalogen* (SBB 23; Stuttgart: Katholisches Bibelwerk, 1991), 90–92.

one species of catalogue among many, notable perhaps for their distinctive content but indistinguishable on stylistic grounds from other sorts of rhythmic lists. One need not get very far into the *Discourses* to see what I mean:[15]

1.1.12
    τὴν δύναμιν ταύτην
        τὴν ὁρμητικὴν   τε καὶ ἀφορμητικὴν
        καὶ ὀρεκτικὴν   τε καὶ ἐκκλιτικὴν
        καὶ ἁπλῶς τὴν χρηστικὴν ταῖς φαντασίαις,
    ἧς ἐπιμελούμενος καὶ ἐν ᾗ τὰ σαυτοῦ τιθέμενος
        οὐδέποτε κωλυθήσῃ
        οὐδέποτ' ἐμποδισθήσῃ
    οὐ στενάξεις   οὐ μέμψῃ   οὐ κολακεύσεις οὐδένα[16]

1.1.14
    θέλομεν πολλῶν ἐπιμελεῖσθαι
        καὶ πολλοῖς προσδεδέσθαι
    καὶ τῷ σώματι   καὶ τῇ κτήσει
    καὶ ἀδελφῷ   καὶ φίλῳ
    καὶ τέκνῳ   καὶ δούλῳ[17]

1.2.36–37
    Ἐπίκτητος κρείσσων Σωκράτους οὐκ ἔσται·
        εἰ δὲ μή, οὐ χείρων, τοῦτό μοι ἱκανόν ἐστιν.
    οὐδὲ γὰρ Μίλων ἔσομαι   καὶ ὅμως οὐκ ἀμελῶ τοῦ σώματος·
    οὐδὲ Κροῖσος   καὶ ὅμως οὐκ ἀμελῶ τῆς κτήσεως[18]

---

15. Compare also Rom 8:38–39, cited above, with Plato, *Menex.* 245D: οὐ γὰρ Πέλοπες οὐδὲ Κάδμοι οὐδὲ Αἰγυπτοί τε καὶ Δαναοὶ οὐδὲ ἄλλοι πολλοὶ φύσει μὲν βάρβαροι ὄντες, νόμῳ δὲ Ἕλληνες, συνοικοῦσιν ἡμῖν.

16. "[T]his faculty of choice and refusal, of desire and aversion, or, in a word, the faculty which makes use of external impressions; if thou care for this and place all that thou hast therein, thou shalt never be thwarted, never hampered, shalt not groan, shalt not blame, shalt not flatter any man" (LCL).

17. "We choose … to care for many things, and to be tied fast to many, even to our body and our estate and brother and friend and child and slave" (LCL).

18. "Epictetus will not be better than Socrates; but if only I am not worse, that suffices me. For I shall not be a Milo, either, and yet I do not neglect my body; nor a Croesus, and yet I do not neglect my property" (LCL).

1.3.7
λύκοις ὅμοιοι γινόμεθα,
    ἄπιστοι   καὶ ἐπίβουλοι   καὶ βλαβεροί
οἱ δὲ λέουσιν,
    ἄγριοι   καὶ θηριώδεις   καὶ ἀνήμεροι[19]

1.6.14
διὰ τοῦτο ἐκείνοις μὲν ἀρκεῖ
    τὸ ἐσθίειν   καὶ πίνειν
    καὶ τὸ ἀναπαύεσθαι καὶ ὀχεύειν
καὶ τἄλλ' ὅσα ἐπιτελεῖ τῶν αὐτῶν ἕκαστον[20]

Clearly the stylistic features Pauline scholars have come to associate with Epictetus's so-called hardship catalogues—assonance, isocolon, homoioteleuton, antithesis, anaphora, patterned use of conjunctions, groups of two or three items—in fact characterize Epictetus's catalogue making style in general.[21] Isolating certain of these catalogues on the basis of their content for comparison with Paul's lists of tribulations gives the misleading impression of unique stylistic resemblance when in fact we are dealing with a much more general phenomenon.

And it is a general phenomenon indeed. As Fitzgerald himself has shown, lists and catalogues constitute a mode of expression ubiquitous in the literature of antiquity.[22] These catalogues share no set form or structure; there are, however, a number of recurrent stylistic features. Particularly characteristic are asyndeton, anaphora, chiasm, alliteration, assonance,

---

19. "[We] become like wolves, faithless and treacherous and hurtful, and others like lions, wild and savage and untamed" (LCL).

20. "And so for them it is sufficient to eat and drink and rest and procreate, and whatever else of the things within their own province the animals severally do" (LCL).

21. The same is true, we might note, with regard to Paul, who also uses catalogues for purposes other than enumerating hardships. E.g., 1 Cor 3:21–22:

πάντα γὰρ ὑμῶν ἐστιν
    εἴτε Παῦλος   εἴτε Ἀπολλῶς   εἴτε Κηφᾶς
    εἴτε κόσμος   εἴτε ζωὴ   εἴτε θάνατος
    εἴτε ἐνεστῶτα   εἴτε μέλλοντα

22. John T. Fitzgerald, "The Catalogue in Ancient Greek Literature," in *The Rhetorical Analysis of Scripture: Essays from the 1995 London Conference* (ed. Thomas H. Olbricht and Stanley E. Porter; JSNTSup 146; Sheffield: Sheffield Academic Press, 1997), 275–93. Cf. O. Regenbogen, "Πίναξ," PW 20:1407–82; Hansrudolf Trüb, *Kataloge in der griechischen Dichtung* (Oberwinterthur, 1952).

homoioteleuton, and the use of rhythm and rhyme[23]—in other words, precisely those stylistic features that Paul's tribulation lists share with so-called Stoic *peristasis* catalogues. A brief survey will illustrate the point.

John Austin's thorough treatment of catalogues in the *Iliad* provides a good overview of the "endless variations and complexities which this form presents" in Homer.[24] I have selected a characteristic example (*Il.* 10.227–232):

> ὣς ἔφαθ', οἳ δ' ἔθελον Διομήδεϊ πολλοὶ ἕπεσθαι.
> ἠθελέτην Αἴαντε δύω θεράποντες Ἄρηος,
> ἤθελε Μηριόνης, μάλα δ' ἤθελε Νέστορος υἱός,
> ἤθελε δ' Ἀτρεΐδης δουρικλειτὸς Μενέλαος,
> ἤθελε δ' ὁ τλήμων Ὀδυσεὺς καταδῦναι ὅμιλον
> Τρώων· αἰεὶ γάρ οἱ ἐνὶ φρεσὶ θυμὸς ἐτόλμα.[25]

The text is, of course, hexametric, so we see none of the staccato terseness of Paul's or Epictetus's catalogues. Still, typical catalogue features like anaphora (ἠθελέτην ... ἤθελε ... ἤθελε) and elaboration of the final item do appear.[26]

Free from the constraints of meter, catalogues in the Hebrew Bible more closely resemble the compressed style we find in Paul. Hosea 1:7 provides an interesting example:[27]

---

23. Fitzgerald, "The Catalogue in Ancient Greek Literature," 282–83 n. 22, 287 n. 45.

24. John N. H. Austin, "Catalogues and the Catalogue of Ships in the *Iliad*" (Ph.D. diss., University of California, Berkeley, 1965), 15. On Homer's catalogues, see also Benjamin Sammons, *The Art and Rhetoric of the Homeric Catalogue* (Oxford: Oxford University Press, 2010); Elizabeth Minchin, "The Performance of Lists and Catalogues in the Homeric Epics," in *Voice into Text: Orality and Literacy in Ancient Greece* (ed. Ian Worthington; Mnemosyne Supplement 157; Leiden: Brill, 1996), 3–20; Jan Felix Gaertner, "The Homeric Catalogues and Their Function in Epic Narrative," *Hermes* 129 (2001): 298–305; Mark W. Edwards, "The Structure of Homeric Catalogues," *TAPA* 110 (1980): 81–105.

25. "So spake he, and many there were that were fain to follow Diomedes. Fain were the two Aiantes, squires of Ares, fain was Meriones, and right fain the son of Nestor, fain was the son of Atreus, Menelaus, famed for his spear, and fain too was the steadfast Odysseus to steal into the throng of the Trojans, for ever daring was the spirit in his breast" (Murray, LCL).

26. See further Austin, "Catalogues and the Catalogue of Ships in the *Iliad*," 16–18.

27. Cited by Hodgson, "First Century Tribulation Lists," 70 n. 35. Cf. Amos 4:6–

I will not save them	ולא אושיעם
by bow or by sword or by war	בקשת ובחרב ובמלחמה
by horses or by horsemen	בסוסים ובפרשים

Here we have the repetitive use of the preposition that is characteristic of Paul. Notice that the catalogue is structured into two groups of items, within each of which the conjunction ו is used consistently. The beginning of the second grouping is signaled by asyndeton. This follows, not coincidentally, upon ובמלחמה, which, with its additional syllable relative to the previous two items, completes the rhythmic unit.

Interestingly, the LXX manifests its own instinct for structure by adding an additional item ("chariots"), thus creating two groups of three items, each of which rhymes the first with the final item:

οὐ σώσω αὐτοὺς
  ἐν τόξῳ   οὐδὲ εν ρομφαία   οὐδὲ ἐν πολέμῳ
  οὐδὲ ἐν ἅρμασιν   οὐδὲ ἐν ἵπποις   οὐδὲ ἐν ἱππεῦσιν

The items in the first group are singular, in the second group plural. As in the Hebrew, here too the consistent use of both the preposition and the conjunction is anaphoric. The repeated use of ἐν, incidentally, is reminiscent of Paul's usage in 2 Cor 6:4–7, 11:23, 27, and 12:10 (cf. Deut 28:48 LXX).

Somewhat more complex is the catalogue in the Chronicler's version of Solomon's prayer at the dedication of the temple (2 Chr 6:28–29):

If there is famine in the land,	רעב כי־יהיה בארץ
if there is pestilence,	דבר כי־יהיה
if blight or mildew,	שדפון וירקון
locust or caterpillar;	ארבה וחסיל
there is	כי יהיה
if his enemies besiege him	כי יצר־לו אויביו
at his gates in the land;	בארץ שעריו
every plague and every disease,	כל־נגע וכל־מחלה
every prayer, every supplication	כל־תפלה כל־תחנה
which there is from every man	אשר יהיה לכל־האדם
or from all your people Israel	ולכל עמך ישראל
which they know	אשר ידעו

10; Isa 8:22; 30:6; Jer 16:4; Ezek 14:21; 2 Chr 20:9. For a thoughtful treatment of catalogues in the Hebrew Bible, see Yair Hoffman, *A Blemished Perfection: The Book of Job in Context* (JSOTSup 213; Sheffield: Sheffield Academic Press, 1996), 84–114.

each one his plague and his pain   איש נגעו ומכאבו
he will stretch out his hands toward this house   ופרש כפיו אל־הבית הזה

The catalogue divides neatly into two parts. The first is bounded by an inclusio created by the repeated use of בארץ. Note the epistrophic repetition of כי יהיה throughout this first section, as well as the pairs of items joined by the conjunction ו, which stand out against the asyndeton that characterizes the remainder of the section. The second part features the anaphoric repetition of כל. Each of these features, which the exception of the inclusio in the first section, is preserved, *mutatis mutandis*, in the LXX.

Catalogues appear in later Jewish literature as well.[28] Indeed, according to Wolfgang Schrage, it is Jewish apocalyptic literature that provides a true analogue to Paul's hardship catalogues, being nearer than the Stoic material to Paul's eschatological perspective on suffering.[29] I will not pause here to consider the merits of this argument; instead, I hope simply to demonstrate the ubiquity in Second Temple Jewish texts of the stylistic features found also in Paul's catalogues.

In the *Testament of Joseph* we find this antithetically structured psalm (1.4–7):

οἱ ἀδελφοί μου οὗτοι ἐμίσησάν με
   καὶ ὁ Κύριος ἠγάπησέ με
αὐτοὶ ἤθελόν με ἀνελεῖν
   καὶ ὁ Θεὸς τῶν πατέρων μου ἐφύλαξέ με
εἰς λάκκον με ἐχάλασαν
   καὶ ὁ ὕψιστος ἀνήγαγέ με

---

28. See esp. Wolfgang Schrage, "Leid, Kreuz und Eschaton: Die Peristasenkataloge als Merkmale paulinischer *theologia crucis* und Eschatologie," in *Kreuzestheologie und Ethik im Neuen Testament: Gesammelte Studien* (FRLANT 205; Göttingen: Vandenhoeck & Ruprecht, 2004), 23–57; repr. from *EvT* 34 (1974); Michael E. Stone, "Lists of Revealed Things in the Apocalyptic Literature," in *Magnalia Dei, the Mighty Acts of God: Essays on the Bible and Archaeology in Memory of G. Ernest Wright* (ed. Frank Moore Cross, Werner E. Lemke, and Patrick D. Miller; Garden City, N.Y.: Doubleday, 1976), 414–52; Albert Wifstrand, "Stylistic Problems in the Epistles of James and Peter," in *Epochs and Styles: Selected Writings on the New Testament, Greek Language and Greek Culture in the Post-classical Era* (ed. Lars Rydbeck and Stanley E. Porter; trans. Denis Searby; WUNT 179; Tübingen: Mohr Siebeck, 2005), 54–55. In addition to texts cited below, see Sir 39:24–30; Wis 8:17–18; *1 En.* 60.11–13; *2 En.* 65.9; 66.6; *2 Bar.* 59.5–11; 73.4; *T. Jud.* 23; *T. Iss.* 6; *T. Dan* 2; *L.A.B.* 3.9; *Sib. Or.* 3.601–603; 4.67–69.

29. Schrage, "Leid, Kreuz und Eschaton," 25–26 and passim.

ἐπράθην εἰς δοῦλον
    καὶ ὁ Κύριος ἐλευθέρωσέ με
εἰς αἰχμαλωσίαν ἐλήφθην
    καὶ ἡ κραταιὰ αὐτοῦ χεὶρ ἐβοήθησέ μοι
ἐν λιμῷ συνεσχέσθην
    καὶ αὐτὸς ὁ Κύριος διέθρεψέ με

μόνος ἤμην
    καὶ ὁ Θεὸς παρεκάλεσέ με
ἐν ἀσθενείᾳ ἤμην
    καὶ ὁ ὕψιστος ἐπεσκέψατό με
ἐν φυλακῇ ἤμην
    καὶ ὁ σωτὴρ ἐχαρίτωσέ με

ἐν δεσμοῖς
    καὶ ἔλυσέ με
ἐν διαβολαῖς
    καὶ συνηγόρησέ μοι
ἐν λόγοις Αἰγυπτίων πικροῖς
    καὶ ἐρρύσατό με
ἐν φθόνοις συνδούλων
    καὶ ὕψωσέ με[30]

The antitheses are reminiscent of what we observed above in Plutarch, *Stoic. abs.* 1057E and 2 Cor 4:8–9. Four distinct patterns characterize each of the four sections, distinguished by changes in the verb form in the first line of each antithetical pair: in the first, the brothers' action is expressed in the third-person plural; in the second, Joseph's situation is

---

30. "These, my brothers, hated me but the Lord loved me. They wanted to kill me, but the God of my fathers preserved me. Into a cistern they lowered me; the Most High raised me up. They sold me into slavery; the Lord of all set me free. I was taken into captivity; the strength of his hand came to my aid. I was overtaken by hunger; the Lord himself fed me generously. I was alone, and God came to help me. I was in weakness, and the Lord showed his concern for me. I was in prison, and the Savior acted graciously in my behalf. I was in bonds, and he loosed me; falsely accused, and he testified in my behalf. Assaulted by bitter words of the Egyptians, and he rescued me. A slave, and he exalted me" (Kee, *OTP*). Cited by Schrage, "Leid, Kreuz und Eschaton," 27; Hodgson, "First Century Tribulation Lists," 68–69; Fitzgerald, *Cracks in an Earthen Vessel*, 198; Karl Theodor Kleinknecht, *Der leidende Gerechtfertigte: Die alttestamentlich-Jüdische Tradition vom "leidenden Gerechten" und ihre Rezeption bei Paulus* (WUNT 2/13; Tübingen: Mohr, 1984), 258.

described with a first-person verb in the passive voice; in the third section, the rhythm is compressed by the use of the simple copulative verb; and, in the even terser final section, the verb is unexpressed, and, in contrast to the variegated use of epithets in the first two sections, so is the divine subject. Epistrophe is created by the use of the first-person pronoun at the end of each clause (με throughout, except twice where Joseph is the indirect object), and anaphora in the second half of the catalogue by the repeated use of the preposition ἐν. As in 2 Cor 4:8–9—and in any number of other catalogues—the same conjunction is used within each clause, and the clauses themselves are asyndetic (cf. Hos 1:7; Wis 7:17–21).

The incorporation of a number of different rhythmic patterns that vary in complexity is a feature *T. Jos.* 1.4–7 shares with 2 Cor 11:21b–30 and 2 Cor 6:4b–10.[31] It appears also in *Jub.* 23.12–14, 17–19, presented here in the Latin version:

Et non est pax, propter quod
    uulnus super uulnus
    et dolor super dolorem
    et tribulatio super tribulationem
    et auditus malus super auditum malum
    et infirmitas super infirmitatem
    et uniuersa iudicia eius[modi]
        maligna secundum hoc ipsud cum
            corruptione et clades et niues et pruinae et glacies et febris et
                frigora
            et prouocatio et famis et mors et gladius et captiuitas
            et uniuersae plaga planctus.
                Et omnia haec superuenit superuenient [sic] super
                    generationem quae est iniqua quae iniquitatem
                    facit in terra
                et inmunditia et fornicationes et pollutiones abomina-
                tiones operum ipsorum. . . .
Propter quod
    uniuersi malignati sunt
    et omne os loquitur maligna
    et omnes operationes eorum inmunditia et odium
    et uniuersae uiae eorum pollution[es] et abominatio et exterminium.

---

31. Cf. Fitzgerald's discussion of 2 Cor 11:21b–30 in "Cracks in an Earthen Vessel: An Examination of the Catalogues of Hardships in the Corinthian Correspondence" (Ph.D. diss., Yale University, 1984), 374–86.

Et ecce
> terra [p]erit
>> propter omnia opera ipsorum
> et non est semen et uinum et oleum
>> propter quod uniuersa m[align]ata sunt opera ipsorum
> et uniuersi [pe]reunt bestiae et animalia et aues et omnes pisces maris
>> a malitia filiorum hominum.

Et litigabunt isti cum illis.
> Nam iubenes cum senioribus
>> et seniores cum iunioribus
> pauper cum diuite
>> infimus cum magno
>> et egenus cum eo qui potestatem exercet
>>> in lege pro testamentom
>>> quoniam obliti sunt
>>>> praeceptum et testamentum
>>>> et diem festum et mensem
>>>> et sabbatum et iubeleum
>>>> et omnia iudicia.[32]

I have replicated this text at length in order to demonstrate the difficulty of categorizing ancient catalogues. This is clearly not a hardship catalogue, although it does include lists of tribulations; and it is no vice catalogue, though it is does elaborate vices. As is true of the other catalogues we have

---

32. "And there is no peace, because (there will be) blow upon blow, wound upon wound, distress upon distress, bad news upon bad news, disease upon disease, and every (kind of) bad punishment like this, one with the other: disease and stomach pains; snow, hail, and frost; fever, cold, and numbness; famine, death, sword, captivity, and every (sort of) blow and difficulty. All this will happen to the evil generation which makes the earth commit sin through sexual impurity, contamination, and their detestable actions…. For all have acted wickedly; every mouth speaks what is sinful. Everything that they do is impure and something detestable; all their ways are (characterized) by contamination, and corruption. The earth will be destroyed because of all that they do. There will be no produce from the vine and no oil because what they do (constitutes) complete disobedience. All will be destroyed together—animals, cattle, birds, and all fish of the sea—because of mankind. One group will struggle with the other—the young with the old, the old with the young; the poor with the rich, the lowly with the great; and the needy with the ruler—regarding the law and the covenant. For they have forgotten commandment, covenant, festival, month, sabbath, jubilee, and every verdict" (trans. VanderKam). Cited by Schrage, "Leid, Kreuz und Eschaton," 25–26.

adduced, there is no form per se, but there certainly are discernable patterns. The more one sees of this sort of thing, the more one is convinced that the stylistic features this text shares with other ancient catalogues derive not from any specific literary tradition, but rather from a general rhetorical sensibility that governs human list-making. We will return to this point in part 3 below.

I will not comment in detail on the stylistic features of this catalogue, which by now should be familiar enough, except to draw attention to the preponderance of emphatic words like *omnis* and *universus*. We have seen this already in 2 Chr 6:28-29 (כל [cf. Jer 25:18-26]), and it is a feature of a number of Pauline catalogues too, wherein we encounter πᾶς, πολύς, πάντοτε, ἀεί, and the like.[33]

This survey could be extended indefinitely. As Robert Hodgson has shown, comparable catalogues are extant from Nag Hammadi (*Great Pow.* 39.21-33) and appear in both Josephus (*B.J.* 2.151-153; 4.165) and the Mishnah (*m. Pesaḥ.* 10:5; *m. Taʿan.* 3:5).[34] There are a number in Philo as well (*Det.* 34; *Somn.* 2.84; *Mos.* 2.16).[35] Anton Fridrichsen has found examples in various Greek novels (Chariton, *Chaer.* 3.8.9; 5.5.2; Achilles Tatius, *Leuc. Clit.* 5.18.4).[36] And I have not even begun to look into the catalogues in Sumerian, Akkadian, Ugaritic, and Egyptian documents, which, apparently, are legion.[37] The point is, the use of catalogues was ubiquitous in the ancient world, and, where we find catalogues, we find a flexible but consistent set of stylistic features. We certainly need not posit any one particular stylistic influence to account for Paul's tribulation lists, and we should avoid begging the question of their interpretation by perpetuating a faux *terminus technicus* like *Peristasenkatalog*.

---

33. Cf. Rom 8:37; 2 Cor 4:8, 10-11; 6:4, 10; Phil 4:12. See further Zmijewski, *Der Stil der paulinischen "Narrenrede,"* 320; Fitzgerald, "The Catalogue in Ancient Greek Literature," 285.

34. Hodgson, "First Century Tribulation Lists," 69-76.

35. Cf. Rudolf Schmitt, "Ist Philo, Vita Moysis (Mos) II 251 ein Peristasenkatalog?" *NovT* 29 (1987): 177-82.

36. Fridrichsen, "Sprachliches und Stilistisches," 288.

37. For bibliography, see Fitzgerald, *Cracks in an Earthen Vessel*, 276-77 n. 5.

Catalogues, *Auxēsis*, and Rhetorical Education

The composition of catalogues is not described as such in ancient rhetorical theory; however, as Fitzgerald has noted in a useful study of catalogues in ancient Greek literature, the rhetorical strategies involved fall under the rubric of *auxēsis* or *amplificatio*.[38] Quintilian describes five different methods of *amplificatio*, of which the final one is "accumulation of words and sentences identical in meaning" (8.4.26 [Butler, LCL]). Although this would appear to exclude catalogues (since items in a catalogue tend not to be strictly synonymous), Quintilian does note the affinity between such *amplificatio* and "the figure styled συναθροισμός by the Greeks," in which "it is a number of different things that are accumulated" (8.4.27).[39] For Quintilian, these figures appear to be functionally equivalent.

The potential of catalogues to fulfill the magnifying function of *auxēsis* is particularly clear in *On the Sublime*. Here "Longinus" cites the consensus position on the nature of *auxēsis*, which holds that amplification is "discourse which invests the subject with grandeur" (μέγεθος [*Subl.* 12.1; trans. Roberts]).[40] But he is not quite content with this definition, since it fails to describe what sets *auxēsis* apart from other figurative language, and so Longinus goes on to provide his own description, emphasizing that amplification consists essentially in multiplicity or abundance (ἐν πλήθει [12.1–2]; cf. 23.1–2; Apsines, *Rhet.* 5.5 [*RG* 1:366]). One means of its execution, then, consists in accumulation of what things are done or suffered (11.2; cf. 23:1–4),[41] the result of which would be difficult to distinguish from what we have been calling a catalogue.

Again, we have no evidence of instruction in how such amplificatory catalogues should be constructed, but, as we have already seen, there are a number of specific figures that do seem to have been associated with catalogues in practice if not explicitly in theory. Most frequently attested are

---

38. Fitzgerald, "The Catalogue in Ancient Greek Literature," 285–93.

39. The clearest description of συναθροισμός is that of Alexander Numenius (mid-2nd century C.E.), who provides as an example Demosthenes, *Cor.* 71, wherein Demosthenes catalogues the offenses of Philip against the Hellenes (1.9 [*RG* 3:17]).

40. Cf. Aristotle, *Rhet.* 1.9.40; Anonymous Seguerianus 4.230 (*RG* 1:457).

41. Roberts translates ἔργων ἢ παθῶν as "of facts or passions," but here I think Longinus refers to the commonplace contrast between the person as subject or object of what occurs. Cf. Plato, *Phaedr.* 245C; Aristotle, *Rhet.* 1.9.15; Philo, *Leg.* 3.88; Plutarch, *Rom.* 12.5.

anaphora and epistrophe, asyndeton and patterned use of conjunctions, and assonance or rhyming. Each of these figures was discussed by ancient rhetorical theorists; moreover, as has been observed at least since the work of Johannes Weiss, Paul's list of hardships in 2 Cor 11 contains them all. So, did he learn such rhetoric at school?

One way to address this question would be to inquire concerning the education of those authors in whose works we have already found analogues to Paul's catalogues. Here we have mixed results: Plutarch considered himself a philosopher, not an orator, and was critical of "sophistic pedantry" (σοφιστικὴ μικροφροσύνη [*Glor. Ath.* 251A]), yet he clearly benefited from a thorough rhetorical education.[42] Josephus had some trouble with Greek diction, apparently, but both he and Philo were educated as befit aristocrats.[43] And, of course, Dio Chrysostom was a famously eloquent orator. So, some of these catalogues were composed by men educated in classical rhetoric.

But others were not. Hosea, for example, clearly benefited from familiarity with the indigenous rhetorical tradition of Hebrew prophecy, but of course had no training in Greek or Roman rhetoric. And the authors of

---

42. Russell, *Plutarch*, 18–41; F. Frazier, "Les visages de las rhétorique contemporaine sous le regard de Plutarque," in *Rhetorical Theory and Praxis in Plutarch* (ed. L. Van der Stockt; Collection d'études classiques 11; Leuven: Peeters, 2000), 183–202.

43. Josephus, *A.J.* 20.236; *C. Ap.* 1.50; *Vita* 1–11. The extent to which Josephus received a specifically rhetorical education is disputed. Cf. Robert G. Hall, "Josephus' Contra Apionem and Historical Inquiry in the Roman Rhetorical Schools," in *Josephus' Contra Apionem: Studies in its Character and Context* (ed. L. H. Feldman and J. R. Levison; AGJU 34; Leiden: Brill, 1996), 229–49; John M. G. Barclay, "Josephus v. Apion: Analysis of an Argument," in *Understanding Josephus: Seven Perspectives* (ed. Steve Mason; Sheffield: Sheffield Academic Press, 1998), 194–221. That Philo was rhetorically educated most seem to agree: Thomas Conley, "Philo's Rhetoric: Argumentation and Style" *ANRW* 22.1:243–71; Manuel Alexandre, *Rhetorical Argumentation in Philo of Alexandria* (BJS 322; Atlanta: Scholars Press, 1999); Burton L. Mack, "Decoding the Scripture: Philo and the Rules of Rhetoric," in *Nourished with Peace: Studies in Hellenistic Judaism in Memory of Samuel Sandmel* (ed. Frederick E. Greenspahn, Earle Hilgert, and Burton L. Mack; Scholars Press Homage Series 9; Chico, Calif.: Scholars Press, 1984), 81–116; J. Leopold, "Philo's Knowledge of Rhetorical Theory," in *Two Treatises of Philo of Alexandria: A Commentary on* De gigantibus *and* Quod Deus sit immutabilis (ed. David Winston and John Dillon; BJS 25; Chico, Calif.: Scholars Press, 1983), 129–36.

Jubilees and the *Testament of Joseph* can at most have had superficial exposure to Greek rhetorical principles.[44]

Epictetus's is an interesting case. Born a slave, he would certainly not have been expected to learn to speak like an aristocrat.[45] As a young man, however, he was permitted to attend philosophical lectures by Musonius Rufus, and eventually became a philosopher in his own right. Still, although literate and clearly well read in philosophy, Epictetus apparently received no formal rhetorical education.[46] What he knew of style would have been learned from his observation of Rufus's practice and from his own experience in persuasion. So, although he was certainly convincing in his own way, those with a taste for refined style seem not to have been impressed (*Diatr.* 3.9.12–14; cf. Origen, *Cels.* 6.2).

Finally, it goes without saying that the catalogues in Homer and Hesiod cannot have resulted from formal rhetorical education. Indeed, recent scholarship has placed these lists on the very threshold of oral and written "literature," associating such stylistic features as rhythm, alliteration, and assonance not only with aesthetic intent but also with mnemonic function.[47]

Clearly, then, the presence of catalogues in Paul's letters is not in itself evidence that he was exposed to techniques of *auxēsis* at rhetorical school. Catalogues and their attendant stylistic features occur too frequently in literature that was not informed by the formal tradition of classical rhetoric for their appearance straightforwardly to be attributed to its influence. Moreover, as we have seen, instruction in the composition of catalogues is not attested in rhetorical sources; at best it can be inferred from Longinus's isolated description of *auxēsis*. This is a perilous foundation upon which to assert that stylistic features associated with catalogues provide evidence of formal rhetorical education.

---

44. See Helmut Koester, *History, Culture, and Religion of the Hellenistic Age* (vol. 1 of *Introduction to the New Testament*; 2nd ed.; Berlin: de Gruyter, 1995), 108–9; Wifstrand, "Stylistic Problems," 54–55.

45. The distinction between the diction of slaves and their masters is put to good use in ancient comedy, wherein it serves a characterizing function. See Evangelos Karakasis, *Terence and the Language of Roman Comedy* (Cambridge Classical Studies; Cambridge: Cambridge University Press, 2005), 1–16, 21–143.

46. According to A. A. Long, although Epictetus was a "virtuoso user of colloquial Greek … he probably did not have the elaborate training in schoolbook rhetoric that was the staple of Roman education" (*Epictetus*, 13).

47. See esp. Minchin, "The Performance of Lists."

Conclusion

As noted in chapter 1, both C. F. G. Heinrici and Johannes Weiss described a wealth of aurally pleasing stylistic features—Heinrici called them *Klangfiguren*—in Paul's list of tribulations in 2 Cor 11.[48] Weiss attributed them to rhetorical education; Heinrici disagreed. And, in many respects, the discussion has remained precisely at the impasse where they left it. Indeed, although the consensus among scholars has shifted in Weiss's favor, this is not because new evidence has been adduced or even because new arguments have been articulated. No, it is the scholarly audience that has changed, not the arguments, which remain, in their essence, undefended assertions regarding whether or not the ability to write with a compelling sense of rhythm presupposes formal rhetorical education.[49] The examples adduced above demonstrate that rhetorical education is neither a necessary nor an adequate explanation for the widespread appearance of catalogues and their attendant stylistic features in the literature of antiquity. Indeed, as we will see in part 3 below, it is difficult to account for the ubiquity of "catalogue style" without positing an origin in the "general rhetoric" of human persuasion.

---

48. Heinrici, *Der zweite Brief an die Korinther*, 313–14; Weiss, "Beiträge zur Paulinischen Rhetorik," 185–88.

49. Compare, e.g., Weiss, "Beiträge zur Paulinischen Rhetorik," 187; Murphy-O'Connor, *Paul: A Critical Life*, 319–21.

6
NOT A FOOL, A FOOL'S MASK:
NARRENREDE AND *PROSŌPOPOIIA*

HANS WINDISCH AND PAUL'S SO-CALLED *NARRENREDE*

Hans Windisch's 1924 commentary on 2 Corinthians spawned, or at least anticipated, a number of key features of the approach to 2 Cor 10–13 that predominates in current scholarship. Among the most influential of his proposals was his designation of the heart of the passage (11:21–12:11) as a *Narrenrede* or "Fool's Speech."[1] On this reading, the peculiarities of the passage result from Paul's deliberate adoption of the role of the foolish braggart (ὁ ἀλαζών), a role presumably familiar to his audience from the mimic theater. In other words, Paul was self-consciously and ironically playacting: "Der 'Narr' [ist] für P[aulus] nur eine 'Rolle'"; indeed, it is "eine seinem Wesen fremde 'Rolle.'"[2]

Response to Windisch's proposal has been somewhat paradoxical. Few have pursued his specific argument—that is, the notion that the role Paul plays comes from the mime. The most prominent exception, a 1999 article by Larry Welborn, shows why: Welborn certainly is able to demonstrate the ubiquity of the mime in contemporary popular culture,[3] but he gets no further than Windisch did in explaining how Paul's hearers would have been able to recognize mimic stock characters—and Welborn identifies

---

1. Windisch, *Der zweite Korintherbrief*, 316.
2. Ibid., 344, 316: "The 'fool' is only a 'role' for Paul … a 'role' alien to his character."
3. L. L. Welborn, "The Runaway Paul," *HTR* 92 (1999): 122–37. Ulrich Heckel argues that it is improbable that Paul could have known "das griechische Theater in der abstoßend obszönen Form des Mimus" but provides no convincing evidence (*Kraft in Schwachheit: Untersuchungen zu 2. Kor 10–13* [WUNT 2/56; Tübingen: Mohr Siebeck, 1993], 194; likewise Thrall, *Second Epistle*, 2:712).

five of them!—in Paul's letter. According to Welborn, Paul's self-referential statements throughout the section—"I speak like a fool," and so forth— "are the linguistic counterpart of the dress and manners by which the fool was identified when he appeared on the mimic stage,"[4] but this assertion only highlights the gulf between the representational mode of the theater and the written discourse of the letter.[5] To make a leap between two such different contexts, Paul's hearers would have needed unambiguous cues indeed. Welborn argues that in the prologue introducing the "Fool's Speech" proper (2 Cor 11:1–21a) "Paul takes pains to identify the role that he is playing as that of the fool."[6] That's true in a way, I suppose, but Paul's concession that he is speaking foolishly (ἐν ἀφροσύνῃ [11:17, 21]) is hardly clear evidence that he had the mime in mind.[7] There may have been a lot of folly in mimic comedy, but presumably Paul's readers had seen some nonfictional fools too.[8]

In any case, if scholars have not been convinced of the particulars of Windisch's argument, nevertheless they have enthusiastically latched on to his characterization of the passage as a "Fool's Speech." Almost every recent discussion of the passage calls it Paul's *Narrenrede* or "Fool's Speech" or "foolish discourse," typically with no explanation of what is meant by

---

4. Welborn, "The Runaway Paul," 138. It does not help Welborn's case that one of these self-referential interjections—παραφρονῶν λαλῶ (11:23)—does not, according to Welborn's scheme, accompany a change in roles, and that the change from "braggart warrior" to "anxious old man" is accompanied by no such interjection. See Lee A. Johnson, "The Epistolary Apostle: Paul's Response to the Challenge of the Corinthian Congregation" (Ph.D. diss., University of St. Michael's College, 2002), 207.

5. See Johnson, "The Epistolary Apostle," 206–8.

6. Welborn, "The Runaway Paul," 137.

7. If Paul were taking on a mimic role here, it is difficult to understand why he would refer ambiguously to boasting ἐν ἀφροσύνῃ (11:17, 21b; cf. 11:1) rather than consistently and straightforwardly naming the role (ὁ ἄφρων [11:16; cf. 11:19]—or, better, ὁ ἀλαζών) he purportedly is playing.

8. Windisch's proposal was modified by Hans Dieter Betz, who argued that the *Narrenrede* was a literary form Paul encountered by way of popular philosophy (*Der Apostel Paulus und die sokratische Tradition*, 79–89). Betz seeks literary precedents in Alcibiades's speech in Plato's *Symposium* (212C–222B) and Seneca's *Apocolocyntosis*— texts that are themselves so different that is difficult to see how they can be adduced as examples of a "literarische Form." Still, Betz has been followed by Strecker, "Die Legitimität des paulinischen Apostolates," 269–70; Stefan Schreiber, *Paulus als Wundertäter: Redaktionsgeschichtliche Untersuchungen zur Apostelgeschichte und den authentischen Paulusbriefen* (BZNW 79; Berlin: de Gruyter, 1996), 215–16.

the designation.[9] And although we are provided with little in the way of detailed treatment of ancient parallels, general assertions that Paul "acts out the fool's role" or is wearing "an assumed disguise" are common.[10]

Given the longstanding tendency of interpreters to seek justification for Paul's foolish boasting, this selective use of Windisch's interpretive proposal should perhaps arouse some suspicion. And, indeed, the use of *Narrenrede* as a quasi-technical term appears to play a consistent function in the rhetoric of Pauline scholarship: it legitimizes an interpretive whim—namely, the assertion that Paul's boasting is not really boasting—by vaguely suggesting some sort of literary precedent where in fact there is no relevant literature to adduce. Murray Harris's recent commentary is typical. With no explanation of what a "Fool's Speech" might be, and no discussion of ancient parallels, he nevertheless uses the designation to sponsor his assertion that Paul himself—that is, his essential nature—is not implicated in his boasting: "Although Paul has censured his rivals for indulging in pointless comparison with one another and in unbridled boasting, he now proceeds to engage in comparisons and boasting himself, *but only in the disguise of a fool*, as he begins the 'Fool's Speech.'"[11]

Thus what we accomplish, it seems, by invoking the dubious form of the "Fool's Speech" is to mute the immediacy of Paul's voice and thereby to

---

9. So Furnish, *II Corinthians*, 498; Martin, *2 Corinthians*, 357; Calvin J. Roetzel, *2 Corinthians* (ANTC; Nashville: Abingdon Press, 2007), 103–14; Holland, "Speaking Like a Fool"; Sundermann, *Der schwache Apostel*, 15 n. 25; Travis, "Paul's Boasting," 529; Watson, "Paul and Boasting," 85; Harris, *Second Corinthians*, 789; David E. Garland, *2 Corinthians* (NAC 29; Nashville: Broadman & Holman, 1999), 487; McCant, *2 Corinthians*, 114–57; Paul Barnett, *The Second Epistle to the Corinthians* (NICNT; Grand Rapids: Eerdmans, 1997), 494–96; Zmijewski, *Der Stil der paulinischen "Narrenrede"*; Vegge, *A Letter about Reconciliation*, 363–65; Fitzgerald, *Cracks in an Earthen Vessel*, 152; M. David Litwa, "Paul's Mosaic Ascent: An Interpretation of 2 Corinthians 12:7–9," *NTS* 57 (2011): 254. Jan Lambrecht calls this a "Fool's Speech," but explicitly denies any connection to the mime ("Paul's Foolish Discourse: A Reply to A Pitta," *ETL* 83 [2007]: 411 n. 28).

10. Here Martin, *2 Corinthians*, 361; McCant, *2 Corinthians*, 127. See also Rudolf Bultmann, *The Second Letter to the Corinthians* (ed. Erich Dinkler; trans. Roy A. Harrisville; Minneapolis: Augsburg, 1985), 210; Mitchell, "Patristic Perspective," 366 n. 63; Harris, *Second Corinthians*, 789; Holland, "Speaking Like a Fool"; Sundermann, *Der schwache Apostel*, 31–39; Garland, *2 Corinthians*, 487.

11. Harris, *Second Corinthians*, 789 (references omitted; my emphasis). Similarly Donald Dale Walker, *Paul's Offer of Leniency (2 Cor 10:1): Populist Ideology and Rhetoric in a Pauline Letter Fragment* (WUNT 2/152; Tübingen: Mohr Siebeck, 2002), 309.

attenuate his unbecoming demeanor. If Paul's willingness to make a fool of himself is not desperate self-promotion but clever rhetorical calculation, then the real Paul, the man behind the fool's mask, can retain his respectability. He remains the sort of man whom we admire, committed to his cause but self-controlled, dispassionately selecting a daring but effective rhetorical strategy.

NARRENREDE, PROSŌPOPOIIA, AND RHETORICAL EDUCATION

No one, to my knowledge, has suggested that ancient rhetorical education involved training in how to write a *Narrenrede* as such, but Windisch's interpretive paradigm has sponsored arguments that the manner of Paul's "Fool's Speech" attests to his knowledge of rhetorical conventions. Specifically, it is claimed that this is an instance of speech-in-character,[12] something Paul must have learned during his rhetorical training.[13]

The figure in question, variously called προσωποποιία and ἠθοποιία by ancient rhetorical theorists,[14] was indeed on the ancient rhetorical curriculum. According to Theon's *Progymnasmata*, προσωποποιία is "the introduction of a person to whom words are attributed that are suitable to the speaker and have an indisputable application to the subject discussed" (8 [*RG* 2:115; trans. Kennedy]). The key element here, it appears, is suitability; for, as Theon goes on to emphasize, in order to be effective one must consider well what manner of speech befits the specific speaker one has in mind. Indeed, as Quintilian insists, when speaking in the voices of others "we shall only carry conviction if we represent them as uttering what they may reasonably be supposed to have had in their minds" (*Inst.* 9.2.30 [Butler, LCL]; cf. Theon, *Progymn.* 1 [RG 2:60]). Without such realism, the figure will fall flat.

---

12. So David E. Aune, "Boasting," in *The Westminster Dictionary of New Testament and Early Christian Literature and Rhetoric* (Louisville, Ky.: Westminster John Knox, 2003), 83; Keener, *1–2 Corinthians*, 231; Walker, *Paul's Offer of Leniency*, 309–12; cf. Mitchell, "Patristic Perspective," 366 n. 63.

13. Cf. Hock, "Greco-Roman Education," 209–12; Vegge, *Paulus und das antike Schulwesen*, 406.

14. Quintilian, *Inst.* 9.2.29–37; *Rhet. Her.* 4.52.65; Theon, *Progymn.* 8 (*RG* 2:115–118); Ps.-Hermogenes, *Progymn.* 9 (Rabe 20–22); Aphthonius, *Progymn.* 11 (*RG* 2:44–46); Nicolaus, *Progymn.* 10 (Felten 63–67). The latter three designate the figure ἠθοποιία.

I do not intend here to enter the dispute regarding other putative instances of *prosōpopoiia* in Paul's letters. Whatever one concludes regarding Paul's use of the figure in Romans,[15] it is beyond dispute that Paul, in various ways, incorporates the voices of opponents real and fictive into his discourse. He even does so in 2 Cor 10–13 (cf. 10:1b, 10; 12:16). Although these may not be examples of *prosōpopoiia* per se, clearly they manifest a similar sensitivity to verisimilitude in inhabiting another voice. I do not think this constitutes evidence of formal rhetorical education, and will explain why in part 3 below. For the present, though, I wish to challenge the notion that Paul's "Fool's Speech" is an instance of speech-in-character by highlighting two key difficulties with this approach. First, it has proven impossible to delineate the extent of Paul's use of the figure: The speech he disowns as "foolish" is not separable from his own voice, nor is it clear where his foolish discourse begins or ends. Second, Paul does not speak consistently of being "a fool" (ἄφρων [11:16]) but in fact introduces the theme by asking indulgence to engage in "a little foolishness" (μικρόν τι ἀφροσύνης [11:1])—a usage that suggests not role-playing but self-consciousness. Allow me to elaborate.

As noted above, recent commentators have been unable to agree where Paul's so-called "Fool's Speech" begins and ends[16]—a lack of agreement that highlights, I think, a fatal problem with the current interpretive paradigm: there is no clear demarcation of Paul's "foolishness" from the remainder of the letter, thus no clear distinction between Paul's own voice and the role he is purported to adopt. If, for example, we assume for the sake of argument that Paul takes on the role of a fool at 11:21a, as is most

---

15. Most influential has been the proposal of Stanley K. Stowers, "Romans 7.7–25 as a Speech-in-Character (προσωποποιία)," in *Paul in His Hellenistic Context* (ed. Troels Engberg-Pedersen; SNTW; London: T&T Clark, 1994), 180–202. Ronald Hock is not fully convinced, noting that if this is an instance of *prosōpopoiia*, the form is "rather irregular" ("Paul and Greco-Roman Education," 212). Dean Anderson, insisting that *prosōpopoiia* must be marked by textual cues, rejects Stowers's suggestion altogether (*Ancient Rhetorical Theory*, 321 n. 89).

16. Proposals for its beginning include 11:16 (Roetzel, *2 Corinthians*, 103–12), 11:21b (Windisch, *Der zweite Korintherbrief*, 315–98; Furnish, *II Corinthians*, 498; Harris, *Second Corinthians*, 729), and 11:22 (Keener, *1–2 Corinthians*, 232), with 11:1f. sometimes considered an introduction of sorts. Various readers propose that it ends with 12:10 (Holland, "Speaking Like a Fool," 251; Zmijewski, *Der Stil der paulinischen "Narrenrede"*), 12:13 (Furnish, *II Corinthians*, 484), or 12:18 (Sundermann, *Der schwache Apostel*, 45).

commonly suggested, his voice thereafter should be clearly distinguishable from what precedes. This is not the case. Paul asks permission to be foolish already in 11:1, and undertakes a comparison of himself with his opponents, which includes an explicit boast (καύχησις [v. 10]), throughout 11:4-15. This material is really of a piece with Paul's "foolishness" later in the chapter.

Well, then, perhaps those readers are correct who believe Paul is already wearing the mask of the fool in 11:1-15. If he is, though, it is difficult to know how one should interpret his solemn assertion in v. 11 ("Why? Because I do not love you? God knows I do!"), not to mention his characterization of his opponents in vv. 13-15. Few would be willing to accept that all this should be consigned to the mouth of a fool.

Indeed, a reading of the "Fool's Speech" in context makes clear that Paul's persona does not in fact change at 11:1, 11:16, or even 11:21a. Specifically, the boastfulness and the comparison with his rivals that generally are associated with his fool's role are entirely in accord with what Paul says throughout in the letter *in propria persona*. Note, particularly, 10:7-8:

> If someone (τις) is confident that he is of Christ (Χριστοῦ), let such a one consider again this, that just as he is of Christ, so also are we. For even if I boast (καυχήσωμαι) a little excessively about our authority ... I will not be ashamed. (my trans.)

Certainly there is less elaboration here than in Paul's subsequent boasting, but this is no different in kind from 11:22-23. In fact, Paul boasts about his authority and his status before, during, and after the so-called "Fool's Speech" (cf. 11:6-12; 12:11b-12), a fact that makes it impossible to distinguish the voice of the fool from Paul's own voice. If this is *prosōpopoiia*, it is not very convincing, for it lacks the clear differentiation of personae stressed by the rhetoricians.

Moreover, if Paul says things *in propria persona* that sound suspiciously like the fool, the converse is also true: the fool says things that sound suspiciously like Paul. According to Glenn Holland, once Paul puts on his fool's mask "he pretends to share his opponents' own foolish behavior as well as their faulty human judgments of things."[17] But is this an apt characterization of Paul's assertion, "If I must boast, I will boast of the things that show

---

17. Glenn S. Holland, *Divine Irony* (Selinsgrove, Pa.: Susquehanna University Press, 2000), 142.

my weakness" (11:30)? Again, according to Holland, "Everything [Paul] says as a fool may be expected to be ... worldly, self-congratulatory, and boastful."[18] But is this really a suitable description of what Paul says in 12:6: "If I wish to boast, I will not be a fool, for I will be speaking the truth. But I refrain from it, so that no one may think better of me than what is seen in me or heard from me"?[19] Indeed, what might a statement like this mean coming from the persona of a fictive boastful fool? Even if we were willing to consider this some sort of role-playing *mise en abyme*, in which Paul the reluctant boaster plays a fool playing a reluctant boaster,[20] we are left with a considerable problem: Paul's putative attempt at credible speech-in-character has been compromised by discourse that is not at all suitable to the character in whose mouth it is supposed to appear.

So, given the difficulty of sustaining a prosopopoetic reading of Paul's boasting, I suggest a simpler explanation: The integration of the so-called "Fool's Speech" with the rest of the passage suggests not that Paul is inhabiting another's voice but rather that he is making a self-referential comment about his own voice. Paul is worried about being considered a fool, and preempts the accusation by accepting it in qualified form.

Not only is this the simplest way to account for the text as it stands, it also gains support from Paul's analogous procedure in the previous chapter. Note the disclaimer in 10:8: "Even if I boast a little too much of our own authority ... I will not be ashamed." Clearly, Paul is aware that his self-referential speech leaves him susceptible to characterization as shameless. He is self-conscious about his boasting, but he insists he will do it anyway. Likewise, in 11:16 Paul clearly anticipates the potential accusation of his addressees ("Let no one think that I am a fool"). Again he is aware that he

---

18. Ibid.

19. Margaret Mitchell resorts to the suggestion that Paul here "pauses between his own voice and that of his 'fool' persona" (*Birth of Christian Hermeneutics*, 89).

20. Here we approach the over-subtle interpretation of Windisch, *Der zweite Korintherbrief*, 316, who is followed by Welborn, "The Runaway Paul," 159–61. See also Glenn Holland's strained attempt to read consistent irony throughout this section. According to Holland, "The claim [in 12:6a] that all his boasts are 'no brag, just fact' is of course typical of a boaster and a fool. Far from being a sober assessment of his apostolic credentials, 12.6a represents the very heights of Paul's 'foolishness'" ("Speaking Like a Fool," 262). But this reading quickly runs aground, for Paul has said essentially the same thing ("we will not boast beyond limits") in 10:13 and 10:15, long before having supposedly put on the mask of the boastful fool. Again, Paul and the fool sound suspiciously alike.

is liable to belittling characterization, and again Paul insists that he will not be cowed: "But if you do, then accept me as a fool, so that I too may boast a little."

Finally, the diverse ways in which Paul refers to his foolishness in 11:1–12:11 are much easier to interpret as self-consciousness than as announcements of a prosopopoetic role. Paul introduces the theme of foolishness not as a description of himself as speaker, but rather as characteristic of his speech itself: ὄφελον ἀνείχεσθέ μου μικρόν τι ἀφροσύνης (11:1). Throughout the passage, his usage alternates between the abstract and the concrete noun (although readers of the NRSV or NIV may be led astray here, as both translations standardize Paul's usage, rendering ἐν ἀφροσύνῃ in 11:17 and 11:21 with the concrete noun: "as a fool"):

11:1—μικρόν τι ἀφροσύνης
11:16—ἄφρονα (twice)
11:17—ἐν ἀφροσύνῃ
11:19—ἀφρόνων
11:21—ἐν ἀφροσύνῃ
11:23—παραφρονῶν λαλῶ
12:6—ἄφρων
12:11—ἄφρων

There simply is no reason to assume that "the fool" is the governing image here. Paul is engaged instead with the general notion of foolishness and, accordingly, uses the word group in various ways. He is disclaiming *his own speech* as foolish. This is not *prosōpopoiia*.

Conclusion

It is time, I suggest, to lay the notion of Paul's *Narrenrede* or "Fool's Speech" to rest. The term signifies nothing—nothing, that is, except an elusive and misleading interpretive tradition, a tradition that began with an unwarranted assertion and continues as an unexamined assumption, and a tradition, I submit, that precludes any understanding of this text. There is no evidence for anything like a literary, let alone epistolary *Narrenrede* in the ancient world, and the suggestion that Paul is playing a role from the mime cannot be sustained from the text. Further, the notion that Paul is engaged in *prosōpopoiia* fails to take account of what he actually says while purportedly speaking in the voice of the fool.

7
Synkrisis in Corinth

The rhetorical features addressed in each of the previous three chapters have been seen, on closer examination, to have a very dubious relationship with the sort of ancient rhetorical theory Paul is alleged to have encountered in school. In fact, we have seen that three *termini technici* held dear by exegetes of 2 Cor 10–13 are, to varying degrees, the invention of modern scholarship: neither *periautologia*, nor the *peristasis* catalogue, nor the *Narrenrede* was discussed by rhetorical theorists prior to the time of Paul; only *periautologia* was discussed by ancient rhetorical theorists at all. Moreover, when we turn to ancient rhetorical practice, it becomes clear that the referents of these terms have little to do with rhetoric: If the term *Narrenrede* could accurately be said to name anything in the ancient world, it is certainly not a rhetorical strategy. So-called *peristasis* catalogues have no distinguishing stylistic features, but instead encode ideal moral values concerning masculinity and freedom. Ancient examples of self-praise and its avoidance evince concern not with rhetoric per se but rather with the mitigation of envy and rivalry.

Assertions of Paul's familiarity with rhetorical conventions for *synkrisis*, however, are an entirely different matter. Already Aristotle had suggested that one should compare (συγκρίνειν) the subject of one's encomium with another estimable person as a form of *auxēsis* (*Rhet.* 1.9.38; cf. *Rhet. Alex.* 3.7–8), and the *Progymnasmata* provide detailed instruction on how this should be done, under the unambiguous heading Περὶ συγκρίσεως.[1] Here, at last, we are clearly in the realm of rhetorical education.

---

1. Theon, *Progymn.* 10 (*RG* 2:112–115); Ps.-Hermogenes, *Progymn.* 8 (Rabe 18–20); Aphthonius, *Progym.* 10 (*RG* 2:42–44); Nicolaus, *Progymn.* 9 (Felten 59–63); Libanius, *Progymn.* 10.

The notion that Paul's boasting constitutes a rhetorical *synkrisis* was proposed by Christopher Forbes and Peter Marshall, two students of E. A. Judge, as an elaboration of Judge's approach to 2 Cor 10–13.[2] Judge had argued that Paul found himself, in Corinth, "a reluctant and unwanted competitor in the field of professional 'sophistry.'"[3] Among the Corinthian sophists, Judge claimed, boasting was "absolutely *de rigeur*," and so Paul, if he was to have any influence, had no choice but to compete.

It is in this social context that Forbes and Marshall too place 2 Cor 10–13. According to Forbes, "the key to the whole 'boasting' passage" comes in 10:12–13, which text he cites as follows:

> Not that we dare to classify (ἐγκρῖναι) or compare (συγκρῖναι) ourselves with some of those who commend themselves. When they measure themselves by themselves, and compare themselves with themselves, they are without understanding. We, however will not boast beyond proper limits ...[4]

Forbes deduces from Paul's statement here that Paul's rivals have been boasting, and, further, that their boasting has included both "mutual comparison (σύγκρισις)" and comparison of themselves with Paul.[5] So, since self-commendatory σύγκρισις was the order of the day, Paul responded by undertaking "a highly ironical comparison of himself with his Corinthian opponents"[6]—that is, he parodied the synkritic form of his rival's boasting by choosing to boast of his incomparable weakness.

This reading, which has been widely influential,[7] rests on the convergence of three pieces of evidence: First, Paul's opponents are thought to

---

2. Marshall, *Enmity in Corinth*, 53–55, 325–28, 348–53; Forbes, "Comparison, Self-Praise, and Irony." Cf. Betz, *Der Apostel Paulus und die sokratische Tradition*, 119–20.

3. Judge, "Paul's Boasting," 67.

4. Forbes, "Comparison, Self-Praise, and Irony," 1–2.

5. Ibid., 2.

6. Ibid.

7. See Winter, *Philo and Paul*, 231–39; Neyrey, "Social Location of Paul," 141–42; Long, *Ancient Rhetoric*, 227; Witherington, *Conflict and Community in Corinth*, 433; Keener, *1–2 Corinthians*, 220; Duling, "2 Corinthians 11:22," 830–34; Vegge, *A Letter about Reconciliation*, 332; Ske-kar Wan, *Power in Weakness: Conflict and Rhetoric in Paul's Second Letter to the Corinthians* (New Testament in Context; Harrisburg, Pa.: Trinity, 2000), 144; Vegge, *Paulus und das antike Schulwesen*, 421–22; cf. Holland, "Speaking Like a Fool," 256–60.

have been engaging in self-commendatory comparison (10:12), which, it is said, corresponds well with what we know of contemporary sophistic activity, not least in Corinth. Second, although he initially disavowed comparative boasting, Paul went on to compare himself with his Corinthian rivals, and, we are told, did so in ways that evince familiarity with rhetorical conventions for σύγκρισις. Finally, Paul placed his own boasting and that of his rivals in rhetorical context by using the common rhetorical term συγκρῖναι (10:12). I will address each of these claims individually.

Sophistry in Corinth?

In his *Philo and Paul among the Sophists*, Bruce Winter depicts Corinth as a city abuzz with sophistic rhetoric and thus permeated by rivalry and self-aggrandizement. "Corinth," he says, "was flush with sophists, orators and poets, and the intense rivalry which seemed to arise wherever two or three were gathered together."[8] For Winter, Paul's difficulties at Corinth must be seen against this background: the Corinthians were fascinated with sophistic display and susceptible to factionalism, hence their preference for Apollos and other "sophists" and their denigration of Paul.[9] It was in such an environment, then, that Paul engaged in a parody of a self-adulating rhetorical *synkrisis*.

There are, I suggest, two problems with this analysis. First, much of the evidence cited by Winter pertains not to Paul's time but rather to the height of the so-called Second Sophistic in the second century. In fact, there is little to suggest that "sophists" as such were of cultural significance in mid-first-century Corinth. Second, the notion that the "boasting" of Paul's rivals had a particularly sophistic flair receives no support from the text of 2 Cor 10–13.

Corinth, in fact, was not one of the "great sophistic centres" of the second century; Athens, Smyrna, Ephesus, and, of course, Rome retained that honor.[10] It did, however, share the usual enthusiasm of provincial

---

8. Winter, *Philo and Paul*, 128–29.
9. Ibid., 172–79.
10. G. W. Bowersock, *Greek Sophists in the Roman Empire* (Oxford: Clarendon, 1969), 17; Ewen Bowie, "The Geography of the Second Sophistic: Cultural Variations," in *Paideia: The World of the Second Sophistic* (ed. Barbara Borg; Millennium Studies 2; Berlin: de Gruyter, 2004), 68. Indeed, the logic of Favorinus's self-description in his *Corinthian Oration* 25–27 makes it clear that whatever aspirations Corinth had

cites, playing occasional host to such luminaries as Favorinus and Herodes Atticus.[11] This, however, was some years after Paul was in town. Herodes Atticus, a fabulously wealthy Athenian, was born in the first few years of the second century.[12] Favorinus was a generation older, which still puts his floruit three-quarters of a century after Paul's.[13] In any case, despite the impression one might get from reading Winter's treatment, neither of the two men had any particular connection to Corinth.

Winter does provide some evidence from the first century, but it is of dubious value. He refers, firstly, to Dio Chrysostom. Although Philostratus demurs from calling Dio a sophist outright (*Vit. soph.* 1.7–8), the latter's career certainly anticipated the movement that Philostratus sought to memorialize.[14] Dio was far more interested in both Rome and his native Prusa than in Corinth,[15] but he does mention the city on occasion, and Jerome Murphy-O'Connor thinks he describes it with the accuracy of an eyewitness.[16]

Winter focuses on Dio's eighth oration (*De virtute*), one of a number of addresses in which Dio uses Diogenes as a mouthpiece. It is generally agreed that Dio's purpose in speaking in the persona of Diogenes is to use the Cynic hero as a lens through which to refract his own experience—in

---

to being a city of *paideia* it had despite the inherent disadvantage of being a Roman colony: Favorinus's personal example proves "that no one even of the barbarians may despair of attaining the culture of Greece" (Crosby, LCL).

11. Winter, *Philo and Paul*, 129–38.

12. Walter Ameling, *Herodes Atticus* (Subsidia epigraphica 11; 2 vols.; Hildesheim: Olms, 1983), 2:2.

13. Philostratus (*Vit. soph.* 1.8) and Cassius Dio (*Hist. rom.* 69.3.4–69.4.1) have Favorinus active under Hadrian (117–38 C.E.). See further Simon Swain, "Favorinus and Hadrian," *ZPE* 79 (1989): 150–58. His *Corinthian Oration* ([Dio Chrysostom], *Or.* 37) is usually thought to have been delivered ca. 130. See L. Michael White, "Favorinus's 'Corinthian Oration': A Piqued Panorama of the Hadrianic Forum," in *Urban Religion in Roman Corinth: Interdisciplinary Approaches* (ed. Daniel N. Schowalter and Steven J. Friesen; HTS 53; Cambridge: Harvard University Press, 2005), 66 n. 19.

14. Graham Anderson, *The Second Sophistic: A Cultural Phenomenon in the Roman Empire* (London: Routledge, 1993), 20–21; Bowersock, *Greek Sophists in the Roman Empire*, 110–12.

15. See Giovanni Salmeri, "Dio, Rome, and the Civic Life of Asia Minor," in *Dio Chrysostom: Politics, Letters, and Philosophy* (ed. Simon Swain; Oxford: Oxford University Press, 2000), 53–92.

16. Jerome Murphy-O'Connor, *St. Paul's Corinth: Texts and Archaeology* (3rd ed.; GNS 6; Wilmington, Del.: Glazier, 2002), 99–103.

particular, his exile.[17] For Winter, this means that what purports to be a description of Diogenes's fourth-century B.C.E. Corinth should in fact be understood as "Dio's assessment of the sophistic movement in Corinth" in the late first century C.E.[18]

What Dio's Diogenes says about sophists in Corinth is rather hackneyed stuff, and hardly bears the weight of Winter's historical reconstruction. The sophists, we learn, are gathered around the temple of Poseidon βοώντων καὶ λοιδορουμένων ἀλλήλοις while their "so-called disciples" quarrel (μάχομαι [9; cf. 36]). For Winter, this is an allusion to the propensity for rivalry and envy among the sophists of Dio's time.[19] Whether or not the leading lights of the Second Sophistic were any more quarrelsome than competitive aristocrats of any other period is debatable.[20] In any case, this is invective, not description, and has more to do with the sort of vilification Dio favors than with the characteristics of sophists, be they contemporaries of Dio or of Diogenes.[21] And, on that note, it is worth considering the possibility that Dio's reference to sophists here is not aimed at his contemporaries at all, but is in fact part of the ethopoetic furniture of Dio's oration, a detail included because it provides the conventional backdrop against which Diogenes's legendary wit should be viewed (cf. Diogenes Laertius, *Vit. phil.* 6.47, 57).

Further, the sophists Dio's Diogenes mentions are visitors to Corinth, not residents. Diogenes, we are told, had gone down to the isthmus with everyone else for the games (6). It was then (τότε)—that is, during the Isthmian games—that one could hear sophists at the temple of Poseidon (9).[22] Thus it sounds very much like these sophists had come to Corinth for the special occasion, an impression that is confirmed a few lines later: Diogenes, apparently, did not attract any Corinthians, since they reasoned

---

17. H. F. A. von Arnim, *Leben und Werke des Dio von Prusa* (Berlin: Weidmann, 1898), 260–67; J. L. Moles, "The Career and Conversion of Dio Chrysostom," *JHS* 98 (1978): 79–100.

18. Winter, *Philo and Paul*, 123–24.

19. Ibid., 125–26.

20. On their rivalries, see Anderson, *The Second Sophistic*, 35–39; Bowersock, *Greek Sophists in the Roman Empire*, 89–100.

21. Dio puts μάχομαι and λοιδορέω together elsewhere too, using the pair to describe the fractiousness of the avaricious man (*4 Regn.* 96), the disagreeable drunk (*Compot.* 3), and ignorant and corrupt humanity in general (*Conc. Apam.* 32).

22. As Winter also notes (*Philo and Paul*, 124 n. 5). Cf. Dio's similar comment in *Dei cogn.* 5, this time referring to the sophists who flocked to the games at Olympia.

that they could see him on their streets at any time (10); the Corinthians were more interested in the novel fare on offer from the visiting sophists. Clearly, then, Dio's brief and stereotyped description cannot be taken as evidence of a sophistic movement in late first-century Corinth.

Plutarch, like Dio, can be critical of σοφισταί, attributing to them the same sort of unworthy motives Dio posits: vanity, φιλοτιμία, and greed.[23] Again, this can hardly be taken as a report of the values of first-century rhetors. These are *topoi*, as old as Plato's dispute with the original sophists,[24] and, by Plutarch's time, useful in denigrating any sort of rival at all (cf. Lucian, *Vit. auct.*; *Peregr.*). Plutarch's usage tells us little more than that he considered some contemporary rhetoricians vacuous and vain.[25]

Moreover, any connection specifically to Corinth is extremely tenuous. Winter notes that two of the symposia described in Plutarch's *Table Talk* take place in Corinth (5.3 [675D–677B]; 8.4 [723A–724F]), and rhetors are among the guests at each.[26] Again, however, it appears these men were in Corinth for the Isthmian games, as was Plutarch himself. And, even if one of these ῥήτορες were local, the appearance of a leading rhetor at a banquet hardly means that Corinth was rash with sophistry. It simply means that Corinth, like any other city, had a rhetorical school or a court of law.

This is approximately the level of banal insight into Corinth we get from the other first-century text Winter discusses, Epictetus's discourse "Of personal adornment" (*Diatr.* 3.1). The discourse is addressed to a young rhetorician who dressed too elaborately for Epictetus's tastes (3.1.1). We can infer, from a passing mention, that he was a Corinthian: "Shall

---

23. *Tu. san.* 131A; *Pyth. orac.* 408D. Cf. Dio Chrysostom, *Virt.* 33; *Dei cogn.* 5; Lucian, *Rhet. praec.* 1–2. Plutarch also uses the word neutrally, and apparently makes no distinction between "rhetors" and "sophists." See G. R. Stanton, "Sophists and Philosophers: Problems of Classification," *AJP* 94 (1973): 151–53.

24. See esp. Håkan Tell, "Wisdom for Sale? The Sophists and Money," *CP* 104 (2009): 13–33.

25. Indeed, first-century use of the philosopher vs. sophist *topos* seems to have amounted to little more than shadow boxing, an exercise in self-definition that allowed everyone to enjoy the esteem of being part of a courageous moral minority— a Socrates or a Diogenes. Hence, in the first century, everyone we might think to call a sophist insists that they are not (see Stanton, "Sophists and Philosophers," 351–58). By the time we clear the room of philosophers, there is no one left to argue the other side. See, e.g., on Dio Chrysostom, Tim Whitmarsh, *The Second Sophistic* (Greece and Rome: New Surveys in the Classics 35; Oxford: Oxford University Press, 2005), 17.

26. Winter, *Philo and Paul*, 138–39.

we make a man like you a citizen of Corinth, and perchance a warden of the city, or superintendent of ephebi, or general, or superintendent of the games?" (3.1.34 [Oldfather, LCL]). Evidently the young man was an aristocrat. Accordingly, he was receiving the rhetorical education that generally was thought necessary for a public career, in Corinth and elsewhere (cf. Quintilian, *Inst.* 1 pr. 9–10; 1.2.18). And his attire has nothing to do with being a sophist; it falls within the spectrum of the ordinary fashion of the Greek elite.[27] Epictetus's problem is simply that it is not very "philosophical" (cf. Quintilian, *Inst.* 1 pr. 15).

In short, then, all of Winter's evidence for "the sophistic movement in Corinth" erodes upon further examination. Reference to Corinth is marginal throughout, and, in the first-century material, there is no clear indication of sophists per se. The most we can say is that first-century Corinth, like any other town, had its fair share of orators—and perhaps more than its fair share during the games.

Of course, sophists or no sophists, rhetoric and its elite practitioners would have been esteemed in Corinth as elsewhere. Surely they were competitive, and perhaps they quarreled. But there is no evidence in Paul's letter that this is the background against which his troubles in Corinth should be viewed. I will restrict my comments here to Winter's exegesis of 2 Cor 10–13.[28] According to Winter, "Paul calls his opponents in 2 Corinthians 10–13 'ignorant' and 'fools' because they engaged in σύγκρισις and boasted about their achievements"—that is to say, they acted like sophists.[29] But let us look more carefully at what Paul actually says about their boasting. First, the notion that what Paul means to specify by his use of συγκρῖναι in 10:12 is that his rivals had a particular affinity for the rhetorical exercise described in the *Progymnasmata* simply is not credible. The

---

27. As Eve D'Ambra explains, "Care taken to maintain one's appearance and to distinguish oneself from the *hoi polloi* by grooming was an essential prerequisite for a man of honor" ("Kosmetai, the Second Sophistic, and Portraiture in the Second Century," in *Periklean Athens and Its Legacy: Problems and Perspectives* [ed. Judith M. Barringer and Jeffrey M. Hurwit; Austin: University of Texas Press, 2005], 207). See also Gleason, *Making Men*, 74–76.

28. On Winter's reading of 2 Cor 10:10 in particular, see ch. 12 below. Also significant in Winter's study, as in much recent scholarship on the Corinthian correspondence, is a reading of 1 Cor 2:1–5 as an engagement of Corinthian preoccupation with rhetoric (*Philo and Paul*, 148–50, 158–64). As I have argued elsewhere ("Rhetorical Terminology in Paul," 186–90), this reading does not withstand scrutiny.

29. Winter, *Philo and Paul*, 231.

word's use alongside such related terms as ἐγκρῖναι, καυχᾶσθαι, and ἑαυτοὺς συνιστάνειν makes it clear that Paul is referring to something considerably more general. And, when Paul goes on to describe more precisely what is bothering him, he says nothing that calls to mind the sophists.[30]

On the contrary, in 2 Cor 10:12–16, Paul makes it clear that the immoderate "boasting" he attributes to his rivals—and insists that he will not undertake—consists of taking credit for the labors of others, harvesting in a field someone else has tilled:

> οὐ γὰρ τολμῶμεν ἐγκρῖναι ἢ συγκρῖναι ἑαυτούς τισιν τῶν ἑαυτοὺς συνιστανόντων ... ἡμεῖς δὲ οὐκ εἰς τὰ ἄμετρα καυχησόμεθα ... οὐκ εἰς τὰ ἄμετρα καυχώμενοι ἐν ἀλλοτρίοις κόποις ... οὐκ ἐν ἀλλοτρίῳ κανόνι εἰς τὰ ἕτοιμα καυχήσασθαι. (10:12, 13, 15, 16)[31]

Clearly, his rivals are intruding on what Paul considers to be his territory. Paul founded the Corinthian community, and he wants the credit for it (cf. 1 Cor 4:15). His rivals' "boasting," then, consists of nothing more than a claim to status in the Corinthian community—which, of course, is precisely the nature of Paul's "boasting," too (2 Cor 10:8). The difference between them is simply that, from Paul's perspective, he has not overstepped his God-ordained limits (vv. 13–14),[32] and thus his boasting is not ἄμετρος.[33] It is he alone who has the commendation of his master, Paul insists, and thus he alone is able to boast, as the Scriptures mandate, ἐν κυρίῳ (vv. 17–18).[34]

---

30. Winter implies (*Philo and Paul*, 235) that they boasted, as sophists were wont to do, in their δόξα, πλοῦτος, τιμή, and ἀρχή, but there is no evidence for this in the text of 2 Corinthians. The only grounds for such an assertion is that such were the things about which sophists boasted. This is clearly a circular argument.

31. On Paul's rather obscure εἰς τὰ ἕτοιμα, see Plummer, *Second Epistle*, 290; Thrall, *Second Epistle*, 2:652. Note that καυχάομαι, particularly in Paul, need not signify boasting per se. It often refers more generally to taking pride in something (cf. 2 Cor 7:14; Gal 6:13). See BDAG s.v.; R. Bultmann, "καυχάομαι κτλ.," *TDNT* 3:645–54; Ashton, *Religion of Paul*, 118.

32. Paul's κατὰ τὸ μέτρον τοῦ κανόνος οὗ ἐμέρισεν ἡμῖν ὁ θεὸς μέτρου is notoriously difficult to translate, although the sense is clear enough from the context: Paul is not "overreaching" (10:14) by working in Corinth, since it is within his God-measured jurisdiction. See Plummer, *Second Epistle*, 287–88; Furnish, *II Corinthians*, 471–72.

33. Cf. Hafemann, "Self-Commendation," 79–80.

34. Paul's citation of Jer 9:23 here is often taken to be a denunciation of all human boasting. So Ulrich Heckel, for example, contrasts Paul's absolute opposition to boast-

The comparative dimension in all of this is, of course, that his rivals have been asserting their own status at the expense of Paul's.[35] Thus Paul insists that he is not their inferior (11:5; 12:11), and emphasizes his own superiority where he can—specifically, in preaching the gospel free of charge—so as to "deny an opportunity to those who want an opportunity to be recognized as our equals in what they boast about" (11:12). There is nothing particularly rhetorical, let alone sophistic, about this sort of comparative dispute.

ΣΥΓΚΡΙΝΩ AND RHETORIC

Much of the credibility of the approach of Winter, Forbes, Marshall, et al. seems to derive from Paul's use in 2 Cor 10:12 of the word συγκρῖναι, a

---

ing with the attitude of "the Greeks": "In Unterschied zu den Griechen geht es dem Apostel jedoch nicht einfach um die Vermeidung von Hybris und das Einhalten des rechten Maßes, sondern um Gottes Ehre als Schöpfer und Erlöser sowie um den völligen Verzicht auf jeglichen Selbstruhm des Menschen vor Gott" (*Kraft in Schwachheit*, 157). But this sounds more like Lutheran theologizing than exegesis of Paul (cf. Bultmann, "καυχάομαι," *TDNT* 3:648–52), and is belied by consideration of the context of the citation in Paul's argument. Perhaps in 1 Cor 1:31, in the midst of a discussion of the futility of wisdom, power, and nobility κατὰ σάρκα (v. 25), we are justified in supposing that Paul's citation of Jer 9:23 is intended to evoke the illegitimate grounds of boasting delimited in Jer 9:22 (σοφία, ἰσχύς, πλοῦτος). Here, however, there are no indications of the relevance of the broader Jeremianic context, *contra* Josef Schreiner, "Jeremia 9,22.23 als Hintergrund des paulinischen 'Sich-Rühmens,'" in *Neues Testament und Kirche: Für Rudolf Schnackenburg* (ed. Joachim Gnilka; Freiburg: Herder, 1974), 530–42; Heckel, *Kraft in Schwachheit*, 191–93; Heckel, "Jer 9,22f. als Schlüssel für 2 Kor 10–13: Ein Beispiel für die methodischen Probleme in der gegenwärtigen Diskussion über den Schriftgebrauch bei Paulus," in *Schriftauslegung im antiken Judentum und im Urchristentum* (ed. Martin Hengel and Hermut Löhr; WUNT 73; Tübingen: Mohr [Siebeck], 1994), 206–25. On the contrary, as Scott Hafemann argues, "Taken together, 10.17–18 are … the last assertions in Paul's argument in 10.12–18 in support of his ability and willingness to 'boast' concerning his own authority (cf. 10.8)" ("Self-Commendation," 74).

35. Paul's initial characterization gives the impression that his rivals are making comparisons among themselves (αὐτοὶ ἐν ἑαυτοῖς ἑαυτοὺς μετροῦντες καὶ συγκρίνοντες ἑαυτοὺς ἑαυτοῖς [10:12]), but his elaboration focuses solely on their comparability with himself. Hence this is probably best interpreted as an attempt by Paul dismissively to portray his rivals' denigration of him as just one instance of characteristically self-promoting behavior. On this point I have an unlikely ally in Peter Marshall, *Enmity in Corinth*, 326–27.

verbal cognate of the rhetorical term σύγκρισις. This is interpreted, often, as straightforward evidence that what Paul's rivals were engaged in, and what he himself reluctantly undertook, was not merely comparison, but comparison as informed by rhetorical theory.[36]

Indeed, both words, σύγκρισις and συγκρίνω, were used frequently by rhetorical theorists;[37] however, as we will see, both were very common words, hardly restricted to this technical sense. A modern English equivalent, I suspect, would be hypothesis, which, as the *Oxford English Dictionary* notes, is used in a technical sense by logicians, but also more generally by the hoi polloi.[38] Its use certainly is not evidence that the speaker is referring to formal logic.

I will focus on the verb συγκρίνω, since Paul nowhere uses the noun. "Compare" is one of four primary senses listed by LSJ. The word occurs only here with this meaning in the NT; in its one other NT occurrence, also in Paul (1 Cor 2:13), it means "interpret," as it frequently does also in the LXX.[39] Elsewhere in the LXX, συγκρίνω means "compare" in the general sense, with no particular rhetorical connotation.[40] Josephus uses it six times, in five of which the word means "compare;"[41] there is no indication in any of these instances that rhetorical *synkrisis* is what he had in mind. LSJ notes two occurrences for Polybius: on one occasion, Polybius does use the word in a setting somewhat reminiscent of the sort of *synkrisis* the rhetoricians recommend,[42] but he also uses it more generally to describe Scipio's meticulous collation of his spies' reports (συνέκρινε καὶ διηρεύνα τὰ

---

36. See, e.g., Marshall, *Enmity in Corinth*, 53.
37. For the noun, see Anderson, *Glossary of Greek Rhetorical Terms*, 110–11. The verb occurs at Aristotle, *Rhet.* 1.9.38; Dionysius of Halicarnassus, *Pomp.* 1.11; *Thuc. id.* 14; *Dem.* 17; 21; Theon, *Progymn.* pr.; 6 (3x); 10 (8x); Ps.-Hermogenes, *Inv.* 3.9; 4.14 (4x); *Progymn.* 7; 8 (3x); Menander Rhetor, *RG* 3:372, 377, 380 (3x), 381 (2x), 383, 386, 402, 417 (3x), 425, 427; Aphthonius, *Progymn.* 10 (3x); Nicolaus, *Progymn.* 9 (4x).
38. *Oxford English Dictionary Online*, s.v. "Hypothesis."
39. Gen 40:8, 16, 22; 41:12, 13, 15; Dan 5:7.
40. 1 Macc 10:71 (of the size of armies); Wis 7:29; 15:18.
41. *A.J.* 5.77; 8.42; 8.99; 13.89; *B.J.* 1.402. In *A.J.* 4.33 the sense is "judge."
42. It is limited, however, to a comparison of historical methods: Σκεψώμεθα δὴ καὶ τὴν αὐτοῦ τοῦ Τιμαίου προαίρεσιν καὶ τὰς ἀποφάσεις συγκρίνωμεν ἐκ παραθέσεως, ἃς πεποίηται περὶ τῆς αὐτῆς ἀποικίας, ἵνα γνῶμεν πότερος ἄξιος ἔσται τῆς τοιαύτης κατηγορίας (12.9.1).

λεγόμενα [14.3.7]). I could go on, but the point is clear: the word simply means "compare."⁴³

Moreover, in this case the context actually tells against the rhetorical sense of the word. As noted above, Paul uses συγκρίνω here alongside such related terms as ἐγκρίνω, καυχάομαι, and ἑαυτοὺς συνιστάνειν, suggesting that the concrete behavior to which he refers is not the sort of thing that is best described by a technical term but instead falls somewhere within the general semantic range circumscribed by these various words and phrases. Indeed, it would be very odd to put together a paronomastic pairing like ἐγκρῖναι ἢ συγκρῖναι⁴⁴ in which one word had a general and the other a

---

43. A crude but telling way to see the scope of this word's nonrhetorical usage is a simple *TLG* search. A lemma search across the entire corpus locates 2635 occurrences of συγκρίνω; of these, only 141 occur in authors to which the editors of the *TLG* have appended the generic epithet *Rhetorici*. For the noun σύγκρισις, the ratio is marginally higher: 335 of 3407 hits occur in authors designated rhetoricians. Even granting that a considerable number of references to rhetorical comparison may occur in non-rhetorical writings, these data are striking, and make it impossible to assume, merely from the word's occurrence, that Paul in 2 Cor 10:12 is referring to the rhetorical practice of *synkrisis*. Finally, a note on the meaning of σύγκρισιν in P.Oxy. XVIII 2190 is order, since Forbes adduces it as an example of rhetorical *synkrisis* used for the purposes of self-advertisement among "popular teachers" ("Comparison, Self-Praise, and Irony," 7). The text in question is a letter from a boy named Neilus, who is pursuing his education, probably in Alexandria, written to his father back in Oxyrhynchus. Neilus has been searching in vain for a teacher he likes. Some friends of his are being urged to attend the classes of one Didymus, who had recently sailed down the river (καταπλεύσαντα [line 19; cf. line 5]) to the city. Neilus is not impressed. I quote from the translation of John Rea: "I for my part ... am depressed by the very fact that this person, who used to be a teacher in the country (ἐπὶ τῆς χώρας), has made up his mind to enter into competition with the others (ἔδοξεν εἰς σύγκρισιν τοῖς ἄλλοις ἔρχεσθαι)" (lines 25–29). The logic of Neilus's argument makes it clear that σύγκρισις here has nothing to do with the rhetorical exercise, but refers to competition in a more general sense. What Nelius criticizes is Didymus's decision to attempt the transition from country teacher, a humble role but one with little competition, to city teacher, where competition for students was evidently intense. It is not orations wherein he compares himself with other teachers but his "sailing down" in the first place that constitute his ill-advised entry εἰς σύγκρισιν τοῖς ἄλλοις.

44. This sort of paronomasia, I might note in passing, is hardly evidence of particular rhetorical sophistication. See, for example the similar pairing οὐδὲ φάσις οὐδὲ βάσις in P.Oxy. XLVIII 3396.5–6, a letter regarding which G. O. Hutchinson notes that "ubiquitous misspellings, limited vocabulary, and unambitious sentence-structure indicate a considerable distance from the world of the previous writer"—a writer whom Hutchison had placed at "the very foot of the rhetorical ladder" ("Down among

technical signification.⁴⁵ And, as noted above, when Paul goes on to elaborate on his rivals' ἄμετρος "boasting," καυχάομαι refers not to rhetorical exercises but to assertions of status or authority. In short, συγκρίνω here has nothing to do with rhetoric.

Paul's Comparison in 2 Corinthians 11:21b–23

If there is no evidence that Paul's rivals in Corinth were engaging in rhetorical *synkrisis*, and no evidence that Paul uses συγκρίνω in its technical rhetorical sense, then any argument that Paul utilizes this figure must rest solely on Paul's prose itself. That is, only if his comparison of himself with his rivals in fact resembles the practice of rhetorical *synkrisis* could one argue that he was familiar with the rhetorical tradition the *Progymnasmata* represent.

There is, of course, some general resemblance. Paul does compare himself with his rivals, and arguably does hit on one of the traditional headings. But I am not at all persuaded, with Forbes, that Paul's "boasting clearly takes the form of a σύγκρισις."⁴⁶ On the contrary, Paul's comparison is far too brief, stylistically far too idiosyncratic, and far too easily explained on other grounds to suggest the influence of rhetorical theory.

Paul's putative *synkrisis*, it should be noted, constitutes only the first few verses of his foolish boasting (11:21b–23):

ἐν ᾧ δ' ἄν τις τολμᾷ, ἐν ἀφροσύνῃ λέγω, τολμῶ κἀγώ·
  Ἑβραῖοί εἰσιν; κἀγώ.
  Ἰσραηλῖταί εἰσιν; κἀγώ.
  σπέρμα Ἀβραάμ εἰσιν; κἀγώ.
  διάκονοι Χριστοῦ εἰσιν; παραφρονῶν λαλῶ, ὑπὲρ ἐγώ·
    ἐν κόποις περισσοτέρως
    ἐν φυλακαῖς περισσοτέρως
    ἐν πληγαῖς ὑπερβαλλόντως
    ἐν θανάτοις πολλάκις.

---

the Documents: Criticism and Papyrus Letters," in *Ancient Letters: Classical and Late Antique Epistolography* [ed. Ruth Morello and A. D. Morrison; Oxford: Oxford University Press, 2007], 28).

45. Note that Marshall disingenuously avoids this problem by providing, in his citation of the text, the Greek for "compare" but not for "class" (*Enmity in Corinth*, 325).

46. Forbes, "Comparison, Self-Praise, and Irony," 18.

The passage begins in an explicitly comparative mode, expressed by the repeated use of κἀγώ. The precise connotations of Ἑβραῖος, Ἰσραηλίτης, and σπέρμα Ἀβραάμ need not detain us here; it is enough to note that each of these items of comparison revolves around authentic Judean ethnicity.[47] With διάκονοι Χριστοῦ, Paul leaves behind his κἀγώ claims and asserts his superiority: ὑπὲρ ἐγώ. When it comes to service of Christ, Paul claims to be peerless.

It is not entirely clear whether the clauses that follow should be considered a continuation of Paul's comparison with his rivals—that is, whether he means to back up his ὑπὲρ ἐγώ by specifying the ways in which his service exceeds theirs.[48] As Plummer notes,

> The comparative form is dropped after the repeated περισσοτέρως, and therefore only in these first two clauses is there even in form any possibility of comparison with [the opponents]. It is possible that after ὑπὲρ ἐγώ they are altogether banished from consideration, and that περισσοτέρως means "very abundantly."[49]

In any case, by the end of v. 23, the comparative aspect of Paul's boasting has disappeared, and all agree that from this point on Paul's boasting no longer resembles a rhetorical *synkrisis*.[50]

Nevertheless, for Marshall and Forbes, the significance of Paul's boasting throughout 11:24–12:10 still derives from its relationship to the conventional form of a *synkrisis*. The argument is as follows: Paul begins his boasting—as Theon's *Progymnasmata* recommends, we are told with a comparison of "birth and racial status"; "next, where one would expect magistracies and honours, or some equivalent, Paul brings forward beatings and dangers on all sides." From this perspective, it is precisely Paul's deviation from the expected synkritic form that signals his aim:

---

47. For an overview of the discussion, see Martin, *2 Corinthians*, 373–75; Thrall, *Second Epistle*, 2:723–30.

48. So Thrall, *Second Epistle*, 2:734; Fitzgerald, "Cracks in an Earthen Vessel," 378 n. 254.

49. Plummer, *Second Epistle*, 322; cf. Denney, *Second Epistle*, 339. Plummer adduces 1 Cor 1:12; 2:4; 7:13, 15; 12:15 as instances where Paul uses περισσοτέρως without obvious comparative intent. Cf. 1 Thess 2:17; Phil 1:14.

50. Forbes, "Comparison, Self-Praise, and Irony," 19; Marshall, *Enmity in Corinth*, 350–51.

Paul "amplifies what he should minimise and minimises what he should amplify," thus constructing a "parody of the self-display of his opponents."[51]

For this sort of parody to work—that is, for the listeners to recognize it as parody—two basic conditions must be met: first, the form in question must have clearly identifiable distinguishing features; second, the parodist must make clear reference to them.[52] Paul's putative synkritic parody meets only one of these conditions. There were, I think, clearly identifiable features of ancient rhetorical comparison, and thus parodic *synkrisis* was certainly possible. Indeed, how else would one make sense of the *synkrisis* of "peas and lentils" reportedly undertaken by the great poet and satirist Meleager of Gadara (Athenaeus, *Deipn.* 4.45)? However, as we will see, Paul's boasting is not sufficiently reminiscent of progymnastic or literary *synkrisis* to function as a parody.

As noted above, Forbes implies that Paul's boasting follows the conventional order of headings for comparison as outlined by Aelius Theon. But his argument here is rather misleading.[53] What Theon in fact says is this:

---

51. Forbes, "Comparison, Self-Praise, and Irony," 19. See also Marshall, *Enmity in Corinth*, 351–52.

52. See Seymour Chatman, "Parody and Style," *Poetics Today* 22 (2001): 28.

53. Note also that contrary to the impression given by Forbes there is no well-defined order of headings to be addressed in *synkrisis*. The *Progymnasmata* differ among themselves (Theon: see below; Ps.-Hermogenes: city of origin (πόλις), family (γένος), nurture (τροφή), pursuits (ἐπιτηδεύματα), deeds (πράξεις), external factors (τὰ ἐκτός), manner of death, and "what comes after"; Aphthonius: not specified; Nicolaus: not specified). They do, however, generally agree that the headings are the same as those of encomium. But that too is a shifting target: Theon (9) has three major headings—goods of the mind and character, goods of the body, and external goods—while Ps.-Hermogenes (7) and Nicolaus (8) follow a chronological or biographical format. There is certainly some common ground here—origin and education are, predictably, at the beginning of each list; πράξεις are the main focus; manner of death, if included, comes at the end—but, beyond that, there is no firmly fixed order. Indeed, these authors explicitly advocate flexibility, in order that speakers may judge what is relevant in any particular case (cf. Nicolaus, *Progymn.* 8). Such flexibility, I might note, is precisely what we see in Plutarch, whose famous *synkriseis* are composed not according to a set order of headings but rather with an eye to what is most interesting—from Plutarch's moralizing perspective, that is—about each pair of heroes. See Duff, *Plutarch's Lives*, 243–86; and, more generally, Timothy W. Seid, "Synkrisis in Hebrews 7: The Rhetorical Structure and Strategy," in *The Rhetorical Interpretation of Scripture: Essays from the 1996 Malibu Conference* (ed. Stanley E. Porter and Dennis L. Stamps; JSNTSup 180; Sheffield: Sheffield Academic Press, 1999), 327, 332.

Whenever we compare persons we shall first put side by side their good birth (τὴν εὐγένειαν) and education (τὴν παιδείαν) and the excellence of their offspring (τὴν εὐτεκνίαν) and the offices they have held (τὰς ἀρχὰς) and their reputation (τὴν δόξαν) and the condition of their bodies (τὴν τοῦ σώματος διάθεσιν) and any other bodily and external good that we mentioned earlier in discussing encomia. After this we shall compare their actions (τὰς πράξεις). (*Progymn*. 10 [*RG* 2:113; trans. Kennedy])

Forbes does the best he can to make Paul's series of κἀγώ statements appear to conform to Theon's description, describing them as reference to "birth and racial status."[54] But Paul's insistence on meeting the criteria of authentic Judean ethnicity (cf. Phil 3:4–6) is certainly not the sort of thing Theon meant by "good birth" (εὐγένεια), which refers, quite unambiguously, to social status or nobility of birth.[55]

And, even if we were to let Forbes fudge here, we would still have only a single point of similarity between Paul's putative *synkrisis* and that described by Theon. Paul says nothing about παιδεία and nothing about εὐτεκνία. There is at most a single shared heading. Is this really sufficient grounds for Paul's listeners to "expect magistracies and honours" to come next? Such an expectation, remember, is key to Forbes's interpretation: If there is no formal expectation that Paul enumerate his honors, his listing of humiliations may constitute a paradox but cannot be a parody.

A further important observation tells against Forbes's reading. Forbes describes the progymnastic method as "point for point" comparison,[56] and, although this certainly is an accurate description, nevertheless it misleads with regard to the relationship between 2 Cor 11:21b–23 and the *synkriseis* composed in rhetorical school. Stylistically, there is no similarity at all.

---

54. Forbes, "Comparison, Self-Praise, and Irony," 19; so also Watson, "Paul's Boasting in 2 Corinthians 10–13," 272.

55. See LSJ, s.v. What Theon meant is clearly visible from Plutarch's *Comp. Demetr. Ant.* 1.1–2 (Perrin, LCL): "Since, then, both these men experienced great reversals of fortune, let us first observe, with regard to their power and fame, that in the one case these were acquired for him by his father and inherited, since Antigonus became the strongest of Alexander's successors, and before Demetrius came of age had attacked and mastered the greater part of Asia; Antony, on the contrary, was the son of a man who, though otherwise gifted, was yet no warrior, and could leave him no great legacy of reputation."

56. Forbes, "Comparison, Self-Praise, and Irony," 19. Cf. Marshall, *Enmity in Corinth*, 351.

Aphthonius helpfully provides a sample composition, which gives us a good sense of what "point for point" means in the case of the *Progymnasmata*:

> They were not born in the same land, but nevertheless each in a land to be praised. The one (ὃ μὲν) came from Phthia, where the eponymous hero of Hellas came from, and the other (ὃ δὲ) from Troy, whose original founders were descendants of gods. To the extent that having been born in similar places is no derogation of praise, Hector is not excelled by Achilles.
>
> And while both were born in a praiseworthy land, both had equal ancestry; for each descended from Zeus. Achilles was son of Peleus (Πηλέως μὲν γὰρ Ἀχιλλεύς), Peleus of Aeacus, and Aeacus of Zeus; similarly, Hector was son of Priam (Ἕκτωρ τε ὁμοίως Πριάμου), and [grandson] of Laomedon, and Laomedon was son of Dardanus, and Dardanus had been a son of Zeus....
>
> When both came to manhood, they acquired equal prestige from one war. First, Hector (πρῶτον μὲν γὰρ Ἕκτωρ) was leader of the Trojans and, while alive, the protector of Troy; during that time he continued to have gods aiding him in the fight and when he fell made Troy fall with him. Achilles (Ἀχιλλεὺς δὲ) was the leader of Greece in arms; terrifying all, he subdued the Trojans and had the help of Athene in the fight, and his death took away the superiority of the Achaeans. (*Progymn.* 10 [trans. Kennedy])

Note that, in contrast to the terseness of 2 Cor 11:21b–23, each heading is introduced, briefly elaborated so as to justify any claim to equality or superiority, and, on occasion, summarized. The same pattern characterizes each heading in the *synkriseis* with which Plutarch concludes most of his paired *Lives*.[57] I quote but two examples:

> As for their outlays of money, Nicias was more public spirited (πολιτικώτερος μὲν ὁ Νικίας) in his noble ambition to make offerings to the gods and provide the people with gymnastic exhibitions and trained choruses; and yet his whole estate, together with his expenditures, was not a tithe of what Crassus expended (ὧν δ' ὁ Κράσσος ἀνήλωσεν) when

---

57. On the influence of rhetorical theory in the construction of Plutarch's *synkriseis*, see Friedrich Focke, "Synkrisis," *Hermes* 58 (1923): 357–58.

he feasted so many myriads of men at once, and then furnished them with food afterwards. (*Comp. Nic. Crass.* 1.4 [Perrin, LCL])

> It is possible, too, to get a glimpse of the character of each in his style of speaking. For that of Demosthenes (ὁ μὲν γὰρ Δημοσθενικός), which had no prettiness or pleasantry, and was condensed with a view to power and earnestness, did not smell of lamp-wicks, as Pytheas scoffingly said, but of water-drinking and anxious thought, and of what men called the bitterness and sullenness of his disposition; whereas Cicero (Κικέρων δὲ) was often carried away by his love of jesting into scurrility, and when, to gain his ends in cases, he treated matters worthy of serious attention with ironical mirth and pleasantry, he was careless of propriety.... (*Comp. Dem. Cic.* 1.3–4 [Perrin, LCL])

Plutarch is less concerned than the progymnast in simple demonstrations of superiority. Instead, his more sophisticated fascination is with the interplay of difference and sameness. But the structural similarity is evident: as in Aphthonius's exemplar, in each case the heading is identified and then elaborated, often with specific examples.

Another stylistic similarity is the frequent use of balanced μέν ... δέ constructions. Such constructions are, of course, eminently suitable to the sort of point-by-point comparison involved in *synkrisis*.[58] Plutarch is a little less bound to this form than Aphthonius, occasionally finding more creative ways of denoting the second side of an opposition. Still, it would be difficult to imagine *synkrisis* without μέν and δέ clauses or their equivalents.

A particularly telling example of the conventions for *synkrisis* is a treatise, falsely attributed to Plutarch, that compares the merits of fire and water:

> ἆρ᾿ οὖν οὐ χρησιμώτερον ἐκεῖνο, οὗ πάντοτε καὶ διηνεκῶς δεόμεθα καὶ πλείστου, καθάπερ ἐργαλεῖον καὶ ὄργανον καὶ νὴ Δία φίλος ὁ πάσης ὥρας καὶ παντὸς καιροῦ παρὼν ἕτοιμος; καὶ μὴν τὸ μὲν πῦρ οὐ πάντοτε χρήσιμον, ἔστι δ᾿ ὅτε καὶ βαρυνόμεθα καὶ ἀποσπώμεθα· τοῦ δ᾿ ὕδατος χρεία καὶ χειμῶνος καὶ θέρους καὶ νοσοῦσι καὶ ὑγιαίνουσι, νυκτὸς καὶ μεθ᾿ ἡμέραν, καὶ οὐκ ἔστιν ὅτ᾿ ἄνθρωπος οὐ δεῖται.... καὶ ἄνευ μὲν πυρὸς ἦν πολλάκις, ὕδατος δ᾿ οὐδέποτ᾿ ἄνθρωπος. (*An ignis* 2 [*Mor.* 955E–956A])[59]

---

58. Cf. Heb 7:5–25, with Seid, "Synkrisis in Hebrews 7," 338–47.

59. "Is not that element the more useful of which most of all, everywhere, invariably, we stand in need as a household tool, and, I swear, a friend, ready to help us at any time, in any emergency? Yet fire is not always useful; sometimes, indeed, we find it

ἔτι μήν, ὃ πολλαπλασιαζόμενον τὴν ὠφέλειαν ἀπόλλυσιν, ἀχρηστότερον· τοιοῦτον δὲ τὸ πῦρ, οἷον θηρίον παμφάγον καὶ δαπανῶν τῶν παρακειμένων, καὶ μεθόδῳ καὶ τέχνῃ μᾶλλον καὶ μετριότητι ἢ τῇ αὑτοῦ φύσει ὠφέλιμον· τὸ δ' ὕδωρ οὐδέποτε φοβερόν. (*An ignis* 6 [*Mor.* 956E])[60]

What makes this *synkrisis* of particular interest is how poorly it is executed. As F. H. Sandbach explains, in addition to "the unusual meagreness of the author's vocabulary," the treatise is marred by unwieldy attempts at rhetorical display: "The author is clearly striving after effect, but hardly achieving it."[61] One manifestation of its amateurish quality is the way in which substance—and logic—has been sacrificed in order to meet formal expectations. This author is intent on picking a winner, thus an observation about the danger of conflagrations produces, by necessity of comparison, the absurd conclusion that water is never to be feared.[62]

Note that despite this author's incompetence the treatment of the headings conforms closely to the pattern we have come to expect: Each heading is briefly introduced and then elaborated, generally using balanced μέν ... δέ clauses. What the *Progymnasmata* teach, and what Plutarch utilizes elegantly, this author bungles. It is difficult to see how Paul's comparison of himself with his rivals in 2 Cor 11 could be said even to belong on the same continuum.

It is true that rhetorical *synkrisis* was not confined to the progymnastic exercise that went by that name. On the contrary, it was also widely used as a means of *auxēsis* in encomiastic oratory.[63] Does such use bear more resemblance to Paul's comparison? Well, no. Compare the *synkrisis* in Xenophon's famous encomia:[64]

---

too much and interrupt our use of it. But water is used both winter and summer, sick and well, night and day: there is no time when a man does not need it....Man has often existed without fire, but without water never" (Perrin, LCL).

60. "Then, too, that which by multiplication destroys its own contribution is the less useful. Such a thing is fire which, like an all-devouring beast, consumes everything near, so that it is useful rather by skilful handling and craft than by its own nature; but water is never dangerous" (Perrin, LCL).

61. F. H. Sandbach, "Rhythm and Authenticity in Plutarch's *Moralia*," *CQ* 33 (1939): 200.

62. See ibid., 201.

63. Aristotle, *Rhet.* 1.9.38; *Rhet. Alex.* 3.7–8; Theon, *Progymn.* 9 (*RG* 2:111)

64. Cf. Isocrates, *De pace* 41–44, which is explicitly labeled a *synkrisis* by Dionysius of Halicarnassus (*Isocr.* 17; *Dem.* 17), and Isocrates, *Evag.* 34–37.

> I will next point out the contrast between [Agesilaus's] behaviour and the imposture of the Persian king. In the first place the Persian (ὁ μὲν) thought his dignity required that he should be seldom seen: Agesilaus (Ἀγησίλαος δὲ) delighted to be constantly visible, believing that, whereas secrecy was becoming to an ugly career, the light shed lustre on a life of noble purpose. In the second place, the one (ὁ μὲν) prided himself on being difficult of approach: the other (ὁ δὲ) was glad to make himself accessible to all.... In the matter of personal comfort, moreover, it is worth noticing how much simpler and much more easily satisfied were the tastes of Agesilaus. The Persian king (τῷ μὲν γὰρ Πέρσῃ) has vintners ... But Agesilaus (Ἀγησίλαος δὲ), thanks to his love of toil, enjoyed any drink that was at hand ... (Xenophon, *Ages.* 9.1–2 [Marchant and Bowersock, LCL])

Immediately evident, again, is the use of balanced μέν ... δέ clauses. Note also that just as in the *synkriseis* cited earlier, the grounds of each comparison are specified before being elaborated. Indeed, the structural similarity of these encomiastic comparisons with what we have seen in the progymnastic tradition is striking. And here, I suspect, we have a clue as to the generic conventions that would allow Meleager to produce a parodic *synkrisis* of peas and lentils. I imagine headings something like this, though certainly more humorous:

> Further, with regard to texture, peas and lentils compete valiantly for the prize: For while the one, when cooked, becomes so mushy as to render teeth unnecessary, the other, upon being boiled in a broth, resembles not so much victuals as sludge.

In fact, I like both lentils and peas. My point is simply that it is this sort of thing, not Paul's brief comparison of himself with his rivals, that would have been recognizable as a parody of the conventions of *synkrisis*.

Paul, of course, was not composing an oration; he was writing a letter. And so one could perhaps argue that the conventions for *synkrisis* I have highlighted would not have been relevant in the case of 2 Cor 10–13. From this perspective, Paul's comparison does not sound like the *synkriseis* of oratory or the *Progymnasmata* because it is presented in a style that befits letter writing, terser and less formal than the stuff of oratory. But this sort of argument does nothing to rehabilitate Forbes's reading of 2 Cor 11:21b–23 as a parodic *synkrisis*, since we have no evidence of epistolary *synkriseis* with defined characteristics predictable enough to make them amenable to parody.

More troublingly, this sort of argument leaves us in the awkward position of having derived our reading of the evidence from a prior conclusion. That is, having concluded that Paul was trained to compose rhetorical *synkriseis*, we have managed to find a way of explaining why he does not in fact do so. Surely it makes more sense first to consider the evidence—Paul compares himself with his rivals, and his comparison does not resemble a formal *synkrisis*—and then to reach our conclusion. A suitable conclusion, I think, would be that Paul's comparison of himself with his rivals does not evince knowledge of formal rhetorical practice.

In fact, there is a much simpler explanation than Paul's putative knowledge of rhetorical conventions for the fact that he compares himself with his rivals: he was competing with them. The situation simply demanded that he assert his superiority, and that is a task for which it is difficult to imagine a more obvious strategy than comparison.

8
Not a Fool, It's (Only) Irony

The assertion that Paul's boasting is (only) ironic is all but universal in current scholarship, and it undergirds a number of the rhetorical-critical readings treated above.[1] Whatever rhetorical measures Paul must resort to, we are told, they cannot be taken at face value; no, it is the deeper ironic meaning of Paul's rhetoric to which we must attend. From this perspective, Paul's boasting becomes anti-boasting, a devastating critique of his rivals—who, one is left to imagine, prattle on shamelessly of their accomplishments, and do so without a trace of irony. In other words, interpreting this text as irony allows Paul to have his cake and eat it too: His ironic self-commendation functions both to demonstrate his superiority as an apostle and to demonstrate the absurdity of the very self-commendation he undertakes.[2]

---

1. So esp. Holland, "Speaking Like a Fool"; Holland, *Divine Irony*, 137–49; Aida Besançon Spencer, "The Wise Fool (and the Foolish Wise): A Study of Irony in Paul," *NovT* 23 (1981): 349–60; J. A. Loubser, "A New Look at Paradox and Irony in 2 Corinthians 10–13," *Neot* 26 (1992): 507–21; McCant, *2 Corinthians*, 101–72; Witherington, *Conflict and Community in Corinth*, 442–64; Walker, *Paul's Offer of Leniency*, 299–318; Watson, "Paul's Boasting in 2 Corinthians 10–13," 265–66; Murphy-O'Connor, *Paul: A Critical Life*, 319–22; Marshall, *Enmity in Corinth*, 349–53; Savage, *Power through Weakness*, 63; Vegge, *A Letter about Reconciliation*, 332–37; Garland, *2 Corinthians*, 421–22.

2. Prior to the rise of this ironic reading, interpreters sought to resolve the apparent contradiction between Paul's own self-commendation and his denouncement of self-commendation by positing a theological dialectic. See Ernst Käsemann, "Die Legitimität des Apostels: Eine Untersuchung zu II Korinther 10–13," *ZNW* 41 (1942): 33–71; John H. Schütz, *Paul and the Anatomy of Apostolic Authority* (2nd ed.; NTL; Louisville: Westminster John Knox, 2007), 165–86; Hafemann, "Self-Commendation." Like the ironic interpretation we will discuss below, this is a needlessly convoluted reading. As I argued in the previous chapter, a simpler explanation—and one that

This would be a clever rhetorical strategy indeed.[3] The trouble is, Paul didn't use it. Although he does make isolated ironic statements in this passage, his boasting as a whole simply does not admit of an ironical reading. Paul explains exactly what he intends to do, and then he does it. This explicitness leaves no compass for irony. In the end, one suspects that the attribution to Paul of ironic intent derives not from cues in the text but rather from interpreters' incredulity that Paul could thus have praised himself in earnest.

Glenn Holland's Boastful Ironist

Undoubtedly the most thorough attempt to read 2 Cor 10–13 as an essentially ironic discourse is that of Glenn Holland. Irony is not easy to define, and Holland begins by taking us on an instructive foray into the nature of irony, wading through the sometimes murky waters of modern literary criticism.[4] Irony, he insists, is better understood through concrete instances than attempts at description. Still, he provides a useful working definition of the sort of irony that most interpreters attribute to Paul:

> As it is most commonly understood, irony is a rhetorical trope, that of saying one thing while meaning another.... The ironic interpretation arises out of a perception (and this perception may be communicated in different ways) that another meaning lies below the surface meaning, and that this second meaning, the ironic one, is the true one.[5]

---

makes better sense of the text—is that Paul sought to discount his rivals' "boasting" because it was his rivals', and thought his own was legitimate because it was his own.

3. According to Christopher Forbes and Tor Vegge, Paul's striking use of irony attests to his rhetorical sophistication—sophistication that can only have been achieved through formal rhetorical education (Forbes, "Comparison, Self-Praise, and Irony," 22–24; Vegge, *Paulus und das antike Schulwesen*, 418–23).

4. Holland, *Divine Irony*, 19–58.

5. Ibid., 20, 37–38. Holland discusses at some length whether irony inheres in authorial intention or in the evaluation of the reader, and, in short, equivocates—as can be seen from the odd notion in the quotation above of "communicating" a "perception." For our purposes, the whole debate is irrelevant: those who assert Pauline irony in 2 Cor 10–13 generally believe that by doing so they are saying something about the historical Paul and his intention. What I am asking is thus not whether the text can be read ironically—any text can—but whether Holland et al. are right to assert that Paul's boasting was self-consciously ironic.

This is a good description of what we may call (stable) verbal irony,[6] and Holland evokes it again when summarizing his reading of Paul's so-called "Fool's Speech":

> In the guise of the fool, Paul is free both to speak ironically and to draw his reader's attention to the fact that he is doing so. The whole concept of "speaking like a fool" invites the reader to look past the surface meaning of the text in order to find its deeper, true meaning.... Throughout these chapters Paul unabashedly presents matters from the divine perspective, exalting humility and suffering over human ideas of glory in an ironic tour de force.[7]

Tellingly, though, in treating Paul's alleged irony in 2 Cor 10–13, Holland does not in fact isolate an ironic from a "surface meaning."

Let me provide an example. Holland asserts that in describing his flight from Damascus (11:32–33) "Paul is being ironic, boasting about the cowardice that is part of his weakness."[8] But what Holland describes as the ironic meaning here is in fact the explicit surface meaning of the passage, for Paul had introduced the episode by explaining: "If I must boast, I will boast of the things that show my weakness" (v. 30). There is no irony here—that is, to use Holland's words, no meaning below the surface meaning—for Paul has flatly declared his intentions, paradoxical though they may be.[9] Glorying in episodes that display one's vulnerability may be counterintuitive, and Paul may indeed be "exalting humility and suffering over human ideas of glory," but he is not using irony to do so.[10]

---

6. Cf. *Rhet. Alex.* 21; Quintilian, *Inst.* 8.6.54. And see Wayne C. Booth, *A Rhetoric of Irony* (Chicago: University of Chicago Press, 1974).

7. Holland, *Divine Irony*, 138–39. I am grateful to Dr. Holland for his charitable and helpful remarks on an earlier draft of this section.

8. Ibid., 144.

9. F. R. Ankersmit provides a useful differentiation of paradox and irony: "When being ironical we ... expect the hearer or reader to see our point and to exchange what we say for what we really intended to express. But here irony differs from paradox. In the case of paradox semantic opposition should *not* be obliterated—as irony expects us to do—but has to be respected.... The secret of ... paradox lies in the requirement that neither of the two opposites yield to the other" (*Aesthetic Politics: Political Philosophy beyond Fact and Value* [Stanford, Calif.: Stanford University Press, 1996], 334).

10. Perhaps there would be irony here if, as E. A. Judge suggested, Paul intended to parody contemporary accounts of military daring: "If it is realised that everyone in antiquity would have known that the finest military award for valour was the *corona*

As Lee Johnson has shown, the same difficulty haunts Holland's broader assertion that Paul's "foolishness" constitutes an ironic stance: there simply is no compass for irony here, for Paul repeatedly makes his intention plain (11:1, 16–17).[11] Indeed, each step of the way, Paul gives his reader explicit guidance as to how his "boasting" should be construed. Paul begins by explaining that he is about to boast κατὰ σάρκα and warning his addressees not to take such boasting as if it were κατὰ κύριον (11:17–18). Then, precisely as in Phil 3:2–6, where too Paul explains his grounds for confidence κατὰ σάρκα, Paul lists his qualifications as an authentic representative of Judean piety.[12] When it comes to being a διάκονος Χριστοῦ, Paul offers yet another disclaimer (παραφρονῶν λαλῶ), and then explains, quite earnestly, just as in 1 Cor 15:10, that he is the hardest working of all the apostles (περισσότερον αὐτῶν πάντων ἐκοπίασα [1 Cor 15:10]; ἐν κόποις περισσοτέρως [2 Cor 11:23]). These κόποι are the grounds, apparently, on which he can claim to excel his rivals. But, in arguing his superiority as a διάκονος Χριστοῦ on these grounds, Paul finds himself making revelations that, he realizes, are hardly compelling indicators of authoritative status. Thus v. 30: "If I must boast, I will boast of the things that show my weakness." There is no irony here, just a man caught between a rock and a hard place.

According to Wayne Booth, the first step in detecting the ironic intent of an author is the recognition that the author cannot mean what he or she seems to mean—that is, the recognition that we are "required to reject the literal meaning."[13] A good example comes from 2 Cor 10–13

---

muralis, for the man who was first up the wall in the face of the enemy, Paul's point is devastatingly plain: he was first down" ("Educational Aims," 708; so also Holland, *Divine Irony*, 144). But this would be rather an opaque reference: the incident is narrated with economy, not the bombast one would expect from such a parody; there is nothing to suggest a military context; and, as Murray Harris notes, "the crucial element of 'firstness' is missing" (*Second Corinthians*, 824).

11. See Johnson, "The Epistolary Apostle," 218–19.

12. Thus, against Holland (*Divine Irony*, 141) there are no grounds for reading κατὰ σάρκα here as a reference to "human standards" in general, let alone the putatively worldly values of his rivals (cf. Winter, *Philo and Paul*, 234). On the telling parallel with Phil 3 here, see esp. Fitzgerald, "Cracks in an Earthen Vessel," 375–77.

13. Booth, *A Rhetoric of Irony*, 10. Booth is referring here to what he calls "stable irony," which he distinguishes from such "unstable irony" as resists the reconstruction of a final authorial perspective. Since Paul clearly expects the Corinthians to be able to reconstruct his perspective well enough—well enough, indeed, to obey him (cf. 13:2,

itself: When Paul asks, "Did I commit a sin by humbling myself so that you could be exalted?" (11:7), we must reject the notion that Paul intends this as a sincere question. Paul cannot really be seeking an answer to the question as stated, for the correct answer, when the issue is framed this way, is so obvious as to be laughable. The preposterousness of the question, then, changes our focus from the literal meaning to a "deeper," ironic meaning: Translated, rather flatly, into literal terms, what Paul is really asking is something like, "How can you treat my work on your behalf with such disdain?"[14]

In order to conclude that Paul's boasting is ironic, then, we should need some compelling reason to reject a literal interpretation. That is, there must be some indication that Paul cannot mean what he seems to mean: first, that he knows boasting is foolish, but that he feels compelled to do it anyway, and, second, that he has nowhere to take refuge except in apostolic labors that turn out, as indicators of his status, to be ambivalent at best. The fact that Paul manages to refigure his weaknesses into marks of divine strength (12:9–10) does not mean the whole passage is ironic. Rather—if I may risk another old saw—Paul has only lemons, so he makes lemonade.

Allow me briefly to elaborate. For many scholars, it seems that what finally renders this passage ironic is Paul's simultaneous claim to status and confession of weakness. From this perspective, the irony reaches a climax in what Holland calls Paul's "claim to superiority through nothingness" in 12:11b.[15] Again, though, it is difficult to locate an ironic signification. The

---

10)—unstable irony need not concern us. Paul knows quite precisely what he wants, and he expects the Corinthians to know too.

14. According to Forbes, Paul's irony here is tinged with what Hermogenes calls indignation (βαρύτης [Περὶ ἰδεῶν 2.8]), and thus reflects his knowledge of rhetorical theory ("Comparison, Self-Praise, and Irony," 17). The basic problem here is chronological: Hermogenes's discussion of style dates from the 2nd c., as does the similar discussion in the *Ars Rhetorica* falsely attributed to Aelius Aristides (1.2.1–2). See Kennedy, *Greek Rhetoric under Christian Emperors*, 70; Malcolm Heath, *Menander: A Rhetor in Context* (Oxford: Oxford University Press, 2004), 45–48. So, as I. Vegge correctly notes, there is no evidence for discussion of βαρύτης as a style of composition in Paul's time (*A Letter about Reconciliation*, 315). Any correspondence between Hermogenes's discussion and Paul's prose must be attributed to the fact that Hermogenes did a good job of his stated goal—namely, to describe what types of style speakers in fact use (1.1).

15. Holland, *Divine Irony*, 147–48.

"surface meaning" of the statement is clear enough. It has two clauses: (1) Paul claims that he is not inferior to his rivals; (2) Paul admits that he is nothing. I think it is quite clear that neither of these clauses demands an ironic interpretation. Paul does in fact think that he is not inferior to his rivals (cf. 2 Cor 10:7, 11:5), and his self-designation as "nothing" (οὐδέν) is not out of keeping with how he describes himself in texts where few would allege ironic intent (1 Cor 3:7; 15:8–10; cf. 1 Cor 1:28; Gal 6:3). Quite simply, in both clauses, Paul means exactly what he says.

Holland's analysis suggests that what he finds ironic here is in fact the relationship between these two clauses: "Paul can claim to be a better apostle precisely because he is more completely a nothing."[16] But I suspect the irony of juxtaposing these two apparently contradictory statements inheres not in Paul's perspective, but in Holland's. As a reader, Holland may find situational irony here—that is, it may be an ironic state of affairs, from Holland's perspective, that Paul can claim, in the same breath, to be both "nothing" and "not inferior"—but that does not mean *Paul* is being ironic.[17] On sober reflection, of course, Paul's statements are logically irreconcilable. But when speaking of matters like identity and dignity one is not usually concerned above all with propositional logic. Rather, these two statements pertain to two different realms wherein Paul negotiates his identity: Paul experiences himself as a Christ-filled "nothing"; he also is convinced that he is an apostle, and expects to be honored as such. Again, comparison with 1 Cor 15:9–10 is instructive:

> I am the least of the apostles, unfit to be called an apostle, because I persecuted the church of God. But by the grace of God I am what I am, and his grace toward me has not been in vain. On the contrary, I worked harder than any of them—though it was not I, but the grace of God that is with me.

Here too Paul is both the least and he is by no means inferior—and he certainly is not being ironic. I submit, then, that the paradoxical nature of Paul's "boasting" in 2 Cor 10–13 derives not from Pauline irony but rather

---

16. Ibid. Notice that Paul does not in fact assert the causal relationship between his superiority and his nothingness that Holland finds in this text (εἰ καὶ οὐδέν εἰμι), which is why his assertion that Paul's engages in Socratic irony here cannot be sustained.

17. On this distinction, see Booth, *A Rhetoric of Irony*, 9; David S. Kaufer, "Irony, Interpretive Form, and the Theory of Meaning," *Poetics Today* 4 (1983): 452.

from Paul's ongoing attempt to negotiate his controverted status as a disreputable apostle.

Disclaiming Boastfulness

Although recent interpreters of 2 Cor 10–13 have various emphases and approaches, the majority share a basic pattern of interpretation, an argumentative structure into which rhetorical criticism was co-opted and which rhetorical criticism now sponsors. It may be summarized as follows: Paul took up the rhetorical toolbox of his opponents in order to beat them at their own game; however, he did so *ironically*, and thereby deconstructed the worldly values of the Corinthians.[18]

This is an attractive interpretation. When we read this text ironically, we get a Paul who not only is sophisticated enough to outsmart his opponents, but also is humble enough to abstain from any straightforward participation in the quest for honor. He is the perfect Christian gentleman, if rather more passionate that most, responding with modesty, wit, and dignity to a challenging situation. But is this really the voice that speaks in 2 Cor 10–13? Given the long exegetical history of attempts to excuse Paul's behavior here, it is useful to remember Richard Levin's observation, cited by Holland himself: ironic interpretation is often suspiciously adept at defending authors from accusations of simple bad taste.[19]

Notice further how this mode of interpretation shapes the characterization of Paul the rhetor in current scholarship: Paul not only knows how to engage in *periautologia* but he can up the rhetorical ante by doing so ironically.[20] Paul is not only capable of composing a striking *peristasis* catalogue, but he can cleverly parody the genre.[21] Paul not only has mastered the art of *prosōpopoiia*, but he ironically has chosen to take on the

---

18. For particularly clear statements of the argument, see Forbes, "Comparison, Self-Praise, and Irony," 20; Harris, *Second Corinthians*, 792–93; Travis, "Paul's Boasting," 529–30.

19. Richard Levin, *New Readings vs. Old Plays: Recent Trends in the Reinterpretation of English Renaissance Drama* (Chicago: University of Chicago Press, 1979), 125–35; cited in Holland, *Divine Irony*, 34–35; cf. Booth, *A Rhetoric of Irony*, 82.

20. So Forbes, "Comparison, Self-Praise, and Irony," 20; Watson, "Paul's Boasting in 2 Corinthians 10–13," 271–74; Duling, "2 Corinthians 11:22," 829.

21. Travis, "Paul's Boasting," 529–30; Witherington, *Conflict and Community in Corinth*, 452.

persona of a fool.[22] Finally, not only can Paul put together a fine *synkrisis*, but he can deconstruct the form by selecting ironic criteria for comparison.[23] In short, the attribution of ironic intent has been used to make Paul not only a gifted rhetor but the consummate rhetor—and, moreover, the only person in Corinth who can see through the superficial formality and the childish boastfulness of the Greco-Roman rhetorical tradition. Indeed, it appears that one reason recent interpreters of 2 Cor 10–13 have found rhetorical criticism so attractive is that it provides, as *Spätjudentum* did until the recent crisis of conscience among New Testament scholars, a foil against which to highlight Paul's moral and intellectual superiority. In other words, the argument that Paul's boasting is ironic is not in fact exegetical but apologetic.

To understand the apologetic logic here, it is important to recognize that among the chief social functions of irony is its ability to allow speakers to say things "off-record" and thereby to save face.[24] Irony disassociates a speaker from his or her own words; it is, in the useful metaphor of Erving Goffmann, a framing device, signaling that a speaker "means to stand in a relation of reduced personal responsibility for what he is saying. He splits himself off from the content of his words by expressing that their speaker is not he himself in a serious way."[25] In other words, irony interrupts the easy assumption of listeners that what a speaker says is illustrative of her or his character. It does not take much time spent reading commentary on 2 Cor 10–13 to notice that, for centuries, interpreters have been eager precisely to distance Paul from the boastful speaker implied by the passage.[26] Attributing to him ironic intent is simply the latest in a series of such strategies.

---

22. Keener, *1–2 Corinthians*, 231.

23. Forbes, "Comparison, Self-Praise, and Irony," 2.

24. Erving Goffman, *Frame Analysis: An Essay on the Organization of Experience* (New York: Harper & Row, 1974), 514–15; Penelope Brown and Stephen C. Levinson, *Politeness: Some Universals in Language Usage* (Studies in Interactional Sociolinguistics 4; Cambridge: Cambridge University Press, 1987), 221–22, 262–65; Shelly Dews, Joan Kaplan, and Ellen Winner, "Why Not Say It Directly? The Social Functions of Irony," *Discourse Processes* 19 (1995): 347–67.

25. Goffman, *Frame Analysis*, 512. For an incisive analysis of irony from this perspective, see Rebecca Clift, "Irony in Conversation," *Language in Society* 28 (1999): 523–53.

26. See the beginning of ch. 4 above.

Notably, Paul himself does seek to disassociate himself from the implication that he is a boastful fool (cf. 2 Cor 11:1, 16–17, 21; 12:6, 11), but he uses a rather more explicit framing device—and one that, apparently, his interpreters have deemed ineffectual: the disclaimer. By repeatedly drawing attention to the fact that he is aware of the foolishness of his boasting, Paul goes, as it were, "off-record."

Disclaimers, as John Hewitt and Randall Stokes have observed, result from a basic element of social interaction: Those who listen to a speaker "typify" that speaker—that is, they make judgments concerning the speaker's character—on the basis of what is said, and, further, the speaker knows that this process of typification is underway.[27] Speakers use disclaimers, then, in an attempt to manipulate how they are typified. Hewitt and Stokes provide the standard definition:

> A disclaimer is a verbal device employed to ward off and defeat in advance doubts and negative typifications [of the speaker] which may result from intended conduct.... In each example, a specific utterance calls the other's attention to a *possible* undesired typification and asks forbearance. Each phrase, in effect, disclaims that the word or deed to follow should be used as a basis for identity challenge and re-typification.[28]

Paul's disclaimers, I submit, are textbook cases. I know boasting is foolish, he insists, but, now that you know I know this, you need not characterize me as a foolish boaster—even though I will go on to boast.[29] As Plummer rightly explained, without the benefit of all this theory, "[Paul] is anxious that the Corinthians should be aware that he recognizes the foolishness of self-praise, and that it is not his fault that he is guilty of it."[30]

Why, then, have interpreters not been content with Paul's own strategy for mitigating the negative characterization that could result from his boasting? Why have they found it necessary to attribute to Paul ironic

---

27. John P. Hewitt and Randall Stokes, "Disclaimers," *American Sociological Review* 40 (1975): 2–3.

28. Ibid., 3. Among their examples are: "I know this sounds stupid, but ..."; "This is just off the top of my head, so ..."; "I realize I'm being anthropomorphic ..."

29. Notice that this provides an explanation for Paul's introduction of the motif of "foolishness" that renders unnecessary Larry Welborn's suggestion that Paul's ἄφρων language was introduced into the discussion by Paul's rival (*An End to Enmity*, 155–58).

30. Plummer, *Second Epistle*, 313.

intent? Here I suspect the answer lies in the relative status that listeners attribute to speakers who use these two different framing strategies.

We have already considered the implications for characterizing Paul's voice of attributing to him ironic intent. Reading Paul's boasting as irony provides us with a Paul confident and secure in his own status. Yes, he is beleaguered, but he is sufficiently self-possessed to avoid the shameful spectacle of sincere self-promotion. Nor is he so vulnerable—so socially weak—that he must sacrifice his principles in order to assert his worth. This Paul remains firmly in control.

This is in keeping with the nature of ironic speech, which tends to project an air of superiority. According to Aristotle, those who speak in earnest get angry with ironists, for irony is inherently disdainful (καταφρονητικός [Rhet. 2.2.24–25]). Indeed, for Aristotle, it is precisely this capacity of irony to host its apparent opposite, ἀλαζονεία, that makes it a vice (Eth. nic. 4.7.15; cf. Quintilian, Inst. 11.1.21)[31]—though, when used in moderation, he sees irony as a mark of superior refinement (Eth. nic. 4.3.28; 4.7.16; Rhet. 3.18.7). Similarly, for more recent theorists, the "ironic position is always one of superior power, knowledge or authority."[32] An ironic speaker is detached or disinterested enough that he or she is willing to risk misunderstanding—that is, to risk that his or her hearers will miss the irony—and thus retains an aura of invulnerability.

In other words, one can boast ironically of weakness only if one can live with the potential consequence that a few boors will miss the irony and simply think that one is weak. Paul is apparently not secure enough in his position to leave such an interpretive option open (cf. 10:7–12; 11:5–6; 12:11; 13:1–4). So Paul uses the disclaimer, a framing strategy that avoids the risk of misinterpretation associated with irony.

The disclaimer, however, has its own risks. First, the repeated or habitual use of disclaimers is often associated by listeners with speakers who lack credibility and authority.[33] This stands to reason: why should speak-

---

31. See further P. W. Gooch, "Socratic Irony and Aristotle's Eiron: Some Puzzles," Phoenix 41 (1987): 97–99.

32. Andreea Ghita, "Negotiation of Irony in Dialogue," in Negotiation and Power in Dialogic Interaction (ed. Edda Weigand and Marcelo Dascal; Current Issues in Linguistic Theory 214; Philadelphia: John Benjamins, 2001), 140. Cf. Holland, Divine Irony, 59–60.

33. Robert A. Bell, Christopher J. Zahn, and Robert Hopper, "Disclaiming: A Test of Two Competing Views," Communication Quarterly 32 (1984): 28–36; Bonnie

ers use disclaimers unless they lack the confidence to say what they are going to say "on-record"? Disclaimers, then, project insecurity or heightened concern with how one will be viewed—precisely the opposite of the detachment and disdainful disregard for the perception of others that ironists project.

Second, it is not at all clear that disclaimers actually work—that is, that they prevent the negative characterization of speakers on the basis of what they say. One recent study suggests that people who preface a statement with "I don't mean to sound arrogant ..." only avoid such characterization if what they go on to say is not, in fact, particularly arrogant.[34] If such a disclaimer is followed by a statement of only modest self-praise, it appears to head off characterizations of arrogance. If, however, it is followed by what would otherwise be deemed shameless self-promotion, the disclaimer backfires, not only failing to prevent negative characterization, but even priming the pump by shaping the listener's expectations.

My point is this: Paul disclaims the foolishness that he fears his audience will attribute to him as a result of his boasting. As the history of interpretation demonstrates, many readers have not found his disclaimers entirely convincing, and have been somewhat troubled by what appears to be Paul's insecurity and concern for his own status. So, as the most recent move in a long apologetic tradition, interpreters have attributed to Paul a more refined rhetorical strategy, one that projects a more detached and self-possessed speaker—namely, irony. This may make for a more palatable Paul, but it obscures the voice that speaks in 2 Cor 10–13.

Conclusion

The burden of part 2 of this study has been to evaluate the evidence put forward by recent scholarship that Paul's rhetoric in 2 Cor 10–13 demonstrates his familiarity with the classical rhetorical tradition. As we have seen, this text does overlap in four limited ways with the theory and practice of the formal tradition of classical rhetoric: (1) Paul's boasting in 2

Erickson et al., "Speech Style and Impression Formation in a Court Setting: The Effects of 'Powerful' and 'Powerless' Speech," *Journal of Experimental Social Psychology* 14 (1978): 266–79.

34. Amani El-Alayli et al., "'I Don't Mean to Sound Arrogant, but ...': The Effects of Using Disclaimers on Person Perception," *Personality and Social Psychology Bulletin* 34 (2008): 130–43.

Cor 10–13 is reminiscent of two general aspects of ancient discussions of self-praise: It is better to be praised by others than to praise oneself; self-praise is appropriate when done in legitimate self-defense. Additionally, Paul uses strategies akin to what the rhetorical theorists referred to as (2) *prodiorthōsis*, and (3) *prosōpopoiia*. Finally, (4) he utilizes a catalogue style that also appears in some rhetorically trained writers.

However, on a close reading, the majority of the putative evidence simply evaporates:

(1) There is no evidence in 2 Cor 10–13 that Paul was familiar with the refinements of formal epistolary theory. What he did know of letter writing cannot be located with any confidence in the *enkyklios paideia* within which rhetorical training was undertaken.

(2) Arguments that Paul's "boasting" in this passage attests to his familiarity with ancient rhetorical conventions for self-praise (περιαυτολογία) fail on two counts: First, they depend upon a superficial and misleading reading of Plutarch's *De laude ipsius*, a reading that misconstrues the text as evidence for rhetorical conventions and thus overlooks the moral structure of Plutarch's argument. Second, and as a result, they fail to observe how different a social role Paul projects from the aristocratic role Plutarch commends. When one does compare Paul's boasting with Plutarch's recommendations, as well as with the practice of exemplary speakers like Demosthenes, it becomes clear that Paul's is not the sort of rhetoric Plutarch admires.

(3) Although Paul does employ stylistic features associated generally with catalogues, this cannot be attributed to his dependence on formal rhetorical tradition. According to some, Paul used the *peristasis* form, conventionally enough, to assert his status as an ideal sage; for others, Paul's boasting in weakness amounts to a parody, a *reductio ad absurdum* of his opponents' boasting in their achievements. The problem with both these interpretations is simple: there was no established form for Paul to utilize or to parody. Stylistic features associated with catalogues were common enough, but they appear in such widely divergent texts and to such widely divergent ends that to speak of a form is meaningless.

(4) There is no evidence that Paul's so-called "Fool's Speech" derives from literary or dramaturgical conventions. Nor it is possible to distinguish Paul's alleged *prosōpopoiia* or speech in the character of a fool from Paul's voice in the rest of the letter.

(5) Paul's comparison of himself with his rivals does not resemble a formal rhetorical *synkrisis*, and his use of the verb συγκρίνω cannot be

taken as a reference to the rhetorical device. Clearly not every comparison is a rhetorical *synkrisis*, and, when we look more carefully at the stylistic features of *synkrisis* in the *Progymnasmata* and encomiastic oratory, it becomes evident that Paul's comparative boasting does not participate in this rhetorical tradition.

(6) There are no cues in the text to suggest that Paul's boasting was intended ironically. Paul uses disclaimers, not irony, in his attempt to disassociate himself from the boastful fool his speech threatens to imply.

A further observation is perhaps of equal significance: We have not found in 2 Cor 10–13 what were for the ancients the essential indicators of *paideia*—refined diction, learned literary references, elegant use of conventional tropes and *topoi*, and elite moral and social values.[35] Indeed, a careful reading of Paul's letter against the backdrop of elite rhetorical discourse has begun to reveal a demeanor—a "voice"—that is strikingly different from that cultivated among the *pepaideumenoi*.

It is difficult, then, to sustain the argument that 2 Cor 10–13 shows Paul to have been the recipient of a formal rhetorical education. Quite simply, little compelling evidence for this proposition has been put forward—certainly nothing compelling enough to overturn the centuries of consensus on the matter we noted in chapter 1. Paul's putative rhetorical education is not a very good explanation for the peculiar nature of this text. How, then, can the long-observed rhetorical characteristics of this letter be explained? That is the question with which we will be concerned in part 3.

---

35. See ch. 3, n. 56 above for documentation.

Part 3
Rhetoric as Informal Social Practice

9
Toward a Theory of General Rhetoric

As part 2 of this study has demonstrated, there is very little evidence to support the claim that Paul received formal education in Greco-Roman rhetoric. Second Corinthians 10–13 is the text most often cited as evidence of Paul's rhetorical prowess, yet an examination of recent claims produced almost exclusively negative results. There are a few points of contact between Paul's letter and ancient rhetorical handbooks and exemplars, but much of the evidence adduced simply does not withstand scrutiny. Moreover, when Paul is read alongside the rhetoricians, it becomes increasingly clear that they are not part of the same discursive world. In sum, attributing to Paul a formal rhetorical education fails to explain the nature of Pauline discourse. It brings to light more idiosyncrasies than it resolves.

This leaves us with a puzzle: If they are not easily explained as resulting from formal rhetorical education, how are we to account for the presence in Paul's letters of rhetorical features like anaphora, *prosōpopoiia*, and *prodiorthōsis*? Further, how do we explain the fact that readers have, for centuries, found his prose peculiarly compelling? Is it possible to address these questions without reverting to romantic notions of "natural" eloquence or resorting to the unsatisfying conclusion that Paul's instinctive aptitude for rhetoric was simply unprecedented?[1]

In what follows, I will demonstrate that if Paul spoke persuasively despite lacking formal rhetorical education, he would by no means be unique. By invoking a number of comparators who clearly did not have formal training in classical rhetoric but nevertheless were forceful speakers and, moreover, used many of the figures and tropes codified in ancient

---

1. Cf. Mitchell, "Le style, c'est l'homme," 387–88: "As much as I agree with the evocative power of Paul's prose (both in antiquity and as attested by its history of reception), I cannot join what must ultimately be an apologetic argument for his complete uniqueness in this regard [by denying Paul's knowledge of contemporary rhetoric]."

rhetorical theory, I will provide the outlines of an alternative explanation for the nature of Paul's rhetoric: like many other such speakers, Paul learned rhetoric not as curriculum but as informal social practice.

A Theory of General Rhetoric

"After spending much of my professional life teaching rhetoric, I began to wonder what I was talking about."[2] So George Kennedy, eminent historian of classical rhetoric and guide for New Testament scholars pursuing the topic,[3] began a late-career odyssey, probing behind the Greek rhetorical tradition and seeking to describe the "general rhetoric" that constitutes all human communication. And not only human communication; no, what particularly fascinated Kennedy was the comparability of human persuasion to the rudimentary rhetorical activity of all living things—rhetoric from growls to birdsong. Rhetoric, Kennedy observed, was favored by evolution because it was less energy-intensive than fight or flight.[4] Two red deer stags competing for a mate could fight it out, but their species would be more likely to survive if they were to roar at each other instead, the stronger eventually convincing the weaker to back down.[5] Human political rhetoric may be more complex than this, but, Kennedy observed, it serves a comparable evolutionary function.

---

2. George A. Kennedy, "A Hoot in the Dark: The Evolution of General Rhetoric," in *Rhetoric: Concepts, Definitions, Boundaries* (ed. William A. Covino and David A. Jolliffe; Boston: Allyn & Bacon, 1995), 105; repr. from *Philosophy and Rhetoric* 25 (1992).

3. Kennedy's authoritative treatments of classical rhetoric include *The Art of Persuasion in Greece* (Princeton, N.J.: Princeton University Press, 1963); *The Art of Rhetoric in the Roman World, 300 B.C.–A.D. 300* (History of Rhetoric 2; Princeton, N.J.: Princeton University Press, 1972); *Greek Rhetoric under Christian Emperors* (History of Rhetoric 3; Princeton, N.J.: Princeton University Press, 1983. He has provided translations of everything from Aristotle (*On Rhetoric: A Theory of Civic Discourse* [2nd ed.; New York: Oxford University Press, 2007]) to the *Progymnasmata* (*Progymnasmata: Greek Textbooks of Prose Composition and Rhetoric* [WGRW 10; Atlanta: Society of Biblical Literature, 2003]). And he helped initiate rhetorically sensitive readings of the New Testament with his *New Testament Interpretation through Rhetorical Criticism* (Studies in Religion; Chapel Hill: University of North Carolina Press, 1984).

4. Kennedy, "A Hoot in the Dark," 112–13.

5. Ibid., 108; Kennedy, *Comparative Rhetoric*, 13–14.

Kennedy followed up an initial exploratory article with *Comparative Rhetoric*, a wide-ranging survey that begins with a reiteration of his discoveries concerning animal communication, continues on to a consideration of various nonliterate cultures, and proceeds to treat ancient Chinese and Indian rhetoric before revisiting the Greco-Roman tradition. Kennedy analyzes all of this material using the categories of the classical tradition—not, he admitted, because they were necessarily the most adequate, but simply because they were what he had been bequeathed.[6]

Thus Kennedy found, for example, that deliberative rhetoric is "a universal genre," whereas Western formulations of judicial and epideictic rhetoric are not particularly helpful for describing speech outside of the Western tradition.[7] Enthymemes are frequently found in traditional societies; however, complex chains of logical arguments seem to appear only in literate societies.[8] Arguments from *ethos*, *pathos*, and *logos* appear in various forms in all societies.[9] And even animals use such rhetorical devices as repetition, anaphora, homoioteleuton, and hyperbole.[10]

What this all amounts to, of course, is a fundamental redefinition of rhetoric.[11] Rhetoric can no longer be thought of as a particular quality *added* to speech—and certainly not as something the Greeks invented. It is in fact *prior* to speech, perhaps identifiable with the "energy" that inheres in a communicative act—"the emotional energy that impels the speaker to speak, the physical energy expended in the utterance, the energy level coded in the message, and the energy experienced by the recipient in decoding the message."[12] Therefore, although rhetoric certainly is culturally conditioned, it also contains universal elements that are shared among humans in general and even with our evolutionary forebears.[13]

---

6. Kennedy, *Comparative Rhetoric*, 5–6; Kennedy, "A Hoot in the Dark," 115. See further the section "Categories for Comparison" that concludes this chapter.

7. Kennedy, *Comparative Rhetoric*, 220–22.

8. Ibid., 224.

9. Ibid., 223–24; see also Kennedy, "A Hoot in the Dark," 116.

10. Kennedy, "A Hoot in the Dark," 117–19.

11. Cf. Christian Meyer, "Precursors of Rhetoric Culture Theory," in *Culture and Rhetoric* (ed. Ivo A. Strecker and Stephen A. Tyler; Studies in Rhetoric and Culture 1; New York: Berghahn Books, 2009), 40–42.

12. Kennedy, "A Hoot in the Dark," 106; see also Kennedy, *Comparative Rhetoric*, 215–16.

13. Kennedy, "A Hoot in the Dark," 115.

The perspective gained from this foray into cross-cultural comparison reaffirmed for Kennedy the conception of the classical tradition that he already had proffered in his *New Testament Interpretation through Rhetorical Criticism*: what was "unique" about the Greco-Roman tradition was not its use of rhetoric but rather its extensive theorization thereof.[14] In other words, the ancients' study of rhetoric was descriptive before it was prescriptive.

But this is not a novel claim. In fact, it coheres perfectly with Aristotle's own description of his project in the *Rhetoric*: to observe and theorize the reasons why speakers succeed in persuasion (1.1). Aristotle takes for granted that rhetoric is, "to a certain extent, within the knowledge of all people" (1.1 [trans. Kennedy]). Some utilize rhetoric "at random" (εἰκῇ), others "through an ability acquired by habit" (διὰ συνήθειαν ἀπὸ ἕξεως [1.2]). Aristotle's theorization is meant to provide a third way, "a path" to eloquence—rhetoric as an art (τέχνη [1.2]; cf. Plato, *Gorg.* 465A).[15]

Aristotle is by no means the only ancient theorist to have recognized that rhetoric is practiced independently of theoretical knowledge. Quintilian has a special interest in insisting that "no man can be an orator untaught" (*Inst.* 2.17.12 [Butler, LCL]);[16] still, his description of the origin of rhetoric parallels what we saw in Aristotle:

> It was ... nature that created speech, and observation that originated the art of speaking. Just as men discovered the art of medicine by observing that some things were healthy and some the reverse, so they observed that some things were useful and some useless in speaking, and noted them for imitation or avoidance. (3.2.3 [LCL])

---

14. Kennedy, *Comparative Rhetoric*, 218; Kennedy, *New Testament Interpretation*, 10–11. So, likewise, Peter L. Osterreich, "Homo Rhetoricus," in *Culture and Rhetoric* (ed. Ivo A. Strecker and Stephen A. Tyler; Studies in Rhetoric and Culture 1; New York: Berghahn Books, 2009), 49–50; Classen, *Rhetorical Criticism*, 28.

15. Mastery of a τέχνη, we might remember, consists for Aristotle not merely of competence, which can also be acquired by experience, but by theoretical knowledge—knowledge of the reasons for success or failure (*Metaph.* 1.981a–b). See further Alan G. Gross, "What Aristotle Meant by Rhetoric," in *Rereading Aristotle's* Rhetoric (ed. Alan G. Gross and Arthur E. Walzer; Carbondale: Southern Illinois University Press, 2000), 27–33. On the ensuing discussion among philosophers and rhetorical theorists, see David Roochnik, "Is Rhetoric an Art?" *Rhetorica* 12 (1994): 127–54.

16. See esp. Michael Winterbottom, "Quintilian and the *vir bonus*," *JRS* 54 (1964): 96.

Moreover, Quintilian grudgingly concedes the observation attributed to Lysias "that uneducated persons, barbarians and slaves, when speaking on their own behalf, say something that resembles an *exordium*, state the facts of the case, prove, refute and plead for mercy just as an orator does in his peroration" (2.17.6; cf. 2.11.7).[17] And, presented with Demades, a real-live example of a boatman cum orator (cf. Sextus Empiricus, *Math.* 2.16–17), Quintilian waffles, making an admission that nearly undercuts the premise of his pedagogical project: "It is quite uncertain that he never studied rhetoric and in any case continuous practice in speaking was sufficient to bring him to such proficiency as he attained: for experience is the best of all schools" (2.17.12).

Cicero sounds the same note in his presentation of his mentor Crassus. In *De Oratore*, Crassus admits that since he entered into the fray of the courtroom at an early age he himself did not receive the sort of rhetorical education he would now recommend: "In fact public life was my education, and practical experience of the laws and institutions of the state and the custom of the country was my schoolmaster" (3.20.74–75 [Sutton and Rackham, LCL]; cf. Isocrates, *Soph.* 14–15). Cicero himself, like Quintilian, is convinced that true eloquence generally derives from careful training, but he acknowledges that prior to the influence of Greek teachers budding orators had no choice but to learn as Crassus had—relying on their own *ingenium* and *cogitatio* (1.4.14; cf. *Inv.* 1.2.2–3).[18]

Moreover, like Aristotle, Cicero takes for granted that the practice of rhetoric precedes its theorization. His Crassus initially dismisses as a matter of mere semantics the contentious question whether oratory is an art (1.23.107), but eventually he opines:

> If ... the actual things noticed in the practice and conduct of speaking have been heeded and recorded by men of skill and experience, if they have been defined in terms, illuminated by classification, and distributed under subdivisions ... I do not understand why this should not be regarded as an art. (1.23.109)

---

17. Quintilian also notes a number of specific figures that occur "naturally" in uneducated speech: emphasis (8.3.86), metaphor (8.6.4), allegory (8.6.51), and hyperbole (8.6.75). See Elaine Fantham, "The Concept of Nature and Human Nature in Quintilian's Psychology and Theory of Instruction," *Rhetorica* 13 (1995): 132.

18. See further Elaine Fantham, *The Roman World of Cicero's* De Oratore (Oxford: Oxford University Press, 2004), 78–82.

In sum, then, for Cicero's Crassus, "Eloquence is not the offspring of the art, but the art of eloquence" (1.32.146; cf. 3.197; Philodemus, *Rhet.* 2.28; Longinus, *Subl.* 18.2; 22.1; Quintilian, *Inst.* 8.3.86).

Some centuries later, Augustine echoed this conclusion (*Doct. chr.* 4.3.4 [PL 34:91]), using the acquisition of grammar as an analogy for the process by which rhetorical capacity can be learned even without formal education:

> As infants cannot learn to speak except by learning words and phrases from those who do speak, why should not men become eloquent without being taught any art of speech? ... For even the art of grammar, which teaches correctness of speech, need not be learnt by boys, if they have the advantage of growing up and living among men who speak correctly. For without knowing the names of any of the faults, they will, from being accustomed to correct speech, lay hold upon whatever is faulty in the speech of any one they listen to, and avoid it. (4.3.5 [PL 34:91; *NPNF*¹ 2:575–76]).

Augustine would, it appears, concur with the conclusion of Mark Edwards:

> To prove that [the New Testament authors] had enjoyed [rhetorical] education, we should need to do more than demonstrate the presence in their writings of such figures as anaphora, hyperbole, asyndeton or litotes; such terms, like those of grammar, merely codify the practices in which most competent speakers of a language will engage before they have learned to give a name to them.[19]

In other words, before it is theory, rhetoric is social practice, and thus is learned as one learns any social practice, through a process of observation and imitation—a process we will explore in more detail in chapter 11 below.

Still, as Peter Osterreich observes, "the universality of rhetoric does not imply that every human being is a well-versed orator."[20] There *is* a difference between the educated and uneducated speaker, not least because the codification of rhetoric, together with the value judgments that attend such codification,[21] creates canons of speech, conventional

---

19. Edwards, "Gospel and Genre," 51.
20. Osterreich, "Homo Rhetoricus," 50.
21. Aristotle's initial codification looks like an attempt to control the unruly power of speech by valuing *logos* above *pathos* (*Rhet.* 1.1.4–6; 2.22.3; 3.14.7–8)—

expectations on the part of auditors. In other words, speech practices are culturally defined—and among the cultural gatekeepers we find teachers of eloquence.

We can, then, theoretically distinguish three sources of rhetorical practice: (1) the general human capacity for persuasive speech—Kennedy's "general rhetoric"; (2) the culturally-conditioned norms, constituent of what Pierre Bourdieu calls the *habitus*,[22] that pervade the speech patterns of any given group—what I will call "informal rhetoric"; (3) the formally codified rhetoric taught by and to the cultural elite, which, it should be noted, can influence rhetorical practice either directly, through formal education, or indirectly, by means of the influence it exerts on broader cultural practices.

Distinguishing what is universal from what is culturally conditioned is no easy matter.[23] Repetition, as its appearance among all manner of living thing indicates, is a device belonging to general rhetoric, whereas the use of asyndeton requires particular grammatical circumstances and thus cannot be universal. Still, perhaps asyndeton is a particular instantiation of a general rhetorical tendency. And what of the *partes orationis*? To what extent did such elite speech patterns influence the "informal rhetoric" of the Greco-Roman world? Or do they too instantiate a universal persuasive tendency, and thus recur outside of the classical tradition? Finally, particularly pressing for an understanding of Paul's rhetoric in 2 Cor 10–13, what about the use of *prodiorthōsis*?

The comparative and synthetic research necessary for a thoroughgoing theory of general rhetoric has not yet been undertaken. But what clearly cannot be sustained is the facile assumption that Paul's use of rhetorical strategies is in itself evidence of formal rhetorical education. To make that argument, one would need first to determine what, particularly, distinguished formal Greco-Roman rhetoric from other instances of human persuasion as well as from the informal rhetoric of the Greco-Roman

---

which is why, as Carol Poster has noted, Aristotle himself repeatedly "disavows the very techniques he explicates" ("Aristotle's *Rhetoric* against Rhetoric: Unitarian Reading and Esoteric Hermeneutics," *AJP* 118 [1997]: 240). Likewise, if Edward Schiappa is correct, the origins of the word *rhetoric* itself. See "Did Plato Coin *Rhētorikē*?" *AJP* 111 (1990): 457–70.

22. See pp. 250–51 below.

23. Cf. Mary Douglas, *Natural Symbols: Explorations in Cosmology* (London: Barrie & Rockliff, 1970), 69.

world, and then to identify these distinguishing factors in Paul's letters. This has not even been tried, let alone accomplished.

In the absence of a more general theory differentiating formal from informal rhetoric, I will use a series of comparators to test, on a case-by-case basis, the claim that what Paul knew about rhetoric must have been learned in school. If the rhetorical strategies to which Pauline scholars have recently drawn our attention are equally attested in uneducated speakers, then they must belong to the realm of either informal or general rhetoric, and thus, in the absence of other indicators of Paul's familiarity with formal classical rhetoric,[24] they provide no evidence that Paul received a formal rhetorical education.

The simplest way to proceed, of course, would be to use comparators from Paul's own milieu, speakers with no formal education but whose usage was shaped by the same informal rhetorical traditions as shaped Paul's. Unfortunately, we are lacking in such comparative material. By far the majority of extant texts—and particularly those that can be said to make an argument—derive from the educated elite. Thus I will introduce comparators from a variety of other speech communities, focusing in particular on the Iroquois orator Red Jacket and the tradition of Native American oratory to which he attests. The disadvantage of such a procedure is that it is unable to give us direct leverage on the informal rhetorical tradition of Paul's world. It does, however, serve as an effective *reductio ad absurdum* of the logic that currently sponsors claims of Paul's rhetorical education: If Red Jacket uses *prodiorthōsis*, for example, as effectively as does Paul, then the figure can hardly serve as evidence of formal training in classical rhetoric.[25]

Rhetoric in the New World

Kennedy is the most systematic student of comparative rhetoric to date; however, as is evident from his own chapter on Native American oratory, he is certainly not the first. With the European "discovery" of the

---

24. As documented above (ch. 3 n. 56), recent work on the nature of *paideia* in the ancient world suggests the following as a list of potential such indicators: specific patterns of refined diction, learned literary references, elegant use of conventional tropes and *topoi*, and elite moral and social values.

25. On the logic and function of these comparisons, see further the introduction to this volume.

New World came exposure to cultures that were at once strange and yet strangely familiar, and, in the resulting protoethnographic discourse of similarity and difference, indigenous rhetoric—and, in particular, its comparability to Western rhetorical practice—often took center stage.[26] Expressions of surprise at the eloquence of the "unschooled savages"—eloquence that was often said to rival the best of the newly rediscovered classical tradition—became commonplace among observers Spanish, French, and British alike.[27]

In his *The Florida of the Inca*, published in 1605, Garcilaso de la Vega, after expressing doubt that the eloquent speeches reported to him could possibly have come from "barbarian" lips, is rebuffed by his informant, who ensures him that the speeches he heard were indeed so eloquent that "many Spaniards well read in history" could not but conclude that the speakers "appeared to have been trained in Athens when it was flourishing in moral letters."[28] The *Jesuit Relations* too are peppered with admiring references to the eloquence of First Nations speakers. Paul le Jeune, for example, praised an Ottawa *capitaine* who spoke "with a keenness and

---

26. See esp. Edna C. Sorber, "The Noble Eloquent Savage," *Ethnohistory* 19 (1972): 227–36. Also Don Paul Abbott, *Rhetoric in the New World: Rhetorical Theory and Practice in Colonial Spanish America* (Studies in Rhetoric/Communication; Columbia: University of South Carolina Press, 1996), 9; and, more generally, Andreas Motsch, *Lafitau et l'émergence du discours ethnographique* (Sillery, Québec: Septentrion, 2001), 7–8.

27. See Kennedy, *Comparative Rhetoric*, 84; Charles Camp, "American Indian Oratory in the White Image: An Analysis of Stereotypes," *Journal of American Culture* 1 (1978): 811–12; William M. Clements, *Oratory in Native North America* (Tucson: University of Arizona Press, 2002), 4–12; Sorber, "The Noble Eloquent Savage," 228–230; Christian Meyer, *"Mahnen, Prahlen, Drohen ...": Rhetorik und politischen Organisation amerikanischer Indianer* (Frankfurt: IKO-Verlag für Interkulturelle Kommunikation, 2005), 38–46. In addition to what follows, other striking examples include Amos Stoddard, *Sketches, Historical and Descriptive, of Louisiana* (Philadelphia: Carey, 1812), 431–33; Elijah M. Haines, *The American Indian (Uh-nish-in-na-ba)* (Chicago: Massinnagan, 1888), 498–517; "Indian Eloquence," *The Knickerbocker, or the New-York Monthly Magazine* 7, no. 4 (April 1836): 385–90; and, more recently, Lois E. Buswell, "The Oratory of the Dakota Indians," *QJS* 21 (1935): 323–27; Louis Thomas Jones, *Aboriginal American Oratory: The Tradition of Eloquence among the Indians of the United States* (Los Angeles: Southwest Museum, 1965).

28. Garcilaso de la Vega, *The Florida of the Inca* (trans. John Grier Varner and Jeannette Johnson Varner; Austin: University of Texas Press, 1951), 160; cited in Kennedy, *Comparative Rhetoric*, 84.

delicacy of rhetoric that might have come out of the schools of Aristotle or Cicero."[29] And Thomas Jefferson famously praised Native American "eminence in oratory," singling out Logan's speech to Lord Dunmore: "I may challenge the whole orations of Demosthenes and Cicero, and of any more eminent orator, if Europe has furnished more eminent, to produce a single passage, superior to the speech of Logan."[30]

None of this, of course, represents disinterested academic appraisal. As Edna Sorber has shown, admiration for "Indian eloquence" in North America remains deeply implicated in the romantic idea of the "Noble Savage."[31] It has also been politically useful. "Aestheticization" of Native American oratory has served to draw attention away from its political content and context—land claims, often—and highlighted instead its nostalgic pathos.[32] Accordingly, surrender speeches and swansongs have long been particularly popular fare.[33] The anonymous writer of "Indian Eloquence," for example, contributing to *The Knickerbocker* in 1836, predicted that these great orations, "heightened ... in impressiveness by the melancholy accompaniment of approaching extermination, will be as enduring as the swan-like music of Attic and Roman eloquence, which was the funeral song of the liberties of those republics."[34]

Paradoxically, then, the motif of "Indian eloquence" has served as justification for dispossession: It was precisely the "primitiveness" of Native American speech, its apparent freedom from the artificial constraints of

---

29. Reuben Gold Thwaites, ed., *The Jesuit Relations and Allied Documents: Travels and Explorations of the Jesuit Missionaries in New France, 1610–1791* (73 vols.; New York: Pageant, 1959), 5:205. See further William M. Clements, *Native American Verbal Art: Texts and Contexts* (Tucson: University of Arizona Press, 1996), 53–72.

30. Thomas Jefferson, *Notes on the State of Virginia* (Richmond, Va.: Randolph, 1853), 67.

31. Sorber, "The Noble Eloquent Savage."

32. See David Murray, *Forked Tongues: Speech, Writing, and Representation in North American Indian Texts* (Bloomington: Indiana University Press, 1991), 40–44; Thomas H. Guthrie, "Good Words: Chief Joseph and the Production of Indian Speech(es), Texts, and Subjects," *Ethnohistory* 54 (2007): 509–46; Barbara Alice Mann, "Introduction," in *Native American Speakers of the Eastern Woodlands: Selected Speeches and Critical Analyses* (ed. Barbara Alice Mann; Westport, Conn.: Greenwood Press, 2001), xiii.

33. See Guthrie, "Good Words," 528–31.

34. "Indian Eloquence," 390.

form, that appealed to many European Americans[35]—and what is primitive, they reasoned, is destined for decay. And so, according to the logic of their European interlocutors, "The more eloquently they spoke, often uttering their own elegies, the more certain was their passing."[36]

So, the notion of Native American eloquence was romanticized, and it was a convenient salve for colonial consciences. That does not mean it was baseless. As William Clements observes, "One obvious reason that the image of the American Indian as a skilled orator appears so often is because it is accurate."[37] Eloquence is, of course, a difficult thing to quantify, but it would be difficult to deny the rhetorical power of the speeches to which we have access, particularly when we are guided by readers who understand the traditional rhetorical practices these speeches reflect, as well as the political exigencies they addressed.[38] And we should not be surprised to encounter rhetorical prowess among the indigenous peoples of North America: as Kennedy notes, a vital tradition of oratory is an important aspect of social organization in many nonliterate cultures, and

---

35. So Stoddard, *Sketches, Historical and Descriptive, of Louisiana*, 432: "Who at this day, except the untutored sons of nature, can utter the language of Ossian and Homer? What man, trammeled with the forms of modern art, can speak like Logan …? The language of nature can alone arrest attention, persuade, convince, and terrify; and such is the language of the Indians." See further Hoxie Neale Fairchild, *The Noble Savage: A Study in Romantic Naturalism* (New York: Columbia University Press, 1928), 441–97; Clements, *Oratory*, 8–9.

36. Guthrie, "Good Words," 536; cf. Mann, "Introduction," xiv; Murray, *Forked Tongues*, 34–47.

37. Clements, *Oratory*, 4.

38. For examples of such culturally, historically, and rhetorically sensitive readings of Native American speeches, see esp. Barbara Alice Mann, ed., *Native American Speakers of the Eastern Woodlands: Selected Speeches and Critical Analyses* (Westport, Conn.: Greenwood Press, 2001); Granville Ganter, "'Make Your Minds Perfectly Easy': Sagoyewatha and the Great Law of the Haudensoaunee," *Early American Literature* 44 (2009): 121–27; Richard A. Ek, "Red Cloud's Cooper Union Address," *Central States Speech Journal* 17 (1966): 257–62; Walter Hochbruck, "'I Ask for Justice': Native American Fourth of July Orations," in *The Fourth of July: Political Oratory and Literary Reactions, 1776–1876* (ed. Paul Goetsch and Gerd Hurm; Tübingen: Nurr, 1992), 155–67. Outstanding analyses of the rhetoric of Native American narrative appear in Joel Sherzer and Anthony C. Woodbury, eds., *Native American Discourse: Poetics and Rhetoric* (Cambridge Studies in Oral and Literate Culture 13; Cambridge: Cambridge University Press, 1987).

particularly in those societies that depend upon consensus and negotiation for political decision-making.[39]

But the majority of early European observers noticed no forest of rhetorical culture, only the individual trees of unexpectedly articulate orators. What they expected from savages was ululation, not argument,[40] hence their ongoing surprise at the power of Native American speech. Seeing no evidence of formal education, and unable to imagine any other rational explanation for the phenomenon, they resorted to romanticism: This was the pure speech of those untainted by the corruptions of formalism or of civilization itself. This was the eloquence of the Noble Savage.

European expressions of surprise at Native American eloquence, like the subsequent romanticizing thereof, are thus emblematic of the discomfiting interruption of the modern Western assumption that culture equals literate culture. In the Western imagination, texts, as Walter Ong explains, "have clamored for attention so peremptorily that oral creations have tended to be regarded generally as variants of written productions, or, if not this, as beneath serious scholarly attention."[41] Only the literate can study;[42] and it is study, we have assumed, that enables the production of meaningful discourse. Already Garcilaso de la Vega had internalized his colonizers' assumption:

> I plead now that this account be received in the same spirit as I present it, and that I be pardoned its errors because I am an Indian. For since we Indians are a people who are ignorant and uninstructed in the arts and sciences, it seems ungenerous to judge our deeds and utterances strictly in accordance with the precepts of those subjects which we have not learned.[43]

---

39. Kennedy, *Comparative Rhetoric*, 63. Cf. Clements, *Oratory*, 5–6; Meyer, *Mahnen, Prahlen, Drohen*, 46. For an excellent introduction to this aspect of Iroquois life, see Alan Taylor, *The Divided Ground: Indians, Settlers, and the Northern Borderland of the American Revolution* (New York: Knopf, 2006), 18–28.

40. See Clements, *Native American Verbal Art*, 4. Cf. J. Niles Hubbard, *An Account of Sa-go-ye-wat-ha, or Red Jacket, and his People, 1750–1830* (Albany, N.Y.: Munsell, 1886), 14.

41. Walter J. Ong, *Orality and Literacy: The Technologizing of the Word* (London: Routledge, 2002), 8.

42. Ibid., 8–9.

43. Vega, *The Florida of the Inca*, xlv.

The response of European observers to Native American oratory parallels tellingly, I think, the history of the (Western) interpretation of Pauline discourse. As noted in part 1, nineteenth-century scholars were well aware that Paul's letters did not belong amid the great literature of the classical tradition. Paul's prose just wasn't literary. It was, however, strangely powerful. Like Europeans encountering Native American oratory, biblical and classical scholars had no rational explanation for this unliterary yet forceful discourse, thus they resorted to romanticism: Paul's was a natural rhetoric, untainted by formalism; Paul's was the "rhetoric of the heart."

Recent Pauline scholarship has decried the romanticism of an earlier era but has failed adequately to question the continuing presupposition that eloquence is the exclusive preserve of formal literate culture. Pauline discourse is striking, we observe, hence Paul must have been formally educated. Like Europeans in the New World, we still have trouble believing that those without formal Western education could say something worthwhile, let alone do so persuasively.

Categories for Comparison

George Kennedy's decision to retain the terminology of Greco-Roman rhetoric has consistently been the most criticized aspect of his comparative project; for, although he insisted that he had no desire to impose Western categories on other cultures,[44] critics have been suspicious of "unexamined ethnocentrism" and of a methodology that "teeters dangerously on the edge of a comparison that smacks of the logic of Orientalism."[45] Indeed, the fledgling discipline of comparative rhetoric appears to be mired in a methodological quagmire: comparison requires the use of a single analytical grid, but the use of a grid external to the culture being analyzed is potentially distorting.[46] (Moreover, in some academic climates,

---

44. Kennedy, *Comparative Rhetoric*, 5–6.

45. Mary M. Garrett, review of George A. Kennedy, *Comparative Rhetoric: An Historical and Cross-Cultural Introduction*, *Rhetorica* 16 (1998): 432; LuMing Mao, "Reflective Encounters: Illustrating Comparative Rhetoric," *Style* 37 (2003): 411. See also Xing Lu, "Studies and Development of Comparative Rhetoric in the U. S. A.: Chinese and Western Rhetoric in Focus," *China Media Research* 2 (2006): 113; Sue Hum and Arabella Lyon, "Recent Advances in Comparative Rhetoric," in *The SAGE Handbook of Rhetorical Studies* (ed. Andrea A. Lunsford; Los Angeles: Sage, 2009), 154–55.

46. See further Mary M. Garrett, "Some Elementary Methodological Reflections on the Study of the Chinese Rhetorical Tradition," in *Rhetoric in Intercultural Contexts*

cross-cultural comparison is itself a minefield: observation of difference is easily interpreted as allegation of deficiency; observation of similarity is seen as an attempt to impose hegemonic universals upon diversity.) It is important, then, for me to be clear about what precisely I intend by using the categories of Greco-Roman rhetoric to frame a comparison between Paul and speakers from other cultures.

As Jonathan Z. Smith observes in his *Drudgery Divine*, a manifesto of sorts on the nature of comparison, "there is nothing 'natural' about the enterprise of comparison. Similarity and difference are not 'given.' They are the result of mental operations."[47] Comparison—or, more broadly, analogical reasoning—is an important mode of human thought,[48] one means of imposing structure and meaning on the world. Similarity and difference, then, inhere not in the things that are being compared but in the conceptualizing processes of the person who compares them. In the academy, that person is the scholar. As Smith explains, "Comparison ... brings differences together within the space of the scholar's mind for the scholar's own intellectual reasons."[49]

My intellectual reasons for undertaking the comparisons I do have been explained repeatedly throughout the course of this study: Current scholarship asserts that Paul was well trained in rhetoric, an assertion built on a comparison between Paul's letters (x) and exemplars of Greco-Roman rhetorical theory and practice (y), where x is shown to resemble y. But such a dyadic expression of resemblance is, as Smith notes, logically incomplete. Its full articulation would demand the introduction of a third term and the explication of the grounds of comparison: Paul's letters (x) resemble exemplars of educated rhetoric (y) *more than* do attempts at persuasion by uneducated speakers (z) *with respect to* the use of rhetorical invention, arrangement, and style.[50] Thus, in the first place, I undertake

---

(ed. Alberto González and Dolores V. Tanno; International and Intercultural Communication Annual 22; Thousand Oaks, Calif.: Sage, 1999), 54.

47. Smith, *Drudgery Divine*, 50–51.

48. For a survey of recent research, see Robert E. Haskell, "The Access Paradox in Analogical Reasoning and Transfer: Whither Invariance?" *Journal of Mind and Behavior* 30 (2009): 36–37. I am indebted here to James Contastine Hanges, "'Severing the Joints and the Marrow': The Double-Edged Sword of Comparison" (paper presented at the annual meeting of the Society of Biblical Literature, Altanta, Ga., 22 November 2010).

49. Smith, *Drudgery Divine*, 51.

50. Ibid.

comparison with other speakers in order to introduce the necessary third term (z) into the comparison, falsifying the argument by demonstrating that, in regard to formal rhetorical conventions, x resembles y no more than z resembles y.

Accordingly, my argument is not that the rhetoric of Red Jacket, for example, is an instance of Greco-Roman rhetorical theory in unconscious application. Rather, I argue that in the same way that Paul's rhetoric is analogous to the formal Greco-Roman tradition, so also is that of Red Jacket and other speakers. This is a subtle but an important distinction, for it creates space for an analysis of the rhetoric of both Paul and Red Jacket on their own terms, without assuming that formal Greco-Roman rhetorical categories best describe their arts of persuasion.

Nevertheless, Greco-Roman rhetorical categories are privileged in this analysis, and they are privileged for a simple reason: they constitute the terms of comparison—the "with respect to"—of the argument I seek to falsify. It is the fact that Paul's letters can be analyzed according to these particular categories that sponsors the argument that Paul was formally educated in rhetoric. Thus I use Greco-Roman rhetorical categories in analyzing Red Jacket's oratory not because they are the most appropriate, but because they are the terms of the conversation in which I seek to participate. If I were to use other categories—Perelman and Olbrechts-Tyteca's "New Rhetoric," say—my comparisons would perhaps be interesting but would not be deemed probative for assessing the historical question of Paul's rhetorical education.

10
Attending to Other Voices

In part 2 of this study we saw that the bulk of the putative evidence for Paul's conformity in 2 Cor 10–13 to the dictates of rhetorical theory did not withstand scrutiny. Nevertheless, I identified four ways in which Paul's rhetoric does correspond to what was recommended and practiced among ancient orators. First, with regard to what later became known as *periautologia*, Paul evidently shares his contemporaries' belief that it is better to be praised by others than to praise oneself, and he concurs with Plutarch et alia that self-praise is less offensive when done in self-defense. Second, Paul utilizes what the rhetoricians called *prodiorthōsis*, warning his addressees in advance that he is about to say something unpleasant. Third, Paul approximates *prosōpopoiia* by speaking in the voice of his opponents in texts like 2 Cor 10:1b, 10, and 12:16. And, finally, Paul's list of tribulations is composed in what has been called "catalogue style" and contains numerous related rhetorical features: rhythm, anaphora, isocolon, asyndeton and patterned use of conjunctions, and assonance or rhyme.

None of this constitutes evidence of formal rhetorical education. By showing that each of these persuasive strategies is also utilized by speakers who have no formal training in classical rhetoric, this chapter will demonstrate that such strategies must be attributed to what Kennedy calls general rhetoric. They are not unique to Greco-Roman society, let alone its formal rhetorical tradition. There is no reason, then, to attribute Paul's use of them to formal rhetorical education.

But I have another task in this chapter as well: by providing a telling set of comparators—specifically, speakers who lack formal education but are, in their various ways, persuasive—I seek to provide an alternative context for conceptualizing Paul's rhetoric and an alternative matrix wherein to describe Paul's persuasive voice.

Red Jacket's Self-Defensive Boasting

In chapter 4, I compared Paul's boasting with the recommendations of Plutarch and Quintilian and the self-praise of speakers like Demosthenes. These comparisons brought mixed results: Paul was found to share with his educated contemporaries some general cultural assumptions; however, attention to the aristocratic social values underlying their mitigation of self-praise highlighted Paul's remoteness from their social and discursive world. Further, I suggested that what similarities do exist between Paul's rhetoric and Plutarch's recommendations are too general to sustain the conclusion that Paul received a formal rhetorical education. Rather, they appear to result from analogous responses to a common social exigency, namely, the tension between the desire for honor and the need to abide by social proscriptions of arrogance.

A final comparison will reinforce this interpretation of the relationship between Plutarch's treatise and Paul's boasting. The Iroquois orator Red Jacket, independently of any knowledge of classical rhetorical precepts for *periautologia*, also stressed that he spoke of his own accomplishments only when compelled to defend himself and only because of his concern for the well-being of others, and Red Jacket too presupposed that it was preferable to let others praise him. In fact, in a number of significant ways, Red Jacket's self-defense is closer to the spirit of Plutarch's treatise and the great orator Demosthenes's exemplary self-praise than is Paul's—a phenomenon that forces us to reconsider what constitutes evidence for Paul's rhetorical training.

Sagoyewatha, or Red Jacket

The Seneca chief Sagoyewatha, whom the British dubbed Red Jacket, was among the most famous of Native American orators. Since a number of my examples of general or informal rhetoric derive from extant records of his speeches, it is worth providing a brief introduction. Probably born in 1758,[1] Red Jacket rose to prominence in the late eighteenth and early nineteenth centuries as the Iroquois' foremost orator.[2] His reputation

---

1. Christopher Densmore, *Red Jacket: Iroquois Diplomat and Orator* (The Iroquois and their Neighbors; Syracuse, N.Y.: Syracuse University Press, 1999), 6.

2. For an excellent account of Red Jacket's role, see Granville Ganter, "'You Are a Cunning People without Sincerity': Sagoyewatha and the Trials of Community Rep-

among English-speaking Americans was considerable. According to William Stone, his first major biographer: "That he was an orator, in the most exalted sense of the term, of great and commanding power, is the universal testimony of all who enjoyed opportunities of forming a just opinion on the subject."[3] "His name," avers J. Niles Hubbard, "like that of Demosthenes, is forever associated with eloquence."[4]

Often speaking on behalf of the Iroquois clan mothers, Red Jacket was a vocal defender of the land rights of his people. Many of his most compelling speeches occurred in the context of treaty negotiations and are thus preserved in treaty records. Other public performances were printed in local newspapers. Neither source is unproblematic, particularly since extant records present not Red Jacket's words but English translations thereof.[5] Still, we may be confident of the fundamental authenticity of many of these speeches. As Granville Ganter explains, Red Jacket "referred to himself as an orator and intended his speeches to be read and discussed in state capitols"; therefore, he concerned himself with ensuring accurate representation of his words.[6] The representatives of the United States were also concerned to ensure accuracy of translation and transcription, since speeches like those of Red Jacket became part of the public record and played a significant role in shaping American policy.

Interpreters were often selected by Red Jacket himself. Two of his principal interpreters, Jasper Parrish and Horatio Jones, were captured as teens by the Seneca and were thus deeply familiar with both Red Jacket's language and his culture.[7] Moreover, by the apex of his political career, Red Jacket "understood English well enough to know when his meaning had

---

resentation," in *Native American Speakers of the Eastern Woodlands: Selected Speeches and Critical Analyses* (ed. Barbara Alice Mann; Westport, Conn.: Greenwood Press, 2001), 165–95.

3. William L. Stone, *Life and Times of Red-Jacket, or Sa-Go-Ye-Wat-Ha* (New York: Wiley & Putnam, 1841), 2.

4. Hubbard, *An Account of Sa-go-ye-wat-ha*, 9.

5. For a detailed treatment of "sources and resources for Native American oratory," see Clements, *Oratory*, 23–78.

6. Ganter, "You Are a Cunning People," 168. See also Harry W. Robie, "Red Jacket's Reply: Problems in the Verification of a Native American Speech Text," *New York Folklore* 12, no. 3–4 (1986): 102–3.

7. Granville Ganter, "Introduction," in *The Collected Speeches of Sagoyewatha, or Red Jacket* (ed. Granville Ganter; The Iroquois and Their Neighbors; Syracuse, N.Y.: Syracuse University Press, 2006), xxiii; Ganter, "You Are a Cunning People," 68.

been misinterpreted."[8] So, although we do not have unmediated access to Red Jacket's oral performance, we do possess, quite frequently, his authentic communication. We have what he meant for English readers to have.

Let me provide an example: On August 3, 1802, Red Jacket spoke in defense of a Seneca named Stiff-Armed George, who had been taken into the custody of the sheriff after allegedly killing a white man, John Hewitt, in a drunken altercation the previous week.[9] Red Jacket and the Seneca did not recognize American legal jurisdiction, arguing that the situation should be resolved according to "the customs and habits of [their] forefathers."[10] Red Jacket also emphasized Stiff-Armed George's drunkenness, and pointedly reminded his white hearers who it was that had introduced liquor among his people. Finally, in a rather astute piece of political rhetoric, he sought to shame President Jefferson into intervening:

> The President of the United States is a Great Man, possessing great power—he may do what he pleases—he may turn men out of office; men who held their offices long before he held his. If he can do these things, can he not even control the laws of this state? Can he not appoint a Commissioner to come forward to our country and settle the present differences?

Red Jacket's speech, as translated by Horatio Jones, was published the following week in the *Ontario Gazette* (Aug. 12, 1802). Although this publication is no longer extant, the speech was reprinted in other newspapers over the following few months, as well as in a pamphlet published by James D. Bemis, who worked for the *Gazette* and thus would have had access to the original published version.[11] Although there was some contemporary dispute concerning the authenticity of the speech, it now appears to be beyond question. In the earliest extant version, published in the Septem-

---

8. Ganter, "You Are a Cunning People," 169.

9. See Ganter, *Collected Speeches*, 118; Taylor, *The Divided Ground*, 317–22. Contemporary accounts of the event, which include resumes of Red Jacket's speech, were recorded in the *Albany Centinel*, March 15, 1803, and the *American State Papers, Indian Affairs* 2:667–68.

10. *Albany Centinel*, September 3, 1802; repr. in Ganter, *Collected Speeches*, 119–21.

11. *Native Eloquence: Being Public Speeches Delivered by Two Distinguished Chiefs of the Seneca Tribe of Indians* (Canandaigua, N.Y.: Bemis, 1811), 18–24. On the transmission history of the speech, see Ganter, *Collected Speeches*, 119.

ber 3, 1802 edition of the *Albany Centinel*, as well as the all but identical text in Bemis's *Native Eloquence*, Red Jacket appeals for his speech to be delivered to the President himself: "We therefore now call upon you to take our Speech in writing, and forward our ideas to the President of the United States." Of course, this in itself does not attest to the speech's authenticity, since such a detail could itself be fabricated. There is, however, clear evidence elsewhere that it was not. In a separate speech on the matter, independently attested, that Red Jacket delivered later that August to the governor of New York, he refers to the documentation of what can only be his August 3 defense of George: "We have sent on our speech to the President of the United States about this business, and now present you with a copy thereof."[12] Not only does this fortuitously preserved cross-reference authenticate these particular texts but it also demonstrates Red Jacket's intention to communicate via written translations of his speeches, which, in turn, motivated both him and his hearers to ensure their faithful translation and transmission. Indeed, in this case, the English translation of Red Jacket's words, sent to the president and delivered to the governor, apparently played a significant role in effecting Stiff-Armed George's pardon.[13]

Still, there are fraudulent speeches purporting to be by Red Jacket, and thus discretion is necessary. In assessing the authenticity of individual speeches, I am generally dependent upon the evaluation of scholars more qualified than I. Where expert evaluation is not available, I follow Harry Robie in considering three measures of authenticity: first, the competence of the interpreter; second, the speech's publication history; and, finally, the coherence of the speech with the rhetorical tradition of which it purports to be a part.[14] In the specific case of Red Jacket, this last measure is particularly useful, for the extant record is extensive enough that it is possible to identify Red Jacket's authentic "voice"—that is, the sort of thing that he was liable to say—as well as deviations from it.[15]

---

12. Text in Ganter, *Collected Speeches*, 124.
13. See ibid., 18.
14. Robie, "Red Jacket's Reply," 100–101. See also Clements, *Oratory*, 31–32.
15. See Ganter, "You Are a Cunning People," 168–69, 184–85; Taylor, *The Divided Ground*, 22–23.

Red Jacket's *Periautologia*

On August 31, 1826, Oliver Forward purchased large tracts of Seneca land, including four entire reserves, on behalf of the Ogden Land Company.[16] Red Jacket was among the chiefs who signed the agreement, but immediately thereafter he began to accuse Forward of bribery and deception, petitioning that the deal be nullified. According to a letter of petition signed by Red Jacket and a number of other Seneca chiefs, in addition to giving out bribes, Forward had resorted to threats: "If they did not sell he should write to the President and Secretary at War, and they would show us the way to the Cherokee country"[17]—a nation whose own looming dispossession attested to the plausibility of the threat. Meanwhile, the Christian Seneca sent a counter-petition in support of the land deal.

The whole controversy angered Thomas McKenney at the Office of Indian Affairs, who wrote a letter to the Christian leaders notifying them that the President would be pleased with the removal of Red Jacket as chief.[18] Putative government support for the deposition of an outspoken critic of Christianity was an offer the Christian chiefs could not resist, and, on September 15, 1827, they met in council and signed a declaration against Red Jacket: "We now renounce you as a Chief, and from this time you are forbid to act as one."[19] Further, in a letter to President John Quincy Adams, they requested the President to "pay no further attention to the communication of Red Jacket.... Red Jacket is an old man, his mind is broken, his memory is short, and he is devoid of truth."[20]

Though beleaguered, Red Jacket still had allies, and, on October 16, he convened his own council, at which chiefs from a number of Seneca tribes spoke on his behalf. Finally, we are told, "after an impressive pause," Red Jacket spoke in his own defense:

---

16. For what follows, see Laurence M. Hauptman, *Conspiracy of Interests: Iroquois Dispossession and the Rise of New York State* (The Iroquois and Their Neighbors; Syracuse, N.Y.: Syracuse University Press, 1999), 152–61.

17. Red Jacket et al., "Petition to Governor Clinton for Inquiry into 1826 Land Sale," in Ganter, *Collected Speeches*, 250–53.

18. Ganter, *Collected Speeches*, 260.

19. *Buffalo Emporium*, September 24, 1827; repr. in Ganter, *Collected Speeches*, 260–61.

20. Repr. in Hauptman, *Conspiracy of Interests*, 158.

You have heard, he said, what my associates in council have said and explained, in regard to the foolish charges against me. This is the legal and proper manner to meet these charges—and the only way in which I could notice them. Charges which I despise; and was it not for the concern which the respected chiefs of my nation feel for the character of their aged chief, now before you, I could fold my arms and sit quietly under these slanders.[21]

There are a number of things to notice here. First, like elsewhere in his speeches, Red Jacket begins with an exordium that clearly lays out the context for his remarks and seeks to win the good will of hearers.[22] Although there is no record here of a direct plea for his hearers' attention, we can presume, on the basis of Red Jacket's speech patterns elsewhere, that if we had a verbatim report rather than a summary of this address we would find something like "Brothers, hear patiently what we have to say" or "I ... beg your attention, and the attention of the Warriors and chief Women while I speak for the Nation"[23]—in other words, something that sounds remarkably like the *captatio benevolentiae* that introduce the rhetorically astute speeches made by the Paul of Acts and

---

21. *Albany Argus*, October 27, 1827; repr. in Ganter, *Collected Speeches*, 262–64. The proceedings are described in such detail that the newspaper article can only have been written by an eyewitness. The general reliability of the account is further corroborated by the quality of the translator, a Seneca leader named Jack Berry, as well as the coherence of the content of the speech with what Red Jacket says elsewhere—in particular, his emphasis on the continuity of his religious practice with that of his ancestors, on which see Ganter, "Make Your Minds Perfectly Easy," 125–27. We do not have a verbatim account of Red Jacket's speech; it is presented in detailed summary. This is, of course, a barrier to accessing Red Jacket's rhetoric, but arguably no more of a barrier than that which we face in accessing Paul's voice in 2 Cor 10–13, which was almost certainly mediated through both a secretary and whoever compiled canonical 2 Corinthians. On the secretarial process, regarding the nature of which we can only make informed speculations, see esp. Richards, *Secretary in the Letters of Paul*.

22. Particularly striking for one familiar with the history of New Testament rhetorical criticism is Red Jacket's famous "Reply to Cram, 1805," which begins with an *exordium*, moves on to a *narratio*, provides a *partitio*, and then presents a loosely connected series of proofs before a closing *peroratio*. Text in Ganter, *Collected Speeches*, 138–43. See George Kennedy's rhetorical analysis in *Comparative Rhetoric*, 92–94.

23. Ganter, *Collected Speeches*, 112, 78. For an insightful and culturally sensitive reading of Red Jacket's introductory invocations, see Ganter, "Make Your Minds Perfectly Easy," 127–30.

his fellow Lukan speechmakers.[24] The fact that we do not see such invocations made by the Paul of the letters is not itself evidence that he lacked rhetorical training—after all, Paul was writing letters, not orations. Here I simply observe that the same logic used to make Paul a trained rhetorician would, in this instance, lead to the erroneous conclusion that Red Jacket had training in formal Greek oratory.

The structure of Red Jacket's request for the indulgence of his hearers is also worthy of remark, particularly because of its striking resemblance to exordia composed by Demosthenes (*1 Phil.* 1; *Exord.* 1.1; 48.1): If matters had been different, both explain, I would have gladly remained silent; but, due to circumstances beyond my control, I must ask your indulgence to speak. Further, in the context of our discussion of self-praise, it is important to note that Red Jacket's argument accomplishes precisely that for which Quintilian praised Demosthenes: it casts the odium of speaking about his own achievements onto the opponents who forced him to do so (*Inst.* 11.1.22; cf. Demosthenes, *Cor.* 4). With no advice from rhetorical theorists, Red Jacket recognized the wisdom of insisting that it was his rivals' slander that forced him to speak in his own defense (cf. *De laude* 540C).

But Red Jacket's argument goes one step further: Even the need to defend himself from slander would not rouse him to speak, were it not for the concern of his allied chiefs. It is to ease *their* minds that he speaks—and here I think the issue is not that he must assuage their doubts about his worthiness to lead; rather, they will be troubled on his behalf so long as there is a shadow upon his reputation. It is for their benefit, then, that he rises to vindicate himself. His boasting, like that Plutarch is willing to tolerate, "[has] in prospect some great advantage to [his] hearers" (Plutarch, *De laude* 547F; cf. Quintilian, *Inst.* 4.1.6).

By insisting that, so far as he is concerned, he would be just as happy ignoring the foolish slander of his opponents, Red Jacket seeks to win his audience's goodwill at the outset of his speech by establishing his own *ethos* as well as by discrediting his opponents—a rhetorical ploy recommended widely by the ancients (Aristotle, *Rhet.* 3.14.7; *Rhet. Her.* 1.8; Quintilian, *Inst.* 4.1.7–12). The hypothetical portrait Red Jacket paints of himself—sitting with arms folded, unmoved by the slander against him—recalls an image,

---

24. Acts 13:16: "You Israelites, and others who fear God, listen." Cf. Acts 2:22; 7:2; 21:22; 26:2–3. For somewhat more elaborate examples, see Demosthenes, *Exord.* 4, 5, 49; Dio Chrysostom, *Alex.* 1–2.

one suspects, that remains fresh in his hearers' memory from his posture during the "impressive pause" before he deigned to speak. It is a portrait of a man dignified and self-possessed, a man "of lofty spirit and greatness of character," who, like Plutarch's Epaminondas, towers above his petty opponents (*De laude* 540D).[25] Red Jacket maintains this demeanor throughout the speech—the sort of demeanor that, according to Plutarch, "by refusing to be humbled humbles and overpowers envy" (540D).[26] Thus his stirring conclusion: "As long as I can raise my voice, I shall oppose such measures; as long as I can stand in my moccasins, I will do all I can for my nation."[27]

The heart of Red Jacket's self-praise—like that of Demosthenes (*Cor.*; *Ep.* 2, 3) and Cicero (*Cat.* 3.1–2)—consists of a reminder of his unparalleled service on behalf of his people:

> It grieves my heart when I look around and see the situation of my people; once united and powerful; now, weak and divided. I feel sorry for my nation—when I am gone to the other world—when the Great Spirit calls me away—who among my people can take my place? Many long years have I guided the nation.

As it does for Demosthenes, such reference to his own solicitous leadership has a dual function. First, it functions ethically, reinforcing the perception of his character as one concerned not with his own interests, but with those of his nation (cf. Demosthenes, *Ep.* 2.1, 11). Second, it functions pathetically, inviting his hearers to consider their own potentially grievous fate (cf. Demosthenes, *Ep.* 2.3; 3.5)—and implying that they had better trust in Red Jacket's leadership while they have the chance.[28] His

---

25. Cf. Isocrates, *Antid.* 2–3: "Although I have known that some of the sophists traduce my occupation ... nevertheless I have never deigned to defend myself against their attempts to belittle me, because I considered that their foolish babble had no influence whatever."

26. On Red Jacket's self-confident *ethos* more generally, see Ganter, "You Are a Cunning People," 72. Cf. Taylor, *The Divided Ground*, 23.

27. Given that what we have here is a summary, it would not be wise to insist that the parallelism of this sentence results from Red Jacket's rhetorical design.

28. Cf. Demosthenes, *Ep.* 3.28, 31 (trans. Goldstein): "In sum, gentlemen of Athens, everyone shares in the disgrace and the entire city suffers a grievous blow when malice is seen to have more influence among you than gratitude for public services.... I am afraid that a time is coming when you will be bereft of men who will be spokesmen for your interests, especially when time and fortune and our common destiny have been carrying off some of the men devoted to the people."

rhetoric renders his own fate and that of his nation one—just as Demosthenes's "basic appeal does not come from merely praising himself but from identifying himself with Athens."[29]

Red Jacket's self-praise is brief, but bold—and particularly so in a culture that, far more than that of Demosthenes or Cicero, was suspicious of self-assertion and expected from its speakers expressions of deference and humility.[30] Its brevity attests to the fact that, like Xenophon (*Mem.* 2.1.31) and Plutarch (*De laude* 539D), Red Jacket recognized that praise from others was more effective than self-praise. Thus he ceded the floor to his allied chiefs until the close of the council, allowing Big Kettle, for example, to recall that it was Red Jacket who "was the companion of the Great Washington" rather than drawing explicit attention to this honor himself.

Finally, it is interesting to note that, much more clearly than Paul, Red Jacket conforms to Plutarch's admonition to avoid rivalrous boasting, contending rather with "unsound policy" than with "the praise and fame of others" (545D–E). Although he bitterly describes the accusations against him as "ridiculous," he does not attack his opponents or accuse them of ill will; he rather asserts that they are "misguided." Rather than trading slander for slander, he undertakes to defend his policy:

> The Lord gave his red children their lands—General Washington said they were sure—the Great Spirit has marked out a clear path for his children—the Christian party, by advice of the white people, have left this path and religion of our fathers. We worship as we always have done.

The argument is subtler than it initially appears. Red Jacket dexterously manages to build his own stature by association with the great (white) "General Washington" while simultaneously discrediting the Christian party for their association with "the white people." Contradictory or not,

---

29. Jon M. Ericson, "Rhetorical Criticism: How to Evaluate a Speech," in *Demosthenes' On the Crown: A Critical Case Study of a Masterpiece of Ancient Oratory* (ed. James J. Murphy; New York: Random House, 1967), 132.

30. The "profound humility" of Iroquois speakers was frequently noted, though perhaps misunderstood, already by the Jesuits. See, e.g., Thwaites, *Jesuit Relations*, 5:205; 9:266. See, more generally, Lois J. Einhorn, *The Native American Oral Tradition: Voices of the Spirit and Soul* (Westport, Conn.: Praeger, 2000), 69–70; Michael K. Foster, *From the Earth to beyond the Sky: An Ethnographic Approach to Four Longhouse Iroquois Speech Events* (Canadian Ethnology Service Paper 20; Ottawa: National Museums of Canada, 1974), 30–31.

this is certainly clever. Moreover, by placing the ultimate blame not on his Seneca opponents but on those predators who mislead them, Red Jacket provides his opponents with a ready excuse, thus giving them an opportunity to back down without losing too much face.[31]

Although Red Jacket's defense certainly merits consideration on its own terms, for our purposes we have seen enough: Red Jacket insisted that he spoke on his own behalf only under compulsion and for the purposes of self-defense; he rose to vindicate himself, he claimed, only because of his concern for his fellow chiefs and his nation; he clearly demonstrated preference for the praise of others over self-praise. None of this is evidence of classical rhetorical education or, of course, knowledge of precepts for *periautologia*. On the contrary, what we have here is an astute man, conscious of the social dynamics of his situation, intuitively negotiating the tension between his need to defend himself and his need to refrain from inordinate self-assertion.

Finally, analysis of Red Jacket's speech has sharpened our observations regarding Paul's remoteness from the sort of speech admired by Plutarch. Red Jacket, though far removed in innumerable ways from the Greek world, provides a much closer analogue to the confident political self-assertion that characterizes the speech of Demosthenes and his ilk than does Paul. That is, with respect to comportment or "voice," Red Jacket, much more than Paul, resembles the elite rhetoricians of the Greco-Roman world. This does not, of course, result from their participation in a shared rhetorical tradition; rather, they inhabit analogous social locations: Red Jacket, like Demosthenes and Plutarch, was accustomed to deference, and comported himself accordingly. Paul, it appears, spoke from a rather more precarious place, and could not rely on the persuasive power of calm and confident dignity. Instead, he speaks, as I will attempt to demonstrate in chapter 12, with the voice of one accustomed to derision.

CONCLUSION

Rhetorical analysis of Red Jacket's self-defense has demonstrated that those rhetorical strategies for self-praise which Paul does share with his educated Greek and Roman contemporaries are too general and too widespread to be compelling as evidence for Paul's formal rhetorical edu-

---

31. Cf. Ps.-Demetrius 18 and the discussion in ch. 3 above.

cation. What Paul shares with Plutarch, he shares also with Red Jacket. Accordingly, we must conclude that these persuasive strategies are not specific to formal classical rhetoric but rather inhere in what Kennedy calls "general rhetoric."

By this I do not mean that "boastful" speech takes the same shape across cultures. It certainly does not.[32] Instead, I would argue that the rhetorical exigency out of which these persuasive strategies arise—namely, the pressure to praise oneself and the countervailing pressure to avoid socially inappropriate self-display—is universal, and therefore it is not surprising that some of the same basic strategies for inoffensive self-praise recur in various cultures. Certainly various societies have specific rhetorical traditions with regard to self-praise, both as aspects of what I have called formal and of informal rhetoric. But Paul, I have shown, does not evince specific familiarity with the rhetorical tradition of self-praise current among the Greco-Roman literati. Moreover, his self-praise is very different both in demeanor and in content from what our elite exemplars would have us expect.

Two conclusions suggest themselves: First, the persuasive competencies to which Paul's manner of self-praise attests derive in the first place from socialization, not from formal education.[33] Second, his socialization appears not to have been socialization into the values of the educated elite. Accordingly, even if precepts for self-praise had been on the curricula of first-century rhetorical schools—something for which we have no evidence—it would be difficult to sustain the argument that Paul learned to praise himself at school.

Informal *Prodiorthōsis*

Among the most memorable features of Paul's boasting in 2 Cor 10–13 are his repeated warnings, prior to beginning his litany in earnest, of the "foolishness" to come: "I repeat, let no one think that I am a fool; but if you do, then accept me as a fool, so that I too may boast a little" (11:16; cf. 11:1; 12:1). The cumulative impression given by these statements is one of hesitancy to do what he is about to do: Chrysostom, as noted above,

---

32. See Karl Reisman, "Contrapuntal Conversations in an Antiguan Village," in *Explorations in the Ethnography of Speaking* (ed. Richard Bauman and Joel Sherzer; 2nd ed.; SSCFL 8; Cambridge: Cambridge University Press, 1989), 117–18.

33. See further ch. 11 below.

compared Paul's reluctant boasting to a horse rearing back from a precipice (*Laud. Paul.* 5.12; *Hom. 2 Cor. 11:1* 4 [PG 51:305]); likewise, F. W. Robertson's impression was that "fact after fact of [Paul's] own experiences is, as it were, wrung out, as if he had not intended to tell it."[34]

The rhetorical term for warnings of unpleasant or unseemly speech to come is *prodiorthōsis*, a word that means essentially what its lexical elements would suggest: straightening out in advance any potentially problematic implications of what one is about to say.[35] This is surely what Paul is doing here, and these verses have long been recognized as instances of this figure.[36] I do not dispute such an identification. However, I would like to emphasize that the use of *prodiorthōsis* is by no means restricted to orators formally educated in the classical tradition. No, *prodiorthōsis* is, as we will see, undoubtedly an element of general rhetoric. Given the nature of Paul's dilemma in 2 Cor 10–13, my focus here will be on *prodiorthōsis* that anticipates potentially offensive self-praise, though, as noted in chapter 4 above, the figure is by no means restricted to such usage.

ANTICIPATING SOCIAL CONSTRAINTS

Evincing hesitation prior to engaging in self-praise is so intuitive and so widespread in ordinary conversation that even the briefest of pauses may be interpreted as a concession to modesty. Prior to the final of the 2010 Australian Open, tennis great Roger Federer commented on his opponent's chances. After noting that the relatively inexperienced Andy Murray would be in for an uphill battle, he added: "Plus he's playing, you know, me, who's won many Grand Slams and has been able to win here three times."[37] "You know, me." Clearly this interjection has the same rhetorical function as formal *prodiorthōsis*, though I doubt Federer is aware of the fact or that he learned it in school. On the contrary, it simply is required by the social dynamics of the situation: unrestrained arrogance is socially unacceptable,

---

34. Robertson, *Sermons*, 418.
35. For ancient descriptions, see Ps.-Herodian, *Fig.* 33 (*RG* 3:95); Alexander, *Fig.* 1.3 (*RG* 3:14–15); Tiberius, *Fig.* 8; Hermogenes, Περὶ ἰδεῶν, 2.4; Apsines, *Rhet.* 10.34 (*RG* 1:399).
36. See further pp. 118–19 above.
37. Joe Drape, "Federer, Making Quick Work of Tsonga, Will Face Murray in Final," *New York Times*, January 30, 2010. Cited 5 March 2010. Online: http://www.nytimes.com/2010/01/30/sports/tennis/30tennis.html.

and Federer asks for our indulgence by expressing, briefly, awareness that he is transgressing ordinary canons of self-reference.[38]

Federer's situation is common enough that English speakers have developed idiomatic shortcuts: "I don't mean to toot my own horn," "If I may say so myself," and the like.[39] These formulae are specific to particular speech communities and thus belong to the realm of what I have called informal rhetoric, but, as we will see, they instantiate a general phenomenon of human communication and social interaction.

The social exigencies that engender such prodiorthotic disclaimers have been thoughtfully examined by pragmatic linguists under the rubric of "politeness theory." The seminal work here is Penelope Brown and Stephen Levinson's *Politeness*. It will be helpful to summarize the basic contours of their argument. According to Brown and Levinson, mutual awareness of "face"—a concept they define, following Erving Goffmann, as "the public self-image that every member wants to claim for himself"—is a human universal.[40] Further, since people are always vulnerable to the loss of face, it "must be constantly attended to in interaction"; indeed, in conversation people generally cooperate to maintain their own face as well as

---

38. Specifically, "you know" seems to function here by alerting Federer's hearers to the fact that what he is about to say is already well known. The implication is that he is not boasting, but merely reminding his hearers of relevant information. Cf. Janet Holmes, "Functions of *You Know* in Women's and Men's Speech," *Language in Society* 15 (1986): 7–10, 16.

39. See further Anita Pomerantz's discussion of "self-praise avoidance" techniques in informal English conversation ("Compliment Reponses: Notes on the Co-operation of Multiple Constraints," in *Studies in the Organization of Conversational Interaction* [ed. Jim Schenkein; Language, Thought, and Culture Series; New York: Academic Press, 1978], 88–92).

40. Brown and Levinson, *Politeness*, 61–62. See Erving Goffman, "On Face-Work: An Analysis of Ritual Elements in Social Interaction," in *Interaction Ritual: Essays on Face-to-Face Behavior* (Garden City, N.Y.: Anchor, 1967), 5–45; repr. from *Psychiatry: Journal for the Study of Interpersonal Processes* 18 (1955). The claim to universality has been contested, but intercultural research has vindicated the usefulness of Brown and Levinson's basic assertion. See, e.g., Maria Sifianou, *Politeness Phenomena in England and Greece: A Cross-Cultural Perspective* (Oxford: Clarendon, 1992); Rosina Márquez-Reiter, *Linguistic Politeness in Britain and Uruguay: A Contrastive Study of Requests and Apologies* (Pragmatics and Beyond 2/83; Amsterdam: Benjamins, 2000); Ming-Chung Yu, "On the Universality of Face: Evidence from Chinese Compliment Response Behavior," *Journal of Pragmatics* 35 (2003): 1679–1710.

that of their interlocutors.⁴¹ But of course people have other interpersonal goals besides face maintenance,⁴² and sometimes the pursuit of these goals conflicts with their basic desire to maintain face—which, of course, leaves them in a bind. Politeness, according to Brown and Levinson, is the means whereby they resolve this dilemma; it is, in other words, a repertoire of strategies people employ to minimize the negative impact of undertaking "face-threatening acts."⁴³

Self-praise is clearly such a "face-threatening act."⁴⁴ As Plutarch explains as well as anyone, it poses a threat to the face both of the speaker and of the listener. The speaker appears to be in shameful violation of cultural proscriptions against hubris (539D; 540A), and the listener is put in a dilemma, stuck between two equally unseemly responses: either he applauds the speaker and looks like a flatterer or he censures the speaker and "appears disgruntled and envious" (539D–E [LCL]). Nevertheless, it is easy to see how other social goals—the desire for honor and recognition, for example, or, with Plutarch, the pursuit of πλειόνων καὶ καλλιόνων πράξεων (539F; cf. 547F)—could compel one to risk face and praise oneself anyway. In such a case, we should expect to see what Brown and Levinson call "redressive actions," communicative strategies that attempt to mitigate the negative consequences of face-threatening acts.

Among the repertoire of common redressive actions they identify is, not surprisingly, the use of "hedges" by which speakers express their reluctance to threaten face. Brown and Levinson describe the use of such hedges in English, Tamil, and Tzeltal; Japanese research demonstrates their use among children as early as the second grade.⁴⁵ In other words, here we clearly are encountering what Kennedy would call general rhetoric.

---

41. Brown and Levinson, *Politeness*, 61; Goffman, "On Face-Work," 27–31.

42. Goffman, "On Face-Work," 12.

43. Note that Brown and Levinson's conception of politeness intersects with but also differs from what the term means in ordinary usage. Thus Paul's *prodiorthōsis*, for example, is clearly *not* polite in any ordinary sense of the term (see esp. 11:16–21), but it nevertheless is illuminated by politeness theory: Paul seeks to maintain his own face by forewarning his readers of his self-praise—an instance of what Rong Chen refers to as "self-politeness" ("Self-Politeness: A Proposal," *Journal of Pragmatics* 33 [2001]: 87–106)—but in fact heightens the threat to the face of his readers.

44. Brown and Levinson, *Politeness*, 67; Geoffrey N. Leech, *Principles of Pragmatics* (Longman Linguistics Library 30; London: Longman, 1983), 136–38.

45. Brown and Levinson, *Politeness*, 145–72, 37. See also the Ilongot examples provided by Michelle Z. Rosaldo, "Words That Are Moving: The Social Meanings

Two of the examples Brown and Levinson provide are of particular interest for describing Paul's expressions of reluctance in 2 Cor 10–13. First, although the authors nowhere speak explicitly of *prodiorthōsis* (or name any other rhetorical devices), they do note the common occurrence of hedges that "function directly as notices of violations of face wants": "to be honest," "I hate to have to say this," and so forth[46]—in other words, notices that function as disclaimers.[47] Paul's "Bear with me" (11:1) is of this nature, mitigating his self-praise by alerting his hearers to the fact that he is aware of and regrets the face-threat. Second, Brown and Levinson note the frequent occurrence of diminutives and vague "quantity hedges" ("roughly," "more or less," "to some extent") as means of moderating a speaker's investment in a face-threatening act.[48] Paul's μικρόν τι (11:1, 16; cf. 10:8) clearly serves this function.[49] That employment of this strategy does not require formal rhetorical education is clear from a particularly colloquial example reproduced by Anita Pomerantz—an example that incorporates quantitative hedging, informal *prodiorthōsis*, and general expressions of hesitancy: "So he—so then, at this—y'see,—I don' like to brag but see he sorta like backed outta the argument then."[50]

In summary, then, expressions of reluctant self-praise are ubiquitous not because of rhetorical training but because of what are apparently transcultural canons of social interaction. As Ian Rutherford notes regarding discussions of appropriate self-praise in antiquity, what occasions them is a "conflict between the social pressure to assert oneself in public and the social criticism of excessive assertiveness."[51] We may define "excessive

---

of Ilongot Verbal Art," in *Dangerous Words: Language and Politics in the Pacific* (ed. Donald Lawrence Brenneis and Fred R. Myers; New York: New York University Press, 1984), 147.

46. Brown and Levinson, *Politeness*, 171–72. Note also their discussion of the organization of speech elements, which demonstrates that redressive action is generally "more polite" when it precedes a face-threatening action than when it appears to be an afterthought (93).

47. See the fuller discussion of disclaimers in ch. 8 above.

48. Brown and Levinson, *Politeness*, 157, 166–67. Cf. Mei-yun Ko and Tzu-fu Wang, "A Politeness Strategy: Downtoners, Hedges and Disclaimers," *International Journal of the Humanities* 5 (2007): 189–98.

49. Cf. Calvin, *Corinthians*, 2:253; Beet, *Corinthians*, 439.

50. Pomerantz, "Compliment Responses," 90.

51. Ian Rutherford, "The Poetics of the *Paraphthegma*: Aeilus Aristides and the *Decorum* of Self-Praise," in *Ethics and Rhetoric: Classical Essays for Donald Russell on*

assertiveness" quite differently than did the ancients, and the pressure to assert oneself may be differently constructed, but the fundamental tension remains—as does its unstable rhetorical resolution.

"You Must Not Think Hard If We Speak Rash"

Whether it pertains to boasting or other potentially offensive speech, *prodiorthōsis* results from a speaker's anticipation and concern for how her or his hearers will respond. Such sensitivity to one's audience is, as noted already by Plato's Socrates, a prerequisite for effective speech (*Phaedr.* 271D–272B). Certainly the formal study of rhetoric may nourish this sensitivity, but, as indicated by my brief survey of politeness theory above, formal study is hardly its origin. A look at the function of *prodiorthōsis* in the rhetoric of Red Jacket will clarify the point.

Among the Iroquois, as Alan Taylor notes, speech was a means not only of communication but also of social governance: "Authority ultimately lay in the constant flow of talk, which regulated reputation through the variations of praise and ridicule, celebration and shaming."[52] The functioning of such an informal system of social control depended on the ability of speakers to anticipate and negotiate the reception of their words, that is, to shape their speech such that it had its intended effect. As a result, Iroquois culture nourished in its speakers just such sensitivity to one's audience as generates *prodiorthōsis*.

This is evident in the rhetoric of Red Jacket, whose speeches often show him dexterously anticipating and manipulating the responses of his hearers, using, among other techniques, *prodiorthōsis*. Red Jacket's speech to the governor of New York regarding the murder trial of Stiff-Armed George provides a fine example: "Altho' the matter we have to communicate with you on this occasion is of a disagreeable and melancholy nature, yet we hope you will open your Ears to what we shall say, and reflect seriously on the subject."[53] Elsewhere, Red Jacket apologizes in advance for reiterating what his auditors have already been told.[54]

His Seventy-Fifth Birthday (ed. Doreen Innes, Harry Hine, and Christopher Pelling; Oxford: Clarendon, 1995), 201.
    52. Taylor, *The Divided Ground*, 21.
    53. Ganter, *Collected Speeches*, 124.
    54. Ibid., 29.

Notably, like modern speakers of English, Red Jacket often uses a formulaic idiom to forewarn his audience of potentially offensive words: "Brothers, you must not think hard if we speak rash"; "You must not think hard of us, when tomoro [sic] we lay before you all we have to say"; "Now if we say any thing not agreeable, have no hard thoughts of it. Keep your mind easy; listen to what we say."[55] The idiom occurs frequently in the extant record, including at least one appearance not in a reported speech but in a letter bearing Red Jacket's signature.[56] Here we are clearly hearing Red Jacket's own voice.

Further, like Paul in 2 Cor 12:11, Red Jacket follows up potentially offensive speech with what Alexander Numenius (*Fig.* 1.4 [*RG* 3:15]; cf. Ps.-Herodian, *Fig.* 34 [*RG* 3:95–96]) calls *epidiorthōsis*—apology after the fact: "Do not think hard of what has been said"; "Now you must not think hard, nor suppose we are disturbed in our own minds, because we have given you the reasons of our surprise"; "Now Brother you must not be offended that at this time we have mentioned some of our ancient ways."[57]

Red Jacket's use of both *prodiorthōsis* and *epidiorthōsis* does not, of course, derive from formal education in classical rhetoric; instead, this is an instantiation of a general rhetorical aptitude as mediated by the rhetorical traditions of his particular speech community. In other words, "do not think hard" is what I have called informal rhetoric; *prodiorthōsis* itself is universal, an aspect of general rhetoric.

"Feigned Reluctance"?

Having demonstrated that *prodiorthōsis* is a general rhetorical aptitude is not, of course, equivalent to having shown that Paul's particular use of it was not shaped by formal rhetorical education. Perhaps his halting self-praise does reflect the calculation of a trained orator, or even "feigned reluctance," as Watson has it.[58] But on what basis could such an assertion be made? Given the ubiquity of the figure, it will not do to jump directly from observation of *prodiorthōsis* to the assumption of studied rhetorical intention. No, to argue that Paul's use of this figure was mediated by the

---

55. Texts from ibid., 3, 6, 24.
56. See ibid., 3.
57. Texts from ibid., 10, 27, 13.
58. Watson, "Paul and Boasting," 90.

formal tradition of classical rhetoric, scholars should have to say something about how he used it, not only that he did so.

This sort of evaluation is complicated by the complex relationship between what we have called formal and general rhetoric: As "Longinus" avers, "Art is perfect when it seems to be nature, and nature hits the mark when she contains art hidden within her" (*Subl.* 22.1 [trans. Roberts]; cf. Cicero, *De or.* 3.215–219). Or, as Quintilian explains, a little more snobbishly: "There is ... a sort of resemblance between certain merits and certain defects [of speech]" (*Inst.* 2.12.4 [Butler, LCL]). Still, it is not impossible to discriminate. I think all will agree that Roger Federer, like Pomerantz's exemplar, expressed himself instinctively and unselfconsciously; but, when Demosthenes, in the elegant proem of *De corona* (4), warns his audience that he will be forced to speak immodestly—and that this puts him at a rhetorical disadvantage vis-à-vis his accuser—that this is a considered rhetorical strategy.

Where does Paul fit on this continuum? Perhaps Longinus and Quintilian can help us map the territory. If Longinus's basic ideal is that art replicates nature, it is nevertheless important to recognize that art is never simply a copy of nature; on the contrary, even "realistic" art is governed by conventional canons of realism. Quintilian provides a useful example in his discussion of comic actors, "whose delivery is not exactly that of common speech, since that would be inartistic, but is on the other hand not far removed from the accents of nature, for if it were their mimicry would be a failure" (2.10.13 [LCL]). Mimesis, then, in order to be artistic, must reveal that it is mimesis—but must manage to do so without evaporating the mimetic spell. What comic actors do in order to accomplish this delicate balance is "exalt the simplicity of ordinary speech by a touch of stage decoration."

For Quintilian, the difference between common speech and its comic imitation is analogous to the relationship between real forensic oratory and declamation: the latter imitates the former but adds a touch of rhetorical showmanship (2.10.12). But from what Quintilian says elsewhere it is clear that this would be an equally apt analogy for his understanding of the relationship between the uneducated speaker and his educated counterpart. Defending educated orators against the accusation that they lack the vigor of untrained speakers, Quintilian explains:

> It must be confessed that learning does take something from oratory, just as the file takes something from rough surfaces or the whet-stone from

blunt edges or age from wine; it takes away the defects, and if the results produced after subjection to the polish of literary studies are less, they are less only because they are better. (*Inst.* 2.12.8 [LCL])

So, education files off the rough edges of untrained speech—the bombast, in particular (cf. 2.12.6; 2.12.9–10). Educated orators reproduce the passion of a "naturally" emoting speaker,[59] but signal that this is mimesis—and thus retain their aristocratic dignity—by doing so with "discrimination and self-restraint" (2.12.6 [LCL]). Indeed, "if [the educated speaker] has any one canon for universal observance, it is that he should both possess the reality and present the appearance of self-control (*modestus*)" (2.12.10 [LCL]).[60]

If Quintilian is at all reliable on this score, what we should be looking for in educated, strategic *prodiorthōsis* is not in fact hesitancy or embarrassment, which would involve the loss of the orator's aristocratic self-possession, but rather the stylized appearance thereof. And this is precisely the sort of thing we see in Demosthenes: "I shall try to [speak about myself] as modestly as I can; but what I am forced to do by the case itself is fairly to be blamed upon the person who set this prosecution in train—my opponent" (*Cor.* 4 [trans. Usher]; cf. Isaeus, *Phil.* 17). The *idea* of reluctance to boast certainly is evoked by this meta-discursive disclaimer, but Demosthenes remains decorously detached from any emotional investment in the issue. He reports on his own situation almost as if he were an outside observer.

This is clearly reflected in Demosthenes's diction. He provides a reasoned and dispassionate explanation for his self-adulation, and does so using well-balanced μέν ... δέ clauses within an elaborate periodic structure:

τούτων τοίνυν δ μέν ἐστι πρὸς ἡδονήν, τούτῳ δέδοται,
ὃ δὲ πᾶσιν ὡς ἔπος εἰπεῖν ἐνοχλεῖ, λοιπὸν ἐμοί.

---

59. See esp. *Inst.* 6.2.26–27 (LCL): "What other reason is there for the eloquence with which mourners express their grief, or for the fluency which anger lends even to the uneducated, save the fact that their minds are stirred to power by the depth and sincerity of their feelings? Consequently, if we wish to give our words the appearance of sincerity, we must assimilate ourselves to the emotions of those who are genuinely so affected, and our eloquence must spring from the same feeling that we desire to produce in the mind of the judge." Cf. Cicero, *De or.* 2.189–96; *Tusc.* 4.43–55. M. Zerba helpfully explores the complexities of this "pantomimic" mode in "Love, Envy, and Pantomimic Morality in Cicero's *De oratore*," *CP* 97 (2002): 299–321.

60. Cf. *Inst.* 6.3.35; 11.3.184. And note Aristotle's characterization of the great-souled man as one who has a "steady voice" (λέξις στάσιμος [*Eth. nic.* 4.3.19]).

κἂν μὲν εὐλαβούμενος τοῦτο μὴ λέγω τὰ πεπραγμέν' ἐμαυτῷ,
    οὐκ ἔχειν ἀπολύσασθαι τὰ κατηγορημένα δόξω,
    οὐδ' ἐφ' οἷς ἀξιῶ τιμᾶσθαι δεικνύναι·
ἐὰν δ' ἐφ' ἃ καὶ πεποίκα καὶ πεπολίτευμαι βαδίζω,
    πολλάκις λέγειν ἀναγκασθήσομαι περὶ ἐμαυτοῦ.
πειράσομαι μὲν οὖν ὡς μετριώτατα τοῦτο ποιεῖν·
ὅ τι δ' ἂν τὸ πρᾶγμα αὔτ' ἀναγκάζῃ
    τούτου τὴν αἰτίαν οὗτός ἐστι δίκαιος ἔχειν ὁ τοιοῦτον ἀγῶν'
    ἐνστησάμενος.⁶¹

Importantly, then, what Demosthenes's *prodiorthōsis* signals to his audience is not uncertainty, nor hesitancy, but, on the contrary, measured self-confidence and solicitousness.

Observe, similarly, Cicero's parenthetical *prodiorthōsis* in a letter to Atticus:

> And it is once more I—for I do not feel as if I were boasting vaingloriously when speaking of myself to you, especially in a letter not intended to be read by others—it was I once more, I say, who revived the fainting spirits of the loyalists ... (*Att.* 1.16.8 [trans. Shuckburgh])

Cicero's interruption of himself perhaps superficially resembles Paul's parenthetical ἐν ἀφροσύνῃ λέγω and παραφρονῶν λαλῶ (11:21, 23), but notice again that whereas Paul *concedes* his foolishness, Cicero and Demosthenes anticipate objections, but, like Plutarch's dignified self-praisers, hold their heads up high and proceed with calmness and confidence. Again, Cicero's diction is telling: his use of a parenthesis gives the impression of sincere spontaneity, while the elegant epanalepsis with which he resumes his account (*idem ego ... idem inquam ego*) projects control and self-possession.⁶²

---

61. "The part that gives pleasure is given to him, while that which vexes practically everyone is left to me. And if I try to avoid this by omitting to recount my deeds, it will be thought that I cannot rebut the accusations or indeed show the grounds on which I think I should be honoured; while if I embark on an account of my political achievements, I shall be forced to make many references to myself. Therefore I shall try to do this as modestly as I can; but what I am forced to do by the case itself is fairly to be blamed upon the person who set this prosecution in train—my opponent" (trans. Usher).

62. Note also Demosthenes's aposiopesis in *Cor.* 3, wherein he manages, despite a break in the grammar and logic of the sentence, to preserve the μέν ... δέ rhythm: ἀλλ'

Contrast Paul's "sudden outburst":[63] ὄφελον ἀνείχεσθέ μου μικρόν τι ἀφροσύνης· ἀλλὰ καὶ ἀνέχεσθέ μου (11:1). These short, abrupt sentences constitute a very different sort of *prodiorthōsis* from that of Demosthenes or Cicero—or, for that matter, Red Jacket. Far from downplaying his emotional investment, Paul's diction highlights it. The word ὄφελον is, as Plummer notes, comparable to the English particle "'Oh,' expressing a wish as to what might happen, but is almost too good to come true."[64] The anguished hope of Namaan's wife captures the sense: "If only (ὄφελον) my lord were with the prophet who is in Samaria! He would cure him of his leprosy" (2 Kgs 5:3). It expresses an earnest plea.[65]

Paul's earnestness—or, as Quintilian might allege, his lack of self-control—is evident also from the repetition of the plea,[66] which, on its second iteration, is expressed in the imperative mood.[67] This sort of repeated entreaty certainly does not attest to the self-possession of this speaker; rather, it bespeaks uncertainty, if not desperation. As noted in chapter 8 above, whereas moderate and confident use of disclaimers may be effective, such repetition *ad nauseum* as we see in Paul (11:1, 16–18, 21, 23; 12:1, 5–6, 11) tends to undermine the credibility of a speaker by projecting insecurity. The fact that Paul goes on to speak pathetically—in the rhetorical, if not also the colloquial sense—about how the Corinthians

---

ἐμοὶ μὲν—οὐ βούλομαι δυσχερὲς εἰπεῖν οὐδὲν ἀρχόμενος τοῦ λόγου, οὗτος δ' ἐκ περιουσίας μου κατηγορεῖ ("For me—but I wish to say nothing untoward at the beginning of my speech—whereas he prosecutes me from a position of advantage" [trans. Usher]). Cf. Athanasius, *Vit. Ant.* 39.

63. Plummer, *Second Epistle*, 292.

64. Ibid. See also BDF §359.1.

65. Cf. LXX Exod 16:3; Num 14:2; 20:3; 2 Kgs 5:3; Ps 118:5; Job 14:13. Elsewhere Paul uses the word with venomous irony (1 Cor 4:8; Gal 5:12), but, as the context indicates, that can hardly be the case here. Paul certainly wants to be taken seriously in 10:13–18, and he is in deadly earnest in 11:2–3, the thrust of which would be completely undermined if 11:1 were ironic. *Pace* Windisch, *Der zweite Korintherbrief*, 317; Harris, *Second Corinthians*, 732; Welborn, *An End to Enmity*, 154–55.

66. Paul's ἀλλὰ καί here is not really adversative, but emphatic, as in Phil 1:18. Cf. BDF § 448.6; Nigel Turner, *Syntax* (vol. 3 of J. H. Moulton, *A Grammar of New Testament Greek*; Edinburgh: T&T Clark, 1963), 330. The sort of reading suggested by Martin (*2 Corinthians*, 327), such that ἀλλά "modifies and corrects" the implied impossibility of the wish expressed by ὄφελον plus the imperfect, is unnecessarily subtle.

67. Grammatically, ἀνέχεσθε in v. 1b can be rendered either as an indicative or imperative, but the connection with vv. 2–3 demands the latter. See Harris, *Second Corinthians*, 733; Thrall, *Second Epistle*, 2:659.

are cheating on him and his gospel (11:2-4) does nothing to alleviate this impression. His authority no longer respected, here Paul uses guilt, shame, and the specter of his own humiliation to win compliance. This may be an effective means of persuasion, but it certainly is not the sort of elite comportment that was taught in rhetorical school.

In sum, then, Paul's *prodiorthōsis* bears little resemblance to the elegant and reasoned justifications we find in Demosthenes or Cicero, and it contains no indicators of the influence of formal rhetorical tradition or training. It looks instead like an impassioned plea. John Chrysostom certainly saw it as such: for him Paul spoke ἀπό τινος ἔρωτος θερμοῦ καὶ μανικοῦ (*Hom. 2 Cor.* 23.1 [PG 61:552]). So did Calvin, who paraphrased 11:2a as follows: "Do not demand that I should show the equable temper of a man that is at ease, and not excited by any emotion, for that vehemence of jealousy, with which I am inflamed towards you, does not suffer me to be at ease."[68] Perhaps Chrysostom and Calvin—along with every other interpreter prior to Betz—were taken in by Paul's masterful rhetoric, his flawless imitation of natural passion; however, before we make confident assertions to that effect, we should need to provide some evidence.

PROSŌPOPOIIA AND THE USE OF INTERLOCUTORS' VOICES

Werner Herzog insisted on filming *Fitzcarraldo* on the Rio Camisea deep in the Peruvian Amazon, using a cast largely comprised of local Machiguenga and Campa (Asháninka) villagers. As a striking interview with a young indigenous extra named Elia reveals, many of these villagers approached their encounter with Herzog and his European crew with considerable anxiety. What I want to highlight here, however, is not the content of the interview but its rhetoric, and, specifically, Elia's colloquial but capable use of what might be called informal *prosōpopoiia*,[69] which I have indicated here with italicized text. (Note that ellipsis marks represent pauses or breaks in Elia's speech, except those in brackets, which mark my own abridgement.)

---

68. Calvin, *Corinthians*, 2:338.
69. Like Paul's use of his interlocutor's voice in 2 Cor 10:1b, 10; 12:16, Elia's speech does not consist of the sort of formal *prosōpopoiia* one encounters in the *Progymnasmata* or in ancient declamation, but her usage does reflect the same sensitivity to verisimilitude in inhabiting another voice, and plays a similar rhetorical function.

Interviewer: ¿Cuando venía aquí tenía miedo de los gringos?
Elia: Yo no tenía miedo porque he comprendido todo lo que ... mi compadre Walter dice,
  [Walter:] *es engaño, es mentira. Mentira es.*
Interviewer: ¿Que le dijeron [...]?
Elia: Sí, pués,
  [Others:] *van a sacar cara,*
  que
  [Others:] *van a sacar su grasa para avión.*
[...]
  Me he venido casi todos los días. Hemos ido por acá, han llegado mis compañeros los que han venido de miedo, de miedo cuando le han visto los campamentos ... de miedo! Yo les he dicho,
    [Elia:] *No tengas miedo! Hay bastante gente que ... como lo demás.*
    [Others:] *No, no les están esperando.*
  Y Atalaina han dicho que
    [Atalaina:] *Hay con este ... este sanitario ... que te van a poner ampolleta y te lo este sacando un sangre, te está poniendo ... veneno en tus venas y cuando regreses en tu pueblo ¡vas a morir!*
  Tenían miedo. Y
    [Atalaina?] *No comes tanto cuando te invitan a comer. Así te dan* [mimes large serving of food]. *No comes para que te engorden, ¡para que te maten!*

Interviewer: Were you afraid of the gringos when you came here?
Elia: No, I wasn't afraid, because I understood all that ... my friend Walter told me
  [Walter:] it's all lies. All lies.
Interviewer: What did they tell you [...]?
Elia: Yes, well,
  [Others:] *they will take off your face,*
  and
  [Others:] *they will uses your grease for airplanes.*
[...]
  I've come to this camp nearly every day. We've been around. When my friends arrived [and saw] those who had come, [they were] afraid, afraid when they visited the camp ... afraid! I told them,
    [Elia:] *Don't be afraid! There are a lot of people that ... like the rest.*
    [Others:] *No, no, they are waiting [to kill] us.*
  And Atalaina said
    [Atalaina:] *The way it is with this ... this health clinic ... they*

> *will give you an injection and taking out your blood and putting ... poison in your veins and when you return to your village you will die!*
>
> They were afraid. And
>
> [Atalaina?] *Don't eat too much when they invite you to eat. They give you this much* [mimes large serving of food]! *Don't eat so much because they'll fatten you up and then kill you.*[70]

I have attempted to clarify the prosopopoetic features here by indicating in brackets the speakers in whose voices Elia expresses herself at various points in the interview: her friend Walter, the other villagers (collectively), one villager named Atalaina, and Elia herself. She uses a variety of cues, especially vocal modulation, to signal her adoption of these voices. Sometimes she designates clearly that she is presenting reported speech ("mi compadre Walter dice"); sometimes context and vocal cues are sufficient to allow her listeners to identify the voice in which she speaks. Particularly noteworthy is the reported dialogue between her and the other villagers, in which the transition between her own (reported) speech and that of her interlocutors is marked only by non-verbal cues.

The basic point is simple: such informal *prosōpopoiia*—and, more generally, the use of others' voices to further one's own persuasive ends—is not unique to the classical rhetorical tradition, and it certainly is not restricted to the speech of those with formal rhetorical education. This is an aspect of general rhetoric: it is transcultural and independent of rhetorical training.[71]

But I would also like to make a few observations regarding the particular characteristics of Elia's voice. Noteworthy here is the coexistence of rhetorically effective *prosōpopoiia* with colloquial and sometimes clumsy

---

70. Text and translation (which I have altered to conform more closely to the structure of the original) from Les Blank and James Bogan, eds., *Burden of Dreams: Screenplay, Journals, Reviews, Photographs* (Berkeley, Calif.: North Atlantic Books, 1984), 38–40. From the scene "Separate Worlds," *Burden of Dreams*, directed by Les Blank (1982; Criterion Collection, 2005).

71. For further examples and documentation, see Kennedy, *Comparative Rhetoric*, 56, 98; Meyer, *Mahnen, Prahlen, Drohen*, 183. Note also Zhuangzi's use of "imputed speech" (*yu yan*), whereby the great Chinese philosopher introduced the fictive voice of interlocutors into his philosophical works. See Xing Lu, *Rhetoric in Ancient China, Fifth to Third Century, B.C.E.: A Comparison with Classical Greek Rhetoric* (Columbia: University of South Carolina Press, 1998), 251, and Zhuagzi's own discussion of the technique in *The Complete Works of Chuang Tzu* (trans. Burton Watson; New York: Columbia University Press, 1968), 303.

use of Spanish. What Elia accomplishes by adopting the role of Atalaina et alia is, in fact, the establishment of *ethos*: At the expense of her fellow villagers, whose voices she imbues with laughable naivety as to the ways of the European visitors, Elia positions herself as uniquely sensible and worldly-wise. That is, by internalizing the evaluation of her visitors—and, by means of her speech-in-character, adopting their external evaluative stance vis-à-vis her compatriots—Elia has made herself an insider.

This is a rhetorically astute move, but its execution could hardly be called eloquent. In fact, there are a number of indicators here that Elia is not particularly articulate. I give but two examples. First, there is the odd turn of phrase, *sacar cara*, which seems to represent what we might call, duly noting the irony, a local "urban legend." In context here, it is clear that what is feared is that the Europeans will remove the faces of the locals and somehow use them to fuel their airplanes (*van a sacar su grasa para avión*).[72] Apart from the missing article, what makes this usage confusing is its resemblance to the common idiom *sacar la cara por alguien*—that is, "to stand up for somebody."[73]

Second, note the broken syntax in her initial description of the fear of her *compañeros*: *Hemos ido por acá, han llegado mis compañeros los que han venido de miedo, de miedo cuando le han visto los campamentos*. There is no grammatical connection between the first clause and the remainder of the sentence. Likewise, *de miedo*, repeated for emphasis, is logically but not grammatically attached to the narration of her fellow villagers' arrival. It is clear enough what Elia means—she was already in the camp, and watched those of her *compañeros* who showed up later gape in fear when they arrived—but she lacks the linguistic resources to articulate it such that grammar and sense coincide.

This is characteristic of Elia's prose. Given contextual cues, we can deduce her meaning, but she does not very well articulate what she communicates. Curiously, then, her rhetorical effectiveness far outstrips her control of the language. Hers is an informal rhetoric, and, regardless of its colloquial force, would never be confused with learned speech.

---

72. Note that correct usage would demand an infinitive after *para* here, or, alternatively, an article with *avión*.

73. Nicholas Rollin, ed., *The Concise Oxford Spanish Dictionary* (Oxford: Oxford University Press, 1998), s.v. "Cara."

Prosōpopoiia in 2 Corinthians 10–13

I argued above that Paul's so-called Fool's Speech is not an instance of *prosōpopoiia*. On the contrary, in his boasting Paul speaks in his own voice, which is precisely why he is concerned that the Corinthians will consider him a fool. There are, however, a number of examples of what I have called informal *prosōpopoiia* in this letter. Indeed, in 2 Cor 10–13 Paul inhabits the voices of his rivals in a variety of ways, utilizing a spectrum of prosopopoetic strategies from verbatim reported speech to subtler allusions to the language of his rivals.[74]

The clearest instance of this appears in 10:10, where Paul uses an explicit citation formula to mark the change in voice: αἱ ἐπιστολαὶ μέν, φησίν, βαρεῖαι καὶ ἰσχυραί, ἡ δὲ παρουσία τοῦ σώματος ἀσθενὴς καὶ ὁ λόγος ἐξουθενημένος. Whoever is the implied subject of φησίν,[75] it is clear that Paul is integrating into his argument a hostile voice.[76]

We hear echoes of this voice elsewhere in the letter. Indeed, Paul interrupts himself in its first extant verse to provide a characterization of himself that clearly derives from the perspective of his rivals:[77] ὃς κατὰ πρόσωπον μὲν ταπεινὸς ἐν ὑμῖν, ἀπὼν δὲ θαρρῶ εἰς ὑμᾶς (10:1b). This opposition between Paul's demeanor when present and when absent clearly recalls the accusation reported in 10:10,[78] but here Paul speaks in the first-person singular throughout, thus putting his opponents' words into his own mouth.[79] This is not technically *prosōpopoiia*, but it is evidently a manifestation of the same rhetorical impulse. As in 10:10, Paul confronts his opponents' charge head on by citing or paraphrasing it and then adding a qualification that reverses its force: Yes, in the past I have not

---

74. For an excellent treatment of these dialogic features in the Corinthian correspondence, see Mitchell, "The Birth of Pauline Hermeneutics," 46–52.

75. On the interpretation of φησίν, see p. 72 above.

76. So Windisch, *Der zweite Korintherbrief*, 305; Plummer, *Second Epistle*, 282; Furnish, *II Corinthians*, 468; Betz, *Der Apostel Paulus und die sokratische Tradition*, 44–45; Mitchell, "Le style, c'est l'homme," 382.

77. So already Chrysostom, *Hom. 2 Cor.* 21.1 (PG 61:542). Cf. Heinrici, *Der zweite Brief an die Korinther*, 312.

78. Windisch, *Der zweite Korintherbrief*, 305; Betz, *Der Apostel Paulus und die sokratische Tradition*, 47; Bultmann, *Second Corinthians*, 190. Cf. Chrysostom, *Hom. 2 Cor.* 21.1 (PG 61:542).

79. See esp. Betz, *Der Apostel Paulus und die sokratische Tradition*, 46.

been so bold in person as I have been in my letters, but that will change if you persist in disobedience (10:2, 11).

Having indicated to his addressees that presence/absence and weak/bold oppositions characterize the voice of his rivals, Paul can use these oppositions and their attendant vocabulary (πάρειμι/ἄπειμι; ταπεινός/θαρρέω or τολμάω) throughout the letter to channel that voice (10:2, 11, 12; 11:7, 21; 13:2, 10). Such rhetorical use of his rivals' voice reconfigures his alleged weakness as a generous decision to "spare" the Corinthians (13:2), to use his God-given ἐξουσία to build up the Corinthians and not to tear them down (10:8; 13:10).[80] Further, it highlights Paul's threat that he will not spare them again (13:2-4). Again, this is not *prosōpopoiia* per se, but it certainly has the same function.[81]

Characteristic, then, of Paul's prosopopoetic discourse is his ability to use his opponents' own language against them. Paul redeploys key elements of his opponents' accusations, rhetorically reshaping them to serve his own very different rhetorical ends. Yes, he is weak, just as his rivals claim (10:10), but what this weakness signifies, he insists, is that he is a perfect vessel of divine power (12:9-10). This is clever rhetoric. But is it a mark of formal rhetorical education?

"The Tree of Friendship"

According to Granville Ganter, surely the preeminent student of Red Jacket's rhetoric, the capacity for "harnessing his opponents' tropes and values to suit his own purpose ... was Sagoyewatha's most characteristic gift as a poet and a politician."[82] Like Paul in 2 Cor 10-13, Red Jacket echoed his

---

80. So, correctly, Welborn, *An End to Enmity*, 63.

81. One final example should briefly be noted: ἔστω δέ, ἐγὼ οὐ κατεβάρησα ὑμᾶς· ἀλλὰ ὑπάρχων πανοῦργος δόλῳ ὑμᾶς ἔλαβον (12:16). As in 10:1b, Paul speaks in the first person, but the voice of his rivals is clearly discernible. As Plummer paraphrases the underlying accusation: "Be it so, we are agreed about that; you did not *yourself* burden us by coming on us for support; but you were cunning enough to catch us and our money in other ways" (*Second Corinthians*, 363). Cf. Windisch, *Der zweite Korintherbrief*, 402; Martin, *2 Corinthians*, 444-46. As Ralph Martin notes, the parenthetical "you say" supplied by the translators of the NRSV should probably be replaced with "they say"—or, perhaps "he says" (cf. 10:10)—to reflect more accurately Paul's ongoing prosopopoetic dialogue with his rival or rivals (445).

82. Granville Ganter, "Red Jacket and the Decolonization of Republican Virtue," *American Indian Quarterly* 31 (2007): 576.

interlocutors' language, first adopting and then subverting their voices. I will restrict myself here to a single example.[83]

In his July 1819 attempt to convince the Seneca to accept President Monroe's recommendation that they sell the majority of their remaining lands, Judge Morris S. Miller used the analogy of a tree to describe what he saw as the Seneca's plight:

> [Your great Father the President] remembers that the tree of your glory and your strength flourished upon the mountain; that its branches extended in every direction; that its root struck deep into the earth, and its top reached to the clouds. He observes with regret, that while some of its branches have fallen in the lapse of time, others have been lopped off by your own improvidence; … and others have been rent by the hand of violence; that what remains shews manifest symptoms of disease and decay; that the trunk itself, once so vigorous and healthful, is now covered with moss; that the top is bending with weakness; and that a destructive canker has fastened on its roots.[84]

Miller's analogy of a once-mighty tree was chosen shrewdly, recalling the Great White Pine that served as a primary symbol of the strength and unity of the Six Nations.[85] What Miller implied thereby was that the glorious days of the Iroquois confederacy were in the past, and the Seneca now had no choice but to depend on the magnanimity of the Americans.

In his response, delivered a few days later and translated by Jasper Parrish,[86] Red Jacket began by adopting—and using to his own advantage—the role laid out for him and his people by Miller's rhetoric. He "played the role of a simpleton,"[87] feigning political naivety and ignorance of American polity:

---

83. See further Ganter, "You Are a Cunning People"; Ganter, "Decolonization"; Matthew Dennis, "Red Jacket's Rhetoric: Postcolonial Persuasions on the Native Frontiers of the Early Republic," in *American Indian Rhetorics of Survivance: Word Medicine, Word Magic* (ed. Ernest Stromberg; Pittsburgh Series in Composition, Literacy, and Culture; Pittsburgh: University of Pittsburgh Press, 2006), 15–33.

84. Text from Ganter, *Collected Speeches*, 203.

85. See Ganter, "Decolonization," 566; William N. Fenton, *The Great Law and the Longhouse: A Political History of the Iroquois Confederacy* (Civilization of the American Indian Series 223; Norman: University of Oklahoma Press, 1998), 103.

86. On the translation and textual history of the speech, see Ganter, *Collected Speeches*, 198–99.

87. Ganter, "Decolonization," 569.

> Brother, We had thought that all the promises made by one President, were handed down to the next. We do not change our Chiefs as you do. Since these treaties were made with us, you have had several changes of your President—And we do not understand why the treaty made by one President is not binding upon the other. On our parts we expect to comply with our engagements.[88]

Miller's speech had represented the Seneca as hapless children, dependent on the benevolence and wisdom of their father the President.[89] By feigning simplicity, Red Jacket ironically accepted the dependent role he and his people were assigned—and, in so doing, highlighted the failure of President Monroe to act as the virtuous father Miller's rhetoric had made him out to be.

Red Jacket carried on in this vein for much of his speech, acting the part with considerable relish:

> We do not think that there is any land, in any of our reservations, but what is useful. Look at the white people around us and back. You are not cramped for seats; they are large. Look at that man (pointing to Mr. Ellicott) he has plenty of land; if you want to buy apply to him. We have none to part with.[90]

Red Jacket's subsequent reference to his hearers' laughter makes clear that the humor of his remark was not lost on the audience—humor that derived, of course, from his ability simultaneously to pretend naivety and to strike at the heart of the matter under discussion. As Ganter explains, "While he pleads for compassion and pity as an ignorant, unlettered Native, he figuratively cuffs his opponent in the head with evidence to the contrary"[91]—evidence, that is, of his political acuity.

Not only did Red Jacket subvert the role provided for him by Miller's rhetoric; he redeployed Miller's tree analogy by echoing its language while redefining its import. Traditionally, Red Jacket and the Iroquois spoke of their relationship with the Americans as a "chain of friendship" from

---

88. Text from Ganter, *Collected Speeches*, 213.
89. E.g.: "Your great Father has cast his paternal eye over your nation"; "Your great Father the President, whose happiness it is, to promote the welfare of all his children, has not been inattentive to you" (Ganter, *Collected Speeches*, 200, 203).
90. Text from Ganter, *Collected Speeches*, 214.
91. Ganter, "You Are a Cunning People," 172.

which it was necessary, from time to time, to remove the rust.[92] The metaphor appears almost invariably throughout Red Jacket's extant speeches. Here, however, when Red Jacket holds up the treaty parchment and speaks of the Iroquois's friendship with the Americans, the metaphorical chain has been replaced by Miller's decaying tree: "Now the tree of friendship is decaying," Red Jacket laments. "Its limbs are fast falling off, and you are at fault."[93] Ganter explains the rhetorical move well: "Inverting Commissioner Miller's metaphor that the Tree of the Six Nations was rotting under their guidance, Sagoyewatha held … the rolled treaty to show that it was the national honor of the United States that was in decay."[94]

In short, like Paul in 2 Cor 10–13, Red Jacket constructed his argument by manipulating the very language and tropes of his interlocutors—and not least the language with which they characterized him. Such a strategy may be evidence of an astute speaker, but it hardly serves as proof of formal rhetorical education.

The Ubiquity of Catalogue Style

Such figures of speech as characterize Paul's tribulation list in 2 Cor 11—anaphora, isocolon, repetition, and assonance or rhyming—are, as George Kennedy explains, among the most widely observed rhetorical features of human speech.[95] What is of interest here, however, is not simply their evi-

---

92. See Fenton, *The Great Law and the Longhouse*, 7; Ganter, "Decolonization," 569–70.
93. Text from Ganter, *Collected Speeches*, 214.
94. Ganter, "Decolonization," 572.
95. Kennedy, *Comparative Rhetoric*, 42, 52–53, 88, 100, 229. See further Christian Meyer, "Rhetoric and Stylistics in Social/Cultural Anthropology," in vol. 2 of *Rhetorik und Stilistik: Ein internationales Handbuch historischer und systematischer Forschung* (ed. Ulla Fix, Andreas Gardt, and Joachim Knape; 2 vols.; Handbücher zur Sprach- und Kommunikationswissenschaft 31; Berlin: de Gruyter, 2009), 1877–78; Meyer, *Mahnen, Prahlen, Drohen*, 178–83. The ubiquity of the more general phenomenon of parallelism, to which all of these figures are closely related, was demonstrated by Roman Jakobson, "Grammatical Parallelism and Its Russian Facet," *Language* 42 (1966): 399–429. Cf. Sherzer and Woodbury, *Native American Discourse*, passim; Deborah Tannen, *Talking Voices: Repetition, Dialogue, and Imagery in Conversational Discourse* (2nd ed.; Studies in Interactional Sociolinguistics 25; Cambridge: Cambridge University Press, 2007), 48–101.

dent universality, but the ubiquity of their use, in combination, to produce catalogue style.

In particular, it is not difficult to document what appears to be a basic human propensity to catalogue hardships using various forms of isocolon and anaphora. The following are firsthand accounts, provided by locals and reported by international journalists, of various recent catastrophes:

> "There is no water, there is no food, no shelter. There are thousands of people living in the field."[96]

> "We have no work, no shelter, no food. People have died because of the terrible conditions we live in."[97]

> "We have no food, no clothes, no home. We have lost everything."[98]

> "These people have no water, no food, no medicine; nobody is helping us."[99]

> "No job, no money, no social welfare, no food."[100]

From Kenya to Haiti to Ireland to Bangladesh, these speakers describe their plight remarkably similarly. None of these incipient catalogues, of course, approaches the length and complexity of Paul's list of tribulations,

---

96. Jorge Barerra, "More than 1,400 Canadians Still Missing in Haiti," *National Post*, January 15, 2010. Cited 20 January 2010. Online: http://www.nationalpost.com/story.html?id=2444958.

97. Associated Press, "International Court Names Suspects in Kenya Attacks," *National Public Radio*, 15 December 2010. Cited 5 January 2011. Online: http://www.npr.org/2010/12/15/132081457/international-court-names-suspects-in-kenya-attacks?.

98. Jonathan Watts, "No Food, No Clothes, No Home: Bangladesh's Poor Who Have Lost Everything," *The Guardian*, 23 November 23 2007. Cited 20 January 2010. Online: http://www.guardian.co.uk/world/2007/nov/23/naturaldisasters.internationalaidanddevelopment.

99. Tom Brown and Andrew Cawthorne, "Mass Burials after Haiti Quake; Aid Jams Airport," *Reuters*, 14 January 2010. Cited 20 January 2010. Online: http://www.reuters.com/article/idUSTRE60B5IZ20100114.

100. Noel Baker, " 'No Job, No Money, No Social Welfare, No Food,' " *Irish Examiner*, 9 April 2009. Cited 5 January 2011. Online: http://www.irishexaminer.com/ireland/idididqloj/.

but they clearly are manifestations of the same rhetorical sensibility. The common impulse for rhythmic itemization is particularly evident from the decision of each to avoid any elaboration until the conclusion of each list.

The same impulse can be observed in a Canadian woman's testimony regarding a more personal tragedy, the diagnosis of her husband with Alzheimer's disease:

> I cannot scarcely think of an aspect of our lives that is not being impacted by this: um, our financial circumstances, our physical circumstances—we're having to sell our home and to move—even our emotional [pause] relationship.[101]

A modern day Quintilian might scorn a few aspects of her usage ("cannot scarcely," "impacted"), but nevertheless this is an interesting example of the rudiments of catalogue style. Note the epistrophic repetition of "circumstances" in the first two items, a usage to which, it seems from her pause, she is tempted to return in formulating the final item until she realizes its inappropriateness and selects a better word.

Interesting here too is the redundancy of this catalogue. The first two items are both comprehended by the more specific detail—the necessity of selling her home—by which they are explained. Clearly, then, it is the catalogue-like features themselves that give the impression of comprehensiveness, regardless of whether the specific items listed substantiate that impression. Indeed, here we meet with the basic rhetorical force of the catalogue: the impression of magnitude it is able to generate. As Yair Hoffman explains, "It seems that a flow of words, all of which have the same syntactical structure and a certain common denominator, … has a cumulative power far beyond the information conveyed in the adding of parts to one another."[102] The catalogue, in other words, has the potential to function metonymically.[103] Even without rhetorical training, speakers apparently recognize this potential, hence the ubiquity of the form.

It would not be surprising to find catalogues in the speech of Red Jacket. Christian Meyer introduces his thorough review of ethnographic

---

101. CBC Radio, *The Story from Here*, 14 July 2010. Cited 5 January 2011. Online: http://www.cbc.ca/thestoryfromhere/episode-update/2010/07/14/july-14-2010/.

102. Hoffman, *A Blemished Perfection*, 88.

103. See John Miles Foley, *The Singer of Tales in Performance* (Voices in Performance and Text; Bloomington: Indiana University Press, 1995), 121–22.

study of indigenous North and South American speech practices by observing, "Die wichtigsten, überall vielfach verwendeten Figuren der amerikanischen Indianer sind Repetitio und Parallelismus."[104] He elaborates in terms reminiscent of what we have been calling catalogue style: "Mit Parallelismus wird z.B. die Wiederholung eines Wortes, Wortteils, Satzes oder Satzteils in einem anderen Kontext (Anapher, Epipher, Alliteration, Reim), [oder] die Wiederholung rhythmischer oder intonationaler Muster ... bezeichnet."[105]

Lacking transcription in the original language, it is difficult to verify the presence of such stylistic features in Red Jacket's speech, but there are tantalizing hints that he used them extensively:

> [The President] told us it would be necessary to quit the mode of Indian living and learn the manner of the White people. And that the US would provide us oxen to plow the ground which would relieve our women from digging—that we should be provided with cows & we must learn our girls to milk & make butter & chees. That we should be furnished with farming utensils for cultivating the ground & raise wheat & other grain—that we must have spinning wheals & learn our children to spin & knitt—We were told we must make use of Cattle instead of Moose Elk etc. & Swine in stead of beans, sheep in place of dear etc etc.[106]

One suspects that Red Jacket was just getting going when the translator or transcriber lost patience.[107] In any case, even in translation, echoes of the rhythmic pattern remain: The government's proposed provision is set out, followed by its putatively salutary result.[108] Notice Red Jacket's affinity for paired items at the end of each clause: butter and cheese, wheat and other

---

104. Meyer, *Mahnen, Prahlen, Drohen*, 178: "The most important, widely and frequently used figures of speech of the American Indian are repetition and parallelism."

105. Ibid., 179: "Parallelism refers to, e.g., the repetition of a word, word-part, sentence or clause in another context (anaphora, epiphora, alliteration, rhyme), or the repetition of rhythmic or tonal pattern."

106. Text from Ganter, *Collected Speeches*, 116. For other examples of isocolon, see pp. 17, 106.

107. For the use of *etc.* to mark elision by a transcriber, see, e.g., Ganter, *Collected Speeches*, 46.

108. Albert Lord's discussion of the usefulness of formulas in the composition of oral epic poetry may help us understand the ubiquity of such repetitive syntax as Red Jacket exemplifies here. The reuse of syntactical structures with substitution of key elements is not only rhetorically effective, but also rather easy to pull off, once one gets

grain, spin and knit. Finally, if it does not result from the summarizing work of the translator, observe his use in the final sentence of simple antithetical clauses reminiscent of texts like 2 Cor 4:8–9.

If the precise nature of Red Jacket's use of these figures remains inaccessible, we are fortunate, thanks to the work of Gary Gossen, to have a significant record of Chamula speech in the original language. Gossen provides the following as an example of the "redundancy and parallelism [that] is repeated throughout the oral tradition." Here a female sheep thief is being chastised in court:[109]

ʾoy ša shayibuk velta ʾelkʿanik.	Many times already you have stolen.
šavelkʿan čihe.	You steal sheep.
šavelkʿan ti ʾalakʿe.	You steal chicken.
šavelkʿan ti ʾisakʿe.	You steal potatoes.
šavelkʿan ti maʾil e.	You steal squash.
šavelkʿan ti kʿuʾil e.	You steal clothing.
šavelkʿan ti ʾitah e.	You steal cabbage.
šavelkʿan ti tulukʿe.	You steal turkeys.
skotol kʿusi šavelkʿan.	You steal anything.
ʾaʾ ša noʾoš muyuk bu šavelkʿan be sbekʿ yat li kirsanoetik;	The only thing you don't steal from people are their testicles;
ʾaʾ ša noʾoš čaloʾ.	And those you only eat.

The anaphoric repetition of *šavelkʿan* here is reminiscent of Paul's repeated use of κινδύνοις in 2 Cor 11:26. An added touch here, though, is the use of rhythmic couplets, the first two of which rhyme. The initial accusation, stealing sheep, stands alone, followed by three pairs of items and then the catch-all "anything"—a common way, as we have already seen, to conclude a catalogue. Notice also the elegant reversal of the syntax, not reproduced in the translation, in the last catalogue item. Finally, in the second "stanza" note the artfulness of the final line, which follows the syntax of the first right up until the devastating final word.

---

the hang of it. See *The Singer of Tales* (Harvard Studies in Comparative Literature 24; Cambridge: Harvard University Press, 1960), 35–36.

109. Text and translation from Gary Gossen, "To Speak with a Heated Heart: Chamula Canons of Style and Good Performance," in *Explorations in the Ethnography of Speaking* (ed. Richard Bauman and Joel Sherzer; 2nd ed.; SSCFL 8; Cambridge: Cambridge University Press, 1989), 401–2.

Another example, for which I am indebted to a useful article by Christian Meyer, comes from Ivo Strecker's ethnographic work among the Hamar people of southern Ethiopia. Though a song rather than an oration, we see here the same pattern of lexical substitution within a fixed syntactic structure,[110] as well as figures of speech such as (informal) *prosōpopoiia* and, in the final line, aposiopesis:

> Are people fathered for the vultures?
>> Fathered for the hyenas?
>> Fathered for the sun?
>
> People are fathered for people.
> A man fathers [a son] so that he may herd cows;
>> that he may herd goats;
>> that he may make fields;
>> that he may herd calves;
>> that he may herd lambs;
>> that he may be sent on an errand:
>>> 'Run and get me that thing from him over there!'
>
> He whom you fathered—[he has been devoured by] vultures.[111]

Finally, a rather different example: Billy Sunday remains one of the most influential of that peculiarly American religious figure, the revivalist preacher. Though frequently scorned by the intellectual and cultural elite, Sunday was enormously popular, not least because of his impassioned and compelling preaching style.[112] What is interesting for our purposes is the means by which he acquired his prowess as a preacher. It was not primarily formal education.

Sunday was the son of an itinerant laborer who died less than a month after his son's birth, in 1862, in rural Iowa. After spending some years in an orphanage, Sunday was working for his living by the age of 14. Although,

---

110. For further examples, see Meyer, *Mahnen, Prahlen, Drohen*, 108–9, 159; Tannen, *Talking Voices*, 58.

111. Ivo Strecker, *Nyabole: Laufgesang—Singing on the Way to the Dancing Ground* (Museum Collection Berlin; Berlin: Wergo, 2003), 74–75; cited in Meyer, "Rhetoric and Stylistics," 1878.

112. The best recent treatments of Sunday and his influence are Lyle W. Dorsett, *Billy Sunday and the Redemption of Urban America* (Library of Religious Biography; Grand Rapids: Eerdmans, 1991); Robert F. Martin, *Hero of the Heartland: Billy Sunday and the Transformation of American Society, 1862–1935* (Bloomington: Indiana University Press, 2002).

thanks to the patronage of a generous employer, he did attend some high school, he did not graduate. As a youth, he was known not for brains but for his speed on the baseball field.[113] Some years later, when, as a professional ball player in Chicago, he tried to court a respectable, middle-class girl, he was, as his letters to her suggest, "sensitive about his impoverished background, his ungrammatical speech, and his lack of polish."[114]

But if Sunday did not have the advantage of extensive formal education, he nevertheless had heard a lot of good preaching. By the late nineteenth century, revivalist preaching was a well-established part of the fabric of American culture and religious life. Sunday himself was converted through the evangelistic sermons of Harry Munroe—sermons that, if Sunday's recollections can be trusted, were typical instances of the genre.[115] And, before hitting the road as an evangelist himself, he spent two years as an assistant to the well-known Presbyterian preacher J. Wilbur Chapman.[116] It was through something akin to apprenticeship, then, that Sunday learned to harness his natural theatricality into the rhythms and cadences of preaching. Moreover, since he met with only limited success in his first decade on the road,[117] we can safely assume that much of his prowess simply derived from practice.

One aspect of rhetorical performance that Sunday mastered was what Quintilian would have called *amplificatio* (*Inst.* 8.4). In Sunday's telling of the tale, for example, the owners of the pigs Jesus dispatched into the sea are described as "peanut-brained, weasel-eyed, hog-jowled, beetle-browned, bull-necked lobsters."[118] In other settings, this propensity for rhythmic elaboration is expressed in catalogue-style itemization. Here Sunday eulogizes the temperance movement:

> They have driven the business from Kansas,
> > they have driven it from Georgia
> > > and Maine and Mississippi
> > > and North Carolina and North Dakota
> > > and Oklahoma and Tennessee and West Virginia.

---

113. Martin, *Hero of the Heartland*, 2–8; Dorsett, *Billy Sunday*, 6–15.
114. Martin, *Hero of the Heartland*, 36.
115. See Dorsett, *Billy Sunday*, 25–27.
116. Martin, *Hero of the Heartland*, 46.
117. See ibid., 47–48.
118. Text from William T. Ellis, *"Billy" Sunday: The Man and His Message* (Philadelphia: Myers, 1914), 86.

> And they have driven it out of 1,756 counties…
>> It is prosperity against poverty,
>> sobriety against drunkenness,
>> honesty against thieving,
>> heaven against hell.
> Don't you want to see men sober? Brutal staggering men transformed into respectable citizens?
> No, said a saloonkeeper, to hell with men. We are interested in our business, we have no interest in humanity.[119]

I have included the final two sentences apropos of our discussion of *prosōpopoiia* in the previous section.[120] As for features of catalogue style, note the consistency of Sunday's use of conjunctions: in the first section, initial asyndeton gives way to consistent use of "and" once Sunday begins to elide the verb phrase; in the second, he uses asyndeton throughout. Either pattern would be at home in Paul's catalogues: such repetition of conjunctions is reminiscent of Rom 8:35–39; the antitheses in 2 Cor 4:8–9 are linked asyndetically. Noteworthy also is the rhythmic isocolon in the second section, centering on the repetition of "against" and building to its rather overwrought climax. Finally, notice Sunday's use of alliteration/anaphora in the organization of the states: Maine and Mississippi; North Carolina and North Dakota.

As a final illustration of Sunday's verbal art, at once tasteless and compelling, note the use of anaphora and isocolon in his declaration of eternal war against the saloon:

> I'll kick it as long as I have a foot
>> and I'll fight it and punch it as long as I have a fist
> I'll bark as long as I have a head
>> I'll bite it as long as I have a tooth
> and when I am old
>> and fistless
>> and footless
>> and toothless

---

119. Ibid., 87–88.

120. This is, in fact, the first of many instances in this sermon of Sunday's attribution of venal first-person speech to those who profit from "booze." A number are accompanied by apostrophe.

I'll gum it
> till I go home to glory
> and it goes home to perdition.[121]

Conclusion

Since the earliest work of Betz on Galatians, it has been recognized that if Paul utilized formal rhetorical conventions, he did so in his own peculiar way. Betz himself observed both the general comparability of Paul's letters with rhetorical sources and a number of specific idiosyncrasies that such comparison placed in sharp relief.[122] His explanation of these data has become standard fare: similarities result from Paul's knowledge of rhetorical conventions; specific differences derive from Paul's philosophical inclination or conscious rhetorical intention.[123] Accordingly, arguments like that of Tor Vegge for Paul's formal rhetorical education have proceeded on the basis of Paul's general affinity to rhetorical theory, and then found ways to explain away specific differences. But this mode of argumentation obscures the nature of the Paul's relation to the formal rhetorical sources.

Consider again, for example, Paul's putative use of *synkrisis*: Yes, Paul certainly makes comparisons, but he does not do so in accordance with the conventions for *synkrisis* as manifested in the *Progymnasmata*, Plutarch's *Parallel Lives*, and encomiastic oratory. Although there are differences in the use of *synkrisis* among these three sources, all clearly share a family resemblance; Paul does not. In short, with respect to his use of *synkrisis*, Paul differs more from the rhetorical sources than they differ among themselves. In the company of such speakers, he is an outlier.

---

121. Transcribed from an audio recording available at *SermonIndex.net*. Cited 6 January 2011. Online: http://media.sermonindex.net/4/SID4499.mp3. Sunday stumbles over the "fight it" in the second line; the disruption of the rhythm appears to be accidental.

122. See Betz, "Literary Composition and Function," 360, 369, 375–79.

123. Ibid., 369; Betz, *Galatians*, 129. See also Vegge, *Paulus und das antike Schulwesen*, 405; C. Jan Swearingen, "The Tongues of Men: Understanding the Greek Rhetorical Sources for Paul's Letters to the Romans and 1 Corinthians," in *Rhetorical Argumentation in Biblical Texts: Essays from the Lund 2000 Conference* (ed. Anders Eriksson, Thomas H. Olbricht, and Walter G. Übelacker; ESEC 8; Harrisburg, Pa.: Trinity, 2002), 233.

This chapter has presented a different group of comparators, consisting of not of speakers formally educated in classical rhetoric but instead of those whose rhetorical capacity was acquired informally. Here Paul is rather more at home—or, to stretch my statistical metaphor, here Paul is within a standard deviation: With respect to the rhetoric of his self-reference (*periautologia*) and his use of *prodiorthōsis*, informal *prosōpopoiia*, and catalogue style, Paul differs from these comparators about as much as they differ from one another. Thus, given the fact that he evinces no greater similarity to the formal rhetorical sources than do these other speakers, there is far more justification for locating Paul in this informal rhetorical matrix than for placing him among the educated elite of the Greco-Roman world.

One related conclusion, central to the argument of this study, should be reiterated: the four rhetorical features treated in this chapter evidently belong to the realm of general rhetoric—the basic human propensity for persuasive speech. Thus there is no evidence that Paul's use thereof evinces familiarity with the specific conventions of formal Greco-Roman rhetoric. Certainly the appearance of these rhetorical features in Paul's letters does not provide grounds for overturning what was for centuries the consensus view of Paul's rhetoric—namely, that it was forceful but unschooled.

Although I have limited myself here to an evaluation of rhetorical features in 2 Cor 10–13, there are indications that this method of analysis, if extended to the remainder of the Pauline corpus, would meet with similar results. Kennedy provides evidence, for example, of the ubiquity of the rhetorical question,[124] and gives diverse examples of the persuasive use of what Aristotle called proof from *logos*, *ethos*, and *pathos*.[125] The division of speeches along the general lines of the formal *partes orationis* is attested in other cultures as well.[126] These data must be taken into account when evaluating Paul's rhetoric. It will not do to make claims about how Paul's rhetoric relates to the formal Greco-Roman tradition without cultivating sensitivity to the general phenomenon of persuasive human speech.

Finally, this chapter has, I hope, illustrated a more general point as well: Compelling speech is not the exclusive preserve of the formally educated. This is hardly a novel observation; still, given the nature of recent

---

124. Kennedy, *Comparative Rhetoric*, 88, 105, 127, 230; also Meyer, "Rhetoric and Stylistics," 1878.
125. Kennedy, *Comparative Rhetoric*, 223–25.
126. Ibid., 92, 148.

discussion of Paul's rhetorical education, it bears repeating. As Antoinette Clark Wire has quipped: "Just as a child can speak her native tongue correctly without schooling, so a man can sell a horse or a conviction very persuasively without reflecting upon how he does it."[127] The process of "language socialization" by which such skills are acquired is the subject of the next chapter.

---

127. Antoinette Clark Wire, *The Corinthian Women Prophets: A Reconstruction through Paul's Rhetoric* (Minneapolis: Fortress, 1990), 2.

11
THE ACQUISITION OF
INFORMAL RHETORICAL KNOWLEDGE

The acquisition of informal rhetorical competence is, in practice, inseparable from the acquisition of language itself.[1] We do not learn first to speak and then to speak persuasively. We learn to speak. This is, in short, because there is no speech in the abstract, only speech as social practice. Accordingly, it is as social practice that we learn the essentials of persuasion—that is, of rhetorical performance.

In the previous chapter, I set forth evidence that the sort of rhetorical aptitude demonstrated by Paul can also be found among those with no formal schooling in rhetoric. In this chapter I will discuss briefly the means by which such informal rhetorical ability is developed. We lack sufficient biographical information about Paul to assert any specific correspondence between Paul's experience and that, for example, of Red Jacket; rather, this is an attempt to map the territory, and, in so doing, to invite us to rethink the privileged place formal education has in our explanatory imagination.

THE NATURE OF LANGUAGE SOCIALIZATION

In the course of his ethnographic fieldwork among the Melanesians of eastern New Guinea, Bronislaw Malinowski was struck by his inability to translate with any degree of adequacy many of the texts he had collected. Or, rather, Malinowski recognized that translation was itself an act of ethnographic description: the only way to render these utterances meaningful was to explain, explicitly or implicitly, their social context and function.[2] From this observation, Malinowski drew the attendant conclusion:

---

[1]. See Hymes, "On Communicative Competence," 61.
[2]. Bronislaw Malinowski, "The Problem of Meaning in Primitive Languages," in

> A statement, spoken in real life, is never detached from the situation in which it has been uttered. For each verbal statement by a human being has the aim and function of expressing some thought or feeling actual at that moment and in that situation, and necessary for some reason or other to be made known to another person or persons ... Without some imperative stimulus of the moment, there can be no spoken statement.[3]

Speech, then, is "a mode of action," and an utterance "a piece of human behaviour."[4] Language, Malinowski concluded, must be studied ethnographically, as one functional element in a social system.[5]

Accordingly, if speech belongs to the realm of social practice, what children learn when they learn their mother tongue is not language in the abstract but rather what Dell Hymes has called "communicative competence,"[6] the ability to use speech according to the linguistic but also the social norms of a particular "speech community." To quote Malinowski once more:

> To the child, words are ... not only means of expression but efficient modes of action. The name of a person uttered aloud in a piteous voice possesses the power of materializing this person. Food has to be called for and it appears—in the majority of cases.[7]

What children learn, in other words, is the effective use of speech in social interaction—and this includes, as Malinowski's examples make clear, the rudimentary ability to persuade.

The Meaning of Meaning, by C. K. Ogden and I. A. Richards (New York: Harcourt, Brace, and Company, 1936), 299–302.

3. Ibid., 307.

4. Ibid., 312. There clearly is considerable similarity between Malinowski's description of language as a "mode of action" and the basic insights of J. L. Austin's speech-act theory some decades later. See *How To Do Things with Words* (Cambridge: Harvard University Press, 1962). Pragmatists continue to debate Malinowski's influence on Austin's work. See Kepa Korta, "Malinowski and Pragmatics: Claim Making in the History of Linguistics," *Journal of Pragmatics* 40 (2008): 1645–60.

5. See also the seminal discussion of Dell Hymes in *Foundations in Sociolinguistics: An Ethnographic Approach* (Philadelphia: University of Pennsylvania Press, 1974).

6. Ibid., 75. See further Hymes, "Competence and Performance in Linguistic Theory," in *Language Acquisition: Models and Methods* (ed. Renira Huxley and Elisabeth Ingram; London: Academic Press, 1971), 3–28.

7. Malinowski, "The Problem of Meaning," 320.

Building on these basic insights, sociolinguists have given considerable thought to the nature of language acquisition—or, as some prefer, "language socialization"—in various speech communities.[8] For present purposes, we need not pursue the discussion in detail. What is significant, though, is the basic insight: effective use of language, which includes facility in the common tropes and conventional genres of one's speech community, is learned primarily through social interaction. As we will see below, the same obtains for the language socialization of adults into more sophisticated rhetorical practices. Formal systems of rhetorical theorization and education are the exception; more commonly, informal rhetorical competence is transmitted as are other social practices, through what Bourdieu describes as "an anonymous, pervasive pedagogic action" by means of which "practical mastery is transmitted in practice, in its practical state, without attaining the level of discourse."[9]

An Analogy: *The Singer of Tales*

Kennedy would likely argue that Malinowksi's crying child is already using rhetoric, (unconsciously?) manipulating pitch and volume, if not yet verbal meaning, for maximum persuasive effect.[10] But even if it is legitimate to call this rhetoric, it is clearly a far cry—no pun intended—from the sort of thing we observe in the letters of Paul. Is the notion of language socialization sufficient to account also for this degree of rhetorical aptitude? Recent research into the ethnography of communication suggests that it is—as, indeed, do my comparative observations above. Before we pursue these studies, however, it will be helpful to consider an analogous process of language socialization, one that attests to the subtlety and complexity of the language practices that can be transmitted independently of formal education.

---

8. See esp. Elinor Ochs, "Linguistic Resources for Socializing Humanity," in *Rethinking Linguistic Relativity* (ed. John J. Gumperz and Stephen C. Levinson; SSCFL 17; Cambridge: Cambridge University Press, 1996), 407–37; Ochs, *Culture and Language Development: Language Acquisition and Language Socialization in a Samoan Village* (SSCFL 6; Cambridge: Cambridge University Press, 1988); Bambi B. Schieffelin and Elinor Ochs, eds., *Language Socialization across Cultures* (SSCFL 3; Cambridge University Press, 1986).

9. Bourdieu, *Theory of Practice*, 87.

10. On various levels of intentionality in the production of rhetoric, see Kennedy, *Comparative Rhetoric*, 25–26.

In *The Singer of Tales*, Albert Lord describes a three-stage process of observation, imitation, and practice by which a young Yugoslav learns the art of oral epic.[11] The first stage he characterizes as an "unconscious process of assimilation":

> From meter and music he absorbs in his earliest years the rhythms of epic, even as he absorbs the rhythms of speech itself and in a larger sense of the life about him. He learns empirically the length of phrase, the partial cadences, the full stops. If the singer is in the Yugoslav tradition, he obtains a sense of ten syllables followed by a syntactical pause, although he never counts out ten syllables, and if asked, might not be able to tell how many syllables there are between pauses. In the same way he absorbs into his own experience a feeling for the tendency toward the distribution of accented and unaccented syllables and their very subtle variations caused by the play of tonic accent, vowel length, and melodic line. These "restrictive" elements he comes to know from much listening to the songs about him and from being engrossed in their imaginative world. He learns the meter ever in association with particular phrases, those expressing the most common and oft-repeated ideas of the traditional story.... His instinctive grasp of alliterations and assonances is sharpened. One word begins to suggest another by its very sound.[12]

The second stage of a singer's "education" involves more intentionality, the conscious decision to attend to and to imitate the singing of the masters. Still, there is no school in which to learn to perform these songs, only the opportunity for immersion in their performance. Even if books of songs exist, most singers are illiterate and cannot put them to any meaningful use.[13]

Finally, Lord emphasizes the decisive role of practice: "Whatever feeling for such sound patterns the boy has absorbed in his pre-singing days is crystallized when he begins to perform."[14] He enters the arena of public performance, unsteadily at first, but with growing confidence and control as he learns to produce the rhythms and formulae in which he has been immersed.

---

11. Lord, *The Singer of Tales*, 20–26.
12. Ibid., 32–33.
13. Ibid., 23.
14. Ibid., 42.

Acquiring aptitude as a singer, then, involves "no definite program of study, of course, no sense of learning this or that formula or set of formulas. It is a process of imitation and of assimilation through listening and much practice of one's own."[15] It is, in other words, a process of socialization into a particular speech practice, albeit one that is at some remove from informal communication and thus is acquired with a greater than usual degree of self-consciousness.[16]

Mexicano Rhetorical "Education"

The process of the acquisition of informal "rhetorical competence" among the Mexicanos of rural New Mexico, as described by ethnographer and folklorist Charles L. Briggs, follows the same three stages as Lord outlined, namely, observation, imitation, and ongoing practice. Briggs's summary is strikingly reminiscent of Lord's discussion:

> The beginning of the acquisition process lies in observation. Frequent exposure to the behavior of one's seniors leads to the internalization of a sense of the pattern underlying what has been seen and heard. This permits the "student" to begin imitating the words and actions of others. Evaluating the success of such attempts is no less important for initial imitations than for other areas of rhetorical competence. Once an individual can adequately reproduce the forms provided by his or her seniors ... the time has come to make one's own judgments as to which utterances are appropriate in which environments. Such attempts to produce original utterances are met with evaluations with respect to his or her success.[17]

---

15. Ibid., 24.
16. As a recent study by Lucy Green demonstrates, popular music provides a similar analogy. Popular music skills and knowledge are acquired primarily through what Green calls "informal music learning practices"; therefore, "despite its widespread provision in a large number of countries, and notwithstanding the recent entrance of popular music into the formal arena, music education has had relatively little to do with the development of the majority of those musicians who have produced the vast proportion of the music which the global population listens to, dances to, identifies with and enjoys" (*How Popular Musicians Learn: A Way Ahead for Music Education* [Ashgate Popular and Folk Music Series; Aldershot, Eng.: Ashgate, 2001], 5).
17. Charles L. Briggs, *Learning How to Ask: A Sociolinguistic Appraisal of the Role of the Interview in Social Science Research* (SSCFL 1; Cambridge: Cambridge University Press, 1986), 63–64.

Again, then, it is through social interaction that the Mexicanos learn to speak appropriately and persuasively. We can elaborate further, thanks to the acuity of Briggs's observations during more than a decade of fieldwork in Córdova, New Mexico.

Córdova is—or was in the 1970s and 80s, when Briggs was there—a town of about 700 inhabitants in rural northern New Mexico. The town, located in the foothills of the Sangre de Cristo Mountains, was populated almost exclusively by Mexicanos, who first settled the area in the first half of the eighteenth century.[18] By the 1980s, a majority of the local workforce did janitorial and construction work in Los Alamos, 30 miles to the southwest.[19] Prior to 1946, however, the community was considerably more isolated: the road into town was little more than a trail; Córdovans relied on sheep herding and seasonal migratory labor for income.[20]

This geographical isolation from mainstream America was paralleled by linguistic isolation. Córdovans speak New Mexico Spanish, which sets them apart not only from the English speakers who represent the majority in Los Alamos, but also from other Hispanics. As Briggs explains:

> Using Castilian or Standard Mexican Spanish in northern New Mexico immediately alerts native speakers of New Mexican Spanish that the person in question has emerged from a vastly different social, cultural, and educational background and, more than likely, a higher social class. A person learns New Mexican Spanish not in formal academic settings but by living with *Mexicanos*.[21]

In short, the Córdovan speakers whom Briggs studied—and especially the elders who were his primary informants[22]—represent a distinct speech community. Fluency in their native speech practices derives not from formal education but from social interaction.

This does not mean that Córdovans take a pedestrian view of language, or that they lack rhetorical sophistication. On the contrary, in Córdova

---

18. See Charles L. Briggs, *Competence in Performance: The Creativity of Tradition in Mexicano Verbal Art* (University of Pennsylvania Press Conduct and Communication Series; Philadelphia: University of Pennsylvania Press, 1988), 30–31.

19. Briggs, *Learning How to Ask*, 33.

20. Ibid., 36; Briggs, *Competence in Performance*, 37–38.

21. Briggs, *Learning How to Ask*, 36–37.

22. According to Briggs, "many residents over fifty know little or no English" (ibid., 36).

"rhetorical competence is highly valued, and an individual's verbal capacity is closely related to her or his reputation in the community."[23] Such competence includes mastery of folkloric material—what the locals refer to as *la plática de los viejitos de antes*[24]—but also the ability to engage in what the classical tradition would call deliberative rhetoric. Briggs explains the social practices that facilitate the development of what he calls "political oratory" in Córdova:

> As they progress from age thirty to sixty, many assume roles of importance in religious voluntary associations, irrigation-ditch associations, parish affairs, domestic water and land-grant associations, and other intracommunity groups. If they prove themselves to be thoughtful and persuasive speakers, their statements with regard to community affairs can come to be taken quite seriously by persons of all ages. These are the years in which men and women who possess *talento* for public speaking are expected to develop and exhibit their rhetorical facility. A great deal of prestige accrues to the community member who can sway an audience in the course of a meeting or other public gathering.... Gaining recognition for one's verbal abilities is an important part of the process of moving through the status of *muchacho* (literally "boy," meaning "young man") and into full-fledged adult status. Speaking out on the affairs of the community is the most important means of establishing one's reputation at this point in life.[25]

Briggs provides an example from a speech delivered at a community meeting regarding water usage. His rhetorical analysis highlights the speaker's ability to establish *ethos* from the outset, as well as effective utilization of key shared values.[26] Further, Briggs explains how the orator's "slow, clear, measured, rhythmic forceful speech" won the attention of his audience. Its rhythmic qualities are clear from the following few lines, chosen apropos of our discussion of catalogue style above. (Note that Briggs uses small uppercase letters to indicate emphasis.)

Y no camine bajo de,
    bajo de POLÍTICA

---

23. Ibid., 38.
24. For a comprehensive discussion, see Briggs, *Competence in Performance.*
25. Briggs, *Learning How to Ask*, 77, 82.
26. Ibid., 79–83

o bajo de ENVÍDIA
o bajo de esto y el OTRO.[27]

Briggs's study is remarkable for its detailed attention to the acquisition of rhetorical ability, but he is hardly alone in his conclusions. In 1975, Maurice Bloch edited a volume entitled *Political Language and Oratory in Traditional Society*.[28] Despite a host of differences in speech practices among the various cultural groups treated, two notes run like a refrain throughout the volume: first, rhetorical competence is both valued and cultivated;[29] second, it is acquired through a process of observation, imitation, and practice, sometimes formalized to varying degrees, but often undertaken through informal social processes.[30] Anne Salmond's account of the acquisition of oratorical ability among the rural Maori is particularly lucid:

> Oratory is learned as a natural process. Children hang around the fringes of the *marae* [speaking-ground] at local gatherings to watch the elders perform. Proverbs, genealogy, and local history soon become familiar, and the formal constraints of speech-making are unconsciously acquired. Young men stand to speak for the first time at a family life crisis ... and after that the ambitious ones take their opportunities where they can.... It is in the informal speeches that they first enter *marae* discussions, and practice for an eventual role as regular speakers.[31]

The *marae* of which Salmond speaks, like the community meeting at which our Mexicano orator held forth, exemplify what Pierre Bourdieu refers to as "structural exercises" that enable the transmission of practical

---

27. Ibid., 78–79. "And not walk under—under [the influence of] politics, or under envy, or under this or that."
28. Maurice Bloch, ed., *Political Language and Oratory in Traditional Society* (London: Academic Press, 1975).
29. Maurice Bloch, "Introduction," 4–5; Anne Salmond, "Mana Makes the Man: A Look at Maori Oratory and Politics," 45, 50; Mark Hobart, "Orators and Patrons: Two Types of Political Leader in Balinese Village Society," 74–75; John Comaroff, "Talking Politics: Oratory and Authority in a Tswana Chiefdom," 143; David Turton, "The Relationship between Oratory and the Exercise of Influence among the Mursi," 176.
30. Bloch, "Introduction," 22–23; Salmond, "Mana Makes the Man," 50; Hobart, "Orators and Patrons," 77. Cf. Turton, "Oratory and the Exercise of Influence," 177–78.
31. Salmond, "Mana Makes the Man," 50, 62.

mastery.³² Bourdieu conceptualizes such exercises as lying in the middle ground between learning through unconscious familiarization and explicit instruction. Like the play wrestling of pups, such activities serve to inculcate at once both practical skills and social roles—or, as Bourdieu would have it, practical mastery of the dispositions constituting the *habitus*. As Bourdieu explains, it is through boys' "silent observance of the discussions in the men's assembly, with their effects of eloquence, their rituals, their strategies,"³³ that they receive informal training both in diction and in disposition.

A similar process of language socialization almost certainly lies at the root of Red Jacket's rhetorical prowess. Political oratory played a key role in Iroquois society, wherein consensus generally was reached through persuasion rather than the exercise of power.³⁴ Red Jacket was fascinated by the political discourse of the council from a young age, and at seventeen was selected as a "runner" and entrusted with "the responsibility of accurately transmitting the words spoken in council" to neighboring tribes.³⁵ Thus he had plenty of opportunity for observation and imitation, and, later, practice.

Conclusion

George Kennedy's study of comparative rhetoric led him to what now should be a familiar conclusion regarding the acquisition of rhetorical competence: excepting the rare instances of formal rhetorical education, oratorical skills are attained through a process of "learning rhetorical conventions by observing older speakers, imitating them, and finding opportunities for practice."³⁶ In other words, most people acquire rhetorical competency the same way they do most of their learning—through social

---

32. Bourdieu, *Theory of Practice*, 88–89.
33. Ibid., 89.
34. See Taylor, *The Divided Ground*, 18–21; Meyer, *Mahnen, Prahlen, Drohen*, 47–77.
35. Densmore, *Red Jacket*, 8. Cf. Meyer, *Mahnen, Prahlen, Drohen*, 83. Michael Foster's ethnographic study of ritual oratory in the contemporary Iroquois Longhouse describes a similar process of acquiring competence (*From the Earth to Beyond the Sky*, 31).
36. Kennedy, *Comparative Rhetoric*, 63.

interaction. I will conclude this chapter with a few observations regarding the applicability of such a model to Paul.

Galatians 1:14 has long been taken as an autobiographical statement referring to Paul's Jewish education: "I advanced in Judaism beyond many among my people of the same age, for I was far more zealous [lit. "a zealot"] for the traditions of my ancestors" (NRSV). For Conybeare and Howson, what we see here is an "eager and indefatigable student"; likewise, more recently, Margaret Mitchell speaks of "Paul's self-portrait in Gal 1:14 of his youthful studious zeal."[37] The interpretation is offered far more often than it is argued; in fact, I have yet to locate an attempt to explain why Paul's progress ἐν τῷ Ἰουδαϊσμῷ should be interpreted as scholastic achievement. In any case, the reading is insupportable.[38] As John Knox rightly insists, Paul "nowhere claims to have been an expert in the law, only zealous of carrying it out."[39]

What then does Paul mean by saying that he "advanced" (προκόπτω) beyond his contemporaries? Josephus does use this word to refer to his own progress εἰς μεγάλην παιδείας (Vita 8), but its usage elsewhere makes clear that there is no inherent connection to education. Josephus also, for example, uses the word to describe Agrippa's growing consolidation of political power (A.J. 18.142; cf. 18.339). And Luke uses it to describe the adolescent Jesus' growth in σοφίᾳ καὶ ἡλικίᾳ καὶ χάριτι (Luke 2:52). Paul's own use of the cognate noun refers to something similarly intangible: he speaks of the Philippians' "progress and joy in faith" (Phil 1:25).

Paul himself connects his "advancement" with the fact that he was more of a zealot than most for "the traditions of his ancestors" (τῶν πατιρκῶν μου παραδόσεων). Again, there is nothing in the phrase to suggest that he is talking about scholarship. In Paul's single other use of παράδοσις (1 Cor 11:2) he is clearly referring not to doctrine but to customary prac-

---

37. Conybeare and Howson, *St. Paul*, 62; Mitchell, *The Heavenly Trumpet*, 241. See also Farrar, *St. Paul*, 23; Hengel, *Pre-Christian Paul*, 41; Bruce, *Paul*, 43; Murphy-O'Connor, *A Critical Life*, 86; Légasse, *Paul apôtre*, 43; Hooker, *Paul*, 35–36; Vegge, *Paulus und das antike Schulwesen*, 440; Hock, "Greco-Roman Education," 216.

38. Note that, despite its frequent occurrence in biographical treatments of Paul, such a reading is conspicuously absent from recent commentaries on Galatians. See, e.g., Betz, *Galatians*, 66–69; Longenecker, *Galatians*, 27–30; James D. G. Dunn, *The Epistle to the Galatians* (Black's New Testament Commentaries; London: Black, 1993), 55–62.

39. John Knox, *Chapters in a Life of Paul* (rev. ed.; Macon, Ga.: Mercer University Press, 1987), 54.

tice (cf. συνήθεια in 11:16). Likewise the similar phrase ἡ παράδοσις τῶν πρεσβυτέρων in the Synoptic Gospels (Matt 15:2; Mark 7:3, 5).[40] Josephus gives us helpful context for understanding what zeal for these traditions might mean:

> The Pharisees have delivered (παρέδοσαν) to the people a great many observances (νόμιμα) by succession from their fathers, which are not written in the law of Moses; and for that reason it is that the Sadducees reject them and say that we are to esteem those observances to be obligatory which are in the written word, but are not to observe (τηρεῖν) what are derived from the tradition (παραδόσεως) of our forefathers. (*A.J.* 13.297 [trans. Whiston]; cf. 10.51; 13.408)

Some, clearly, are more zealous for the traditions than others, but what sets them apart is not knowledge of these customs, let alone classroom study thereof, but zeal for practical observance. Indeed, such traditions are, by their very nature, not esoteric; they are matters of practice well known, as Josephus explains, among the people (δῆμος). What Paul is reminding the Galatians, then, is that in his former life he had been among the most scrupulous observers of ancestral tradition—κατὰ νόμον Φαρισαῖος, as he puts it in Phil 3:5. Further, the context of Paul's remarks in Galatians makes clear that he associates this former zeal for tradition with his persecution of those who strayed from traditional practice on account of their Christ faith (1:13).[41] This is rather a different sort of zeal from the "intense commitment to his studies" of which Jerome Murphy O'Connor speaks.[42]

---

40. Note also the frequent use of παραδίδωμι, not least by Paul himself, to refer not to formal education but to transmission of customary knowledge or practice: Luke 1:2; Acts 6:14; 16:4; Rom 6:17; 1 Cor 11:2, 23; 15:3; 2 Pet 2:21; Jude 3; Josephus, *A.J.* 15.268. Cf. Plato, *Charm.* 157E; *Phileb.* 16C; Aristotle, *Poet.* 1451b; *Pol.* 5.1313a; Demosthenes, *Aristocr.* 65 (noted by LSJ, s.v. I.4).

41. Further clarification of Paul's meaning here comes from Steve Mason's recent work on the significance of Ἰουδαϊσμός in its rare pre-Christian usage ("Jews, Judaeans, Judaizing, Judaism: Problems of Categorization in Ancient History," *JSJ* 38 [2007]: 460–71). Although almost universally translated "Judaism," Mason clearly demonstrates that prior to the 3rd c. C.E. the word "is not a general term for 'Judaism,' but rather a certain kind of *activity* over against a pull in another, foreign direction" (p. 466). This makes admirable sense in the context of Gal 1: Paul is not simply stating that he was a Judean, but rather that he fought against the dilution of Judean custom—in this case by persecuting the church.

42. Murphy-O'Connor, *A Critical Life*, 86.

So, Gal 1:13–14 gives us no indication that Paul was striving to be at the top of his class nor indeed that he spent any time in class at all. It does, however, demonstrate the extent of the youthful Paul's participation in a particular community with particular social practices. Such participation would have provided one forum within which Paul would have had opportunity to observe and to imitate effective speakers—particularly such speakers, I would suspect, as nourished his zeal.

Such an understanding of Paul's acquisition of rhetorical competence fits well with the evidence presented so far. Second Corinthians 10–13 does include, as recent scholars have noted, some rhetorical figures and strategies discussed by ancient theorists, but these are also attested in speakers with no formal rhetorical training, and Paul's use thereof lacks the specific markers associated with formal education. Therefore, they are best understood as deriving from informal social practice. If this is correct, we may conclude that Paul, like the majority of speakers in most human societies, learned what he knew of persuasive speech not through formal education but through an informal process of observation, imitation, and practice.

12
ΙΔΙΩΤΗΣ ΤΩ ΛΟΓΩ

There is no evidence in 2 Cor 10–13 that Paul received formal training in rhetoric. Many of the alleged correspondences between Paul and the rhetoricians derive from superficial or misleading treatments of the evidence; others are too general to be compelling, for we find the same figures, tropes, and rhetorical strategies among speakers who demonstrably have no training in formal rhetoric. To put it crudely, the presence of *prosōpopoiia*, *prodiorthōsis*, elements of catalogue style, and sensitivity to charges of boastfulness in Paul's letters tells us nothing more than that Paul was a relatively adept speaker, and that he had a basic sense of the social dynamics of his situation.

In other words, our foray into comparative rhetoric has demonstrated that the presence of these rhetorical figures cannot in itself be adduced as evidence of rhetorical education. Neither does it constitute evidence of eloquence. In the course of our analysis, we have seen these rhetorical devices used by speakers artful and tasteless alike. Red Jacket, though not formally educated, uses *prosōpopoiia* to powerful ironic effect. Elia, speaking Spanish as a second language and not fully in control of her grammar, does so clumsily—though she still manages to get her point across with a certain colloquial force. Billy Sunday is uneducated but artful, as well as bombastic. The Mexicano orator we overheard was reported to be powerful, though not eloquent by learned standards. His speech derived its rhetorical force from adept use of prosodic variation as well as invocation of his audience's shared values.

I expect none of these characterizations to be controversial, although, depending on our own tastes and our own social locations, we may value such rhetorical styles differently. What I want to draw attention to are the indicators that enable such characterizations. Rhetorical figures per se do not help us much, although the specific manner of their use may be telling.

Instead, two discursive features are particularly significant. First and most fundamental is the speaker's control of grammatical and syntactical conventions. It is failure here that immediately marks Elia and our Mexicano orator as uneducated speakers. However much we might admire various aspects of their speech, they cannot attain to what generally is considered—at least by their cultured despisers—to be eloquence.

Second, our characterization of these speakers owes much to what I have called their "voice," the particular way in which each speaker negotiates the dynamics of his or her own identity vis-à-vis his or her audience and within a particular social location. Late in his career, Red Jacket, accustomed to deference and respect, defends himself by adopting a dignified posture of immovable superiority; he disdains his accusers. Elia, an indigenous Peruvian, casually insinuates herself to her European interviewer by laughing at the naivety of her co-ethnics, highlighting the knowledge that she alone among her peers shares with her interlocutor. Billy Sunday occupies a dual—one might say duplicitous—location as cultural insider and cultural outsider, projecting at once both power and alienation. Each of these speakers seeks room to maneuver within the constraints of a given social location; each adopts a persuasive *ethos* that is available within those bounds.

How, then, shall we characterize Paul's rhetoric? Or—again to paraphrase Rudy Wiebe's question—where is his voice coming from? The question is far too large to receive a complete answer here. I will, however, follow up on a number of specific leads that the comparisons undertaken in the present study have provided. To do so will necessitate further consideration of Paul's prose style, as well as sustained exegesis of two key verses, 2 Cor 10:10 and 11:6. I will also reprise the comparison begun in chapter 4 of Paul's self-praise with that recommended by Plutarch, before concluding by reflecting on the significance of Paul's boasting in weakness.

Untempered Vigor

As noted briefly in chapter 1, prior to the recent rise of rhetorical criticism, it was generally agreed that Paul's letters were forceful, in their own peculiar way, but hardly represented the sort of eloquent discourse cultivated in the schools of rhetoric. For decades, even centuries, competent readers came to more or less the same conclusion, namely, that "dieses Griechisch mit gar keiner Schule, gar keinem Vorbilde etwas zu tun hat,

ΙΔΙΩΤΗΣ ΤΩ ΛΟΓΩ

sondern unbeholfen in überstürztem Gesprudel direkt aus dem Herzen strömt."[1]

Such evaluations may appear impressionistic and may be couched in romantic language, but in fact they derive from three well-founded observations regarding Paul's prose, each of which will be demonstrated at greater length below. First, grammatical and syntactical irregularities are numerous. By Benjamin Jowett's estimation, "more numerous anacolutha occur in St. Paul's writings ... than in the writings of any other Greek author of equal length."[2] Second, his train of thought is often difficult to follow. According to Ernest Renan: "His language is, if I dare express myself so, hackled, not a connected phrase."[3] Finally, when Paul does attempt paronomasia, the results are often far from elegant.[4] In sum, then, if for Quintilian the three virtues of style are correctness, lucidity,

---

1. Ulrich von Wilamowitz-Moellendorff, "Die griechische Literatur des Altertums," in *Die griechische und lateinische Literatur und Sprache* (ed. Paul Hinneberg; 3rd ed.; Die Kultur der Gegenwart 1.8; Leipzig: Teubner, 1912), 232. For similar evaluations, see below and Calvin, *Corinthians*, 2:345; Baur, *Paul*, 2:280–81; Farrar, *St. Paul*, 1:619–25; Beet, *Corinthians*, 439; Heinrici, *Der zweite Brief an die Korinther*, 453; Heinrici, *Der litterarische Charakter der neutestamentlichen Schriften*, 65–66; Deissmann, *Light from the Ancient East*, 70; Deissmann, *Paul*, 59; W. M. Ramsay, *The Teaching of Paul in Terms of the Present Day* (2nd ed.; London: Hodder & Stoughton, 1914), 330 n. 2, 423 (but cf. 418); Carl von Weizsäcker, *The Apostolic Age of the Christian Church* (trans. James Millar; 2 vols.; 3rd ed.; London: Williams & Norgate, 1907), 1:224–26, 311; Philipp Vielhauer, *Geschichte der urchristlichen Literatur: Einleitung in das Neue Testament, die Apokryphen und die apostolischen Väter* (Berlin: de Gruyter, 1975), 68; Bruce, *Paul*, 15–16; Knox, *Chapters in a Life of Paul*, 78. More recently, Reiser, *Sprache und literarische Formen*, 69–77.

2. Benjamin Jowett, *The Interpretation of Scripture and Other Essays* (London: Routledge, 1907), 51. Cf. John Calvin, *Commentaries on the Epistle of Paul the Apostle to the Romans* (trans. John Owen; Edinburgh: Calvin Translation Society, 1849), 206, 211. For numerous specific examples, see Nigel Turner, *Style* (vol. 4 of *A Grammar of New Testament Greek*; ed. J. H. Moulton; Edinburgh: T&T Clark, 1976), 85–86; BDF §466–470.

3. Ernest Renan, *Saint Paul* (trans. Ingersoll Lockwood; New York: Carleton, 1875), 155. Cf. Jowett, *The Interpretation of Scripture*, 165; Norden, *Die antike Kunstprosa*, 2:499. In 1975, Hans Dieter Betz observed, "Scholars of the later twentieth century seem in basic agreement that Paul's letters are 'confused', disagreeing only about whether the confusion is caused by emotional disturbances, 'Diktierpausen' or 'rabbinic' methodology" ("Literary Composition and Function," 354).

4. See esp. Norden, *Die antike Kunstprosa*, 2:502–3.

and elegance (*Inst.* 1.5.1), it is no wonder Paul was seldom thought to have benefited from the sort of education on offer from Quintilian's ilk.

What positive things were said about Paul's powers of expression also display a striking uniformity. He was, above all, praised for his vigor: "There are no formal periods," concedes A. D. Nock, "but there is a rhetorical movement and energy which express a powerful personality."[5] Similarly, for Calvin, Paul is "not an eloquent orator," yet he sends forth "thunderbolts, not mere words."[6] Such untempered vigor, we might note, is the one (dubious) virtue Quintilian is willing to grant the unschooled (*indoctus*) speaker (*Inst.* 2.12; cf. Lucian, *Somn.* 8).[7]

Epistolary Style: A Red Herring

It remains the case that no one attributes oratorical diction to Paul. Weiss's century-old description would still be uncontroversial:

> Es ist anerkannt, dass Paulus nicht periodisch schreibt. Man braucht nur den Hebräerbrief zu vergleichen, … und man wird den Unterschied merken. Das Grundelement der Rede des Apostels ist der einzelne kurze Satz, der nur selten mit anderen zu einer grösseren, wirklichen Periode verbunden wird. Die Regel ist entweder das asyndetische Nebeneinander, das namentlich in der lebhaften Rede sehr häufig ist oder die lockere Anreihung durch Copula, antithetische oder vergleichende Partikeln, Appositionen, oft mit Participiis conjunctis, sehr selten mit absoluten Genitiven. Zur anreihenden, nicht periodisierten Rede gehören auch die Sätze mit ὅτι, ἵνα, ὅπως, ὥστε etc., wenn, was fast immer der Fall ist, der Hauptsatz sie nicht periodisierend umklammert

---

5. Nock, *St. Paul*, 27, 235. Cf. already Theodore of Mopsuestia, *Comm. ep. Paul.* 1:93.

6. Calvin, *Corinthians*, 2:344–45.

7. This characteristic of Paul's prose has occasionally been attributed to a propensity for "Asianic" rhetoric. So, tentatively, Norden, *Die antike Kunstprosa*, 507; and, more emphatically, Friedrich Blass, *Die Rhythmen der asianischen und römischen Kunstprosa (Paulus-Hebräerbrief-Pausanias-Cicero-Seneca-Curtius-Apuleius)* (repr. ed.; Hildesheim: Gerstenberg, 1972). The latter work, originally published in 1905, was not well received. See J. E. Sandys, "Rhythm in Greek and Latin Prose" (review of Blass, *Die Rhythmen der asianischen und römischen Kunstprosa*), *CR* 21 (1907): 85–88. And recent studies suggest that so-called "Asianic" rhetoric gets us no closer to Paul than its Attic counterpart. See Fairweather, "Galatians and Classical Rhetoric," 233–34; Anderson, *Ancient Rhetorical Theory*, 283.

und so zu einem runden Schluss führt. Auch die längeren Satzgefüge bestehen nur aus locker aneinander geknüpften Sätzen, die beliebig vermehrt werden könnten.[8]

Whatever one makes of such a style, this is certainly not what was taught in rhetorical school—which is why Pseudo-Demetrius, for example, can take for granted that the use of periods sounds σοφιστικός and the lack thereof ἰδιωτικός (*Eloc.* 15).[9] Apparently, the argument for Paul's formal rhetorical education has proceeded not because of his diction, but despite it.

At this point it will surely be objected that I am comparing apples and oranges: Paul wrote letters, not orations, and therefore can hardly be evaluated on the basis of his conformity to oratorical stylistic conventions. Letter writers were expected, after all, to employ a "looser," nonperiodic style (Ps.-Demetrius, *Eloc.* 229; cf. Quintilian, *Inst.* 9.4.19). Margaret Mitchell has taken Marius Reiser to task recently for precisely this error, namely, considering style independently of genre.[10] But when one looks

---

8. Weiss, "Beiträge zur Paulinischen Rhetorik," 167: "It is generally accepted that Paul does not write in periodic style. One need only compare the letter to the Hebrews … and one will notice the difference. The basic element of the speech of the apostle is the individual short sentence, which is only rarely bound with others into a larger, genuine period. The rule is either asyndetic juxtaposition, which, particularly in lively speech, is very common, or loose parataxis using the copula, antithetical or comparative particles, apposition, often with the conjunctive participle, very rarely with the genitive absolute. The sentences with [subordinating conjunctions] also belong to paratactic, not periodic, speech when, as is almost always the case, the main clause does not embrace them in periodic style and thus lead to a conclusion that rounds off the sentence. Even the longer complex sentence consists only of loosely connected clauses that can be multiplied at will." Cf., more recently, Anderson, *Ancient Rhetorical Theory*, 185 n. 125. Also BDF §464.

9. Of course, stylistic theory was more complicated than this simple dichotomy would suggest, with some preferring to avoid periodic composition in certain situations. See esp. Dionysius of Halicarnassus, *Comp.* 22. Still, the basic point is indisputable: The style most associated with rhetorical education and prowess was periodic. Note that short sentences and asyndeton are what characterize the speech attributed to ignorant slaves and rustics by Menander. See A. G. Katsouris, *Linguistic and Stylistic Characterization: Tragedy and Menander* (Dodone Supplement 5; Ioanina, 1975), 108, 121; W. Geoffrey Arnott, "Menander's Manipulation of Language for the Individualisation of Character," in *Lo spettacolo delle voci* (ed. Francesco de Martino and Alan H. Sommerstein; vol. 2; Le Rane 14; Bari: Levante, 1995), 157.

10. Mitchell, "Le style, c'est l'homme," 376–77; cf. Reiser, *Sprache und literarische Formen*, 69–77.

more carefully at the texts she adduces, her appeal to the conventions of epistolary style looks rather like a red herring.

Mitchell turns our attention here to Pseudo-Demetrius's "valuable and ... still largely unappreciated discussion," which does indeed advocate a looser, more conversational style (*Eloc.* 223–235).[11] What she fails to mention is that Pseudo-Demetrius in fact expressly forbids treatises disguised as letters or letters that are overly didactic. Moral exhortation, he opines, is not fitting in a letter (232), nor is philosophizing: "If anybody should write of logical subtleties or questions of natural history in a letter, he writes indeed, but not a letter" (231 [trans. Roberts]; cf. 230, 234; Gregory of Nazianzus, *Ep.* 51.4; Ps.-Libanius 50). Pseudo-Demetrius is similarly opposed to letters of excessive length:[12] "Those that are too long, and further are rather stilted in expression, are not in sober truth letters but treatises with the heading 'My dear So-and-So" (συγγράμματα τὸ χαίρειν ἔχοντα προσγεγραμμένον [228; trans. Roberts]). A true letter, he explains, is a περὶ ἁπλοῦ πράγματος ἔκθεσις καὶ ἐν ὀνόμασιν ἁπλοῖς (231). Clearly, if Paul knew anything about conventional epistolary style, he flagrantly violated its strictures. It seems rather odd, then, to look here for an explanation of his nonperiodic prose. Why should he have taken to heart just this one piece of advice?

Quintilian follows Pseudo-Demetrius closely on this matter, distinguishing periodic from nonperiodic style and noting that the latter generally is appropriate for letters (*Inst.* 9.4.19). Notice, though, his qualification: "... except when [the letters] deal with some subject above their natural level, such as philosophy, politics or the like" (Butler, LCL). From Quintilian's perspective, then, it is the conversational content of the letter that makes its conversational diction appropriate. Once outside the natural purview of the epistolary genre—as Paul's letters clearly are—epistolary stylistic considerations are no longer relevant.[13] In any case, Paul hardly can be said to abide by them.

Letters, according to Pseudo-Demetrius, are to be a mixture of plain and elegant style (235), neither of which has any room for the sort of untempered vigor readers have long seen in Paul (cf. 128; 193; Gregory of Nazianzus, *Ep.* 51.5–7). Further, if there was one stylistic virtue all but

---

11. Mitchell, "Le style, c'est l'homme," 376.

12. On the unusual length of Paul's letters relative to contemporary conventions, see Richards, *Secretary in the Letters of Paul*, 213.

13. Cf. Anderson, *Ancient Rhetorical Theory*, 186 n. 131.

unanimously deemed appropriate to the letter, it was clarity (σαφήνεια).[14] Thus Pseudo-Libanius, quoting Philostratus of Lemnos, remarks, "One should adorn the letter, above all, with clarity ... for while clarity is a good guide for all discourse, it is especially so for the letter" (48 [trans. Malherbe]; cf. Gregory of Nazianzus, *Ep.* 51.4; Julius Victor, *Rhet.* 27.19–21; Ps.-Demetrius, *Eloc.* 190–235). Few would suggest that Paul's letters have been thus adorned. Now, I agree wholeheartedly with Mitchell's assertion that Paul "is not only to be measured by the singular virtue of 'clarity,' but also by other elements, such as profundity, passion, brevity, power, etc."[15] But is this not simply to admit that Paul is not to be measured by the stylistic conventions of epistolography—at least not the conventions current among those with literary education?

Το εν Λογω Ιδιωτικον του Αποστολου

Until recent decades, modern scholars generally assumed that Paul was formally educated, but not, as we have seen, specifically trained in rhetoric. As I have demonstrated elsewhere, patristic interpreters did not attribute formal *paideia* to Paul at all.[16] In Chrysostom's evaluation, Paul "did not demonstrate the power of eloquence, but, to the utter contrary, was unlearned, to the lowest degree of poor learning."[17] To support this claim, Chrysostom, like other early exegetes, frequently cited Paul's concession in 2 Cor 11:6 that he was an ἰδιώτης τῷ λόγῳ.[18]

---

14. See Jeffrey T. Reed, "Using Ancient Rhetorical Categories to Interpret Paul's Letters: A Question of Genre," in *Rhetoric and the New Testament: Essays from the 1992 Heidelberg Conference* (ed. Stanley E. Porter and Thomas H. Olbricht; JSNTSup 90; Sheffield: JSOT Press, 1993), 310–11.

15. Mitchell, "Le style, c'est l'homme," 387.

16. On patristic evaluations of Paul's learning, see further my "τὸ ἐν λόγῳ ἰδιωτικὸν τοῦ Ἀποστόλου: Revisiting Patristic Testimony on Paul's Rhetorical Education," *NovT* 54 (2012): 354–68. Cf. Norden, *Die antike Kunstprosa*, 2:501–5; Deissmann, *Light from the Ancient East*, 71; James W. Voelz, "The Language of the New Testament," *ANRW* 25.2:895–96; Judge, "Paul's Boasting," 58–62; Maurice F. Wiles, *The Divine Apostle: The Interpretation of St. Paul's Epistles in the Early Church* (Cambridge: Cambridge University Press, 1967), 16–18; Kern, *Rhetoric and Galatians*, 167–203.

17. *Laud. Paul.* 4.10 (trans. Mitchell): οὐ λόγων ἰσχὺν ἐπιδεικνύμενος, ἀλλὰ καὶ τοὐναντίον ἅπαν, τὴν ἐσχάτην ἀμαθίαν ἀμαθὴς ὤν.

18. *Laud. Paul.* 4.10; *Hom. Rom.* pr. (PG 60:394); *Hom. 1 Cor.* 3.4 (PG 61:27

Notably, Chrysostom and his peers came to this conclusion despite their recognition that Paul's letters contained identifiable rhetorical tropes and figures. Augustine, like Chrystostom, devoted considerable attention to Paul's rhetoric and discussed his use of a number of specific figures (*Doct. chr.* 4.7).[19] Still, he insisted that the learned and unlearned alike would laugh if anyone were such an *imperite peritus*—perhaps *pedant* captures the sense—to claim that Paul was following the rules of rhetoric (4.7.11).

Apparently these readers did not consider the use of rhetorical figures decisive evidence of rhetorical education (cf. Augustine, *Doct. chr.* 4.4.6)—and this is no wonder, seeing as they also identified such figures in the writings of Amos, Isaiah, and Jesus.[20] Instead, like Jowett, Renan, and Norden, their estimation of Paul's education derived from his failure to fulfill learned expectations regarding clarity of grammar and syntax. Here patristic readers found unambiguous indicators of untutored speech.

This is clear already in the exegesis of Origen. Significantly, it is the comparably elevated style of the book of Hebrews that convinced Origen that this text came from a different hand than Paul's (*Fr. Heb.* [PG 14:1308–1309]). According to Origen, anyone who knows how to make stylistic distinctions (πᾶς ὁ ἐπιστάμενος κρίνειν φράσεων διαφοράς) is able to recognize that Hebrews lacks τὸ ἐν λόγῳ ἰδιωτικὸν τοῦ Ἀποστόλου. This text is simply "Greeker," says Origen, than we should expect from Paul (συνθέσει τῆς λέξεως ἑλληνικωτέρα). His detailed exegesis of Romans provides specific examples to support this general evaluation of Paul's style.[21]

Admittedly, early interpreters managed to get considerable apologetic and theological mileage from Paul's lack of worldly eloquence, refiguring this apparent weakness into a mark of unique and divine power.[22] Peter

---

[ἀμαθής, ἰδιώτης, ἀπαίδευτος]); *Sac.* 4.6. See also Origen, *Fr. Eph.* 13; *Comm. Rom.* 6.3.2 (PG 14:1059); Jerome, *Comm. Eph.* 2.586 (PL 26:477); Gregory of Nyssa, *Eun.* 3.1.106.

19. On Chrysostom's "rhetorical criticism," see Mitchell, *The Heavenly Trumpet*, 244–45, 278–91; Mitchell, "Patristic Perspective"; Malcolm Heath, "John Chrysostom, Rhetoric and Galatians," *BibInt* 12 (2004): 369–400; Lauri Thurén, "John Chrysostom as a Rhetorical Critic: The Hermeneutics of an Early Father," *BibInt* 9 (2001): 180–218; Fairweather, "Galatians and Classical Rhetoric," 2–22.

20. Augustine, *Doct. chr.* 4.7.16–21; Chrystostom, *Comm. Isa.* 3.10; 5.5 (PG 56:54, 63); *Hom. Matt.* 22.4 (PG 57.304). The latter are noted in Mitchell, "Patristic Perspective," 366 n. 62.

21. See esp. *Comm. Rom.* 1.9.6 (PG 14:853); 3.1.2–3 (PG 14:921); 6.3.2 (PG 14:1059).

22. See Origen, *Cels.* 1.62; 3.39; 6.1–2; 7.37, 41; *Comm. Jo.* 4.2; Augustine, *Conf.*

Brown rightly speaks of "a long tradition that reached back to the apologists of the second and third centuries [in which] Christian writers insisted that the miraculous character of their religion was proved by the manner in which it had been spread throughout the Roman world by humble men, without *paideia*."[23] But it will not do to claim, as does Margaret Mitchell, that their assessment of Paul's diction should therefore be discounted,[24] for early commentators used this apologetic *topos* to account for specific exegetical problems arising from these less than perspicuous letters. Moreover, it is clear that they did so in response to persistent critique from hostile readers who mocked the vulgarity of their sacred texts.[25] Paul's letters evidently were susceptible to such critique, thus alternative evaluations of rhetoric were deployed according to which, to quote Chrysostom, "this accusation becomes an encomium" (*Hom. 1 Cor.* 3.4 [PG 61:27]). Paul's defenders—like Paul himself, I would argue—did their best to make a virtue of necessity.

"Confused and Insufficiently Explicit"

Alfred Plummer describes 2 Cor 10–13 in accordance with the general evaluations of Paul's diction noted above: Although the language is "powerful" and "sometimes has a rhythmical and rhetorical swing that sweeps one along in admiration of its impassioned intensity … at the same time [it] bewilders

---

3.5.9; *Ep.* 137.5.18 (PL 33:524); Ambrosiaster, *Comm.* 199 (PL 17:321); Jerome, *Comm. Eph.* 2.587–588 (PL 26:478); Chrysostom, *Hom. 1 Cor.* 3.4 (PG 61:27–28); *Hom. 2. Cor.* 21.4 (PG 61:546); *Laud. Paul.* 4.13.

23. Peter Brown, *Power and Persuasion in Late Antiquity: Towards a Christian Empire* (Madison: University of Wisconsin Press, 1992), 73. See also Mitchell, *The Heavenly Trumpet*, 200–50.

24. Margaret M. Mitchell, "Reading Rhetoric with Patristic Exegetes: John Chrysostom on Galatians," in *Antiquity and Humanity: Essays on Ancient Religion and Philosophy* (ed. Adela Yarbro Collins and Margaret M. Mitchell; Tübingen: Mohr Siebeck, 2001), 333–55; Mitchell, "Patristic Perspective," 369–70; Mitchell, *The Heavenly Trumpet*, 242 n. 198.

25. See esp. Celsus 1.27; 6.2; Chrysostom, *Hom. 1 Cor* 3.4 (PG 61:27); Ambrose, *Ep.* 8.1 (PL 16:911); Arnobius, *Gent.* 1.58–59 (PL 5:796–97); Augustine, *Doct. chr.* 4.7.14; Lactantius, *Inst.* 5.2.17 (PL 6:555–556). Cf. Xavier Levieils, *Contra Christianos: La critique sociale et religieuse du christianisme des origines au concile de Nicée (45–325)* (BZNW 146; Berlin: de Gruyter, 2007), 257–74.

us as to the exact aim of this or that turn of expression."[26] Indeed, there are a number of instances in our text of language that is, to quote Origen, "confused and insufficiently explicit" (*Comm. Rom.* pr. 1 [trans. Scheck]). In their rush to locate Paul's use of tropes and figures of speech, rhetorical critics generally have ignored these features of his prose. But if, as Quintilian has it, "the first of all virtues is the avoidance of faults" (*Inst.* 8.3.41), we cannot evaluate Paul's rhetoric without attending to his grammar.

Commenting on 2 Cor 10:2, Ralph Martin notes, "The sentence is convoluted and hard to unravel, but the meaning is tolerably plain."[27] It is convoluted indeed: δέομαι δὲ τὸ μὴ παρὼν θαρρῆσαι τῇ πεποιθήσει ᾗ λογίζομαι τολμῆσαι ἐπί τινας τοὺς λογιζομένους ἡμᾶς ὡς κατὰ σάρκα περιπατοῦντας. A few problems are worthy of note. First, from the outset, the sentence is hampered by Paul's failure to articulate what, precisely, he is asking of the Corinthians. As it stands, he begs that he should not be bold—an entreaty he is presumably in a better position to oblige than are his addressees. In lieu of a discussion of the problem, most commentators elect to refer us to Blass's treatment of the accusative articular infinitive (BDF §399.3).[28] Fine. But the construction still fails to express what Paul is trying say—that is, that he does not want to *feel forced* to "show boldness." Barrett adds "to compel me" here, noting that the "words are not in the Greek but bring out the force of Paul's request."[29] The NRSV elects for "*need* not show boldness." It is not difficult to determine what Paul must mean, but it is important to recognize that he does not in fact say it.

Second, the awkwardness of θαρρῆσαι τῇ πεποιθήσει ᾗ λογίζομαι τολμῆσαι is exacerbated by the inexplicable redundancy of the clause: "be bold with the confidence with which I propose to be courageous" (NASB). There is no good reason not to take θαρρέω and τολμάω as synonyms here,[30] so, if Paul wanted to reuse τολμάω (cf. v. 1), perhaps in order to echo his rival's language, why not skip θαρρέω altogether? Indeed, the whole of θαρρῆσαι τῇ πεποιθήσει ᾗ λογίζομαι could be dropped from the sentence without

---

26. Plummer, *Second Epistle*, xlviii.
27. Martin, *2 Corinthians*, 304.
28. Windisch, *Der zweite Korintherbrief*, 294; Furnish, *II Corinthians*, 456; Bultmann, *Second Corinthians*, 183. The use of the nominative participle παρών is correct; it agrees with the implied subject of δέομαι. See BDF §409.5.
29. C. K. Barrett, *A Commentary on the Second Epistle to the Corinthians* (Black's New Testament Commentaries; London: Black, 1973), 248.
30. So Windisch, *Der zweite Korintherbrief*, 294; Thrall, *Second Epistle*, 2:605 n. 64.

losing anything but confusion.³¹ Unlike the NASB—a translation bold and confident and courageous enough to render the text as it stands—most recent English versions resort to paraphrase: "be as bold as I expect to be" (NIV); "show boldness by daring to oppose" (NRSV).

Third, this absolute use of τολμάω with ἐπί is perhaps comprehensible, but certainly not idiomatic. The only approximate parallel is from the Greek version of *1 Enoch*³²—hardly evidence for its currency among fluent speakers. In every other occurrence of ἐπί with τολμάω I have examined, the prepositional phrase either sets out the motivation for one's boldness, or modifies not τολμάω but an infinitive that is dependent on it.³³ Harris solves the problem by supplying χρᾶσθαι as a complement to τολμάω, thus conforming the phrase to this latter usage ("the confidence that I reckon I will dare *to use*").³⁴ Others point us to the occurrence of τολμάω with κατά in a few papyri: BGU III 909.18 has τὰ τολμηθέντα ὑπ' αὐτῶν κατ' ἐμοῦ.³⁵ But even if this is a good guide to what Paul means, it only highlights the oddity of his usage.

It is difficult to be certain whether the repetition of λογίζομαι here is a conscious play on words.³⁶ As recent research demonstrates, such repetition is often unintentional, since it is normal for speakers to gravitate toward recently used words.³⁷ But even if this is intentional paronomasia, it is not

---

31. Cf. Jean Héring, *The Second Epistle of Saint Paul to the Corinthians* (trans. A. W. Heathcote and P. J. Allcock; London: Epworth, 1967), 69–70.

32. οἱ γίγαντες ἐτόλμησαν ἐπ' αὐτούς, καὶ κατησθίοσαν τοὺς ἀνθρώπους (*1 En.* 7:4). Cited in BDAG, s.v. τολμάω.

33. For the former, see Philo, *Ios.* 225. For the latter, Thucydides 6.86.4; Herodotus, *Hist.* 7.158; Lysias, *1 Alc.* 10; Diodorus Siculus 14.24.7; Dionysius of Halicarnassus, *Ant. rom.* 5.62.3; Josephus, *B.J.* 4.391; *A.J.* 17.230; 17.278; 18.266; 20.181; Lucian, *Tox.* 54.

34. Harris, *Second Corinthians*, 673 (my emphasis).

35. Cited in MM 638. See also P.Lips. I 39.8, cited by Philip Bachmann, *Der zweite Brief des Paulus an die Korinther* (4th ed.; ZKNT 8; Leipzig: Scholl, 1922), 342; Windisch, *Der zweite Korintherbrief*, 295.

36. So Barnett, *Second Epistle*, 460; Furnish, *II Corinthians*, 456–57; Harris, *Second Corinthians*, 673–74; H. A. W. Meyer, *Critical and Exegetical Handbook to the Epistles to the Corinthians* (trans. David Hunter; 2 vols.; KEK 5–6; Edinburgh: T&T Clark, 1879), 2:392. Bultmann's suggestion (*Second Corinthians*, 184; cf. Georgi, *Opponents of Paul*, 235) that Paul is taking up the wording of his rivals is pure speculation, and is not really necessary: Paul employs such paronomasia frequently enough. See esp. Norden, *Die antike Kunstprosa*, 2:502–3; Anderson, *Ancient Rhetorical Theory*, 283–88.

37. Willem J. M. Levelt, "Accessing Words in Speech Production: Stages, Pro-

particularly effective. In this context, with all the distracting static generated by the obscurity of the sentence, it merely muddies the waters further.[38] Moreover, as Dean Anderson notes, ancient theorists considered paronomasia inappropriate for solemn or emotionally charged subject matter.[39] Even at their best, such figures produce charm, says Pseudo-Demetrius, not forcefulness (*Eloc.* 27–29; cf. *Rhet. Her.* 4.32). Compare an example of paronomastic repetition that Pseudo-Demetrius does favor, an otherwise unattested quip from Aristotle: ἐγὼ ἐκ μὲν Ἀθηνῶν εἰς Στάγειρα ἦλθον διὰ τὸν βασιλέα τὸν μέγαν, ἐκ δὲ Σταγείρων εἰς Ἀθήνας διὰ τὸν χειμῶνα τὸν μέγαν (29, 154; cf. 211).[40] Here it is the simplicity and lucidity of the antithetical construction that creates an appropriate backdrop for the elegant repetition of μέγαν. Even excusing the clutter of his sentence, what Paul does with λογίζομαι in 2 Cor 10:2 is, if intentional, more reminiscent of the trite wordplay Quintilian censures as "a poor trick even when employed in jest": *Amari iucundum est, si curetur ne quid insit amari* (*Inst.* 9.3.70 [Butler, LCL]).[41] Perhaps a more charitable comparison could be made with the folksy wit exemplified by Jay-Z in a recent radio interview: "You have to either know how to deal with that situation, or it deals with you."[42]

Tellingly, in his homily on the passage, Chrysostom does us the favor of a paraphrase, explaining what Paul means but is not quite able to articulate: δέομαι γὰρ ὑμῶν, φασὶ, μή με ἀναγκάσητε δεῖξαι, ὅτι καὶ παρὼν ἰσχυρός

---

cesses and Representations" in *Lexical Access in Speech Production* (ed. Willem J. M. Levelt; Cambridge, Mass.: Blackwell, 1993), 8; repr. from *Cognition* 42 (1992); Tannen, *Talking Voices*, 92–100.

38. It remains possible that the first occurrence of λογίζομαι is passive, not middle, hence "the confidence with which I am reckoned to dare ..." Though out of favor now, this is how the Vulgate understood it, as also, reports Meyer, did Anselm, Luther, Beza, Bengel, and Semler, among others (*Corinthians*, 2:392). The reading has the advantage of cohering with the motif, frequently repeated throughout this section, that Paul is aware of being considered too bold (cf. vv. 1, 8–11). Whatever voice of the verb Paul intended, he has clearly left himself open to misunderstanding.

39. Anderson, *Ancient Rhetorical Theory*, 283–85.

40. "I went from Athens to Stageira because of the great king, and from Stageira to Athens because of the great storm" (trans. Roberts).

41. For a thoughtful treatment of ancient discussions of repetition, see P. E. Pickering, "Did the Greek Ear Detect 'Careless' Verbal Repetitions?" *CQ* 2/53 (2003): 490–99.

42. National Public Radio, *Fresh Air*, "The Fresh Air Interview: Jay-Z 'Decoded,'" 16 November 2010. Cited 2 February 2011. Online: http://www.npr.org/templates/transcript/transcript.php?storyId=131334322.

εἰμι καὶ δύναμιν ἔχω (*Hom. 2 Cor.* 21.1 [PG 61:542]). And again: ὃ γὰρ θέλει εἰπεῖν, τοῦτό ἐστι· δέομαι ὑμῶν, μή με ἀναγκάσητε, μηδὲ ἀφῆτε χρήσασθαι τῇ δυνάμει μου κατὰ τῶν ἐξευτελιζόντων ἡμᾶς, καὶ νομιζόντων σαρκικοὺς ἄνδρας εἶναι (21.1 [PG 61:541]). After the murkiness of Paul's prose, the clarity of Chrysostom's is striking. He resolves all of the problems noted above: The addition of με ἀναγκάσητε clarifies the content of Paul's request, and the confusing string of datives and infinitives has found a suitable replacement. Further, the awkward τολμάω plus ἐπί has given way to the clearer χρήσασθαι τῇ δυνάμει μου κατά....[43]

Notice again what has happened here: Paul has written an awkward but comprehensible sentence; Chrysostom has drawn out its essence—that is, "what he wishes to say" (ὃ θέλει εἰπεῖν).[44] Significantly, this is just what we noted in the speech of Elia: The sense could be deciphered—we could read it between the lines, so to speak—but it did not sit on the surface of the text. The grammar and the logic were not coterminous. This disjuncture between grammar and logic is, I submit, characteristic of Paul's prose and is a significant indicator of the level of his rhetorical aptitude.

Plummer's comment on 2 Cor 10:8–9 sounds the same tone as Martin's on 10:2: "The constr[uction], though not quite regular, is intelligible enough."[45] Here I think he is overly optimistic: ἐάν [τε] γὰρ περισσότερόν τι καυχήσωμαι περὶ τῆς ἐξουσίας ... οὐκ αἰσχυνθήσομαι. ἵνα μὴ δόξω ὡς ἂν ἐκφοβεῖν ὑμᾶς διὰ τῶν ἐπιστολῶν. The basic problem here is accounting for the ἵνα: There simply is no logical connection between Paul's refusal to be ashamed and the purpose or result clause that follows. As Windisch observes: "Wenn zwischen V. 8 und V. 9 nichts ausgefallen ist, dann ist V. 9 wieder ein Beispiel für den außerordentlich brachylogischen Stil des P[aulus]."[46] There are two quite credible "solutions," but neither leaves us with a particularly coherent text.[47]

---

43. Notice also the addition of ὑμῶν to δέομαι, which eliminates the ambiguity that had led some commentators to view the verse as a prayer. See Thrall, *Second Epistle*, 2:605 n. 63.

44. See also *Hom. 2 Cor.* 24.2 (PG 61:566), where Chrysostom uses a similar phrase (ὃ γὰρ βούλεται εἰπεῖν) to introduce a paraphrase of the "obscure" (ἀσαφής) 11:21b.

45. Plummer, *Second Epistle*, 281.

46. Windisch, *Der zweite Korintherbrief*, 305: "If nothing has fallen out between v. 8 and v. 9, then v. 9 is an example of the extraordinarily brachylogical style of Paul."

47. For a thorough survey of the exegetical options, see Harris, *Second Corinthians*, 696–98; Thrall, *Second Epistle*, 2:626–29.

First, v. 9 can be taken as the protasis of a construction that is resumed in v. 11, with v. 10 forming a parenthesis.[48] This would be analogous to what we see in 10:1-2, with Paul breaking off in order to interject the words of his rivals: "In order that I may not seem as though I were [merely] trying to frighten you with my letters—[v. 10: 'for this is what he is saying, that I am bold in my letters but weak in person']—let such a one consider this, that just as we are in word through letters when absent, thus also [will we be] when present in deed." This reading makes decent sense of the flow of thought here, but it leaves us with rather garbled syntax. Verse 10 cannot be a true parenthesis, since, on this interpretation, it provides the antecedent of the τοιοῦτος in v. 11.[49] Moreover, this interpretation results in an odd disjuncture between the protasis and the apodosis: "In order that I should not seem ... let such a one consider."[50] Finally, we are still left with a "very palpably abrupt" transition between v. 8 and v. 9.[51]

The other possibility, more frequently advocated by recent commentators, is that v. 9 connects with v. 8 "by means of some intermediate thought that remains unexpressed."[52] But which thought, precisely? Perhaps what is elided here is an implicit decision not to boast any further, in which case Barrett's addition of "I forbear to do this" prior to ἵνα captures the sense.[53] Moule suggests supplying a verb of volition prior to ἵνα.[54] Harris prefers to add τοῦτο λέγω.[55] In any case, Paul has not made himself clear; that is,

---

48. So Martin, *2 Corinthians*, 310-11; BDF §483. Meyer reports this as the interpretation of Calvin, Rückert, de Wette, and Ewald (*Corinthians*, 2:402).

49. So Thrall, *Second Epistle*, 2:627; cf. Plummer, *Second Epistle*, 281.

50. Such a construction would be awkward, but by no means exceptional in Paul's letters. Nigel Turner provides a number of examples from Paul (Rom 2:17; 16:27; Gal 2:4-6) of "the anacoluthon whereby the original construction is forgotten after an insertion." *Syntax* (vol. 3 of *A Grammar of New Testament Greek*; ed. J. H. Moulton; Edinburgh: T&T Clark, 1963), 343. See also Marius Reiser, "Paulus als Stilist," *SEÅ* 66 (2001): 158-61.

51. Meyer, *Corinthians*, 2:402. Note the addition of δέ after ἵνα in Chrysostom's reported text (*Hom. 2 Cor.* 22.2 [PG 61:548]) and of *autem* in the Vulgate.

52. Thrall, *Second Epistle*, 2:626.

53. Barrett, *Second Corinthians*, 259. Cf. Plummer, *Second Corinthians*, 281; Chrysostom, *Hom. 2 Cor.* 22.2 (PG 61:548).

54. C. F. D. Moule, *An Idiom Book of New Testament Greek* (2nd ed.; Cambridge: Cambridge University Press, 1959), 145.

55. Harris, *Second Corinthians*, 697; also Thrall, *Second Epistle*, 2:626.

his syntax does not conform to the logic of the sentence, however it is we reconstruct that logic.

One could argue, I suppose, that this is intentional ellipsis for stylistic purposes,[56] but it is difficult to see what Paul would gain thereby. For his part, Pseudo-Demetrius acknowledges that admission of hiatus and even "disconnected composition" (ἡ διαλελυμένη σύνθεσις) befit a forceful style (*Eloc.* 299–301; cf. Dionysius of Halicarnassus, *Comp.* 22). But what he means here is *nonperiodic* composition, as is evident from his earlier discussion (12). He certainly is not advocating such ellipses as obscure the sense of a passage. Indeed, he specifically censures prose that is downright disjointed (διεσπασμένος), complaining about cola that "resemble fragmentary pieces" (303 [trans. Roberts]; cf. Quintilian, *Inst.* 2.11.7).[57] In any case, the notion that this is an intentional stylistic choice becomes increasingly untenable when we observe the extent of the syntactical irregularities and ambiguities in this text.[58]

---

56. Cf. Mitchell, "Le style, c'est l'homme," 384. Mitchell notes Dionysius of Halicarnassus's displeasure with Plato's sometime lack of clarity (*Dem.* 5), suggesting that Paul, like Plato, sometimes chose to use language "cryptically" (384–88). But such a comparison is hardly relevant here: Dionysius is complaining about exotic figures, not disjointed prose, and 2 Cor 10:7–11 is hardly a passage of such esoteric content that it requires cryptic language.

57. Notice that it is not only the transition between vv. 8 and 9 that is abrupt; rather, the whole section is disjointed. Observes Windisch regarding the transition from v. 7 to v. 8: "Nicht leicht ist der logische Zusammenhang ... zu bestimmen" (*Der zweite Korintherbrief*, 303).

58. A few additional problems in these verses are worthy of note: First, if Paul intended by his use of περισσότερον in v. 8 to suggest that he could boast of more than simply being equally Χριστοῦ (cf. v. 7; so Barrett, *Second Corinthians*, 258; Meyer, *Corinthians*, 2:401), he has not made himself clear. Alternatively, he may have used the word without comparative force (so Plummer, *Second Epistle*, 280; Harris, *Second Corinthians*, 692), which usage is acceptable, but, in this context, introduces the sort of ambiguity that has led Barrett and Meyer astray. Chrysostom clarifies the matter by substituting the simply adjective περισσόν (*Hom. 2 Cor.* 22.1 [PG 61:547–548]). Second, Paul's use of ὡς ἄν (or ὡσάν) in v. 9 is both unusual and, with δοκέω, pleonastic, prompting Moule to suggest that two distinct modes of expression have been conflated here (*Idiom Book*, 152). Finally, a number of manuscripts, including ℵ, have καυχήσομαι in place of καυχήσωμαι (B D 1739) here. The two words appear consecutively in P46, an oddity that is best attributed to conflation of variant readings already preserved in its *Vorlage*. See Zuntz, *Text*, 254–56. Both readings, then, are very early. The aorist subjunctive, unlike the future indicative, is grammatically correct with ἐάν, and thus generally is deemed the original. So Thrall, *Second Epistle*, 2:623 n. 210;

The chart below lists a number of additional difficulties that commentators have identified in 2 Cor 10–13. In most cases—for example, the lack of explicit negation to explain the γάρ in 10:3—we can discern the sense with confidence. That is, despite inexplicitness on the level of syntax, we know what Paul must have meant. Occasionally, however, there is sharp disagreement among commentators—and, as the state of the text attests, among early scribes—regarding how to render the text. Regardless of the merits of Paul's usage in any one particular instance, the cumulative effect, I submit, is to obscure the logic of the passage. This sort of writing may facilitate the proliferation of exegetical commentaries; it does not facilitate comprehension, let alone effective persuasion.

10:2	see above	
10:3 – γάρ	negation elided	Plummer 275; Harris 275; Bultmann 184
10:4 – δυνατὰ τῷ θεῷ	questionable use of dative ("Semitism"?)	Turner, *Style*, 90–91; Plummer 276; Thrall 2:609–10
10:4–6 – καθαιροῦντες … αἰχμαλωτίζοντες … ἔχοντες	anacoluthic nominative absolute with finite sense (or v. 4 is a difficult parenthesis)	Turner, *Syntax*, 343; Plummer, 276; Allo 244; Harris 680–81; Meyer 2:394; cf. BDF §468
10:7 – πέποιθεν ἑαυτῷ	a use of dative "rare in Hellenistic prose"	MM 501; Lambrecht 156
10:8–10	see above	
10:12 – τισιν τῶν ἑαυτοὺς συνιστανόντων	more regular would be τισιν ἑαυτοὺς συνιστάνουσιν	Windisch 308
10:12 – ἀλλὰ αὐτοί*	implies contrast with οὐ γὰρ τολμῶμεν that would demand Paul as the continued referent	Thrall 2:637–39; Windisch 309; Bultmann 192

Harris, *Second Corinthians*, 665. But is a scribal error a priori more likely than an error by Paul himself? Admittedly, scribal confusion of omega and omicron is not uncommon (cf. Rom 5:1; Luke 16:25), but neither are scribal attempts to smooth out perceived errors and irregularities in Paul. For examples, see Turner, *Style*, 86; Zuntz, *Text*, 187.

ΙΔΙΩΤΗΣ ΤΩ ΛΟΓΩ

* This difficulty, and the next on our chart, are ameliorated in the Western text, which omits οὐ συνιᾶσιν ἡμεῖς δὲ, thereby making Paul the referent of αὐτοί and preserving the contrastive sense of ἀλλά. See Plummer, *Second Epistle*, 284–85; Meyer, *Corinthians*, 2:408; Thrall, *Second Epistle*, 2:636–39. The longer text is surely correct: it has better external attestation, and is difficult to account for if not original. Plummer suggests that the shorter reading results from an attempt to clarify a text that even early readers (e.g., Theodoret, *Int. Paul.* [PG 82:437]) recognized as unclear. Cf. Barrett, *Second Corinthians*, 264.

10:12 – οὐ συνιᾶσιν	"flat and obscure"	Thrall 2:638; cf. Bultmann 195; Windisch 309
10:13 – τὸ μετρόν τοῦ κανόνος οὗ ἐμερισεν ἡμῖν ὁ θεός μέτρου	1) redundant; 2) referent of genitive relative pronoun contested	1) final μέτρου omitted in Vulgate; cf. Windisch 310; 2) BDF §294.5; Barrett 266; Harris 714; Héring 74; Lambrecht 166
10:13 – ἐφικέσθαι	for infinitive of result τοῦ ἐφικέσθαι would be expected	Bultmann 194; Windisch 310; cf. BDF §391.4
10:14 – ἐφικνούμενοι	the apparent sense demands aorist, not present, participle	Windisch 310–11; Thrall 2:648; cf. Meyer 2:411; Lambrecht 166
10:14 – ἐφθάσαμεν	if comparative sense ("preceded") is intended, insufficiently clear	Meyer 2:411; Harris 718; cf. explicit comparison with φθάνω in 1 Thess 4:15
10:15 – καυχώμενοι ... ἔχοντες	anacoluthic nominative absolute with finite sense (or v. 14 is a difficult parenthesis)	Turner, *Syntax*, 343, Thrall 2:649 n. 385; Plummer 289; Meyer 2:410–12; Martin 322; cf. BDF §468
10:15 – ἐν ὑμῖν	ambiguous, depending (awkwardly) on either αὐξανομένης or μεγαλυνθῆναι	Plummer 289; Bultmann 196; Windisch 312–13; Meyer 2:413 n. 3; cf. Thrall 2:651 n. 397
10:15 – μεγαλυνθῆναι	context seems to demand unusual sense of passive	Meyer 2:412 n. 1; Harris 720; cf. BDAG s.v.; MM 392
10:15–16 – εἰς ... εἰς ... εἰς	"gehackten, grimmig hingeworfenen Satzbrocken"	Lietzmann 143; cf. Windisch 312–13; Martin 323–24

10:16 – ὑπερέκεινα	"vulgarism"? coinage?	Plummer 289; Meyer 2:414; MM 653
10:16 – εὐαγγελίσασθαι ... καυχήσασθαι	connection of asyndetic infinitive clauses unclear	Bultmann 196–97; Windisch 313–14; Thrall 2:651 n. 399; Meyer 2:414; ; Allo 253; Furnish 473–74; Héring 75
10:16 – εἰς τὰ ἕτοιμα	obscure	Plummer 290; Windisch 314; Héring 75
11:1 – ἀνείχεσθέ μου μικρόν τι ἀφροσύνης	amphibolous μου	Meyer 2:419; Lietzmann 144; Windisch 317–18; Héring 78; Plummer 292–93; Thrall 2:658
11:3 – φθαρῆναι ἀπό	awkward use of preposition	BDF §211; Thrall 2:662 n. 51
11:4 –ἀνέχεσθε/ ἠνείχεσθε	scribal corrections to create coherent conditional sentence?	Meyer 2:417, 424–25; Lietzmann 145; Plummer 297–98; Thrall 2:665–66; Zmijewksi 93
11:5 – γάρ	unclear transition	Meyer 2:426; Windisch 329–30; Thrall 2:671; Martin 342; cf. Lambrecht 174
11:6	see section "Boorish in Speech" below	
11:12 – ὃ ποιῶ καὶ ποιήσω	unclear whether complex subject (conjunctive καὶ; cf. v. 9) with verb elided, or relative clause + main verb (adjunctive καὶ)	Meyer 2:433–44; Windisch 339; Allo 284; Harris 768; Martin 348; Thrall 2:690 n. 247
11:12 – ἀφορμήν ... ἀφορμήν	redundant	
11:12 – ἵνα ... ἵνα	false parallel	Meyer 2:435–437; Windisch 339; Bultmann 207; Allo 284–85; Plummer 307; Lambrecht 177–78

ΙΔΙΩΤΗΣ ΤΩ ΛΟΓΩ

11:17 – ἐν ταύτῃ τῇ ὑποστάσει τῆς καυχήσεως	difficult usage of ὑπόστασις	Windisch 346; Héring 82
11:21 – κατὰ ἀτιμίαν λέγω ὡς ὅτι ἡμεῖς ἠσθενήκαμεν	"obscure"	Plummer 317; cf. Meyer 2:444–46; Thrall 2:718–21
11:28 – χωρὶς τῶν παρεκτός	unclear	Meyer 2:451–53; Plummer 329; Bultmann 217; Thrall 2:748–49; Martin 381
11:32 – ἐν Δαμασκῷ ... τὴν πόλιν Δαμασκηνῶν	redundant	Meyer 2:457; Plummer 334
12:1	relationship between three clauses? (note variants)	Meyer 2:459–62; Windisch 367; Furnish 523
12:2 – ἄνθρωπον ἐν Χριστῷ	expect ἄνθρωπον τὸν ἐν Χριστῷ	Turner, *Syntax*, 221; Harris 834; cf. Plummer 340
12:2 – πρὸ ἐτῶν δεκατεσσάρων	awkward use of genitive (of time?) with πρό	Moule 74; Harris 835
12:3–4 – οἶδα τὸν τοιοῦτον ἄνθρωπον ... ὅτι ἡρπάγη	hyperbaton	Harris 842
12:6 – γάρ	unclear transition	Meyer 2:472; Windisch 381; Martin 408
12:6 – φείδομαι	unusual absolute usage	Meyer 2:472; Plummer 346; cf. Barrett 312
12:6 – μή τις εἰς ἐμὲ λογίσηται	awkward construction	Plummer 346; Thrall 2:800–801; Harris 849–50
12:6 – τι	apparently superfluous (if original)	Meyer 2:473; Harris 850; Thrall 2:801 n. 228
12:7 – καὶ τῇ ὑπερβολῇ τῶν ἀποκαλύψεων	anacoluthic connection either with what precedes or with what follows	Lietzmann 155; Plummer 347; Bultmann 224; Thrall 2:802–5

12:7 – ἵνα μὴ ὑπεραίρωμαι	redundant (note variants)	Lietzmann 155; Bultmann 225; Allo 310; Lambrecht 202
12:9 – μᾶλλον	force of comparison unclear	Barrett 317; Martin 421
12:14 – τρίτον τοῦτο ἑτοίμως ἔχω ἐλθεῖν	word order introduces ambiguity	Meyer 2:486; Plummer 360–61; Allo 326; Martin 439–40; Thrall 2:843; Barrett 323; Lambrecht 213
12:14 – οὐ καταναρκήσω	transitive verb used as intransitive, or adverbial genitive elided (note variants)	Harris 882; Plummer 361–62; cf. Lambrecht 212
12:17 – τινα ... δι' αυτοῦ	anacoluthic resumption	BDF §466.1; Meyer 2:488; Lietzmann 159; Plummer 364; Windisch 403; Harris 890; Moule 176; Barrett 325
12:18 – παρεκάλεσα Τίτον	verbal idea incomplete	Windisch 403; Harris 891
12:19 – πάλαι	unusual usage (note variants)	Meyer 2:490; Plummer 367; Harris 893
12:19 – τὰ δὲ πάντα κτλ.	verb elided (or amphibolous)	Meyer 2:491; Plummer 368; Thrall 2:861
12:20 – μή πως ἔρις κτλ.	verb elided	Windisch 408; Plummer 369; Harris 897–98; Lambrecht 214–15
12:21 – ἐλθόντος μου	incorrect genitive absolute (note variants)	BDF §423.2; Thrall 2:865 n. 703; Furnish 562; but cf. Allo 334
12:21 – πάλιν	ambiguous reference	Windisch 409; Barrett 330; Thrall 2:865 n. 704; Bultmann 238–39; Allo 334
12:21 – πολλοὺς κτλ.	cumbersome	Windisch 409; Harris 902

12:21 – πολλοὺς τῶν προημαρτηκότων	misleading use of genitive	Lietzmann 159–160; Windisch 410; Bultmann 239; Barrett 332; Furnish 562; Lambrecht 215
13:2-7 – προείρηκα ... ἡμεῖς ἀσθενοῦμεν ... ἐλπίζω ... ἡμεῖς οὐκ ἐσμέν ... εὐχόμεθα	inconsistent use of first/third person (note variants)	Plummer 337; Thrall 2:892 n. 165, 893 n. 172; Furnish 572; Harris 922; cf. Meyer 2:508–9
13:4 – καὶ γάρ	repetition (for parallel?) obscures connection	Bultmann 243; Thrall 2:885
13:4 – εἰς ὑμᾶς	awkward (note variants)	Meyer 2:498; Thrall 2:887 n. 125; Barrett 336–37; Harris 905
13:5 – Ἰησοῦς Χριστὸς ἐν ὑμῖν	awkward ellipsis of copula (note variants)	Thrall 2:890 n. 152; Harris 918
13:7 – ὑμᾶς	ambiguous (subject or object?)	Lietzmann 161; Windisch 422; Bultmann 247; Allo 339; Thrall 2:893–94
13:7 – ἵνα ... ἵνα κτλ.	unclear (verbal complements [of εὐχόμεθα] or final clauses?)	Meyer 2:509–10; Windisch 422; Allo 339; Thrall 2:894–95; Barrett 923–24
13:8 – οὐ γὰρ κτλ.	explanatory force unclear	Bultmann 247–48; cf. Barrett 339; Harris 925

Again, it is important to note that such difficulties can hardly be explained as resulting from an intentional stylistic decision.[59] The only possible benefit that could arise from the use of such disjointed syntax is the impression of unrestrained vehemence (cf. "Longinus," *Subl.* 8.4;

---

59. In only a few cases have stylistic explanations been proposed. With regard to Paul's amphibolous use of ἐν ὑμῖν in 10:15, Thrall proposes that its location before rather than after μεγαλυνθῆναι is chiastic (*Second Epistle*, 2:651 n. 397). But cf. Quintilian, *Inst.* 7.9.9–12, who assumes that such ambiguity is a fault that should be remedied. Similarly, some suggest the duplication of ἵνα μὴ ὑπεραίρωμαι in 12:7 is intended to form an emphatic chiasm. So Zmijewski, *Der Stil der paulinischen "Narrenrede,"* 366; Martin, *2 Corinthians*, 393.

22.1–4; Ps.-Demetrius, *Eloc.* 300 [but cf. 303]). But being overly forceful from afar is precisely what Paul knows he is accused of in Corinth (cf. 10:1, 8–11), and it would be a strange rhetorical move indeed to fan the flames by intentionally selecting such a style. Surely a more straightforward explanation is that Paul's irregular syntax arises from a lack of articulateness, exacerbated, perhaps, by real anger and distress.[60] It was widely recognized already in antiquity that redundancy and frequent anacolutha and parentheses signaled speakers possessed of strong emotion.[61] Thus to explain Paul's uneven diction by appeal to conscious stylistic choice is both far-fetched and unnecessary.[62]

What, then, does this analysis of Paul's syntax indicate with regard to his rhetorical education? First, it must be admitted that such diction does not itself necessarily rule out formal rhetorical training. Pseudo-Plutarch's *synkrisis* of fire and water (*An ignis*), discussed in chapter 7 above, is evidence enough that the rudiments of a rhetorical education provide no guarantee of articulateness, let alone eloquence. But notice what shape Pseudo-Plutarch's incorporation of rhetorical theory takes: a clumsy and rather wooden adherence to formal expectations. He clearly has some rhetorical education, but not enough to be fully fluent. All agree that such wooden application of rhetorical forms is not what we find in Paul, which is why Betz and his followers consistently have argued that if Paul knew rhetorical theory, he had so thoroughly digested it that he could benefit from its insights without being bound by mere imitation of its forms.[63] But

---

60. So already Calvin, *Corinthians*, 2:318; cf. Plummer, *Second Epistle*, xlviii, 270.

61. This is clear from the representation of angry and agitated speech in ancient comedy. For Menander's use of anacolutha in such circumstances see Karakasis, *Terence and the Language of Roman Comedy*, 4. For repetition, see Katsouris, *Linguistic and Stylistic Characterization*, 107.

62. Aware of the difficulty, apparently, Ben Witheringon lays the blame at the feet of Paul's secretary: "Paul has composed [1 Corinthians] by dictation … This explains why there are infelicities of grammar, syntax, structure, and anacoluthon along the way. The poor scribe could not entirely always keep up—hence some incomplete sentences" (review of Kenneth E. Bailey, *Paul through Mediterranean Eyes: Cultural Studies in 1 Corinthians*, Review of Biblical Literature [http://www.bookreviews.org] [2012]). For Witheringon, then, stylistic assets can be attributed to Paul, and deficiencies to his scribe—a convenient arrangement indeed.

63. See Betz, "Literary Composition and Function," 356, 369; Vegge, *Paulus und das antike Schulwesen*, 405; Swearingen, "The Tongues of Men," 233. Cf. Kraftchick, "Πάθη in Paul," 39.

here Paul's syntax becomes a fatal problem, for the degree of rhetorical proficiency Betz posits can hardly be reconciled with the clumsiness of expression and inelegant diction we find in 2 Cor 10–13. Perhaps neither Paul's uneven syntax nor his failure to abide by formal conventions is, on its own, irreconcilable with the claim that he received a formal rhetorical education. But taken together they point rather straightforwardly, I think, to a different world of discourse altogether.

2 Corinthians 10:10; 11:6

Our survey of 2 Cor 10–13 has substantiated the evaluations of Norden, Jowett, et alia: Paul's diction is, to quote Windisch, "wirklich holperig,"[64] and frequently renders his train of thought difficult to follow. There is often a disjuncture between Paul's apparent flow of thought and his syntax. Sometimes we can discern the intended sense with confidence; sometimes we cannot.

There is an old habit of attributing this lack of clarity to the profundity of Paul's thought. Already F. C. Baur opined that "the peculiar stamp of the apostle's language" was a sign that "the thought is too weighty for the language, and can scarcely find fit forms for the superabundant matter it would fain express."[65] But such an explanation hardly accounts for 2 Cor 10, where there is no "thought" to speak of, let alone "superabundant matter." Why should it be so difficult for Paul to articulate with clarity his conviction that his opponents' boasting is vacuous, and that he will be as powerful when present as he is in his absence?

So, if Baur's explanation is unconvincing, perhaps we should revisit the possibility that Paul simply was not, by any conventional standard, an eloquent man. This is, after all, what Paul's rivals in Corinth seem to have thought—and, as we will see, Paul himself admitted as much.

"His Letters Are Forceful and Bold"

Together with 2 Cor 11:6, which will be considered in detail below, 2 Cor 10:10 has become a central text in discussions regarding Paul's rhetorical ability. As noted in chapter 2 above, the verse preserves a characterization of Paul that derives from his rivals in Corinth. It is, one might say, the earliest record of the reception history of Paul's letters. Therefore, its

---

64. Windisch, *Der zweite Korintherbrief*, 313.
65. Baur, *Paul*, 2:280–81.

interpretation is pivotal in our attempt to locate Paul's voice. The report in question is as follows:

αἱ ἐπιστολαὶ μέν ... βαρεῖαι καὶ ἰσχυραί
ἡ δὲ παρουσία τοῦ σώματος ἀσθενὴς
καὶ ὁ λόγος ἐξουθενημένος

All agree this is a highly significant text, but what exactly it signifies is disputed. One interpretive crux concerns the meaning of the twin adjectives βαρεῖαι and ἰσχυραί. Are they complimentary in their intent ("weighty and strong"), or, on the contrary, disdainful ("tyrannical and oppressive")?[66]

Of course, those who see Paul as well trained in rhetoric advocate the former interpretation. In its essence, the argument runs as follows:[67] What this passage preserves is the perceived difference in rhetorical capacity between Paul the letter writer and Paul the extempore orator. Paul's letters, his detractors admit, are rhetorically effective and powerful. (In fact, βαρεῖαι and ἰσχυραί, we are told, are words that derive from rhetorical theory, wherein they designate positive stylistic traits.) What Paul lacks is the capacity for compelling rhetorical delivery (ὑπόκρισις), something cultivated among professional orators and sophists—and sought by the Corinthians. So, Paul was well trained in rhetoric and used it capably in his letters, but, for whatever reason, was either incapable or unwilling to deliver in person.

I have explained in chapter 7 above why I am not persuaded by the notion that the trouble in Corinth spawned from the rhetorical sensitivities of a community infatuated with oratorical performance. But, however one conceives of the context in Corinth, what is troubling about the reading summarized above is that an external interpretive lens—in this case, rhetorical theory—is allowed to trump clear indicators in the text itself that point decisively to a different interpretation.

---

66. These alternatives are taken, respectively, from the NRSV and Harris, *Second Corinthians*, 698.

67. See esp. Winter, *Philo and Paul*, 204–23; Winter, "Philodemus and Paul on Rhetorical Delivery (ὑπόκρισις)," in *Philodemus and the New Testament World* (ed. John T. Fitzgerald, Dirk Obbink, and Glenn S. Holland; NovTSup 111; Leiden: Brill, 2004), 323–43; Welborn, *An End to Enmity*, 101–22; Marshall, *Enmity in Corinth*, 384–86; Witherington, *Conflict and Community in Corinth*, 433–36; Mitchell, "Le style, c'est l'homme," 382. Cf. Betz, "Rhetoric and Theology," 154–55.

It must be admitted from the outset that the words βαρεῖαι and ἰσχυραί can, in various contexts, signify either positive or negative qualities:[68] The word βαρύς most commonly means heavy, oppressive, or grievous (LSJ s.v.), but the closely related βάρος is also used by Dionysius of Halicarnassus to refer to the stylistic virtue of "gravity" (*Thuc.* 23 [Usher, LCL]). The term ἰσχυρός is occasionally used in reference to positively forceful prose (Dionysius of Halicarnassus, *Comp.* 22; *Thuc.* 31), but can also designate severity or violence (LSJ s.v., I.3). Clearly, then, the sense of both words must be determined from their context in 2 Cor 10–13.[69]

Here it will be helpful to work outward, in concentric circles, from 10:10 itself. Notice how Paul introduces the accusation in v. 9: "I do not want to seem as though I am trying to frighten you with my letters." This alone is not decisive, but does seem to suggest that "threatening" would be more apt than "powerful" as a description of how Paul's letters are perceived.[70]

Even more telling is v. 11: "Let such a one [as says this about me] consider this, that just as we are in word through letters when absent (τῷ λόγῳ δι' ἐπιστολῶν ἀπόντες), so also will we be in deed when present (παρόντες τῷ ἔργῳ)" (my trans.).[71] The appropriateness of this as a rebuttal to the accusation in v. 10 is not at all clear if we follow the rhetorical interpretive model.[72] On that model, remember, the discrepancy between the present Paul and the absent Paul is one of rhetorical aptitude: he writes with eloquent power, but speaks poorly. But v. 11, where Paul insists that his words-from-afar and deeds-when-present will in fact coincide, makes no sense as a response to such an accusation—unless, perhaps, Paul is saying that he is on his way to Corinth to deliver his oratorical *pièce de résistance*, which, inexplicably, he characterizes not as λόγος but as ἔργον. No, what

---

68. For the range of significations, see esp. Corin Mihaila, *The Paul-Apollos Relationship and Paul's Stance toward Greco-Roman Rhetoric: An Exegetical and Socio-Historical Study of 1 Corinthians 1–4* (LNTS 402; London: T&T Clark, 2009), 155–60; Vegge, *A Letter about Reconciliation*, 310–16.

69. It should be noted, however, that neither is a common rhetorical term. See Anderson, *Ancient Rhetorical Theory*, 278. The fact that Dionysius occasionally uses both with reference to prose style does not alter this fact, for, as he himself explains, his descriptive vocabulary is not technical but metaphorical (*Comp.* 21). Cf. Vegge, *A Letter about Reconciliation*, 314–16.

70. Cf. Harris, *Second Corinthians*, 699.

71. The future tense I have used in the second clause is not explicit, but is surely implied. See ibid., 702–3.

72. Cf. Vegge, *A Letter about Reconciliation*, 321–22.

Paul's rebuttal evidently addresses is a perceived discrepancy in how Paul asserts his authority when present versus when absent: whatever he is bold enough to say from afar, he insists, he will henceforth be bold enough to follow through on in person. So there is no evidence here that his letters were admired for their rhetorical force. Rather, the sense of the accusation in 10:10 is that Paul's bark is bigger than his bite: from a safe distance, he poses as strong and authoritative, but, when in Corinth, his abject weakness is manifest.

This interpretation is confirmed when we look at the broader context. The characterization of Paul in 10:10 is, as is widely acknowledged, reflected also in v. 1b:[73] "I who am humble (ταπεινός) when face to face with you, but bold toward you (θαρρῶ εἰς ὑμᾶς) when I am away." Again, the perceived discrepancy is hardly one of rhetorical competence. It rather concerns the authority (ἐξουσία) in which Paul boasts (v. 8; cf. 13:10), but which, apparently, he has not (yet) been able to exercise.[74] On his proximate visit, he insists at the letter's close, he will not be lenient (οὐ φείσομαι) but will manifest the disciplinary power of God (13:1–4; cf. 10:2, 6).[75]

---

73. So Chrysostom, *Hom. 2 Cor.* 21.1 (PG 61:542); Calvin, *Corinthians*, 2:330; Meyer, *Corinthians*, 2:403; Windisch, *Der zweite Korintherbrief*, 305; Harris, *Second Corinthians*, 698; Jan Lambrecht, "Dangerous Boasting: Paul's Self-Commendation in 2 Cor 10–13," in *The Corinthian Correspondence* (ed. Reimund Bieringer; BETL 125; Leuven: Leuven University Press, 1996), 329; Martin, *The Corinthian Body*, 53; Vegge, *A Letter about Reconciliation*, 260–62. Betz's interpretation of v. 1b (*Der Apostel Paulus und die sokratische Tradition*, 45–57), wherein both ταπεινός and θαρρεῖν have positive connotations as characteristics of a true (Cynic) philosopher, tears the fabric of the text, failing in particular to cohere with v. 11. Moreover, as Margaret Thrall observes, Betz adduces but one example of the use of ταπεινός in this sense (Lucian, *Somn.* 9–13), and it is unconvincing (*Second Epistle*, 2:604 n. 62). Similarly, it is telling that 2 Cor 10:11 is nowhere to be found in Donald Walker's treatment of "Paul's offer of leniency," and 13:1–4 is given only perfunctory treatment (*Paul's Offer of Leniency*). This results in a failure to recognize the straightforward sincerity of Paul's threatened discipline, and thus seriously undermines Walker's reading.

74. Cf. Jennifer Larson, "Paul's Masculinity," *JBL* 123 (2004): 91–92; Savage, *Power through Weakness*, 65–66.

75. How, exactly, Paul expected to manifest this power remains obscure. We may find a clue, however, in 1 Cor 5:4, where he uses similar language—exercising power (δύναμις) with (σύν) Christ—in speaking of the role of his spirit in handing over the sexually immoral man to Satan: συναχθέντων ὑμῶν καὶ τοῦ ἐμοῦ πνεύματος σὺν τῇ δυνάμει τοῦ κυρίου ἡμῶν Ἰησοῦ. See Thrall, *Second Epistle*, 2:887, following Karl Prümm, *Diakonia pneumatos: Der zweite Korintherbrief als Zugang zur apostolischen Botschaft*,

This language would have sounded familiar to the Corinthians, for, in a previous letter, he had issued a similar ultimatum:[76]

> But some of you, thinking I am not coming to you, have become arrogant. But I will come to you soon, if the Lord wills, and I will find out not the talk of these arrogant people but their power. For the kingdom of God depends not on talk but on power. What would you prefer? Am I to come to you with a stick, or with love in a spirit of gentleness? (1 Cor 4:18–21; cf. 2 Cor 13:2)

One wonders whether Paul is now reaping the consequences of having made but not followed through on such threats. Paul had indeed gone to Corinth prior to writing 2 Cor 10–13, and, he says, this had been "a painful visit" (2 Cor 2:1)—painful not for the Corinthians, however, as Paul had threatened, but instead for Paul himself (cf. 2:5–10; 7:12; 13:1–4). We do not know precisely what occurred, but it stands to reason that the insulting characterization of Paul as bold from afar but weak in person derives at least in part from his failure on that visit to exercise authority as promised.[77] (Perhaps we catch a glimpse of this in 2 Cor 12:21, where Paul speaks of having been humiliated by God [ταπεινώσῃ με ὁ θεός] before the Corinthians [πρὸς ὑμᾶς]).[78]

Auslegung und Theologie (3 vols.; Rome: Herder, 1960–1967), 1:712. Presumably what is expected is a charismatic display with decisive social consequences. Chrysostom, interestingly, read 1 Cor 4:21 (see below) in conjunction with the account of the death of Ananias and Sapphira in Acts 5:1–11 (*Hom. 1 Cor.* 14.2 [PG 61:116–117]).

76. Cf. Chrysostom, *Hom. 2 Cor.* 21.1 (PG 61:541), who connects 2 Cor 10:1–2 to 1 Cor 4:18–21, noting that Paul's threat (ἀπειλή) in 2 Cor 10:2 is even more severe (βαρύτερον [!]) than in the previous letter.

77. Cf. Plummer, *Second Epistle*, 283.

78. Note that πάλιν in 12:21 can taken be taken with ἐλθόντος (i.e., "lest when I come again") or with ταπεινωσῃ (i.e. "lest God should humble me again"). The latter is almost certainly intended. See Meyer, *Corinthians*, 2:493; Plummer, *Second Epistle*, 369; Furnish, *II Corinthians*, 562; Barrett, *Second Epistle*, 330–31; Martin, *2 Corinthians*, 464–65; Philip E. Hughes, *Paul's Second Epistle to the Corinthians* (2nd ed.; NICNT; Grand Rapids: Eerdmans, 1967), 472 n. 166; Harris, *Second Corinthians*, 901. Paul associates his humiliation—though rather obscurely—with unrepented sin in the community. But what would it mean for him to be humiliated *by God* before them? The context in Corinth makes one wonder if this is a reference to failure on Paul's part to manifest spiritual power, a failure that he interprets as resulting from divine inaction as a response to sin. To my knowledge, no satisfactory interpretation of the verse

In any case, this much is clear: Paul is being treated with derision: ἡ δὲ παρουσία τοῦ σώματος ἀσθενὴς καὶ ὁ λόγος ἐξουθενημένος. Two recent studies have sought, in complementary ways, to uncover the connotations of this characterization of Paul, both indebted, in various ways, to Maud Gleason's Bourdieu-inflected discussion of physiognomy and self-presentation in the Roman Empire.[79] For Jennifer Larson, what is at issue for Paul— as, somewhat differently, for Gleason's Favorinus—is masculinity: Paul's status as a powerful and virile male has been challenged. Viewed in the light of Roman preoccupation with vigilant "performance" of manhood, this is a serious impugnation of his honor indeed.[80] Albert Harrill thinks rather that Paul is being characterized in accordance with "the ancient physiognomic principle that a weak bodily presence signifies a slave."[81] His citation of Lucian, wherein the satirist reflects autobiographically on the choice between παιδεία and a manual trade (τέχνη τῶν βαναύσων [*Somn.* 1]), is particularly instructive:

> On the other hand, if you turn your back upon these men so great and noble, upon glorious deeds and sublime words, upon a dignified appearance (σχῆμα εὐπρεπές), upon honor, esteem, praise, precedence, power (δύναμιν) and offices ... then you will put on a filthy tunic, assume a servile appearance (σχῆμα δουλοπρεπές), and hold bars and gravers and sledges and chisels in your hands, with your back bent over your work; you will be a groundling, with groundly ambitions, altogether humble (πάντα τρόπον ταπεινός); you will never lift your head, or conceive a single manly or liberal thought, and ... you will make yourself a thing of less value than a block of stone. (*Somn.* 13 [Harmon, LCL])

---

has been proffered. Bultmann's notion (*Second Corinthians*, 238–39), similar to that of Chrysostom (*Hom. 2 Cor.* 28.2 [PG 61:591–592]; cf. Meyer, *Corinthians*, 2:493), that Paul feared the "humiliation" of having to exercise his authority for tearing down, not building up (cf. 13:10), fails to account for Paul's previous humiliation, or makes it of a different order altogether. Cf. Martin, *2 Corinthians*, 465–66. Larry Welborn compellingly links Paul's humiliation with the dissention and mutual disfavor Paul highlights in v. 20, but does not offer an adequate explanation for the unrepented sin in v. 21 (*An End to Enmity*, 181, 186–87).

79. Gleason, *Making Men*.
80. Larson, "Paul's Masculinity."
81. J. Albert Harrill, "Invective against Paul (2 Cor 10:10), the Physiognomics of the Ancient Slave Body, and the Greco-Roman Rhetoric of Manhood," in *Antiquity and Humanity: Essays on Ancient Religion and Philosophy* (ed. Adela Yarbro Collins and Margaret M. Mitchell; Tübingen: Mohr Siebeck, 2001), 192.

Harrill and Larson are to be commended, certainly, for helping us locate terms like ἀσθενής and ταπεινός: weak, abject, inarticulate, servile, emasculate—this is the sort of characterization of Paul that is reflected in 2 Cor 10–13 generally and 2 Cor 10:10 specifically. But both Larson and Harrill sidestep what would appear to be the evident conclusion, namely, that Paul was indeed a man susceptible to derision and contempt. Larson's Paul looks and acts weak and servile, but the implication throughout is that this is (merely) voluntary behavior and therefore not indicative of Paul's essential identity. Though the Corinthians mistook his behavior for actual weakness, Paul and his interpreters know better. The prince remains the prince even when playing the pauper. That is, what Larson seems to imagine is that Paul, secure in his apostolic identity, simply stands above the fray.[82] He visits Corinth, but he is not really implicated in the precariousness of his position there.

Harrill has a more explicit means of evading what would seem to be the consequences of his own study. For him, it's all just rhetoric: "The language conforms to conventions and techniques of character assassination common in Greco-Roman invective."[83] Such invective, we are told, "was rarely directed at slaves, *per se*, but rather at freeborn men, often political enemies."[84] Paul had a more philosophical attitude toward the whole thing than did his sophistic rivals in Corinth, who apparently were taken in by the pseudoscience of physiognomy, and thus Paul responded to their invective by intentionally taking on the slavish σχῆμα of a Cynic.[85] The implication, then, is that behind the abject appearance effected by Paul's filthy tunic and work-bent back stands a noble Odysseus or Antisthenes. His ταπεινότης is merely a disguise.

What Harrill seems to have overlooked is that what allows the *topos* of the servile body to function effectively as elite invective is, in fact, the actual body of the slave. In other words, physiognomy is compelling pre-

---

82. See also, far more egregiously, Lars Aejmelaeus, "'Christ is Weak in Paul': The Opposition to Paul in Corinth," in *The Nordic Paul: Finnish Approaches to Pauline Theology* (ed. Lars Aejmelaeus and Antti Mustakallio; LNTS 374; London: T&T Clark, 2008), 129: "His weakness is in reality, if rightly understood, nothing but the greatest spiritual strength.... Because it is so, he is able to accept with calmness [!] the Corinthian evaluation of him."
83. Harrill, "Invective against Paul," 209.
84. Ibid., 201.
85. Ibid., 208–13.

cisely to the extent that it articulates the *habitus*. If the literary record preserves elite men calling each other slavish in appearance, that is because they agreed—indeed, it generally went without saying—that the somatic characteristics of slaves were despicable. Therefore to imply, as Harrill does, that Paul cannot really have been slavish because he was called slavish is, if not absurd, at least profoundly arbitrary.

No, if Paul was called slavish, it was because he really was susceptible to such characterization: his ταπεινότης was embodied.[86] Indeed, what 2 Cor 10:10 reveals, I submit, is that it was his somatic vulnerability that constituted the interpretive matrix through which Paul's failure convincingly to exercise authority in Corinth was seen. Although 2 Cor 10:10 may be invective, it is not merely so: Paul, to all appearances, is weak and derisible—utterly unlike the man who issues bold threats from afar.

But we have still to consider the final clause: ὁ λόγος ἐξουθενημένος. As indicated above, there are no grounds for restricting the sense of λόγος here such that it refers to Paul's rhetorical ὑπόκρισις. What, then, does the word mean in this context?

There are, I suggest, two credible readings. The first fits admirably with the context, but, to my knowledge, has not previously been proposed. If, as I have argued, 2 Cor 10:10 preserves the charge that Paul wrote boldly, even threatening to come to Corinth with a rod of discipline (cf. 1 Cor 4:21), but could not follow through in person, it is attractive to read ὁ λόγος

---

86. In addition to the Corinthians' reported evaluation in 10:10, there are a number of significant indicators in the Pauline corpus of the ignominy of Paul's bodily appearance. First, he was repeatedly whipped, beaten, and deprived (2 Cor 11:23–27), and, as Jennifer Glancy has emphasized, the resulting scars would have been humiliating indicators that he lacked the power of self-determination ("Boasting of Beatings"). Similarly, Paul's work as a manual laborer (1 Thess 2:9; 1 Cor 4:11–12; cf. Acts 18:3) would surely have taken its toll on his body, earning him the soiled clothes and slavish posture that, as Lucian attests, generally accompanied such work. Cf. Hock, *Social Context*, 35–36. Timothy Savage argues that Paul's Corinthian converts can hardly have despised him on the grounds of his labor, since many of them would have been manual laborers themselves (*Power through Weakness*, 84–86). But to invite disdain for Paul on this account, his rivals need not in fact belittle laborers; they need only remind the Corinthians that the demeanor of a laborer ill-befits one who would exercise authority. Finally, see Gal 4:13–14, where Paul recollects that the Galatians did not express disdain nor disgust (οὐκ ἐξουθενήσατε οὐδὲ ἐξεπτύσατε) at his bodily weakness (ἀσθένεια τῆς σαρκός), though they may have been expected to. The similarity of the vocabulary here to that in 2 Cor 10:10 is striking, and makes it impossible to argue that the Corinthians were spinning invective out of whole cloth.

ἐξουθενημένος here as a related taunt: "He talks big, but what he says comes to nothing." Ὁ λόγος, then, would refer specifically to what Paul had said in his βαρεῖαι καὶ ἰσχυραί letters, thus completing the contrastive sense of the sentence. This is a perfectly reasonable way to render λόγος (cf. BDAG s.v., 1.γ), and, importantly, coheres well with the next verse, wherein τῷ λόγῳ corresponds not with παρόντες, as we should expect if it were a reference to Paul's speech in general, but rather with δι' ἐπιστολῶν ἀπόντες.[87]

A possible objection to this interpretation is that it seems to require reading ἐξουθενέω in terms of its etymology and not its established usage. The word generally means "despise" or "disdain," or, in the passive voice used here, "be despised or contemptible." "Come to nothing" appears to be a stretch. Interestingly, though, in the only instances I could locate of ἐξουθενέω (or the equivalent ἐξουδενέω) with reference to λόγος, the word has precisely the connotation required by the interpretation I have proposed. In both 1 Macc 3:14 and 2 Chr 36:16, the active participle is used of those who scorn the command(s) (λόγος/λόγοι) of someone who attempts to exercise authority. Thus Judas Maccabeus and his companions, by virtue of refusing to comply with Antiochus's notorious prohibition, become τοὺς ἐξουδενοῦντας τὸν λόγον τοῦ βασιλέως (cf. 1:50). We have the same situation, *mutatis mutandis* for the participle in the passive voice, in 2 Cor 10:10: Paul has sought to exercise authority, but his threats, commands, and instructions are deemed worthy only of scorn.

If this reading is correct, 2 Cor 10:10 tells us nothing about Paul's knowledge of rhetoric per se. Alternatively, if, as most think, λόγος should be construed more generally as "speech,"[88] what we have here is a damning report indeed. The word ἐξουθενημένος, like ἀσθενής and ταπεινός, belongs to the vocabulary of honor and shame. Second Maccabees apposes the passive participle to βδελυκτός ("abominable" [1:27]). Paul himself famously sets it alongside μωρός, ἀσθενής, and ἀγενής and over against σοφός and

---

87. Contrast Bultmann, *Second Corinthians*, 191, who resorts to the conclusion that "the λόγος of verse 10 belongs precisely to the ἔργον [of v. 11]." Cf. Windisch, *Der zweite Korintherbrief*, 307.

88. So ibid., 306; Plummer, *Second Epistle*, 279; Harris, *Second Corinthians*, 700; Furnish, *II Corinthians*, 468. Lacking anything in the context to demand such a reading, "rhetoric" is too technical a translation for the word as it is used here, contra Martin, *2 Corinthians*, 311. Others argue that λόγος refers to Paul's message or teaching in toto, not merely its form. Cf. Bultmann, *Second Corinthians*, 190; Barrett, *Second Epistle*, 261.

ἰσχυρός (1 Cor 1:27–28). If this is a description of Paul's speech, the implication is that it is not only unskilled, but derisible.

I should clarify that I am not arguing that the characterization of Paul preserved in 2 Cor 10:10 can be taken as an objective historical observation. Clearly it derives from those who would belittle him. But in order to generate such an impassioned response from Paul, it must have hit close to home. In other words, Paul was at least susceptible to such a characterization, which is itself a telling indicator both of his voice and of his social location.

"Boorish in Speech"

Prior to the rise of rhetorical criticism, scholars frequently accounted for Paul's anacolutha and difficult syntax by citing his apparent concession in 2 Cor 11:6 that he was an ἰδιώτης τῷ λόγῳ.[89] In recent decades, however, the significance of this phrase has been contested. No longer considered straightforward attestation of Paul's lack of literary education, it is now frequently read as itself a sophisticated rhetorical figure—namely, *asteismos* or *urbanitas*, a figure wherein, to quote E. A. Judge, who first, though tentatively, proposed this interpretation, "one urbanely displayed one's own skill by affecting the lack of it."[90] On this reading, the concession is an ironic one, akin to that of the eloquent and sophisticated Dio Chrysostom:

---

89. E.g., Norden, *Die antike Kunstprosa*, 2:492–93; Nock, *St. Paul*, 234; BDF §464. For patristic examples, see ch. 12 n. 18 above.

90. Judge, "Paul's Boasting," 57; cf. Watson, "Paul and Boasting," 86; Murphy-O'Connor, *A Critical Life*, 50; Pogoloff, *Logos and Sophia*, 136; DiCicco, *Ethos, Pathos, and Logos*, 24; Classen, *Rhetorical Criticism*, 44; Forbes, "Comparison, Self-Praise, and Irony," 17. H. D. Betz has proposed an alternative reading, suggesting that by emphasizing his knowledge over his verbal prowess Paul is positioning himself on the philosophical side of the philosophy vs. sophistry divide. See *Der Apostel Paulus und die sokratische Tradition*, 57–69; cf. Keener, *1-2 Corinthians*, 227–28; Walker, *Paul's Offer of Leniency*, 275 n. 41. This is not convincing. First, as argued in ch. 7 above, there is no evidence that Paul was contending with sophistry in Corinth. Second, this interpretation requires a more precise signification for both λόγος and γνῶσις than the words can bear in this context (cf. 2 Cor 2:14; 4:6; 8:7). See further below, and Barrett, *Second Epistle*, 279–80; E. A. Judge, "St Paul and Socrates," in *The First Christians in the Roman World: Augustan and New Testament Essays* (ed. James R. Harrison; WUNT 229; (Tübingen: Mohr Siebeck, 2008), 670–83.

ὅταν μὲν γὰρ εἰς ἐμαυτὸν ἀπίδω καὶ τὴν ἀπειρίαν τὴν ἐμαυτοῦ, περὶ πάντα μὲν ἁπλῶς, μάλιστα δὲ τὴν περὶ τοὺς λόγους, ὡς ἰδιώτης ὢν διανοοῦμαι καὶ τὸ λοιπὸν ἰδιώτου βίον βιωσόμενος· ὅταν δὲ εἰς τοὺς σπουδάζοντας καὶ παρακαλοῦντας, ὑπονοεῖν ἐμαυτὸν ἀναγκάζομαι, μὴ ἄρα τι τῶν ἐμῶν λόγου ἄξιον ... (*Dial.* 3; cf. Lucian, *Bis acc.* 33)[91]

The comparison is more telling than Judge and his followers have seen and does not support their reading. Notice Dio's stature: he credibly can claim that he is being eagerly urged to make a speech (cf. 1-2, 4) by those who expect to hear from him τι θαυμαστόν (1). In this situation a show of modesty is indeed well advised. It has the potential to head off not only envy but also the sort of criticism that can arise from a failure to live up to exalted expectations. What possible objection remains for his audience to raise, except perhaps that Dio's modesty is itself ostentation (cf. Quintilian, *Inst.* 11.1.21)? But no, Dio has thought of that too, and disarmed the accusation simply by naming it (*Dial.* 2).

Paul's situation is strikingly different. His competence as a proclaimer of the gospel has been at issue in Corinth for some time (cf. 1 Cor 1:18-2:16). Indeed, it is often argued that the dismissive phrase ἰδιώτης τῷ λόγῳ derives not from Paul himself but rather from his rivals in Corinth.[92] The claim, I think, goes beyond the evidence; however, it is clear that the basic thrust of the characterization had currency in Corinth. Paul, then, is in no position to indulge in faux modesty. An ironic concession would be rather ill advised and liable to be taken as a real admission of inarticulateness[93]— especially given the clumsiness of expression manifested in this very letter, and, indeed, in this very verse.

The central antithesis of 11:6a is clear enough, even if the omission of both εἰμί and a clarifying personal pronoun is unusual:[94] εἰ δὲ καὶ ἰδιώτης τῷ λόγῳ, ἀλλ᾿ οὐ τῇ γνώσει. "Now even though I am an ἰδιώτης with

---

91. "For on the one hand, whenever I consider myself and my inexperience, my inexperience in simply everything, but especially in speaking, recognizing that I am only a layman, I am minded for the future to live the life of a layman; on the other hand, when I consider those who take me seriously and invite me to make a speech, I am constrained to feel suspicious of myself, lest some quality of mine may after all be worth while ..." (Crosby, LCL).

92. Windisch, *Der zweite Korintherbrief*, 331; Martin, *2 Corinthians*, 342-43; Harris, *Second Corinthians*, 748-49; Winter, *Philo and Paul*, 223.

93. Cf. Thrall, *Second Epistle*, 2:677.

94. Cf. BDF §128.2, and notice the addition of εἰμί in a few manuscripts (D* E).

respect to speech, nevertheless I am not with respect to knowledge."⁹⁵ The trouble comes in the next clause, which, concedes Bultmann, is "scarcely intelligible":⁹⁶ ἀλλ' ἐν παντὶ φανερώσαντες ἐν πᾶσιν εἰς ὑμᾶς. This is likely another instance of Paul using a participle where the syntax demands a finite verb,⁹⁷ the difficulty of which is exacerbated, in this case, by the transition from a singular verb in v. 5 to a plural participle in v. 6b, then back to a singular verb in v. 7. If what is to be supplied in v. 6a is ἐσμέν, not εἰμί, this is rather late notice—not to mention the solecism that would result (ἐσμέν [pl.] + ἰδιώτης [sg.]).⁹⁸

In any case, even if we simply take φανερώσαντες to mean ἐφανερώσαμεν, we are still left with an impenetrable turn of phrase. Plummer's rendering, which takes πᾶσιν as masculine, is a decent attempt to make sense of the apparent redundancy of the prepositional phrases ἐν παντί ... ἐν πᾶσιν: "in all things ... among all men."⁹⁹ But more likely this is simply poorly executed emphasis (cf. Phil 4:12: ἐν παντὶ καὶ ἐν πᾶσιν).¹⁰⁰

Finally, and most confoundingly, the sentence is lacking an object. Following Paul's train of thought, it seems most probable, despite being grammatically untenable, that he is referring to the manifestation of his γνῶσις, which is to be supplied from the previous clause.¹⁰¹ Alternatively, one could resolve the problem by adding something like an αὐτήν or, with

---

95. My trans. On this sense of ἀλλά in conditional sentences, see BDF §448.5; LSJ s.v., I.2. The datives are construed as datives of respect with Bultmann, *Second Corinthians*, 203; Harris, *Second Corinthians*, 748. Notice that the syntax suggests a real concession—that is, the protasis is assumed to be factual—as per a "first-class" condition. See Turner, *Syntax*, 115; Plummer, *Second Epistle*, 299; Harris, *Second Corinthians*, 748.

96. Bultmann, *Second Corinthians*, 204.

97. So Turner, *Syntax*, 343; Plummer, *Second Epistle*, 300; Barrett, *Second Epistle*, 280; Harris, *Second Corinthians*, 749–50.

98. The appearance of the singular participle in D* appears to be an attempt to resolve this problem. So Plummer, *Second Corinthians*, 300.

99. Plummer, *Second Epistle*, 300; cf. Bultmann, *Second Corinthians*, 204; Meyer, *Corinthians*, 2:429; Windisch, *Der zweite Korintherbrief*, 332.

100. So Furnish, *II Corinthians*, 491; and, tentatively, Thrall, *Second Epistle*, 2:678; Barrett, *Second Epistle*, 281. Welborn asserts here that Paul "makes intentionally clumsy use of a rhetorical flourish" and thereby "simultaneously mocks the ineptitude of his own delivery and undermines the rhetorical pretensions of his apostolic rivals" (*An End to Enmity*, 131).

101. Cf. Windisch, *Der zweite Korintherbrief*, 333; Plummer, *Second Epistle*, 300.

a number of ancient witnesses, an ἑαυτούς.¹⁰² The scribe who brought us P46 stumbled upon another solution: he omitted the offending clause entirely. However we make sense of the text, Paul certainly has not made all things clear. This is hardly the sort of rhetorical display in the context of which an admission of untutored speech is likely to be taken ironically.

Contrast Dio Chrysostom's sparklingly clear yet expressive diction. As Paul also frequently does, Dio admits a parenthesis (περὶ πάντα μὲν ἁπλῶς, μάλιστα δὲ τὴν περὶ τοὺς λόγους); however, in contrast to what we have seen in Paul, Dio's is clearly structured and brief, and, above all, does not disturb the syntax of the period. It adds a nice touch of spontaneity and authenticity without sacrificing eloquence. Again, like but very unlike Paul, Dio indulges in ellipsis: we must supply ἀπίδω from the μέν clause into the δέ clause. But, again, the clear structure of the sentence precludes any ambiguity or obscurity. Finally, as Paul also often does, Dio utilizes repetition, reusing, to elegant effect, the words ὅταν, ἐμαυτοῦ, and ἰδιώτης. Paul's ἐν παντί ... ἐν πᾶσιν may also be repetition, but it hardly has a comparable rhetorical effect. In short, Dio's is the sort of elegant diction that provides an apt setting for an ironic confession of ineptitude; Paul's is not.

So this is a sincere concession, albeit one that may be prompted by the uncharitable evaluation of his rivals. But what does it mean? The word ἰδιώτης is very common, and its meaning is not really in doubt, but there has been some debate of late regarding the sense in which it should be taken in this context. Dale Martin well articulates the interpretation currently in vogue: "When Paul calls himself a 'layman with regard to speech,' ... he is saying that he is not a professional orator or teacher of rhetoric; but he is not denying that he has had a rhetorical education."¹⁰³ But such a reading cannot be sustained: It misconstrues both ἰδιώτης and λόγος, and it fails to attend to the context of Paul's concession. It is, in short, an egregious case of special pleading.

---

102. For the former option, see Barrett, *Second Epistle*, 280–81; Harris, *Second Corinthians*, 750; Thrall, *Second Epistle*, 2:656 n. 147. The latter can be observed in 0121 0243 630 1739 1881. A roughly equivalent emendation is replacing the active with a passive participle, as in P34 ℵ² D Ψ 0278.

103. Martin, *The Corinthian Body*, 49; cf. Peterson, *Eloquence and the Proclamation of the Gospel*, 109; Harris, *Second Corinthians*, 748–49; Keener, *1–2 Corinthians*, 227. And see already Ramsay, *Teaching of Paul*, 420–22.

Derived from ἴδιος, ἰδιώτης means, firstly, a private individual, one who tends to his own affairs.[104] Accordingly, the word is often used to designate those who play no active role in political life or public service—that is, those outside the political class or aristocracy.[105] By extension, apparently, it came to have two related but distinct significations: First, it could be used of a layperson, someone who was not an expert or professional in a given field.[106] Second, it could be used with reference to the plebs—ordinary folk—in implied opposition to the noble classes.[107] It is this latter sense that allows Lucian to appose "laymen" (ἰδιῶται) to "workingmen" (βάναυσοι) and "tradesmen" (ἀγοραῖοι [*Vit. auct.* 27; Harmon, LCL]).

Given the widespread equation of *paideia* with power and elite status, it is not surprising that these two senses frequently were conflated in the Koine such that the word came to signify the rustic or the ignorant commoner. Hence Josephus contrasts the foolish masses (ἰδιῶται) with οἱ λόγιοι (*B.J.* 6.295). For Lucian, ἰδιῶται are characterized by ἀπαιδευσία (*Nigr.* 24; cf. *Ind.* 29), and can thus be set in opposition to the πεπαιδευμένοι (*Dom.* 2; *Lex.* 24)[108] and the σοφοί (*Symp.* 35). Reflecting these same assumptions, Luke puts ἰδιῶται in apposition to ἀγράμματοι (Acts 4:13).[109] And, for Dionysius of Halicarnassus, ἰδιῶται, more ignorant even than farmers and artisans, are those who do not know how to pay attention to an ordinary, well-composed speech (*Dem.* 15; cf. *Lys.* 3; Epictetus, *Diatr.* 2.12.2–4, 11–13).

It remained possible to refer to those in private life as ἰδιῶται without implying boorishness, but only when the context demanded this more technical sense. Dio Chrysostom, for example, spoke of ἰδιῶται—by which,

---

104. For numerous examples, see LSJ s.v., I, II; MM 299. Also Josephus, *A.J.* 5.344; 9.227; *B.J.* 4.602.

105. E.g., Plato, *Symp.* 185B; Herodotus, *Hist.* 1.59.1; Lysias, *Call.* 5.3 (οὔτ' ἰδιώτης ... οὔτε ἄρχων); Josephus, *A.J.* 3.332; 8.24; 19.213; Lucian, *Vit. auct.* 10.3; Aristides, *Or.* 2.189, 195.

106. For varied examples, see BDAG s.v; LSJ, s.v., III.1. Note also Paul's use of the word to refer to the uninitiated in 1 Cor 14:16, 23, 24.

107. LSJ s.v., II.2. See esp. Plutarch, *Thes.* 24.2 (τῶν μὲν ἰδιωτῶν καὶ πενήτων ... τοῖς δὲ δυνατοῖς); Herodotus, *Hist.* 1.32.1; Herodian, *Excess. div. Marc.* 4.10.2; Josephus, *B.J.* 6.300; Lucian, *Dom.* 3.

108. So also Gregory of Nazianzus, *Ep.* 51.4; Sextus Empiricus, *Math.* 1.155; Philostratus, *Vit. Apoll.* 3.43 (σοφὸς μὲν ... δόξειν ἐξ ἰδιώτου τε καὶ ἀσόφου, πεπαιδευμένος δὲ ἐκ βαρβάρου). Cf. Origen, *Cels.* 7.41 (PG 11:1480).

109. So also Didymus, *Fr. 2 Cor.* 4.7 (Staab 25); Theophilus, *Autol.* 2.35; John Chrysostom, *Hom. Gen.* 28.3 (PG 53:258).

in this context, he simply meant individuals as opposed to πόλεις (see LSJ s.v., I)—who possessed good breeding and education (*Nicom.* 29). But it is only the clarity of Dio's antithetical construction that, in this instance, activates a nonderogatory signification.[110] When the context of its usage does not specify such an opposition, the word consistently implies low social status and the vulgarity assumed to attend it.[111]

It is misleading, then, to adduce texts like Isocrates's *Antidosis*, in which he characterizes trained but nonpracticing orators as ἰδιῶται, as parallels for Paul's usage.[112] Isocrates differentiates those who retire into private life (ἰδιώτας ἀπαλλαττομένους) from those who pursue careers in declamation or forensic rhetoric (ἀγωνιστὰς γιγνομένους [201]; cf. ἰδιωτεύειν ἐβουλήθησαν [204]). The context here leaves no room for doubt regarding in which sense these men are ἰδιῶται: they are, to borrow a phrase from Dionysius of Halicarnassus, ἰδιώτην βίον ζῆν (*Ant. rom.* 5.5.3; cf. Isocrates, *Soph.* 14). Nevertheless it would be an affront to their sophistication to refer to them as ἰδιῶται τῷ λόγῳ.[113]

In addition to demanding an unlikely rendering of the word ἰδιώτης here, the "nonprofessional" interpretation makes no sense in the immediate context. This is an antithetical construction—"but not [an ἰδιώτης] with respect to knowledge," Paul insists—and it will not do to interpret the first half of the antithesis in a way that renders the second half incoherent. Whatever Paul means by saying that he is not an ἰδιώτης τῇ γνώσει, he is

---

110. Cf. Dio Chrysostom, *Regn.* 12; Aristides, *Or.* 1.311; 11.17. Likewise, Dionysius of Halicarnassus, *Dem.* 56, differentiating between speeches that concern private vs. public interests; Epictetus, *Diatr.* 3.15.13 (φιλοσόφον στάσιν ἔχειν ἢ ἰδιώτου); 3.16; 3.19.

111. See also LSJ, s.v. ἰδιωτεία, ἰδιωτεύω, ἰδιωτικός, ἰδιῶτις, and ἰδιωτισμός.

112. Cf. Martin, *The Corinthian Body*, 48; Pogoloff, *Logos and Sophia*, 149; Winter, *Philo and Paul*, 224–25; Peterson, *Eloquence and the Proclamation of the Gospel*, 109.

113. Bruce Winter also cites Philo, *Agr.* 160 as evidence that the ἰδιῶται could "include not only students of rhetoric, but also those who have graduated from such schools" (*Philo and Paul*, 102). What Winter fails to see is that Philo's use of the word ἰδιώτης here derives from an extended military metaphor wherein sophists are experienced, professional soldiers (ἐμπειροπόλεμοι) while their would-be combatants are civilians or private recruits (ἰδιῶται). For ἰδιῶται as civilians (vs. soldiers), see Xenophon, *Eq. mag.* 8.1; and, as privates (vs. men of military rank), P.Hamb. I 26.11 (BGU X 1958); P.Hib. I 30.12; I 89.2; Xenophon, *Anab.* 1.3.11; Polybius, *Hist.* 1.69.11. Thus Philo's usage tells us nothing about the rhetorical knowledge of an ἰδιώτης τῷ λόγῳ.

not claiming to be a professional γνῶσις practitioner. What Paul insists on here is not that he has made a career out of γνῶσις, but that he possesses it.

Two further considerations tell against the reading of Martin et alia. First, it demands a more specific signification for λόγος than the context allows. The word may occasionally mean "rhetoric," but that is hardly its usual sense. In order to translate it as such, we should need some contextual indication that Paul means something more specific than "speech." In this case, there is no such evidence; there is only the recent habit of reading the text through the lens of ancient rhetorical theory. I have demonstrated above the inappropriateness of such a reading.

Second, this interpretation of Paul's concession fails to account for these scholars' own reading of 2 Cor 10:10, where Paul cites the specific accusation to which he is usually thought to be responding in 11:6. Paul's rivals do not accuse him of being, like Isocrates's students, a well-trained orator living a private life; they characterize his rhetorical delivery—at least according to these scholars—as despicable (ὁ λόγος ἐξουθενημένος). According to these scholars' own claims, then, the terms of the dispute have already been established such that an admission that one is an ἰδιώτης τῷ λόγῳ is necessarily a concession of ineloquence, even rudeness of speech.[114]

Indeed, given the pattern of usage elucidated above, translations like "layman" and "untrained" fail to capture the full connotations of the phrase. If Paul were merely conceding that he was untrained, normal usage would require an objective genitive here in place of his dative of reference.[115] Rather, what Paul concedes is that he is an ἰδιώτης—a boor, a plebian, an "ignoramus" (LSJ s.v., III.3)—with regard to speech. His use of the language, he cannot deny, is uncultured and unrefined.

A particularly illuminating glimpse into the characteristics associated with such λόγος ἰδιωτικός is afforded by Sextus Empiricus. Sextus digresses to consider Dionyius Thrax's definition of grammar as "expertness in the language of poets and composers" (*Math.* 1.63 [Bury, LCL]). He notices a contradiction here, for this definition restricts the grammarian to learned language, yet, in practice, grammarians often enough take aim at the common usage of τῶν ἰδιωτῶν καὶ ἀνεπιστημόνων (1.64). And notice what

---

114. The objection holds on my own preferred reading of 2 Cor 10:10 also, since we have evidence elsewhere that the manner of Paul's proclamation was under critique—on which see ch. 2 above.

115. See LSJ s.v., III.2. Cf. Plato, *Prot.* 345A; Xenophon, *Oec.* 3.9.

such grammatical activity involves: καὶ τὸ βάρβαρον καὶ τὸ Ἑλληνικὸν τό τε σόλοικον καὶ τὸ μὴ τοιοῦτον ἐξελέγχουσαν. In other words, the ἰδιῶται are those who, precisely by speaking vulgarly, generate an ample store of raw material for pedantic grammatical analysis.[116]

Our image of the ancient plebs and their defective *Umgangsprache* is enriched later in the treatise, when Sextus goes on to describe the usefulness of graciously adjusting one's vocabulary so as to avoid ridicule from one's audience:

> Aiming at propriety and clearness and the avoidance of ridicule from our serving lads and ordinary folk (τῶν διακονούντων ἡμῖν παιδαρίων καὶ ἰδιωτῶν),[117] we shall use the [term] πανάριον (even if it is barbarous), not ἀρτοφορίς ... And again, in serious discussion, having regard to the company present, we shall put aside commonplace phrases (ἰδιωτικὰς λέξεις) and pursue after a more refined (ἀστειοτέραν) and cultured (φιλολόγον) manner of speech. (*Meth.* 1.234–235 [Bury, LCL])

In the discursive gap that separates slaves and aristocracy, the ἰδιῶται, apparently, belong with the slaves, speaking in language unfit for serious discussion.[118]

---

116. For his part, Dionysius of Halicarnassus insists that composition that resembles the prose of the ἰδιώτης—he specifies the ἀδολέσχης ("prater") and the φλύαρος ("babbler")—is unworthy of critical attention (*Comp.* 26).

117. In his Teubner edition, J. Mau brackets καὶ ἰδιωτῶν here, referencing an emendation suggested by Richard Harder. More recently, Harder's proposed emendation has been rejected by D. L. Blank (Sextus Empiricus, *Against the Grammarians* [Clarendon Later Ancient Philosophers; Oxford: Oxford University Press, 1998], 47 n. 49). For our purposes, the question is immaterial: the following sentence makes clear that Sextus does, in any case, associate ἰδιωτικὰς λέξεις with the speech of "serving lads" et al.

118. Sextus concludes with a remark that should invite us to rethink recent interpretation of 1 Cor 2:1–5: ὡς γὰρ ἡ φιλόλογος γελᾶται παρὰ τοῖς ἰδιώταις, οὕτως ἡ ἰδιωτικὴ παρὰ τοῖς φιλολόγοις (*Math.* 1.235). Notice that what is attested here is neither a "rhetorical [disavowal] of rhetorical activity" (Martin, *Corinthian Body*, 49), nor philosophical disapproval thereof (Betz, "Rhetoric and Theology," 137–52). Rather, it appears that in antiquity, as today, the non-elite were able to take paradoxical satisfaction precisely in what was, from an elite perspective, their deficiency. Indeed, it does not take a philosopher to be dismissive of elite speech. Cf. William Labov, *Sociolinguistic Patterns* (Philadelphia: University of Pennsylvania Press, 1972), 311–13; and, more generally, Pierre Bourdieu, *Distinction: A Social Critique of the Judgement of Taste* (trans. Richard Nice; Cambridge: Harvard University Press, 1984), 193–200.

To sum up, then, when Paul concedes that he is an ἰδιώτης τῷ λόγῳ, he is not merely admitting that he is a nonprofessional orator, or even that he lacks rhetorical education, although certainly that can be inferred. What he is admitting is, rather, that his speech locates him among those liable to be deemed ταπεινός (10:1) and ἀσθενής (10:10). His is an abject voice, and, I submit, the drama of 2 Cor 10–13 derives from his vehement and sometimes vulgar attempt to refigure his degradation into a mark of status and authority—or, more specifically, into a representation of the crucified yet powerful body of Christ (12:9–10; 13:3–4).

Envy and Foolishness: The Social Locations of Self-Praise

As demonstrated in detail in chapter 4 above, the idea that Plutarch's *De laude ipsius* provides us with an inventory of the rhetorical precepts that shaped Paul's boasting derives from a misreading both of Paul and of Plutarch and cannot be sustained. However, that does not render comparison of the two unfruitful. On the contrary, as was noted repeatedly, *De laude ipsius* provides a telling contrast with Paul's boasting, as it appears to be predicated on a very different set of values and social assumptions. These differences, I will suggest here, can be distilled into a single opposition: whereas Plutarch is concerned with the social consequences of envy, Paul is worried about being derided as a fool. Further, this distinction attests to two different social realities inhabited by Plutarch and Paul: Plutarch's concerns presuppose the constraints of an aristocratic social milieu; Paul's attest to his marginality, and the tenuousness of his claim to status.

For his part, Plutarch is negotiating a fundamental tension inherent in his social and political reality, what Ian Rutherford describes as "a problem of *decorum* created by a conflict between the social pressure to assert oneself in public and the social criticism of excessive assertiveness."[119] In other words, everyone wants honor, and everyone is reluctant to grant too much of it to others. This dynamic is most explicit in Plutarch's description of how hearing the praise of others begets self-praise. The passage is worth reproducing in full:

> First, when others are praised, our rivalry (φιλότιμον) erupts, as we said, into praise of self (περιαυτολογίαν); it is seized with a certain barely controllable yearning and urge for glory (ὁρμὴ πρὸς δόξαν) that stings and

---

119. Rutherford, "Poetics of the *Paraphthegma*," 201.

tickles like an itch, especially when the other is praised for something in which he is our equal or inferior. For just as in the hungry the sight of others eating makes the appetite sharper and keener, so the praise of others not far removed inflames with jealousy (ζηλοτυπίᾳ) those who are intemperate in seeking glory. (546C–D [De Lacy and Einarson, LCL]; cf. 540A–C)[120]

Elsewhere in the tractate Plutarch's descriptions of the negative effects of unseemly self-praise tend to mystify this social tension. His terminology is diverse, but generally revolves around two corporeal symbols: disgust and burden-bearing. Unmitigated self-praise is heavy, burdensome, and oppressive (ἐπαχθής [539A; 541B; 541D; 543F; 547A; 547D]; φορτικός [539B; 547A]; βαρύς [547D; cf. 542F; 543E]; cf. ἄχθομαι [539D; 542C]);[121] moreover, it is nauseating (ἀηδής [547D]; cf. ἀηδία [539B; 539C]) and it disgusts us (δυσχεραίνομεν [539D; cf. 540A]). This is not very perspicuous, but what all of this body language seems to effect is the elevation of Plutarch's socially constructed conception of decorum to the level of a natural aversion: when we encounter self-praise, we feel discomfort in our guts—"as if by nature" (ὥσπερ φύσει), as Plutarch has it (547D; cf. Demosthenes, Cor. 3).[122]

Like most arguments from nature, Plutarch's serves his larger interest in preserving stability and social order.[123] The point here is that restraint from self-praise—and restraint of ambition generally (cf. *Praec. ger. rei pub.* 809C; 819F–820B)—attenuates the envy and rivalry that always

---

120. On Plutarch's conception of the relationship between envy and the search for honor, see also *Inv. od.* 537B. On Plutarch's Platonic understanding of the passions more generally, see esp. *Virt. mor.* and Duff, *Plutarch's Lives*, 72–98.

121. Plutarch's vocabulary here is not unique. Laurant Pernot identifies in discussions of self-praise "une série de termes, toujours les mêmes" that depict the burdensome experience of enduring another's boasting: ἐπαχθής, φορτικός, ἐπίφθονος ("Periautologia," 107).

122. Cf. Fields, "Aristides and Plutarch on Self-Praise," 156–57. Note also Plutarch's use of the constraining language of shame: It is seemly to be embarrassed (αἰδεῖσθαι προσῆκον) even when others praise us, hence boasters are derided as "shameless" (ἀναισχύντους [539D]). Cf. 547B: δεῖ γὰρ ἐρυθριᾶν ἐπαινούμενον.

123. So ibid., 157–60. On the political context which lends this task particular urgency—that of an aristocrat in the Greek East under Rome—see Simon Swain, *Hellenism and Empire: Language, Classicism, and Power in the Greek World, AD 50–250* (Oxford: Clarendon, 1996), 135–86.

threaten to disrupt a harmonious society.[124] In short, self-praise is a problem because it incites envy; the solution is decorous modesty.

Hence when Plutarch approves a particular occasion as appropriate for self-praise, it is almost invariably the unlikelihood that boasting in such a situation will arouse envy that provides his rationale. When one is speaking in answer to an accusation, Plutarch notes that bold self-defense, in its refusal to be humiliated, "humbles and overpowers envy" (540D [De Lacy and Einarson, LCL]). Likewise, when one boasts in the midst of hardship, the boaster's peril removes all thought of envy (ἀφῄρει τὸν φθόνον ὁ κίνδυνος [541A]). Blending praise of one's audience with praise of oneself makes self-praise unlikely to incite envy (ἀνεπίφθονος) since the audience is allowed to take some credit for the great deeds that are recited (542B–C). Further, statesmen can remove φθόνος by praising fortune or the gods— the logic being that people "would rather be bested by luck than by merit" (542F). Conspicuous rejection of flattery from others makes room for inoffensive self-praise, since ὁ φθόνος οὐκ ἀηδῶς τῷ τὰ μείζονα παραιτουμένῳ τὰ μετριώτερα δίδωσι (543D). Finally, envy can be averted by confession of minor shortcomings (544B). For good reason, then, the work is entitled Περὶ τοῦ ἑαυτὸν ἐπαινεῖν ἀνεπιφθόνως—or, as Dana Fields paraphrases: "On praising oneself without engendering the odium that accompanies too-eminent success."[125]

Again, then, it is profoundly misleading to speak as if Plutarch were reiterating abstract rhetorical rules, enumerating the occasions when, in ancient society, boasting was "permissible."[126] Instead, his recommendations—and they are but a single take on the matter[127]—derive from social observation. Tautologous as it might sound, self-praise is acceptable when it is well received, that is, when it arouses emulation rather than envy—

---

124. See esp. Dimos Spatharas, "Self-Praise and Envy: From Rhetoric to the Athenian Courts," *Arethusa* 44 (2011): 199–219.

125. Fields, "Aristides and Plutarch on Self-Praise," 159.

126. Watson, "Paul's Boasting in 2 Corinthians 10–13," 270; cf. Betz, *Der Apostel Paulus und die sokratische Tradition*, 78.

127. For example, Plutarch and Quintilian disagree outright regarding the appropriateness of Cicero's self-praise (*De laude* 541A; *Inst.* 11.1.17–18), and different perspectives altogether are evidenced by Aristides and Pliny, e.g., both of whom are rather more forthright about their own virtues than Plutarch would countenance. See Fields, "Aristides and Plutarch on Self-Praise," 160–72; Rutherford, "Poetics of the *Paraphthegma*"; Gibson, "(In)offensive Self-Praise."

and Plutarch's keen analysis into the workings of envy enables him to give a sound estimate of when that might be.

Plutarch's emphasis on the dangerous nexus of self-praise and envy is not novel. In Plato's *Phaedo*, Socrates, having been praised for undertaking a brilliant argument, demurred, attentive to the possibility that such speech should arouse an evil eye (βασκανία [95B]). As noted above, Aristotle too recognized the proclivity of speaking about oneself (περὶ αὑτοῦ λέγειν) to perpetuate envious rivalry (ἐπίφθονος [*Rhet.* 3.17.16]). The same sensitivity is evident in the Homeric scholia: in book 18 of the *Iliad*, Achilles avers that no Achaean is his equal in the art of war, yet concedes that others perform better in council (18.105–106). One ancient commentator notes that by divvying up the praise thus Achilles steers clear of envy (τῷ διελεῖν τὸν ἔπαινον ἀπελύσατο τὸν φθόνον [schol. T. *Il.* 18:105–106a]).[128] Finally, Isocrates remarks, at the outset of his *Antidosis*, that he has adopted the form of a fictional defense speech because if he were to have undertaken his own encomium (εἰ ... ἐπαινεῖν ἐμαυτὸν ἐπιχειροίην) he could not have avoided arousing displeasure and envy (οὔτ᾽ ἐπιχαρίτως οὐδ᾽ ἀνεπιφθόνως εἰπεῖν ... δυνησόμενος [8]).[129]

Evidently, the recognition that self-praise had a dangerous tendency to incite envy was widespread. It is striking, then, that this concern is entirely lacking from Paul's expressions of hesitancy to boast.[130] What worries Paul is the possibility not that he will be envied but that he will appear to be a fool—an evaluation he repeatedly seeks to preempt by using a series of disclaimers (2 Cor 11:1, 16–17, 21, 12:6, 11). How are we to account for this difference in perspective?

For Ulrich Heckel, the explanation for Paul's concern with foolishness is his dependence on "the Jewish wisdom tradition," in which "the fool" (ἄφρων) is the principal antagonist.[131] Foolishness, Heckel concludes, thus consists in "Gegensatz zum Herrn," and Paul manifests it—though

---

128. See further Fish, "Giving Credit Where Credit is Due," 470–72.

129. See also Demosthenes, *Ep.* 2.4, 24; Pliny, *Ep.* 1.8.5–6; 9.23.5–6; Thucydides 2.35.2; Pindar, *Pyth.* 1.81–85.

130. The closest Paul comes is a single mention of jealousy (11:2), but here he is describing his own "righteous zeal" (ζηλῶ γὰρ ὑμᾶς θεοῦ ζήλῳ) for the Corinthians (11:2) which has been aroused by his rivals' intrusion. There is no connection to self-praise. Cf. 11:12, where there is perhaps recognition that envy leads to boasting, but no sensitivity to the inverse possibility.

131. Heckel, *Kraft in Schwachheit*, 194–202.

only in parody of his opponents—by boasting in 11:16–12:10 according to "äußerlich-weltlichen Maßstäben."[132] The trouble here is that it is Heckel's theology, not anything in the texts themselves, that provides the link between Paul's foolishness and the wisdom tradition. Though the fool of the Proverbs is often characterized as loud and brash,[133] there is not much talk of boastfulness (only Sir 20:7), and nothing at all about pride in one's own *äußerlich-weltlichen* accomplishments. Moreover, there is nothing in 2 Cor 10–13 that brings to mind that willful rejection of God that is, as Heckel correctly notes, fundamental to the characterization of the fool in Psalms 13 and 52 LXX.[134] Only if we ourselves provide the middle term—namely, the theological conviction that pride in one's own accomplishments *is* rejection of God—can we link Paul's foolishness with the wisdom tradition.

To appreciate the significance of Paul's concern with foolishness rather than envy, we must look, I suggest, not to a particular theological—or dramaturgical[135]—tradition, but rather to two different mechanisms of social control by which any number of groups seek to restrain the disruptive self-assertion of their individual members. Here Quintilian provides us with a helpful starting point, describing the varied responses of an audience to one who boasts:

> There is ever in the mind of man a certain element of lofty and unbending pride that will not brook superiority: and for this reason we take delight in raising the humble and submissive to their feet, since such an act gives us a consciousness of our superiority, and as soon as all sense of rivalry disappears, its place is taken by a feeling of humanity. But the man who exalts himself beyond reason is looked upon as depreciating and showing a contempt for others and as making them seem small rather than himself seem great. As a result, those who are beneath him

---

132. Ibid., 194, 202: "opposition to the Lord … external-worldly standards." Thus Heckel sees two different kinds of boasting here, boasting "in the Lord" in ch. 10, and foolish boasting in the *Narrenrede* (p. 202). Cf. Travis, "Paul's Boasting," 529, who thinks that with the "fool's speech" Paul deliberately crosses the line from Hebrew "boasting in the Lord" to Greek rhetorical performance—though, again, only as a parody.

133. See Prov 9:13; 12:23; 15:2; 18:6–7, 13; 20:3; 29:11, 20; Eccl 5:3; 10:13–14.

134. Heckel, *Kraft in Schwachheit*, 196.

135. On Windisch's suggestion that Paul's foolishness derives from his imitation of the Greek mime, see the discussion beginning in the first section of ch. 6 above.

feel a grudge (*invident*) against him (for those who are unwilling to yield and yet have not the strength to hold their own are always liable to this failing), while his superiors laugh at him and the good disapprove. (*Inst.* 11.1.16–17 [Butler, LCL])

As Quintilian explains, boasting engenders different responses from different groups within one's audience, with the significant criterion, apparently, being the hearers' social status relative to the speaker: his inferiors envy him (*invident humiliores*), while his superiors laugh (*rident superiores* [*Inst.* 11.1.17]). What we have here, then, are two different ways of dealing with an overambitious status claim: Those who aspire to similar status but find themselves overshadowed by the boaster (*qui nec cedere volunt nec possunt contendere*) feel slighted and cannot resist envy. Those whose recognized status exceeds that of the boaster merely laugh, deriding his claim to honor by treating it as unworthy of serious response.

Quintilian's observation accords with Hesiod's old quip: potter strives with potter, artisan with artisan; beggar envies beggar and singer singer (*Op.* 25–26). Indeed, the notion that envy obtains primarily among relative equals in status was widespread in the ancient world.[136] According to Aristotle:

> The kind of people who feel envy are those who have, or seem to themselves to have [more fortunate acquaintances among] those like themselves. I mean those like themselves in terms of birth, relationship, age, disposition, reputation, possessions, as well as those who just fall short of having all these on an equal basis. (*Rhet.* 2.10.1–2 [trans. Kennedy]; cf. 2.10.5–7)

This is Plutarch's basic assumption too: Envy attaches itself in particular to those who are increasing in virtue and honor and fame, but only if they are within range of competitors. The truly resplendent, like Alexander or Cyrus, are immune to envy; they are in a category all their own (*Inv. od.* 538A–B). Plutarch uses shadow analogies to explain how this works: Those who reach the heights of good fortune are like the noontime

---

136. See Peter Walcot, *Envy and the Greeks: A Study of Human Behaviour* (Warminster, Eng.: Aris & Phillips, 1978), 11–12; D. L. Cairns, "The Politics of Envy: Envy and Equality in Ancient Greece," in *Envy, Spite and Jealousy: The Rivalrous Emotions in Ancient Greece* (ed. David Konstan and N. Keith Rutter; Edinburgh Levantis Studies 2; Edinburgh: Edinburgh University Press, 2003), 240 n. 15.

sun—they shine from far above our head and thus cast hardly a shadow (538A–B); the thing that irritates us is dwelling in the shade of our neighbor's house when it rises above our own (538E).

It is not difficult to transpose this conception of envy onto Plutarch's own political milieu: Roman imperial power is ultimately beyond envy, but rivalry among the local aristocracy is a perpetual threat (cf. *Praec. ger. rei pub.* 815A–B; 825E–F). Indeed, Plutarch's use of the pronoun "we" throughout *De laude ipsius* suggests that what concerns him about immoderate self-praise is precisely its potential to incite envy among people like himself—his circle of provincial aristocrats and statesmen[137]—and thus disrupt the harmonious status quo.[138] Plutarch's entire discussion, then, is predicated on particular aristocratic values and indeed presupposes a particular social location. That is, his "voice" locates him as a man accustomed to a particular set of social constraints.

Paul's concern with appearing foolish is remote from Plutarch's interests; however, it does recall the response to immoderate boasting that Quintilian ascribes to a boaster's superiors, namely, derision. The function of derision as a response to an inordinate status claim is well illustrated by Lucian's account of Peregrinus Proteus. According to Lucian, Peregrinus was so eager for fame (*Peregr.* 38; cf. 1, 2, 4, 8, 20, 22, 42, 43) that he immolated himself by leaping onto a pyre at the Olympic Games. Lucian's one-dimensional diagnosis—φιλόδοξος (38)—tells us more, I suspect, about Lucian himself than about Peregrinus: perhaps Peregrinus's action was misguided, but there really is no reason to suspect that his motives were insincere.[139] In any case, Lucian interpreted his behavior as a status claim—Peregrinus "[dared] to exalt himself as an authority figure independent of the constraints of received culture"[140]—but not one to be taken seriously. No, for Lucian, the only appropriate response to the man's madness (ἀπόνοια [2]) was laughter: "I think I can see you laughing heartily at the old man's drivelling idiocy (ἐπὶ τῇ κορύζῃ τοῦ γέροντος)," Lucian tells his addressee. "Pray, what else … are we to do when we hear utterances so

---

137. See Swain, *Hellenism and Empire*, 135–86.

138. So Fields, "Aristides and Plutarch on Self-Praise," 159–60.

139. So already Eduard Zeller, "Alexander und Peregrinus: Ein Betrüger und ein Schwärmer," in *Vorträge und Abhandlungen: Zweite Sammlung* (Leipzig: Fues, 1877), 173–74.

140. James A. Francis, *Subversive Virtue: Asceticism and Authority in the Second-Century Pagan World* (University Park: Pennsylvania State University Press, 1995), 54.

ridiculous (οὕτω γελοίων ῥήσεων), and see old men all but standing on their heads in public for the sake of a little despicable notoriety?" (2, 8 [Harmon, LCL]). This is the behavior of fools and vainglorious men (μωροὺς καὶ κενοδόξους ἀνθρώπους [25]) and merits only ridicule (34).

Lucian's strained insistence on the authenticity of his laughter (ἐγέλα καὶ δῆλος ἦν νειόθεν αὐτὸ δρῶν [7]) makes one suspect that he is, despite himself, entering into rivalry with Peregrinus for cultural influence and secretly fighting off envy—an emotion, after all, that no one admits to feeling (so Plutarch, *Inv. od.* 537E). Still, he is clearly working from the assumption that when a status claim is unlikely to get much traction it can simply be laughed off. Pierre Bourdieu observed the same phenomenon among the Kabyle, where boastfulness is routinely met with ridicule: "'Only dung swells,' they say."[141]

Bourdieu's related observation has become a commonplace in biblical studies due to the work of Bruce Malina: "Only a challenge issued (or an offence caused) by one's equal in honour deserves to be taken up.... An affront from an inferior in humanity or honour recoils upon the presumptuous person who makes it."[142] But this principle must be modified slightly. As Zeba Crook recently has demonstrated, "inter-status honor challenges" did occur in the ancient world; indeed, even the honor of emperors and gods was vulnerable.[143] What finally makes an honor challenge—or, accordingly, a boast—worthy of a rivalrous response is not, *pace* Bourdieu and Quintilian, the antagonist's relative status per se, but rather the credibility of the challenge in the eyes of a "public court of reputation"[144]—and it just so happens that challenges and boasts from people of inferior status are seldom credited. An insult or a boast only engenders rivalry if it is perceived to hit close to home; if not, it can be met with laughter and ridicule.

And laughter and ridicule, we should remember, constitute precisely the sort of treatment to which those deemed "fools" in the ancient world were susceptible. This is evident above all from the theater, where, as Larry Welborn explains, the "fool" (μωρός), who represented those in society most susceptible to derision and abuse, became a stock character:

---

141. Bourdieu, "Sentiment of Honour," 198.
142. Ibid., 200; cf. Malina, *The New Testament World*, 35.
143. Crook, "Honor, Shame, and Social Status Revisited," 599–604.
144. Cf. Ibid., 609–10.

The "foolishness" of this social type consisted in a weakness or deficiency of intellect, often coupled with a physical grotesqueness. Because the concept of the laughable in the Greco-Roman world was grounded in contemplation of the ugly and defective, those who possessed these characteristics were deemed to be "foolish."[145]

But, of course, the association of foolishness and derision was by no means limited to the mime. Dionysius of Halicarnassus, for example, reports the discovery of the Sibylline oracles by telling of a woman who, oddly, burnt six of the books she had for sale, then came back and tried to sell the remaining three for the same price she had asked for the whole set. Not surprisingly, all thought her a fool (ἄφρων) and derided her (γελασθεῖσα [Rom. ant. 4.62.2]; cf. Cicero, De or. 2.61; Diodorus Siculus 17.101.4–5).

Here the fool is someone who cannot put two and two together (cf. Diodorus Siculus 12.12.1; 12.14.2; Polybius 33.20; Hesiod, Op. 210), and thus incites mockery. More relevant to Paul's usage, perhaps, is the assumed connection between foolishness and silly babble (cf. Plutarch, Garr. 510A), and the association of foolishness with groundless boasting or ἀλαζονεία (Dionysius of Halicarnassus, Ant. rom. 14.9.4; Plutarch, Def. orac. 419B; Dio Chrysostom, Virt. [Or. 69] 7). Note that it appears not to be boasting itself that makes one a fool, but rather the making of self-assertions that one is not able to realize or substantiate (Diodorus Siculus 16.70.2; cf. 2 Cor 12:6). Clearly, then, as Dio Chrysostom's usage attests, being considered a fool is a shameful thing indeed (In cont. 16).

Accordingly, it is of great significance for understanding Paul's hesitant boasting that it is the perception of foolishness that Paul seeks specifically to preempt (11:1, 16–18; 12:6, 12; cf. 1 Cor 4:10). His status is apparently tenuous enough that his claim to apostolic authority teeters on the verge of being derisible. He cannot assume that his status claim will be taken seriously or confronted head on; he fears that it will simply be ridiculed, that he will become a laughingstock. Indeed, who insists that

---

145. L. L. Welborn, *Paul, the Fool of Christ: A Study of 1 Corinthians 1-4 in the Comic-Philosophic Tradition* (JSNTSup 293; London: T&T Clark, 2005), 32–33. Welborn treats the word μωρός, but the observation is relevant to the ἄφρων as well—despite his own overdrawn distinction between μωρός as a social term and ἄφρων as a cognitive one (*An End to Enmity*, 156–62). In addition to the texts cited below, for the correlation of foolishness and physical defect, see Plutarch, *Lyc.* 15.8; Galen, *Quod qual. incorp.* 19.479. For the correlation of foolishness and low social status, see Dionysius of Halicarnassus, *Ant. or.* 1; *Ant. rom.* 5.67.1–2.

he is "not inferior" (11:5), except a man who knows that he is liable to be considered so?

Paul's sensitivity to this possibility is evident from the way he speaks of the perceived gap between the authoritative tone of his letters and the weakness of his personal presence (10:8–11; cf. 10:1–2; 13:2). He will not be ashamed, he insists, for being excessively boastful of his authority (10:8)—that is, for making status claims that overreach the Corinthians' rather belittling estimation of him.[146] We tend to miss his reference to shame here, assuming that what he really means is that he is not *apologetic* for boasting,[147] but such a reading obscures the social dynamics of the situation: Paul is being accused of making himself ridiculous, thus he must defiantly insist that his status claim be taken seriously: "If I wish to boast, I will not be a fool, for I will be speaking the truth" (12:6).[148]

This is a voice remote from that of Plutarch, Quintilian, and Demosthenes, and also from that of Red Jacket, who, in keeping with his own social location as a man accustomed to deference, grounds his self-defense precisely on his dignified demeanor and thus his immunity to his interlocutors' derisive characterization. Tellingly, we find a closer analogue to Paul in Elia, who, like Paul, speaks from a place of marginality. Indeed, although these two speakers make what are in many respects very different rhetorical moves, their strategies are in one key way alike.

Elia, remember, was asked if she had been afraid of the *gringos*. No, not me, she insisted, but you should have seen how scared Atalaina and the others were. Thus she fends off the threat that she herself will be perceived as a naïf. By internalizing the evaluation of the Europeans, and laughing *through* it at her peers, Elia insinuates herself with her interviewer and ensures that she will be laughed with, not laughed at. Clearly,

---

146. Cf. Arthur J. Dewey, "A Matter of Honor: A Social-Historical Analysis of 2 Corinthians 10," *HTR* 78 (1985): 212.

147. So Harris, *Second Corinthians*, 692; Roetzel, *2 Corinthians*, 100; cf. Ragnar Leivestad, "'The Meekness and Gentleness of Christ' II Cor. x. 1," *NTS* 12 (1966): 164; Barnett, *Second Epistle*, 473. Garland recognizes the social dynamics at play here ("shame comes when one exceeds one's social boundaries") but is too embedded in Paul's own view of his status ("he has certainly not exceeded his") to notice the implications (*2 Corinthians*, 443).

148. See also 2 Cor 7:14, where the fact that Paul's boasting in Titus has been shown to be truthful prevents him from being shamed, and 9:3, where the possibility that Paul's boasting in the Corinthians should prove empty creates the potential for his humiliation.

in the particular social space constituted by this interaction, it is her European interviewer who possesses symbolic capital and thus whose evaluative perspective is decisive. Elia occupies a subaltern position, and, in this context, exercises control over her identity only to the extent that she is able to inhabit and then to manipulate this European perspective.

Paul's relationship with his addressees is assuredly quite different; still, like Elia, he knows that he is susceptible to ridicule, and he apparently occupies a marginal position. Indeed, according to the dominant evaluative perspective—that is, the common sense that governs the social space of the Corinthian community—Paul is ἀσθενής and ταπεινός. Like Elia, then, in order to get any traction, he must inhabit and then seek to manipulate that dominant perspective. For Paul, this involves a rather tortured admission of weakness, then an attempt to refigure that weakness as a mark of divine strength. In short, he seeks to resolve his ambivalent status by making a virtue of necessity.

Boasting in Weakness

It is surely an indicator of the inadequacy of the underlying interpretive approach that Paul's boasting in 2 Cor 10–13 has, by various recent scholars, been considered both a sincere attempt at a *peristasis* catalogue and a parody of (self-)encomiastic conventions. In fact, neither proposal does a very good job of explaining the peculiarities of this text.

The latter reading can be traced to the work of Anton Fridrichsen, who, positing formal parallels between Paul's boasting in 2 Cor 11 and Augustus's *Res gestae*, concluded:

> Wenn der Apostel trotz dieser christlichen Grundstimmung des Martyriums und der Schwäche sich dem Stil der Ruhmeschronik anschließt, zeugt das von einer gewissen Spannung in seinem Wesen zwischen menschlichem Selbstbewußtsein und christlicher Selbstentäußerung; einer Spannung, die in der paradoxalen Diskrepanz zwischen Form und Inhalt des Peristasenkatalogs hervorbricht.[149]

---

149. Anton Fridrichsen, "Zum Stil des paulinischen Peristasenkatalogs 2 Cor. 11, 23ff.," *SO* 7 (1928): 29: "That the apostle, despite this Christian sentiment of martyrdom and weakness, follows the style of the chronicle of glorious deeds testifies to a certain tension in his character between human self-confidence and Christian self-renunciation—a tension that erupts through the paradoxical discrepancy between the form and content of the hardship catalogue."

If, for Fridrichsen himself, formal comparison with the *Ruhmeschronik* highlighted the tension both in the text and in the one who wrote it, subsequent interpreters, building on his work, have resolved this tension by suggesting that Paul uses the form only for the purposes of parody. In any case, the stylistic parallels noted by Fridrichsen are insufficient to suggest formal imitation, amounting, essentially, to the use of the first-person aorist, repeated use of πολλάκις, and enumeration of deeds. These are hardly unique to the *Res gestae*.[150] Moreover, the isolated similarities Fridrichsen identifies occur in the context of texts that are, on the whole, hardly comparable.[151] If Paul was attempting to pillory the sort of self-display the *Res gestae* represent, he seems to have missed his target.

The fundamental problem with the former explanation is perhaps best summarized by Scott Andrews: In contrast to what we should expect on the basis of John Fitzgerald's discussion of the meaning of *peristaseis* for the ancient sage, "the apostle boasts of hardships that reveal his weak status and not of the fact that he has overcome or endured the hardships."[152] Indeed, Paul says this explicitly: τὰ τῆς ἀσθενείας μου καυχήσομαι (11:30).

---

150. See Fitzgerald, *Cracks in an Earthen Vessel*, 19–20.

151. The sentences cited by Fridrichsen that, stylistically, have the most in common with 2 Cor 11:23–28 are these: Δὶς ἐπὶ κέλητος ἐθριάμβευσα, τρὶς ἐφ' ἅρματος. Εἰκοσάκις καὶ ἅπαξ προσηγορεύθην αὐτοκράτωρ (*Res. gest. divi. Aug.* 4 [2.9–10]). This does, indeed, look rather like Paul's enumeration of his beatings: ὑπὸ Ἰουδαίων πεντάκις τεσσεράκοντα παρὰ μίαν ἔλαβον, τρὶς ἐραβδίσθην, ἅπαξ ἐλιθάσθην, τρὶς ἐναυάγησα (vv. 24–25). But, as one reads on, all stylistic similarities cease: "Although the Senate decreed me additional triumphs I set them aside. When I had performed the vows which I had undertaken in each war, I deposited upon the Capitol the laurels which had adorned my fasces" (4 [2.10–14; Shipley, LCL]). And so on. Unfortunately for Fridrichsen's thesis, it is this latter sort of prose, devoid of the rhythmic qualities that characterize Paul's catalogue, that predominates in the *Res gestae*. An unsympathetic reader might accuse the Emperor of droning on, an accusation that Paul's catalogue would hardly incite. F. W. Shipley characterizes Augustus's style as one of "studied simplicity": "There is no attempt at literary embellishment…. The superlative is purposefully avoided, and there is also an absence of the usual descriptive adjectives and adverbs" (*Velleius Paterculus, Compendium of Roman History; Res gestae divi Augusti* [LCL; London: Heinemann, 1924], 336). This sort of style is difficult to reconcile with Paul's overwrought descriptions (νυχθήμερον ἐν τῷ βυθῷ [11:25]; ἐν λιμῷ καὶ δίψει [11:27]) and hyperbolic adverbs (περισσοτέρως … περισσοτέρως … ὑπερβαλλόντως [11:23]).

152. Andrews, "Too Weak Not to Lead," 272. Cf. Fitzgerald, *Cracks in an Earthen Vessel*, 203–4.

The importance of Andrews's distinction is clear from what Aelius Theon has to say about hardships in his discussion of encomia (*Progymn.* 9 [*RG* 2:111–112]). Theon adheres to the view, emphasized by Fitzgerald, that "virtue shines brightest in misfortunes" (trans. Kennedy).[153] But notice what sort of rhetorical use of hardships he recommends: "One should say that he was not brought low by his misfortunes (ἀτυχῶν ταπεινὸς οὐκ ἦν) nor unjust in poverty nor servile (ἀνδραποδώδης) when in want."[154] Clearly, what was considered praiseworthy among Theon's ilk was not undergoing hardships per se but enduring them with one's head held high.[155] Indeed, as Andrews correctly insists, whereas endurance of hardship could be adduced as evidence of ἀνδρεία or *constantia*, succumbing to difficulty was simply humiliating.[156]

The ignominy of Paul's self-presentation is particularly evident from his willingness to boast of his beatings. As Jennifer Glancy has shown, the ancients were keenly aware of the difference between honorable war wounds and the humiliating scars of corporal punishment.[157] Whereas one could unveil one's battle-scarred chest as attestation of martial valor,[158] uncovering a back marred by whips and rods was an admission of servile status;[159] for, in the moral logic of antiquity, "dishonorable bodies were whippable; honorable bodies were not."[160] Therefore, as Glancy insists, "in boasting of beatings, Paul boasts not of his ἀνδρεία but of his humiliating corporal vulnerability."[161] So, although Paul might insist that his weakness means something different from what the Corinthians think it means,

---

153. See Fitzgerald, *Cracks in an Earthen Vessel*, 42–44.
154. See also Plutarch, *De laude* 544B–C and the discussion in ch. 4 above.
155. See esp. Fitzgerald, *Cracks in an Earthen Vessel*, 59–65; Stephen D. Moore and Janice Capel Anderson, "Taking It like a Man: Masculinity in 4 Maccabees," *JBL* 117 (1998): 249–73.
156. Andrews, "Too Weak Not to Lead," 268–69.
157. Glancy, "Boasting of Beatings." Cf. Marshall, *Enmity in Corinth*, 363 n. 83.
158. Cf. Livy 45.39.16; Xenophon, *Ages.* 6.2; Sallust, *Bell. Jug.* 85.29–30; Quintilian, *Inst.* 2.15.7. See further Matthew Leigh, "Wounding and Popular Rhetoric at Rome," *Bulletin of the Institute of Classical Studies* 40 (1995): 192–215.
159. Cf. Philo, *Flacc.* 10.75; Aelian, *Var. hist.* 12.21; Livy 2.23.4–7. See further Jonathan Walters, "Invading the Roman Body: Manliness and Impenetrability in Roman Thought," in *Roman Sexualities* (ed. Judith P. Hallett and Marilyn B. Skinner; Princeton, N.J.: Princeton University Press, 1997), 29–43.
160. Glancy, "Boasting of Beatings," 109.
161. Ibid., 101.

nevertheless this sort of self-presentation has little in common with the Stoic values Fitzgerald has described.[162]

But Paul's self-confessed ἀσθένεια does not only constitute a failure to live up to the standards of the austere Stoics; it represents a more fundamental deficiency as well: Paul's "weakness" signifies his inability to act as befits a freeborn man—specifically, to possess ἀνδρεία and autonomy.[163] In Greco-Roman antiquity, as Jennifer Larson explains, "masculinity was all but identified with social and political dominance"—that is to say, with power.[164] Clement of Alexandria pithily expresses what was the conventional view on the distinction between the genders: It is given to man to act (τὸ δρᾶν), to woman to be acted upon (τὸ πάσχειν [*Paed.* 3.3.19.2; cf. Philo, *QE* 1.8]). Slaves were tossed in with latter.[165] Thus Paul's weakness—that is, precisely his inability to act or to dominate—was not something about which a self-respecting freeborn man would boast.

Of all the possible explanations for Paul's failure to conform to such expectations, the one least often considered is that Paul was, in fact, no self-respecting freeborn man. But it is precisely when we make this interpretive move—that is, when we recognize that Paul's voice comes not from a body accustomed to mastery and autonomy but rather from a body that bears the scars of subjugation—that we are in a position to make sense of this text. The voice that speaks here is abject yet defiant, and presents us with what can only be considered a shameless spectacle of persuasion.

Plutarch speaks admiringly of those noble unfortunates who, like the Stoics discussed by Fitzgerald, brave adversity without resort to piteous appeals or self-abasement (φεύγειν ὅλως τὸ ἐλεεινὸν καὶ συνεπιθρηνοῦν τοῖς ἀβουλήτοις καὶ ταπεινούμενον [*De laude* 541A]). What is interesting about this comment is that it presupposes that self-abasement is in fact a tempting rhetorical move, which is why a self-respecting freeborn man must steel himself and flee it. But for someone without such scruples—some-

---

162. Fitzgerald himself is aware of the tension here, though he fails to see its extensive implications for his interpretive proposal. See esp. "Cracks in an Earthen Vessel," 387 n. 267.

163. For shameful ἀσθένεια contrasted with virtuous and honorable ἀνδρεία, see Plutarch, *Cor.* 15.5; Menander Rhetor, *RG* 3:379; Athanasius, *C. Gent.* 16.5. Cf. 1 Cor 16:13; 1 Pet 3:7; 2 Tim 3:6.

164. Larson, "Paul's Masculinity," 86; see also Moore and Anderson, "Taking It like a Man," 250; Harrill, "Invective against Paul," 191.

165. See Harrill, "Invective against Paul," 192–201; Larson, "Paul's Masculinity," 92–94; Moore and Anderson, "Taking It like a Man," 262.

one, for example, for whom it is more important that his master stop whipping him than that he appear to possess ἀνδρεία—self-abasement might be an attractive means of persuasion indeed. Here, I submit, we begin to hear Paul's voice.

Conclusion
"Where Is the Voice Coming From?"

When I began this project, I expected part 2 to be considerably shorter. I had done enough work with speakers like Red Jacket and Elia to know, as demonstrated in chapter 10, that many of the rhetorical figures attributed to Paul could securely be placed in the realm of "general rhetoric." But what I did not expect was to find that much of the alleged correspondence between Paul and the theorists and practitioners of formal Greco-Roman rhetoric would turn out to be unsubstantiated and illusory. I did not expect to find blatant but pervasive misreadings of the ancient rhetorical sources, not to mention of 2 Cor 10–13, or recently invented *termini technici* being used as if they designated ancient rhetorical concepts.

So we have spent much more time than I anticipated clearing away the overgrowth, as it were, of a methodology that seems to have taken on a life of its own. Apparently, once elevated to the level of one of New Testament scholarship's many "criticisms," rhetorical criticism has quickly morphed from scholarly query to methodological presupposition, and, accordingly, much recent scholarship has approached our text having already decided that the ancient rhetorical sources constitute the lens through which Pauline persuasion should be analyzed. As part 2 of this study has amply demonstrated, this presupposition has not facilitated clarity of analysis. The rhetorical-critical model that has dominated the landscape of Pauline scholarship fails to account for what we find in 2 Cor 10–13, and, moreover, misconstrues the rhetorical sources themselves.

Chapters 9–11 tested another model for explaining Paul's rhetoric, one that had been anticipated quite frequently by scholars chafing at the confines of the dominant model but had not been subjected to critical analysis. Using George Kennedy's work on comparative rhetoric and the insights of sociolinguists on language socialization, we examined the possibility that what Paul knew of persuasion derived not from formal education but from informal social practice. Here, amid a diverse assortment of speakers from a variety of social and cultural locations, we found a compelling context within which to apprehend the nature of Pauline persuasion.

Finally, in chapter 12 we took a few key steps toward a redescription of what I have been calling Paul's "voice." First, we observed that Paul's control of grammatical and syntactical conventions is at times unsteady, a fact that points decisively away from the only sort of formal rhetorical competence that could explain his widely observed independence from formal conventions, namely, fully integrated fluency.[1] This point is important, and bears repeating: Since the earliest rhetorical-critical work of Betz and his followers, it has been widely agreed that Paul's letters do not in fact closely conform to the formal prescriptions of the rhetorical handbooks. Betz's explanation for this fact has become commonplace: Paul, like any good rhetor, does not slavishly follow schoolbook forms but creatively adapts them to his own persuasive ends. And certainly it is true that the best ancient exemplars attest not to mechanistic adherence to formal prescriptions but rather, as Mitchell puts it, to "the fluidity and variety of possibilities of rhetorical composition."[2] But note that such fluency is predicated on a degree of skill considerably beyond that achieved through only rudimentary rhetorical training; indeed, such basic training, we have seen, is likely to result in precisely such wooden, formally correct productions as all agree we do not find in Paul.[3] Accordingly, if the rhetorical features of Paul's letters are to be attributed to formal education, we must impute to him considerable mastery of the subject, not just elementary exposure. And this is where Paul's unsteady prose is telling, for, so long as formal education remains our explanatory paradigm, such mastery of rhetoric simply is not compatible with Paul's failure to master grammar and syntax. No, here Paul resembles the Mexicano orator we met in chapter 10—rhetorically astute, in his own way, but lacking the niceties of polished prose—far more than either Demosthenes, on one end of the scale of formal rhetoric, or Pseudo-Plutarch, on the other. In other words, informal rhetorical socialization provides a far more credible explanation than does formal education for the nature of Paul's rhetoric.

---

1. See further the section "Confused and Insufficiently Explicit" in ch. 12 above.
2. Mitchell, *Rhetoric of Reconciliation*, 9.
3. See esp. the discussion of Ps.-Plutarch's *An ignis* in the last section of ch. 7 above.

This conclusion received confirmation from exegesis of two key verses in our text, 2 Cor 10:10 and 11:6. Although neither verse directly addresses the question of Paul's rhetorical education, both imply that he speaks unimpressively, and, moreover, attest to a voice that inhabits a very different position in Corinth than does the authoritative apostle generated by the rhetorical-critical model. Paul evidently is susceptible to characterization as weak, derisible, and vulgar. Importantly, he is in no position to refute these characterizations; instead, he seeks to redeploy his evident weakness as a mark of divine commission.

Finally, comparison of Paul's rhetorical demeanor with that of Plutarch, Demosthenes, Red Jacket, and Elia highlighted the abjectness of Paul's rhetoric in 2 Cor 10–13. Paul cannot rely on the persuasive power of calm and dignified self-possession. His voice comes from a more tenuous place. His is a rhetoric that arises from vulnerability, desperation, and defiance.

Voice, *Habitus*, and the Individual Speaker

I have referred throughout this study to what I have been calling Paul's "voice," a term I have often glossed as "rhetorical comportment." It may seem odd to reserve a theoretical discussion of this concept for this concluding chapter; nevertheless, it will be most effective, I think, to explain now, in retrospect, how the notion of voice has functioned and what are its theoretical underpinnings.

As noted in the introduction, my starting point here is the correlation between voice, as a mode of comportment, and social location—a correlation we have observed repeatedly throughout this study. There was something particularly "aristocratic," remember, about Plutarch's voice—and, differently, Red Jacket's—but not Paul's. But what exactly was it, and why should this be? Here sociolinguistic theory can provide a framework for conceptualizing what we have seen. Let us begin with a striking article by Edward Sapir, first published in 1927.

Sapir introduces the concept of "voice" with a discussion of a number of characteristics of speech for which the term commonly serves as a metonym: intonation, rhythm, pronunciation, and, more significantly for our purposes, vocabulary and style.[4] As Sapir observed, these features together

---

4. Edward Sapir, "Speech as a Personality Trait," in *Selected Writings of Edward*

constitute a "form of gesture,"⁵ which, like other modes of comportment, derives from and thus attests to both cultural patterns and the particularity of an individual speaker: "Society has its patterns, its set ways of doing things," Sapir noted, "while the individual has his method of handling those particular patterns of society, giving them just enough of a twist to make them 'his' and no one else's."⁶ For Sapir, then, "voice" serves as an indicator both of social location and of individual identity.⁷

What interested Sapir was how people spoke, not what they said. In other words, to use Dell Hymes's distinction, he was interested in "stylistic" as opposed to "referential" aspects of speech.⁸ But, as Hymes's own work in particular has shown, the content of speech, not only its style, derives its meaning from its relationship to conventional social norms.⁹ So, when I speak of voice, I refer not only to vocabulary and style, but also to referential content insofar as it pertains to Sapir's two domains of analysis, namely, social patterns and individual negotiation thereof.

Sapir's basic insight can be extended in both directions, toward consideration of voice as an indicator of social location and toward analysis of the particularity of individual speech. In conceptualizing the former, the work of Pierre Bourdieu is particularly useful. For Bourdieu, social interaction is structured not by "rules" but by *habitus*, "systems of durable, transposable *dispositions*"¹⁰ that are, quite literally, the embodiment of (social) history: "Biological individuals carry with them, at all times and in all places," he explains, "their present and past positions in the social structure ... in the form of dispositions which are so many marks of *social position*."¹¹ These are "values given body, *made* body" in keeping with what

---

Sapir in Language, Culture, and Personality (ed. David G. Mandelbaum; Berkeley: University of California Press, 1949), 533–43; repr. from *American Journal of Sociology* 32 (1927).

5. Ibid., 535.
6. Ibid., 538.
7. See also Hymes, "Ways of Speaking," 436.
8. Ibid., 435–39.
9. See esp. Dell Hymes, "Sociolinguistics and the Ethnography of Speaking," in *Social Anthropology and Language* (ed. Edwin Ardener; London: Tavistock, 1971), 56.
10. Bourdieu, *Theory of Practice*, 72.
11. Ibid., 82. Relevant here is Richard Rohrbaugh's helpful clarification that social location is "a *structural* term describing a position in a social system," not a reference to group membership ("'Social Location of Thought' as a Heuristic Construct in New Testament Study," *JSNT* 30 [1987]: 114).

Bourdieu refers to as bodily *hexis*: "a permanent disposition, a durable manner of standing, speaking, and thereby of *feeling* and *thinking.*"[12] In other words, an individual's bodily *hexis* or comportment represents the somatic reinscription of his or her social location and attendant history of social interaction.

It follows, then, that discursive elements of social interaction—in a word, speech—take place in accordance with the dispositions inculcated by and constitutive of the *habitus*.[13] Communication, as social practice, is structured not only by grammar and syntax—let alone by literary forms and genres, which are merely the tip of the iceberg of discursive conventions—but by a "durably installed generative principle of regulated improvisations."[14] What I am calling voice, then, is one instance of such regulated improvisation, one aspect of the embodiment of the structuring dispositions of the *habitus*—namely, their vocalization. A voice comes from a particular body, and a particular body comports itself in accordance with its particular social location—that is, in accordance with a repertoire of past experiences specific to its particular place in society.[15]

But this is not to say that each individual who occupies a comparable position in society will speak or act identically. On the contrary, although it is often suppressed in both linguistic and sociological theory—including that of Bourdieu—individual variation and idiosyncrasy are, in actual occurrence, constant features of social practice. As Hymes has repeatedly insisted, their analysis is fundamental to any adequate empirical account of human communication.[16] Individuals have different resources—different

---

12. Bourdieu, *Theory of Practice*, 93–94.

13. See esp. Ochs, "Linguistic Resources for Socializing Humanity." Cf. William F. Hanks, "Pierre Bourdieu and the Practices of Language," *Annual Review of Anthropology* 34 (2005): 72.

14. Description of the *habitus* from Bourdieu, *Theory of Practice*, 78.

15. No one has demonstrated this more compellingly than William Labov, who, in his studies of English usage and pronunciation in New York City, correlated such features of spoken English as post-vocalic *r* and diphthong variation with both social location and personal aspiration. See esp. *The Social Stratification of English in New York City* (Washington, D.C.: Center for Applied Linguistics, 1966).

16. See esp. Dell Hymes, "Sapir, Competence, Voices," in *Individual Differences in Language Ability and Behavior* (ed. Charles J. Fillmore, Daniel Kempler, and William S-Y. Wang; Perspectives in Neurolinguistics and Psycholinguistics; New York: Academic Press, 1979), 33–45. Also Hymes, "Sociolinguistics and the Ethnography of Speaking," 51–59; Hymes, *"In Vain I Tried to Tell You": Essays in Native Ameri-*

sorts of "communicative competence"—at their disposal, and they do different things with what they have. In other words, within the constraints of the *habitus*, persons speak and act with varying degrees of skill, appropriateness, and creativity.¹⁷ Each has his or her own "personal voice."¹⁸ Or, as Albert Vanhoye puts it, intuiting, apparently, the theoretical insight of Sapir and Hymes:

> Quoi que je dise, c'est avec ma voix que je le dis et ma voix n'est identique à aucune autre. Elle a des inflexions et des modulations, qui correspondent à mon caractère et à mon éducation, à ma sensibilité, à mes capacités de décision et de relations, bien plus elle reflète ma situation physique et psychologique du moment.¹⁹

This, then, is what I mean by the evaluation of voice: the attempt to elucidate the social location of a speaker as well as his or her particular negotia-

---

can Ethnopoetics (Studies in Native American Literature 1; Philadelphia: University of Pennsylvania Press, 1981), 8–10. The point has recently been taken up by Barbara Johnstone, "The Individual Voice in Language," *Annual Review of Anthropology* 29 (2000): 405–24.

17. Bourdieu explicitly downplays the significance of individual variation, stating that "sociology treats as identical all the biological individuals who, being the product of the same objective conditions, are the supports of the same habitus" (*Theory of Practice*, 85; and cf. 79). But of course he cannot deny such variation outright. For Bourdieu, then, "it is in a relation of homology, of diversity within homogeneity ... that the singular habitus of the different members of the same class are united; the homology of world-views implies the systematic differences which separate singular world-views, adopted from singular but concerted standpoints" (86). In other words, personal style is analogous to an individual specimen: it can meaningfully be characterized only in relation to its genus. What is personal is, in Bourdieu's terms, a "structural variant" (86; cf. Hanks, "Practices of Language," 71). On Bourdieu's reification of the *habitus* here, and his consequent failure adequately to account for human agency, see Brenda Farnell, "Getting Out of the Habitus: An Alternative Model of Dynamically Embodied Social Action," *Journal of the Royal Anthropological Institute* 6 (2000): 397–418.

18. Hymes, "Sapir, Competence, Voices," 43.

19. Albert Vanhoye, "Personnalité de Paul et exégèse paulinienne," in *L'apôtre Paul: Personnalité, style et conception du ministère* (ed. Albert Vanhoye; BETL 73; Leuven: Leuven University Press, 1986), 4: "Whatever I say, it is with my voice that I say it, and my voice is not identical to any other. It has inflections and modulations that correspond to my character and my education, to my sensibilities, to my decision-making and relational capacities—even more it reflects my physical and psychological situation of the moment."

tion of what we might call, alluding to Bourdieu, the "habitual" constraints of that location. So, when I speak of Paul's voice, I mean to indicate the discursive dispositions, correlative of his social location but also distinctly his own, that characterize his letters as artifacts of social practice. Paul's voice comes from Paul's body; Paul's body inhabits a particular social location, and it does so in its own peculiar way.

Toward a Reading of 2 Corinthians 10–13

Although the primary focus of this study has been the question of Paul's rhetorical education, the use of 2 Cor 10–13 as a case study has involved sustained exegesis as well. Indeed, scattered throughout the previous pages lie the basic contours of a reading of 2 Cor 10–13, a reading that runs counter to the interpretive model that currently prevails. My aim here, by way of conclusion, is to provide a brief synthesis of these exegetical insights, and thus to suggest an alternative model.

First, I have been at pains to show that the crisis that occasioned Paul's "Letter of Tears" was not a dispute concerning rhetoric—though certainly it was, in the broadest sense of the phrase, a rhetorical dispute. There is no evidence that the Corinthian community was especially enamored of rhetorical display, and no reason to imagine that words in 2 Cor 10–13 like λόγος and συγκρῖναι refer to the practice of formal rhetoric. If 2 Cor 11:6 reflects criticism of Paul's manner of speech, this is not because Paul was deemed a rhetorical amateur but because his unrefined speech was derisible and thus served for the Corinthians as one further indicator that he was, as his rivals said openly, ταπεινός and ἀσθενής.

Thus 2 Cor 10–13 represents Paul's attempt to reassert his status in Corinth by confronting the demeaning characterization to which he was evidently susceptible. Paul's response, I have argued, was not a parody of the boasting of his opponents. Indeed, a close reading here suggests that their so-called boasting consisted not in verbal (let alone rhetorical) bragging but simply in their willingness to claim apostolic status *and to do so in Corinth*, where Paul—by divine commission, he believes—had been the first to arrive with the gospel.[20] Nor is Paul's response essentially ironic, although it does include isolated moments of irony. Rather, Paul straight-

---

20. See now James C. Hanges, *Paul, Founder of Churches: A Study in Light of the Evidence for the Role of "Founder-Figures" in the Hellenistic-Roman Period* (WUNT 292; Tübingen: Mohr Siebeck, 2012), 388–89, 391–97.

forwardly insists that he is not inferior to his rivals, and, with all sincerity, threatens the Corinthians with disciplinary tokens of his authority when he arrives.

But Paul was, apparently, in no position straightforwardly to deny his ἀσθένεια, hence the tortured and tortuous "boasting" wherein he attempts to refigure his ignominious weakness into a mark of divine power. The passage is, as C. K. Barrett once remarked, a "puzzling mixture of humility and aggression, of self-abasement and authority."[21] Indeed, as we have seen, one important aspect of Paul's "boasting" in 2 Cor 10-13 is the shameless display of his own humiliation. But there is defiance in Paul's voice too, and this complicates the rhetoric of the text considerably: at one and the same time he abases himself and insists on his status (cf. 11:21; 12:11; 1 Cor 15:8-10)—two rhetorical moves that may appear to be mutually exclusive, but in fact occur in concert often enough (though not, to be sure, in the mouths of powerful speakers).[22] In other words, Paul is willing to forfeit any normal claim to self-respect in an attempt to win status of a different sort: Yes, I am shamefully weak and I have no claim to ἀνδρεία; nevertheless, as one in whose body dwells the spirit-power of Christ, I merit your respect and fear (cf. 13:3-4). Receive me as a fool if you must, but you must receive me (cf. 11:16).

This apparently paradoxical self-presentation derives, I suggest, from the profound ambivalence of Paul's self-understanding. Paul is at once convinced of his status as an apostle in whom Jesus Christ is manifest (Gal 1:1, 15-16) and cognizant of his equally manifest humiliation (Gal 4:12; 2 Cor 10:1, 10). This conflicted self-understanding finds a manner of resolution in Paul's conviction regarding the conformity of his embodied existence to that of Jesus. "[We are] always carrying around the dying [νέκρωσιν] of Jesus in the body," he says, "so that the life of Jesus also may be made manifest in our body" (2 Cor 4:10 [my trans.]; cf. 13:3-4; Phil 3:10-11, 21). But such resolution is necessarily unstable, for this sort of

---

21. C. K. Barrett, "Boasting (καυχᾶσθαι, κτλ.) in the Pauline Epistles," in *L'apôtre Paul: Personnalité, style et conception du ministère* (ed. Albert Vanhoye; BETL 73; Leuven: Leuven University Press, 1986), 368.

22. For two striking examples, see Joanna Brooks, ed., *The Collected Writings of Samson Occom, Mohegan: Leadership and Literature in Eighteenth-Century Native America* (Oxford: Oxford University Press, 2006), 52-58; Bertram Wyatt-Brown, "The Mask of Obedience: Male Slave Psychology in the Old South," *American Historical Review* 93 (1988): 1228-29.

conviction is difficult to sustain unless it is recognized and affirmed by those to whom one imagines oneself to be manifesting Christ. In their *Portraits of Paul*, Malina and Neyrey helpfully discuss the need, particularly acute in "collectivist cultures," to maintain conformity between the privately defined self and the self as defined by one's in-group.[23] But they fail to note the extent to which, in Paul's case, these two selves are in conflict: both in Corinth and in Galatia, after an initial period of enthusiasm, Paul's converts—his in-group, to use Malina and Neyrey's term—have ceased to validate the honorable identity he claims for himself.

Again, Malina and Neyrey correctly note that Paul's "'independence' of any group authorization would have been a major liability for him,"[24] but, presumably because their rigid schematization makes little room for Paul even to possess a discrete sense of self, they fail to consider how Paul negotiates the resulting tension: on the one hand, Paul insists that he is Παῦλος ἀπόστολος οὐκ ἀπ' ἀνθρώπων οὐδὲ δι' ἀνθρώπου ἀλλὰ διὰ 'Ιησοῦ Χριστοῦ (Gal 1:1; cf. 1:10–11); on the other hand, his very insistence on this point attests to his need for this status to be recognized ἐν ἀνθρώποις. It is this same tension, I submit, that animates 2 Cor 10–13: not least in his relationship with the Corinthians, Paul experiences himself both as weak and as strong, as derisible and as glorious, and he struggles to give an account of himself as nevertheless a coherent self.[25]

If, then, as George Kennedy suggests, rhetoric is the energy that inheres in a communicative act, Paul's "boasting" in 2 Cor 10–13 is precisely the energy he must expend in his effort to hold together two (socially constructed) conceptions of himself, the man he knows himself to be from habitual experiences of public derision and subjugation and his own internalization thereof, and the man he knows himself to be from experiences of Christ-glory and erstwhile in-group ratification thereof.

"Where Is the Voice Coming From?"

I began by posing a question derived from the title of a short story by novelist Rudy Wiebe: "Where is Paul's voice coming from?" I intended the question to be evocative and exploratory, to open up space for reflecting

---

23. Bruce J. Malina and Jerome H. Neyrey, *Portraits of Paul: An Archaeology of Ancient Personality* (Louisville: Westminster John Knox, 1996), 213.
24. Ibid., 217.
25. Cf. Shantz, *Paul in Ecstasy*, 128–29.

on the alternative to the prevailing assumption that Paul's letters represent intellectual discourse.

I know of at least one compelling attempt to name this alternative, one I cited in the opening sentence of this study: In his *Paulus*, Adolf Deissmann insisted that Paul's was the mission of an artisan, not the mission of a scholar; that, although incidentally interested in Χριστολόγος, he was, "above all and in everything," a Χριστοφόρος; that the center of gravity of Pauline discourse was religion, not theology.[26] Unlike the majority of Pauline interpreters then and since, Deissmann attended to the way Paul's voice arose from and attested to his embodied experience.[27] In other words, he conceptualized Paul as a human subject, not merely as a cipher for a theological system.

Deissmann's *Paulus* generally is dismissed as a romantic flight of fancy rather than serious scholarship.[28] This is not least, I imagine, because of his fondness for a vivid phrase. But interpreters of Paul have perceived a more serious difficulty with his emphases as well, one aptly summarized by Albert Vanhoye in a neglected rumination not on Deissmann but on the place of "personality" in exegesis of Paul: "Il n'y a pas de science de l'individuel [cf. Aristotle, *Metaph.* 13.1086b]. En s'intéressant à ce qu'il y a d'unique dans une personne, l'exégèse risque de devenir subjective et de n'être donc plus scientifique."[29]

The guild's collective fear of such subjectivity, of losing our status as objective historians,[30] is invoked to powerful effect by advocates of rhetorical criticism. Observe, for example, Troy Martin's rebuttal to Michael Cosby's "Red-Hot Rhetoric." Cosby had taken issue with the tendency of rhetorical critics—Lauri Thurén is the focus of his ire—to read "every emotional sounding outburst" in Galatians as the fruit of a dispassionate

---

26. Deissmann, *Light from the Ancient East*, 385; Deissmann, *Paul*, 136–37; 6, 79–81, 135–57.

27. See esp. Deissmann, *Paul*, x, 13, 63–64.

28. E.g., Albrecht Gerber, *Deissmann the Philologist* (BZNW 171; Berlin: de Gruyter, 2010), 149; Ramsay, *Teaching of Paul*, 446; Malherbe, *Social Aspects*, 32; Meeks, *First Urban Christians*, 51.

29. Vanhoye, "Personnalité de Paul," 10: "There is no science of the individual. By focusing on what is unique about a person, exegesis risks becoming subjective and thus no longer being scientific."

30. On which see the insightful comments of Ward Blanton, *Displacing Christian Origins: Philosophy, Secularity, and the New Testament* (Religion and Postmodernism; Chicago: University of Chicago Press, 2007), 11.

CONCLUSION

rhetorical strategy: "To relegate Paul's emotional language to a calculated use of rhetorical techniques," he insists, "is to miss a vital source of the letter's power."[31] Notably, Martin responds not by assessing the evidence, but simply by raising the daunting specter of a "methodological void": the mark of the "judicious" scholar, we are told, is the recognition "that Paul was probably not overwhelmed by emotions but as an effective rhetorician knew exactly what he was doing."[32]

I must confess this baffles me. Is it not precisely as arbitrary to presume Paul to be dispassionate as to presume him to be under the sway of intense emotion? Surely neither conclusion is judicious if it cannot be demonstrated from a reading of the text.[33] Whether we like it or not, Paul's letters derive from a human subject, and thus his discourse must be interpreted as human behavior.[34] We cannot simply evade the question of Paul's subjectivity because it is methodologically inconvenient. As Vanhoye goes on to say, "Ce risque inverse consiste à stériliser les textes bibliques en les

---

31. Michael Cosby, "Galatians: Red-Hot Rhetoric," in *Rhetorical Argumentation in Biblical Texts: Essays from the Lund 2000 Conference* (ed. Anders Eriksson, Thomas H. Olbricht, and Walter G. Übelacker; ESEC 8; Harrisburg, Pa.: Trinity, 2002), 299; cf. Lauri Thurén, "Was Paul Angry? Derhetorizing Galatians," in *The Rhetorical Interpretation of Scripture: Essays from the 1996 Malibu Conference* (ed. Stanley E. Porter and Dennis L. Stamps; JSNTSup 180; Sheffield: Sheffield Academic Press, 1999), 302–20.

32. Troy W. Martin, "Invention and Arrangement in Recent Pauline Rhetorical Studies: A Survey of the Practices and the Problems," in *Paul and Rhetoric* (ed. J. Paul Sampley and Peter Lampe; New York: T&T Clark, 2010), 110.

33. Moreover, Martin's comment surely poses a false alternative: The assumption that persuasive intention is incompatible with the expression of emotion surely reflects a remarkably superficial conception of what it is that people do when they speak. And note that it is precisely on the basis of this false alternative that Thurén and his ilk posit a dispassionate Paul: If Paul can be shown to be using a rhetorical figure, the argument goes, then we must assume that he is not in fact expressing emotion. See esp. *Derhetorizing Paul: A Dynamic Perspective on Pauline Theology and the Law* (Harrisburg, Pa.: Trinity, 2002), 59–64.

34. Peter Lampe offers another way to circumvent consideration of Paul's subjectivity by advocating that scholars of Pauline rhetoric join the march of "secular studies of literature" toward consideration of the text and its reception apart from authorial intention ("Rhetorical Analysis of Pauline Texts—Quo Vadit? Methodological Reflections," in *Paul and Rhetoric* [ed. J. Paul Sampley and Peter Lampe; New York: T&T Clark, 2010], 20–21). I am in no position to tell Lampe he cannot undertake such a reading. But one cannot make such a move and still claim, as most are wont, to be saying something about Paul.

soumettant à des analyses incomplètes, qui ne tiennent pas suffisamment compte de leur aspect personnel."[35] Indeed,

> Est-il possible d'exposer correctement la christologie de Paul, sans analyser la relation personnelle de Paul avec le Christ, telle qu'il l'exprime en parlant de lui-même, et de sa vie dans le Christ? Peut-on rendre compte de l'ecclésiologie de Paul sans analyser avec soin la place que prend la personnalité de l'apôtre dans ses rapports avec les communautés au moment de leur fondation, lors de leur croissance, dans les périodes de tension et de crise?[36]

My intent here is not to vindicate Deissmann's portrayal of Paul—though I am, in fact, persuaded by each of his three proposals noted above. Rather, my intent is to highlight the crucial significance of addressing the fundamental question of Paul's voice. Who speaks? What sort of discourse do we have here? As long as we persist in avoiding this question, all our attempts at methodological rigor have us straining out gnats while swallowing a camel.

Il n'y a pas de science de l'individuel. Perhaps. But, as I hope this study has begun to demonstrate, what confronts us is not, as Martin would have it, a methodological void but rather a void of methodological imagination.

A Weak Apostle in Corinth

If the Corinthian correspondence is not our only opportunity to observe the diachronic development of Paul's relationship with a community of his founding, it is certainly the most substantive. Indeed, to my knowledge, there is no other moment in the history of earliest Christianity that is so well attested as Paul's relationship with the Corinthian community in the mid-50s of the first century.

---

35. Vanhoye, "Personnalité de Paul," 10: "The opposite risk consists in sterilizing the biblical texts by subjecting them to incomplete analyses that do not take sufficient account of their personal aspect."

36. Ibid., 9: "Is it possible adequately to explain Paul's Christology without analyzing Paul's personal connection with Christ, as he himself expresses it, and his life in Christ? Can one give an account of Paul's ecclesiology without analyzing carefully the role of the apostle's personality in his relationship with the communities at the time of their foundation, during their growth, in the periods of tension and crisis?"

That does not mean we know all we should like to know; for, although we have tantalizing clues, they do not always admit of confident historical reconstruction. Even the fundamental question of the number and sequence of letters contained in canonical 1 and 2 Corinthians continues to defy consensus. Still, with regard to one key element of the story all seem to be in agreement: Paul initially had significant success in Corinth; thereafter, his influence was increasingly uncertain. Explaining "this deterioration of Paul's relationship with the Corinthians" may be, to quote Margaret Mitchell, "the largest puzzle on the landscape of Corinthian studies."[37]

For F. C. Baur, the roots of Paul's difficulties in Corinth were twofold: First, the introduction of the Gospel to "the classic ground of ancient Greece" inevitably brought with it cultural complications: "How," asked Baur, "could the Greek spirit disown its original nature, even when newborn in Christianity?"[38] Second, and more famously, Baur posited that Paul's "Judaising opponents ... introduced a new and most disturbing element into the life of this Greek Christian Church, when still in the first stage of its development."[39] Specifically, his opponents asserted that Paul was disqualified from true apostleship because he had not had direct interaction with Jesus.[40]

Although the details of Baur's reconstruction no longer exert much influence, these have remained the two dominant modes of explanation: Paul's waning influence in Corinth is attributed, on the one hand, to perduring Corinthian characteristics—their profligacy, their factiousness, their "worldly values," or, more recently, their sophistic orientation—and, on the other, to the influence of intruders, whose specific identity has long been a preoccupation of Pauline scholarship.[41] Seldom, then, have we framed this as a question about Paul himself: What was it about Paul that made him initially so compelling and then, within a few years, all but disposable? Why was he susceptible to this sudden loss of stature?

---

37. Mitchell, "The Birth of Pauline Hermeneutics," 23.
38. Baur, *Paul*, 1:258.
39. Ibid., 1:259.
40. Ibid., 1:267–74.
41. For the latest permutation, see Thomas R. Blanton, "Spirit and Covenant Renewal: A Theologoumenon of Paul's Opponents in 2 Corinthians," *JBL* 129 (2010): 129–51.

There appear to have been multiple factors at play, and it is beyond my scope here to give a full explanation.[42] Nevertheless, the abject voice we have heard in 2 Cor 10–13 provides a telling clue, as does our exegesis of 2 Cor 10:10 and 11:6: Paul was not a man whose dignity commanded respect; rather, he was weak and servile, subject to derision and subjugation.

I have not attempted in this study to isolate the biographical details correlative of this characterization but rather have been content with the more general observation that Paul evidently did not occupy an elevated social location. He was not, as I concluded above, a respectable freeborn man. Still, it may be useful at least to list those aspects of his precarious and ignominious existence to which the letters, more or less arguably, attest: Paul was, to use Glancy's term, "whippable";[43] he was frequently imprisoned;[44] he was a manual laborer;[45] he was itinerant;[46] he seems to have suffered from some sort of bodily infirmity;[47] and, as the present study has emphasized, his speech was rude and uncultured.

If this is Paul, perhaps the real puzzle is not why the Corinthians wavered in their loyalty, but why they attended to Paul and his gospel in the first place. This is a problem of some moment, and one that has received surprisingly little attention. In general, the implicit assumption seems to be that Paul drew in converts through convincingly reasoned articulation of (proto-)Christian theology. He expounded the truth.

If this is our starting point, it is easy to see why we have been so quick to assume that the source of Paul's difficulty in Corinth was some form of "false teaching," for, on this model, only the intrusion of an alluringly deceptive doctrinal alternative can explain why Paul's teaching,

---

42. For a number of valuable recent contributions, see Mitchell, "The Birth of Pauline Hermeneutics," 23, 26–30; Shantz, *Paul in Ecstasy*, 182–84; Ron Cameron and Merrill P. Miller, eds., *Redescribing Paul and the Corinthians* (SBLECL 5; Atlanta: Society of Biblical Literature, 2011).

43. Glancy, "Boasting of Beatings." See esp. 2 Cor 11:24–25.

44. Rom 16:7; Phlm 1, 9, 23; Phil 1:12–17.

45. 1 Thess 2:9; 1 Cor 4:12. See further Hock, *Social Context*.

46. On the precariousness and ignominy associated with Paul's traveling, see my "'Danger in the Wilderness, Danger at Sea': Paul and the Perils of Travel," in *Travel and Religion in Antiquity* (ed. Philip A. Harland; Studies in Christianity and Judaism/Études sur le christianisme et le judaisme 21; Waterloo, Ont.: Wilfred Laurier University Press, 2011), 141–61.

47. Illness or infirmity is clearly in view in Gal 4:13–14. And there is, of course, much speculation on the nature of Paul's "thorn in the flesh."

once so convincing, had now lost its luster. A basic difficulty here, as we have seen, is that when the chips are down this is not the level on which Paul engages his rivals in Corinth. Indeed, when Paul does talk about his own foundational proclamation, he says nothing to suggest that it was comprised primarily of intellectual activity—unless, perhaps, in the attenuated sense of "intellectual" employed in the excellent recent work of Stanley Stowers.[48] On the contrary, as Colleen Shantz has insisted, what he refers to is "unequivocal experience of the spirit."[49]

And notice that such powerful charismatic display is precisely what appears to have been absent on Paul's second and painful visit to Corinth.[50] Paul had promised to come with a rod of discipline, to demonstrate that the kingdom of God consisted not in word but in power. He did not follow through. Instead, he was humiliatingly "lenient"—or, as his rivals in Corinth put it, less charitably, he who had been bold and overbearing from afar turned out to be powerless and derisible in person.

In the face of such derision, Paul the weak apostle insists, like Aesop the whippable slave, "My worthless body is my instrument, by which I utter wise words to benefit the lives of mortals" (*Vit. Aesop.* 99 [trans. Wills])—or, more in keeping with Paul's own self-understanding: My worthless body is God's instrument, in which—and for your benefit, you Corinthians!—Christ-power dwells. This is a voice at once abject and defiant—a voice, I submit, that arises from a decidedly precarious "social location."

---

48. See esp. Stanley K. Stowers, "Kinds of Myth, Meals, and Power: Paul and the Corinthians," in *Redescribing Paul and the Corinthians* (ed. Ron Cameron and Merrill P. Miller; SBLECL 5; Atlanta: Society of Biblical Literature, 2011), 115, 117: "Paul was certainly not a sophist legitimated in the dominant fraction of the field [of *paideia*] (as some have supposed), but belonged to one of the aspiring, competing illegitimate fractions that were every bit as necessary to the existence of the field as a field of cultural-production-as-contestation.... One must view Paul as a producer and distributor of an alternative esoteric *paideia* different from the dominant sophistic or philosophical kinds, yet still recognizable as a form of the same broader game of specialized literate learning."

49. Shantz, *Paul in Ecstasy*, 178–81; citing 1 Cor 2:4–5; Gal 3:1–5; 1 Thess 1:4–5. Cf. Rom 1:9; 15:19; 2 Cor 12:12.

50. See the exegetical discussion in section "His Letters are Forceful and Bold" of ch. 12.

Bibliography

1. Ancient Texts and Translations

Most citations of primary sources are from the editions of the Loeb Classical Library or those available online through the *Thesaurus linguae graecae* (http://www.tlg.uci.edu). Exceptions are listed here, as are additional translations and editions to which I have made express reference. Papyri are cited in accordance with John F. Oates et al., eds., *Checklist of Greek, Latin, Demotic and Coptic Papyri, Ostraca and Tablets*. Cited 15 May 2011. Online: http://scriptorium.lib.duke.edu/papyrus/texts/clist.html. Inscriptions are cited and abbreviated in accordance with the online database compiled by the Packard Humanities Institute. Cited 15 May 2011. Online: http://epigraphy.packhum.org/inscriptions.

Ambrosiaster. *Commentaries on Romans and 1–2 Corinthians*. Translated by Gerald L. Bray. Ancient Christian Texts. Downers Grove, Ill.: IVP Academic, 2009.

Aristotle. *On Rhetoric: A Theory of Civic Discourse*. Translated by George A. Kennedy. 2nd ed. New York: Oxford University Press, 2007.

Augustine. "Latin Text, Translation, and Commentary of Book IV of *De Doctrina Christiana*." Translated by Thérèse Sullivan. Pages 33–185 in *The Rhetoric of St. Augustine of Hippo:* De Doctrina Christiana *and the Search for a Distinctly Christian Rhetoric*. Edited by Richard Leo Enos et al. Studies in Rhetoric and Religion 7. Waco, Tex.: Baylor University Press, 2008.

Aelius Théon. *Progymnasmata*. Edited and translated by Michel Patillon. Budé. Paris: Les belles lettres, 1997.

Bertalotto, Pierpaolo, Ken M. Penner, and Ian W. Scott, eds. "1 Enoch." Prepublication edition. In *The Online Critical Pseudepigrapha*. Edited by Ken M. Penner, David M. Miller, and Ian W. Scott. Atlanta: Society of Biblical Literature, 2006. Cited 15 May 2011. Online: http://ocp.tyndale.ca/1-ethiopic-apocalypse-of-enoch.

Charlesworth, James H., ed. *The Old Testament Pseudepigrapha*. 2 vols. Garden City, N.Y.: Doubleday, 1983.

Demetrius. *On Style*. Translated by W. Rhys Roberts. Cambridge: Cambridge University Press, 1902.

Dilts, Mervin R., and George A. Kennedy, eds. and trans. *Two Greek Rhetorical Treatises from the Roman Empire: Introduction, Text, and Translation of the* Arts of Rhetoric, Attributed to Anonymous Seguerianus and to Apsines of Gadara. Mnemosyne Supplement 168. Leiden: Brill, 1997.

Elliger, K., W. Rudolph, and A. Schenker, eds. *Biblia Hebraica Stuttgartensia*. 4th ed. Stuttgart: Deutsche Bibelgesellschaft, 1983.

Erbse, Hartmut, ed. *Scholia Graeca in Homeri Iliadem (scholia Vetera)*. 7 vols. Berlin: de Gruyter, 1969.

Galen. *Opera omnia*. Edited by K. G. Kühn. 22 vols. Leipzig: Knobloch, 1821–1833.

Hermogenes. *Opera*. Edited by Hugo Rabe. BSGRT. Rhetores Graeci 6. Leipzig: Teubner, 1913.

John Chrysostom. "English Translation of *De laudibus sancti Pauli* 1–7." Pages 440–87 in *The Heavenly Trumpet: John Chrysostom and the Art of Pauline Interpretation*, by Margaret M. Mitchell. HUT 40. Tübingen: Mohr Siebeck, 2000.

Josephus. *The Works of Josephus: Complete and Unabridged*. Translated by William Whiston. New updated ed. Peabody, Mass.: Hendrickson, 1987.

Longinus. *On the Sublime*. Translated by W. Rhys Roberts. Cambridge: University Press, 1899.

Malherbe, Abraham J., ed. and trans. *Ancient Epistolary Theorists*. SBLSBS 19. Atlanta: Scholars Press, 1988.

Migne, J.-P., ed. Patrologia latina. 217 vols. Paris, 1857–1886.

Migne, J.-P., ed. Patrologiae graeca. 162 vols. Paris, 1857–1886.

Mullach, F. W. A., ed. *Fragmenta philosophorum graecorum*. 3 vols. Paris: Didot, 1867.

Nicolaus. *Progymnasmata*. Edited by Joseph Felten. BSGRT. Rhetores Graeci 11. Leipzig: Teubner, 1913.

Origen. *Commentary on the Epistle to the Romans*. Translated by Thomas P. Scheck. 2 vols. Fathers of the Church 104. Washington, D.C.: Catholic University of America Press, 2001–2002.

Philodemus. *Volumina rhetorica*. Edited by Siegfried Sudhaus. BSGRT. Leipzig: Teubner, 1892–1896.

———. Περὶ τοῦ καθ' Ὅμηρον ἀγαθοῦ βασιλέως *libellus*. Edited by Alexander Olivieri. BSGRT. Leipzig: Teubner, 1909.

Progymnasmata: Greek Textbooks of Prose Composition and Rhetoric. Translated by George A. Kennedy. WGRW 10. Atlanta: Society of Biblical Literature, 2003.

Pseudo-Hermogenes. *Invention and Method: Two Rhetorical Treatises from the Hermogenic Corpus.* Translated by George A. Kennedy. WGRW 15. Atlanta: Society of Biblical Literature, 2005.

Pseudo-Herodian. *De figuris: Überlieferungsgeschichte und kritische Ausgabe.* Edited by Kerstin Hajdú. SGLG 8. Berlin: de Gruyter, 1998.

Rahlfs, Alfred, ed. *Septuaginta: Id est Vetus Testamentum graece iuxta LXX interpretes.* Stuttgart: Deutsche Bibelgesellschaft, 1935.

Rea, John. "A Student's Letter to His Father: P. Oxy. XVIII 2190 Revised." *ZPE* 99 (1993): 75–88.

Rose, Valentinus, ed. *Aristotelis qui ferebantur librorum fragmenta.* BSGRT. Leipzig: Teubner, 1886.

Schaff, Philip, ed. *The Nicene and Post-Nicene Fathers*, Series 1. 1886–1889. 14 vols. Repr., Peabody, Mass.: Hendrickson, 1994.

Sextus Empiricus. *Adversus mathematicos, libros I–VI continens.* Edited by Jürgen Mau. Vol. 3 of *Sexti Empirici Opera*. Edited by Hermann Mutschmann. BSGRT. Leipzig: Teubner, 1961.

———. *Against the Grammarians.* Translated by D. L. Blank. Clarendon Later Ancient Philosophers. Oxford: Oxford University Press, 1998.

Spengel, Leonhard von, ed. *Rhetores Graeci.* 3 vols. BSGRT. Leipzig: Teubner, 1854–1885.

Staab, Karl, ed. *Pauluskommentare aus der griechischen Kirch aus Katenenhandschriften.* Neutestamentliche Apokryphen 15. Münster: Aschendorff, 1933.

Theodore of Mopsuestia. *The Commentaries on the Minor Epistles of Paul.* Translated by Rowan A. Greer. WGRW 26. Atlanta: Society of Biblical Literature, 2010.

VanderKam, James C., ed. and trans. *The Book of Jubilees.* CSCO 510–511. Scriptores aethiopici 87–88. Louvain: Peeters, 1989.

White, John L. *Light from Ancient Letters.* FF. Philadelphia: Fortress, 1986.

Wills, Lawrence M., trans. "English Translation of the *Life of Aesop*." Pages 177–224 in *The Quest of the Historical Gospel: Mark, John, and the Origins of the Gospel Genre.* London: Routledge, 1997.

2. Secondary Literature

Abbott, Don Paul. *Rhetoric in the New World: Rhetorical Theory and Practice in Colonial Spanish America*. Studies in Rhetoric/Communication. Columbia: University of South Carolina Press, 1996.

Adam, Karl. "Der Junge Paulus." Pages 9–21 in *Paulus-Hellas-Oikumene: An Ecumenical Symposium*. Athens: Student Christian Association of Greece, 1951.

Adams, Edward, and David G. Horrell, eds. *Christianity at Corinth: The Quest for the Pauline Church*. Louisville: Westminster John Knox, 2004.

Aejmelaeus, Lars. "'Christ is Weak in Paul': The Opposition to Paul in Corinth." Pages 117–31 in *The Nordic Paul: Finnish Approaches to Pauline Theology*. Edited by Lars Aejmelaeus and Antti Mustakallio. LNTS 374. London: T&T Clark, 2008.

Alexandre, Manuel. *Rhetorical Argumentation in Philo of Alexandria*. BJS 322. Atlanta: Scholars Press, 1999.

Allen, Walter. "Cicero's Conceit." *TAPA* 85 (1954): 121–44.

Alles, Gregory D. *The Iliad, the Rāmāyaṇa, and the Work of Religion: Failed Persuasion and Religious Mystification*. Hermeneutics: Studies in the History of Religions. University Park: Pennsylvania State University Press, 1994.

Ameling, Walter. *Herodes Atticus*. 2 vols. Subsidia epigraphica 11. Hildesheim: Olms, 1983.

Anderson, Graham. *The Second Sophistic: A Cultural Phenomenon in the Roman Empire*. London: Routledge, 1993.

Anderson, R. Dean. *Ancient Rhetorical Theory and Paul*. Rev. ed. CBET 18. Leuven: Peeters, 1998.

———. *Glossary of Greek Rhetorical Terms*. CBET 24. Leuven: Peeters, 2000.

Andrews, Scott B. "Too Weak Not to Lead: The Form and Function of 2 Cor 11.23b–33." *NTS* 41 (1995): 263–76.

Ankersmit, F. R. *Aesthetic Politics: Political Philosophy beyond Fact and Value*. Stanford, Calif.: Stanford University Press, 1996.

Anon. *The Life and Travels of the Apostle Paul*. Boston: Lilly, Wait, Colman & Holden, 1833.

Arnim, H. F. A. von. *Leben und Werke des Dio von Prusa*. Berlin: Weidmann, 1898.

Arnott, W. Geoffrey. "Menander's Manipulation of Language for the Individualisation of Character." Pages 147–64 in *Lo spettacolo delle voci*, vol. 2. Edited by Francesco de Martino and Alan H. Sommerstein. Le Rane 14. Bari: Levante, 1995.
Ascough, Richard S. *Paul's Macedonian Associations: The Social Context of Philippians and 1 Thessalonians*. WUNT 2/161. Tübingen: Mohr Siebeck, 2003.
———. "The Thessalonian Christian Community as a Professional Voluntary Association." *JBL* 119 (2000): 311–28.
Ashton, John. *The Religion of Paul the Apostle*. New Haven: Yale University Press, 2000.
Aune, David E. "Boasting." Pages 81–84 in *The Westminster Dictionary of New Testament and Early Christian Literature and Rhetoric*. Louisville: Westminster John Knox, 2003.
———. Review of Hans Dieter Betz, *Galatians: A Commentary on Paul's Letter to the Churches in Galatia*. *RelSRev* 7 (1981): 323–28.
Austin, J. L. *How to Do Things with Words*. Cambridge: Harvard University Press, 1962.
Austin, John N. H. "Catalogues and the Catalogue of Ships in the *Iliad*." Ph.D. diss., University of California, Berkeley, 1965.
Bachmann, Philip. *Der zweite Brief des Paulus an die Korinther*. 4th ed. ZKNT 8. Leipzig: Scholl, 1922.
Ball, Charles R. *The Apostle of the Gentiles: His Life and Letters*. London: SPCK, 1885.
Barclay, John M. G. "Josephus v. Apion: Analysis of an Argument." Pages 194–221 in *Understanding Josephus: Seven Perspectives*. Edited by Steve Mason. Sheffield: Sheffield Academic Press, 1998.
Barnett, Paul. *The Second Epistle to the Corinthians*. NICNT. Grand Rapids: Eerdmans, 1997.
Barrett, C. K. "Boasting (καυχᾶσθαι, κτλ.) in the Pauline Epistles." Pages 363–68 in *L'apôtre Paul: Personnalité, style et conception du ministère*. Edited by Albert Vanhoye. BETL 73. Leuven: Leuven University Press, 1986.
———. *A Commentary on the Second Epistle to the Corinthians*. BNTC. London: Black, 1973.
Bartchy, S. Scott. "'When I'm Weak, I'm Strong': A Pauline Paradox in Cultural Context." Pages 49–60 in *Kultur, Politik, Religion, Sprach—Text: Wolfgang Stegemann zum 60. Geburtstag*. Edited by Christian Strecker. Vol. 2 of *Kontexte der Schrift*. Stuttgart: Kohlhammer, 2005.

Basso, Keith H. "The Ethnography of Writing." Pages 425–32 in *Explorations in the Ethnography of Speaking*. Edited by Richard Bauman and Joel Sherzer. 2nd ed. SSCFL 8. Cambridge: Cambridge University Press, 1989.

Baur, Ferdinand Christian. *Paul the Apostle of Jesus Christ: His Life and Work, His Epistles and His Doctrine*. Edited by Eduard Zeller. Translated by Allan Menzies. 2 vols. 2nd ed. London: Williams & Norgate, 1876.

Becker, Jürgen. *Paul: Apostle to the Gentiles*. Translated by O. C. Dean. Louisville: Westminster John Knox, 1993.

Beet, Joseph Agar. *A Commentary on St. Paul's Epistles to the Corinthians*. London: Hodder & Stoughton, 1882.

Bell, Robert A., Christopher J. Zahn, and Robert Hopper. "Disclaiming: A Test of Two Competing Views." *Communication Quarterly* 32 (1984): 28–36.

Bengel, Johann Albrecht. *Gnomon of the New Testament*. Translated by Andrew R. Fausset. 5 vols. 7th ed. Edinburgh: T&T Clark, 1873.

Betz, Hans Dieter. *2 Corinthians 8 and 9: A Commentary on Two Administrative Letters of the Apostle Paul*. Edited by George W. MacRae. Hermeneia. Philadelphia: Fortress, 1985.

———. *Der Apostel Paulus und die sokratische Tradition: Eine exegetische Untersuchung zu seiner "Apologie" 2 Korinther 10–13*. BHT 45. Tübingen: Mohr, 1972.

———. "De laude ipsius (Moralia 539A–547F)." Pages 367–93 in *Plutarch's Ethical Writings and Early Christian Literature*. Edited by Hans Dieter Betz. SCHNT 4. Leiden: Brill, 1978.

———. *Galatians: A Commentary on Paul's Letter to the Churches in Galatia*. Hermeneia. Philadelphia: Fortress, 1979.

———. "The Literary Composition and Function of Paul's Letter to the Galatians." *NTS* 21 (1975): 353–79.

———. *Paul's Apology II Corinthians 10–13 and the Socratic Tradition*. Edited by Wilhelm H. Wuellner. Colloquy 2. Berkeley: Center for Hermeneutical Studies, 1975.

———. "The Problem of Rhetoric and Theology according to the Apostle Paul." Pages 126–62 in *Paulinische Studien*. Gesammelte Aufsätze 3. Tübingen: Mohr Siebeck, 1994.

Blank, Les, and James Bogan, eds. *Burden of Dreams: Screenplay, Journals, Reviews, Photographs*. Berkeley, Calif.: North Atlantic Books, 1984.

Blanton, Thomas R. "Spirit and Covenant Renewal: A Theologoumenon of Paul's Opponents in 2 Corinthians." *JBL* 129 (2010): 129–51.

Blanton, Ward. *Displacing Christian Origins: Philosophy, Secularity, and the New Testament*. Religion and Postmodernism. Chicago: University of Chicago Press, 2007.

Blass, Friedrich. *Die Rhythmen der asianischen und römischen Kunstprosa (Paulus-Hebräerbrief-Pausanias-Cicero-Seneca-Curtius-Apuleius)*. Repr., Hildesheim: Gerstenberg, 1972.

Blass, F., A. Debrunner, and R. W. Funk. *A Greek Grammar of the New Testament and Other Early Christian Literature*. Chicago: University of Chicago Press, 1961.

Bloch, Maurice, ed. *Political Language and Oratory in Traditional Society*. London: Academic Press, 1975.

Bloomer, W. Martin. "Schooling in Persona: Imagination and Subordination in Roman Education." *ClAnt* 16 (1997): 57–78.

Böhlig, Hans. *Die Geisteskultur von Tarsos im augusteischen Zeitalter: Mit Berücksichtigung der paulinischen Schriften*. FRLANT 2/2. Göttingen: Vandenhoeck & Ruprecht, 1913.

Booth, Alan D. "Elementary and Secondary Education in the Roman Empire." *Florilegium* 1 (1979): 1–14.

———. "The Schooling of Slaves in First-Century Rome." *TAPA* 109 (1979): 11–19.

Booth, Wayne C. *A Rhetoric of Irony*. Chicago: University of Chicago Press, 1974.

Borg, Marcus J., and John Dominic Crossan. *The First Paul: Reclaiming the Radical Visionary Behind the Church's Conservative Icon*. New York: HarperOne, 2009.

Bornkamm, Günther. "The History of the Origin of the So-Called Second Letter to the Corinthians." *NTS* 8 (1962): 258–64.

Bourdieu, Pierre. *Distinction: A Social Critique of the Judgement of Taste*. Translated by Richard Nice. Cambridge: Harvard University Press, 1984.

———. *Outline of a Theory of Practice*. Translated by Richard Nice. Cambridge Studies in Social Anthropology 16. Cambridge: Cambridge University Press, 1977.

———. "The Sentiment of Honour in Kabyle Society." Pages 191–242 in *Honour and Shame: The Values of Mediterranean Society*. Edited by J. G. Peristiany. Chicago: University of Chicago Press, 1966.

Bowersock, G. W. *Greek Sophists in the Roman Empire*. Oxford: Clarendon, 1969.
Bowie, Ewen. "The Geography of the Second Sophistic: Cultural Variations." Pages 65–83 in *Paideia: The World of the Second Sophistic*. Edited by Barbara Borg. Millennium Studies 2. Berlin: de Gruyter, 2004.
Brawley, Robert L. "Paul in Acts: Lucan Apology and Conciliation." Pages 129–47 in *Luke-Acts: New Perspectives from the Society of Biblical Literature*. Edited by C. H. Talbert. New York: Crossroad, 1984.
Briggs, Charles L. *Competence in Performance: The Creativity of Tradition in Mexicano Verbal Art*. University of Pennsylvania Press Conduct and Communication Series. Philadelphia: University of Pennsylvania Press, 1988.
———. *Learning How to Ask: A Sociolinguistic Appraisal of the Role of the Interview in Social Science Research*. SSCFL 1. Cambridge: Cambridge University Press, 1986.
Brooks, Joanna, ed. *The Collected Writings of Samson Occom, Mohegan: Leadership and Literature in Eighteenth-Century Native America*. Oxford: Oxford University Press, 2006.
Brown, Penelope, and Stephen C. Levinson. *Politeness: Some Universals in Language Usage*. Studies in Interactional Sociolinguistics 4. Cambridge: Cambridge University Press, 1987.
Brown, Peter. *Power and Persuasion in Late Antiquity: Towards a Christian Empire*. Madison: University of Wisconsin Press, 1992.
Bruce, F. F. *Paul, Apostle of the Heart Set Free*. Grand Rapids: Eerdmans, 1977.
———. "Is the Paul of Acts the Real Paul?" *BJRL* 58 (1976): 282–305.
Bultmann, Rudolf. *Exegetische Probleme des zweiten Korintherbriefes*. 2nd ed. Darmstadt: Wissenschaftliche Buchgesellschaft, 1963.
———. *The Second Letter to the Corinthians*. Edited by Erich Dinkler. Translated by Roy A. Harrisville. Minneapolis: Augsburg, 1985.
———. *Der Stil der paulinischen Predigt und die kynisch-stoische Diatribe*. FRLANT 13. Göttingen: Vandenhoeck & Ruprecht, 1910.
Bürgi, E. "Ist die dem Hermogenes zugeschriebene Schrift Περὶ μεθόδου δεινότητος echt?" *Wiener Studien* 48 (1930): 187–97; 49 (1931): 40–69.
Buswell, Lois E. "The Oratory of the Dakota Indians." *QJS* 21 (1935): 323–27.
Cairns, D. L. "The Politics of Envy: Envy and Equality in Ancient Greece." Pages 235–52 in *Envy, Spite and Jealousy: The Rivalrous Emotions in Ancient Greece*. Edited by David Konstan and N. Keith Rutter. Edin-

burgh Levantis Studies 2. Edinburgh: Edinburgh University Press, 2003.

Calvin, John. *Commentaries on the Epistle of Paul the Apostle to the Romans*. Translated by John Owen. Edinburgh: Calvin Translation Society, 1849.

———. *Commentary on the Epistles of Paul the Apostle to the Corinthians*. Translated by John Pringle. 2 vols. Edinburgh: Calvin Translation Society, 1849.

Cameron, Ron, and Merrill P. Miller, eds. *Redescribing Paul and the Corinthians*. SBLECL 5. Atlanta: Society of Biblical Literature, 2011.

Camp, Charles. "American Indian Oratory in the White Image: An Analysis of Stereotypes." *Journal of American Culture* 1 (1978): 811–17.

Campbell, Douglas A. *The Rhetoric of Righteousness in Romans 3.21–26*. JSNTSup 65. Sheffield: JSOT Press, 1992.

Chadwick, H. "'All Things to All Men' (1 Cor. IX. 22)." *NTS* 1 (1955): 261–75.

Chatman, Seymour. "Parody and Style." *Poetics Today* 22 (2001): 25–39.

Chen, Rong. "Self-Politeness: A Proposal." *Journal of Pragmatics* 33 (2001): 87–106.

Chilton, Bruce. *Rabbi Paul: An Intellectual Biography*. New York: Doubleday, 2004.

Church, F. Forrester. "Rhetorical Structure and Design in Paul's Letter to Philemon." *HTR* 71 (1978): 17–33.

Classen, Carl Joachim. "Kann die rhetorische Theorie helfen, das Neue Testament, vor allem die Briefe des Paulus, besser zu verstehen?" *ZNW* 100 (2009): 145–72.

———. "Philologische Bemerkungen zur Sprache des Apostels Paulus." *Wiener Studien* 107–8 (1994–1995): 321–35.

———. *Rhetorical Criticism of the New Testament*. WUNT 128. Tübingen: Mohr Siebeck, 2000.

———. "St. Paul's Epistles and Ancient Greek and Roman Rhetoric." *Rhetorica* 10 (1992): 319–44.

Clements, William M. *Native American Verbal Art: Texts and Contexts*. Tucson: University of Arizona Press, 1996.

———. *Oratory in Native North America*. Tucson: University of Arizona Press, 2002.

Clift, Rebecca. "Irony in Conversation." *Language in Society* 28 (1999): 523–53.

Clines, David J. A. "Paul, the Invisible Man." Pages 181–92 in *New Testament Masculinities*. Edited by Stephen D. Moore and Janice Capel Anderson. SemeiaSt 45. Atlanta: Society of Biblical Literature, 2003.
Conley, Thomas. "Philo's Rhetoric: Argumentation and Style." ANRW 22.1:243–71.
Connolly, Joy. "Problems of the Past in Imperial Greek Education." Pages 339–72 in *Education in Greek and Roman Antiquity*. Edited by Yun Lee Too. Leiden: Brill, 2001.
Conybeare, W. J., and J. S. Howson. *The Life and Epistles of St. Paul*. New ed. London: Longmans & Green, 1870.
Cosby, Michael. "Galatians: Red-Hot Rhetoric." Pages 296–309 in *Rhetorical Argumentation in Biblical Texts: Essays from the Lund 2000 Conference*. Edited by Anders Eriksson, Thomas H. Olbricht, and Walter G. Übelacker. ESEC 8. Harrisburg, Pa.: Trinity, 2002.
Cribiore, Raffaella. *Gymnastics of the Mind: Greek Education in Hellenistic and Roman Egypt*. Princeton, N.J.: Princeton University Press, 2001.
———. *The School of Libanius in Late Antique Antioch*. Princeton, N.J.: Princeton University Press, 2007.
———. *Writing, Teachers, and Students in Graeco-Roman Egypt*. ASP 36. Atlanta: Scholars Press, 1996.
Crook, Zeba. "Honor, Shame, and Social Status Revisited." *JBL* 128 (2009): 591–611.
D'Ambra, Eve. "Kosmetai, the Second Sophistic, and Portraiture in the Second Century." Pages 201–16 in *Periklean Athens and Its Legacy: Problems and Perspectives*. Edited by Judith M. Barringer and Jeffrey M. Hurwit. Austin: University of Texas Press, 2005.
Dahl, Nils A. *Studies in Paul: Theology for the Early Christian Mission*. Minneapolis: Augsburg, 1977.
Danker, Frederick W. "Paul's Debt to the *De Corona* of Demosthenes: A Study of Rhetorical Techniques in 2 Corinthians." Pages 262–80 in *Persuasive Artistry: Studies in New Testament Rhetoric in Honor of George A. Kennedy*. Edited by Duane F. Watson. JSNTSup 50. Sheffield: Sheffield Academic Press, 1991.
Danker, Frederick W., Walter Bauer, William F. Arndt, and F. Wilbur Gingrich. *Greek-English Lexicon of the New Testament and Other Early Christian Literature*. 3rd ed. Chicago: University of Chicago Press, 1999.
Deissmann, Adolf. *Bible Studies*. Translated by Alexander Grieve. Edinburgh: T&T Clark, 1901.

———. *Light from the Ancient East: The New Testament Illustrated by Recently Discovered Texts of the Graeco-Roman World*. Translated by Lionel R. M. Strachan. London: Hodder & Stoughton, 1927.

———. *Paul: A Study in Social and Religious History*. Translated by William E. Wilson. New York: Harper & Row, 1957.

———. *Paulus: Eine kultur- und religionsgeschichtliche Skizze*. Tübingen: Mohr, 1911.

Delia, Jesse G. "The Logic Fallacy, Cognitive Theory, and the Enthymeme: A Search for the Foundations of Reasoned Discourse." *QJS* 56 (1970): 140–48.

Denney, James. *The Second Epistle to the Corinthians*. Expositor's Bible. London: Hodder & Stoughton, 1894.

Dennis, Matthew. "Red Jacket's Rhetoric: Postcolonial Persuasions on the Native Frontiers of the Early Republic." Pages 15–33 in *American Indian Rhetorics of Survivance: Word Medicine, Word Magic*. Edited by Ernest Stromberg. Pittsburgh Series in Composition, Literacy, and Culture. Pittsburgh: University of Pittsburgh Press, 2006.

Densmore, Christopher. *Red Jacket: Iroquois Diplomat and Orator*. The Iroquois and their Neighbors. Syracuse, N.Y.: Syracuse University Press, 1999.

Dewey, Arthur J. "A Matter of Honor: A Social-Historical Analysis of 2 Corinthians 10." *HTR* 78 (1985): 209–17.

Dews, Shelly, Joan Kaplan, and Ellen Winner. "Why Not Say It Directly? The Social Functions of Irony." *Discourse Processes* 19 (1995): 347–67.

Dibelius, Martin. *Paul*. Edited by Werner Georg Kümmel. Translated by Frank Clarke. Philadelphia: Westminster, 1953.

DiCicco, Mario M. *Paul's Use of Ethos, Pathos, and Logos in 2 Corinthians 10–13*. Mellen Biblical Press Series 31. Lewiston, N.Y.: Mellen Biblical Press, 1995.

Dilts, Mervin R., and George A. Kennedy, eds. *Two Greek Rhetorical Treatises from the Roman Empire: Introduction, Text, and Translation of the Arts of Rhetoric, Attributed to Anonymous Seguerianus and to Apsines of Gadara*. Mnemosyne Supplement 168. Leiden: Brill, 1997.

Dodd, C. H. *New Testament Studies*. Manchester: Manchester University Press, 1953.

Dorsett, Lyle W. *Billy Sunday and the Redemption of Urban America*. Library of Religious Biography. Grand Rapids: Eerdmans, 1991.

Douglas, Mary. *Natural Symbols: Explorations in Cosmology*. London: Barrie & Rockliff, 1970.

Downing, F. Gerald. "A Bas Les Aristos: The Relevance of Higher Literature for the Understanding of the Earliest Christian Writings." *NovT* 30 (1988): 212–30.
Dubay, Ronald. "Paul, Citizen and Prince." Ph.D. diss., University of California, Irvine, 2009.
Duff, Timothy E. *Plutarch's Lives: Exploring Virtue and Vice*. Oxford: Oxford University Press, 2002.
Duling, Dennis C. "2 Corinthians 11:22: Historical Context, Rhetoric, and Ethnicity." *HvTSt* 64 (2008): 819–43. Reprint of pages 65–89 in *The New Testament and Early Christian Literature in Greco-Roman Context: Studies in Honor of David E. Aune*. Edited by John Fotopoulos. NovTSup 122. Leiden: Brill, 2006.
Dunn, James D. G. *The Epistle to the Galatians*. BNTC. London: Black, 1993.
Edwards, Mark J. "Gospel and Genre: Some Reservations." Pages 51–62 in *The Limits of Ancient Biography*. Edited by Brian McGing and Judith Mossman. Swansea: Classical Press of Wales, 2006.
Edwards, Mark W. "The Structure of Homeric Catalogues." *TAPA* 110 (1980): 81–105.
Einhorn, Lois J. *The Native American Oral Tradition: Voices of the Spirit and Soul*. Westport, Conn.: Praeger, 2000.
Ek, Richard A. "Red Cloud's Cooper Union Address." *Central States Speech Journal* 17 (1966): 257–62.
El-Alayli, Amani, Christoffer J. Myers, Tamara L. Petersen, and Amy L. Lystad. "'I Don't Mean to Sound Arrogant, but…': The Effects of Using Disclaimers on Person Perception." *Personality and Social Psychology Bulletin* 34 (2008): 130–43.
Ellis, William T. *"Billy" Sunday: The Man and His Message*. Philadelphia: Myers, 1914.
Erickson, Bonnie, E. Allan Lind, Bruce C. Johnson, and William M. O'Barr. "Speech Style and Impression Formation in a Court Setting: The Effects of 'Powerful' and 'Powerless' Speech." *Journal of Experimental Social Psychology* 14 (1978): 266–79.
Ericson, Jon M. "Rhetorical Criticism: How to Evaluate a Speech." Pages 127–36 in *Demosthenes' On the Crown: A Critical Case Study of a Masterpiece of Ancient Oratory*. Edited by James J. Murphy. New York: Random House, 1967.
Eriksson, Anders. "Enthymemes in Pauline Argumentation: Reading between the Lines in 1 Corinthians." Pages 243–59 in *Rhetorical Argu-*

mentation in Biblical Texts: Essays from the Lund 2000 Conference. Edited by Anders Eriksson, Thomas H. Olbricht, and Walter G. Übelacker. ESEC 8. Harrisburg, Pa.: Trinity, 2002.

Exler, Francis Xavier J. *The Form of the Ancient Greek Letter of the Epistolary Papyri (3rd c. B.C.-3rd c. A.D.): A Study in Greek Epistolography.* Chicago: Ares, 1976.

Fairchild, Hoxie Neale. *The Noble Savage: A Study in Romantic Naturalism.* New York: Columbia University Press, 1928.

Fairweather, Janet. "The Epistle to the Galatians and Classical Rhetoric." *TynBul* 45 (1994): 1–38, 213–43.

Fantham, Elaine. "The Concept of Nature and Human Nature in Quintilian's Psychology and Theory of Instruction." *Rhetorica* 13 (1995): 125–36.

―――. *The Roman World of Cicero's* De Oratore. Oxford: Oxford University Press, 2004.

Farnell, Brenda. "Getting Out of the Habitus: An Alternative Model of Dynamically Embodied Social Action." *Journal of the Royal Anthropological Institute* 6 (2000): 397–418.

Farrar, Frederic W. *The Life and Work of St. Paul.* 2 vols. New York: Dutton, 1879.

Fee, Gordon D. *The First Epistle to the Corinthians.* NICNT. Grand Rapids: Eerdmans, 1987.

Fenton, William N. *The Great Law and the Longhouse: A Political History of the Iroquois Confederacy.* Civilization of the American Indian Series 223. Norman: University of Oklahoma Press, 1998.

Fields, Dana. "Aristides and Plutarch on Self-Praise." Pages 151–72 in *Aelius Aristides Between Greece, Rome, and the Gods.* Edited by W. V. Harris and Brooke Holmes. Columbia Studies in the Classical Tradition 33. Leiden: Brill, 2008.

Firth, Raymond. "Speech-Making and Authority in Tikopia." Pages 29–43 in *Political Language and Oratory in Traditional Society.* Edited by Maurice Bloch. London: Academic Press, 1975.

Fish, Jeffrey. "The Good King's Giving Credit Where Credit is Due: *P.Herc.* 1507, Col. 34." Pages 469–74 in vol. 1 of *Atti del XXII Congresso internazionale di papirologia: Firenze, 23–29 agosto 1998.* Edited by Isabella Andorlini, Guido Bastianini, Manfredo Manfredi, and Giovanna Menci. 3 vols. Florence: Istituto papirologico G. Vitelli, 2001.

Fitzgerald, John T. "The Catalogue in Ancient Greek Literature." Pages 275–93 in *The Rhetorical Analysis of Scripture: Essays from the 1995*

London Conference. Edited by Thomas H. Olbricht and Stanley E. Porter, 275–93. JSNTSup 146. Sheffield: Sheffield Academic Press, 1997.

———. *Cracks in an Earthen Vessel: An Examination of the Catalogues of Hardships in the Corinthian Correspondence*. SBLDS 99. Atlanta: Scholars Press, 1988.

———. "Cracks in an Earthen Vessel: An Examination of the Catalogues of Hardships in the Corinthian Correspondence." Ph.D. diss., Yale University, 1984.

———. "Paul, the Ancient Epistolary Theorists, and 2 Corinthians 10–13." Pages 190–200 in *Greeks, Romans, and Christians: Essays in Honor of Abraham J. Malherbe*. Edited by David L. Balch, Everett Ferguson, and Wayne A. Meeks. Minneapolis: Fortress, 1990.

Foakes-Jackson, F. J. *The Acts of the Apostles*. MNTC 5. London: Hodder & Stoughton, 1931.

———. *The Life of Saint Paul: The Man and the Apostle*. New York: Boni & Liveright, 1926.

Focke, Friedrich. "Synkrisis." *Hermes* 58 (1923): 327–68.

Foley, John Miles. *The Singer of Tales in Performance*. Voices in Performance and Text. Bloomington: Indiana University Press, 1995.

Forbes, Christopher. "Ancient Rhetoric and Ancient Letters: Models for Reading Paul, and Their Limits." Pages 143–79 in *Paul and Rhetoric*. Edited by J. Paul Sampley and Peter Lampe. New York: T&T Clark, 2010.

———. "Comparison, Self-Praise, and Irony: Paul's Boasting and the Conventions of Hellenistic Rhetoric." *NTS* 32 (1986): 1–30.

Foster, Michael K. *From the Earth to beyond the Sky: An Ethnographic Approach to Four Longhouse Iroquois Speech Events*. Canadian Ethnology Service Paper 20. Ottawa: National Museums of Canada, 1974.

Francis, James A. *Subversive Virtue: Asceticism and Authority in the Second-Century Pagan World*. University Park: Pennsylvania State University Press, 1995.

Frazier, F. "Les visages de las rhétorique contemporaine sous le regard de Plutarque." Pages 183–202 in *Rhetorical Theory and Praxis in Plutarch*. Edited by L. Van der Stockt. Collection d'études classiques 11. Leuven: Peeters, 2000.

Fridrichsen, Anton. "Sprachliches und Stilistisches zum Neuen Testament." Pages 282–91 in *Exegetical Writings: A Selection*. Edited by Chrys C. Caragounis and Tord Fornberg. WUNT 76. Tübingen: Mohr

Siebeck, 1994. Reprint from *Kungliga Humanistiska Vetenskaps-Samfundet i Uppsala, Årsbok* 1 (1943): 24–36.

———. "Zum Stil des paulinischen Peristasenkatalogs 2 Cor. 11, 23ff." *SO* 7 (1928): 25–29.

———. "Zum Thema 'Paulus und die Stoa': Ein stoische Stilparallele zu 2 Kor 4,8f." *ConBNT* 9 (1944): 27–31.

Friesen, Steven J. "After the First Urban Christians: The Social Scientific Study of Pauline Christianity Twenty Five Years Later." Panel discussion at the annual meeting of the Society of Biblical Literature. New Orleans, La., November 21, 2009.

———. "Paul and Economics: The Jerusalem Collection as an Alternative to Patronage." Pages 27–54 in *Paul Unbound: Other Perspectives on the Apostle*. Edited by Mark D. Given. Peabody, Mass.: Hendrickson, 2010.

———. "Poverty in Pauline Studies: Beyond the So-Called New Consensus." *JSNT* 26 (2004): 323–61.

Furnish, Victor Paul. *II Corinthians*. AB 32A. Garden City, N.Y.: Doubleday, 1984.

Gaertner, Jan Felix. "The Homeric Catalogues and Their Function in Epic Narrative." *Hermes* 129 (2001): 298–305.

Ganter, Granville. "Introduction." Pages xxi–xxxvii in *The Collected Speeches of Sagoyewatha, or Red Jacket*. Edited by Granville Ganter. The Iroquois and Their Neighbors. Syracuse, N.Y.: Syracuse University Press, 2006.

———. "'Make Your Minds Perfectly Easy': Sagoyewatha and the Great Law of the Haudensoaunee." *Early American Literature* 44 (2009): 121–27.

———. "Red Jacket and the Decolonization of Republican Virtue." *American Indian Quarterly* 31 (2007): 559–81.

———. "'You Are a Cunning People without Sincerity': Sagoyewatha and the Trials of Community Representation." Pages 165–95 in *Native American Speakers of the Eastern Woodlands: Selected Speeches and Critical Analyses*. Edited by Barbara Alice Mann. Westport, Conn.: Greenwood Press, 2001.

Ganter, Granville, ed. *The Collected Speeches of Sagoyewatha, or Red Jacket*. The Iroquois and Their Neighbors. Syracuse, N.Y.: Syracuse University Press, 2006.

Garland, David E. *2 Corinthians*. NAC 29. Nashville: Broadman & Holman, 1999.

Garrett, Mary M. Review of George A. Kennedy, *Comparative Rhetoric: An Historical and Cross-Cultural Introduction*. *Rhetorica* 16 (1998): 431–33.

———. "Some Elementary Methodological Reflections on the Study of the Chinese Rhetorical Tradition." Pages 53–63 in *Rhetoric in Intercultural Contexts*. Edited by Alberto González and Dolores V. Tanno. International and Intercultural Communication Annual 22. Thousand Oaks, Calif.: Sage, 1999.

Georgi, Dieter. *The Opponents of Paul in Second Corinthians: A Study of Religious Propaganda in Late Antiquity*. Philadelphia: Fortress, 1986.

Gerber, Albrecht. *Deissmann the Philologist*. BZNW 171. Berlin: de Gruyter, 2010.

Ghita, Andreea. "Negotiation of Irony in Dialogue." Pages 139–48 in *Negotiation and Power in Dialogic Interaction*. Edited by Edda Weigand and Marcelo Dascal. Current Issues in Linguistic Theory 214. Philadelphia: John Benjamins, 2001.

Gibson, Roy K. "Pliny and the Art of (In)offensive Self-Praise." *Arethusa* 36 (2003): 235–54.

Given, Mark D. *Paul's True Rhetoric: Ambiguity, Cunning, and Deception in Greece and Rome*. ESEC 7. Harrisburg, Pa.: Trinity, 2001.

Glancy, Jennifer A. "Boasting of Beatings (2 Corinthians 11:23–25)." *JBL* 123 (2004): 99–135.

Gleason, Maud W. *Making Men: Sophists and Self-Presentation in Ancient Rome*. Princeton, N.J.: Princeton University Press, 1995.

Gnilka, Joachim. *Paulus von Tarsus: Apostel und Zeuge*. HTKNTSup 6. Freiburg: Herder, 1996.

Goffman, Erving. *Frame Analysis: An Essay on the Organization of Experience*. New York: Harper & Row, 1974.

———. "On Face-Work: An Analysis of Ritual Elements in Social Interaction." Pages 5–45 in *Interaction Ritual: Essays on Face-to-Face Behavior*. Garden City, N.Y.: Anchor, 1967. Reprint from *Psychiatry: Journal for the Study of Interpersonal Processes* 18 (1955): 213–31.

Gooch, P. W. "Socratic Irony and Aristotle's *Eiron*: Some Puzzles." *Phoenix* 41 (1987): 95–104.

Goodspeed, Edgar J. *An Introduction to the New Testament*. Chicago: University of Chicago Press, 1937.

———. *Paul*. Nashville: Abingdon, 1947.

Gossen, Gary. "To Speak with a Heated Heart: Chamula Canons of Style and Good Performance." Pages 389–413 in *Explorations in the Ethnog-

raphy of Speaking. Edited by Richard Bauman and Joel Sherzer. 2nd ed. SSCFL 8. Cambridge: Cambridge University Press, 1989.

Gottschalk, H. B. "Diatribe Again." *Liverpool Classical Monthly* 7 (1982): 91–92.

———. "More on DIATRIBAI." *Liverpool Classical Monthly* 78 (1983): 91–92.

Grant, Robert M. "Hellenistic Elements in 1 Corinthians." Page 60–66 in *Early Christian Origins: Studies in Honor of Harold R. Willoughby*. Edited by Allen Paul Wikgren. Chicago: Quadrangle, 1961.

Green, Lucy. *How Popular Musicians Learn: A Way Ahead for Music Education*. Ashgate Popular and Folk Music Series. Aldershot, Eng.: Ashgate, 2001.

Gross, Alan G. "What Aristotle Meant by Rhetoric." Pages 24–37 in *Rereading Aristotle's* Rhetoric. Edited by Alan G. Gross and Arthur E. Walzer. Carbondale: Southern Illinois University Press, 2000.

Guthrie, Thomas H. "Good Words: Chief Joseph and the Production of Indian Speech(es), Texts, and Subjects." *Ethnohistory* 54 (2007): 509–46.

Haacker, Klaus. "Zum Werdegang des Apostels Paulus: Biographische Daten und ihre theologische Relevanz." *ANRW* 26.2:815–938.

Haenchen, Ernst. *The Acts of the Apostles: A Commentary*. Translated by Bernard Noble and Gerald Shinn. Oxford: Blackwell, 1971.

Hafemann, Scott J. "'Self-Commendation' and Apostolic Legitimacy in 2 Corinthians: A Pauline Dialectic?" *NTS* 36 (1990): 66–88.

Haines, Elijah M. *The American Indian (Uh-nish-in-na-ba)*. Chicago: Massinnagan, 1888.

Hajdú, Kerstin. *Ps.-Herodian, De figuris: Überlieferungsgeschichte und kritische Ausgabe*. SGLG 8. Berlin: de Gruyter, 1998.

Hall, Robert G. "Josephus' *Contra Apionem* and Historical Inquiry in the Roman Rhetorical Schools." Pages 229–49 in *Josephus'* Contra Apionem*: Studies in its Character and Context*. Edited by L. H. Feldman and J. R. Levison. AGJU 34. Leiden: Brill, 1996.

Hanges, James C. *Paul, Founder of Churches: A Study in Light of the Evidence for the Role of "Founder-Figures" in the Hellenistic-Roman Period*. WUNT 292. Tübingen: Mohr Siebeck, 2012.

———. "'Severing the Joints and the Marrow': The Double-Edged Sword of Comparison." Paper presented at the annual meeting of the Society of Biblical Literature. Altanta, Ga., November 22, 2010.

Hanks, William F. "Pierre Bourdieu and the Practices of Language." *Annual Review of Anthropology* 34 (2005): 67–83.
Harrill, J. Albert. "Invective against Paul (2 Cor 10:10), the Physiognomics of the Ancient Slave Body, and the Greco-Roman Rhetoric of Manhood." Pages 189–213 in *Antiquity and Humanity: Essays on Ancient Religion and Philosophy*. Edited by Adela Yarbro Collins and Margaret M. Mitchell. Tübingen: Mohr Siebeck, 2001.
Harris, Murray J. *The Second Epistle to the Corinthians: A Commentary on the Greek Text*. NIGTC. Grand Rapids: Eerdmans, 2005.
Harris, William V. *Ancient Literacy*. Cambridge: Harvard University Press, 1989.
Haskell, Robert E. "The Access Paradox in Analogical Reasoning and Transfer: Whither Invariance?" *Journal of Mind and Behavior* 30 (2009): 33–66.
Hauptman, Laurence M. *Conspiracy of Interests: Iroquois Dispossession and the Rise of New York State*. The Iroquois and Their Neighbors. Syracuse, N.Y.: Syracuse University Press, 1999.
Hausrath, Adolf. *A History of New Testament Times: The Time of the Apostles*. Translated by L. Huxley. 4 vols. London: Williams & Norgate, 1895.
———. *Der Vier-Capitel-Brief des Paulus an die Korinther*. Heidelberg: Bassermann, 1870.
Heath, Malcolm. "John Chrysostom, Rhetoric and Galatians." *BibInt* 12 (2004): 369–400.
———. *Menander: A Rhetor in Context*. Oxford: Oxford University Press, 2004.
———. "Theon and the History of the Progymnasmata." *GRBS* 43 (2002): 129–60.
Heath, Shirley Brice. *Ways with Words: Language, Life, and Work in Communities and Classrooms*. Cambridge: Cambridge University Press, 1983.
Heckel, Ulrich. "Jer 9,22f. als Schlüssel für 2 Kor 10–13: Ein Beispiel für die methodischen Probleme in der gegenwärtigen Diskussion über den Schriftgebrauch bei Paulus." Pages 206–25 in *Schriftauslegung im antiken Judentum und im Urchristentum*. Edited by Martin Hengel and Hermut Löhr. WUNT 73. Tübingen: Mohr Siebeck, 1994.
———. *Kraft in Schwachheit: Untersuchungen zu 2. Kor 10–13*. WUNT 2/56. Tübingen: Mohr Siebeck, 1993.

Heinrici, C. F. Georg. *Der litterarische Charakter der neutestamentlichen Schriften*. Leipzig: Dürr, 1908.

———. *Der zweite Brief an die Korinther: Mit einem Anhang, Zum Hellenismus des Paulus*. 8th ed. KEK 6. Göttingen: Vandenhoeck & Ruprecht, 1900.

Hellholm, David. "Enthymemic Argumentation in Paul: The Case of Romans 6." Pages 119–79 in *Paul in His Hellenistic Context*. Edited by Troels Engberg-Pedersen. SNTW. Minneapolis: Fortress, 1995.

Hengel, Martin. *The Pre-Christian Paul*. Translated by John Bowden. London: SCM, 1991.

Héring, Jean. *The Second Epistle of Saint Paul to the Corinthians*. Translated by A. W. Heathcote and P. J. Allcock. London: Epworth, 1967.

Hester Amador, J. David. "Revisiting 2 Corinthians: Rhetoric and the Case for Unity." *NTS* 46 (2000): 92–111.

———. "The Unity of 2 Corinthians: A Test Case for a Re-discovered and Re-invented Rhetoric." *Neot* 33 (1999): 411–32.

Hewitt, John P., and Randall Stokes. "Disclaimers." *American Sociological Review* 40 (1975): 1–11.

Hezser, Catherine. *Jewish Literacy in Roman Palestine*. TSAJ 81. Tübingen: Mohr Siebeck, 2001.

Hochbruck, Walter. "'I Ask for Justice': Native American Fourth of July Orations." Pages 155–67 in *The Fourth of July: Political Oratory and Literary Reactions, 1776–1876*. Edited by Paul Goetsch and Gerd Hurm. Tübingen: Nurr, 1992.

Hock, Ronald F. "Paul and Greco-Roman Education." Pages 198–227 in *Paul in the Greco-Roman World: A Handbook*. Edited by J. Paul Sampley. Harrisburg, Pa.: Trinity, 2003.

———. "Paul's Tentmaking and the Problem of his Social Class." *JBL* 97 (1978): 555–64.

———. "The Problem of Paul's Social Class: Further Reflections." Pages 7–18 in *Paul's World*. Edited by Stanley E. Porter. PaSt 4. Leiden: Brill, 2008.

———. *The Social Context of Paul's Ministry: Tentmaking and Apostleship*. Philadelphia: Fortress, 1980.

———. "The Workshop as a Social Setting for Paul's Missionary Preaching." *CBQ* 41 (1979): 438–50.

Hodge, Charles. *An Exposition of the Second Epistle to the Corinthians*. New York: Hodder & Stoughton, 1858.

Hodgson, Robert. "Paul the Apostle and First Century Tribulation Lists." *ZNW* 74 (1983): 59–80.

Hoffman, Yair. *A Blemished Perfection: The Book of Job in Context.* JSOTSup 213. Sheffield: Sheffield Academic Press, 1996.

Holland, Glenn S. *Divine Irony.* Selinsgrove, Pa.: Susquehanna University Press, 2000.

———. "Speaking Like a Fool: Irony in 2 Corinthians 10–13." Pages 250–63 in *Rhetoric and the New Testament: Essays from the 1992 Heidelberg Conference.* Edited by Stanley E. Porter and Thomas H. Olbricht. JSNTSup 90. Sheffield: Sheffield Academic Press, 1993.

Holloway, Paul A. "The Enthymeme as an Element of Style in Paul." *JBL* 120 (2001): 329–43.

Holmes, Janet. "Functions of *You Know* in Women's and Men's Speech." *Language in Society* 15 (1986): 1–22.

Holtzmann, H. J. *Die Apostelgeschichte.* 3rd ed. Hand-Commentar zum Neuen Testament 1.2. Tübingen: Mohr Siebeck, 1901.

Holzner, Josef. *Paul of Tarsus.* Translated by Frederic C. Eckhoff. St. Louis: Herder, 1946.

Hooker, Morna D. "'Beyond the Things Which Are Written': An Examination of 1 Cor. iv. 6." *NTS* 10 (1963): 127–32.

———. *Paul: A Short Introduction.* Oxford: Oneworld, 2003.

Horrell, David G. "Pauline Churches or Early Christian Churches? Unity, Disagreement, and the Eucharist." Pages 185–203 in *Einheit der Kirche im Neuen Testament.* Edited by Anatoly A. Alexeev, Christos Karakolis, and Ulrich Luz. WUNT 218. Tübingen: Mohr Siebeck, 2008.

Horsfall, Nicholas. "The Cultural Horizons of the 'Plebs Romana.'" *Memoirs of the American Academy in Rome* 41 (1996): 101–19.

———. "Statistics or States of Mind?" Pages 59–76 in *Literacy in the Roman World.* Edited by J. H. Humphrey. Journal of Roman Archaeology Supplement Series 3. Ann Arbor: University of Michigan, 1991.

———. "'The Uses of Literacy' and the 'Cena Trimalchionis.'" *GR* 2/36 (1989): 74–89, 194–209.

Hubbard, J. Niles. *An Account of Sa-go-ye-wat-ha, or Red Jacket, and His People, 1750–1830.* Albany, N.Y.: Munsell, 1886.

Hughes, Philip E. *Paul's Second Epistle to the Corinthians.* 2nd ed. NICNT. Grand Rapids: Eerdmans, 1967.

Hum, Sue, and Arabella Lyon. "Recent Advances in Comparative Rhetoric." Pages 153–65 in *The SAGE Handbook of Rhetorical Studies.* Edited by Andrea A. Lunsford. Los Angeles: Sage, 2009.

Hurd, John Coolidge. *The Origin of 1 Corinthians.* New York: Seabury, 1965.

Hutchinson, G. O. "Down among the Documents: Criticism and Papyrus Letters." Pages 17–36 in *Ancient Letters: Classical and Late Antique Epistolography*. Edited by Ruth Morello and A. D. Morrison. Oxford: Oxford University Press, 2007.

Hymes, Dell. "Competence and Performance in Linguistic Theory." Pages 3–28 in *Language Acquisition: Models and Methods*. Edited by Renira Huxley and Elisabeth Ingram. London: Academic Press, 1971.

———. *Foundations in Sociolinguistics: An Ethnographic Approach*. Philadelphia: University of Pennsylvania Press, 1974.

———. *"In Vain I Tried to Tell You": Essays in Native American Ethnopoetics*. Studies in Native American Literature 1. Philadelphia: University of Pennsylvania Press, 1981.

———. "On Communicative Competence." Pages 53–73 in *Linguistic Anthropology: A Reader*. Edited by Alessandro Duranti. 2nd ed. Malden, Mass.: Blackwell, 2001.

———. "Sapir, Competence, Voices." Pages 33–45 in *Individual Differences in Language Ability and Behavior*. Edited by Charles J. Fillmore, Daniel Kempler, and William S-Y. Wang. Perspectives in Neurolinguistics and Psycholinguistics. New York: Academic Press, 1979.

———. "Sociolinguistics and the Ethnography of Speaking." Pages 47–94 in *Social Anthropology and Language*. Edited by Edwin Ardener. London: Tavistock, 1971.

———. "Ways of Speaking." Pages 433–54 in *Explorations in the Ethnography of Speaking*. Edited by Richard Bauman and Joel Sherzer. 2nd ed. SSCFL 8. Cambridge: Cambridge University Press, 1989.

"Indian Eloquence." *The Knickerbocker, or the New-York Monthly Magazine* 7, no. 4 (April 1836): 385–90.

Jakobson, Roman. "Grammatical Parallelism and Its Russian Facet." *Language* 42 (1966): 399–429.

Jefferson, Thomas. *Notes on the State of Virginia*. Richmond, Va.: Randolph, 1853.

Jocelyn, H. D. "Diatribes and Sermons." *Liverpool Classical Monthly* 7 (1982): 3–7.

———. "'Diatribes' and the Greek Book-Title Διατριβαί." *Liverpool Classical Monthly* 8 (1983): 89–91.

Johanson, Bruce C. *To All the Brethren: A Text-Linguistic and Rhetorical Approach to I Thessalonians*. ConBNT 16. Stockholm: Almqvist & Wiksell, 1987.

Johnson, Lee A. "The Epistolary Apostle: Paul's Response to the Challenge of the Corinthian Congregation." Ph.D. diss., University of St. Michael's College, 2002.

Johnson, Luke Timothy. *The Writings of the New Testament: An Interpretation*. Rev. ed. Minneapolis: Fortress, 1999.

Johnson, William A. *Readers and Reading Culture in the High Roman Empire: A Study of Elite Communities*. New York: Oxford University Press, 2010.

Johnstone, Barbara. "The Individual Voice in Language." *Annual Review of Anthropology* 29 (2000): 405–24.

Jones, C. P. *Plutarch and Rome*. Oxford: Clarendon, 1971.

———. "Towards a Chronology of Plutarch's Works." *JRS* 56 (1966): 61–74.

Jones, Ivor H. "Rhetorical Criticism and the Unity of 2 Corinthians: One 'Epilogue', or More?" *NTS* 54 (2008): 496–524.

Jones, Louis Thomas. *Aboriginal American Oratory: The Tradition of Eloquence among the Indians of the United States*. Los Angeles: Southwest Museum, 1965.

Jowett, Benjamin. *The Interpretation of Scripture and Other Essays*. London: Routledge, 1907.

Judge, E. A. "The Conflict of Educational Aims in the New Testament." Pages 693–708 in *The First Christians in the Roman World: Augustan and New Testament Essays*. Edited by James R. Harrison. WUNT 229. Tübingen: Mohr Siebeck, 2008. Reprint from *Journal of Christian Education* 9 (1966): 32–45.

———. "Cultural Conformity and Innovation in Paul: Some Clues from Contemporary Documents." Pages 157–74 in *Social Distinctives of the Christians in the First Century: Pivotal Essays*. Edited by David M. Scholer, 157–74. Peabody, Mass.: Hendrickson, 2008. Reprint from *TynBul* 35 (1984): 3–24.

———. "The Early Christians as a Scholastic Community." Pages 526–52 in *The First Christians in the Roman World: Augustan and New Testament Essays*. Edited by James R. Harrison. WUNT 229. Tübingen: Mohr Siebeck, 2008. Reprint from *JRH* 1 (1960–1961): 5–15, 125–37.

———. "Ethical Terms in St Paul and the Inscriptions of Ephesus." Pages 368–77 in *The First Christians in the Roman World: Augustan and New Testament Essays*. Edited by James R. Harrison. WUNT 229. Tübingen: Mohr Siebeck, 2008.

———. *The First Christians in the Roman World: Augustan and New Testament Essays*. Edited by James R. Harrison. WUNT 229. Tübingen: Mohr Siebeck, 2008.

———. "First Impressions of St Paul." Pages 410–15 in *The First Christians in the Roman World: Augustan and New Testament Essays*. Edited by James R. Harrison. WUNT 229. Tübingen: Mohr Siebeck, 2008. Reprint from *Prudentia* 2 (1970): 52–58.

———. "Paul's Boasting in Relation to Contemporary Professional Practice." Pages 57–71 in *Social Distinctives of the Christians in the First Century: Pivotal Essays*. Edited by David M. Scholer. Peabody, Mass.: Hendrickson, 2008. Reprint from *ABR* 16 (1968): 37–50.

———. "The Reaction against Classical Education in the New Testament." Pages 709–16 in *The First Christians in the Roman World: Augustan and New Testament Essays*. Edited by James R. Harrison. WUNT 229. Tübingen: Mohr Siebeck, 2008. Reprint from *Journal of Christian Education* 77 (1983): 7–14.

———. *Social Distinctives of the Christians in the First Century: Pivotal Essays*. Edited by David M. Scholer. Peabody, Mass.: Hendrickson, 2008.

———. "The Social Pattern of the Christian Groups in the First Century." In *Social Distinctives of the Christians in the First Century: Pivotal Essays*. Edited by David M. Scholer, 1–56. Peabody, Mass.: Hendrickson, 2008. Reprint from *The Social Pattern of the Christian Groups in the First Century: Some Prolegomena to the Study of New Testament Ideas of Social Obligation*. London: Tyndale, 1960.

———. "St Paul and Socrates." Pages 670–83 in *The First Christians in the Roman World: Augustan and New Testament Essays*. Edited by James R. Harrison. WUNT 229. Tübingen: Mohr Siebeck, 2008. Reprint from *Interchange* 14 (1973): 106–16.

———. "St. Paul and Classical Society." Pages 73–97 in *Social Distinctives of the Christians in the First Century: Pivotal Essays*. Edited by David M. Scholer. Peabody, Mass.: Hendrickson, 2008. Reprint from *Jahrbuch für Antike und Christentum* 15 (1972): 19–36.

———. "St. Paul as a Radical Critic of Society." Pages 99–115 in *Social Distinctives of the Christians in the First Century: Pivotal Essays*. Edited by David M. Scholer. Peabody, Mass.: Hendrickson, 2008. Reprint from *Interchange* 16 (1974): 191–203.

Jülicher, Adolf. *Einleitung in das Neue Testament*. 5th & 6th ed. Grundriss der theologischen Wissenschaften 3.1. Tübingen: Mohr Siebeck, 1906.

Karakasis, Evangelos. *Terence and the Language of Roman Comedy*. Cambridge Classical Studies. Cambridge: Cambridge University Press, 2005.
Käsemann, Ernst. "Die Legitimität des Apostels: Eine Untersuchung zu II Korinther 10–13." *ZNW* 41 (1942): 33–71.
Kaster, Robert A. "Controlling Reason: Declamation in Rhetorical Education at Rome." Pages 317–37 in *Education in Greek and Roman Antiquity*. Edited by Yun Lee Too. Leiden: Brill, 2001.
———. "Notes on 'Primary' and 'Secondary' Schools in Late Antiquity." *TAPA* 113 (1983): 323–346.
———. "Self-Aggrandizement and Praise of Others in Cicero." *Princeton/Stanford Working Papers in Classics*, no. 120502 (2005). Online: http://www.princeton.edu/~pswpc/pdfs/kaster/120502.pdf.
Katsouris, A. G. *Linguistic and Stylistic Characterization: Tragedy and Menander*. Dodone Supplement 5. Ioanina, 1975.
Kaufer, David S. "Irony, Interpretive Form, and the Theory of Meaning." *Poetics Today* 4 (1983): 451–64.
Keener, Craig S. *1–2 Corinthians*. New Cambridge Bible Commentary. Cambridge: Cambridge University Press, 2005.
Kennedy, George A. *The Art of Persuasion in Greece*. Princeton, N.J.: Princeton University Press, 1963.
———. *The Art of Rhetoric in the Roman World, 300 B.C.–A.D. 300*. History of Rhetoric 2. Princeton, N.J.: Princeton University Press, 1972.
———. *Comparative Rhetoric: An Historical and Cross-Cultural Introduction*. New York: Oxford University Press, 1998.
———. *Greek Rhetoric under Christian Emperors*. History of Rhetoric 3. Princeton, N.J.: Princeton University Press, 1983.
———. "A Hoot in the Dark: The Evolution of General Rhetoric." Pages 105–21 in *Rhetoric: Concepts, Definitions, Boundaries*. Edited by William A. Covino and David A. Jolliffe. Boston: Allyn & Bacon, 1995. Reprint from *Philosophy and Rhetoric* 25 (1992): 1–21.
———. *New Testament Interpretation through Rhetorical Criticism*. Studies in Religion. Chapel Hill: University of North Carolina Press, 1984.
———. *Quintilian*. New York: Twayne, 1969.
Kennedy, George A., trans. *Progymnasmata: Greek Textbooks of Prose Composition and Rhetoric*. WGRW 10. Atlanta: Society of Biblical Literature, 2003.
Kennedy, James Houghton. *The Second and Third Epistles of St. Paul to the*

Corinthians: With Some Proofs of Their Independence and Mutual Relation. London: Methuen, 1900.
Ker, Donald. "Paul and Apollos—Colleagues or Rivals?" *JSNT* 77 (2000): 75–97.
Kern, Philip H. *Rhetoric and Galatians: Assessing an Approach to Paul's Epistle.* SNTSMS 101. Cambridge: Cambridge University Press, 1998.
Kittel, Gerhard, and Gerhard Friedrich, eds. *Theological Dictionary of the New Testament.* Translated by Geoffrey W. Bromiley. 10 vols. Grand Rapids: Eerdmans, 1964–1976.
Klauck, Hans-Josef. *Ancient Letters and the New Testament: A Guide to Context and Exegesis.* Translated by Daniel P. Bailey. Waco, Tex.: Baylor University Press, 2006.
Kleinknecht, Karl Theodor. *Der leidende Gerechtfertigte: Die alttestamentlich-Jüdische Tradition vom "leidenden Gerechten" und ihre Rezeption bei Paulus.* WUNT 2/13. Tübingen: Mohr, 1984.
Knox, John. *Chapters in a Life of Paul.* Rev. ed. Macon, Ga.: Mercer University Press, 1987.
Knox, Wilfred L. *St Paul and the Church of Jerusalem.* Cambridge: Cambridge University Press, 1925.
Ko, Mei-yun, and Tzu-fu Wang. "A Politeness Strategy: Downtoners, Hedges and Disclaimers." *International Journal of the Humanities* 5 (2007): 189–98.
Koester, Helmut. *History, Culture, and Religion of the Hellenistic Age.* Vol. 1 of *Introduction to the New Testament.* 2nd ed. Berlin: de Gruyter, 1995.
Korta, Kepa. "Malinowski and Pragmatics: Claim Making in the History of Linguistics." *Journal of Pragmatics* 40 (2008): 1645–60.
Koskenniemi, Heikki. *Studien zur Idee und Phraseologie des griechischen Briefes bis 400 n. Chr.* Helsinki, 1956.
Kraftchick, Steven J. "Πάθη in Paul: The Emotional Logic of 'Original Argument.'" Pages 39–68 in *Paul and Pathos.* Edited by Thomas H. Olbricht and Jerry L. Sumney. SBLSymS 16. Atlanta: Society of Biblical Literature, 2001.
Kraus, Thomas J. "Schooling and School System in (Late) Antiquity and Their Influence on Paul" (review of Tor Vegge, *Paulus und die antike Schulwesen: Schule und Bildung des Paulus*). *ExpTim* 118 (2007): 617.
Kremendahl, Dieter. *Die Botschaft der Form: Zum Verhältnis von antiker Epistolographie und Rhetorik im Galaterbrief.* NTOA 46. Freiburg: Universitätsverlag, 2000.

Krenkel, Max. *Paulus: Der Apostel der Heiden.* Leipzig: Duncker & Humblot, 1869.
Labov, William. *The Social Stratification of English in New York City.* Washington, D.C.: Center for Applied Linguistics, 1966.
———. *Sociolinguistic Patterns.* Philadelphia: University of Pennsylvania Press, 1972.
Lake, Kirsopp. *The Earlier Epistles of St. Paul: Their Motive and Origin.* London: Rivingtons, 1911.
Lambrecht, Jan. "Dangerous Boasting: Paul's Self-Commendation in 2 Cor 10–13." Pages 325–46 in *The Corinthian Correspondence.* Edited by Reimund Bieringer. BETL 125. Leuven: Leuven University Press, 1996.
———. "The Fool's Speech and Its Context: Paul's Particular Way of Arguing in 2 Cor 10–13." *Bib* 82 (2001): 305–24.
———. "Paul's Foolish Discourse: A Reply to A Pitta." *ETL* 83 (2007): 407–11.
Lampe, Peter. "Rhetorical Analysis of Pauline Texts—Quo Vadit? Methodological Reflections." Pages 3–21 in *Paul and Rhetoric.* Edited by J. Paul Sampley and Peter Lampe. New York: T&T Clark, 2010.
———. "Theological Wisdom and the 'Word About the Cross': The Rhetorical Scheme in 1 Corinthians 1–4." *Int* 44 (1990): 117–31.
Larson, Jennifer. "Paul's Masculinity." *JBL* 123 (2004): 85–97.
Lausberg, Heinrich. *Handbook of Literary Rhetoric: A Foundation for Literary Study.* Edited by David E. Orton and R. Dean Anderson. Leiden: Brill, 1998.
Leech, Geoffrey N. *Principles of Pragmatics.* Longman Linguistics Library 30. London: Longman, 1983.
Légasse, Simon. *Paul apôtre: Essai de biographie critique.* 2nd ed. Paris: Cerf, 2000.
Leigh, Matthew. "Wounding and Popular Rhetoric at Rome." *Bulletin of the Institute of Classical Studies* 40 (1995): 192–215.
Leivestad, Ragnar. "'The Meekness and Gentleness of Christ' II Cor. x. 1." *NTS* 12 (1966): 156–64.
Lentz, John Clayton. *Luke's Portrait of Paul.* SNTSMS 77. Cambridge: Cambridge University Press, 1994.
Leopold, J. "Philo's Knowledge of Rhetorical Theory." Pages 129–36 in *Two Treatises of Philo of Alexandria: A Commentary on* De gigantibus *and* Quod Deus sit immutabilis. Edited by David Winston and John Dillon. BJS 25. Chico, Calif.: Scholars Press, 1983.

Levelt, Willem J. M. "Accessing Words in Speech Production: Stages, Processes and Representations." Pages 1–22 in *Lexical Access in Speech Production*. Edited by Willem J. M. Levelt. Cambridge, Mass.: Blackwell, 1993. Reprint from *Cognition: International Journal of Cognitive Science* 42 (1992): 1–22.

Levieils, Xavier. *Contra Christianos: La critique sociale et religieuse du christianisme des origines au concile de Nicée (45–325)*. BZNW 146. Berlin: de Gruyter, 2007.

Levin, Richard. *New Readings vs. Old Plays: Recent Trends in the Reinterpretation of English Renaissance Drama*. Chicago: University of Chicago Press, 1979.

Liddell, Henry George, Robert Scott, and Henry Stuart Jones. *A Greek-English Lexicon*. 9th ed. with revised supplement. Oxford: Oxford University Press, 1996.

Lietaert Peerbolte, Bert Jan. "Paul and the Practice of *Paideia*." Pages 261–80 in *Jesus, Paul, and Early Christianity: Studies in Honour of Henk Jan de Jonge*. Edited by Rieuwerd Buitenwerf, Harm W. Hollander, and Johannes Tromp. NovTSup 130. Leiden: Brill, 2008.

Lietzmann, Hans. "Paulus." Pages 380–409 in *Das Paulusbild in der neueren deutschen Forschung*. Edited by Karl Heinrich Rengstorf. Wege der Forschung 24. Darmstadt: Wissenschaftliche Buchgesellschaft, 1964.

Lincoln, Andrew T. "'Paul the Visionary': The Setting and Significance of the Rapture to Paradise in II Corinthians XII.1–10." *NTS* 25 (1979): 204–20.

Lis, Catharina. "Perceptions of Work in Classical Antiquity: A Polyphonic Heritage." Pages 33–68 in *The Idea of Work in Europe from Antiquity to Modern Times*. Edited by Josef Ehmer and Catharina Lis. Burlington, Vt.: Ashgate, 2009.

Litfin, A. Duane. *St. Paul's Theology of Proclamation: 1 Corinthians 1–4 and Greco-Roman Rhetoric*. SNTSMS 79. Cambridge: Cambridge University Press, 1994.

Litwa, M. David. "Paul's Mosaic Ascent: An Interpretation of 2 Corinthians 12:7–9." *NTS* 57 (2011): 238–57.

Long, A. A. *Epictetus: A Stoic and Socratic Guide to Life*. Oxford: Clarendon, 2002.

Long, Fredrick J. *Ancient Rhetoric and Paul's Apology: The Compositional Unity of 2 Corinthians*. SNTSMS 131. Cambridge: Cambridge University Press, 2004.

Longenecker, Bruce W. "Exposing the Economic Middle: A Revised Economy Scale for the Study of Early Christianity." *JSNT* 31 (2009): 243–78.
———. *Remember the Poor: Paul, Poverty, and the Greco-Roman World*. Grand Rapids: Eerdmans, 2010.
Longenecker, Richard N. *Galatians*. WBC 41. Nashville: Thomas Nelson, 2003.
Lord, Albert B. *The Singer of Tales*. Harvard Studies in Comparative Literature 24. Cambridge: Harvard University Press, 1960.
Loubser, J. A. "A New Look at Paradox and Irony in 2 Corinthians 10–13." *Neot* 26 (1992): 507–21.
Lu, Xing. *Rhetoric in Ancient China, Fifth to Third Century, B.C.E.: A Comparison with Classical Greek Rhetoric*. Columbia: University of South Carolina Press, 1998.
———. "Studies and Development of Comparative Rhetoric in the U.S.A.: Chinese and Western Rhetoric in Focus." *China Media Research* 2 (2006): 112–16.
Lyons, George. *Pauline Autobiography: Toward a New Understanding*. SBLDS 73. Atlanta: Scholars Press, 1985.
Mack, Burton L. "Decoding the Scripture: Philo and the Rules of Rhetoric." Pages 81–116 in *Nourished with Peace: Studies in Hellenistic Judaism in Memory of Samuel Sandmel*. Edited by Frederick E. Greenspahn, Earle Hilgert, and Burton L. Mack. Scholars Press Homage Series 9. Chico, Calif.: Scholars Press, 1984.
———. *Rhetoric and the New Testament*. GBS. Minneapolis: Fortress, 1990.
Malherbe, Abraham J. *Social Aspects of Early Christianity*. Baton Rouge: Louisiana State University Press, 1977.
Malherbe, Abraham J., ed. *Ancient Epistolary Theorists*. SBLSBS 19. Atlanta: Scholars Press, 1988.
Malina, Bruce J., and Jerome H. Neyrey. "First-Century Personality: Dyadic, Not Individualistic." Pages 67–96 in *The Social World of Luke-Acts: Models for Interpretation*. Edited by Jerome H. Neyrey. Peabody, Mass.: Hendrickson, 1991.
———. *Portraits of Paul: An Archaeology of Ancient Personality*. Louisville: Westminster John Knox, 1996.
Malina, Bruce J. *The New Testament World: Insights from Cultural Anthropology*. 3rd ed. Louisville: Westminster John Knox, 2001.
Malinowski, Bronislaw. "The Problem of Meaning in Primitive Languages." Pages 296–336 in *The Meaning of Meaning*, by C. K. Ogden and I. A. Richards. New York: Harcourt, Brace, and Company, 1936.

Mann, Barbara Alice. "Introduction." Pages xiii–xvii in *Native American Speakers of the Eastern Woodlands: Selected Speeches and Critical Analyses*. Edited by Barbara Alice Mann. Westport, Conn.: Greenwood Press, 2001.

Mann, Barbara Alice, ed. *Native American Speakers of the Eastern Woodlands: Selected Speeches and Critical Analyses*. Westport, Conn.: Greenwood Press, 2001.

Mao, LuMing. "Reflective Encounters: Illustrating Comparative Rhetoric." *Style* 37 (2003): 401–25.

Márquez-Reiter, Rosina. *Linguistic Politeness in Britain and Uruguay: A Contrastive Study of Requests and Apologies*. Pragmatics and Beyond 2/83. Amsterdam: Benjamins, 2000.

Marrou, Henri I. *A History of Education in Antiquity*. Translated by George Lamb. New York: Sheed & Ward, 1956.

Marshall, Peter. *Enmity in Corinth: Social Conventions in Paul's Relations with the Corinthians*. WUNT 2/23. Tübingen: Mohr Siebeck, 1987.

Martin, Dale B. *The Corinthian Body*. New Haven: Yale University Press, 1995.

———. "Justin J. Meggitt, Paul, Poverty and Survival." *JSNT* 84 (2001): 51–64.

———. *Slavery as Salvation: The Metaphor of Slavery in Pauline Christianity*. New Haven: Yale University Press, 1990.

Martin, Ralph P. *2 Corinthians*. WBC 40. Waco, Tex.: Word, 1986.

Martin, Raymond A. *Studies in the Life and Ministry of the Early Paul and Related Issues*. Lewiston, N.Y.: Mellen Biblical Press, 1993.

Martin, Robert F. *Hero of the Heartland: Billy Sunday and the Transformation of American Society, 1862–1935*. Bloomington: Indiana University Press, 2002.

Martin, Troy W. "Invention and Arrangement in Recent Pauline Rhetorical Studies: A Survey of the Practices and the Problems." Pages 48–118 in *Paul and Rhetoric*. Edited by J. Paul Sampley and Peter Lampe. New York: T&T Clark, 2010.

———. "The Voice of Emotion: Paul's Pathetic Persuasion (Gal 4:12–20)." Pages 181–202 in *Paul and* Pathos. Edited by Thomas H. Olbricht and Jerry L. Sumney. Atlanta: Society of Biblical Literature, 2001.

Mason, Steve. "Jews, Judaeans, Judaizing, Judaism: Problems of Categorization in Ancient History." *JSJ* 38 (2007): 457–512.

McCant, Jerry W. *2 Corinthians*. Readings. Sheffield: Sheffield Academic Press, 1999.

McNelis, Charles A. "Greek Grammarians and Roman Society during the Early Empire: Statius' Father and His Contemporaries." *Classical Antiquity* 21 (2002): 67–94.
Meeks, Wayne A. *The First Urban Christians: The Social World of the Apostle Paul*. New Haven: Yale University Press, 1983.
Meggitt, Justin J. *Paul, Poverty and Survival*. SNTW. Edinburgh: T&T Clark, 1998.
———. "Response to Martin and Theissen." *JSNT* 84 (2001): 85–94.
———. "Sources: Use, Abuse and Neglect." Pages 241–53 in *Christianity at Corinth: The Scholarly Quest for the Corinthian Church*. Edited by Edward Adams and David G. Horrell. Louisville: Westminster John Knox, 2004.
Meyer, Christian. *"Mahnen, Prahlen, Drohen...": Rhetorik und politischen Organisation amerikanischer Indianer*. Frankfurt: IKO-Verlag für Interkulturelle Kommunikation, 2005.
———. "Precursors of Rhetoric Culture Theory." Pages 31–48 in *Culture and Rhetoric*. Edited by Ivo A. Strecker and Stephen A. Tyler. Studies in Rhetoric and Culture 1. New York: Berghahn Books, 2009.
———. "Rhetoric and Stylistics in Social/Cultural Anthropology." Pages 1871–85 in vol. 2 of *Rhetorik und Stilistik: Ein internationales Handbuch historischer und systematischer Forschung*. Edited by Ulla Fix, Andreas Gardt, and Joachim Knape. 2 vols. Handbücher zur Sprach- und Kommunikationswissenschaft 31. Berlin: de Gruyter, 2009.
Meyer, Eduard. *Ursprung und Anfänge des Christentums*. 3 vols. Stuttgart: Cotta, 1923.
Meyer, H. A. W. *Critical and Exegetical Handbook to the Epistles to the Corinthians*. Translated by David Hunter. 2 vols. KEK 5–6. Edinburgh: T&T Clark, 1879.
Mihaila, Corin. *The Paul-Apollos Relationship and Paul's Stance toward Greco-Roman Rhetoric: An Exegetical and Socio-Historical Study of 1 Corinthians 1–4*. LNTS 402. London: T&T Clark, 2009.
Minchin, Elizabeth. "The Performance of Lists and Catalogues in the Homeric Epics." Pages 3–20 in *Voice into Text: Orality and Literacy in Ancient Greece*. Edited by Ian Worthington. Mnemosyne Supplement 157. Leiden: Brill, 1996.
Mitchell, Margaret M. "The Corinthian Correspondence and the Birth of Pauline Hermeneutics." Pages 17–53 in *Paul and the Corinthians: Studies on a Community in Conflict; Essays in Honour of Margaret Thrall*.

Edited by Trevor J. Burke and J. K. Elliott. NovTSup 109. Leiden: Brill, 2003.

———. *The Heavenly Trumpet: John Chrysostom and the Art of Pauline Interpretation*. HUT 40. Tübingen: Mohr Siebeck, 2000.

———. "Le style, c'est l'homme: Aesthetics and Apologetics in the Stylistic Analysis of the New Testament." *NovT* 51 (2009): 369–88.

———. "A Patristic Perspective on Pauline περιαυτολογία." *NTS* 47 (2001): 354–71.

———. *Paul and the Rhetoric of Reconciliation: An Exegetical Investigation of the Language and Composition of 1 Corinthians*. HUT 28. Tübingen: Mohr Siebeck, 1991.

———. *Paul, the Corinthians and the Birth of Christian Hermeneutics*. Cambridge: Cambridge University Press, 2010.

———. "Paul's Letters to Corinth: The Interpretive Intertwining of Literary and Historical Reconstruction." Pages 307–38 in *Urban Religion in Roman Corinth: Interdisciplinary Approaches*. Edited by Daniel N. Schowalter and Steven J. Friesen. HTS 53. Cambridge: Harvard University Press, 2005.

———. "Reading Rhetoric with Patristic Exegetes: John Chrysostom on Galatians." Pages 333–55 in *Antiquity and Humanity: Essays on Ancient Religion and Philosophy*. Edited by Adela Yarbro Collins and Margaret M. Mitchell. Tübingen: Mohr Siebeck, 2001.

Moe, Olaf. *The Apostle Paul: His Life and His Work*. Translated by L. A. Vigness. Grand Rapids: Baker, 1968.

Moles, J. L. "The Career and Conversion of Dio Chrysostom." *JHS* 98 (1978): 79–100.

Momigliano, Arnaldo. *The Development of Greek Biography*. Cambridge: Harvard University Press, 1971.

Mommsen, Theodor. "Die Rechtsverhältnisse des Apostels Paulus." *ZNW* 2 (1901): 81–96.

Moore, Stephen D., and Janice Capel Anderson. "Taking It Like a Man: Masculinity in 4 Maccabees." *JBL* 117 (1998): 249–73.

Morgan, Teresa. *Literate Education in the Hellenistic and Roman Worlds*. Cambridge Classical Studies. Cambridge: Cambridge University Press, 1998.

———. "Rhetoric and Education." In *A Companion to Greek Rhetoric*. Edited by Ian Worthington, 303–19. Blackwell Companions to the Ancient World. Malden, Mass.: Blackwell, 2007.

Motsch, Andreas. *Lafitau et l'émergence du discours ethnographique.* Sillery, Québec: Septentrion, 2001.
Moule, C. F. D. *An Idiom Book of New Testament Greek.* 2nd ed. Cambridge: Cambridge University Press, 1959.
Moulton, James Hope and George Milligan. *The Vocabulary of the Greek Testament Illustrated from the Papyri and Other Non-Literary Sources.* London: Hodder & Stoughton, 1930.
Muir, John. *Life and Letters in the Ancient Greek World.* London: Routledge, 2009.
Murphy-O'Connor, Jerome. *Paul: A Critical Life.* Oxford: Oxford University Press, 1997.
———. *St. Paul's Corinth: Texts and Archaeology.* 3rd ed. GNS 6. Wilmington, Del.: Glazier, 2002.
Murray, David. *Forked Tongues: Speech, Writing, and Representation in North American Indian Texts.* Bloomington: Indiana University Press, 1991.
Murray, Oswyn. "Philodemus on the Good King according to Homer." *JRS* 55 (1965): 161–82.
Nanos, Mark D., ed. *The Galatians Debate: Contemporary Issues in Rhetorical and Historical Interpretation.* Peabody, Mass.: Hendrickson, 2002.
Native Eloquence: Being Public Speeches Delivered by Two Distinguished Chiefs of the Seneca Tribe of Indians. Canandaigua, N.Y.: Bemis, 1811.
Neusner, Jacob. *The Rabbinic Traditions about the Pharisees before 70.* 3 vols. Leiden: Brill, 1971.
Neyrey, Jerome H. "Luke's Social Location of Paul: Cultural Anthropology and the Status of Paul in Acts." Pages 268–76 in *History, Literature, and Society in the Book of Acts.* Edited by Ben Witherington. Cambridge: Cambridge University Press, 1996.
———. "The Social Location of Paul: Education as the Key." Pages 126–64 in *Fabrics of Discourse: Essays in Honor of Vernon K. Robbins.* Edited by David Gowler, Gregory Bloomquist, and Duane F. Watson. Harrisburg, Pa.: Trinity, 2003.
———. "'Teaching You in Public and from House to House' (Acts 20.20): Unpacking a Cultural Stereotype." *JSNT* 26 (2003): 69–102.
Nock, A. D. *St. Paul.* London: Butterworth, 1938.
Norden, Eduard. *Die antike Kunstprosa vom VI. Jahrhundert V. Chr. bis in die Zeit der Renaissance.* 2 vols. 5th ed. Stuttgart: Teubner, 1958.
O'Mahony, Kieran J. *Pauline Persuasion: A Sounding in 2 Corinthians 8–9.* JSNTSup 199. Sheffield: Sheffield Academic Press, 2000.

Ochs, Elinor. *Culture and Language Development: Language Acquisition and Language Socialization in a Samoan Village*. SSCFL 6. Cambridge: Cambridge University Press, 1988.

———. "Linguistic Resources for Socializing Humanity." Pages 407–37 in *Rethinking Linguistic Relativity*. Edited by John J. Gumperz and Stephen C. Levinson. SSCFL 17. Cambridge: Cambridge University Press, 1996.

Omerzu, Heike. *Der Prozeß des Paulus: Eine exegetische und rechtshistorische Untersuchung der Apostelgeschichte*. BZNW 115. Berlin: de Gruyter, 2002.

Ong, Walter J. *Orality and Literacy: The Technologizing of the Word*. London: Routledge, 2002.

Osterreich, Peter L. "Homo Rhetoricus." Pages 49–58 in *Culture and Rhetoric*. Edited by Ivo A. Strecker and Stephen A. Tyler. Studies in Rhetoric and Culture 1. New York: Berghahn Books, 2009.

Padilla, Osvaldo. "Hellenistic παιδεία and Luke's Education: A Critique of Recent Approaches." *NTS* 55 (2009): 416–37.

Patillon, Michel, ed. *Aelius Théon: Progymnasmata*. Budé. Paris: Les belles lettres, 1997.

Pauly, A. F. *Paulys Realencyclopädie der classischen Altertumswissenschaft*. New edition by Georg Wissowa and Wilhelm Kroll. 50 vols. in 84 parts. Stuttgart: Metzler and Druckenmüller, 1894–1980.

Pernot, Laurant. "*Periautologia*: Problèmes et méthodes de l'éloge de soi-même dans la tradition éthique et rhétorique gréco-romaine." *REG* 111 (1998): 101–24.

Pervo, Richard I. *The Making of Paul: Constructions of the Apostle in Early Christianity*. Minneapolis: Fortress, 2010.

———. *Profit with Delight: The Literary Genre of the Acts of the Apostles*. Philadelphia: Fortress, 1987.

Peterson, Brian K. *Eloquence and the Proclamation of the Gospel in Corinth*. SBLDS 163. Atlanta: Scholars Press, 1998.

Phillips, Thomas E. *Paul, His Letters, and Acts*. Library of Pauline Studies. Peabody, Mass.: Hendrickson, 2009.

Pickering, P. E. "Did the Greek Ear Detect 'Careless' Verbal Repetitions?" *CQ* 2/53 (2003): 490–99.

Pitta, Antonio. "Il 'discorso del pazzo' o periautologia immoderata? Analisi retoricoletteraria di 2 Cor 11,1–12,18." *Bib* 87 (2006): 493–510.

Pitts, Andrew W. "Hellenistic Schools in Jerusalem and Paul's Rhetorical

Education." Pages 19–50 in *Paul's World*. Edited by Stanley E. Porter. PaSt 4. Leiden: Brill, 2008.

Plummer, Alfred. *A Critical and Exegetical Commentary on the Second Epistle of St. Paul to the Corinthians*. ICC. Edinburgh: T&T Clark, 1915.

Pogoloff, Stephen M. *Logos and Sophia: The Rhetorical Situation of 1 Corinthians*. SBLDS 134. Atlanta: Scholars Press, 1992.

Pomerantz, Anita. "Compliment Reponses: Notes on the Co-operation of Multiple Constraints." Pages 79–112 in *Studies in the Organization of Conversational Interaction*. Edited by Jim Schenkein. Language, Thought, and Culture Series. New York: Academic Press, 1978.

Porter, Stanley E. "The Argument of Romans 5: Can a Rhetorical Question Make a Difference?" *JBL* 110 (1991): 655–77.

———. *Paul in Acts*. Library of Pauline Studies. Peabody, Mass.: Hendrickson, 2001.

———. "Paul of Tarsus and His Letters." Pages 533–85 in *Handbook of Classical Rhetoric in the Hellenistic Period, 330 B.C.–A.D. 400*. Edited by Stanley E. Porter. Leiden: Brill, 1997.

———. "The Theoretical Justification for Application of Rhetorical Categories to Pauline Epistolary Literature." Pages 100–122 in *Rhetoric and the New Testament: Essays from the 1992 Heidelberg Conference*. Edited by Stanley E. Porter and Thomas H. Olbricht. JSNTSup 90. Sheffield: JSOT Press, 1993.

Poster, Carol. "Aristotle's *Rhetoric* against Rhetoric: Unitarian Reading and Esoteric Hermeneutics." *AJP* 118 (1997): 219–49.

———. "A Conversation Halved: Epistolary Theory in Greco-Roman Antiquity." Pages 21–51 in *Letter-Writing Manuals and Instruction from Antiquity to the Present: Historical and Bibliographic Studies*. Edited by Carol Poster and Linda C. Mitchell. Studies in Rhetoric/Communication. Columbia: University of South Carolina Press, 2007.

———. "The Economy of Letter Writing in Graeco-Roman Antiquity." Pages 112–24 in *Rhetorical Argumentation in Biblical Texts: Essays from the 2000 Lund Conference*. Edited by Anders Eriksson, Thomas H. Olbricht, and Walter Ubelacker. ESEC. Harrisburg, Pa.: Trinity, 2002.

Prümm, Karl. *Diakonia pneumatos: Der zweite Korintherbrief als Zugang zur apostolischen Botschaft, Auslegung und Theologie*. 2 vols. Rome: Herder, 1960–1967.

Radermacher, L. "Studien zur Geschichte der greichischen Rhetorik, II: Plutarchs Schrift de se ipso citra invidiam laudando." *RhM* 2/52 (1897): 419–24.

Rahn, Helmut. *Morphologie der antiken Literatur: Eine Einführung*. Die Altertumswissenschaft. Darmstadt: Wissenschaftliche Buchgesellschaft, 1969.

Ramsay, W. M. *St. Paul the Traveller and the Roman Citizen*. London: Hodder & Stoughton, 1895.

———. *The Teaching of Paul in Terms of the Present Day*. 2nd ed. London: Hodder & Stoughton, 1914.

Rapske, Brian. *The Book of Acts and Paul in Roman Custody*. Vol. 3 of *The Book of Acts in Its First Century Setting*, ed. Bruce W. Winter. Grand Rapids: Eerdmans, 1994.

Reed, Jeffrey T. "Using Ancient Rhetorical Categories to Interpret Paul's Letters: A Question of Genre." Pages 292–324 in *Rhetoric and the New Testament: Essays from the 1992 Heidelberg Conference*. Edited by Stanley E. Porter and Thomas H. Olbricht. JSNTSup 90. Sheffield: JSOT Press, 1993.

Reinhardt, Tobias, and Michael Winterbottom, eds. *Quintilian, Institutio Oratoria, Book 2*. Oxford: Oxford University Press, 2006.

Reiser, Marius. "Paulus als Stilist." *SEÅ* 66 (2001): 151–65.

———. *Sprache und literarische Formen des Neuen Testaments: Eine Einführung*. UTB 2197. Paderborn: Schöningh, 2001.

Reisman, Karl. "Contrapuntal Conversations in an Antiguan Village." Pages 110–24 in *Explorations in the Ethnography of Speaking*. Edited by Richard Bauman and Joel Sherzer. 2nd ed. SSCFL 8. Cambridge: Cambridge University Press, 1989.

Reitzenstein, Richard. *Die hellenistischen Mysterienreligionen nach ihren Grundgedanken und Wirkungen*. 3rd ed. Leipzig: Teubner, 1927.

Renan, Ernest. *Saint Paul*. Translated by Ingersoll Lockwood. New York: Carleton, 1875.

Richards, E. Randolph. *Paul and First-Century Letter Writing: Secretaries, Composition, and Collection*. Downers Grove, Ill.: InterVarsity Press, 2004.

———. *The Secretary in the Letters of Paul*. WUNT 2/42. Tübingen: Mohr Siebeck, 1991.

Richardson, Peter. "The Thunderbolt in Q and the Wise Man in Corinth." Pages 91–111 in *From Jesus to Paul: Studies in Honour of Frank Wright*

Beare. Edited by Peter Richardson and John C. Hurd. Waterloo, Ont.: Wilfred Laurier University Press, 1984.

Riesner, Rainer. *Paul's Early Period: Chronology, Mission Strategy, Theology.* Translated by Doug Stott. Grand Rapids: Eerdmans, 1998.

Robertson, F. W. *Sermons on St. Paul's Epistles to the Corinthians.* Boston: Ticknor & Fields, 1860.

Robie, Harry W. "Red Jacket's Reply: Problems in the Verification of a Native American Speech Text." *New York Folklore* 12. 3-4 (1986): 99-117.

Roetzel, Calvin J. *2 Corinthians.* ANTC. Nashville: Abingdon Press, 2007.

———. *Paul: The Man and the Myth.* Studies on Personalities of the New Testament. Columbia, S.C.: University of South Carolina Press, 1998.

Rohrbaugh, Richard L. "'Social Location of Thought' as a Heuristic Construct in New Testament Study." *JSNT* 30 (1987): 103-19.

Roochnik, David. "Is Rhetoric an Art?" *Rhetorica* 12 (1994): 127-54.

Rosaldo, Michelle Z. "Words That Are Moving: The Social Meanings of Ilongot Verbal Art." Pages 131-60 in *Dangerous Words: Language and Politics in the Pacific.* Edited by Donald Lawrence Brenneis and Fred R. Myers. New York: New York University Press, 1984.

Russell, D. A. *Plutarch.* London: Duckworth, 1973.

Russell, D. A. "On Reading Plutarch's 'Moralia.'" *GR* 2/15 (1968): 130-46.

Rutherford, Ian. "The Poetics of the *Paraphthegma*: Aeilus Aristides and the *Decorum* of Self-Praise." Pages 193-204 in *Ethics and Rhetoric: Classical Essays for Donald Russell on His Seventy-Fifth Birthday.* Edited by Doreen Innes, Harry Hine, and Christopher Pelling. Oxford: Clarendon, 1995.

Saldarini, Anthony J. *Pharisees, Scribes and Sadducees in Palestinian Society: A Sociological Approach.* Biblical Resource. Grand Rapids: Eerdmans, 2001.

Salmeri, Giovanni. "Dio, Rome, and the Civic Life of Asia Minor." Pages 53-92 in *Dio Chrysostom: Politics, Letters, and Philosophy.* Edited by Simon Swain. Oxford: Oxford University Press, 2000.

Sammons, Benjamin. *The Art and Rhetoric of the Homeric Catalogue.* Oxford: Oxford University Press, 2010.

Sampley, J. Paul. "Paul, His Opponents in 2 Corinthians 10-13, and the Rhetorical Handbooks." Pages 162-77 in *The Social World of Formative Christianity and Judaism.* Edited by Jacob Neusner,. Philadelphia: Fortress, 1988.

Sandbach, F. H. "Rhythm and Authenticity in Plutarch's *Moralia.*" *CQ* 33 (1939): 194-203.

Sanders, E. P. *Paul. Past Masters.* Oxford: Oxford University Press, 1991.
Sandys, J. E. "Rhythm in Greek and Latin Prose" (review of Friedrich Blass, *Die Rhythmen der asianischen und römischen Kunstprosa*). *Classical Review* 21 (1907): 85–88.
Sapir, Edward. "Speech as a Personality Trait." Pages 533–43 in *Selected Writings of Edward Sapir in Language, Culture, and Personality.* Edited by David G. Mandelbaum. Berkeley: University of California Press, 1949.
Savage, Timothy B. *Power through Weakness: Paul's Understanding of the Christian Ministry in 2 Corinthians.* SNTSMS 86. Cambridge: Cambridge University Press, 1996.
Scenters-Zapico, J. "The Social Construct of Enthymematic Understanding." *RSQ* 24 (1994): 71–87.
Scheidel, Walter, and Steven J. Friesen. "The Size of the Economy and the Distribution of Income in the Roman Empire." *JRS* 99 (2009): 61–91.
Schellenberg, Ryan S. "'Danger in the Wilderness, Danger at Sea': Paul and the Perils of Travel." Pages 141–61 in *Travel and Religion in Antiquity.* Studies in Christianity and Judaism/Études sur le christianisme et la judaisme 21. Waterloo, Ont.: Wilfred Laurier University Press, 2011.
———. "Rhetorical Terminology in Paul: A Critical Reappraisal." *ZNW* 104 (2013): 177–91.
———. "τὸ ἐν λόγῳ ἰδιωτικὸν τοῦ Ἀποστόλου: Revisiting Patristic Testimony on Paul's Rhetorical Education." *NovT* 54 (2012): 354–68.
———. "'Where is the Voice Coming from?': Querying the Evidence for Paul's Rhetorical Education in 2 Corinthians 10–13." Ph.D. diss., University of St. Michael's College, 2012.
Schiappa, Edward. "Did Plato Coin *Rhētorikē*?" *AJP* 111 (1990): 457–70.
Schiefer Ferrari, Markus. *Die Sprache des Leids in den paulinischen Peristasenkatalogen.* SBB 23. Stuttgart: Katholisches Bibelwerk, 1991.
Schieffelin, Bambi B., and Elinor Ochs, eds. *Language Socialization across Cultures.* SSCFL 3. Cambridge University Press, 1986.
Schmitt, Rudolf. "Ist Philo, Vita Moysis (Mos) II 251 ein Peristasenkatalog?" *NovT* 29 (1987): 177–82.
Schmitz, Thomas. *Bildung und Macht: Zur sozialen und politischen Funktion der zweiten Sophistik in der griechischen Welt der Kaiserzeit.* Zetemata 97. Munich: Beck, 1997.
Schnelle, Udo. *Apostle Paul: His Life and Theology.* Translated by Eugene M. Boring. Grand Rapids: Baker Academic, 2005.

Schrage, Wolfgang. *Der erste Brief an die Korinther.* 4 vols. EKKNT 7. Zürich: Benziger, 1991–2001.

———. "Leid, Kreuz und Eschaton: Die Peristasenkataloge als Merkmale paulinischer *theologia crucis* und Eschatologie." Pages 23–57 in *Kreuzestheologie und Ethik im Neuen Testament: Gesammelte Studien.* FRLANT 205. Göttingen: Vandenhoeck & Ruprecht, 2004. Reprint from *EvT* 34 (1974): 141–75.

Schreiber, Stefan. *Paulus als Wundertäter: Redaktionsgeschichtliche Untersuchungen zur Apostelgeschichte und den authentischen Paulusbriefen.* BZNW 79. Berlin: de Gruyter, 1996.

Schreiner, Josef. "Jeremia 9,22.23 als Hintergrund des paulinischen 'Sich-Rühmens.'" Pages 530–42 in *Neues Testament und Kirche: Für Rudolf Schnackenburg.* Edited by Joachim Gnilka. Freiburg: Herder, 1974.

Schütz, John H. *Paul and the Anatomy of Apostolic Authority.* 2nd ed. NTL. Louisville: Westminster John Knox, 2007.

Schweitzer, Albert. *The Mysticism of Paul the Apostle.* Translated by William Montgomery. London: Black, 1931.

Seid, Timothy W. "Synkrisis in Hebrews 7: The Rhetorical Structure and Strategy." Pages 322–47 in *The Rhetorical Interpretation of Scripture: Essays from the 1996 Malibu Conference.* Edited by Stanley E. Porter and Dennis L. Stamps. JSNTSup 180. Sheffield: Sheffield Academic Press, 1999.

Sellin, Gerhard. "Das 'Geheimnis' der Weisheit und das Rätsel der 'Christuspartei' (zu 1 Kor 1–4)." *ZNW* 73 (1983): 69–96.

Semler, Johann Salomo. *Paraphrasis II: Epistolae ad Corinthios.* Halle: Hemmerde, 1776.

Shantz, Colleen. *Paul in Ecstasy: The Neurobiology of the Apostle's Life and Thought.* Cambridge: Cambridge University Press, 2009.

Sherzer, Joel, and Anthony C. Woodbury, eds. *Native American Discourse: Poetics and Rhetoric.* Cambridge Studies in Oral and Literate Culture 13. Cambridge: Cambridge University Press, 1987.

Shipley, Frederick W., ed. *Velleius Paterculus, Compendium of Roman History; Res gestae divi Augusti.* LCL. London: Heinemann, 1924.

Sifianou, Maria. *Politeness Phenomena in England and Greece: A Cross-Cultural Perspective.* Oxford: Clarendon, 1992.

Smit, Joop F. M. "'What Is Apollos? What Is Paul?' In Search for the Coherence of First Corinthians 1:10–4:21." *NovT* 44 (2002): 231–51.

Smith, Jonathan Z. *Drudgery Divine: On the Comparison of Early Christi-*

anities and the Religions of Late Antiquity. CSHJ. Chicago: University of Chicago Press, 1990.

Sorber, Edna C. "The Noble Eloquent Savage." *Ethnohistory* 19 (1972): 227–36.

Spatharas, Dimos. "Self-Praise and Envy: From Rhetoric to the Athenian Courts." *Arethusa* 44 (2011): 199–219.

Spencer, Aida Besançon. "The Wise Fool (and the Foolish Wise): A Study of Irony in Paul." *NovT* 23 (1981): 349–60.

Stanton, G. R. "Sophists and Philosophers: Problems of Classification." *AJP* 94 (1973): 350–64.

Stegemann, Wolfgang. "War der Apostel Paulus ein römischer Bürger?" *ZNW* 78 (1987): 200–229.

———. "Zwei sozialgeschichtliche Anfragen an unser Paulusbild." *Der evangelische Erzieher* 37 (1985): 480–490.

Steinmann, Alphons A. *Zum Werdegang des Paulus: Die Jugendzeit in Tarsus*. Freiburg: Herder, 1928.

Still, Todd D. "Did Paul Loathe Manual Labor? Revisiting the Work of Ronald F. Hock on the Apostle's Tentmaking and Social Class." *JBL* 125 (2006): 781–95.

Stoddard, Amos. *Sketches, Historical and Descriptive, of Louisiana*. Philadelphia: Carey, 1812.

Stone, Michael E. "Lists of Revealed Things in the Apocalyptic Literature." Pages 414–52 in *Magnalia Dei, the Mighty Acts of God: Essays on the Bible and Archaeology in Memory of G. Ernest Wright*. Edited by Frank Moore Cross, Werner E. Lemke, and Patrick D. Miller. Garden City, N.Y.: Doubleday, 1976.

Stone, William L. *Life and Times of Red-Jacket, or Sa-Go-Ye-Wat-Ha*. New York: Wiley & Putnam, 1841.

Stowers, Stanley K. "Apostrophe, ΠΡΟΣΩΠΟΠΟΙΙΑ and Paul's Rhetorical Education." Pages 351–69 in *Early Christianity and Classical Culture*. Edited by Thomas H. Olbricht and L. M. White. NovTSup 110. Leiden: Brill, 2003.

———. *The Diatribe and Paul's Letter to the Romans*. SBLDS 57. Chico, Calif.: Scholars Press, 1981.

———. "Kinds of Myth, Meals, and Power: Paul and the Corinthians." Pages 105–49 in *Redescribing Paul and the Corinthians*. Edited by Ron Cameron and Merrill P. Miller. SBLECL 5. Atlanta: Society of Biblical Literature, 2011.

———. *Letter Writing in Greco-Roman Antiquity*. LEC 5. Philadelphia: Westminster, 1986.

———. *A Rereading of Romans: Justice, Jews, and Gentiles*. New Haven: Yale University Press, 1994.

———. Review of Hans Dieter Betz, *2 Corinthians 8 and 9: A Commentary on Two Administrative Letters of the Apostle Paul*. *JBL* 106 (1987): 727–30.

———. "Romans 7.7–25 as a Speech-in-Character (προσωποπιία)." Pages 180–202 in *Paul in His Hellenistic Context*. Edited by Troels Engberg-Pedersen. SNTW. London: T&T Clark, 1994.

———. "Social Status, Public Speaking and Private Teaching: The Circumstances of Paul's Preaching Activity." *NovT* 26 (1984): 58–82.

———. "Social Typification and the Classification of Ancient Letters." Pages 78–90 in *The Social World of Formative Christianity and Judaism*. Edited by Jacob Neusner. Philadelphia: Fortress, 1988.

Strachan, R. H. *The Second Epistle of Paul to the Corinthians*. MNTC. London: Hodder & Stoughton, 1935.

Strecker, Georg. "Die Legitimität des paulinischen Apostolates nach 2 Korinther 10–13." *NTS* 38 (1992): 566–86.

Street, Brian V. *Literacy in Theory and Practice*. Cambridge Studies in Oral and Literate Culture. Cambridge: Cambridge University Press, 1984.

Sumney, Jerry L. *Identifying Paul's Opponents: The Question of Method in 2 Corinthians*. JSNTSup 40. Sheffield: JSOT Press, 1990.

———. "Paul and His Opponents: The Search." Pages 55–70 in *Paul Unbound: Other Perspectives on the Apostle*. Edited by Mark D. Given. Peabody, Mass.: Hendrickson Publishers, 2010.

———. "Paul's Use of Πάθος in His Argument against the Opponents of 2 Corinthians." Pages 147–60 in *Paul and Pathos*. Edited by Thomas H. Olbricht and Jerry L. Sumney. SBLSymS 16. Atlanta: Society of Biblical Literature, 2001.

Sundermann, Hans-Georg. *Der schwache Apostel und die Kraft der Rede: Eine rhetorische Analyse von 2 Kor 10–13*. Europäische Hochschulschriften 23, Theologie 575. Frankfurt: Lang, 1996.

Swain, Simon. "Favorinus and Hadrian." *ZPE* 79 (1989): 150–58.

———. *Hellenism and Empire: Language, Classicism, and Power in the Greek World, AD 50–250*. Oxford: Clarendon, 1996.

Swearingen, C. Jan. "The Tongues of Men: Understanding the Greek Rhetorical Sources for Paul's Letters to the Romans and 1 Corinthians." Pages 232–42 in *Rhetorical Argumentation in Biblical Texts: Essays from the Lund 2000 Conference*. Edited by Anders Eriksson, Thomas H. Olbricht, and Walter G. Übelacker. ESEC 8. Harrisburg, Pa.: Trinity, 2002.

Talbert, Charles H. *Reading Corinthians: A Literary and Theological Commentary on 1 and 2 Corinthians*. New York: Crossroad, 1987.

Tannen, Deborah. *Talking Voices: Repetition, Dialogue, and Imagery in Conversational Discourse*. 2nd ed. Studies in Interactional Sociolinguistics 25. Cambridge: Cambridge University Press, 2007.

Taylor, Alan. *The Divided Ground: Indians, Settlers, and the Northern Borderland of the American Revolution*. New York: Knopf, 2006.

Taylor, N. H. "The Composition and Chronology of Second Corinthians." *JSNT*, no. 44 (1991): 67–87.

Tell, Håkan. "Wisdom for Sale? The Sophists and Money." *CP* 104 (2009): 13–33.

Theissen, Gerd. *The Social Setting of Pauline Christianity: Essays on Corinth*. Translated by John H. Schütz. SNTW. Edinburgh: T&T Clark, 1982.

———. "The Social Structure of the Pauline Communities: Some Critical Remarks on J. J. Meggitt, *Paul, Poverty, and Survival*." *JSNT* 84 (2001): 65–84.

Thrall, Margaret E. *A Critical and Exegetical Commentary on the Second Epistle to the Corinthians*. 2 vols. ICC. Edinburgh: T&T Clark, 1994–2000.

Thurén, Lauri. *Derhetorizing Paul: A Dynamic Perspective on Pauline Theology and the Law*. Harrisburg, Pa.: Trinity, 2002.

———. "John Chrysostom as a Rhetorical Critic: The Hermeneutics of an Early Father." *BibInt* 9 (2001): 180–218.

———. "Was Paul Angry? Derhetorizing Galatians." Pages 302–20 in *The Rhetorical Interpretation of Scripture: Essays from the 1996 Malibu Conference*. Edited by Stanley E. Porter and Dennis L. Stamps. JSNTSup 180. Sheffield: Sheffield Academic Press, 1999.

Thwaites, Reuben Gold, ed. *The Jesuit Relations and Allied Documents: Travels and Explorations of the Jesuit Missionaries in New France, 1610–1791*. 73 vols. New York: Pageant, 1959.

Toorn, Karel van der. "Parallels in Biblical Research: Purposes of Comparison." Pages 1–8 in *Proceedings of the Eleventh World Congress of Jewish Studies, Jerusalem, June 22–29, 1993: Division A, The Bible and Its World*. Jerusalem: World Union of Jewish Studies, 1994.

Travis, S. H. "Paul's Boasting in 2 Corinthians 10–12." Pages 527–32 in *Studia Evangelica VI*. Edited by Elizabeth A. Livingstone. TUGAL 112. Berlin: Akademie-Verlag, 1973.

Trüb, Hansrudolf. *Kataloge in der griechischen Dichtung*. Oberwinterthur, 1952.

Turner, Nigel. *Style*. Vol. 4 of *A Grammar of New Testament Greek*. Edited by J. H. Moulton. Edinburgh: T&T Clark, 1976.

———. *Syntax*. Vol. 3 of *A Grammar of New Testament Greek*. Edited by J. H. Moulton. Edinburgh: T&T Clark, 1963.

Ulmer, Rivka. "The Advancement of Arguments in Exegetical Midrash Compared to that of the Greek ΔΙΑΤΡΙΒΗ." *JSJ* 28 (1997): 48–91.

Unnik, W. C. van. *Tarsus or Jerusalem, the City of Paul's Youth*. Translated by George Ogg. London: Epworth, 1962.

Vanhoye, Albert. "Personnalité de Paul et exégèse paulinienne." Pages 3–15 in *L'apôtre Paul: Personnalité, style et conception du ministère*. Edited by Albert Vanhoye. BETL 73. Leuven: Leuven University Press, 1986.

Vega, Garcilaso de la. *The Florida of the Inca*. Translated by John Grier Varner and Jeannette Johnson Varner. Austin: University of Texas Press, 1951.

Vegge, Ivar. *2 Corinthians—a Letter about Reconciliation: A Psychagogical, Epistolographical and Rhetorical Analysis*. WUNT 2/239. Tübingen: Mohr Siebeck, 2008.

Vegge, Tor. *Paulus und das antike Schulwesen: Schule und Bildung des Paulus*. BZNW 134. Berlin: de Gruyter, 2006.

Vielhauer, Philipp. *Geschichte der urchristlichen Literatur: Einleitung in das Neue Testament, die Apokryphen und die apostolischen Väter*. Berlin: de Gruyter, 1975.

Voelz, James W. "The Language of the New Testament." *ANRW* 25.2:893–977.

Vos, Johan S. "Die Argumentation des Paulus in 1 Kor 1,10–3,4." Pages 87–119 in *The Corinthian Correspondence*. Edited by Reimund Bieringer. BETL 125. Leuven: Leuven University Press, 1996.

———. "Der ΜΕΤΑΣΧΗΜΑΤΙΣΜΟΣ in 1 Kor 4,6." *ZNW* 86 (1995): 154–72.

Walcot, Peter. *Envy and the Greeks: A Study of Human Behaviour*. Warminster, Eng.: Aris & Phillips, 1978.

Walker, Donald Dale. *Paul's Offer of Leniency (2 Cor 10:1): Populist Ideology and Rhetoric in a Pauline Letter Fragment*. WUNT 2/152. Tübingen: Mohr Siebeck, 2002.

Wallace, Richard, and Wynne Williams. *The Three Worlds of Paul of Tarsus*. London: Routledge, 1998.

Wallach, Barbara Price. *Lucretius and the Diatribe against the Fear of Death: De rerum natura III 830–1094*. Mnemosyne Supplement 40. Leiden: Brill, 1976.

Walters, Jonathan. "Invading the Roman Body: Manliness and Impenetrability in Roman Thought." Pages 29–43 in *Roman Sexualities*. Edited by Judith P. Hallett and Marilyn B. Skinner. Princeton, N.J.: Princeton University Press, 1997.

Walzer, Arthur E. "Moral Philosophy and Rhetoric in the Institutes: Quintilian on Honor and Expediency." *RSQ* 36 (2006): 263–80.

———. "Quintilian's 'Vir Bonus' and the Stoic Wise Man." *RSQ* 33 (2003): 25–41.

Wan, Ske-kar. *Power in Weakness: Conflict and Rhetoric in Paul's Second Letter to the Corinthians*. New Testament in Context. Harrisburg, Pa.: Trinity, 2000.

Wanamaker, Charles A. "'By the Power of God': Rhetoric and Ideology in 2 Corinthians 10–13." Pages 194–221 in *Fabrics of Discourse: Essays in Honor of Vernon K. Robbins*. Edited by David Gowler, Gregory Bloomquist, and Duane F. Watson. New York: Trinity, 2003.

———. "A Rhetoric of Power: Ideology and 1 Corinthians 1–4." Pages 115–37 in *Paul and the Corinthians: Studies on a Community in Conflict; Essays in Honour of Margaret Thrall*. Edited by Trevor J. Burke and J. K. Elliott. NovTSup 109. Leiden: Brill, 2003.

Watson, Duane F. "Paul and Boasting." Pages 77–100 in *Paul in the Greco-Roman World: A Handbook*. Edited by J. Paul Sampley. Harrisburg, Pa.: Trinity, 2003.

———. "Paul's Boasting in 2 Corinthians 10–13 as Defense of His Honor: A Socio-Rhetorical Analysis." Pages 260–75 in *Rhetorical Argumentation in Biblical Texts: Essays from the 2000 Lund Conference*. Edited by Anders Eriksson, Thomas H. Olbricht, and Walter G. Übelacker. ESEC 8. Harrisburg, Pa.: Trinity, 2002.

———. "Second Corinthians 10–13 as the Best Evidence that Paul Received a Rhetorical Education." Paper presented at the annual meeting of the Society of Biblical Literature. Chicago, November 17, 2012.

———. "The Three Species of Rhetoric and the Study of the Pauline Epistles." Pages 25–47 in *Paul and Rhetoric*. Edited by J. Paul Sampley and Peter Lampe. New York: T&T Clark, 2010.

Watson, Francis. "2 Cor. X–XIII and Paul's Painful Letter to the Corinthians." *JTS* 35 (1984): 324–46.
Watson, Nigel M. "'Physician, Heal Thyself'? Paul's Character as Revealed in 2 Corinthians, and the Congruence between Word and Deed." Pages 671–78 in *The Corinthian Correspondence*. Edited by Reimund Bieringer. BETL 125. Leuven: Leuven University Press, 1996.
Webb, Ruth. "The *Progymnasmata* as Practice." Pages 289–316 in *Education in Greek and Roman Antiquity*. Edited by Yun Lee Too. Leiden: Brill, 2001.
Weiss, Johannes. "Beiträge zur Paulinischen Rhetorik." Pages 165–247 in *Theologische Studien*. Edited by Caspar René Gregory. Göttingen: Vandenhoeck & Ruprecht, 1897.
———. *Earliest Christianity: A History of the Period A.D. 30–150*. Edited by Rudolf Knopf. Translated by Frederick C. Grant. 2 vols. New York: Harper & Row, 1959.
———. *Der erste Korintherbrief*. 9th ed. KEK 5. Göttingen: Vandenhoeck & Ruprecht, 1910.
Weizsäcker, Carl von. *The Apostolic Age of the Christian Church*. Translated by James Millar. 2 vols. 3rd ed. London: Williams & Norgate, 1907.
Welborn, L. L. "'By the Mouth of Two or Three Witnesses': Paul's Invocation of a Deuteronomic Statute." *NovT* 52 (2010): 207–20.
———. *An End to Enmity: Paul and the "Wrongdoer" of Second Corinthians*. BZNW 185. Berlin: de Gruyter, 2011.
———. "The Identification of 2 Corinthians 10–13 with the 'Letter of Tears.'" *NovT* 37 (1995): 138–53.
———. *Paul, the Fool of Christ: A Study of 1 Corinthians 1–4 in the Comic-Philosophic Tradition*. JSNTSup 293. London: T&T Clark, 2005.
———. "The Runaway Paul." *HTR* 92 (1999): 115–63.
Wendt, Hans Hinrich. *Die Apostelgeschichte*. 9th ed. KEK 3. Göttingen: Vandenhoeck & Ruprecht, 1913.
White, John L. *Light from Ancient Letters*. FF. Philadelphia: Fortress, 1986.
White, L. Michael. "Favorinus's 'Corinthian Oration': A Piqued Panorama of the Hadrianic Forum." Pages 61–110 in *Urban Religion in Roman Corinth: Interdisciplinary Approaches*. Edited by Daniel N. Schowalter and Steven J. Friesen. HTS 53. Cambridge: Harvard University Press, 2005.
Whitmarsh, Tim. "Reading Power in Roman Greece: The *paideia* of Dio Chrysostom." Pages 192–213 in *Pedagogy and Power: Rhetorics of*

Classical Learning. Edited by Yun Lee Too and Niall Livingstone. Ideas in Context 50. Cambridge: Cambridge University Press, 1998.

———. *The Second Sophistic*. Greece and Rome: New Surveys in the Classics 35. Oxford: Oxford University Press, 2005.

Wiebe, Rudy. *Where Is the Voice Coming From?* Toronto: McClelland & Stewart, 1974.

Wifstrand, Albert. "Stylistic Problems in the Epistles of James and Peter." Pages 46–58 in *Epochs and Styles: Selected Writings on the New Testament, Greek Language and Greek Culture in the Post-Classical Era*. Edited by Lars Rydbeck and Stanley E. Porter, translated by Denis Searby. WUNT 179. Tübingen: Mohr Siebeck, 2005.

Wikenhauser, Alfred. *New Testament Introduction*. Translated by Joseph Cunningham. New York: Herder & Herder, 1958.

Wilamowitz-Moellendorff, Ulrich von. "Die griechische Literatur des Altertums." In *Die griechische und lateinische Literatur und Sprache*. Edited by Paul Hinneberg. 3rd ed. Die Kultur der Gegenwart 1.8. Leipzig: Teubner, 1912.

Wiles, Maurice F. *The Divine Apostle: The Interpretation of St. Paul's Epistles in the Early Church*. Cambridge: Cambridge University Press, 1967.

Windisch, Hans. *Der zweite Korintherbrief*. 9th ed. KEK 6. Göttingen: Vandenhoeck & Ruprecht, 1924.

Winter, Bruce W. *Philo and Paul among the Sophists: Alexandrian and Corinthian Responses to a Julio-Claudian Movement*. 2nd ed. Grand Rapids: Eerdmans, 2002.

———. "Philodemus and Paul on Rhetorical Delivery (ὑπόκρισις)." Pages 323–43 in *Philodemus and the New Testament World*. Edited by John T. Fitzgerald, Dirk Obbink, and Glenn S. Holland. NovTSup 111. Leiden: Brill, 2004.

———. "The Toppling of Favorinus and Paul by the Corinthians." Pages 291–306 in *Early Christianity and Classical Culture: Comparative Studies in Honor of Abraham J. Malherbe*. Edited by John T. Fitzgerald, Thomas H. Olbricht, and L. Michael White. NovTSup 110. Leiden: Brill, 2003.

Winterbottom, Michael. "Quintilian and the *vir bonus*." JRS 54 (1964): 90–97.

———. "Quintilian the Moralist." Pages 317–34 in vol. 1 of *Quintiliano: Historia y actualidad de la retórica*. Edited by Tomás Albaladejo, Emilio del Río, and José Antonio Caballero. 3 vols. Logroño: Ediciones Instituto de Estudios Riojanos, 1998.

Wire, Antoinette Clark. *The Corinthian Women Prophets: A Reconstruction through Paul's Rhetoric*. Minneapolis: Fortress, 1990.
Witherington, Ben. *Conflict and Community in Corinth: A Socio-Rhetorical Commentary on 1 and 2 Corinthians*. Grand Rapids: Eerdmans, 1995.
———. *The Paul Quest: The Renewed Search for the Jew of Tarsus*. Downers Grove, Ill.: InterVarsity Press, 1998.
———. Review of Kenneth E. Bailey, *Paul through Mediterranean Eyes: Cultural Studies in 1 Corinthians*. *Review of Biblical Literature* (2012). No pages. Online: http://bookreviews.org/pdf/8357_9407.pdf.
Wojciechowski, Michael. "Paul and Plutarch on Boasting." *Journal of Greco-Roman Christianity and Judaism* 3 (2006): 99–109.
Wrede, William. *Paulus*. 2nd ed. Tübingen: Mohr Siebeck, 1907.
Wuellner, Wilhelm H. "Greek Rhetoric and Pauline Argumentation." Pages 177–88 in *Early Christian Literature and the Classical Intellectual Tradition*. Edited by William R. Schoedel and Robert L. Wilken. ThH 54. Paris: Beauschesne, 1979.
———. "Der vorchristliche Paulus und die Rhetorik." Pages 133–65 in *Tempelkult und Tempelzersörung (70 n. Chr.): Festschrift für Clemens Thoma zum 60. Geburtstag*. Edited by Simon Lauer and Hanspeter Ernst. Judaica et Christiana 15. Bern: Lang, 1995.
Wyatt-Brown, Bertram. "The Mask of Obedience: Male Slave Psychology in the Old South." *AHR* 93 (1988): 1228–52.
Young, Frances M., and David F. Ford. *Meaning and Truth in 2 Corinthians*. BFT. London: SPCK, 1987.
Youtie, Herbert C. "ΑΓΡΑΜΜΑΤΟΣ: An Aspect of Greek Society in Egypt." *HSCP* 75 (1971): 161–76.
———. "Βραδέως γράφων: Between Literacy and Illiteracy." *GRBS* 12 (1971): 239–61.
Yu, Ming-Chung. "On the Universality of Face: Evidence from Chinese Compliment Response Behavior." *Journal of Pragmatics* 35 (2003): 1679–1710.
Zeller, Eduard. "Alexander und Peregrinus: Ein Betrüger und ein Schwärmer." Pages 154–213 in *Vorträge und Abhandlungen: Zweite Sammlung*. Leipzig: Fues, 1877.
Zerba, Michelle. "Love, Envy, and Pantomimic Morality in Cicero's *De oratore*." *CP* 97 (2002): 299–321.
Zhuangzi. *The Complete Works of Chuang Tzu*. Translated by Burton Watson. New York: Columbia University Press, 1968.

Zmijewski, Josef. *Der Stil der paulinischen "Narrenrede": Analyse der Sprachgestaltung in 2Kor 11,1-12,10 als Beitrag zur Methodik von Stiluntersuchungen neutestamentlicher Texte*. BBB 52. Cologne: Hanstein, 1978.

Zuntz, Günther. *The Text of the Epistles: A Disquisition upon the* Corpus Paulinum. London: Oxford University Press, 1953.

Index of Ancient Texts

Old Testament/Hebrew Bible

Genesis
- 40:8, 16, 22 — 158 n. 39
- 41:12–15 — 158 n. 39

Exodus
- 16:3 — 222 n. 65

Numbers
- 14:2 — 222 n. 65
- 20:3 — 222 n. 65

Deuteronomy
- 19:15 — 72 n. 44
- 28:48 — 131

2 Kings
- 5:3 — 222

2 Chronicles
- 6:28–29 — **131–32**, 136
- 20:9 — 130–31 n. 27
- 36:16 — 285

Job
- 14:13 — 222 n. 65

Psalms
- 13 LXX — 298
- 52 LXX — 198
- 118:5 LXX — 222 n. 65

Proverbs
- 9:13 — 298 n. 133
- 12:23 — 298 n. 133
- 15:2 — 298 n. 133
- 18:6–7, 13 — 298 n. 133
- 20:3 — 298 n. 133
- 29:11, 20 — 298 n. 133

Ecclesiastes
- 5:3 — 298 n. 133
- 10:13–14 — 298 n. 133

Isaiah
- 8:22 — 130–31 n. 27

Jeremiah
- 9:22 LXX — 157 n. 34
- 9:23 LXX — 156–57 n. 34
- 16:4 — 130–31 n. 27
- 25:18–26 — 136

Ezekiel
- 14:21 — 130–31 n. 27

Daniel
- 5:7 — 158 n. 39

Hosea
- 1:7 — **130–31**, 134

Amos
- 4:6–10 — 130–31 n. 27

Jewish Apocrypha and Pseudepigrapha

1 Maccabees
  1:50   285
  3:14   285
  10:71   158 n. 40

2 Maccabees
  1:27   285

Sirach
  20:7   298
  39:24–30   132 n. 28

Wisdom of Solomon
  7:17–21   134
  7:29   158 n. 40
  8:17–18   132 n. 28
  15:18   158 n. 40

2 Baruch
  59.5–11   132 n. 28
  73.4   132 n. 28

1 Enoch
  7.4   265
  60.11–13   132 n. 28

2 Enoch
  65.9   132 n. 28
  66.6   132 n. 28

Jubilees
  23.12–19   **134–36**

Liber antiquitatum biblicarum
  3.9   132 n. 28

Sibylline Oracles
  3.601–603   132 n. 28
  4.67–69   132 n. 28

Testament of Dan
  2   132 n. 28

Testament of Issachar
  6   132 n. 28

Testament of Joseph
  1.4–7   **132–34**

Testament of Judah
  23   132 n. 28

Ancient Jewish Writers

Josephus, *Antiquitates judaicae*
  3.332   290 n. 105
  4.33   158 n. 41
  5.77   158 n. 41
  5.344   290 n. 104
  8.24   290 n. 105
  8.42   158 n. 41
  8.99   158 n. 41
  9.227   290 n. 104
  10.51   253
  13.89   158 n. 41
  13.297   253
  13.408   253
  15.268   253 n. 40
  17.230   265 n. 33
  17.278   265 n. 33
  18.142   252
  18.266   265 n. 33
  18.339   252
  19.213   290 n. 105
  20.121   265 n. 33
  20.236   138 n. 43

Josephus, *Bellum judaicum*
  1.402   158 n. 41
  2.151–153   136
  4.165   136
  4.391   265 n. 33
  4.602   290 n. 104
  6.295   290
  6.300   290 n. 107

Josephus, *Contra Apionem*
  1.50   138 n. 43

Josephus, *Vita*		6:14	253 n. 40
1–11	138 n. 43	7:2	208 n. 24
8	252	13:16	208 n. 24
		16:4	253 n. 40
Philo, *De agricultura*		17:16–34	21
160	**291 n. 113**	18:3	21, 284 n. 86
		21:22	208 n. 24
Philo, *Quod deterius potiori insidari soleat*		21:39	20
34	136	22:3	46
		22:25–39	20
Philo, *In Flaccum*		23:27	20
10.75	306 n. 159	26:2–3	208 n. 24
		27	21 n. 15
Philo, *De Iosepho*			
225	265 n. 33	Romans	
		1:9	323 n. 49
Philo, *Legum allegoriae*		2:17	268 n. 50
3.88	137 n. 41	5:1	269–70 n. 58
		6:17	253 n. 40
Philo, *De vita Mosis*		7	145
2.16	136	8:35–39	238
		8:35b	127 n. 12
Philo, *Quaestiones et solutiones in Exodum*		8:37	136 n. 33
1.8	307	8:38–39	124, 128 n. 15
		15:19	323 n. 49
Philo, *De somniis*		16:7	322 n. 44
2.84	136	16:27	268 n. 50
NEW TESTAMENT		1 Corinthians	
		1–4	**70–71**
Matthew		1:10	61 n. 17
15:2	253	1:12	70, 161 n. 49
		1:17	71, 73
Mark		1:17–2:13	70
7:3–5	253	1:18–23	73
		1:18–2:16	287
Luke		1:25	157 n. 34
1:2	253 n. 40	1:27–28	285–86
2:52	252	1:28	174
16:25	269–70 n. 58	1:31	157 n. 34
		2:1–5	71, 73, 155 n. 28
Acts		2:4–5	323 n. 49
2:22	208 n. 24	2:4	70, 161 n. 49
4:13	290	2:5	60
5:1–11	280–81 n. 75	2:13	158

1 Corinthians (cont.)		13	23 n. 23
2:14–3:3	70	14:16	290 n. 106
3:6	111	14:23–24	290 n. 106
3:7	174	15:3	253 n. 40
3:8, 9	71	15:8–10	**174**, 316
3:10–17	71	15:10	172
3:21–22	128 n. 21	16:13	307 n. 163
4:8	222 n. 65		
4:10	302	2 Corinthians	
4:10–13a	127	1–7	64 n. 24, 83
4:11–12	284 n. 86	1–9	63–64, 66, 68
4:12	41, 322 n. 45	1:1–2:13	64 n. 24, 69
4:15	111, 156	1:15–2:1	67
4:18–21	**281**	1:15–2:4	63
4:20	70	1:15–2:13	67
4:20–21	72	1:17	67
4:21	71, 280–81 n. 75, 284	1:23	63–64
5:4	280–81 n. 75	2:1	69, 281
6:12	62 n. 17	2:1–5	72
7	**47–50**	2:3–4	63
7:1	49	2:4	63, 69
7:2	62 n. 17	2:5–10	281
7:2–4	48	2:5–11	69
7:2–5	49	2:9	64
7:3–4	48–49	2:14	286 n. 90
7:5	48, 62 n. 17	2:14–6:13	64 n. 24
7:9	62 n. 17	2:14–7:4	64 n. 24
7:13, 15	161 n. 49	3:1	63, 64 n. 24
7:26–35	62 n. 17	4:6	286 n. 90
7:28b	48	4:8	136 n. 33
7:34	48	4:8–9	**126–27**, 133–34, 235, 238
7:35	62 n. 17	4:10	316
7:35a	48	4:10–11	136 n. 33
7:36–37	62 n. 17	5:12	63, 64 n. 24
8	73–74 n. 47	6:4	136 n. 33
8:4	37	6:4–7	131
9:3–18	73–74	6:4b–5	127 n. 12
9:19	41	6:4b–10	134
10:20	37	6:8–10	127
10:23, 33	62 n. 17	6:10	136 n. 33
11:2	252–53	6:14–7:1	64 n. 24
11:14	48	7:2–4	64 n. 24
11:16	253	7:5–16	64 n. 24, 69
11:23	253 n. 40	7:8–12	63
12:15	161 n. 49	7:12	69, 72, 75–76, 281

INDEX OF ANCIENT TEXTS 377

7:14	156 n. 31, 303
7:14–15	68 n. 36
8	64 n. 24, 75 n. 50
8:6	64 n. 24, 75
8:7	286 n. 90
8:18	75
8:20–21	75 n. 51
8:22	64 n. 24
9	64 n. 24, 65 n. 24
9:3	303
10–13	2, 5–7, 25, 30, 31, 34, 51, **57–77**, 81–84, 86, 88, 96, 97–98, 102 n. 19, 107–109, 113–14, 150, 155–57, 174–75, 179–81, 185, 201, 207 n. 21, 227–28, 231, **263–77**, 304, **315–17**
10:1	67, **73**, 264, 266 n. 38, 276, 294, 316
10:1–2	63, 69, 83, 87, 268, 281 n. 76, 303
10:1–11:15	66
10:1b	145, 201, 223 n. 69, 227, 228 n. 81, 280
10:2	69, 228, **264–67**, 280, 281 n. 76
10:2–4	67
10:3	270
10:3–5	70–71
10:4	270
10:4–6	270
10:6	64, 71, 102 n. 19, 280
10:7	71, 72, 174, 270
10:7–8	146
10:7–11	87, 269 n. 56
10:7–12	178
10:8	114, 147, 156, 157 n. 34, 216, 228, 280, 303
10:8–9	**267–69**
10:8–11	69, 266 n. 38, 276, 303
10:9	279
10:9–11	63, 67, 73
10:10	7, 31, 34, **72–73**, 145, 155 n. 28, 201, 223 n. 69, 227, 228, 256, 268, **277–86**, 292, 294, 311, 316, 322
10:10–11a	69
10:11	72, 73, 228, 268, 279–80, 285 n. 87
10:11b–12	69
10:12	34–35, 63, 87, 110, 111, 112, 150–51, 155–56, **157–60**, 228, 270–71
10:12–13	150
10:12–16	71, 156
10:12–18	157 n. 34
10:13	147 n. 20, 271
10:13–14	156
10:13–16	110, 112
10:13–18	222 n. 65
10:14	111, 156 n. 32, 271
10:14–18	87
10:15	71, 147 n. 20, 271, 275 n. 59
10:15–16	271
10:16	272
10:17–18	156, 157 n. 34
10:18	63, 112
11	125 n. 9, 138, 140, 166, 231, 304
11:1	118–19, 142 n. 7, 145–46, 148, 172, 177, 212, 216, **222–23**, 272, 297, 302
11:1–15	146
11:1–21a	142
11:1–12:10	76
11:1–12:11	148
11:1–12:13	60
11:1b	222 n. 67
11:2–3	113, 222 nn. 65 and 67
11:2–4	112, 222–23
11:3	272
11:4	70, 71, 113, 272
11:4–15	146
11:5	69, 71–72, 73, 112, 157, 177, 272, 288, **302–3**
11:5–6	71, 87, 178
11:6	7, 31, 34, 60, 73, 256, 261, 277, **286–94**, 311, 315, 322
11:6–12	146
11:6a	**73**, 287–88
11:6b	288
11:7	41, 74, 173, 228, 288
11:7–9	74

2 Corinthians (cont.)
- 11:7–12 87
- 11:9 74, 272
- 11:10 74, 146
- 11:11 146
- 11:12 71, 157, 272
- 11:12–13 87
- 11:12–15 69
- 11:13–15 71, 112, 113, 146
- 11:16 142 n. 7, 145–46, 147–48, 212–13, 216, 316
- 11:16–17 172, 177, 297
- 11:16–18 222, 302
- 11:16–21 215 n. 43
- 11:16–12:10 66, 77, 297–98
- 11:17 118–19, 142, 148, 273
- 11:17–18 172
- 11:17–12:10 87
- 11:18 69, 172 n. 12
- 11:19 142 n. 7, 148
- 11:20 69
- 11:21 142, 148, 177, 221, 222, 228, 273, 297, 316
- 11:21–12:11 141
- 11:21a 69, 145–46
- 11:21b 69, 142 n. 7, 145 n. 16, 267 n. 44
- 11:21b–23 **160–64**, 167
- 11:21b–30 134
- 11:22 145 n. 16
- 11:22–23 112, 146
- 11:22–23a 69
- 11:23 131, 142 n. 7, 148, 161, 172, 221, 222, 305 n. 151
- 11:23–27 284 n. 86
- 11:23–28 123, 305 n. 151
- 11:23–30 76
- 11:23b–29 127 n. 12
- 11:24–25 305 n. 151, 322 n. 43
- 11:24–12:10 161–62
- 11:26 235
- 11:27 131, 305 n. 151
- 11:28 273
- 11:30 103, 146–47, 171, 172, 305
- 11:32 272
- 11:32–33 171–72
- 12:1 103, 114–15, 118–19, 212, 222, 273
- 12:1–4 115 n. 45
- 12:2 273
- 12:2–4 114
- 12:3–4 273
- 12:5–6 222
- 12:6 147, 148, 177, 273, 297, 302, 303
- 12:7 273–74, 275 n. 59
- 12:8 64 n. 24
- 12:9 274
- 12:9–10 173, 228, 294
- 12:10 131, 145 n. 16
- 12:11 63, 69, 71–72, 87, 103, 115, 148, 157, 177, 178, 218, 222, 297, 316
- 12:11–13 87
- 12:11–13:10 66
- 12:11b **173–74**
- 12:11b–12 146
- 12:12 323 n. 49
- 12:12–14 74
- 12:13 74, 145 n. 16
- 12:14 74, 274
- 12:15–19 87
- 12:16 **73–75**, 145, 201, 223 n. 69, 228 n. 81
- 12:16–18 75
- 12:17 274
- 12:18 75 n. 50, 145 n. 16, 274
- 12:19 74, 106, 274
- 12:20 274, 281–82 n. 78
- 12:21 69, 274–75, **281–82**
- 13:1–2 69
- 13:1–4 63, 71, 178, 280, 281
- 13:1a 72 n. 44
- 13:2 69, 72 n. 44, 73, 172–73 n. 13, 228, 281, 303
- 13:2–4 67, 72 n. 44, 228
- 13:2–7 275
- 13:3–4 87, 294, 316
- 13:4, 5 275
- 13:6–8 87

13:7, 8	275	Hebrews	258–59
13:10	67, 69, 71, 73, 172–73 n. 13, 228, 280, 281–82 n. 78	7:5–25	165 n. 58
		1 Peter	
Galatians	32–33, 57–59	3:7	307 n. 163
1:1	316, 317		
1:10–11	317	2 Peter	
1:13	253	2:21	253 n. 40
1:13–14	254		
1:14	**252–54**	Jude	
1:15–16	316	3	253 n. 40
2:4–6	268 n. 50		
3–4	32, 58	GREEK AND ROMAN LITERATURE	
3:1–5	323 n. 49		
4:12	316	Achilles Tatius, *Leucippe et Clitophon*	
4:13–14	284 n. 86, 322 n. 47	5.18.4	136
4:19	3		
5–6	58	Aelian, *Varia historia*	
5:12	222 n. 65	12.21	306 n. 159
6:3	174		
6:13	156 n. 31	Aelius Theon, *Progymnasmata*	
		pr.	158 n. 37
Philippians		1	144
1:12–17	322 n. 44	6	158 n. 37
1:14	161 n. 49	8	90–91, 144
1:18	222 n. 66	9	162 n. 53, 166 n. 63, 306
1:25	252	10	149 n. 1, 158 n. 37, **162–63**
3:2–6	172	11	47–49
3:4–6	163		
3:5	253	Alexander Numenius, *De figuris*	
3:10–11, 21	316	1.3	119, 213 n. 35
4:12	127, 136 n. 33, 288	1.4	218
		1.9	137 n. 39
1 Thessalonians			
1:4–5	323 n. 49	Alexander Numenius, Περὶ ῥητορικῶν ἀφορμῶν	
2:9	284 n. 86, 322 n. 45		
2:17	161 n. 49	*RG* 3:4	100–101
4:15	271	*RG* 4:9	102 n. 20
2 Timothy		Anaximenes, *Rhetorica ad Alexandrum*	
3:6	307 n. 163	3.7–8	149, 166 n. 63
		21	171 n. 6
Philemon			
1, 9, 23	322 n. 44	Anonymous Seguerianus, *Ars rhetorica*	
		4.230	137 n. 40

Apsines, *Ars rhetorica*
5.5   137
10.34   119, 213 n. 35

Apthonius, *Progymnasmata*
10   149 n. 1, 158 n. 37, 162 n. 53, **164**
11   144 n. 14

Aristides, *Orationes*
1.311   291 n. 110
2.189   290 n. 105
2.195   290 n. 105
11.17   291 n. 110

Ps.-Aristides, *Ars rhetorica*
1.2.1–2   173 n. 14
1.12.2.7   119 n. 55

Aristotle, *Ethica nichomachea*
4.3.19   220 n. 60
4.3.28   178
4.7.15–16   178

Aristotle, *Fragmenta varia*
669   266

Aristotle, *Metaphysica*
1.981a–b   188 n. 15
13.1086b   318

Aristotle, *Poetica*
1451b   253 n. 40

Aristotle, *Politica*
5.1313a   253 n. 40

Aristotle, *Rhetorica*
1.1–2   **188**
1.1.4–6   190–91 n. 21
1.6.29   74 n. 47
1.7.32   101
1.9.15   137 n. 41
1.9.38   149, 158 n. 37, 166 n. 63
1.9.40   137 n. 40
2.2.24–25   178

2.10.1–2   299
2.10.5–7   299
2.22.3   190–91 n. 21
3.14.7   208
3.14.7–8   190–91 n. 21
3.17.16   101–2, 117, 297
3.18.7   178

Athenaeus, *Deipnosophistae*
4.45   162, 167

Cassius Dio, *Historiae romanae*
69.3.4–69.4.1   152 n. 13

Celsus, Ἀληθὴς λόγος
1.27   263 n. 25
3.55   17
6.2   263 n. 25

Chariton, *De Chaerea et Callirhoe*
3.8.9   136
5.5.2   136

Cicero, *In Catalinam*
3:1–2   209

Cicero, *De domo suo*
92–95   105

Cicero, *Epistulae ad Atticum*
1.16.8   117 n. 49, **221**

Cicero, *De haruspicum responso*
17   105, 106

Cicero, *De inventione rhetorica*
1.2.2–3   189
1.16.22   102

Cicero, *Orationes philippicae*
14.13   106

Cicero, *De oratore*
1.4.14   189
1.23.107–109   **189**

1.32.146	190	Demosthenes, *Epistulae*	
2.61	302	2.1	209
2.189–196	220 n. 59	2.3	209
3.20.74–75	189	2.4	297 n. 129
3.197	190	2.11	209
3.215–219	219	2.24	297 n. 129
		3.5	209
Cicero, *Tusculanae disputationes*		3.28–31	209 n. 28
4.43–55	220 n. 59		
		Demosthenes, *Exordia*	
Ps.-Demetrius, *De elocutione*		1.1	208
12	269	4, 5	208 n. 24
15	259	48.1	208
27–29	266	49	208 n. 24
29	266		
128	260	Demosthenes, *Philippica i*	
154	266	1	208
190–235	261		
193	260	Dio Chrysostom, *Ad Alexandrinos*	
211	266	1–2	208 n. 24
223–235	**260–61**		
229	259	Dio Chrysostom, *De compotatione*	
299–301	269	3	153 n. 21
300	275–76		
303	269, 275–76	Dio Chrysostom, *De concordia cum Apamensibus*	
		32	153 n. 21
Ps.-Demetrius, Τύποι ἐπιστολικοί			
pr.	85, 91	Dio Chrysostom, *In contione*	
1	86 n. 15	16	302
4, 6, 7–9	83		
11	86 n. 15	Dio Chrysostom, *De dei cognitione*	
12	83	5	153 n. 21, 154 n. 23
17	83, 84 n. 8		
18	83, **84–88**, 211 n. 31	Dio Chrysostom, *Dialexis*	
20	83 n. 5	1–2	287
		3	**286–87**, **289**
Demosthenes, *In Aristocratem*		4	287
65	253 n. 40		
		Dio Chrysostom, *Nestor*	103
Demosthenes, *De corona*	209–10	3, 4–8, 9	109
3	106, 221–22 n. 62, 295		
4	105, 208, 219, **220–21**	Dio Chrysostom, *Ad Nicomedienses*	
10	108	29	290–91
71	137		

Dio Chrysostom, *Politica*
2   105
12   108

Dio Chrysostom, *De regno*
12   291 n. 110

Dio Chrysostom, *De regno iv*
96   153 n. 21

Dio Chrysostom, *De virtute*
(*Or.* 8)   **152–53**
6, 9   153
10   153–54
15–16   127 n. 14
33   154 n. 23
36   153

Dio Chrysostom, *De virtute* (*Or.* 69)
7   302

Diodorus Siculus, *Bibliotheca historica*
12.12.1   302
12.14.2   302
14.24.7   265 n. 33
15.66–72   107 n. 30
16.70.2   302
17.101.4–5   302

Diogenes Laertius, *Vitae philosophorum*
6.47   153
6.57   153

Dionysius of Halicarnassus, *De antiquis oratoribus*
1   302 n. 145

Dionysius of Halicarnassus, *Antiquitates romanae*
4.62.2   302
5.5.3   291
5.62.3   265 n. 33
5.67.1–2   302 n. 145
14.9.4   302

Dionysius of Halicarnassus, *De compositione verborum*
21   279 n. 69
22   259 n. 9, 269, 279
26   293 n. 116

Dionysius of Halicarnassus, *De Demosthene*
5   269 n. 56
15   290
17   158 n. 37, 166 n. 64
21   158 n. 37
56   291 n. 110

Dionysius of Halicarnassus, *Epistula ad Pompeium Geminum*
1.11   158 n. 37

Dionysus of Halicarnassus, *De Isocrate*
17   166 n. 63

Dionysus of Halicarnassus, *De Lysia*
3   290

Dionysius of Halicarnassus, *De Thucydide*
23   279
31   279

Dionysius of Halicarnassus, *De Thucydidis idiomatibus*
14   158 n. 37

Ps.-Dionysius, *Ars rhetorica*
5.6   102

Epictetus, *Diatribai*
1.1.12   128
1.1.14   128
1.1.22–24   127 n. 14
1.2.36–37   128
1.3.7   129
1.6.14   129
1.11.33   124, 127 n. 14
1.18.21–22   **125–26**, 127 n. 14

1.24.1	127	Ps.-Herodian, *De figuris*	
2.1.35	127 n. 14	33	118–19, 213 n. 35
2.10.17	127 n. 12	34	218
2.12.2–4	290		
2.12.11–13	290	Herodotus, *Historiae*	
2.16.42	127 n. 14	1.32.1	290 n. 107
2.19.18	127 n. 14	1.59.1	290 n. 105
2.19.24	127	7.158	265 n. 33
3.1	**154–55**		
3.1.1	154	Hesiod, *Opera et dies*	
3.1.34	154–55	25–26	299
3.9.12–14	139	210	302
3.15.13	291 n. 110		
3.16	291 n. 110	Homer, *Ilias*	
3.19	291 n. 110	1.260–268	109
		1.273–274	109
Favorinus, *Corinthiaca*	152 n. 13	10.227–232	130
25–27	151–52 n. 10	11.655–762	103
		18.105–106	297
Galen, *Quod qualitates incorporeae sint*			
19.479	302 n. 145	Homer, scholiast T	
		Il. 18:105–106	297
Hermogenes, Περὶ ἰδεῶν λόγου			
1.1	173 n. 14	Horace, *Satirae*	
2.4	119, 213 n. 35	2.7.83–87	127 n. 14
2.8	173 n. 14		
		Isaeus, *De Philoctemone*	
Ps.-Hermogenes, *De Inventione*		17	220
3.5	123–4 n. 2		
3.9	158 n. 37	Isocrates, *Antidosis*	
4.12	119	1–8	105
4.14	158 n. 37	2–3	209 n. 25
		8	297
Ps.-Hermogenes, Περὶ μεθόδου δεινότητος		201–204	291
25	101		
		Isocrates, *Evagoras*	
Ps.-Hermogenes, *Progymnasmata*		34–37	166 n. 64
7	158 n. 37, 162 n. 53		
8	149 n. 1, 158 n. 37, 162 n. 53	Isocrates, *De pace*	
9	144 n. 14	41–44	166 n. 64
24–25	49 n. 135		
		Isocrates, *In sophistas*	
Herodian, *Ab excessu divi Marci*		14	291
4.10.2	290 n. 107	14–15	189

Isocrates, *Trapeziticus*
1   106

Julius Victor, *Ars rhetorica*
27.19–21   261

Libanius, *Progymnasmata*
10   149 n. 1

Ps.-Libanius, Ἐπιστολιμαῖοι χαρακτῆρες
7, 9, 13, 24   83 n. 5
48   261
50   260
54, 56, 60   83 n. 5
64   83 n. 5, 84 n. 8
69, 71   83 n. 5
92   **83–84 n. 5**

Livy, *Ab urbe condita libri*
2.23.4–7   306 n. 159
45.39.16   306 n. 158

[Longinus, *De sublimitate*]
8.4   275
11.2   137
12.1–2   137
18.2   190
22.1   190, 219
22.1–4   275–76
23.1–4   137

Lucian, *Bis accusatus*
33   287

Lucian, *De domo*
2   290
3   290 n. 107

Lucian, *Adversus indoctum*
29   290

Lucian, *Lexiphanes*
24   290

Lucian, *De morte Peregrini*   154
1   300
2   **300–301**
4   300
7   301
8   **300–301**
20, 22   300
25, 34   301
38, 42, 43   300

Lucian, *Nigrinus*
24   290

Lucian, *Rhetorum praeceptor*
1–2   154 n. 23

Lucian, *Somnium*
1   282
8   258
9–13   280 n. 73
13   282

Lucian, *Symposium*
35   290

Lucian, *Toxaris*
54   265 n. 33

Lucian, *Vitarum auctio*   154
10.3   290 n. 105
27   290

Lysias, *In Alcibiadem i*
10   265 n. 33

Lysias, *Pro Callia*
5.3   290 n. 105

Menander Rhetor, Περὶ ἐπιδεικτικῶν
RG 3:372   158 n. 37
RG 3:377   158 n. 37
RG 3:380   158 n. 37
RG 3:381   158 n. 37
RG 3:383   158 n. 37
RG 3:386   158 n. 37

INDEX OF ANCIENT TEXTS

RG 3:397	307 n. 163	Plato, *Gorgias*	
RG 3:402	158 n. 37	465A	188
RG 3:417	158 n. 37		
RG 3:425	158 n. 37	Plato, *Menexenus*	
RG 3:427	158 n. 37	245D	128 n. 15

Nepos, *Epaminondas*
7–8   107 n. 30
8.2–5   107

Nicolaus, *Progymnasmata*
8   162 n. 53
9   149 n. 1, 158 n. 37, 162 n. 53
10   91 n. 32, 144 n. 14

Philodemus, *De bono rege secundum Homerum*
col. 16   102, 103 n. 22
col. 18   102, 103 n. 22
col. 20   102, 103 n. 22
col. 21   102
col. 22   102–3
fr. 9   103, 109–10

Philodemus, *Volumina rhetorica*
2.28   190

Philostratus, *Vita Apollonii*
3.43   290 n. 108

Philostratus, *Vitae sophistarum*
1.7–8   152
1.8   152 n. 13

Pindar, *Pythionikai*
1.81–85   297 n. 129

Plato, *Charmides*
157E   253 n. 40

Plato, *Epistulae*
3   86 n. 16
7   86 n. 16

Plato, *Phaedo*
95B   297

Plato, *Phaedrus*
245C   137 n. 41
271D–272B   217

Plato, *Philebus*
16C   253 n. 40

Plato, *Protagoras*
345A   292 n. 115

Plato, *Respublica*
361E–362A   127 n. 14

Plato, *Symposium*
185B   290 n. 105
212C–222B   142 n. 8

Pliny, *Epistulae*
1.8.5–6   297 n. 129
9.23.5–6   117, 297 n. 129

Plutarch, *Quomodo adolescens poetas audire debeat*
29B   102 n. 20

Plutarch, *An seni respublica gerenda sit*
783C–E   99 n. 10

Plutarch, *Comparatio Demetrii et Antonii*
1.1–2   163 n. 55

Plutarch, *Comparatio Demosthenis et Ciceronis*
1.3–4   **165**
2.1   102 n. 20
2.3   100

Plutarch, *Comparatio Niciae et Crassi*
  1.4   164–65

Plutarch, *De defectu oraculorum*
  419B   302

Plutarch, *Demosthenes*
  2   116 n. 46

Plutarch, *De garrulitate*
  510A   302

Plutarch, *De gloria Atheniensium*
  251A   138

Plutarch, *De invidia et odio*
  537B   295 n. 120
  537E   301
  538A–B   299–300
  538E   300

Plutarch, *De laude ipsius*
  539A   295
  539B   295
  539A–B   104
  539C   102 n. 20, 295
  539D   210, 215, 295
  539D–E   215
  539E   102 n. 20, 103
  539E–F   109
  539F   99, 215
  540A   215, 295
  540A–C   **110–12**, 295
  540B   102 n. 20
  540C   105, 112, 208
  540D   **106–7**, 108, 209, 296
  540E   107
  540F   102 n. 20, 103
  541A   103, 108, 296, **307–8**
  541A–C   108–9
  541B   108, 295
  541B–D   103
  541D   295
  542B–C   296
  542C   295

  542C–D   114
  542E   103, 114
  542F   295, 296
  543D   296
  543E   295
  543F   295
  543F–544B   103
  544B   109 n. 33, 296
  544B–C   306 n. 154
  544C   102 n. 20
  544D   103, 109
  544D–F   110
  545D   112
  545D–E   210
  545E   112
  546B   100
  546C   102 n. 20
  546C–D   **294–97**
  546D   102 n. 20
  546E   102 n. 20
  547A   295
  547B   295 n. 122
  547C   102 n. 20
  547D   295
  547F   109, 208, 215

Plutarch, *Lycurgus*
  15.8   302 n. 145

Plutarch, *Marcius Coriolanus*
  15.5   307 n. 163

Plutarch, *Pelopidas*
  25.1–2   107 n. 30

Plutarch, *Praecepta gerendae rei publicae*
  798A–825F   99 n. 10
  809C   295
  815A–B   300
  819F–820B   295
  825E–F   300

Plutarch, *De Pythiae oraculis*
  408D   154 n. 23

INDEX OF ANCIENT TEXTS 387

Plutarch, *Quaestionum convivialum libri IX*		2.12.6	220
		2.12.8	219–20
5.3	154	2.12.9–10	220
8.4	154	2.15	116
		2.15.7	306 n. 158
Plutarch, *De recta ratione audiendi*		2.15.34	118
41C	102 n. 20	2.17.6	189
44A	102 n. 20	2.17.12	**188–89**
		3.2.3	**188**
Plutarch, *Romulus*		3.5.5–18	123–4 n. 2
12.5	137 n. 41	4.1.6	208
		4.1.7–12	208
Plutarch, *Stoicos absurdiora poetis dicere*		6.2.26–27	220 n. 59
1057E	**126–27**, 133	6.3.35	220 n. 60
		7.9.9–12	275 n. 59
Plutarch, *Theseus*		8.3.41	264
24.2	290 n. 107	8.3.86	189 n. 17, 190
		8.4	237
Plutarch, *De tuenda sanitate praecepta*		8.4.26–27	137
131A	154 n. 23	8.6.4	189 n. 17
		8.6.51	189 n. 17
Plutarch, *De virtute morali*	295 n. 120	8.6.54	171 n. 6
		8.6.75	189 n. 17
Ps.-Plutarch, *Aquane an ignis utilior*	276, 310 n. 3	9.2.29–37	144 n. 14
		9.2.30	144
2–6	**165–66**	9.3.70	266
		9.4.19	259, 260
Polybius, *Historiae*		10.1.105–114	116 n. 48
1.69.11	291 n. 113	10.1.123	116 n. 48
12.9.1	158	11.1.1	116
14.3.7	158–59	11.1.8–9	116
33.20	302	11.1.11	116, 118
		11.1.14	116
Quintilian, *Institutio oratoria*		11.1.15	116
1 pr. 9–10	155	11.1.15–26	**116–18**
1 pr. 10–18	118	11.1.16	110
1 pr. 15	155	11.1.16–17	**298–300**
1.2.18	155	11.1.17	107 n. 31, 117, 299
1.5.1	257–58	11.1.17–18	296 n. 127
1.10.1	92 n. 39	11.1.17–26	117
2.10.12	219	11.1.18	105, 117
2.10.13	219	11.1.21	117, 178, 287
2.11.7	189, 269	11.1.22	208
2.12	258	11.1.22–23	105
2.12.4	219	11.1.23	117

Quintilian, *Institutio oratoria (cont.)*		1.155	290 n. 108
11.1.29	117	2.16–17	189
11.1.30	117		
11.1.57	117	Strabo, *Geographica*	
11.1.91	117	14.5.13	46–47
11.3.184	220 n. 60		
12 pr. 2–4	118	Thucydides, *Historiae*	
12.1.1	118	2.35.2	297 n. 129
12.1.16–21	116 n. 48	6.86.4	265 n. 33
12.2.6–9	118		
		Tiberius, *De figuris Demosthenicis*	
Res gestae divi Augusti	**304–5**	8	119, 213 n. 35
4	305 n. 151		
		Vita Aesopi	
Rhetorica ad Herennium		99	323
1.5.8	102		
1.8	208	Xenophon, *Agesilaus*	
4.32	266	6.2	306 n. 158
4.52.65	144 n. 14	9:1–2	**166–67**
Sallust, *Bellum jugurthinum*		Xenophon, *Anabasis*	
85.29–30	306 n. 158	1.3.11	291 n. 113
Seneca, *Apocolocyntosis divi Claudii*	142 n. 8	Xenophon, *De equitum magistro*	
		8.1	291 n. 113
Seneca, *De clementia*			
1.10.3	107 n. 31	Xenophon, *Memorabilia*	
		2.1.31	210
Seneca, *De constantia sapientis*			
6.3	127 nn. 12 and 14	Xenophon, *Oeconomicus*	
8.3	127 n. 14	3.9	292 n. 115
13.5	107 n. 31		
14.3	107 n. 31	Xenophon of Ephesus, *Ephesiaca*	
		5.1.4–5.1.11	41
Seneca, *Epistulae morales*			
71.25–29	127 n. 14	**INSCRIPTIONS AND PAPYRI**	
82.10–14	127 n. 14		
		BGU III 909.18	265
Seneca, *De ira*		P.Bon. 5	83 n. 5, 90
3.25.3	107 n. 31	P.Bon. 5 col 11.6–27	83 n. 5
		P.Hamb. I 26.11	291 n. 113
		P.Hib. I 30.12	291 n. 113
Sextus Empiricus, *Adversus mathematicos*		P.Hib. I 89.2	291 n. 113
1.63–64	**292–93**	P.Lips. I 39.8	265 n. 35
1.234–235	**293**	P.Oxy. XVIII 2190	**159 n. 43**

INDEX OF ANCIENT TEXTS

P.Oxy. XLVIII 3396 — 159–60 n. 44
P.Paris 63.1–7 — 90 n. 28

Rabbinic Works

m. 'Abot
2:2 — 19

m. Pesaḥim
10:5 — 136

m. Taʻanit
3:5 — 136

t. Qiddušin
1:11 — 19

Early Christian Literature

Ambrose, *Epistulae*
8.1 — 263 n. 25

Ambrosiaster, *Commentaria in xiii epistolas beati Pauli*
199 — 262–63 n. 22
200 — 97

Arnobius, *Disputationum adversus gentes*
1.58–59 — 263 n. 25

Athanasius, *Contra gentes*
16.5 — 307 n. 163

Athanasius, *Vita Antonii*
39 — 222 n. 62

Augustine, *Confessionum libri XIII*
3.5.9 — 262–63 n. 22

Augustine, *De doctrina christiana*
4.3.4–5 — **190**
4.4.6 — 262
4.7 — 262
4.7.11 — 55 n. 159, 262
4.7.14 — 263 n. 25
4.7.16–21 — 262 n. 20

Augustine, *Epistulae*
137.5.18 — 262–63 n. 22

Clement of Alexandria, *Paedagogus*
3.3.19.2 — 307

Didymus, *Fragmenta in Epistulam ii ad Corinthios*
4.7 — 290 n. 109

Gregory of Nazianzus, *Epistulae*
51.4 — 260, 261, 290 n. 108
51.5–7 — 260

Gregory of Nyssa, *Epistulae*
17.11 — 17 n. 1

Gregory of Nyssa, *Contra Eunomium*
3.1.106 — 262 n. 18

Jerome, *Commentariorum in Epistulam ad Ephesios libri III*
2.586 — 262 n. 18
2.587–588 — 262–63 n. 22

John Chrysostom, *Commentarius in Isaiam*
3.10 — 262 n. 20
5.5 — 262 n. 20

John Chrysostom, *Homiliae in epistulam i ad Corinthios*
3.4 — 17 n. 1, 55 n. 159, 261–62 n. 18, 262–63 n. 22, 263
14.2 — 280–81 n. 75

John Chrysostom, *Homiliae in epistulam ii ad Corinthios*
21.1 — 227 nn. 77–78, 266–67, 280 n. 73, 281 n. 76
22.1 — 269 n. 58
22.2 — 268 nn. 51 and 53
23.1 — 119 n. 52, 223

John Chrysostom, *Homiliae in epistulam ii ad Corinthios* (cont.)
24.1 119 n. 52, 262–63 n. 22
24.2 267 n. 44
25.1 119 n. 52
28.2 281–82 n. 78

John Chrysostom, *In illud: Utinam sustineretis modicum*
4 108, 119 n. 52, 212–13

[John Chrysostom, *In illud: Sufficit tibi gratia mea*]
1 17 n. 1

John Chrysostom, *Homiliae in epistulam ad Hebraeos*
1.2 17 n. 1

John Chrysostom, *Homiliae in epistulam ad Romanos*
pr. 261 n. 18

John Chrysostom, *Homiliae in epistulam ii ad Timotheum*
4.3 17
4.4 17 n. 1
5.2 17 n. 1

John Chrysostom, *Homiliae in Genesim*
28.3 290 n. 109

John Chrysostom, *Homiliae in Matthaeum*
22.4 262 n. 20

John Chrysostom, *De laudibus sancti Pauli apostoli*
4.10 17 n. 1, 261
4.13 17, 55 n. 159, 262–63 n. 22
5.12 108, 114 n. 44, 119 n. 52, 212–13
5.15 114 n. 44

John Chrysostom, *Ad populum Antiochenum de statuis*
5.6 17 n. 1

John Chrysostom, *De sacerdotio*
4.6 262 n. 18

John Chrysostom, *Ad eos qui scandalizati sunt*
20.10 17 n. 1

Lactantius, *Divinarum institutionum libri VII*
5.2.17 263 n. 25

Origen, *Contra Celsum*
1.62 262 n. 22
3.39 262 n. 22
6.1–2 262 n. 22
6.2 139
7.37 262 n. 22
7.41 262 n. 22, 290 n. 108

Origen, *Commentarii in evangelium Joannis*
4.2 55 n. 159, 262 n. 22

Origen, *Commentarii in Romanos*
pr. 1 264
1.9.6 262 n. 21
3.1.2–3 262 n. 21
6.3.2 262 nn. 18 and 21

Origen, *Fragmenta ex commentariis in epistulam ad Ephesios*
13 262 n. 18

Origen, *Fragmenta ex homiliis in epistulam ad Hebraeos* 262

Theodoret, *Graecarum affectionum curatio*
5.67 17 n. 1

Theodoret, *Interpretatio in xiv epistulas sancti Pauli*
PG 82:437   271

Theophilus, *Ad Autolycum*
2.35   290 n. 109

Texts from Nag Hammadi

VI,4 *Concept of our Great Power*
39.21–33   136

Index of Modern Authors

Abbott, Don Paul 193 n. 26
Adam, Karl 18 n. 4
Adams, Edward 1 n. 3
Aejmelaeus, Lars 283 n. 82
Alexandre, Manuel 138 n. 43
Allen, Walter 116 n. 48
Alles, Gregory D. 9 n. 22, 10 n. 24
Ameling, Walter 152 n. 12
Anderson, Graham 152 n. 14
Anderson, Janice Capel 3 n. 10, 306 n. 155, 307 nn. 164–65
Anderson, R. Dean 53–54, 61–62 n. 17, 155 n. 15, 266
Andrews, Scott B. 305–306, 61 n. 16
Ankersmit, F. R. 171 n. 9
Arnim, H. F. A. 153 n. 17
Arnott, W. Geoffrey 259 n. 9
Ascough, Richard S. 1 n. 3
Ashton, John 3 n. 10, 9 n. 22, 156 n. 31
Aune, David E. 32, 86 n. 16, 144 n. 12
Austin, J. L. 244 n. 4
Austin, John N. H. 130
Bachmann, Philip 265 n. 35
Ball, Charles R. 22 n. 20
Barclay, John M. G. 138 n. 43
Barnett, Paul 143 n. 9, 265 n. 36, 303 n. 147,
Barrett, C. K. 264, 268, 269 n. 58, 271, 273–75, 281 n. 78, 285 n. 88, 286 n. 90, 288 nn. 97 and 100, 289 n. 102, 316
Bartchy, S. Scott 113 n. 43
Basso, Keith H. 90 n. 30

Baur, Ferdinand Christian 2–3, 97, 98 n. 3, 120 n. 56, 257 n. 1, 277, 321
Becker, Jürgen 26 n. 39
Beet, Joseph Agar 104 n. 27, 120 n. 56, 216 n. 49, 257 n. 1
Bell, Robert A. 178 n. 33
Bengel, Johann Albrecht 266 n. 38
Betz, Hans Dieter 31–32, 50, 57–59, 62 n. 18, 86 n. 16, 99, 100, 103 n. 24, 105 n. 28, 108 n. 32, 109 n. 34, 110 n. 36, 113 n. 42, 114, 115, 121, 124, 142 n. 8, 150, 223, 227 nn. 76 and 78–79, 239, 252 n. 38, 257 n. 3, 276–77, 278 n. 67, 280 n. 73, 286 n. 90, 293 n. 118, 296 n. 126, 310
Blank, D. L. 293 n. 117
Blank, Les 225 n. 70
Blanton, Thomas R. 321 n. 41
Blanton, Ward 318 n. 30
Blass, Friedrich 258 n. 7, 264
Bloch, Maurice 51 n. 143, 250
Bloomer, W. Martin 96 n. 56
Bogan, James 225 n. 70
Böhlig, Hans 22
Booth, Alan D. 92 n. 38, 94 n. 49
Booth, Wayne C. 171 n. 6, 172, 174 n. 17, 175 n. 19
Borg, Marcus J. 36 n. 76
Bornkamm, Günther 63 n. 20, 64 n. 24
Bourdieu, Pierre 1, 12, 103, 120 n. 57, 191, 245, 250–51, 293 n. 118, 301, 312–13, 314 n. 17, 315
Bowersock, G. W. 151 n. 10, 152 n. 14, 153 n. 20

INDEX OF MODERN AUTHORS

Bowie, Ewen 151 n. 10
Brawley, Robert L. 20 n. 14
Briggs, Charles L. 247–50
Brooks, Joanna 316 n. 22
Brown, Penelope 176 n. 24, 214–16
Brown, Peter 263
Bruce, F. F. 21 n. 17, 252 n. 37, 257 n. 1
Bultmann, Rudolf 42, 43 n. 112, 64 n. 24, 98 n. 5, 124–27, 143 n. 10, 156 n. 31, 157 n. 34, 227 n. 78, 264 n. 28, 265 n. 36, 270–75, 282 n. 78, 285 n. 87–88, 288
Bürgi, E. 101 n. 15
Buswell, Lois E. 193 n. 27
Cairns, D. L. 299 n. 136
Calvin, John 26 n. 39, 104, 129 n. 56, 216 n. 49, 223, 257 nn. 1–2, 258, 268 n. 48, 276 n. 60, 280 n. 73
Cameron, Ron 322 n. 42
Camp, Charles 193 n. 27
Campbell, Douglas A. 33 n. 66
Chadwick, H. 49, 50 n. 137
Chatman, Seymour 162 n. 52
Chen, Rong 215 n. 43
Chilton, Bruce 20 n. 12, 22 n. 20
Church, F. Forrester 32
Classen, Carl Joachim 4 n. 15, 27, 33 n. 66, 34 n. 68, 54 nn. 153–54, 57, 188 n. 14, 286 n. 90
Clements, William M. 193 n. 27, 194 n. 29, 195, 196 nn. 39–40, 203 n. 5, 205 n. 14
Clift, Rebecca 176 n. 25
Clines, David J. A. 3 n. 10
Conley, Thomas 138 n. 43
Connolly, Joy 95 n. 56
Conybeare, W. J. 21, 22 nn. 18 and 20, 252
Cosby, Michael 318, 319 n. 31
Cribiore, Raffaella 46 n. 123, 90 n. 27, 91 n. 32, 93 nn. 42–43, 94
Crook, Zeba 129 n. 57, 301

Crossan, John Dominic 36 n. 76
D'Ambra, Eve 155 n. 27
Dahl, Nils A. 26 n. 39
Danker, Frederick W. 61 n. 16
Deissmann, Adolf 1–2, 3 n. 10, 4, 9, 18, 257 n. 1, 261 n. 16, 318, 320
Delia, Jesse G. 51
Denney, James 104 n. 27, 161 n. 49
Dennis, Matthew 229 n. 83
Densmore, Christopher 202 n. 1, 251 n. 35
Dewey, Arthur J. 303 n. 146
Dews, Shelly 176 n. 24
Dibelius, Martin 19 n. 5
DiCicco, Mario M. 36 n. 76, 100 n. 13, 103 n. 24, 105 n. 28, 286 n. 90
Dilts, Mervin R. 101 n. 15
Dodd, C. H. 97 n. 1
Dorsett, Lyle W. 236 n. 112, 237 nn. 113 and 115
Douglas, Mary 1, 191 n. 23
Downing, F. Gerald 53 n. 150
Dubay, Ronald 20 n. 12
Duff, Timothy E. 99 n. 10, 162 n. 53, 295 n. 120
Duling, Dennis C. 100 n. 13, 103 n. 24, 150 n. 7, 175 n. 20
Dunn, James D. G. 252 n. 38
Edwards, Mark J. 5, 190
Edwards, Mark W. 130 n. 24
Einhorn, Lois J. 210 n. 30
Ek, Richard A. 195 n. 38
El-Alayli, Amani 179 n. 34
Ellis, William T. 237 n. 118
Ericson, Jon M. 210 n. 29
Eriksson, Anders 51 n. 143
Exler, Francis Xavier J. 88 n. 19
Fairchild, Hoxie Neale 195 n. 35
Fairweather, Janet 53 n. 163, 258 n. 7, 262 n. 19
Fantham, Elaine 189 n. 17
Farnell, Brenda 314 n. 17
Farrar, Frederic W. 19, 22, 257 n. 1

Fee, Gordon D. 50
Fenton, William N. 231 n. 92, 229 n. 85
Fields, Dana 99 n. 10, 295 n. 122, 296, 300 n. 138
Firth, Raymond 51 n. 143
Fish, Jeffrey 103 n. 22, 297 n. 128
Fitzgerald, John T. 61 n. 16, 82–84, 89–90, 123 n. 2, 124 nn. 2–3, 125, 126, 129, 130 n. 23, 133 n. 30, 134 n. 31, 136 nn. 33 and 37, 137, 143 n. 9, 161 n. 48, 172 n. 12, 305–7
Foakes-Jackson, F. J. 19 nn. 4–5, 20 nn. 10–11 and 13
Focke, Friedrich 164 n. 57
Foley, John Miles 233 n. 103
Forbes, Christopher 31 n. 55, 34–36, 38, 52, 60, 100 n. 13, 101, 109 n. 35, 150, 157, 159 n. 43, 160–63, 167, 170 n. 3, 173 n. 14, 175 nn. 18 and 20, 176 n. 23, 286 n. 90
Ford, David F. 65 n. 25
Foster, Michael K. 210 n. 30, 251 n. 35
Francis, James A. 300 n. 140
Frazier, F. 138 n. 42
Fridrichsen, Anton 59 n. 9, 106, 126 n. 10, 304–5
Friesen, Steven J. 21 n. 16, 52 n. 146, 65 n. 24, 95, 111 n. 38, 152 n. 13
Furnish, Victor Paul 73 n. 46, 103 n. 24, 105 n. 28, 115 n. 45, 119 n. 53, 143 n. 9, 145 n. 16, 156 n. 32, 264 n. 28, 265 n. 36, 272–75, 281 n. 78, 285 n. 88, 288 n. 100
Gaertner, Jan Felix 130 n. 24
Ganter, Granville 49 n. 134, 195 n. 38, 202 n. 2, 203, 204 nn. 8–11, 205 nn. 12 and 15, 206 nn. 17–19, 207 nn. 21–23, 209 n. 26, 217 n. 53, 228, 229 nn. 83–87, 230–231, 234 nn. 106–107
Garland, David E. 143 nn. 9–10, 169 n. 1, 303 n. 147

Garrett, Mary M. 197 nn. 45–46
Georgi, Dieter 64 n. 24, 66 n. 29, 70 n. 40, 113 n. 41, 265 n. 36
Gerber, Albrecht 318 n. 28
Ghita, Andreea 178 n. 32
Gibson, Roy K. 117 n. 49, 296 n. 127
Given, Mark D. 29 n. 46
Glancy, Jennifer A. 3 n. 10, 109 n. 33, 284 n. 86, 306, 322
Gleason, Maud W. 96 n. 56, 155 n. 27, 282
Gnilka, Joachim 20 n. 9, 26 n. 39, 27 n. 40, 36 n. 46, 157 n. 34
Goffman, Erving 176, 214, 215 nn. 41–42
Gooch, P. W. 178 n. 31
Goodspeed, Edgar J. 18 n. 4, 19 n. 5, 22 n. 20, 59
Gossen, Gary 235
Gottschalk, H. B. 44, 45 n. 120
Grant, Robert M. 23 n. 23
Green, Lucy 247 n. 16
Gross, Alan G. 188 n. 15
Guthrie, Thomas H. 194 nn. 32–32, 195 n. 36
Haacker, Klaus 23 n. 22, 27 n. 40
Haenchen, Ernst 21 n. 15
Hafemann, Scott J. 61 n. 16, 97 n. 2, 156 n. 33, 157 n. 34, 169 n. 2
Haines, Elijah M. 193 n. 27
Hajdú, Kerstin 119 n. 54
Hall, Robert G. 138 n. 43
Hanges, James C. 198 n. 48, 315 n. 20
Hanks, William F. 313 n. 13, 314 n. 17
Harrill, J. Albert 282–84, 307 nn. 164–65
Harris, Murray J. 33 n. 66, 110 n. 36, 143, 145 n. 16, 172 n. 10, 175 n. 18, 222 nn. 65 and 67, 265, 267 n. 47, 268, 269 n. 58, 270–75, 279 nn. 66 and 70, 280 n. 73, 281 n. 78, 285 n. 88, 287 n. 92, 288 nn. 95–97, 289 nn. 102–3, 303 n. 147

Harris, William V. 94
Haskell, Robert E. 198 n. 48
Hauptman, Laurence M. 206 nn. 16 and 20
Hausrath, Adolf 19 n. 5, 62–63, 66
Heath, Malcolm 91, 173 n. 14, 262 n. 19
Heath, Shirley Brice 94 n. 48
Heckel, Ulrich 141 n. 3, 154 n. 34, 156 n. 34, 297–98
Heinrici, C. F. Georg 23–25, 26 n. 38, 59 n. 9, 77 n. 53, 106 n. 29, 108 n. 32, 119, 140, 257 n. 1, 227 n. 77
Hellholm, David 36 n. 46, 45, 51
Hengel, Martin 20 nn. 9 and 12, 22 n. 18, 23 n. 22, 24 n. 30, 26 n. 39, 27 n. 43, 33 n. 66, 35 n. 73, 252 n. 37
Héring, Jean 265 n. 31, 271–73
Hester Amador, J. David 65–66
Hewitt, John P. 177, 204
Hezser, Catherine 20 n. 8, 96 n. 56
Hochbruck, Walter 195 n. 38
Hock, Ronald F. 3 n. 10, 19, 20 n. 8, 26 n. 39, 27 n. 40, 29, 39–43, 47, 52–53, 74 n. 48, 93 nn. 40–41, 144 n. 13, 145 n. 15, 252 n. 37, 284 n. 86, 322 n. 45
Hodge, Charles 104 n. 27, 120
Hodgson, Robert 127 n. 12, 130 n. 27, 133 n. 30, 136
Hoffman, Yair 131 n. 27, 233
Holland, Glenn S. 61 n. 16, 143 nn. 9–10, 145 n. 16, 146–47, 150 n. 7, 169 n. 1, 170–75, 178 n. 32
Holloway, Paul A. 51 n. 141
Holmes, Janet 214 n. 38
Holtzmann, H. J. 19 n. 5
Holzner, Josef 19 n. 4, 20 n. 10, 22 n. 20
Hooker, Morna D. 26 n. 39, 27 n. 40, 36 n. 76, 252 n. 37
Hopper, Robert 178 n. 33
Horrell, David G. 1 n. 3, 10 n. 23, 111

Horsfall, Nicholas 53 n. 150, 93 n. 42, 94 n. 47
Howson, J. S. 21, 22 nn. 18 and 20, 252
Hubbard, J. Niles 196 n. 40, 203
Hughes, Philip E. 281 n. 78
Hum, Sue 197 n. 45
Hurd, John Coolidge 49 n. 136, 50 n. 138, 75 nn. 49 and 51
Hutchinson, G. O. 159 n. 44
Hymes, Dell 6 nn. 18–19, 243 n. 1, 244, 312–14
Jakobson, Roman 231 n. 95
Jefferson, Thomas 194 n. 30, 204
Jocelyn, H. D. 44 n. 118
Johanson, Bruce C. 36 n. 76
Johnson, Lee A. 144 nn. 4–5, 172
Johnson, Luke Timothy 98 n. 5
Johnson, William A. 92 n. 36
Johnstone, Barbara 314 n. 16
Jones, C. P. 101 n. 16, 116 n. 46
Jones, Ivor H. 66–67
Jones, Louis Thomas 193 n. 27
Jowett, Benjamin 257, 262, 277
Judge, E. A. 28–31, 34, 60, 97 n. 1, 113 n. 42, 119, 150, 171 n. 10, 261 n. 16, 286–87
Jülicher, Adolf 18 n. 4, 19 n. 5
Karakasis, Evangelos 139 n. 45, 276 n. 61
Käsemann, Ernst 169 n. 2
Kaster, Robert A. 94 nn. 49–51, 96 n. 56, 116 n. 48
Katsouris, A. G. 259 n. 9, 276 n. 61
Kaufer, David S. 174 n. 17
Kaplan, Joan 176 n. 24
Keener, Craig S. 111 n. 37, 144 n. 12, 145 n. 16, 150 n. 7, 176 n. 22, 286 n. 90, 289 n. 103
Kennedy, George A. 6, 11, 33–34, 51 n. 143, 54 n. 155, 63, 66, 88 n. 18, 91 n. 32, 116 n. 46, 173 n. 14, 186–88, 191, 192, 193 n. 27–28, 195, 196 n.

Kennedy, George A. (cont.)
  39, 197, 201, 207 n. 22, 212, 215, 225 n. 71, 231, 240, 245, 251, 101 n. 15, 309, 317
Kennedy, James Houghton 62–63
Kern, Philip H. 53 n. 152, 54 n. 153, 57 n. 2, 261 n. 16
Klauck, Hans-Josef 85 nn. 11 and 13, 86 n. 15, 88 n. 18, 90 n. 28, 91 n. 34
Kleinknecht, Karl Theodor 133 n. 30
Knox, John 252, 257 n. 1
Ko, Mei-yun 216 n. 48
Koester, Helmut 139 n. 44
Korta, Kepa 244 n. 4
Koskenniemi, Heikki 88 n. 19
Kraftchick, Steven J. 276 n. 63
Kraus, Thomas J. 45, 46 n. 123
Kremendahl, Dieter 36 n. 76
Krenkel, Max 19 n. 5
Labov, William 293 n. 118, 313 n. 15
Lake, Kirsopp 63 nn. 21–22, 66, 67 n. 34, 70 n. 40, 113 n. 41
Lambrecht, Jan 82 n. 1, 143 n. 9, 270–72, 274–75, 280 n. 73
Lampe, Peter 319 nn. 32 and 34
Larson, Jennifer 280 n. 74, 282–83, 307
Leech, Geoffrey N. 215 n. 44
Légasse, Simon 27 n. 39, 252 n. 37
Leigh, Matthew 306 n. 158
Leivestad, Ragnar 303 n. 147
Lentz, John Clayton 20 n. 14, 21 nn. 15–17
Leopold, J. 138 n. 43
Levelt, Willem J. M. 265 n. 37, 266 n. 37
Levieils, Xavier 263 n. 25
Levin, Richard 175
Levinson, Stephen C. 176 n. 24, 214–16, 245 n. 8
Lietaert Peerbolte, Bert Jan 26 n. 39
Lietzmann, Hans 19 n. 4, 271–75

Lincoln, Andrew T. 114 n. 44
Lis, Catharina 42 n. 111
Litfin, A. Duane 33 n. 66
Litwa, M. David 143 n. 9
Long, A. A. 44 n. 119, 139 n. 46
Long, Fredrick J. 65–68, 114 n. 44, 150 n. 7
Longenecker, Bruce W. 26 n. 39, 27 n. 43, 33, 42 n. 108, 52 n. 146
Longenecker, Richard N. 252 n. 38
Lord, Albert B. 234 n. 108, 246–47
Loubser, J. A. 169 n. 1
Lu, Xing 197 n. 45, 225 n. 71
Lyon, Arabella 197 n. 45
Lyons, George 99 n. 9
Mack, Burton L. 33 n. 66, 138 n. 43
Malherbe, Abraham J. 27–28 n. 43, 29, 83 n. 6, 85 nn. 10 and 13, 88–90, 91 nn. 33–34, 318 n. 28
Malina, Bruce J. 1, 120 n. 57, 301, 317
Malinowski, Bronislaw 243–44
Mann, Barbara Alice 194 n. 32, 195 nn. 36 and 38
Mao, LuMing 197 n. 45
Márquez-Reiter, Rosina 214 n. 40
Marrou, Henri I. 93 nn. 40–41, 95 n. 56
Marshall, Peter 35 n. 69, 36 n. 76, 60, 74 n. 48, 99 n. 8, 100 n. 13, 105 n. 28, 112 n. 39, 113 n. 43, 150, 157, 158 n. 36, 160 n. 45, 161, 162 n. 51, 163 n. 56, 169 n. 1, 278 n. 67, 306 n. 157
Martin, Dale B. 1 n. 3, 4–5, 26 n. 39, 27 nn. 40 and 43, 36–37, 38, 41–42 n. 108, 50, 52 n. 145, 280 n. 73, 289, 291 n. 112, 292, 293 n. 118
Martin, Ralph P. 73 n. 46, 143 nn. 9–10, 161 n. 47, 222 n. 66, 228 n. 81, 264, 268 n. 48, 271–74, 275 n. 59, 281 n. 78, 282 n. 78, 285 n. 88, 287 n. 92
Martin, Raymond A. 22–23 n. 22
Martin, Robert F. 236 n. 112, 237 nn. 113–14 and 116

Martin, Troy W. 3, 318–320
Mason, Steve 138 n. 43, 253 n. 41
McCant, Jerry W. 114 n. 44, 143 nn. 9–10, 169 n. 1
McNelis, Charles A. 96 n. 56
Meeks, Wayne A. 1, 26 n. 39, 61 n. 16, 318 n. 28
Meggitt, Justin J. 10 n. 23, 26 n. 39, 40 n. 103, 42, 52–53, 95 n. 54
Meyer, Christian 187 n. 11, 193 n. 27, 196 n. 39, 225 n. 71, 231 n. 95, 233–34, 236, 240 n. 124, 251 nn. 34–35
Meyer, Eduard 19 n. 4, 20 n. 10
Meyer, H. A. W. 265 n. 36, 266 n. 38, 268 nn. 48 and 51, 269 n. 58, 270–75, 280 n. 73, 281–82 n. 78, 288 n. 99
Mihaila, Corin 279 n. 68
Miller, Merrill P. 322 n. 42
Minchin, Elizabeth 130 n. 24, 139 n. 47
Mitchell, Margaret M. 8–9, 17 n. 1, 36 n. 76, 55 n. 160, 58, 59 n. 8, 61 n. 16, 61–62 n. 17, 64 n. 24, 70 n. 42, 72 n. 44, 74 n. 47, 75 n. 50, 96 n. 56, 100 n. 13, 114 n. 44, 119, 143 n. 10, 144 n. 12, 147 n. 19, 185 n. 1, 227 nn. 74 and 76, 252, 259–61, 262 nn. 19–20, 263, 269 n. 56, 278 n. 67, 310, 321, 322 n. 42
Moe, Olaf 18 n. 4, 22 n. 20, 257 n. 1
Moles, J. L. 153 n. 17
Momigliano, Arnaldo 86 n. 16
Mommsen, Theodor 18 n. 4
Moore, Stephen D. 3 n. 10, 306 n. 155, 307 nn. 164–65
Morgan, Teresa 46 n. 123, 92 nn. 36–37 and 39, 93
Motsch, Andreas 193 n. 26
Moule, C. F. D. 268, 269 n. 58, 273–74
Moulton, James Hope 222 n. 66
Muir, John 90
Murphy-O'Connor, Jerome 19 n. 39, 27 nn. 40 and 43, 37–38, 42 n. 108, 46 n. 125, 60, 152, 169 n. 1, 253
Murray, David 194 n. 32, 195 n. 36
Murray, Oswyn 102 n. 21, 103 n. 22
Nanos, Mark D. 58 n. 2
Neusner, Jacob 19
Neyrey, Jerome H. 20 n. 14, 21 n. 16, 26 n. 39, 38–40, 42–43, 52, 58, 82 n. 2, 93 n. 40, 120 n. 57, 123, 150 n. 7, 317,
Nock, A. D. 19 nn. 4–5, 22 n. 20, 258, 286 n. 89
Norden, Eduard 23, 25, 47 n. 127, 106 n. 29, 257 nn. 3–4, 258 n. 7, 261 n. 16, 262, 265 n. 36, 277, 286 n. 89
Ochs, Elinor 245 n. 8, 313 n. 13
O'Mahony, Kieran J. 36 n. 76
Omerzu, Heike 27 n. 40
Ong, Walter J. 196
Osterreich, Peter L. 188 n. 14, 196
Padilla, Osvaldo 96 n. 56
Patillon, Michel 48 n. 132, 91 n. 32
Pernot, Laurant 100 n. 11, 101 n. 16, 295 n. 121
Pervo, Richard I. 21 nn. 14 and 17
Peterson, Brian K. 82 n. 1, 289 n. 103, 291 n. 112
Phillips, Thomas E. 21 n. 17, 26 n. 76
Pickering, P. E. 266 n. 41
Pitta, Antonio 61 n. 16, 100 n. 13, 119 n. 53
Pitts, Andrew W. 24 n. 30, 35 n. 73
Plummer, Alfred 59–60, 63 nn. 20–22, 66 n. 29, 67 n. 34, 73 n. 46, 97–98, 104 n. 27, 156 nn. 31–32, 161, 177, 222 n. 63, 227 n. 76, 228 n. 81, 263, 264 n. 26, 267, 268 nn. 49 and 53, 269 n. 58, 270–75, 276 n. 60, 281 nn. 77–78, 285 n. 88, 288
Pogoloff, Stephen M. 286 n. 90, 291 n. 112
Pomerantz, Anita 214 n. 39, 216, 219

Porter, Stanley E.   21 n. 17, 33 n. 66, 44 nn. 118–19, 57 n. 2
Poster, Carol   85–86, 89, 91 n. 34, 92 n. 35, 95, 191 n. 21
Prümm, Karl   280 n. 75
Radermacher, L.   99–101
Rahn, Helmut   44 n. 119
Ramsay, W. M.   18 n. 4, 21 n. 15, 289 n. 227, 257 n. 1, 318 n. 28
Rapske, Brian   26 n. 39
Reed, Jeffrey T.   261 n. 14
Regenbogen, O.   129 n. 22
Reinhardt, Tobias   116 n. 46
Reiser, Marius   54 n. 157, 257 n. 1, 259, 268 n. 50
Reisman, Karl   212 n. 32
Reitzenstein, Richard   22 n. 21
Renan, Ernest   257, 262
Richards, E. Randolph   33 n. 66, 54 n. 158, 90 n. 31, 92 n. 35, 207 n. 21, 260 n. 12
Richardson, Peter   71 n. 43
Riesner, Rainer   20 n. 9
Robertson, F. W.   104, 120 n. 56, 213
Robie, Harry W.   203 n. 6, 205
Roetzel, Calvin J.   26 n. 39, 40 n. 103, 53 n. 151, 143 n. 9, 145 n. 16, 303 n. 147
Rohrbaugh, Richard L.   312 n. 11
Roochnik, David   188 n. 15
Rosaldo, Michelle Z.   215 n. 45
Russell, D. A.   99 n. 10, 116 n. 46, 138 n. 42
Rutherford, Ian   216, 294, 296 n. 127
Saldarini, Anthony J.   26
Salmeri, Giovanni   152 n. 15
Sammons, Benjamin   130 n. 24
Sampley, J. Paul   102 n. 19
Sandbach, F. H.   166
Sanders, E. P.   26 n. 29, 42 n. 108
Sandys, J. E.   258 n. 7
Sapir, Edward   311–12, 314
Savage, Timothy B.   42 n. 110, 169 n. 1, 280 n. 74, 284 n. 86

Scenters-Zapico, J.   51 n. 144
Scheidel, Walter   52 n. 156
Schellenberg, Ryan S.   17 n. 2, 27 n. 42, 155 n. 28, 261 n. 16, 322 n. 46
Schiappa, Edward   191 n. 21
Schiefer Ferrari, Markus   127 n. 14
Schieffelin, Bambi B.   245 n. 8
Schmitt, Rudolf   136 n. 35
Schmitz, Thomas   96 n. 56
Schnelle, Udo   20 n. 9, 27 nn. 40 and 43, 36 n. 76
Schrage, Wolfgang   132, 133 n. 30, 135 n. 32
Schreiber, Stefan   142 n. 8
Schreiner, Josef   157 n. 34
Schütz, John H.   1 n. 3, 169 n. 2
Schweitzer, Albert   4 n. 14
Seid, Timothy W.   162 n. 53, 165 n. 58
Sellin, Gerhard   71 n. 43
Semler, Johann Salomo   62, 266 n. 38
Shantz, Colleen   2 n. 4, 3 n. 10, 115 n. 45, 317 n. 25, 322 n. 42, 323
Sherzer, Joel   195 n. 38, 231 n. 95
Shipley, Frederick W.   305 n. 151
Sifianou, Maria   214 n. 40
Smit, Joop F. M.   71 n. 43
Smith, Jonathan Z.   9–10, 13, 198
Sorber, Edna C.   193 nn. 26–27, 194
Spatharas, Dimos   296 n. 124
Spencer, Aida Besançon   169 n. 1
Stanton, G. R.   154 nn. 23 and 25
Stegemann, Wolfgang   20 n. 8, 26 n. 39, 27 n. 39
Steinmann, Alphons A.   22 n. 21
Still, Todd D.   40 n. 103, 42
Stoddard, Amos   193 n. 27, 195 n. 35
Stone, Michael E.   132 n. 28
Stone, William L.   203
Stokes, Randall   177
Stowers, Stanley K.   29, 42–45, 54 n. 154, 84–85 n. 9, 85 n. 12, 86 n. 14, 88, 145 n. 15, 323
Strachan, R. H.   98, 120 n. 56

Strecker, Georg   36 n. 76, 142 n. 8
Street, Brian V.   94 n. 48
Sumney, Jerry L.   3 nn. 8–9, 34 n. 66, 70 n. 41, 113 n. 40
Sundermann, Hans-Georg   82 n. 1, 100 n. 13, 105 n. 28, 119 n. 53, 143 nn. 9–10, 145 n. 16
Swain, Simon   152 n. 13, 295 n. 123, 300 n. 137
Swearingen, C. Jan   239 n. 123, 276 n. 63
Talbert, Charles H.   105 n. 28, 112 n. 39
Tannen, Deborah   231 n. 95, 236 n. 110, 266 n. 37
Taylor, Alan   196 n. 39, 204 n. 9, 205 n. 15, 209 n. 26, 217, 251 n. 34
Taylor, N. H.   64 n. 24
Tell, Håkan   154 n. 24
Theissen, Gerd   1 n. 3, 26 n. 39, 37, 52 n. 145, 74 n. 48
Thrall, Margaret E.   62 n. 18, 70 n. 31, 105 n. 28, 115 n. 45, 119 n. 53, 141 n. 3, 156 n. 31, 161 nn. 47–48, 222 n. 67, 264 n. 30, 267 nn. 43 and 47, 268 nn. 49 and 52 and 55, 269 n. 58, 270–75, 280 nn. 73 and 75, 287 n. 93, 288 n. 100, 289 n. 102
Thurén, Lauri   262 n. 19, 318, 319 nn. 31 and 33
Thwaites, Reuben Gold   194 n. 29, 210 n. 30
Toorn, Karel van der   9 n. 22
Travis, S. H.   97 n. 1, 143 n. 9, 175 nn. 18 and 21, 298 n. 132
Trüb, Hansrudolf   129 n. 22
Turner, Nigel   222 n. 66, 257 n. 2, 268 n. 51, 270–71, 273, 288 nn. 95 and 97
Ulmer, Rivka   45 n. 121
Unnik, W. C.   22, 46
Vanhoye, Albert   314, 318–19, 320 n. 35

Vega, Garcilaso de la   193, 196
Vegge, Ivar   33 n. 66, 54 n. 154, 63 n. 18, 68 n. 36, 143 n. 9, 150 n. 7, 169 n. 1, 173 n. 14, 279 nn. 68–69 and 72, 280 n. 73
Vegge, Tor   27 n. 40, 45–52, 60, 144 n. 13, 150 n. 7, 170 n. 3, 239, 252 n. 37, 276 n. 63
Vielhauer, Philipp   257 n. 1
Voelz, James W.   261 n. 16
Vos, Johan S.   33 n. 66
Walker, Donald Dale   143 n. 11, 144 n. 12, 169 n. 1, 280 n. 73, 286 n. 90
Wallace, Richard   47 n. 127
Wallach, Barbara Price   44 n. 119, 45 n. 121
Walters, Jonathan   306 n. 159
Walzer, Arthur E.   116 n. 47, 118 n. 51, 188 n. 15
Wan, Ske-kar   150 n. 7
Wanamaker, Charles A.   61 n. 16, 71 n. 43
Wang, Tzu-fu   216 n. 48, 313 n. 16
Watson, Duane F.   2 n. 7, 57 n. 2, 60 n. 12, 100 n. 13, 103, 105 n. 28, 108 n. 32, 109 n. 35, 110, 117 n. 50, 121, 143 n. 9, 163 n. 54, 169 n. 1, 175 n. 20, 218, 286 n. 90, 296 n. 126
Watson, Francis   63 nn. 18 and 20, 64 n. 23
Watson, Nigel M.   97 n. 2
Webb, Ruth   96 n. 56
Weiss, Johannes   23–25, 64 n. 24, 77, 124, 127, 138, 140, 258, 259 n. 8
Weizsäcker, Carl von   257 n. 1
Welborn, L. L.   62 n. 18, 63 nn. 19–20 and 22, 64 n. 23, 69, 72 nn. 44–45, 75 n. 51, 76 n. 52, 141–42, 147 n. 20, 177 n. 29, 222 n. 65, 228 n. 80, 278 n. 67, 282 n. 78, 288 n. 100, 301, 302 n. 145
Wendt, Hans Hinrich   19 n. 5

White, John L.   88 n. 19
White, L. Michael   152 n. 13
Whitmarsh, Tim   95 n. 56, 154 n. 25
Wiebe, Rudy   3, 256, 317
Wifstrand, Albert   132 n. 28, 139 n. 44
Wikenhauser, Alfred   19 n. 4
Wilamowitz-Moellendorff, U. von 257 n. 1
Wiles, Maurice F.   261 n. 16
Williams, Wynne   47
Windisch, Hans   59, 83, 98–99, 103 n. 24, 115, 141–43, 145 n. 16, 147 n. 20, 222 n. 65, 227 nn. 76 and 78, 228 n. 81, 264 nn. 28 and 30, 267, 269 n. 57, 270–75, 277, 280 n. 73, 285 n. 87, 287 n. 92, 288 nn. 99 and 101, 298 n. 138
Winner, Ellen   176 n. 24
Winter, Bruce W.   26 n. 39, 82 n. 1, 113 n. 42, 150 n. 7, 151–55, 156 n. 30, 157, 278 n. 67, 287 n. 92, 291 nn. 112–13
Winterbottom, Michael   116 n. 46, 118 n. 51, 188 n. 16
Wire, Antoinette Clark   241
Witherington, Ben   26 n. 39, 27 nn. 40 and 43, 38, 59 n. 8, 65 n. 25, 99 n. 9, 150 n. 7, 169 n. 1, 175 n. 21, 278 n. 67
Wojciechowski, Michael   61 n. 16, 100 n. 13, 103 n. 24, 105 n. 28
Woodbury, Anthony C.   195 n. 38, 231 n. 95
Wrede, William   18 n. 3
Wuellner, Wilhelm H.   31 n. 57, 33 n. 66
Wyatt-Brown, Bertram   316 n. 22
Young, Frances M.   65 n. 25
Youtie, Herbert C.   46 n. 123, 93 n. 42
Yu, Ming-Chung   214 n. 40
Zahn, Christopher J.   178 n. 33
Zeller, Eduard   300 n. 139
Zerba, Michelle   220 n. 59

Zmijewski, Josef   77 n. 53, 136 n. 33, 143 n. 9, 145 n. 16, 275 n. 59
Zuntz, Günther   269 n. 58, 270 n. 58

Index of Subjects

alliteration, 129, 139, 234, 238, 246
amplificatio. See *auxēsis*
anacolutha, 54 n. 158, 257, 268 n. 50, 270, 271, 273, 274, 276, 286
anaphora, 7, 77, 123, 129, 130, 131, 132, 134, 138, 185, 187, 190, 201, 231, 232, 234, 235, 238
ἀνδρεία. See Paul: masculinity of
antithesis, 127, 129, 132–33, 235, 238, 266, 287, 291. See also parallelism
Apollos, 71, 151
apologetic letter, 31, 66–67, **83-88**. See also epistolography
aposiopesis, 221–22 n. 62, 236
apostrophe, 238 n. 120
ἀσθενής/ἀσθενεία, 72, 283, 284 n. 86, 285, 294, 303, 304, 305, 307, 311, 315, 316, 323
assonance, 123, 129, 138, 139, 201, 231, 246
asteismos, 286–87
asyndeton, 7, 123, 127, 129, 131, 132, 134, 138, 190, 191, 201, 238, 258, 259 n. 9, 272
auxēsis, 123, 137, 139, 149, 166, 233, 237–38
βαρύς, **278-79**, 281 n. 76, 284–85, 295
βαρύτης, 173 n. 14
Billy Sunday, 236–39, 255–56
boasting, 2, 30, 34–35, 97–98, 119–21, 143, 146–47, 161, 169–70, 177–79, 212, 227, 255, 280. See also foolishness: boasting and; *periautologia*
of eloquence, 116–17

envy and, **294-300**
in letters, 117 n. 49
of Paul's rival(s), 150–151, 155–57, 160, 169–70, 315
κατὰ σάρκα, 157 n. 34, 172 n. 12
as status claim, 299, 300–301, 302–3
of weakness, 146–47, 150, 171, 172–75, 178, **304-8**, 316–17
captatio benevolentia, 207–8
catalogue style, 7, 77, **129-36**, 137, 139, 140, 180, 201, **231-39**, 240, 249–50, 255, 305 n. 151. See also *peristasis catalogue*
chiasm, 129, 275 n. 59
chreia, 25
Chrysostom. See Dio Chrysostom; John Chrysostom
Cicero, 43, 88, 91, 94, 101 n. 16, 105, 116–18, 165, 189–90, 194, 209–10, 221–23, 296 n. 127
clarity. See σαφήνεια
communicative competence, 6, 243, 244, 313–14
comparative rhetoric, 6, 10, 187–88, 192, 197–99, 240, 251, 255, 309
comparison. See also *synkrisis*
analogical versus genealogical, 9–12
historiographical method and, 4, **8-13**, 192, **198-99**, 201, 309–10
Corinth. See also under Paul's letters
characterization of Paul in, 30, **72-76**, 147–48, 177, 227–28, 264, 265 n. 36, 276, **277-86**, 287, 289, 292, 303–4, 311, 315–17, 322–23

-401-

Corinth (cont.)
  factionalism in, 61–62 n. 17, 70, 151
  Paul's rival(s) in, 30, 34–35, **69–72**, 73, 75–76, 84, 87, 97–98, 110–13, 150–51, 155–57, 158, 160, 168, 169, 172 n. 12, 227–28, 268, 277, 283, 288 n. 100, 297 n. 130, 321, 323. *See also under* boasting
  Paul's visits to, 63, 64–65 n. 24, 66–67, 69, 70, 72, 280, 281, 322–23
  social context of, 1, 37, 50, 304, 320
  sophists in, 150, **151–57**, 278, 283, 286 n. 90, 321
curricula. See under *paideia*
Cynics, 29, 43 n. 114, 152–53, 280 n. 73, 283
Demosthenes, 7, 58, 101 n. 16, 105, 165, 180, 194, 202, 203, 208–211, 219, 220–23, 303, 310, 311
diatribe, 24, **42–45**, 72, 76, 124
Dio Chrysostom, 29, 105, 109–10, 138, 152–54, 286–87, 289
disclaimer, 6, 147–48, 172, **177–79**, 181, 214, 216, 220, 222, 297
dispositio. See rhetorical arrangement
education. See *paideia*; rhetorical education
Elia (Peruvian girl), **223–26**, 255–56, 267, 303–4, 309, 311
ellipsis, 269, 270, 272, 274, 275, 287, 289
elocutio. See Paul's letters: style of
emphasis, 189 n. 17, 288
encomium, 39, 101, 149, 162 n. 53, 163, 166–67, 181, 239, 297, 304, 306
enkyklios paideia. See *paideia*: curricula
enthymeme, 51–52, 187
envy, 106–7, 109 n. 33, 110, 112, 115, 149, 153, 209, 215, 287, **294–300**, 301
Epaminondas, 107–8, 209

epanalepsis, 221
Epictetus, 29, 125, 127–29, 130, 139
epidiorthōsis, 218
epistolography, 76, 180. See also apologetic letter
  documentary papyri, 44, 45, 93, 159–60 n. 44
  epistolary style, 88–89, 167, **259–61**
  handbooks for, 39, 82, 83–86, 89, 91, 96
  rhetoric and, 86, 88–92, 167
  training in, 39, 43–44, 82, **88–96**, 180
epistrophe, 132, 134, 138, 233, 234
ēthopoiia. See *prosōpopoiia*
ethos, 13, 101–2, 187, 208, 209, 222, 226, 240, 249, 256
examples. See παραδείγματα
exordium, 102 n. 19, 189, 207–8
Favorinus, 151–52, 282
foolishness, 73, 120, 142, 145–46, 148, 172, 209 n. 25, **297–98**, **300–303**, 316
  boasting and, 173, 177, 179, 212, 221, 297–98, 302–3
"Fool's Speech," 60, 76, 121, **141–48**, 149, 171, 180, 227, 298 nn. 132 and 135
friendship, 86–87, 117 n. 49, 230–31
general rhetoric. See *under* rhetoric
habitus, 12, 191, 250–51, 284, 312–15
historiography, 9–10, 318–20. See also *under* comparison
homoioteleuton, 77, 129, 130, 187
hyperbaton, 273
hyperbole, 187, 189 n. 17, 190, 305 n. 151
ἰδιώτης, 17, 31, 59, 60, 73, 113, 261–62, 286, 287, **289–94**, 315
indignation. See βαρύτης
informal rhetoric. See *under* rhetoric
intonation, 24, 225, 234, 245, 249, 255, 311

INDEX OF SUBJECTS

inventio. See rhetorical invention
irony, 35, 77, 141, 147 n. 20, 150, 165, **169-76**, 177-78, 179, 181, 222 n. 65, 230, 255, 286-89, 315
isocolon, 7, 77, 129, 201, 231, 232, 234 n. 106, 238
John Chrysostom, 17, 55, 261-63, 266-67
Klangfiguren, 24, 25, 140
language socialization. *See under* rhetorical education
"letter of tears," 2, **63-64**, 65, 69, 315. *See also under* Paul's letters
letter writing. *See* epistolography
literacy, 39, 82, 92, 93, 94, 95, 196-97
logos (rhetorical proof), 187, 190 n. 21, 240
λόγος (Greek word), 70, 72, 279, 284-85, 286 n. 90, 289, 292, 315
metaphor, 189 n. 17
Mexicano orator. *See* rhetoric: Mexicano
Narrenrede. See "Fool's Speech"
oral epic, 139, 234-25 n. 108, 246-47
paideia, 17, 45-46, 82, 85, 151-52 n. 10, 163, 252, 261, 263, 282, 290, 323 n. 48. *See also* rhetorical education
  curricula, 39-40, 45, 53, 82, 89, **92-95**, 180, 212
  indicators of, 43 n. 115, **95-96**, 181, 192, 219-21
παραδείγματα, 54, 61 n. 17, 74 n. 47
parallelism, 24, 77, 209 n. 27, 231 n. 95, 234-35, 272, 275. *See also* antithesis
parataxis. *See* periodic style
parenthesis, 221, 228 n. 81, 268, 270, 271, 276, 289
parody, 35, 76, 150, 151, **161-63**, 167, 171-72 n. 10, 175, 180, 297-98, 304, 305, 315
paronomasia, 159-60, 257, 265-66
partes orationis. See rhetorical arrangement

pathos, 2-3, 187, 190 n. 21, 209, 222, 240
patristic exegesis. *See under* Paul's letters
Paul. *See also* Paul's letters
  authority of, 67, 69, 72, 97-98, 110, 111, 113, 146, 147, 157 n. 35, 169-70 n. 2, 172, 223, 280-81, 281-82 n. 78, 284-85, 294, 302-3, 311, 316
  body of, 3, 13, 31, 282-84, 306-7, 315, 316, 318, 322, 323. *See also* ἀσθενής; ταπεινός
  collection project of, 64-65 n. 24, 75
  education of, 17-18, 22-23, 30, 43-44, 46, **252-54**, 261 (*see also under* rhetorical education)
  financial support for, 37, 73-75, 113, 157, 228 n. 81
  Judean identity of, 18, 22, 43, 161, 163, 172, 252-53
  Luke's portrait of, **20-21**, 46, 207-8
  manual labor of, 4, 5, 17, **18-22**, 26-27, 36, 37, **40-42**, 43, 52-53, 56, 282, 284 n. 86, 318, 322
  masculinity of, 282-83, 306-8, 316
  opponents of (*see under* Corinth)
  as Pharisee, 19, 253
  popular philosophy and, 4, 39, 43, 45, 51-52, 76, 123, 127, 142 n. 8, 239, 286 n. 90, 323 n. 48
  Roman citizenship of, 5, 17-19, 20, 27, 36, 38, 41, 52-53, 56
  social location of, 1-2, 4-5, 7, 13, 17-22, 26-27, 29-30, 36, 37-42, 43, 45-47, 52-53, 55-56, 211, 286, 302-3, **307-8**, 311, 317, 321-23. *See also* voice: of Paul
  rhetorical delivery of, 31, 278, 279, 284, 288 n. 100, 292
  zeal of, 252-54, 297 n. 130
Pauline communities, 2, 111

Paul's letters
  patristic evaluation of, 5, 17–18, 55, **261–63**, 264, 266–67
  presence versus absence motif in, 63, 67, 69, 72–73, 227–28, 279–80, 281, 284, 303, 323
  2 Corinthians, partition theories of, **62–68**, 321 (*see also* "letter of tears")
  style of, 23–25, 43, 54, 59–60, 198, 256–59, 260, 261, 262, 263–64, 269, 275–76, 305 n. 151. *See also* βαρύς
  syntax of, 7, 54 n. 158, 257, 262–63, **263–77**, 287–89, 310
Peregrinus, 29, 300–301
periautologia, 6, 35, 76, **98–118**, 119, 120–21, 149, 175, 179–80, 201, 202, **206–12**, 213–17, 221, 240, 256, 294–300. *See also* boasting
periodic style, 24, 54, 220–21, 258–59, 260, 269
peristasis catalogue, 41, 76, 77, **123–30**, 132, 135–36, 149, 175, 180, 232, 304, 305, 306–7. *See also* catalogue style
physiognomy, 282–84
Plutarch, 7, 9, 35, 51, 98, 99–100, 103, 107, 120, 138, 211–212, 294–97, 300, 303, 311
politeness theory, 214–16, 217
prodiorthōsis, 6, 11, **118–20**, 180, 185, 191, 192, 201, **212–23**, 240, 255
Progymnasmata, 39, 40 n. 99, 44, 46, 48–50, 91, 149, 160, 162–67, 181, 239. *See also* Rhetoric: handbooks of
prosōpopoiia, 6, 39, 40 n. 99, 91, 114 n. 44, **144–48**, 175–76, 180, 185, 201, **223–31**, 236, 238, 240, 255
Quintilian, 7, 31, 43, 46, 88, 93, 105, 116–18, 120, 188–89, 222, 233, 257–58, 303
Red Jacket, 8, 9, 49 n. 134, 192, 199, **202–5**, 206–12, 217, 218, 222, 228–31, 233, 234, 235, 243, 255, 256, 303, 309
  education of, 7, 11, 208, 218, 231, **251**
  voice of (*see under* voice)
repetition, 131, 132, 187, 191, 222, 231, 233, 234–35, 238, 265–66, 275, 276 n. 61, 289
rhetoric. *See also* rhetorical education
  as art, 188, 189–90, 219
  Asianic (versus Attic), 258 n. 7
  Chinese, 187, 214 n. 40, 225 n. 71
  comparative (*see* comparative rhetoric)
  comportment and (*see* voice)
  deliberative, 61–62 n. 17, 74 n. 47, 187, 195–96, 249, 251
  emotion and, 2–3, 23, 25, 59–60, 187, 220–21, 223, 257 n. 3, 266, 276, 318–19
  epideictic, 199 n. 55, 187
  forensic, 32, 66, 116, 187, 219, 291
  formal versus informal, 6–7, 10, 11–12, 25, 28, 32–33, **190–92**, 212, 214, 218, 219, 226, 240, 245, 254, 309–10
  general, 6–7, 11, 34, 54, 61 n. 17, 136, 140, **186–92**, 201, 212, 213, 214, 215, 218–19, 225, 240, 309
  Greco-Roman theory of, 6, 8–9, 11, 33–34, 53–54, 57–59, 149, 158, 176, 179–80, 187–90, 191–92, 197–99, 212, 239, 276, 309
  handbooks of, 5, 31–33, 58, 185, 310. *See also Progymnasmata*
  "of the heart," 5, 23, 55, 197, 256, 257
  Mexicano, 247–50, 255–56, 310
  Native American, **192–97**, 203 n. 5, 233–34, 251
  "New Rhetoric," 199
  "natural," 25, 32, 55, 185, 189 n. 17, 194–95, 196, 197, 219–20

INDEX OF SUBJECTS 405

letters and (*see under* epistolography)
Paul and (*see under* Paul's letters)
rhetorical arrangement, 38, 39, 40 n. 99, 53–54, 58–59, 81–82, 189, 191, 198, 207 n. 22, 240
rhetorical criticism, 1–3, 7–8, 13, 31–33, 39, 57–61, 81, 175–76, 256, 264, 309, 310, 311, 318–20
rhetorical education, 58–59, 92, 123, 138–39, 144, 149, 155, 219–20, 236–37. See also *paideia*
  formal, 7, 11, 46, 47, 50, 53, 82, 120, 140, 145, 185, 190, 191–92, 196–97, 201, 212, 216, 218, 225, 228, 231, 236, 243, 245, 248, 254, 251, 276–77, 310
  grammar as indicator of, 226, 255–56, 262, 264, 267, 310
  Judeans and, 24, 35, 138–39
  as observation and imitation, 32, 139, 188, 190, 237, **246–51**, 254
  of Paul, 4–7, 18, 23–25, 27, 30–42, 44–56, 58–61, 81–82, 90, 95–96, 99, 139, 140, 145, 170 n. 3, 181, 185–86, 192, 197, 198–99, 201, 202, 208, 211–12, 218, 223, 239–40, 254, 255, 276–77, 294, **309–11** (*see also* Paul: education of)
  social location and, 4–5, 27–28, 36–42, 53, 55–56, 92, 94 n. 48
  as socialization, 5–6, 30, 33–34, 186, 189–90, 212, 241, **243–52**, 254, 309–10 (*see also* rhetoric: formal versus informal)
rhetorical invention, 54, 198
rhetorical terminology, 27, 34 n. 68, 159–60, 197
rhyme, 130, 131, 138, 201, 231, 234, 235
rhythm, 23–24, 60, 125 n. 7, 127, 128, 130, 131, 134, 139, 140, 201, 233, 234, 235, 237, 238, 239 n. 121, 246, 249, 263, 305 n. 151, 311

Sagoyewatha. *See* Red Jacket
σαφήνεια, 54, 257–58, 260–61, 267, 269 n. 56, 277, 289
secretary, 85, 90, 91–92, 95, 207 n. 21, 276 n. 62
self-defense, 67–68, 72 n. 44, 84, 87, 97, **105–8**, 109, 115, 117, 118, 121, 180, 201, 202, 206, 208, 209 n. 25, 211, 256, 296, 297, 303, 305 n. 151
self-praise. See *periautologia*
social class. *See under* Paul; rhetorical education
sociolinguistics, 6, 10, 245, 309, 311–12
sophists, 28–29, 95, 138, 209 n. 25, 291 n. 113, 323 n. 48. *See also* Corinth: sophists in
  philosophers and, 154 n. 25, 286 n. 90
speech community, 6, 192, 214, 218, 244, 248
speech-in-character. See *prosōpopoiia*
Stoics, 29, 123, 124–25, 126, 130, 132, 306–7
συναθροισμός, 137
"super-apostles." *See* Corinth: Paul's rivals in
synkrisis, 34–35, 39, 76, 149–51, 155–56, **157–68**, 176, 180–81, 239, 276, 315
syntax. *See under* Paul's letters
τάξις. *See* rhetorical arrangement
ταπεινός, 41, 73, 106, 108–9, 228, 280, 281, 282–85, 294, 304, 306, 307–8, 315
Tarsus, 20, 22, 30, 31, 38, **46–47**, 52
tentmaking. *See* Paul: manual labor
thesis, 47–50, 61–62 n. 17
Titus, 63, 64 nn. 23–24, 68 n. 36, 75, 303 n. 148
ὑπόκρισις. *See* Paul: rhetorical delivery of
urbanitas, 286–87
voice, 3, 12–13, 181, 244, 251, 255–56, **311–15**

voice (cont.)
   aristocratic, 7, 88, 106–7, 181, 211, 219–21, 300, 303, 311
   of Elia, 225–26, 256, 303–4, 311
   of Paul, 3–4, 7–8, 81, 88, 107–8, 143–44, 175, 178–79, 181, 201, 211, 222–23, 256, 278, 286, 294, 303–4, 307–8, 310–11, 315, 316, 317–18, 320, 322–23
   of Red Jacket, 7, 205, 208–9, 211, 256, 303, 311

www.ingramcontent.com/pod-product-compliance
Lightning Source LLC
Chambersburg PA
CBHW021814300426
44114CB00009BA/174